European Perspectives on AI and AR Applications in Learning

Jan Vrba
https://orcid.org/0000-0002-8404-5091
Akademia Jagiellońska w Toruniu, Poland

Enrico Moch
https://orcid.org/0009-0005-4722-0961
GrandEdu Research School, Germany

Tobias Oberdieck
https://orcid.org/0009-0002-2017-4991
GrandEdu Research School, Germany

IGI Global
Scientific Publishing
Publishing Tomorrow's Research Today

Vice President of Editorial | Melissa Wagner
Director of Acquisitions | Mikaela Felty
Director of Book Development | Jocelynn Hessler
Production Manager | Mike Brehm
Cover Design | Jose Rosado

Published in the United States of America by
IGI Global Scientific Publishing
701 East Chocolate Avenue
Hershey, PA, 17033, USA
Tel: 717-533-8845 | Fax: 717-533-7115
Website: https://www.igi-global.com E-mail: cust@igi-global.com

Library of Congress Cataloging-in-Publication Data

Names: Vrba, Jan, 1990- editor | Moch, Enrico, 1978- editor | Ritter, Lars Arnold, 1996- editor | Oberdieck, Tobias, 1991- editor
Title: European perspectives on AI and AR applications in learning / Edited by Jan Vrba, Enrico Moch, Lars Arnold Ritter, and Tobias Oberdieck.
Description: Hershey, PA : IGI Global Scientific Publishing, [2027] | Includes bibliographical references and index. | Summary: "This book articulates diverse European interpretations of AI and AR in education. It examines human-rights, democratic, and ethical commitments in technology-enhanced learning"-- Provided by publisher.
Identifiers: LCCN 2026017427 (print) | LCCN 2026017428 (ebook) | ISBN 9798337398839 hardcover | ISBN 9798337398846 paperback | ISBN 9798337398853 ebook
Subjects: LCSH: Artificial intelligence--Educational applications--Europe | Augmented reality in education--Europe | Education--Effect of technological innovations on--Europe
Classification: LCC LB1028.43 .E937 2026 (print) | LCC LB1028.43 (ebook)
LC record available at https://lccn.loc.gov/2026017427
LC ebook record available at https://lccn.loc.gov/2026017428

British Cataloguing in Publication Data
A Cataloguing in Publication record for this book is available from the British Library.

Dedicated to the pioneers of the digital frontier and the students who will inhabit it; as AI and AR redefine the boundaries of what is possible, we dedicate this work to those who strive to ensure that technology serves as a bridge, not a barrier, to knowledge. To everyone working to transform European education into a vibrant, interactive, and personalized journey – may your vision continue to inspire the classrooms of tomorrow.

Table of Contents

Detailed Table of Contents

This chapter examines how artificial intelligence (AI) and augmented reality (AR) are transforming education across Europe within the continent's unique regulatory, ethical, and cultural context. It explores the interplay between technological innovation and Europe's human-centric, rights-based vision of education. The analysis traces key policy instruments - including the EU Artificial Intelligence Act, the Digital Education Action Plan (2021–2027), the European Commission's Ethical Guidelines on AI and Data in Teaching and Learning, and the UNESCO Recommendation on the Ethics of AI, showing how they shape opportunities and limits for AI and AR integration in schools, universities, and lifelong learning. Reviewing emerging evidence on AI-driven personalised learning and AR-supported experiential environments, the chapter also addresses challenges of data protection, bias, automation, inequality, and learner agency. It concludes by mapping the current state of research and policy and outlining directions for future inquiry.

This chapter examines how artificial intelligence is reshaping lifelong learning and adult education across Europe, not simply as a technical innovation, but as a response to deeper social, economic, and demographic pressures. As European societies face rapid labour-market change, ageing populations, migration, and widening skills gaps, AI-supported learning offers new possibilities for flexible pathways, personalized guidance, and continuous reskilling. Yet these possibilities are never neutral. They raise urgent questions about inclusion, learner autonomy, data ethics, institutional readiness, and the risk of reducing adult education to measurable competencies alone. The chapter explores European strategies and emerging practices in AI-enhanced adult learning, with attention to policy frameworks, workplace learning, community-based education, and digital platforms. It argues for a human-centred approach in which AI strengthens, rather than replaces, the reflective, emancipatory, and socially rooted purposes of lifelong learning.

This chapter develops a human-centred conceptual framework for integrating AI and AR as mutually related components of higher education learning ecosystems. It argues that AI and AR should not be treated as separate innovation streams: AI is associated with tutoring, feedback, prediction, personalisation, and automation, whereas AR is associated with visualisation, contextualisation, embodiment, and immersive engagement. Drawing on OECD perspectives on generative AI, teaching, and immersive technologies, European regulatory frameworks, human-centred design, and technology governance, the chapter proposes a five-dimensional framework: human-centred pedagogy, immersive learning design, learner and teacher agency, inclusion and access, and governance and trust. The framework supports researchers, curriculum designers, academic developers, and higher education leaders in evaluating when AI and AR are educationally warranted, how they can be designed responsibly, and what institutional policy and evidence standards are needed to move beyond technology-first adoption narratives.

This chapter investigates the integration of artificial intelligence (AI) into architectural education between 2023 and 2025 through a systematic mapping review of fifteen peer-reviewed studies indexed in WoS and Scopus. Following a PRISMA-informed approach, the chapter examines the different ways AI tools are used across pedagogical frameworks. The findings suggest that while AI significantly accelerates idea generation and increases visual variety, its influence on deeper cognitive aspects, particularly design thinking and spatial reasoning, appears to be more uneven and less conclusive. The review identifies five key dimensions of transformation: ideation and representation, cognitive augmentation, pedagogical integration, student perception and ethics, and methodological constraints. It reveals persistent gaps, including the lack of longitudinal evidence, limited cross-cultural perspectives, and insufficient evaluation metrics. Overall, the chapter contributes a structured framework for understanding current trajectories and proposes directions for AI in architectural pedagogy.

This chapter examines the role of augmented reality (AR) and artificial intelligence (AI) in promoting inclusive and adaptive education in European educational settings. This chapter's goal is to examine how new technologies can improve student engagement, teaching efficacy, and fair access to learning materials. The conversation examines pedagogical frameworks, European educational regulations, and technical advancements that influence the incorporation of AI and AR in educational settings. Accessibility, ethical issues, teacher digital competency, and institutional preparedness are among the major topics covered. Additionally, the chapter offers workable ways to incorporate AI and AR into professional development programs and pedagogical design. Lastly, future research possibilities are described, with a focus on immersive technologies, inclusive digital innovation, and adaptable learning ecosystems in modern educational systems.

Schools, colleges, and universities across the United Kingdom are now confronted with a convergence of pressures—deepening attainment inequalities, overstretched SEND provision, and a persistent recruitment crisis among teaching staff—that has sharpened the professional and policy interest in Artificial Intelligence (AI) and Augmented Reality (AR) as instructional technologies. This chapter provides

The aim of this study is to present a general map of the studies on the use of artificial intelligence in chemistry education to date. The articles were analyzed with Scopus database using bibliometric analysis method. The studies were examined with various keywords and maps of citations were created according to the results of the analysis. Bibliometric analysis results were visualized with VOSviewer program. In this study, 1,538 results were found. The research results were limited to the last ten years between 2014 and 2024, various publication names, subject areas and language options were used, and analysis studies were carried out on 772 research results. As a result of the analysis, they were classified according to keywords, countries, publications, authors and citations. According to this classification; it was determined that the most studies on the concept of artificial intelligence in chemistry education were conducted in the USA. This research covers the results of studies on the use of artificial intelligence in chemistry education.

Artificial Intelligence (AI) application in education is changing the teaching, learning, and institutional management by providing personalized learning systems, automated assessment, and intelligent analytics. Nevertheless, this fast-paced adoption comes with alarming issues regarding the privacy of data, legal conformance, copyright, and ethical governance. The FERPA, GDPR, and COPPA frameworks have stringent conditions on the manner in which student data is gathered, processed, and stored, and adherence to these standards has become a major concern among educational institutions. Also, AI tools create complications in upholding academic integrity and ownership of intellectual work. To solve these dilemmas, it is necessary to take a middle ground so that technological innovation and ethical responsibility and legal obligation can be closely linked. The chapter addresses the use of AI in education, regulatory measures, intellectual property issues, ethical issues, and responsible AI implementing approaches.

Preface

The rapid and profound integration of emerging technologies into the educational fabric of Europe marks a truly pivotal moment in pedagogical history, one that may be compared to the invention of the printing press in its potential to reshape knowledge.

This volume, "European Perspectives on AI and AR Applications in Learning," arrives at a critical juncture – a time when the dual forces of Artificial Intelligence (AI) and Augmented Reality (AR) are rapidly shifting from speculative, theoretical possibilities discussed in laboratories to tangible, daily realities in the contemporary classroom.

We are currently witnessing a paradigm shift where the boundaries between the physical and digital learning environments are becoming increasingly shifted. Across the diverse landscape of the continent – from the tech-integrated primary schools of Portugal to the specialized higher education research laboratories of the United Kingdom – educators, researchers, and policymakers are collectively grappling with a fundamental, era-defining question:

> *"How can we strategically harness these powerful computational tools to enhance human potential and cognitive development, while simultaneously safeguarding the core educational values of equity, privacy, and critical thinking that define the European traditions?"*

This transition is not merely about the adoption of new hardware or software; it is a fundamental reimagining of the relationship between the educator, the student, and the medium of instruction. As AI begins to offer unprecedented levels of personalization and AR provides immersive, multi-sensory experiences that were previously unimaginable, we must ensure that these innovations serve as a bridge to deeper understanding rather than a barrier to authentic human connection.

This book seeks to document this journey, capturing the successes, the ethical frictions, and the visionary frameworks that are currently shaping the future of European learning.

PART I: STRATEGY, THEORY, AND FOUNDATIONS

The first section explores the integration, pedagogical transformation, and ethical governance of Artificial Intelligence (AI) and Augmented Reality (AR) within European education, spanning adult learning, higher education, and specialized fields such as architecture; it outlines European strategies for lifelong learning, proposes human-centred conceptual frameworks for immersive learning design, and identifies current research gaps in AI pedagogy. These chapters synthesize how emerging technologies are reshaped by policy and practice to drive the future of learning while balancing human oversight with technological innovation.

PART II: FRAMEWORKS FOR ADAPTIVE LEARNING AND SUPPORT SYSTEMS

The second section examines the development of adaptive learning environments and support systems powered by AI and Augmented Reality (AR) to enhance both teacher assistance and student engagement across Europe; it focuses on practical frameworks for inclusive education, personalized learning paths, and specialized tools such as gamified, AR-integrated platforms with controlled multimedia consumption. By analyzing various regional approaches, these chapters demonstrate how technology can actively support educators, optimize individual learning experiences, and foster highly engaging, accessible educational ecosystems.

PART III: PRACTICAL CLASSROOM APPLICATIONS AND TEACHER PERCEPTIONS

The third part focuses on teacher perceptions, emotional dynamics, and specialized subject applications of AI, specifically examining how educators navigate generative tools and emotional learning frameworks. It explores pre-service and primary school teachers' experiences and uncertainties regarding AI-generated materials, particularly in Portugal, alongside data-driven insights from a bibliometric analysis of AI in chemistry education. Additionally, the section introduces a practical framework linking teachers' emotions and social-emotional learning to high achievement in mathematics classrooms, highlighting the intersection of human psychology and technological integration.

PART IV: ETHICS, REGULATION, AND COMPLIANCE

The last section addresses the legal, regulatory, and ethical challenges of integrating AI into academic environments, focusing on data privacy, intellectual property, and regional governance; it examines compliance with critical international frameworks – including FERPA, GDPR, COPPA, and copyright laws – to ensure secure and lawful technology adoption. Additionally, the section provides a comparative European analysis of the ethical frictions that arise in AI-enhanced learning, balancing technological advancement with student privacy, fairness, and institutional responsibility.

This collection is intended for researchers, policymakers, and practitioners who recognize that the future of learning is already here; it is our hope that these pages provide the clarity needed to navigate this complex but exhilarating new era of European education.

CHAPTER OVERVIEW

Chapter 1: European Perspectives on Artificial Intelligence and Augmented Reality in Education: Pedagogical Transformation, Ethical Governance, and the Future of Learning

This chapter examines how artificial intelligence (AI) and augmented reality (AR) are transforming education across Europe within the continent's unique regulatory, ethical, and cultural context. It explores the interplay between technological innovation and Europe's human-centric, rights-based vision of education. The analysis traces key policy instruments - including the EU Artificial Intelligence Act, the Digital Education Action Plan (2021–2027), the European Commission's Ethical Guidelines on AI and Data in Teaching and Learning, and the UNESCO Recommendation on the Ethics of AI, showing how they shape opportunities and limits for AI and AR integration in schools, universities, and lifelong learning. Reviewing emerging evidence on AI-driven personalised learning and AR-supported experiential environments, the chapter also addresses challenges of data protection, bias, automation, inequality, and learner agency. It concludes by mapping the current state of research and policy and outlining directions for future inquiry.

Chapter 2: Artificial intelligence for Lifelong Learning and Adult Education: European Strategies and Practices

This chapter examines how artificial intelligence is reshaping lifelong learning and adult education across Europe, not simply as a technical innovation, but as a response to deeper social, economic, and demographic pressures. As European societies face rapid labour-market change, ageing populations, migration, and widening skills gaps, AI-supported learning offers new possibilities for flexible pathways, personalized guidance, and continuous reskilling. Yet these possibilities are never neutral. They raise urgent questions about inclusion, learner autonomy, data ethics, institutional readiness, and the risk of reducing adult education to measurable competencies alone. The chapter explores European strategies and emerging practices in AI-enhanced adult learning, with attention to policy frameworks, workplace learning, community-based education, and digital platforms. It argues for a human-centred approach in which AI strengthens, rather than replaces, the reflective, emancipatory, and socially rooted purposes of lifelong learning.

Chapter 3: Human-Centred AI and Immersive Learning Design in Higher Education - A Conceptual Framework for Artificial Intelligence and Augmented Reality: Human-Centred AI and Immersive Learning Design in Higher Education

This chapter develops a human-centred conceptual framework for integrating AI and AR as mutually related components of higher education learning ecosystems. It argues that AI and AR should not be treated as separate innovation streams: AI is associated with tutoring, feedback, prediction, personalisation, and automation, whereas AR is associated with visualisation, contextualisation, embodiment, and immersive engagement. Drawing on OECD perspectives on generative AI, teaching, and immersive technologies, European regulatory frameworks, human-centred design, and technology governance, the chapter proposes a five-dimensional framework: human-centred pedagogy, immersive learning design, learner and teacher agency, inclusion and access, and governance and trust. The framework supports researchers, curriculum designers, academic developers, and higher education leaders in evaluating when AI and AR are educationally warranted, how they can be designed responsibly, and what institutional policy and evidence standards are needed to move beyond technology-first adoption narratives.

Chapter 4: Artificial Intelligence in Architectural Education: AI Pedagogy and Research Gaps

This chapter investigates the integration of artificial intelligence (AI) into architectural education between 2023 and 2025 through a systematic mapping review of fifteen peer-reviewed studies indexed in WoS and Scopus. Following a PRISMA-informed approach, the chapter examines the different ways AI tools are used across pedagogical frameworks. The findings suggest that while AI significantly accelerates idea generation and increases visual variety, its influence on deeper cognitive aspects, particularly design thinking and spatial reasoning, appears to be more uneven and less conclusive. The review identifies five key dimensions of transformation: ideation and representation, cognitive augmentation, pedagogical integration, student perception and ethics, and methodological constraints. It reveals persistent gaps, including the lack of longitudinal evidence, limited cross-cultural perspectives, and insufficient evaluation metrics. Overall, the chapter contributes a structured framework for understanding current trajectories and proposes directions for AI in architectural pedagogy.

Chapter 5: AI and Augmented Reality for Teacher and Learner Support: European Approaches to Adaptive and Inclusive Education

This chapter examines the role of augmented reality (AR) and artificial intelligence (AI) in promoting inclusive and adaptive education in European educational settings. This chapter's goal is to examine how new technologies can improve student engagement, teaching efficacy, and fair access to learning materials. The conversation examines pedagogical frameworks, European educational regulations, and technical advancements that influence the incorporation of AI and AR in educational settings. Accessibility, ethical issues, teacher digital competency, and institutional preparedness are among the major topics covered. Additionally, the chapter offers workable ways to incorporate AI and AR into professional development programs and pedagogical design. Lastly, future research possibilities are described, with a focus on immersive technologies, inclusive digital innovation, and adaptable learning ecosystems in modern educational systems.

Chapter 6: AI and Augmented Reality for Enhancing Teacher and Learner Support in the UK Educational System

Schools, colleges, and universities across the United Kingdom are now confronted with a convergence of pressures—deepening attainment inequalities, overstretched

SEND provision, and a persistent recruitment crisis among teaching staff—that has sharpened the professional and policy interest in Artificial Intelligence (AI) and Augmented Reality (AR) as instructional technologies. This chapter provides a critical and evidence-grounded examination of how AI and AR function within UK educational settings, drawing on published evaluations, case studies, and policy analyses from primary, secondary, further, and higher education. The discussion spans adaptive learning systems and intelligent tutoring, AR-mediated immersive environments, teacher-facing analytics and assessment tools, and the deployment of simulation for professional development. Equity, data governance, and the risk of teacher de-professionalisation receive sustained attention. The chapter closes by advancing a four-phase implementation framework and identifying productive directions for further empirical inquiry.

Chapter 7: Teacher and Learner Support: European Perspectives on AI and AR in Learning

Over the past decade, debates on effective teaching have shifted, especially with the rise of Artificial Intelligence (AI) and Augmented Reality (AR) in education. This chapter examines these technologies not as standalone solutions but as resources shaped by institutional, pedagogical, and ethical conditions. It highlights their role in supporting teacher professional development and personalising student learning across diverse contexts. The discussion draws on recent empirical and theoretical scholarship, covering generative AI tools, intelligent tutoring systems, adaptive learning architectures, immersive VR-based teacher preparation, and AR-enhanced classroom environments. A European perspective frames the analysis, influenced by regulatory frameworks such as the EU AI Act and GDPR, which impose governance obligations not present in many other regions. The chapter concludes that neither optimism nor scepticism is sufficient; instead, a critical, evidence-informed engagement with the practical realities and limitations of these technologies is essential.

Chapter 8: Teacher and Learner Support for Artificial Intelligence Augmented Reality Applications in Education

The rapid integration of Artificial Intelligence (AI) and Augmented Reality (AR) into European educational landscapes has created a profound shift in pedagogical structures. While these technologies offer unprecedented opportunities for immersive and personalized learning, their success is contingent upon the robust support systems provided to both teachers and learners. This chapter explores the multifaceted dimensions of support required to effectively implement AI and AR in educational settings. Drawing on European frameworks such as DigCompEdu and the Digital

Education Action Plan (2021-2027), the chapter analyzes the technical, pedagogical and emotional support mechanisms necessary for stakeholders. Through a synthesis of literature and case studies, the chapter outlines how AI-driven tutoring systems and AR-enhanced visualizations can be scaffolded to prevent cognitive overload in students and professional burnout in educators. A strategic roadmap for European higher education institutions and K-12 schools to foster a sustainable ecosystem for emerging technologies is provided.

Chapter 9: Personalized Learning and Teacher Assistance Using AI and AR: A European Perspective

This chapter examines how artificial intelligence and augmented reality are reshaping classrooms and teaching practices across Europe. Drawing on peer-reviewed studies published between 2018 and 2026, it analyses applications including personalised learning systems, learning analytics, AI chatbots, generative tools, and AR-enhanced environments, along with the professional development required for effective use. A four-layer convergent framework—data collection, AI processing, AR environment, and personalised output—is presented to explain how these technologies interact. The chapter also addresses unresolved challenges, including digital equity, uneven GDPR compliance, limited teacher preparation, and assessment practices disrupted by generative AI. It concludes with recommendations for institutional leaders, educators, curriculum designers, and policy makers.

Chapter 10: Pre-service teachers' perceptions of developing educational materials using generative artificial intelligence tools

The rapid expansion of generative artificial intelligence (GAI) tools is transforming educational material development processes. This study examines the anxiety and acceptance levels of Special Education and Turkish pre-service teachers regarding the pedagogical use of GAI. Employing a mixed-methods, single-group pre-test/post-test design, 82 participants completed an eight-week structured GAI training. Data were collected through validated anxiety and acceptance scales and semi-structured interviews. Quantitative findings revealed no statistically significant change in overall anxiety or acceptance levels. However, a significant decrease was observed in job replacement anxiety, while effort expectancy showed a meaningful shift after training. Qualitative results indicated that participants adopted a cautiously optimistic stance, recognizing efficiency and productivity benefits while expressing ethical and professional concerns. Overall, pre-service teachers positioned GAI as a supportive instructional tool rather than a substitute for the human-centered nature of teaching.

Chapter 11: Between Promise and Uncertainty: Portuguese Primary Teachers Navigating Generative AI in Education

This chapter explores how Portuguese primary school teachers perceive the integration of generative artificial intelligence in educational contexts. Set against the rapid expansion of AI in society, it discusses both the opportunities these technologies offer and the challenges they raise for teaching and learning in early schooling. Drawing on an exploratory mixed-methods case study with teachers following a professional development workshop, the chapter examines their views on AI's potential to support personalised learning, feedback, and the creation of teaching materials. At the same time, it highlights key concerns related to teacher preparedness, ethical use, data protection, and the impact on students' cognitive development. The findings reveal a stance of cautious optimism, where interest in innovation coexists with uncertainty and the need for guidance. The chapter argues that meaningful integration of AI depends on continuous teacher training, clear policy frameworks, and thoughtful pedagogical mediation, offering reflections and recommendations for educators.

Chapter 12: Bibliometric Analysis of the Use of Artificial Intelligence in Chemistry Education with Vosviewer

The aim of this study is to present a general map of the studies on the use of artificial intelligence in chemistry education to date. The articles were analyzed with Scopus database using bibliometric analysis method. The studies were examined with various keywords and maps of citations were created according to the results of the analysis. Bibliometric analysis results were visualized with VOSviewer program. In this study, 1,538 results were found. The research results were limited to the last ten years between 2014 and 2024, various publication names, subject areas and language options were used, and analysis studies were carried out on 772 research results. As a result of the analysis, they were classified according to keywords, countries, publications, authors and citations. According to this classification; it was determined that the most studies on the concept of artificial intelligence in chemistry education were conducted in the USA. This research covers the results of studies on the use of artificial intelligence in chemistry education.

Chapter 13: AI in Education: Compliance with FERPA, GDPR, COPPA, and Intellectual Property in Academic Environments

Artificial Intelligence (AI) application in education is changing the teaching, learning, and institutional management by providing personalized learning systems, automated assessment, and intelligent analytics. Nevertheless, this fast-paced adoption comes with alarming issues regarding the privacy of data, legal conformance, copyright, and ethical governance. The FERPA, GDPR, and COPPA frameworks have stringent conditions on the manner in which student data is gathered, processed, and stored, and adherence to these standards has become a major concern among educational institutions. Also, AI tools create complications in upholding academic integrity and ownership of intellectual work. To solve these dilemmas, it is necessary to take a middle ground so that technological innovation and ethical responsibility and legal obligation can be closely linked. The chapter addresses the use of AI in education, regulatory measures, intellectual property issues, ethical issues, and responsible AI implementing approaches.

Chapter 14: Ethical Frictions in AI-Enhanced Learning Environments A Comparative European Analysis

The integration of artificial intelligence in education is often framed as a technical implementation problem, overlooking the institutional decision-making processes in which its effects emerge. This article analyses how these structures change under conditions of technological uncertainty. Drawing on institutional and governance theory, it develops a mechanism-based model that conceptualises transformation as a sequence: technological triggers (T) generate conflicts (K), which are processed through institutional mechanisms (M) and stabilised in governance structures (G). Three core mechanisms are identified: diffusion of responsibility, coordination tension, and legitimacy reconstruction. Based on a theory-driven reconstruction of empirical studies and comparative analysis, the findings show a stable mechanism sequence across contexts, while variation in outcomes depends on governance configurations. The study shifts the focus from technological effects to institutional mechanisms and highlights conflict processing as the key condition for successful integration.

On behalf of all the co-editors,

Jan Vrba
Akademia Jagiellońska w Toruniu, Poland

Enrico Moch
GrandEdu Research School, Germany

Tobias Oberdieck
GrandEdu Research School, Germany

Acknowledgement

As editors, we wish to express our profound gratitude to all the contributors, mentors, and peers whose stimulating discussions and critical insights have fundamentally shaped the perspectives shared within these pages; their intellectual rigor and dedication to the field of educational technology have been indispensable.

A special mention belongs to the many students and learners across Europe and the World whose active engagement with AI and AR tools provided the essential practical foundation and real-world evidence for this research.

We are also deeply appreciative of the institutional support and collaborative spirit that made this cross-border exchange of knowledge possible; this work is a testament to the collective effort of all those striving to redefine the future of learning.

Editorial Advisory Board

The Editorial Advisory Board comprises distinguished scholars and practitioners whose expertise has guided the conceptual direction and academic rigor of this edited book. Their insights, critical perspectives, and ongoing support have been instrumental aspect in ensuring the quality and relevance of the contributions. We gratefully acknowledge their commitment to advancing responsible and impactful research in this field.

BSc. Quang Long Huynh, MBA, DBA

Mgr. Ondřej Bortlík, MBA

Ing. Josef Skokan, MBA

On behalf of all the co-editors and contributors,

Prof. PhDr. Mgr. Bc. Jan Vrba, Ph.D., D.B.A., MBA

Introduction

The landscape of modern education is undergoing a shift, driven by the rapid evolution of Artificial Intelligence (AI) and Augmented Reality (AR); as these technologies move from experimental novelties to integral educational tools, there is a pressing need to examine their impact through a localized, European lens. This volume, "European Perspectives on AI and AR Applications in Learning," seeks to bridge the gap between technological potential and pedagogical practice, offering a comprehensive look at how these innovations are being integrated across diverse European educational systems.

Europe's unique educational heritage – rooted in linguistic diversity, inclusivity, and a strong emphasis on critical thinking – provides a rich context for exploring digital transformation; this book brings together a collection of research, case studies, and theoretical frameworks that highlight how AI and AR are not merely augmenting traditional methods, but are fundamentally redefining the relationship between the learner, the educator, and the curriculum.

From personalized AI-driven tutoring systems that cater to diverse student needs to immersive AR environments that bring complex scientific concepts to life, the contributions within these pages showcase the ingenuity of the European research community.

By balancing technological enthusiasm with a critical eye toward ethics and accessibility, this work serves as both a roadmap and a catalyst for the future of learning in the digital age.

On behalf of all the co-editors and contributors,

Prof. PhDr. Mgr. Bc. Jan Vrba, Ph.D., D.B.A., MBA

"The best way to predict the future is to create it."

- Abraham Lincoln

Chapter 1
European Perspectives on Artificial Intelligence and Augmented Reality in Education:
Pedagogical Transformation, Ethical Governance, and the Future of Learning

Simon Baradziej
http://orcid.org/0009-0000-6561-6904
UiT - The Arctic University of Norway, Norway

ABSTRACT

This chapter examines how artificial intelligence (AI) and augmented reality (AR) are transforming education across Europe within the continent's unique regulatory, ethical, and cultural context. It explores the interplay between technological innovation and Europe's human-centric, rights-based vision of education. The analysis traces key policy instruments - including the EU Artificial Intelligence Act, the Digital Education Action Plan (2021–2027), the European Commission's Ethical Guidelines on AI and Data in Teaching and Learning, and the UNESCO Recommendation on the Ethics of AI, showing how they shape opportunities and limits for AI and AR integration in schools, universities, and lifelong learning. Reviewing emerging evidence on AI-driven personalised learning and AR-supported experiential environments, the chapter also addresses challenges of data protection, bias, automation, inequality, and learner agency. It concludes by mapping the current state of research and policy and outlining directions for future inquiry.

DOI: 10.4018/979-8-3373-9883-9.ch001

1. INTRODUCTION

The integration of artificial intelligence (AI) and augmented reality (AR) in education is one of the most significant changes in pedagogy. These technologies are increasingly integrated into teaching and learning globally. From intelligent tutoring systems that adapt to individual learner profiles in real time to immersive AR simulations that bring abstract scientific concepts into tangible, interactive experience. Yet the European approach to these technologies is fundamentally shaped by a set of values, norms, and regulatory traditions that distinguish it from developments elsewhere in the world. The European Union (EU) has positioned itself as a global leader in ethical frameworks ensuring AI serves humanity, pointing out principles of transparency, fairness, accountability, and respect for fundamental human rights.

This chapter maps the evolving European policy, governing AI and AR in education, tracing its' progress and trajectory from early ethical guidelines to legislation. It reviews the current state of empirical evidence regarding how AI and AR are being deployed to support personalised learning, adaptive assessments, immersive instructions, and teacher professional development across European educational contexts. Also, it critically examines the tensions, risks, and unresolved questions that come with the adoption of these technologies. For instance, it includes concerns about data privacy under the General Data Protection Regulation (GDPR), the algorithmic bias with the erosion of critical thinking, and the growing gap in access to technology within and across European nations.

1.1 A Bibliometric Perspective

To understand where European scholarship fits within the global field, it is worth looking at what bibliometric studies tell us about the increase of AI-in-education (AIEd) research. The evidence is clear. Delen et al. (2024), analysing 4,673 articles published between 1975 and 2023 in the Web of Science, found that the number of AIEd studies grew exponentially after 2010, with higher education research more popular than K-12 studies throughout the period. Their analysis also noted quite limited cooperation among the most productive authors and countries - a collaboration deficit that European research networks are well placed to address. A complementary analysis by Prokopyev et al. (2024) of 1,563 SCOPUS articles on AI in higher education confirmed a dramatic increase after 2019, matching with the popularization of generative AI tools, but found similarly limited interactions among research communities.

Looking more specifically at the discipline's composition of the field, Özdemir et al. (2024) examined 1,726 studies published between 2013 and 2023 and found that the USA and China dominate both publication volume and citation impact, with

European institutions classifying lower in global output. This geographic skew is also visible in AI literacy research; Kumar (2025), reviewing 902 peer-reviewed publications from 2021 to early 2025, identified uneven collaboration patterns, with Europe, Africa, and Southeast Asia all underrepresented relative to their share of global higher education enrolment. Guo et al. (2024), in what is the most complete bibliometric survey of the decade, covering AIEd research from 2013 to 2023, documented similar patterns of geographic concentration alongside rapid citation growth across the period.

2. THE EUROPEAN COMMITMENT TO HUMAN-CENTRIC TECHNOLOGY IN EDUCATION

2.1 Historical and Philosophical Foundations

Europe's approach to educational technology is deeply informed by its intellectual traditions of humanism, democracy, and individual rights. The European model consistently positions the learner and the educator at the centre of the technological equation. The European Commission's first AI strategy, published in 2018, stated the ambition of making the EU "a world-class hub for AI" while ensuring that AI remains "human-centric and trustworthy" (European Commission, 2018). This dual focus on excellence and trust has become the fundament of the European approach - distinguishing it from more market-driven, and commercial strategies in North America or the state-directed models that can be found in parts of Asia.

The philosophical base of this approach can be traced to the EU's foundational commitment to human dignity, freedom, democracy, equality, the rule of law, and respect for human rights, as written in the Treaty on European Union (Article 2). When applied to the domain of educational technology, these values translate into specific expectations. AI systems used in teaching must be transparent in their operations, fair in their outcomes, accountable to human oversight, and respectful of individual privacy. The High-Level Expert Group on Artificial Intelligence (AI HLEG) – a group created by the European Commission in 2018, operationalised these principles through its "Ethics Guidelines for Trustworthy AI,". These were published in April 2019 and identified seven key requirements for trustworthy AI:

(1) human agency and oversight; (2) technical robustness and safety; (3) privacy and data governance; (4) transparency; (5) diversity, non-discrimination, and fairness; (6) societal and environmental well-being; and (7) accountability (AI HLEG, 2019).

2.2 Transition From Principles to Practice

The transition from ethical principles to enforceable practice has been a core mission of European policymakers throughout the 2020s. While the AI HLEG guidelines were non-binding, they established a normative vocabulary and assessment framework that influenced subsequent legislative action. The accompanying Assessment List for Trustworthy AI (ALTAI) provided practical tools for organisations to evaluate whether their AI systems met the seven requirements. Simultaneously, the Erasmus+ funded "Trustworthy AI" project aimed to translate the guidelines into higher education curricula across disciplines, reflecting the EU's digital strategy emphasis on training professionals who can "shape technology in a way that respects European values" (European Commission, 2020).

Figure 1. European Policy Timeline (2016–2027)

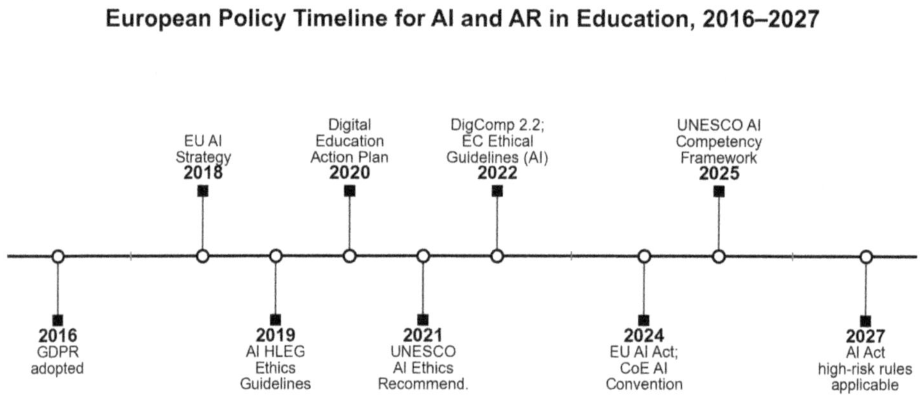

This ethical approach has significant implications for how AI and AR are adopted in educational institutions across Europe. Instead of treating technology adoption as a purely technical or economic decision, European frameworks oblige educators, administrators, and technology developers to take part in ongoing ethical discussion. The European approach positions education not just as a sector for technology deployment but as a domain where the responsible governance of AI is modelled, taught, and practised.

3. THE EUROPEAN REGULATORY AND POLICY FRAMEWORK

3.1 The EU Artificial Intelligence Act

The EU Artificial Intelligence Act (Regulation (EU) 2024/1689), adopted in 2024 and entering into force on 1 August 2024, marks a turning point in the global AI governance. As the first such comprehensive legal framework for regulating artificial intelligence across sectors. The Act establishes a classification system based on risk, that has direct implications for the education. The Act classifies AI systems used in education and vocational training as "high-risk," subjecting them to rigorous requirements for transparency, human oversight, data governance, risk assessment, and quality management.

Under the Act, providers of high-risk AI systems in education must disclose data sources, model logic, and decision outputs. They must implement quality-management systems, perform ongoing risk assessments and maintain human oversight for every high-risk AI system deployed in educational settings. Failure to comply, is subject to substantial fines and market withdrawal. The Act introduces a prohibition on AI systems designed to infer student emotions from facial, vocal, or biometric cues, classifying such systems as "unacceptable risk" and banning them in EU educational settings, except where such use is intended for medical or safety reasons (European Parliament and Council, 2024).

The Act also creates a framework for AI regulatory sandboxes under Articles 57 to 59, intended to foster innovation by providing controlled testing environments in which innovators and regulators work together to identify risks and ensure compliance. These sandboxes are particularly significant for educational technology (EdTech) startups and small and medium-sized enterprises (SMEs), which may otherwise struggle to navigate the complex compliance requirements. The EU Regulatory Sandboxes for AI (EUSAiR) project, funded by the Digital Europe programme, supports the implementation of these sandboxes across Member States, developing common frameworks and enhancing technical and legal capacities (European Commission, 2025).

The implications of the Act for teaching and learning are broad. Adaptive learning platforms, automated grading systems, and AI-driven admissions tools must now meet high standards for data quality, non-discrimination, and explainability. Universities deploying generative AI tools such as ChatGPT must assess whether their usage qualifies them as "deployers" under Article 3(4) of the Act, with corresponding obligations for transparency and human oversight. The Act transforms what was previously a voluntary ethical compliance into enforceable obligation. Marking a shift from "trust me" to "show me and prove it" approach (Swiss Cyber Institute, 2025).

3.2 The Digital Education Action Plan (2021-2027)

The Digital Education Action Plan (2021-2027), adopted by the European Commission on 30 September 2020, provides the overarching strategic framework for digital education in Europe. The Action Plan sets out a common vision of "high-quality, inclusive and accessible digital education" and identifies two strategic priorities: (1) fostering the development of a high-performing digital education system and (2) enhancing the digital skills and competences of learners and educators.

Among the Action Plan's 14 actions, several are directly relevant to AI and AR in education. Action 6 committed the Commission to developing ethical guidelines on the use of AI and data in teaching and learning for educators, which were published in October 2022. Action 8 called for updating the European Digital Competence Framework (DigComp) to include AI and data-related skills, resulting in the DigComp 2.2 update that now includes more than 70 examples of AI-related competences. Action 3 established the European Digital Education Content Framework, while Actions 4 and 5 addressed connectivity, digital equipment, and digital transformation plans for educational institutions.

The Action Plan serves as a connection between high-level EU strategies and the practical aspects of teaching. It recognises that the digital transformation of education requires not only technological infrastructure but also pedagogical changes, innovation, ethical awareness, and sustainable professional development for educators.

3.3 Ethical Guidelines for AI Use in Education

In October 2022, the European Commission published its "Ethical guidelines on the use of artificial intelligence (AI) and data in teaching and learning for educators." Developed by an Expert Group on AI and Data in Education and Training, which operated between July 2021 and June 2022, the guidelines provide practical support and guidance primarily for primary and secondary teachers, including those with little or no prior experience in using AI.

The guidelines serve multiple purposes - clarify common misconceptions about AI that may cause anxiety among educators; address the ethical considerations and requirements that should support the use of AI in schools. Also, offer practical advice on how to integrate AI into school education. A revision of the guidelines was announced for end of 2025, intended to address the latest developments in generative AI and provide improved practical materials. The guidelines also aim to nurture emerging competences for the ethical use of AI among teachers and educators, suggesting ways of raising awareness and engaging with the educational community.

3.4 The UNESCO Framework and International Alignment

While the EU has pursued its own legislative path, European approaches to AI in education are also shaped by international frameworks. Most notably the UNESCO Recommendation on the Ethics of Artificial Intelligence, adopted by 193 Member States in November 2021. The Recommendation is the first global instrument with standard for ethical AI. It establishes four foundational values (human rights and human dignity; peaceful, just, and interconnected societies; diversity and inclusiveness; and environment and ecosystem flourishing). Also, it has ten guiding principles, including proportionality, safety, fairness, sustainability, privacy, human oversight, transparency, responsibility, awareness, and multi-stakeholder governance (UNESCO, 2021).

In the domain of education, UNESCO has further developed the AI Competency Framework for Teachers, introduced during Digital Learning Week 2024, defining 15 competencies across five key areas. Human-centered mindset, ethics of AI, AI foundations and applications, AI pedagogy, and AI for professional learning. The framework establishes three progression levels (acquire, deepen, create) and provides a global reference for national competency development and teacher training programmes. A complementary AI Competency Framework for Students guides policymakers, educators, and curriculum developers in equipping students with the skills, knowledge, and values needed to engage with AI effectively.

The Council of Europe's Framework Convention on Artificial Intelligence and Human Rights, Democracy and the Rule of Law, adopted on 5 September 2024, adds another layer to the European regulatory architecture. As the first international legally binding treaty in the field of AI, the Convention aims to ensure the compatibility of AI systems with core values of human rights, democracy, and the rule of law, and was drafted with the participation of 46 Council of Europe member states alongside the European Union, the United States, and Israel (Council of Europe, 2024).

3.5 National and Institutional Responses

European regulatory influence extends beyond the supranational level into national education systems and individual institutions. Ireland's Higher Education Authority (HEA), for example, published a national policy framework on generative AI in teaching and learning in December 2025, grounded in five core principles: academic integrity, transparency, and accountability; equity and inclusion; critical engagement, human oversight, and AI literacy; privacy and data governance; and sustainable pedagogy (Higher Education Authority, 2025). The Coimbra Group, a network of European research-intensive universities, held its sixth High-Level Seminar on Education Policy on the theme of generative AI in higher education in

November 2024, engaging rectors, vice-rectors, students, and industry representatives in discussions on institutional policies and practices.

At the national level, the Bologna Process Implementation Report (2024) documents how European higher education systems are incorporating digital transformation into their strategic frameworks, with multiple countries developing national programmes focused on digital skills, blended learning, and AI integration. France launched the "Digital Demonstrators in Higher Education" initiative, supporting 17 institutional projects with a total budget of EUR 100 million. Finland's "Digivisio 2030" programme involves all Finnish higher education institutions in building flexible, digitally enabled learning opportunities. The Netherlands' "Npuls" programme (2022-2030) addresses technological improvements and the establishment of teaching and learning centres across institutions.

Estonia offers a particularly instructive case of how national policy and classroom reality can advance together. A large-scale survey by Granström and Oppi (2025) of 15,631 students across 91 Estonian schools, conducted in 2024, found that 74.2% of lower secondary students (grades 6-9) and 90.2% of upper secondary students (grades 10-12) were already using AI tools for learning, with approximately 70% relying on ChatGPT. Upper secondary students rated AI as effective learning tools ($M = 4.41/5$, $SD = 1.43$). The study also identified an implementation gap: student AI practices were evolving faster than pedagogical frameworks, which the authors described as an urgent policy challenge. Estonia responded by formally introducing AI literacy into its national curriculum from the 2025 academic year, making it one of the first countries in Europe to do so at scale. This sequence, from documented organic adoption to curricular formalisation, may offer a model for other European nations navigating the same transition.

4. ARTIFICIAL INTELLIGENCE IN EUROPEAN EDUCATION: APPLICATIONS AND EVIDENCE

4.1 Personalised Learning and Adaptive Systems

One of the most transformative applications of AI in education is the development of personalised learning systems that adapt (instructional content, pace, and assessment types) to individual learner needs. AI-driven personalised learning systems use techniques such as machine learning, natural language processing, knowledge representation, and learning analytics to dynamically adjust instruction based on learner interactions and performance data. These systems continuously analyse data derived from students' learning activities, behaviours, past performances, and individual characteristics, enabling the identification of patterns and insights into learning strengths, weaknesses, and preferences.

A systematic review of AI-driven adaptive learning systems in higher education, analysing 15 empirical studies published between 2020 and 2024, found that the predominant AI technologies include machine learning (40%), natural language processing (33%), and hybrid systems (27%), supporting real-time personalisation and adaptive feedback mechanisms. The review reported academic performance gains of 15 to 25% and improved learner engagement of up to 40% in contexts where adaptive AI systems were implemented. Specific algorithms employed in intelligent tutoring systems include Bayesian networks, decision trees, and deep learning models, which continuously update and refine learner models to allow for real-time adaptation of instructional strategies.

Figure 2. AI in Education Market Growth (2024–2030)

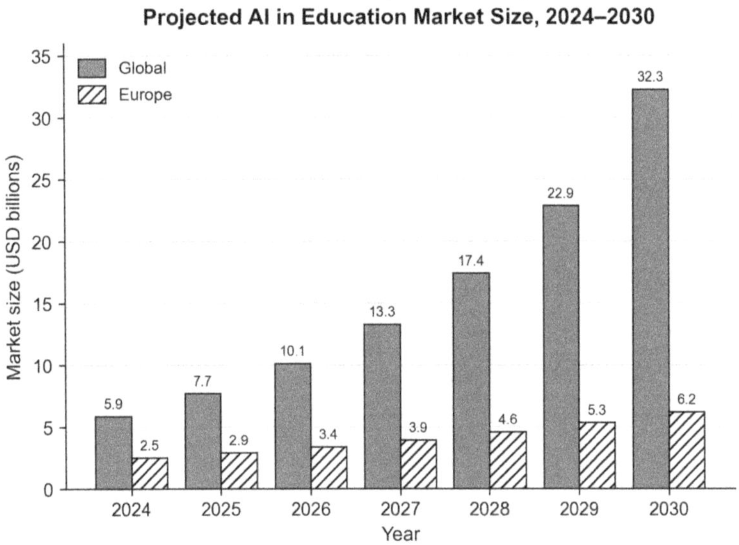

Market analyses indicate that the global AI in education market was estimated at approximately USD 5.88 billion in 2024, with projections reaching USD 32.27 billion by 2030, representing a compound annual growth rate (CAGR) of approximately 31.2%. Within Europe specifically, the education AI market is currently valued at approximately USD 2.5 billion, with projections reaching USD 6.2 billion by 2030. The broader European EdTech market was valued at USD 47.98 billion in 2024 and is projected to reach USD 142.44 billion by 2033, growing at a CAGR of 12.85%.

These systems offer several pedagogical affordances. They provide immediate, personalised feedback, helping students recognise and correct mistakes while giving educators valuable insights to refine their teaching strategies. They support continuous knowledge assessment, ensuring that concepts are well understood before progressing to subsequent material. They create individual learning pathways that engage each learner in activities customised to their specific needs. A meta-analysis of AI-based interventions on self-regulated learning demonstrated a large and statistically significant positive effect, with interventions producing moderate improvements in cognitive and metacognitive dimensions and meaningfully enhancing learners' capacity to plan, monitor, and regulate their learning activities (Achuthan et al., 2025).

Figure 3. Meta-Analytic Effect Sizes of AR and AI Interventions

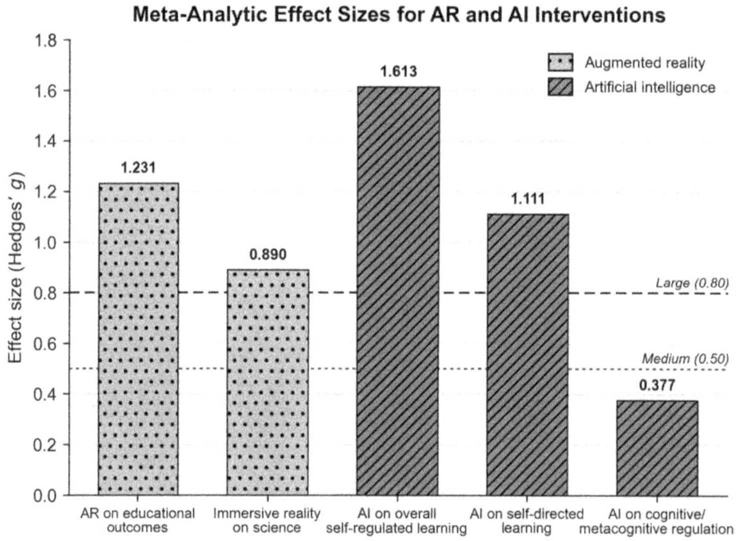

4.2 Intelligent Tutoring Systems

Intelligent tutoring systems (ITS) are a relatively mature area of AI in education research. Having enough evidence supporting their effectiveness. These systems employ machine learning, natural language processing, and explainable AI to enhance the learning experience through improved student engagement, timely feedback, and adaptive instructional strategies. A thorough review of AI-based ITS identified multiple pedagogical strategies, including expert systems utilising predefined rules and domain knowledge, case-based reasoning systems referencing past cases to solve new problems, and cognitive tutors modelling students' cognitive processes to provide individualised instruction.

In the European context, ITS have been deployed across multiple disciplines, with particular strength in STEM fields, language learning, and hybrid learning environments. The integration of generative AI, particularly large language models (LLMs), into ITS has expanded capabilities for dynamic content generation, real-time feedback, and interactive dialogue systems that respond to individual learner needs (Khan et al., 2024). Research on personalised AI tutoring has demonstrated that personalised, active learning AI-powered systems can achieve completion rates and learning gains 2 to 2.5 times higher than those achieved by students on conventional platforms or in control groups without personalised feedback (St-Hilaire et al., 2022).

Education 4.0 research, synthesising 20 high-quality studies published between 2020 and 2025, has identified three major insights: (i) ITS and LLMs enhance learner motivation and performance while supporting teachers with adaptive feedback; (ii) persistent gaps remain in long-term evaluation, ethical design, and implementation in under-resourced settings; and (iii) most studies are limited to short-term or well-resourced contexts, raising concerns about generalisability. This last point is particularly relevant for the European context, where educational resources vary significantly across and within Member States.

4.3 Generative AI Impact on European Higher Education

The emergence of generative AI (GenAI) tools, particularly ChatGPT, has introduced new dynamics into European higher education. European universities have adopted a range of responses, from an experimental integration to proactive policy development. The Coimbra Group's November 2024 seminar brought together institutional leaders and students to discuss opportunities, challenges, and institutional policies for GenAI adoption, with particular emphasis on AI literacy, equity and inclusion, and ethical considerations.

The EU AI Act creates specific regulatory obligations for generative AI. Providers of general-purpose AI (GPAI) models, such as those underlying ChatGPT, face transparency obligations and restrictions that began applying in August 2025. Universities using such models must determine their status as "deployers" under the Act, with corresponding obligations for transparency, human oversight, and risk assessment. Providers located outside the EU who wish to make general purpose AI models available in the EU market must appoint representatives within the Union (European Parliament and Council, 2024, Article 54).

At the institutional level, growing numbers of European universities are developing GenAI policies that balance innovation with academic integrity. Ireland's HEA framework is a good example of this, providing a national reference point grounded in principles of academic integrity, equity, critical engagement, privacy, and sustainable pedagogy. The framework emphasises the need to "move beyond both uncritical adoption and uncritical rejection" toward a principled approach that maintains academic judgement and educational excellence at the centre of teaching and learning (O'Sullivan, 2025; Mosha et al., 2026).

5. AUGMENTED REALITY IN EUROPEAN EDUCATION

5.1 Theoretical Foundations and Pedagogical Affordances

Augmented reality is a technology that combines the physical world with computer-generated virtual elements by superimposing information on the real environment through devices such as tablets, smartphones, or specialised visors. AR has attracted increasing research attention in European education. The theoretical basis for AR in education draws on constructivist and experiential learning theories, which emphasise the importance of active engagement, contextual learning, and the construction of knowledge through interaction with the environment.

Research from the Universitat Oberta de Catalunya (UOC) has characterised AR as a "crucial catalyst for interactive learning," demonstrating positive impacts on student engagement and participation in the classroom. The study further highlighted the need for resources and the importance of developing teaching staff's digital skills to maximise the educational potential of AR. AR technologies "not only allow content to be visualized more attractively, but also facilitate the understanding of complex concepts through interactive three-dimensional models" (Duart et al., 2024).

A systematic review analysing 53 articles from the past decade, drawn from six major academic databases (Scopus, Web of Science, ScienceDirect, ERIC, IEEE Xplore, and the ACM Digital Library), found that the adoption of AR and VR in education has produced mostly positive outcomes, especially in improving learning, enhancing student engagement, and developing both cognitive and non-cognitive skills. The integration of AR and VR technologies has been shown to improve spatial reasoning capabilities, with studies reporting 35 to 45% better performance in three-dimensional conceptualisation tasks (AREdu, 2025).

5.2 The ARETE Project: A Pan-European Case Study

The Augmented Reality Interactive Educational System (ARETE), a Horizon 2020 project coordinated by University College Dublin and involving 10 partners from seven countries (Ireland, Spain, the Netherlands, Germany, Belgium, Italy, and the United Kingdom), is one of the most ambitious European efforts to develop and evaluate AR for educational purposes. Running from November 2019 to April 2023, ARETE aimed to build a pan-European educational platform providing AR learning content to a wide audience.

The project conducted four large-scale pilot studies involving more than 3,000 students and teachers across European countries. Pilot 1 investigated the effects of AR on English literacy attainment using an interactive AR mobile application for primary school students, while Pilot 2 studied the impact of AR technologies on STEM skills learning and retention through immersive AR applications for geography and geometry. The pilots were implemented across multiple countries, including Ireland, Sweden, Luxembourg, Italy, and the United Kingdom.

ARETE's evaluation, led by the University of Wurzburg, examined impacts on student motivation, learning outcomes, and engagement. The project received the CEN/CENELEC Standards+Innovation Award 2022 for Best Research Project, recognising its contribution to establishing standards for AR in learning and performance augmentation. The Open University's Institute of Educational Technology (IET) led the technical development, building interactive AR toolkits and working on formal standards for XR (extended reality) learning, teaching, and training activities, including policy and regulatory guidance for XR ethics, safety, and user experience (Wild, 2022).

5.3 AR in STEM and Medical Education

AR has shown particular promise in STEM education and healthcare training across Europe. A case study from Sofia, Bulgaria, showed the effectiveness of AR for delivering STEM content in secondary schools, with positive impacts on student understanding and engagement over a full school year of implementation (Terzieva et al., 2020). In STEAM education, research from European institutions has shown that combining STEM subjects with the arts using AR-based active learning formats provides a more holistic and engaging educational experience (Achuthan, 2025).

In medical and nursing education, AR applications are gaining interest and traction across European healthcare training institutions. A meta-analysis demonstrated that AR and mixed reality (MR) have been applied in medical education across Europe and other regions, with findings indicating that AR/MR improves medical skill performance in terms of accuracy and speed, particularly for spatial-visual tasks such as surgery (Li et al., 2025). The ALIAS (Augmented Reality in Intensive Care Education for Nursing Students) project, an Erasmus+ funded initiative involving the University of West Attica (Greece), the University of Parma (Italy), University College Dublin (Ireland), and Metropolitano College (Greece), uses AR simulations to prepare nursing students for real-life situations in intensive care units. A German initiative at the Pflegebildungszentrum in Siegen, supported by the EDIH Sudwestfalen, developed and tested AR-based learning scenarios for care students, demonstrating the potential of interactive technologies to consolidate practical knowledge through new methods.

5.4 Quantitative Evidence: Meta-Analytic Findings

The empirical evidence supporting AR's educational effectiveness is substantial and growing. A meta-analysis of quasi-experimental studies examining the impact of AR on educational achievements found a considerable average estimated effect size of 1.231 with an exceedingly low *p*-value ($p < 0.001$), indicating a highly significant statistical association between AR use and heightened educational outcomes (Hunaepi et al., 2023). A separate meta-analysis on the effect of immersive reality applications on science achievement, with 32 effect size values from 23 studies, revealed a statistically significant effect with Hedges' $g = 0.89$, indicating a high effect on students' science achievement.

The evolution of AR/VR in education has followed a noticeable growth. The period from 2018 onwards saw enhanced immersive tools, particularly with mixed-reality platforms such as Microsoft HoloLens integrating AR and VR technologies. The COVID-19 pandemic accelerated adoption of immersive technologies to simulate in-person experiences, driven by increased demand for virtual classrooms and online education. By 2024, the integration of generative AI with AR and VR brought these technologies to new heights, enabling the creation of interactive and immersive learning materials including simulations and virtual labs that enhanced student engagement through game-based learning environments.

6. ETHICAL CONCERNS AND PERSISTENT CHALLENGES

6.1 Data Protection and Privacy

The processing of student data by AI systems in education raises fundamental questions about privacy and data protection that are governed by the General Data Protection Regulation (GDPR) in the European context. The GDPR, which can impose fines of up to EUR 20,000,000 or 4% of global annual turnover for infractions, establishes principles of lawfulness, fairness, transparency, purpose limitation, data minimisation, accuracy, storage limitation, integrity, confidentiality, and accountability (European Parliament and Council, 2016).

AI-driven personalised learning systems, by their nature, require processing of personal data, including learner interactions, performance records, behavioural patterns, and individual characteristics. Under GDPR, if AI providers process student or staff data, educational institutions must establish clear controller-processor relationships and ensure processing agreements are in place. When AI projects are likely to impact privacy, such as profiling students or processing data at scale, institutions must perform a Data Protection Impact Assessment (DPIA) to identify and mitigate risks, including risks of re-identification of anonymised data, unintended bias affecting protected groups, or potential violations if outputs are misused (8allocate, 2026).

The Information and Data Protection Commissioner (IDPC) of Malta has specifically highlighted the high risk of AI applications in education; including biased admissions systems, automated grading, and behavioural monitoring, which can significantly affect students' future and violate their fundamental right to data protection. Educators have been urged to critically assess AI-driven decision-making, particularly regarding progression or access to support, and to comply with Article 22 of the GDPR by avoiding decisions made solely by automated or autonomous means. The Commissioner stressed that AI should support, not replace, human judgement, ensuring human intervention to prevent long-term academic or professional prejudice.

6.2 Algorithmic Bias and Fairness

The risk of algorithmic bias in educational AI systems has been as a central concern in European policy discussion. AI systems can preserve biases present in their training data, amplifying stereotypes and disadvantaging certain groups unfairly. In education, this is particularly concerning because biased AI systems can undermine the pluralism, equity, and inclusion that European educational values seek to foster.

The European Commission has taken significant steps to address discriminatory bias in AI, as documented through an analysis of 21 EU regulatory and ethical guidelines spanning the period from GDPR to the AI Act, from which 152 measures were extracted, differentiated between design, governance, and end-user recommendations (Cerezo-Martinez et al., 2024). The EU AI Act obliges developers to use representative datasets and explicitly prohibits models that discriminate by race, gender, or socioeconomic status in educational settings. Article 10(5) of the Act introduces a novel provision allowing providers to collect sensitive data specifically for the purpose of bias detection and correction, reflecting the recognition that addressing bias may require access to the very categories of data that discrimination law typically restricts (European Parliament and Council, 2024).

At the research level, the NoBIAS project, a Marie Sklodowska-Curie Innovative Training Network, trained 15 doctoral students from six countries in "fairness awareness," aiming to reduce biases in machine learning at all stages: understanding bias in data, mitigating bias in algorithms, and accounting for bias in results. The project adopted an interdisciplinary approach, combining perspectives from computer science, law, and social science, with each doctoral student connected to a partner organisation applying AI in specific fields (Nejdl, 2024).

6.3 Over-Reliance on AI and the Erosion of Critical Thinking

A growing body of evidence suggests that excessive dependence on AI tools may erode critical thinking skills and promote cognitive offloading, raising concerns about the long-term impact on learner development. A study by Gerlich (2025) at SBS Swiss Business School, involving 666 participants in the United Kingdom, demonstrated a significant negative correlation between AI tool usage and critical thinking scores ($r = -0.68$, $p < 0.001$). Frequent AI users exhibited diminished ability to critically evaluate information and engage in reflective problem-solving. Cognitive offloading was strongly correlated with AI tool usage ($r = +0.72$) and inversely related to critical thinking ($r = -0.75$), with mediation analysis revealing that cognitive offloading partially explains the negative relationship between AI reliance and critical thinking performance.

These findings are in line with broader concerns about "deskilling" in AI-mediated environments. Verghis et al. (2025), synthesising empirical evidence through the lenses of Cognitive Load Theory and Bloom's Taxonomy, found that AI-assisted students sometimes solved significantly more problems correctly yet showed lower scores on subsequent concept-understanding tests, pointing to a trade-off between immediate performance gains and deeper conceptual learning. Fan et al. (2024) have introduced the term "metacognitive laziness" to describe how generative AI reduces students' self-monitoring and self-regulation, a concern that is especially acute in higher education where developing these capacities is a core goal. More broadly, students who rely on AI-generated summaries, solutions, or analyses may bypass the essential cognitive processes of forming hypotheses, analysing results, and drawing independent conclusions. Medical education research has raised parallel concerns, noting that overreliance on generative AI risks weakening clinical reasoning skills among medical students and newly qualified doctors through automation bias, cognitive offloading, and the blunting of skills that are still being developed.

The challenge for European educators and policymakers is to find an appropriate balance. AI should serve as a tool that enhances learning without replacing the cognitive work essential to intellectual development. This requires careful pedagogical design, explicit instruction in critical AI literacy, and institutional policies that promote reflective engagement with technology rather than passive consumption.

6.4 The Digital Divide in European Education

Despite Europe's advanced technological infrastructure relative to other world regions, significant digital divides persist within and across EU Member States. It creates a threat of turning AI and AR into instruments of inequality rather than equity. A cross-national survey across seven European countries found that 42% of low-income students do not have stable access to hybrid learning models, whether due to poor broadband, outdated devices, or lack of digital literacy support (Cooper, 2025). In Southern Italy, Eastern Poland, and rural Romania, many students still lack basic digital infrastructure.

The scale of this problem becomes clearer when viewed through EU-level data. Holmarsdottir et al. (2023), drawing on EU-SILC data from 32 European countries, found that an average of 5.4% of school-aged children (ages 6-16) are digitally deprived, meaning those living in households that cannot afford a computer and/or internet connection. The gap between the best and worst performers was stark: digital deprivation affected just 0.7% of Estonian children but 23.1% of Romanian children and 20.8% of Bulgarian children. Children from severely materially deprived households were 6.9 times more likely to be digitally excluded, and those from low-educated family backgrounds 3.3 times more likely, confirming that the digital divide is not a separate problem from poverty but rather one of its clearest expressions.

A European-level study of AI in secondary schools reported that 51% of students experience insufficient internet access, and only 46% report being able to use AI in their schools without difficulties. Access disparities are particularly pronounced in certain national contexts: 74% of Greek students reported a lack of access to digital devices at school, well above the European average of 59%, while both Greek and Portuguese schools reported internet connectivity challenges (65% and 62% respectively). Furthermore, the lower the parents' income, the less access students have to AI tools in schools.

In Europe, 49% of students fear that AI could create inequalities in success among peers, and 34% worry about having fewer opportunities than their classmates to leverage the advantages of AI in their education. These concerns are not merely hypothetical; they reflect lived experiences of differential access to technologies that increasingly shape educational outcomes.

Addressing the digital divide requires multi-level intervention. Amongst other, it may be investing in rural internet access and campus-level digital infrastructure; providing targeted subsidies for devices and connectivity for low-income students; embedding digital literacy and AI governance into curricula so that access translates into capability; and strengthening cross-border collaboration to share best practices and scale solutions. The European Commission's EdTech support mechanisms, including European Digital Innovation Hubs (EDIHs), which operate as over 150 regional centres delivering AI expertise and innovation support to businesses and educational institutions, are one part of this effort.

7. TEACHER AND LEARNER AGENCY IN AI-AFFECTED EDUCATION

7.1 Redefining the Role of the Teacher

The integration of AI into educational settings is fundamentally transforming the teacher-student relationship into what UNESCO has described as a "teacher-AI-student dynamic" (UNESCO, 2024). This change requires a re-assessment of teachers' roles and the competencies they need in an era of AI enhanced education. Yet, few countries have defined these competencies or developed national programmes to train teachers in AI competencies, leaving many educators without guidance.

The UNESCO AI Competency Framework for Teachers addresses this gap by defining 15 competencies across five dimensions: human-centred mindset, ethics of AI, AI foundations and applications, AI pedagogy, and AI for professional learning. The European Digital Competence Framework for Educators (DigCompEdu), developed by the European Commission's Joint Research Centre, complements this international framework by describing 22 competences organised in six areas: professional engagement, digital resources, teaching and learning, assessment, empowering learners, and facilitating learners' digital competence. The AI Pioneers project has developed a supplement to the DigCompEdu framework that integrates critical competencies relating to AI in education, recognising that AI is transforming teaching and learning processes and that educators need skills to understand, evaluate, and utilise AI technologies effectively and responsibly.

The PAIDEIA (Preparing Teachers for the AI Development in Education as an Innovative Asset) project, funded under Erasmus+, has developed a Teacher Competence Framework for Working with AI based on the European Digital Competence Framework, addressing the question of what key AI competencies non-ICT teachers should possess to effectively use AI in the educational process. Evidence from the AREdu 2025 workshop revealed nuanced adoption patterns: while 63.6% of educators deemed interactive technologies appropriate for their courses, 100% required methodological assistance, highlighting the critical gap between tool availability and pedagogical integration.

7.2 Learner Agency and Self-Regulated Learning

A fundamental concern in the deployment of AI in education is its impact on learner agency, understood as students' capacity for self-directed, autonomous learning. Self-regulated learning (SRL) with goal setting, performance monitoring, and reflection, is widely recognised as essential for educational success and lifelong learning. The question of whether AI supports or undermines this capacity is one of the most critical issues in the field.

A systematic review exploring the intersection of AI applications and SRL in higher education, adhering to PRISMA guidelines, identified 14 distinct studies that leveraged AI applications, including chatbots, adaptive feedback systems, serious games, and e-textbooks, to support student autonomy. The findings revealed a picture where AI shows potential in facilitating SRL's planning, performance, and reflection phases. Yet, also highlights tensions between human-centred and AI-centred agency, leading to variations in the SRL model. The review underscored the importance for balanced AI integration, "ensuring technological advantages are harnessed without undermining student self-efficacy" (Achuthan et al., 2025).

A meta-analysis of 32 empirical studies containing 92 effect sizes and 3,029 participants found that AI interventions demonstrated a large and statistically significant positive effect on overall SRL (Hedges' $g = 1.613$, $p = 0.032$) and self-directed learning (Hedges' $g = 1.111$, $p = 0.043$). These results indicate that well-designed AI tools can meaningfully enhance learners' capacity to plan, monitor, and regulate their learning activities while fostering autonomy and persistence. Across SRL dimensions, AI produced moderate improvements in cognitive and metacognitive dimensions (Hedges' $g = 0.377$, $p = 0.0004$).

But these positive findings must be read alongside the evidence on over-reliance and cognitive offloading discussed in Section 6.3. The European Data Protection Supervisor has noted a growing trend towards developing systems that aim to enhance skills like self-regulation and creativity, "rather than merely optimising knowledge delivery based on past data," and has emphasised the importance of fostering human-AI collaboration to "support, not replace, human cognition and social learning" (EDPS, 2024). Personalised learning systems that look ahead could build on developments in agentic AI, AI companions, and automated monitoring. Still, these possibilities carry corresponding risks that require careful ethical governance.

7.3 AI for Democratic Education

Apart from individual learning outcomes, European discussion on the role of AI in education for democracy is popular. The Democrat project, a European initiative, is experimenting with approaches to embed democratic values, competencies, and practices into learning environments across education. The project recognises that AI is not just a tool for automating tasks but is transforming how information flows, and how learners acquire knowledge about citizenship, society and participation in it.

From this perspective, democratic competence in the digital age must include a critical understanding of AI itself: learners need to recognise how AI shapes their exposure to information, how biases can be added to systems, or how automated tools can affect civic engagement. AI can also serve as a tool for teaching critical thinking: AI-powered platforms can simulate scenarios involving misinformation, enabling learners to distinguish between credible and misleading content, and provide real-time feedback on reasoning to help students analyse arguments and identify logical fallacies.

The risk that students and educators rely too heavily on AI outputs and treat them as authoritative is real. Democracy thrives on human judgement, debate, and reflection, not on automated answers. Educational AI systems should therefore be presented as assistive tools that complement, rather than replace, the human capacities for reasoning and ethical consideration on which democracy depends. To harness the potential of AI for education for democracy while mitigating its risks, technological innovation must be deliberately aligned with democratic values, requiring the integration of AI literacy into curricula and the establishment of clear ethical and governance frameworks.

8. FUTURE DIRECTIONS

Several trends will shape the future of AI and AR in European education. The combination of AI and immersive technologies is creating new possibilities for hybrid learning environments. The integration of generative AI with AR and VR made the creation of increasingly sophisticated interactive and immersive learning materials possible. Including simulations, virtual labs, and game-based learning environments that foster active participation. This convergence is likely to accelerate, with future systems offering more seamless integration of AI-driven personalisation with immersive spatial experiences.

The implementation of the EU AI Act will drive a significant transformation in how educational technology is developed, evaluated, and deployed across Europe. As the Act's provisions concerning high-risk AI systems in education become fully applicable by August 2027, institutions will need to develop robust compliance frameworks, including registration in the EU database, ongoing risk assessments, and mechanisms for human supervision. This will require investment in institutional capacity and development of new relationships between educational institutions and technology providers.

Also, the growing emphasis on AI literacy, both for educators and learners, points to the need for thorough, curriculum-integrated approaches to understanding AI. The DigComp 2.2 framework's inclusion of more than 70 AI-related competence examples reflects this priority. Future research should examine how AI literacy programmes are implemented across diverse European educational contexts and what impacts they have on learners' critical engagement with technology.

The digital divide remains a critical concern that threatens to undermine the equity objectives of European education policy. With 42% of low-income students lacking stable access to hybrid learning and significant variations in digital infrastructure across Member States, addressing inequality must remain a central priority. Future research should investigate the effectiveness of targeted interventions, including infrastructure investment, device subsidies, and digital literacy programmes, in reducing disparities.

Questions of long-term impacts on cognitive development, critical thinking, and learner autonomy requires sustained empirical investigation. The evidence on cognitive offloading and deskilling suggests that the design of AI systems for education must attend not only to immediate learning outcomes but also to the development of enduring intellectual capacities. Longitudinal studies tracking the impact of AI-mediated learning on students' cognitive and metacognitive development are urgently needed.

9. CONCLUDING REMARKS

The European approach to AI and AR in education is characterised by a tension between technological ambition and ethics in mind. On one hand, European institutions are investing in the development and deployment of AI-driven personalised learning systems, intelligent tutoring platforms, and immersive AR learning environments - recognising their potential to enhance educational quality, equity, and access. On the other hand, the regulatory architecture being constructed through the EU AI Act, the Digital Education Action Plan, the Ethical Guidelines for Educators, and complementary international instruments reflects a fundamental conviction that technological innovation in education must be governed by principles of transparency, fairness, accountability, and respect for human dignity.

This dual orientation creates both challenges and opportunities. The compliance requirements of the EU AI Act impose significant burdens on educational institutions and technology developers, particularly smaller organisations with limited resources. The digital divide within and across European nations means that the benefits of AI and AR are not evenly distributed, with students from lower-income backgrounds and less-connected regions at risk of being left behind. The evidence on over-reliance and cognitive offloading raises questions about the long-term cognitive effects of AI-mediated learning.

Yet the European model also offers quite a compelling vision of what responsible technology integration in education may look like. By insisting that AI systems in education are transparent, accountable, and subjected to human oversight, European frameworks create the conditions for trust between technology and its users. By investing in teacher professional development and AI literacy, these frameworks acknowledge that technology adoption without pedagogical transformation is unlikely to deliver meaningful educational improvement. By engaging with questions of equity, access, and democratic values, European approaches ensure that the conversation about AI in education goes beyond technical capabilities, to take into consideration wider societal considerations that education serves.

Declarations

The ChatUiT AI-editing tool, provided by the University of Tromsø - The Arctic University of Norway, was used for professional language editing services of this chapter, aligned with all AI ethical editing guidelines. Author has checked and validated all the outputs manually.

REFERENCES

8allocate. (2026). FERPA/GDPR for AI in education: A practical deployment checklist. 8allocate Blog. https://8allocate.com/blog/ferpa-gdpr-for-ai-in-education-a-practical-deployment-checklist/

Achuthan, K.. (2025). Artificial intelligence and learner autonomy: A meta-analysis of self-regulated and self-directed learning. *Frontiers in Education*, *10*, 1738751. DOI: 10.3389/feduc.2025.1738751

AI HLEG. (2019). Ethics guidelines for trustworthy AI. European Commission, High-Level Expert Group on Artificial Intelligence. https://digital-strategy.ec.europa.eu/en/library/ethics-guidelines-trustworthy-ai

ARETE Project. (2023). D6.5 Pilots performance analysis. *Zenodo*. DOI: 10.5281/zenodo.7940994

Cerezo-Martinez, P., Nicolas-Sanchez, A., & Castro-Toledo, F. J. (2024). Analyzing the European institutional response to ethical and regulatory challenges of artificial intelligence in addressing discriminatory bias. *Frontiers in Artificial Intelligence*, *7*, 1393259. DOI: 10.3389/frai.2024.1393259 PMID: 38983275

Coimbra Group. (2025). Generative artificial intelligence in higher education: Literacy and inclusion. Report from the Sixth High-Level Seminar on Education Policy. https://www.coimbra-group.eu/generative-artificial-intelligence-in-higher-education-literacy-and-inclusion/

Cooper, M. (2025). Bridging the digital divide in European higher education. LinkedIn. https://www.linkedin.com/posts/matthew-cooper-university_bridging-the-digital-divide-in-european-higher

Council of Europe. (2024). Framework Convention on Artificial Intelligence and Human Rights, Democracy and the Rule of Law. Council of Europe Treaty Series. https://www.coe.int/en/web/artificial-intelligence/the-framework-convention

Delen, I., Şen, N., Ozudogru, F., & Biasutti, M. (2024). Understanding the growth of artificial intelligence in educational research through bibliometric analysis. *Sustainability (Basel)*, *16*(16), 6724. DOI: 10.3390/su16166724

Democrat Project. (2026). How AI can shape education for democracy: Opportunities and risks. https://democrat-horizon.eu/how-ai-can-shape-education-for-democracy/

Duart, J. M., Cufuna, D. S. A., & Rangel-de Lazaro, G. (2024). Augmented reality, a tool to encourage participatory learning and student involvement. Universitat Oberta de Catalunya. https://www.uoc.edu/en/news/2025/augmented-reality-a-tool-to-encourage-participatory-learning-and-student-involvement

European Commission. (2018). *Artificial intelligence for Europe. Communication from the Commission, COM(2018) 237 final.* European Commission.

European Commission. (2020). *Digital Education Action Plan 2021-2027. Communication from the Commission, COM(2020) 624 final.* European Commission.

European Commission. (2022). Ethical guidelines on the use of artificial intelligence (AI) and data in teaching and learning for educators. Publications Office of the European Union. https://education.ec.europa.eu/node/2285

European Commission. (2025). European approach to artificial intelligence. Digital Strategy. https://digital-strategy.ec.europa.eu/en/policies/european-approach-artificial-intelligence

European Data Protection Supervisor. (2024). AI-driven personalised learning. TechSonar. https://www.edps.europa.eu/data-protection/technology-monitoring/techsonar/ai-driven-personalised-learning_en

European Parliament and Council. (2016). Regulation (EU) 2016/679 of the European Parliament and of the Council of 27 April 2016 on the protection of natural persons with regard to the processing of personal data (General Data Protection Regulation). *Official Journal of the European Union, L, 119*, 1–88.

European Parliament and Council. (2024). *Regulation (EU) 2024/1689 of the European Parliament and of the Council laying down harmonised rules on artificial intelligence (Artificial Intelligence Act).* Official Journal of the European Union.

EUSAiR. (2025). EU Regulatory Sandboxes for AI: Roadmap. Digital Europe Programme. https://eusair-project.eu/

Fan, Y., Tang, L., Le, H., Shen, K., Tan, S., Zhao, Y., Shen, Y., Li, X., & Gašević, D. (2024). Beware of metacognitive laziness: Effects of generative artificial intelligence on learning motivation, processes, and performance. *British Journal of Educational Technology*. Advance online publication. DOI: 10.1111/bjet.13544

Gerlich, M. (2025). AI tools in society: Impacts on cognitive offloading and the future of critical thinking. *Societies (Basel, Switzerland), 15*(1), 6. DOI: 10.3390/soc15010006

Granström, M., & Oppi, P. (2025). Student engagement with AI tools in learning: Evidence from a large-scale Estonian survey. *Frontiers in Education*, *10*, 1688092. DOI: 10.3389/feduc.2025.1688092

Guo, S., Zheng, Y., & Zhai, X. (2024). Artificial intelligence in education research during 2013-2023: A review based on bibliometric analysis. *Education and Information Technologies*, *29*(13), 16387–16409. Advance online publication. DOI: 10.1007/s10639-024-12491-8

Higher Education Authority. (2025). Generative AI in higher education teaching and learning: Policy framework. HEA Ireland. https://hea.ie/2025/12/22/hea-publishes-national-policy-framework-on-generative-ai-in-teaching-and-learning/

Holmarsdottir, H. B., Ayllón, S., & Lado, S. (2023). Digitally deprived children in Europe. *Child Indicators Research*, *16*(3), 643–668. DOI: 10.1007/s12187-022-10006-w PMID: 36618273

Hunaepi, H., Sudiatmika, A. A. I. A., & Fadly, W. (2023). Augmented reality in education: A meta-analysis of (quasi) experimental investigations. Retorika. *Jurnal Ilmu Bahasa*, *9*(3), 78–91. DOI: 10.22225/jr.9.3.9066.78-91

Joint Research Centre. (2017). European Framework for the Digital Competence of Educators (DigCompEdu). [EN, Publications Office of the European Union.]. *EUR*, •••, 28775.

Joint Research Centre. (2022). Digital Competence Framework (DigComp). Publications Office of the European Union. https://joint-research-centre.ec.europa.eu/digcompedu_en

Khan, M. A., ... (2024). Generative AI and its impact on personalized intelligent tutoring systems. arXiv preprint arXiv:2410.10650.

Kumar, J. A. (2025). The global landscape of research on AI literacy: A bibliometric analysis of trends, collaborations, and emerging themes. *Proceedings of the IEEE Frontiers in Education Conference*. DOI: 10.1109/FIE63693.2025.11328420

Li, Y.. (2025). The effectiveness of augmented reality/mixed reality in medical education. *BMC Medical Education*, *25*(1), 1–15. PMID: 39743510

Malta, I. D. P. C. (2025). IDPC raises awareness on AI data protection concerns for students including higher education settings. https://idpc.org.mt/news-latest/idpc-raises-awareness-on-ai-data-protection-concerns-for-students-including-higher-education-settings

Market Data Forecast. (2025). Europe Edtech market size, share and growth report, 2033. https://www.marketdataforecast.com/market-reports/europe-edtech-market

Mosha, N. F. V., Chigwada, J., Ketchiwou, G. F., & Ngulube, P. (2026). A systematic review of artificial intelligence in higher education institutions (HEIs): Functionalities, challenges, and best practices. *Education Sciences*, *16*(2), 185. DOI: 10.3390/educsci16020185

Nejdl, W. (2024). Fairness awareness training helps researchers reduce AI bias. NoBIAS Project, Marie Sklodowska-Curie Innovative Training Network. https://cordis.europa.eu/article/id/454703-fairness-awareness-training-helps-researchers-reduce-ai-bias

O'Sullivan, J. (2025). *Generative AI in higher education teaching and learning: Policy framework*. Higher Education Authority.

Özdemir, D., Durak, G., Can, S., & Çankaya, S. (2024). Artificial intelligence in education: A bibliometric study on its role in transforming teaching and learning. *International Review of Research in Open and Distance Learning*, *25*(3), 219–244. DOI: 10.19173/irrodl.v25i3.7757

PAIDEIA Project. (2024). D 3.2: AI&EDcomp Framework: Teacher competence framework for working with AI. Erasmus+ Project 101132955.

Precedence Research. (2026). AI in education market size to surpass USD 136.79 billion by 2035. Yahoo Finance. https://finance.yahoo.com/news/ai-education-market-size-surpass-095500912.html

Prokopyev, A., Kalmazova, N. A., Molodozhnikova, N. M., Akhmadieva, R. S., Belova, T., & Spichak, V. Yu. (2024). Research trends in the use of artificial intelligence in higher education. *Frontiers in Education*, *9*, 1438715. DOI: 10.3389/feduc.2024.1438715

Skills Upload Jr. (2024). AI in European schools: A European report comparing seven countries. https://skillsuploadjr.eu/docs/contents/AI_in_European_schools.pdf

St-Hilaire, F., Vu, D.D., Frau, A., Burns, N., Faraji, F., Potochny, J., Robert, S., Roussel, A., Zheng, S., Glazier, T., Romano, J.V., Belfer, R., Shayan, M., Smofsky, A., Delarosbil, T., Ahn, S., Eden-Walker, S., Sony, K., Ching, A.O., Elkins, S., Stepanyan, A.Z., Matajová, A., Chen, V., Sahraei, H., Larson, R., Markova, N., Barkett, A., Charlin, L., Bengio, Y., Serban, I., & Kochmar, E. (2022). A new era: Intelligent tutoring systems will transform online learning for millions. ArXiv, abs/2203.03724.

Swiss Cyber Institute. (2025). The EU AI Act: Implications for ethical AI in education. https://swisscyberinstitute.com/research/eu-ai-act-implications-ethical-ai-education/

Terzieva, V.. (2020). The effect of augmented reality on students' learning performance in STEM education. *Information (Basel)*, *11*(4), 209. DOI: 10.3390/info11040209

Trustworthy, A. I. Project. (2022). Framework for Trustworthy AI Education. Erasmus+ Programme. https://www.trustworthyaiproject.eu/framework-for-trustworthy-ai-education/

UNESCO. (2021). Recommendation on the ethics of artificial intelligence. UNESCO General Conference, 41st session. https://www.unesco.org/en/artificial-intelligence/recommendation-ethics

UNESCO. (2024). AI competency framework for teachers. UNESCO Publishing. https://www.unesco.org/en/articles/ai-competency-framework-teachers

Verghis, A. M., Jose, B., Cherian, J., Mumthas, S., Joseph, S., & Varghise, S. M. (2025). The cognitive paradox of AI in education: Between enhancement and erosion. *Frontiers in Psychology*, *16*, 1550621. DOI: 10.3389/fpsyg.2025.1550621 PMID: 40297599

Wang, X. (2025). A review of the Council of Europe Framework Convention on Artificial Intelligence and Human Rights, Democracy and the Rule of Law. *Journal of Politics and Law*, *18*(4), 68. DOI: 10.5539/jpl.v18n4p68

Wild, F. (2022). *Remarks at CEN/CENELEC Standards+Innovation Award ceremony*. Open University, Institute of Educational Technology.

Yildirim, B., Sahin-Topalcengiz, E., Arikan, G., & Timur, S. (2020). Using virtual reality in the classroom: Reflections of STEM teachers on the use of teaching and learning tools. *Journal of Education in Science, Environment and Health*, *6*(1), 1–18. DOI: 10.21891/jeseh.711779

Chapter 2

Artificial intelligence for Lifelong Learning and Adult Education:

European Strategies and Practices

Mustafa Kayyali
http://orcid.org/0000-0003-3300-262X
Maaref University of Applied Sciences, Syria

ABSTRACT

This chapter examines how artificial intelligence is reshaping lifelong learning and adult education across Europe, not simply as a technical innovation, but as a response to deeper social, economic, and demographic pressures. As European societies face rapid labour-market change, ageing populations, migration, and widening skills gaps, AI-supported learning offers new possibilities for flexible pathways, personalized guidance, and continuous reskilling. Yet these possibilities are never neutral. They raise urgent questions about inclusion, learner autonomy, data ethics, institutional readiness, and the risk of reducing adult education to measurable competencies alone. The chapter explores European strategies and emerging practices in AI-enhanced adult learning, with attention to policy frameworks, workplace learning, community-based education, and digital platforms. It argues for a human-centred approach in which AI strengthens, rather than replaces, the reflective, emancipatory, and socially rooted purposes of lifelong learning.

DOI: 10.4018/979-8-3373-9883-9.ch002

INTRODUCTION

Lifelong learning has never been a quiet idea in Europe. It has always carried a larger promise: that learning should not be confined to childhood, formal schooling, or the early years of professional preparation, but should remain available throughout the whole arc of human life (Holford & Milana, 2023). In its most generous sense, lifelong learning is not merely a policy phrase attached to employability, nor a convenient response to labour-market instability. It is a social commitment. It suggests that adults, whatever their age, occupation, educational background, migration history, or social position, should continue to have meaningful chances to grow intellectually, adapt professionally, participate civically, and reinterpret their own lives. Yet this promise is becoming harder to sustain in a world where knowledge changes quickly, work is reorganized by automation, public services are increasingly digitized, and social inequalities often deepen precisely at the point where education is supposed to reduce them.

Artificial intelligence has entered this landscape with unusual force. In adult education and lifelong learning, AI is often presented as a solution to familiar problems: limited time, uneven access, fragmented learning pathways, lack of individual support, skills mismatch, and the difficulty of designing education for highly diverse groups of learners. At first glance, the appeal is clear. AI-based systems can recommend learning materials, diagnose skills gaps, provide instant feedback, translate content, support learners with disabilities, generate adaptive exercises, guide career planning, and help institutions identify learners at risk of disengagement. For adults balancing employment, family responsibilities, financial pressures, and sometimes the emotional burden of returning to education after years away from formal learning, such tools may offer a degree of flexibility that traditional provision has struggled to provide.

However, the story is not as simple as technological optimism would like it to be. Adult education is not just about efficient content delivery. It is also about confidence, identity, dignity, trust, and social belonging. Many adults return to learning with memories of earlier educational exclusion, failure, or discomfort. Others enter adult education because their jobs have disappeared, their qualifications are no longer recognized, or their lives have been disrupted by migration, displacement, illness, or economic instability. In such contexts, AI cannot be treated as a neutral instrument that merely accelerates learning. It becomes part of a wider human encounter (Kamalov et al, 2023). The way it is designed, introduced, explained, governed, and evaluated matters deeply. A recommendation system that personalizes learning may help one learner progress more confidently, while quietly narrowing another learner's possibilities. An automated assessment may save time, yet miss the hesitant but important signs of growth that only a sensitive teacher notices. A digital platform may widen access, but only for those who already possess the devices, connectivity, language skills, and digital confidence needed to use it.

This chapter examines AI for lifelong learning and adult education within the European context, where the conversation is shaped by a distinctive mixture of policy ambition, social responsibility, economic necessity, and ethical caution. Europe has invested heavily in digital skills, adult reskilling, and lifelong learning strategies, particularly as economies respond to demographic change, green transitions, automation, and the demand for more adaptable workforces. At the same time, European debates around AI tend to be strongly marked by concerns about rights, transparency, data protection, inclusion, and human oversight. This creates a productive tension. On one side, there is pressure to modernize education systems and prepare adults for rapidly changing forms of work and citizenship. On the other, there is a clear recognition that technological change must not weaken human agency, democratic participation, or social justice.

The European case is especially important because adult education across the continent is not one single system (Tamozhska et al, 2023). It includes formal higher education, vocational education and training, workplace learning, municipal adult education centres, migrant language programmes, digital literacy initiatives, open universities, community learning projects, professional micro-credentials, and informal learning networks. AI may appear differently in each of these spaces. In a workplace, it may be used to map employee competencies and recommend reskilling pathways. In a public adult education centre, it may assist teachers in creating accessible materials for mixed-ability groups. In higher education, it may support modular learning for adult professionals returning to study. In migrant education, it may provide translation, pronunciation support, or individualized language practice. In community settings, it may help learners access public services, understand health information, or participate more fully in civic life. These differences matter because AI does not have one educational meaning. Its value depends on the purposes it serves and the relationships it reshapes.

A central argument of this chapter is that AI in lifelong learning should be understood less as a replacement for existing adult education practices and more as a test of their underlying values. If adult education is reduced to rapid reskilling alone, AI will likely be used to sort, measure, accelerate, and optimize (Ogbu, 2025). If adult education is understood as a broader human and social project, AI can be positioned more carefully: as a support for access, reflection, multilingual learning, inclusion, formative feedback, and learner autonomy. The question, therefore, is not whether AI should be used in adult education. That question is already being overtaken by practice. The more important question is what kind of adult education AI is being asked to serve.

This is where European strategies and practices deserve close attention. Across Europe, lifelong learning is increasingly linked to digital transformation, employability, social cohesion, and democratic resilience. Yet policies often carry a double language. They speak of human-centred learning while also emphasizing productivity, skills forecasting, and competitiveness. They call for inclusion while relying on digital infrastructures that may exclude those most in need. They promote personalization while sometimes overlooking the collective, dialogic, and community-based nature of adult learning. These contradictions are not signs of failure; rather, they reveal the complexity of governing education in an age when technological systems move faster than institutions, regulations, and pedagogical cultures.

Adult learners themselves must remain at the centre of this discussion. They are not abstract "users" of educational technology. They are workers trying to remain employable, parents trying to support their children, migrants rebuilding professional identities, older adults seeking digital independence, unemployed individuals hoping to regain confidence, and citizens trying to understand a world increasingly mediated by algorithms. Their learning needs are often practical, but they are rarely only practical. They involve emotion, memory, aspiration, frustration, and sometimes fear. AI tools that ignore this human thickness may function technically while failing educationally.

For this reason, the chapter approaches AI in lifelong learning through a reflective and critical lens. It explores how AI can support adult education through personalization, flexible access, learner analytics, multilingual tools, adaptive platforms, career guidance, and skills development. It also considers the risks: surveillance, algorithmic bias, over-standardization, commercial dependency, weak digital inclusion, and the possible erosion of teacher judgment. The chapter argues that responsible AI in adult education requires more than compliance with technical standards. It requires institutional wisdom, participatory design, educator preparation, transparent governance, and a renewed commitment to the public value of lifelong learning.

Ultimately, AI will not determine the future of adult education by itself. Its impact will depend on the choices made by policymakers, educators, institutions, employers, communities, and learners. Europe's challenge is not simply to adopt AI, but to adopt it without forgetting why adult education matters in the first place. Lifelong learning is not only preparation for the next job, the next credential, or the next technological disruption. It is also a way of keeping human beings intellectually alive, socially connected, and capable of shaping the conditions of their own lives. AI may contribute to that aim, but only if it is placed in service of human development rather than administrative convenience or market speed.

REIMAGINING LIFELONG LEARNING IN EUROPE: FROM POLICY AMBITION TO HUMAN DEVELOPMENT

Lifelong learning in Europe has often been spoken of with a certain noble confidence, almost as if the phrase itself could solve the uneasiness it names. It appears in policy papers, ministerial speeches, university strategies, labour-market forecasts, and digital transformation agendas, carrying with it the promise of a society in which learning does not end at graduation, retirement, displacement, or professional exhaustion. Yet beneath this polished language lies a more unsettled reality. Europe is ageing, work is becoming less predictable, migration has redrawn the social and linguistic texture of many communities, and technological change keeps rearranging the ground under people's feet. In such a landscape, lifelong learning is no longer a pleasant educational ideal. It has become a civic necessity, a social safeguard, and, for many adults, a deeply personal act of survival.

The European commitment to lifelong learning has always contained two impulses that do not sit together easily. One is economic: the need to maintain competitiveness, close skills gaps, raise productivity, and prepare citizens for industries that are changing faster than traditional education systems can comfortably absorb (de Viron & Davies, 2022). The other is humanistic: the belief that education should enlarge a person's world, strengthen democratic participation, cultivate dignity, and allow individuals to remain intellectually and socially alive across the full span of life. These two impulses are not enemies, of course. Adults need work, income, competence, and professional relevance. Still, when lifelong learning is narrowed into a mechanism for employability alone, something important slips away. The learner becomes a unit of human capital rather than a person with memory, uncertainty, imagination, and a right to flourish beyond the demands of the labour market.

This tension is especially visible in the age of artificial intelligence. AI has entered European lifelong learning debates with a strong practical appeal. It promises personalized learning routes, rapid feedback, skills diagnostics, multilingual support, automated tutoring, career guidance, and flexible access to educational resources. For adults who cannot attend conventional classes because of work schedules, caregiving responsibilities, disability, geography, or financial limits, such tools may open doors that were previously half-closed or firmly locked. A worker in mid-career can receive tailored reskilling recommendations. A migrant learner can practise language skills with immediate correction. An older adult can receive patient, repeated support while learning to navigate digital public services. A vocational provider can identify patterns of disengagement before a learner quietly disappears. These are not abstract possibilities; they point toward real educational relief.

And yet, relief is not the same as transformation. The danger in many AI-driven lifelong learning strategies is that they treat complexity as a design inconvenience.

Adult learners are rarely tidy. Their needs do not always fit into dashboards, competency maps, or predictive categories (Susnjak et al, 2022). A forty-eight-year-old factory worker returning to education after redundancy does not simply need "upskilling." He may need confidence after humiliation, time after exhaustion, recognition of prior knowledge that was never certified, and a teacher who understands that silence in the classroom is not always a lack of interest. A refugee doctor learning a new language in order to re-enter a profession does not merely need vocabulary exercises. She needs institutional guidance, social trust, legal clarity, and a pathway that does not reduce her previous life to an administrative gap. AI can help in both cases, but only if it is woven into a wider educational ecology that respects biography as much as data.

Reimagining lifelong learning in Europe, then, means moving beyond the familiar language of access and skills. Access to what? Skills for whom? Learning under whose terms? These questions matter because educational policy can sound generous while quietly placing the burden of adaptation almost entirely on individuals. Adults are told to reskill, update themselves, remain flexible, embrace change, and prepare for futures that others have designed. There is something unfair, even slightly cold, in this arrangement when it is not accompanied by serious institutional responsibility. If automation displaces workers, if digital bureaucracy excludes older citizens, if platform economies create unstable careers, lifelong learning should not become a polite way of saying: "adjust yourself." It should also ask how societies, employers, universities, municipalities, and governments must adjust their structures to protect human development.

The European context offers both resources and contradictions for this task. On one hand, Europe has a rich tradition of public education, social partnership, vocational training, adult learning centres, open universities, and community-based education. These traditions remind us that learning is not only individual acquisition but also social participation. On the other hand, adult education remains uneven across countries and regions. Participation is often highest among those who are already educated, already confident, already employed in sectors that reward continuous training. Those who might benefit most—low-skilled workers, rural adults, migrants, unemployed people, people with disabilities, and older learners with fragile digital confidence—are often the hardest to reach. AI may either reduce this inequality or decorate it with a smarter interface.

This is where the idea of human development becomes indispensable. Human development does not ask only whether adults have acquired measurable competencies (Lamri & Lubart, 2023). It asks whether they have gained real freedoms: the freedom to understand, to choose, to participate, to move between roles, to speak with confidence, to interpret the world rather than merely endure it. A human-development approach to lifelong learning would treat AI as a possible amplifier of capability, not as an educational authority in its own right. It would value digital skills, certainly, but also critical judgment, ethical awareness, civic literacy, creativity, emotional resilience, and the capacity to learn with others. It would see the adult learner not as an unfinished worker but as an unfinished human being, which is something far richer and less administratively convenient.

To reach that point, European strategies must pay closer attention to the lived texture of adult learning. Policy documents often speak in smooth verbs: enhance, promote, support, accelerate, empower. Real learning is usually rougher. Adults hesitate. They miss classes. They feel embarrassed asking basic questions. They compare themselves with younger learners and sometimes feel defeated before they begin. They bring practical intelligence that formal systems fail to notice. They may resist technology not because they are backward, but because previous institutions have made them feel small. If AI systems are introduced without tenderness toward these realities, they may become yet another layer of distance between learners and education. But when used carefully, they can also soften entry points, allow private practice, reduce shame, and help learners proceed without the constant fear of public failure.

The role of educators becomes crucial here. In some versions of the AI future, teachers appear as supervisors of platforms, almost peripheral figures standing beside the machine (Shah, 2023). That is a thin and rather depressing vision. Adult educators are not merely content deliverers; they are interpreters of hesitation, builders of trust, negotiators of difference, and witnesses to forms of growth that no metric fully captures. AI may help them prepare materials, identify patterns, translate resources, or offer supplementary practice, but it cannot replace the ethical and relational intelligence that gives adult education its human depth. Europe's lifelong learning future will depend not only on better systems, but on better-supported educators who can use AI critically, creatively, and sometimes disobediently when the tool misreads the learner.

There is also a democratic question running quietly through all of this. As AI enters learning environments, adults need to understand not only how to use digital systems but how such systems shape opportunity, visibility, and judgment. Lifelong learning should include the ability to question algorithmic recommendations, recognize bias, protect personal data, and understand the social consequences of automation. Otherwise, learners may become competent users of technologies they do not truly understand. That would be a poor bargain. A European vision of AI-supported adult education should cultivate not passive adaptation, but informed agency.

Reimagining lifelong learning in Europe therefore requires a shift in tone and architecture (Benavot et al, 2022). The tone must become less managerial and more humane. The architecture must connect policy ambition with local realities: workplaces, libraries, community centres, universities, online platforms, migrant support services, vocational schools, and civil society organizations. AI can travel across these spaces, but it should not flatten them. A workplace reskilling programme is not the same as a community literacy class; an online micro-credential is not the same as a second-chance education pathway; a language-learning app is not the same as belonging. Each context asks different questions of technology.

The real promise of AI in lifelong learning is not that it will make education perfectly efficient. Perfect efficiency is not always desirable in human development, because people grow unevenly, circuitously, sometimes stubbornly. The promise is more modest and more profound: AI may help Europe build learning systems that are more responsive, more inclusive, and more capable of accompanying adults through unstable times. But this will happen only if policy ambition is disciplined by ethical imagination. Lifelong learning must not become a race in which adults are endlessly urged to catch up with machines, markets, and metrics. It should be a public commitment to ensure that, even amid disruption, human beings are not treated as obsolete versions of themselves.

AI IN ADULT EDUCATION: PERSONALIZATION, FLEXIBILITY, AND THE NEW LEARNING CONTRACT

Adult education has always carried a strange kind of urgency. Unlike childhood schooling, it rarely unfolds in a protected space where learning is the central duty of the day. Adults learn between shifts, after putting children to bed, during unemployment, through professional anxiety, in migration centres, on trains, in public libraries, in workplace training rooms, or late at night in front of a glowing screen when the rest of the house has gone quiet (Alanzi et al, 2024). Their learning is often squeezed into the cracks of life. This is precisely why artificial intelligence has gained such appeal in adult education: it seems to offer a form of learning that can bend around the learner rather than forcing the learner to bend completely around the institution.

The promise is powerful. AI-supported adult education can offer personalized pathways, immediate feedback, adaptive exercises, automated translation, skill diagnostics, career guidance, and learning resources that respond to pace, level, preference, and performance. For an adult learner who has not studied formally for years, this can feel less like a technological novelty and more like a small mercy. A system that repeats without irritation, explains without embarrassment, and adjusts without public comparison may reduce some of the emotional weight that adult learners often carry. Many adults do not fear learning itself; they fear being seen failing at it. AI, when used well, can create private rehearsal spaces where learners test themselves, make mistakes, and return again without shame.

Personalization, however, is not a simple educational good. It depends on what is being personalized, who controls the process, and what assumptions sit beneath the design (John, 2025). A platform may personalize the sequence of grammar tasks, coding exercises, digital literacy modules, or vocational simulations. It may recommend easier or harder materials based on learner performance. It may identify gaps in numeracy, literacy, or professional knowledge. These functions can be genuinely useful. Yet adult learning is not only a matter of matching content to current ability. Adults also need to be stretched, surprised, unsettled, and invited into forms of knowledge they did not know they needed. If personalization becomes too narrow, it may quietly build a learning corridor around the adult: efficient, comfortable, measurable, and slightly claustrophobic.

Figure 1. Core AI Support Functions in Adult Learning Programmes

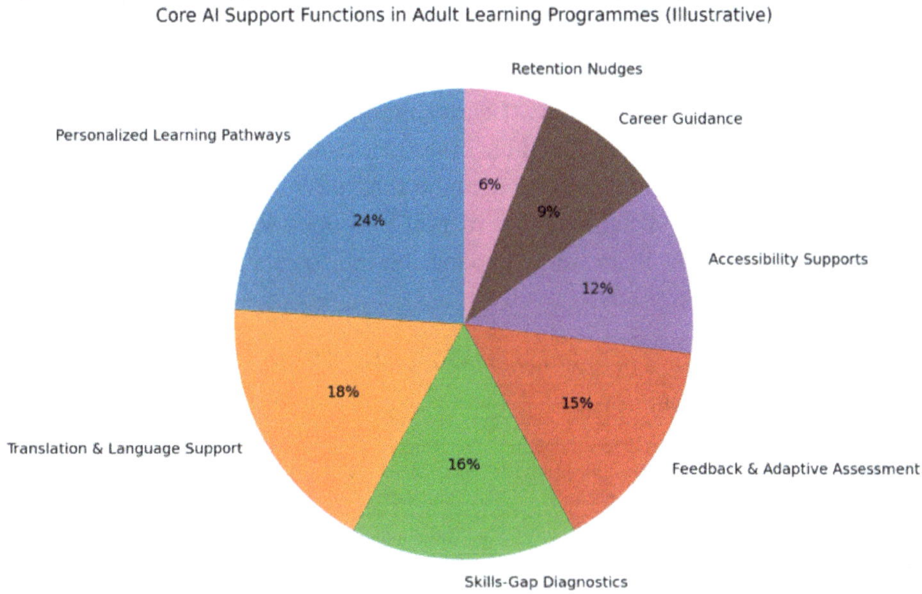

This is one of the paradoxes of AI in adult education. The more precisely a system claims to know the learner, the more carefully educators must ask what kind of knowing is taking place. A learner's data trail does not equal the learner. It may show hesitation on a quiz, repeated errors in pronunciation, irregular attendance, or slow progress through a module. But it may not reveal that the learner is exhausted from night work, anxious about immigration paperwork, embarrassed by earlier school failure, or caring for an ill parent. It may not know that a woman who pauses before submitting an answer is not confused but cautious, shaped by years in workplaces where mistakes were punished. Human beings exceed their patterns. Adult education must remember this stubborn fact.

Flexibility is another central promise of AI-supported learning. European adult education systems have long struggled with the practical realities of participation (Mansur, 2025). Timetables are rigid. Transport is costly. Rural access is uneven. Work schedules change. Care responsibilities fall heavily, often unequally, on women. For migrants and refugees, language barriers may delay entry into education. For older adults, digital systems can appear both necessary and intimidating. AI-supported platforms, especially when combined with mobile access and multilingual resources, can help loosen some of these constraints. Learning can become more modular, more portable, more responsive to interrupted lives.

Still, flexibility can be double-edged. There is a humane version of flexibility, and there is a neoliberal one, though policy language often blurs the distinction. Humane flexibility recognizes that adults live complicated lives and deserve educational arrangements that respect those complications. It offers support, choice, guidance, and second chances. The harsher version transfers responsibility to the learner while institutions withdraw: "Learn anytime" can become "You are on your own." "Personalized pathways" can become fragmented self-management. "Flexible reskilling" can become a polite demand that individuals continuously repair the damage caused by unstable labour markets. AI does not automatically choose between these versions. Its meaning depends on the social contract around it.

Table 1. AI Practices in Lifelong Learning and Adult Education

Practice Area	Why It Matters	Typical AI Uses	Main Watch-Out
Personalization Engines	Support diverse adult learning histories and pacing needs	Adaptive content sequencing; skills-gap recommendations	May narrow options or over-steer learners
Language & Translation Tools	Widen access for migrants and multilingual adults	Instant translation; bilingual glossaries; speech-to-text	Literal or culturally weak translations
Accessibility-Oriented AI	Reduce barriers for adults with disabilities	Captioning, alt text, text simplification, reading supports	Uneven quality if outputs are not reviewed
Career & Skills Mapping	Align learning with changing labour-market demands	Competency mapping; pathway suggestions; CV support	Can over-prioritize employability over broader human development
Early-Support Analytics	Help providers identify disengagement risk	Alerts, nudges, follow-up prompts	Privacy concerns; possible stigma
Educator Co-Pilots	Reduce workload and improve material design	Lesson drafting, quiz generation, feedback support	Risk of over-automation or loss of pedagogical nuance

This is why the idea of a new learning contract is so important. In adult education, AI changes the relationship among learners, educators, institutions, employers, and technology providers (Edwards-Fapohunda & Adediji, 2024). The old contract, at least in its traditional form, assumed that the institution organized knowledge, the educator mediated it, and the learner entered a structured process of instruction and assessment. AI complicates this arrangement. It may recommend content before the teacher does. It may assess performance before the institution has formally reviewed progress. It may suggest career pathways based on labour-market data. It may generate learning materials, summarize texts, translate explanations, or simulate dialogue. The adult learner no longer interacts only with a teacher or curriculum, but with a whole ecology of algorithmic guidance.

That shift requires negotiation. Learners need to know what AI is doing, what data it collects, how recommendations are produced, and where human judgment remains available (Bagunaid et al, 2022). Educators need to know when to trust the tool, when to question it, and when to ignore it entirely. Institutions need to define responsibility clearly. If an AI system misclassifies a learner's level, recommends an unsuitable pathway, reinforces a stereotype, or discourages a person from pursuing a more ambitious goal, who answers for that harm? Responsibility cannot be scattered so thinly across vendors, administrators, designers, and teachers that no one remains accountable.

The new learning contract must also protect adult agency. There is a subtle but serious risk that AI systems may begin to speak with the voice of inevitability. A recommendation can feel like a judgment. A predicted skills gap can feel like a verdict. A dashboard can turn a living learner into a set of coloured indicators. Adults who already feel uncertain may accept these outputs too passively, especially when they come wrapped in institutional authority. Adult education should resist this quiet surrender. AI should help learners understand options, not decide their futures for them. It should widen choice, not disguise sorting as guidance.

At the same time, it would be unfair to treat AI only as a threat. For many adult educators, AI can relieve pressure. It can help prepare differentiated materials for mixed-level groups, create practice tasks, simplify texts without removing meaning, support learners with disabilities, and provide formative feedback between sessions (Aldamen et al, 2026). In classrooms where one teacher supports learners with different literacy levels, languages, ages, and professional goals, such assistance can be invaluable. Used thoughtfully, AI may free educators to focus less on repetitive explanation and more on dialogue, encouragement, interpretation, and the delicate work of building confidence.

European adult education, with its varied traditions of vocational training, community learning, workers' education, open universities, and public digital inclusion programmes, is well placed to develop a more balanced model (Holford, 2023).

The most promising approach will not be one that celebrates AI as an educational miracle, nor one that rejects it as a cold intrusion. A mature approach will treat AI as a powerful but partial instrument. It can personalize, but not fully understand. It can adapt, but not care. It can recommend, but not carry responsibility for another person's becoming. That responsibility remains human.

The new learning contract, then, should be built around reciprocity rather than automation. Learners bring their histories, ambitions, fears, and practical intelligence. Educators bring judgment, relational awareness, and pedagogical imagination. Institutions bring structure, recognition, protection, and continuity. AI brings speed, pattern recognition, generative capacity, and scalable support. None of these elements should swallow the others. When one dominates, adult education becomes distorted: too bureaucratic, too technological, too market-driven, or too informal to provide genuine opportunity.

The deepest question is not whether AI can make adult education more personalized or flexible. It can. The harder question is whether such personalization and flexibility will serve human growth or merely make adaptation more efficient. Europe's challenge is to ensure that AI-supported adult education does not produce solitary learners endlessly optimizing themselves for uncertain markets, but capable adults who can learn with dignity, question systems intelligently, and participate more fully in the worlds they inhabit. That is the contract worth writing.

EUROPEAN STRATEGIES FOR DIGITAL INCLUSION, RESKILLING, AND RESPONSIBLE AI ADOPTION

European strategies for artificial intelligence in lifelong learning are being built on a difficult triangle: digital inclusion, reskilling, and responsible adoption. Each side of this triangle looks reasonable on paper (Bogoslov et al, 2024). Adults need digital skills. Economies need workers who can move across changing sectors. Public institutions need rules so that AI does not become a silent machine of exclusion. Yet, when these ambitions meet the everyday lives of adult learners, the matter becomes more complicated, more human, and frankly less obedient to policy neatness.

Europe's digital agenda has set a clear direction. The Digital Decade framework aims for 80% of adults to have at least basic digital skills by 2030, alongside a target of 20 million employed ICT specialists. The same policy space recognizes that only 55.6% of the EU population currently has at least basic digital skills, showing that the continent's digital future is not merely a technological project but a large social learning challenge. This gap matters because digital competence is no longer a decorative addition to adult life. It is increasingly bound to employment, public administration, healthcare access, banking, mobility, education, and participation in ordinary civic routines. A person who cannot confidently use digital systems may not only miss a course or a job advertisement; they may gradually lose access to the social infrastructure around them.

Digital inclusion, then, should not be mistaken for the simple distribution of devices or the expansion of broadband. These are necessary, yes, but not sufficient. Inclusion also requires language support, accessible design, trust-building, patient guidance, local learning spaces, and recognition of the emotional barriers that often accompany digital exclusion. Many adults who are described as "low-skilled" are not lacking intelligence; they are navigating systems that have become fast, abstract, password-heavy, and unforgiving. To ask such learners to enter AI-supported platforms without support is like inviting someone into a library where all the books are moving shelves. The problem is not only access. It is orientation.

This is why European reskilling initiatives have become so central. The Union of Skills places regular upskilling and reskilling within people's professional lives and connects this aim to micro-credentials, vocational education and training, and a strengthened Pact for Skills (Flintberg, 2022). The Pact for Skills itself brings public and private organizations together around concrete commitments to adult upskilling and reskilling, particularly in relation to the green and digital transitions. Its principles include lifelong learning for all, skill partnerships, anticipation of skill needs, and action against discrimination. There is a certain pragmatism here that should not be dismissed. Labour markets are shifting. Entire occupations are being reorganized by automation, data systems, environmental regulation, and new business models. Adults cannot be expected to remain professionally secure with knowledge acquired once, long ago, under different economic weather.

Figure 2. European Strategy Levers: Policy Priority vs Implementation Reach

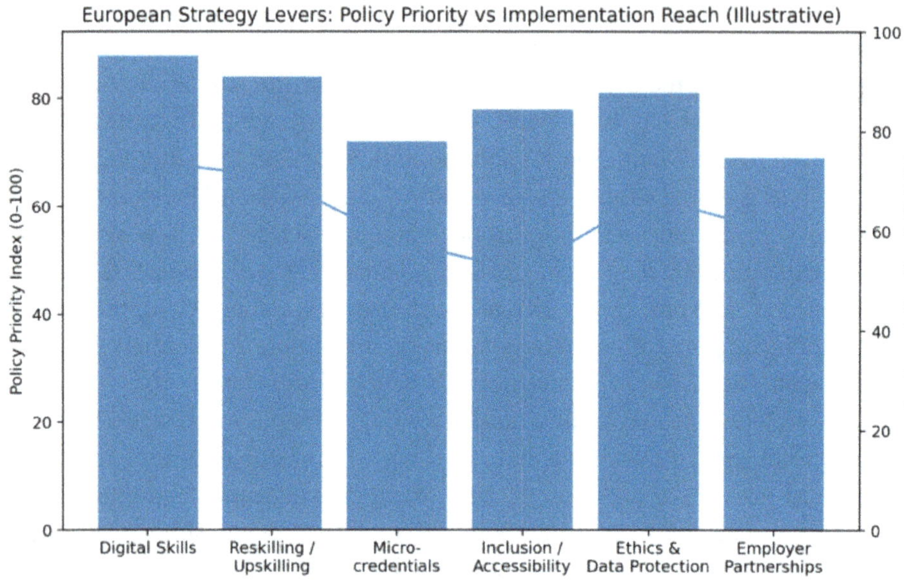

Still, reskilling is not a magic word. It can sound clean while concealing messy realities. Who has time to reskill? Who pays? Who receives guidance? Who gets a credential that employers actually respect? Who is pushed into short training because their old profession has been made invisible by economic change? These questions are uncomfortable, but adult education must ask them. A reskilling strategy that works mainly for confident professionals already attached to stable institutions will not repair inequality. It may even polish it. Those with stronger educational backgrounds often know how to find opportunities, interpret credentials, apply for funding, and translate new skills into career movement. Adults at the margins may encounter the same policy as a maze.

AI can support reskilling in valuable ways. It can map existing competencies, suggest learning pathways, produce adaptive exercises, support career counselling, and translate complex training materials into more accessible language (Vadisetty & Polamarasetti, 2024). It can help vocational providers identify regional skill demands and design courses that respond more quickly to labour-market signals. In theory, this allows adult learning systems to become less sluggish, less generic, and more attentive to individual need. Yet the danger lies in allowing prediction to become prescription. When an AI system recommends a pathway, it may appear objective, but its recommendation is shaped by available data, design assumptions, historical labour patterns, and institutional priorities. If past inequality is buried inside the data, it can return wearing the respectable face of guidance.

Responsible AI adoption is therefore not an optional ethical ornament. It is the condition under which AI can be trusted in adult education. The EU AI Act has placed education and vocational training among areas where certain AI systems may be classified as high-risk, especially when they determine access or admission, evaluate learning outcomes, assess the level of education a person may receive, or monitor behaviour during tests. This matters profoundly for adult learners, because educational decisions can alter life chances. A misplaced assessment may limit entry to a programme. A biased recommendation may steer a learner away from a more ambitious pathway. Automated monitoring may create suspicion where trust is already fragile. In adult education, harm is not always dramatic; sometimes it is a quiet narrowing of possibility.

The European Commission's updated guidance on ethical AI and data use in education responds to this broader climate by emphasizing AI literacy, careful compliance with the AI Act, and practical support for educators making context-sensitive decisions (Dragomir, 2025). Although much of the guidance is framed around formal schooling, its logic travels well into adult education: educators need confidence, not just tools; learners need transparency, not just access; institutions need principles that can survive contact with everyday practice. Responsible AI cannot be reduced to a checklist signed somewhere in the procurement office. It must become part of pedagogical culture.

There is another issue, slightly quieter but just as important: the relationship between European strategies and local realities. Brussels may set targets, frameworks, and funding priorities, but adult learning happens in particular places: a municipal classroom in rural Spain, a digital skills centre in Latvia, a workplace training scheme in Germany, a migrant language programme in Sweden, an open university module in Ireland, a community library in Greece. These settings have different histories, capacities, and learners. A responsible European strategy must leave room for this unevenness. Standardization can help coordinate systems, but too much of it can suffocate the delicate local knowledge that makes adult education work.

Micro-credentials offer a useful example. They are often presented as flexible learning solutions, and they can indeed help adults accumulate recognized evidence of learning without committing immediately to long programmes. For workers who need targeted reskilling, parents with limited study time, or professionals seeking gradual career transition, this flexibility can be liberating. But micro-credentials also raise questions about fragmentation. Does the learner gain a coherent educational pathway, or merely a pocketful of small certificates? Are these credentials portable across borders and sectors? Do employers understand them? Do they support human development, or do they simply slice learning into market-friendly fragments? AI may help organize and recommend micro-credentials, but it cannot answer these value questions by itself.

A humane European strategy would treat digital inclusion, reskilling, and responsible AI as interconnected rather than separate policy boxes (Wright, 2025). Digital inclusion without reskilling may help adults use tools but leave them economically exposed. Reskilling without inclusion may favour those already near opportunity. AI adoption without responsibility may accelerate both access and harm at the same time. The wiser approach is slower, more relational, and more demanding: build digital confidence, provide meaningful learning pathways, protect learners from opaque automated judgments, support educators, and ensure that the adults most affected by technological change have a voice in shaping the systems designed for them.

The language of European policy often speaks of competitiveness, innovation, resilience, and transformation. These words have their place. Yet adult education requires a warmer vocabulary too: dignity, patience, recognition, repair, belonging. AI will enter lifelong learning whether institutions feel ready or not. The real question is whether Europe can make this entry serve democratic and human purposes rather than simply managerial ones (Hutson, 2025). The strongest strategies will be those that refuse to separate technological modernization from social justice. They will understand that an adult learning to use AI, to work with data, to change profession, or to return to education after years away is not merely responding to the economy. That person is renegotiating a place in the world. Policy should be serious enough, and humble enough, to honour that.

ETHICAL TENSIONS AND FUTURE DIRECTIONS: EQUITY, AGENCY, AND TRUST IN AI-SUPPORTED ADULT LEARNING

The ethical debate around AI-supported adult learning cannot be treated as a neat appendix to innovation. It sits at the centre of the whole question. Whenever artificial intelligence enters lifelong learning, it does not simply bring new tools into an old educational field; it changes the conditions under which adults are seen, measured, guided, and sometimes judged. That is why the ethical tensions are so persistent. They are not technical glitches waiting to be repaired by better software. They are signs of a deeper struggle over what adult education is for, who it serves, and how much power should be given to systems that classify human possibility through data.

Equity is the first and perhaps most visible tension. AI is often praised for its capacity to widen access, and in many cases this claim has substance. Adaptive platforms can support learners who need flexible pacing. Translation tools can assist migrants and multilingual learners (Sharma, 2025). Speech-to-text, captioning, and text simplification can help adults with disabilities or limited literacy. AI tutors can provide practice outside formal class hours, which is especially valuable for adults who work irregular shifts or live far from educational centres. These are real gains, not decorative promises. Yet equity is never achieved by access alone. A door may be open, and still many people may not feel able to enter.

The digital divide remains stubbornly social. Adults who lack reliable internet, suitable devices, private study space, digital confidence, or basic literacy may be formally "included" in AI-supported learning while practically left behind. The more adult education depends on intelligent platforms, automated guidance, and digital credentials, the more exclusion may become invisible (Goger et al, 2022). No one is explicitly denied entry; they simply fail to navigate the system. That kind of exclusion is quieter, harder to protest, and often blamed on the learner. In this sense, AI may create a polished version of inequality, one in which opportunity appears abundant but is genuinely usable only by those already equipped to claim it.

Bias adds another layer of concern. AI systems learn from existing data, and existing data carries the sediment of social history: gendered expectations, racialized labour markets, class-based educational pathways, linguistic hierarchies, disability exclusions, and age-related assumptions about competence. If such systems are used to recommend courses, evaluate skills, predict success, or guide career transitions, they may reproduce old patterns under the authority of technological neutrality. A mid-career woman may be nudged toward care-related training rather than advanced technical fields. A migrant learner may be assessed through language deficiencies rather than professional expertise. An older worker may be treated as a risky investment. The system may not intend harm, but harm does not always need intention. Sometimes it only needs inherited patterns and insufficient questioning.

Agency is equally important, though less often discussed with the seriousness it deserves. Adult learning is meaningful partly because adults choose, interpret, resist, revise, and negotiate their own development (Broek et al, 2023). AI complicates this freedom. Recommendation systems can be useful, but they can also become quietly directive. A learner who receives an automated suggestion may experience it as advice, but also as judgment. "This pathway suits you" may sound supportive; it may also shrink ambition. Adults who are already uncertain about their abilities may defer too easily to algorithmic authority, especially when it is embedded in an institutional platform or linked to employment services. The result is not coercion in the old sense. It is softer than that. It is a kind of guided self-limitation.

For this reason, AI-supported adult education must preserve the learner's right to understand and question. Adults should know when AI is being used, what data it draws upon, how recommendations are produced, and what alternatives remain available (Jin & Zhang, 2025). They should be able to refuse certain forms of data use without being punished through reduced access. They should have routes to human review when automated assessments or recommendations affect their learning pathways. Agency is not protected by giving learners a checkbox at the beginning of a platform. It requires an educational culture in which questioning the system is treated as part of learning, not as resistance to progress.

Trust is the third essential pillar, and perhaps the most fragile. Adult learners often enter education carrying complicated relationships with institutions (Dumont & Ready, 2023). Some have experienced school failure. Some have been ignored by employers. Some have had qualifications dismissed because they came from another country. Some distrust digital systems because data collection has been associated with bureaucracy, surveillance, welfare control, migration status, or workplace monitoring. When AI enters these spaces, trust cannot be assumed. It must be earned slowly, through transparency, human mediation, and visible accountability.

Figure 3. Readiness for Responsible AI in Adult Education: Baseline vs Target

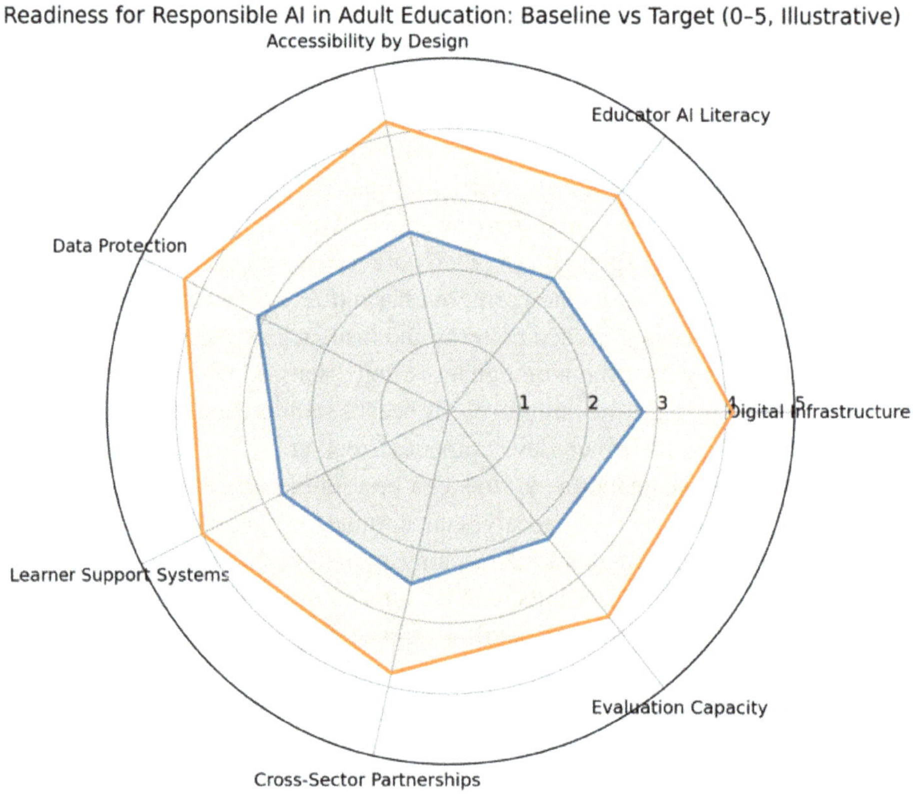

Trust also depends on educators. Teachers, trainers, mentors, and community facilitators need to understand AI well enough to explain it, challenge it, and use it with discretion. If educators are expected merely to operate platforms they do not understand, their professional authority is weakened. Worse, learners may be left with no trusted human interpreter between themselves and the machine. Responsible AI adoption in adult education therefore requires serious investment in educator development. Not superficial workshops that celebrate tools, but sustained professional learning about data ethics, bias, accessibility, pedagogy, and the limits of automation. Educators do not need to become engineers, but they do need enough critical fluency to avoid becoming servants of systems they cannot question.

Future directions for AI-supported adult learning should begin from this ethical ground (Kaya, 2025). The most promising future is not the most automated one. It is the one that combines intelligent tools with strong human relationships, public accountability, and inclusive design. AI should support adult learners in ways that are explainable, contestable, and adaptable to context. It should help teachers notice patterns without replacing their judgment. It should make pathways clearer without trapping learners inside predictive categories. It should expand access without assuming that access alone solves inequality. It should support reskilling without turning adults into endlessly upgradeable labour-market units.

Participatory design will become increasingly important. Adult learners, especially those from marginalized groups, should not be treated only as users of AI systems after decisions have already been made (Judijanto, 2025). They should be involved in shaping the tools, testing their assumptions, identifying risks, and defining what meaningful support actually looks like. A platform designed for unemployed adults without listening to unemployed adults will almost certainly misunderstand something essential. A language-learning tool for migrants that ignores their professional histories, emotional pressures, and legal uncertainties will remain educationally thin, however technically impressive it may be. Design is never neutral; it is a form of power.

There is also a need to rethink assessment. AI can assess rapidly, but adult learning often develops in subtle, uneven, and deeply contextual ways. Confidence, participation, resilience, civic understanding, digital independence, and the ability to make informed choices do not always fit neatly into automated scoring systems. If future adult education becomes overly dependent on machine-readable evidence, it may undervalue precisely those forms of growth that matter most in lifelong learning. Assessment must remain broad enough to recognize human development, not merely platform performance.

The future should also include stronger public governance. Many AI tools used in education are developed by private companies whose priorities may not always align with adult learners' interests (Edwards-Fapohunda & Adediji, 2024). Data ownership, commercial dependency, procurement standards, algorithmic transparency, and long-term accountability must be taken seriously. Public institutions cannot simply purchase tools and hope that ethics has been built into them. They must ask difficult questions before adoption, monitor impacts after implementation, and create mechanisms for redress when things go wrong. In adult education, where learners may already face social vulnerability, weak governance is not a minor administrative flaw. It is an ethical failure.

Table 2. 12-Month Roadmap for AI in Lifelong Learning

Phase	Focus	Key Activities
Q1	Governance & Mapping	Audit adult learner needs; map existing digital infrastructure; define ethical and inclusion principles
Q2	Pilot Design	Launch pilots in translation support, accessibility tools, and adaptive learning pathways; set measurable KPIs
Q3	Capacity Building	Train educators; build guidance for prompt use, review, and data protection; involve employers and local partners
Q4	Evaluation & Scaling	Assess outcomes, retention, and inclusion impact; refine models; scale strongest practices institution-wide

A more humane direction would place AI within an ecosystem of support: community learning spaces, workplace protections, public libraries, vocational institutions, universities, civil society organizations, and digital platforms that remain answerable to human purposes (Mandiá-Rubal, 2026). Such an ecosystem would recognize that adult learners need more than content. They need guidance, recognition, time, encouragement, affordability, and sometimes someone patient enough to sit beside them while they try again. AI can contribute to this ecosystem, but it should not become its soul.

The ethical future of AI-supported adult learning will depend on whether Europe can hold three commitments together: equity, so that technological progress does not widen old fractures; agency, so that adults remain authors of their own learning rather than objects of prediction; and trust, so that innovation grows through openness rather than quiet control (Kruckel, 2025). These commitments are demanding. They slow things down. They complicate implementation. They ask institutions to listen before they scale. But perhaps that is exactly what adult education needs in an age intoxicated by speed. Learning across a lifetime has never been only about catching up with change. It is also about refusing to let change strip human beings of dignity, voice, and the right to become more than any system can forecast.

CONCLUSION

The future of AI in lifelong learning and adult education in Europe will not be decided by technology alone. It will be decided by the educational imagination that surrounds it. AI can certainly make adult learning more flexible, responsive, and accessible. It can help learners identify gaps in their knowledge, receive immediate feedback, translate unfamiliar language, move through content at a suitable pace, and locate learning opportunities that match their goals. It can support institutions in designing better pathways, recognizing prior learning, monitoring participation, and responding earlier when learners begin to disengage. These are not small contributions. For many adults, especially those who have limited time, interrupted educational histories, or complex responsibilities, such support may make the difference between participation and exclusion.

Yet the chapter has argued that these possibilities must be handled with care. Adult education has always been more than the transfer of skills. It is a deeply human field, shaped by biography, social inequality, motivation, confidence, and the search for meaning. Adults do not enter learning as empty containers waiting to be filled with updated competencies. They arrive with histories, wounds, strengths, doubts, obligations, and aspirations. Some are trying to survive economic transition. Some are rebuilding after displacement. Some are seeking dignity after years of low-paid or invisible work. Some simply want to understand the world more fully. If AI systems are introduced into adult education without sensitivity to these realities, they may improve efficiency while narrowing the moral and social purpose of learning.

This is one of the central tensions in European approaches to AI-supported lifelong learning. Europe needs reskilling at scale. The labour market is changing quickly, and adults need opportunities to adapt throughout their working lives. Digital and green transitions require new forms of knowledge, new professional identities, and new institutional responses. From this perspective, AI appears attractive because it promises speed, personalization, and scalability. However, Europe also has a strong tradition of linking education to citizenship, social rights, cultural participation, and democratic life. Adult education is not merely a repair mechanism for labour-market disruption. It is also a space where people regain voice, agency, and confidence. The danger is that AI may pull lifelong learning toward a narrower model: one in which the adult learner is treated mainly as a bundle of skills to be diagnosed, updated, and redeployed.

Avoiding that danger requires a human-centred approach that is more than a slogan. Human-centred AI in adult education must mean that learners understand when and how AI is being used. It must mean that human educators remain able to question, override, reinterpret, and contextualize automated recommendations. It must mean that data is collected carefully, explained clearly, protected rigorously, and never used to quietly rank, stigmatize, or limit learners. It must mean that personalization does not become isolation, and that adaptive pathways do not trap adults inside narrow profiles built from incomplete data. Above all, it must mean that AI supports human judgment rather than displacing it.

Teachers, trainers, tutors, mentors, and community educators remain essential in this future. Their role may change, but it should not disappear. In fact, AI may make their role more important, not less. As automated systems become better at producing content, generating exercises, and tracking performance, educators will be needed to interpret the meaning of learning, notice emotional barriers, encourage persistence, build trust, and create spaces where adults can think together. An AI tutor may explain a grammar point, recommend a coding exercise, or summarize a policy document. But it cannot fully understand the embarrassment of an adult learner who has avoided classrooms for twenty years, or the fragile courage of a migrant professional trying to study in a new language, or the quiet pride of an older learner sending an email independently for the first time. These moments are small, but adult education is made of such moments.

The European context also reminds us that access cannot be assumed. AI-supported lifelong learning may easily benefit those who are already digitally confident, already well educated, already connected to institutions, and already able to navigate complex systems. Meanwhile, adults with low literacy, limited digital access, precarious employment, disabilities, language barriers, or distrust of institutions may remain outside the very systems designed to help them. This is why digital inclusion must be treated as a foundation, not an afterthought. Providing AI tools without addressing connectivity, affordability, accessibility, language diversity, and local support risks deepening inequality under the attractive language of innovation.

Policy, therefore, has a difficult task. It must encourage experimentation without surrendering education to market-driven platforms. It must support innovation while protecting public values. It must help institutions use AI responsibly while recognizing that many adult education providers lack the funding, infrastructure, and technical expertise available to large universities or corporations. Smaller community organizations, municipal centres, and vocational providers need guidance, investment, and practical support. Otherwise, responsible AI will remain a polished phrase in policy documents while everyday educators struggle with uneven tools, unclear regulations, and insufficient training.

A mature European strategy for AI in adult education should also resist the temptation to measure everything simply because more things have become measurable. Learner analytics can be helpful, but not all learning announces itself through neat data points. Adult learning may appear as renewed confidence, a changed sense of possibility, better participation in community life, improved communication with a child's school, or the courage to apply for a new job. These outcomes are real, even when they are difficult to quantify. If AI systems privilege only what can be tracked, scored, and predicted, adult education may lose some of its richest meanings. Measurement should illuminate learning, not shrink it.

The chapter has also emphasized the importance of trust. Without trust, AI-supported lifelong learning will struggle to gain legitimacy. Adult learners need to know that systems are not exploiting their data, misjudging their abilities, or pushing them into pathways chosen by employers, platforms, or institutions rather than by themselves. Educators need to trust that AI tools are pedagogically sound, transparent, and aligned with their professional values. Institutions need governance models that make responsibility visible. Trust cannot be produced by technical performance alone. It grows through openness, dialogue, accountability, and the willingness to admit uncertainty.

Looking ahead, the most promising uses of AI in lifelong learning may be those that remain modest in their claims but meaningful in their effects. AI can help make learning materials more accessible. It can support multilingual education. It can assist adults in navigating fragmented learning opportunities. It can provide practice without shame, feedback without delay, and guidance without requiring every learner to already know how the system works. It can help teachers prepare differentiated materials and reduce some administrative burdens. It can support recognition of prior learning and more flexible educational pathways. These are valuable contributions, especially when embedded in thoughtful educational design.

However, the deeper future of lifelong learning in Europe depends on whether AI is used to expand human possibility or merely to manage adaptation. There is a difference. Expanding human possibility means helping adults participate more fully in social, cultural, economic, and civic life. Managing adaptation means moving people efficiently through changing labour-market demands, often without questioning the conditions that created insecurity in the first place. Europe's challenge is to keep the first vision alive while responding realistically to the second.

In the end, AI should not become the new centre of adult education. The centre should remain the adult learner: unfinished, capable, pressured, curious, vulnerable, resilient. Technology should gather around that human reality with humility. The strongest future for AI in lifelong learning will not be the most automated one, nor the most data-rich, nor the most dazzling in technical terms. It will be the future in which adults are given better chances to learn with dignity, to choose with understanding, to participate with confidence, and to remain more than the economic functions assigned to them. That is the real test of European strategies and practices. Not whether AI can make learning faster, but whether it can help make lifelong learning more just, more humane, and more worthy of the lives it seeks to serve.

REFERENCES

Alanzi, T. M., Arif, W., Aqeeli, R., Alnafisi, A., Qumosani, T., Alreshidi, A., Alhawsawi, S., Alnakli, R., Alotaibi, A., AlOthman, M., Khamisi, M., & Alanzi, N. (2024). Examining the impact of digital detox interventions on anxiety and depression levels among young adults. *Cureus*, *16*(12). Advance online publication. DOI: 10.7759/cureus.75625 PMID: 39803084

Aldamen, H., Alnemrat, A., Al-Deaibes, M., & Alsharefeen, R. (2026, April). Using AI to adapt reading input for mixed-proficiency EFL learners. []. Frontiers Media SA.]. *Frontiers in Education*, *11*, 1737903. DOI: 10.3389/feduc.2026.1737903

Bagunaid, W., Chilamkurti, N., & Veeraraghavan, P. (2022). Aisar: Artificial intelligence-based student assessment and recommendation system for e-learning in big data. *Sustainability (Basel)*, *14*(17), 10551. DOI: 10.3390/su141710551

Benavot, A., Hoppers, C. O., Lockhart, A. S., & Hinzen, H. (2022). Reimagining adult education and lifelong learning for all: Historical and critical perspectives. *International Review of Education*, *68*(2), 165–194. DOI: 10.1007/s11159-022-09955-9 PMID: 35668894

Bogoslov, I. A., Corman, S., & Lungu, A. E. (2024). Perspectives on artificial intelligence adoption for European union elderly in the context of digital skills development. *Sustainability (Basel)*, *16*(11), 4579. DOI: 10.3390/su16114579

Broek, S., Linden, J. V. D., Kuijpers, M. A. C. T., & Semeijn, J. H. (2023). What makes adults choose to learn: Factors that stimulate or prevent adults from learning. *Journal of Adult and Continuing Education*, *29*(2), 620–642. DOI: 10.1177/14779714231169684

de Viron, F., & Davies, P. (2022). New impulses for a lifelong learning university: critical thinking, learning time, and space. In *Third international handbook of lifelong learning* (pp. 1–20). Springer International Publishing. DOI: 10.1007/978-3-030-67930-9_37-1

Dragomir, A. (2025). The role of the European Union in shaping an ethical and legal framework for artificial intelligence (AI) in education. Review of Artificial Intelligence in Education, 6.

Dumont, H., & Ready, D. D. (2023). On the promise of personalized learning for educational equity. *NPJ Science of Learning*, *8*(1), 26. DOI: 10.1038/s41539-023-00174-x PMID: 37542046

Edwards-Fapohunda, M. O., & Adediji, M. A. (2024). Sustainable development of distance learning in continuing adult education: The impact of artificial intelligence. *Iconic Research and Engineering Journals*, *8*(1), 113–114.

Flintberg, B. (2022). Digital micro-credentials for upskilling and reskilling in the vocational sector: A study on the potential use of a blockchain-based ICT system for micro-credentials in Sweden.

Goger, A., Parco, A., & Vegas, E. (2022). *Learning and working in the digital age: Advancing opportunities and identifying the risks*. Brookings Institution.

Holford, J. (2023). Lifelong learning, the European Union, and the social inclusion of young adults: Rethinking policy. In *Lifelong learning, young adults and the challenges of disadvantage in Europe* (pp. 3–39). Springer International Publishing. DOI: 10.1007/978-3-031-14109-6_1

Holford, J., & Milana, M. (2023). The European Union and lifelong learning policy. In *Third international handbook of lifelong learning* (pp. 499–522). Springer International Publishing. DOI: 10.1007/978-3-031-19592-1_27

Hutson, J. (2025). Cultivating Identity, Workforce Readiness, and Heutagogical Lifelong Learning: The Case for Student-Trained AI Agents in Postsecondary Education. FAR Journal of Education and Sociology, 2(3).

Jin, F., & Zhang, X. (2025). Artificial intelligence or human: When and why consumers prefer AI recommendations. *Information Technology & People*, *38*(1), 279–303. DOI: 10.1108/ITP-01-2023-0022

John, B. (2025, January). Personalized Learning through Software Design Critiquing Tools: Tailoring Feedback to Individual Student Needs.

Judijanto, L. (2025). Beyond access: Cultural, ethical, and infrastructural challenges of AI in marginalised education contexts. *European Journal of Contemporary Education and E-Learning*, *3*(6), 83–98. DOI: 10.59324/ejceel.2025.3(6).07

Kamalov, F., Santandreu Calonge, D., & Gurrib, I. (2023). New era of artificial intelligence in education: Towards a sustainable multifaceted revolution. *Sustainability (Basel)*, *15*(16), 12451. DOI: 10.3390/su151612451

Kaya, Y. (2025). The potential of artificial intelligence as the learning ecosystem of the future in adult religious education. Eskişehir Osmangazi Üniversitesi İlahiyat Fakültesi Dergisi, 12(Din ve Yapay Zeka), 127-156.

Kruckel, J. (2025). Recalibrating the Social Contract: The Case for Lifelong Free Education in the Age of AI.

Lamri, J., & Lubart, T. (2023). Reconciling hard skills and soft skills in a common framework: The generic skills component approach. *Journal of Intelligence*, *11*(6), 107. DOI: 10.3390/jintelligence11060107 PMID: 37367509

Mandiá-Rubal, S. (2026). Artificial intelligence and the library as Third Place: Cognitive automation and the reconfiguration of labour. *The Journal of Documentation*, *82*(2), 1–14. DOI: 10.1108/JD-11-2025-0346

Mansur, S. (2025). AI As A Catalyst in Education, Adult Learning, and Digital Literacy. [IJFMR]. *International Journal for Multidisciplinary Research*, *7*(4), 54198. DOI: 10.36948/ijfmr.2025.v07i04.54198

Ogbu, E. (2025). Re-skilling for the future: An innovative approach in the nigerian adult education for sustainable development in the era of automation. Journal on Innovation and Sustainability RISUS, 16(1), 04-17.

Shah, P. (2023). *AI and the Future of Education: Teaching in the Age of Artificial Intelligence*. John Wiley & Sons.

Sharma, S. (2025). Empowering Multilingual Learners: A Framework for Technology Integration in Diverse Classrooms. *Schools*, *22*(2), 257–278. DOI: 10.1086/737545

Susnjak, T., Ramaswami, G. S., & Mathrani, A. (2022). Learning analytics dashboard: A tool for providing actionable insights to learners. *International Journal of Educational Technology in Higher Education*, *19*(1), 12. DOI: 10.1186/s41239-021-00313-7 PMID: 35194560

Tamozhska, I., Lehan, I., Shcherbak, I., Suprun, D., & Hryhorenko, T. (2023). FUNCTIONING AND DEVELOPMENT OF NATIONAL AND EUROPEAN ADULT EDUCATION SYSTEMS: A COMPARATIVE ASPECT. *Conhecimento & Diversidade*, *15*(40), 45–61. DOI: 10.18316/rcd.v15i40.11275

Vadisetty, R., & Polamarasetti, A. (2024, December). AI-Augmented Skill Development Roadmaps: Tailoring 12-Month Learning Paths for Future-Ready Careers in Education 4.0 and Industry 4.0. In 2024 13th International Conference on System Modeling & Advancement in Research Trends (SMART) (pp. 655-661). IEEE.

Wright, S. (2025). Artificial intelligence and work: A review of the European policy landscape. *The Journal of Industrial Relations*, *67*(5), 794–805. DOI: 10.1177/00221856251394780

KEY TERMS AND DEFINITIONS

Adult Education: organized learning opportunities designed for adults returning to, continuing, or reshaping their educational journeys.

Digital Inclusion: ensuring that adults can access, understand, and effectively use digital tools and learning platforms.

Lifelong Learning: continuous learning across the whole life course for personal, professional, and civic development.

Micro-credentials: short, focused, certifiable learning units that validate specific knowledge or competencies.

Reskilling: acquiring new competencies to move into new roles or adapt to structural economic change.

Responsible AI: the development and use of AI in ways that protect rights, fairness, transparency, and human oversight.

Upskilling: strengthening existing skills to improve performance, flexibility, and employability in current roles.

Chapter 3 Human-Centred AI and Immersive Learning Design in Higher Education: A Conceptual Framework for Artificial Intelligence and Augmented Reality

Fatih Kaleci
http://orcid.org/0000-0001-6823-3773
Necmettin Erbakan University, Turkey

ABSTRACT

This chapter develops a human-centred conceptual framework for integrating AI and AR as mutually related components of higher education learning ecosystems. It argues that AI and AR should not be treated as separate innovation streams: AI is associated with tutoring, feedback, prediction, personalisation, and automation, whereas AR is associated with visualisation, contextualisation, embodiment, and immersive engagement. Drawing on OECD perspectives on generative AI, teaching, and immersive technologies, European regulatory frameworks, human-centred design, and technology governance, the chapter proposes a five-dimensional framework: human-centred pedagogy, immersive learning design, learner and teacher agency, inclusion and access, and governance and trust. The framework supports researchers, curriculum designers, academic developers, and higher education

DOI: 10.4018/979-8-3373-9883-9.ch003

leaders in evaluating when AI and AR are educationally warranted, how they can be designed responsibly, and what institutional policy and evidence standards are needed to move beyond technology-first adoption narratives.

1. INTRODUCTION

Artificial intelligence (AI) and augmented reality (AR) now occupy a prominent place in debates about the future of higher education. AI is increasingly embedded in writing support, tutoring systems, automated feedback, learning analytics, adaptive platforms, research assistance and administrative decision-making. AR, meanwhile, is used to overlay digital objects, data, simulations, annotations and interactive representations onto physical or contextually meaningful environments. Together, these technologies promise to expand access to complex phenomena, personalise support and enrich the forms of evidence through which learning can be observed. However, the central question for higher education is no longer whether these technologies can be adopted. The more important question is under what educational, ethical and institutional conditions their adoption is justified.

The urgency of this question has increased with the rapid diffusion of generative AI. General-purpose AI tools can produce text, code, images, explanations, plans and feedback with unprecedented fluency. This fluency creates new possibilities for support, but it also produces a persistent pedagogical risk: students may appear to perform better while engaging less deeply with the cognitive, disciplinary and reflective work that education is supposed to cultivate. OECD analyses of digital education therefore emphasise that generative AI can support learning when guided by clear pedagogical principles, but warn that task performance and learning gain are not equivalent outcomes (OECD, 2026a). This distinction is especially significant in higher education, where advanced learning requires epistemic judgement, methodological rigour, disciplinary argumentation and the capacity to evaluate knowledge claims. A similar caution applies to AR and immersive technologies. Research on AR and immersive learning has shifted from asking whether immersive tools are engaging to asking how representation, interaction, sequencing, feedback and teacher mediation shape learning outcomes (Bower et al., 2014; Radianti et al., 2020; Radu, 2014).

This chapter responds to these challenges by developing a human-centred conceptual framework for AI and immersive learning design in higher education. The core argument is that AI and AR should not be understood as isolated tools or parallel innovation trends. Both reshape how learners encounter knowledge, how teachers orchestrate learning, how evidence of learning is generated, how institutions manage risk and how educational responsibility is distributed across human and technological actors. A shared conceptual language is therefore needed. The chapter makes three contributions. First, it brings AI and AR into a common conceptual space by treating them as components of broader learning ecosystems. Second, it clarifies human-centredness as an educational principle: the design of learning environments that preserve professional judgement, protect learner autonomy, support meaningful participation and ensure that technological mediation remains subordinate to educational purposes. Third, it reframes AR as immersive learning design, foregrounding instructional purpose, epistemic access, interaction and assessment rather than novelty or spectacle.

2. WHY AI AND AR REQUIRE A SHARED CONCEPTUAL LANGUAGE IN HIGHER EDUCATION

AI and AR are often discussed in separate literatures. AI in education is typically associated with intelligent tutoring systems, adaptive learning environments, automated assessment, recommender systems, learning analytics and generative AI (Crompton & Burke, 2023; Zawacki-Richter et al., 2019). AR and immersive technologies are usually located within scholarship on visualisation, simulation, embodiment, spatial learning and experiential design (Bower et al., 2014; Radu, 2014). This separation is analytically convenient, but it obscures an important educational reality: both technologies mediate the relation between learners, teachers, knowledge, evidence and institutional systems.

In AI-supported environments, learners receive automated explanations, feedback, hints, worked examples, quiz items, translations, or analytics-driven recommendations. These forms of support can extend learning opportunities when used to scaffold inquiry and formative assessment. Yet they also raise questions about dependency, authorship, bias, opacity and the displacement of cognitive effort. In AR-supported environments, learners interact with layered representations, three-dimensional models, location-aware prompts, simulated procedures, or mixed physical-digital objects. These affordances can support learning by making invisible, abstract, hazardous, or remote phenomena more accessible. However, AR also reorganises what learners see, what they manipulate and what counts as relevant evidence in the learning situation. A learner may be highly engaged by a visually rich AR experience and still fail to develop the intended conceptual understanding if the experience is not carefully sequenced and mediated.

AI and AR become particularly significant when considered together. AI can personalise, generate, interpret, or adapt content within AR environments; AR can provide the situated or embodied context in which AI support becomes meaningful. A medical student might use AR to visualise anatomical structures while an AI tutor generates prompts requiring diagnostic reasoning. An engineering student might interact with an AR model of a mechanical system while AI-generated feedback identifies misconceptions in the student's explanation. In such cases, the educational value lies not in AI or AR alone but in the designed relationship among representation, interaction, feedback, reflection and teacher mediation. This chapter therefore treats AI and AR as co-mediating technologies whose integration demands a unified conceptual framework.

3. METHODOLOGICAL ORIENTATION: CONCEPTUAL SYNTHESIS

This chapter uses conceptual synthesis as its methodological orientation. Conceptual synthesis is appropriate when a field is characterised by rapid technological development, fragmented terminology and uneven integration between empirical studies, policy discourse and educational theory. The purpose is not to aggregate effect sizes or to provide a systematic review of all AI and AR studies in higher education. Instead, the chapter constructs an integrative framework by interpreting converging themes across five clusters of literature: (1) international policy documents (primarily OECD, UNESCO and European Commission publications on AI, digital education and immersive technologies); (2) AI in higher education, including scholarship on intelligent tutoring, generative AI, learning analytics, assessment and educational AI ethics; (3) AR and immersive learning, covering simulation, embodiment, spatial learning, presence and immersive design; (4) human-centred design, including human-centred AI theory, universal design for learning and participatory design approaches; and (5) technology governance in education, covering data protection, algorithmic accountability, educational integrity and regulatory frameworks.

Sources were selected according to four criteria: conceptual relevance to the integration of AI and AR in higher education; recency, with priority given to publications from 2019 onwards and particular emphasis on OECD and European policy materials from 2024–2026; higher education relevance, favouring sources that explicitly address university-level learning, teaching, assessment, or institutional governance; and policy significance, prioritising internationally recognised frameworks that carry normative weight for education system decision-making. Foundational theoretical works—including Mayer's (2021) multimedia learning theory, Milgram and Kishino's (1994) reality-virtuality continuum and Azuma's (1997) AR definition—were included irrespective of date given their enduring theoretical relevance.

The framework was produced by clustering recurring themes identified across these literature groups. Themes that appeared consistently across policy, design and empirical scholarship—pedagogical purpose, epistemic access, professional agency, equitable participation and institutional accountability—were refined into the five framework dimensions. The resulting framework is both normative and analytical: normative in arguing that educational technologies should serve human development and institutional responsibility; analytical in offering dimensions, design questions and indicators for examining concrete cases. A limitation of this approach is discussed explicitly before the conclusion of this chapter.

4. OECD AND EUROPEAN PERSPECTIVES ON HUMAN-CENTRED AI AND IMMERSIVE TECHNOLOGIES

The convergence of international policy and scholarly attention on AI and AR in higher education is particularly evident in recent OECD and European analyses. The OECD Principles on Artificial Intelligence establish that trustworthy AI should be inclusive, human-centred, transparent, robust and accountable (OECD, 2023). These principles provide a normative foundation applicable across all sectors, including education. More recently, OECD publications on generative AI in education and immersive technologies have specified the educational, professional and governance dimensions of these principles with increasing precision.

The OECD Digital Education Outlook 2026 examines three themes of particular relevance. First, the distinction between task performance and learning: AI-assisted outputs may appear competent without evidence that learners have engaged in the cognitive, disciplinary, or reflective work that produces durable understanding (OECD, 2026a). Second, the reconfiguration of teaching: educators must be able to evaluate AI outputs, design pedagogically coherent tasks and maintain the relational and ethical dimensions of instruction that AI cannot replicate. Third, the need for policy coherence: AI adoption in education should be guided by institutional strategies that integrate pedagogical goals, data governance, professional development and accountability. Schleicher (2026) extends this analysis by calling for the design of safe AI systems in education—systems that are transparent, aligned with educational values and subject to human oversight rather than commercial optimisation.

OECD (2026b) argues that the integration of AI into education does not diminish the importance of teacher expertise but intensifies it. UNESCO's AI Competency Framework for Teachers (2024) similarly identifies five dimensions of teacher AI competency: a human-centred mindset, AI ethics, AI foundations, AI pedagogy and professional development through AI. Together, these frameworks position teachers not as passive users of AI tools but as critical professionals who exercise oversight and design judgement. For immersive technologies, OECD (2026c) identifies both pedagogical promise and significant governance challenges: concerns about the collection of spatial, biometric and behavioural data; digital security; physical safety; and the risk of adoption outpacing regulatory readiness.

European perspectives add regulatory specificity to this normative landscape. The European Digital Education Action Plan 2021–2027 prioritises the development of digital competences, the promotion of digital education research and support for inclusive and accessible digital learning (European Commission, 2020). The European AI Act (European Parliament and Council of the European Union, 2024) introduces a risk-based regulatory framework that designates AI systems used in education as high-risk when they influence access, assessment, or educational progression. High-risk AI systems must meet requirements for transparency, accuracy, human oversight and data governance—making institutional governance literacy a professional necessity rather than an optional competency. UNESCO's (2023) Guidance for Generative AI in Education and Research foregrounds human agency, academic integrity, equity and the importance of institutional validation before AI is embedded in formal educational processes, extending these frameworks to a global level.

The concept of human-centred AI has also received important theoretical elaboration. Shneiderman (2022) argues that human-centred AI should increase human control while enabling high levels of automation where appropriate: in educational contexts, this implies that AI should augment rather than replace pedagogical judgement, disciplinary reasoning and learner responsibility. AR and immersive design theory adds further nuance. Research on presence and plausibility in immersive environments (Makransky & Lilleholt, 2018; Slater, 2009) demonstrates that the subjective sense of being in an environment—while pedagogically relevant—is neither sufficient nor synonymous with learning. The convergence of OECD, European and scholarly frameworks provides the analytical foundation for the five-dimensional framework presented in the following section.

5. A FIVE-DIMENSIONAL FRAMEWORK FOR HUMAN-CENTRED AI AND IMMERSIVE LEARNING DESIGN

Existing AI-in-education frameworks often privilege adaptivity, automation, analytics and feedback, whereas AR and immersive learning frameworks tend to privilege presence, spatial interaction, embodiment and simulation. The proposed framework contributes by treating AI and AR not as separate technological affordances but as co-mediating elements of human-centred learning ecosystems governed by pedagogy, agency, inclusion and trust. This positioning departs from technology-centred adoption frameworks by locating the educational value of both AI and AR not in their respective technical capabilities but in the conditions of design, professional judgement, equity and institutional accountability under which they are deployed.

The proposed framework consists of five interrelated dimensions: human-centred pedagogy, immersive learning design, learner and teacher agency, inclusion and access and governance and trust. These dimensions form an ecosystem in which decisions about learning design, technological affordances, assessment, data, infrastructure and institutional policy mutually influence one another.

Figure 1. Five-Dimensional Conceptual Framework for Human-Centred AI and Immersive Learning Design in Higher Education

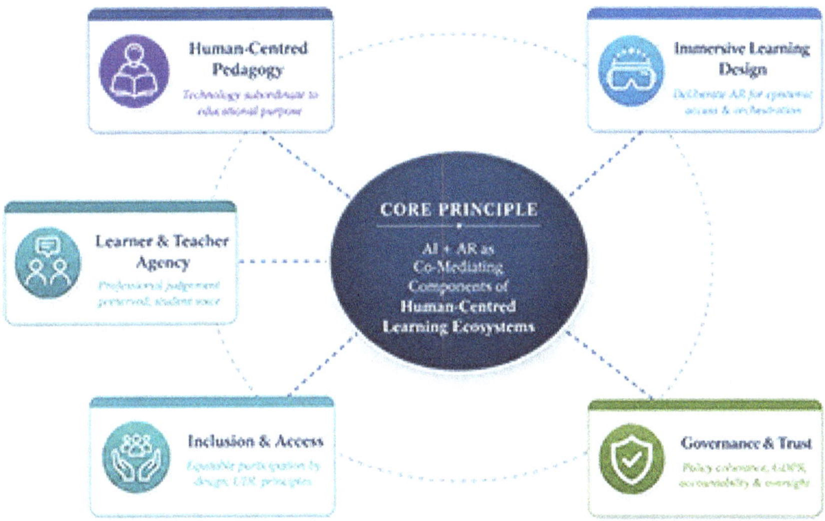

Sources: OECD (2023, 2026a, 2026b, 2026c); UNESCO (2023, 2024); European Parliament and Council of the European Union (2024).

Figure 1 presents the overall framework; Table 1 provides a structured summary of each dimension's core question and design implication. It is important to note that the five dimensions are not always in harmony: inclusion and governance, for example, can represent competing institutional priorities, with efforts to widen access sometimes outpacing the data protection infrastructure needed to support it responsibly. The framework does not resolve such tensions algorithmically; rather, it makes them visible so that institutional decision-makers can navigate them through deliberate professional and ethical judgement. Researchers and practitioners applying the framework analytically should also note that the dimensions are intended as a basis for developing context-specific, measurable indicators: the question "to what extent is this dimension addressed?" can only be answered through institution- and discipline-level operationalisation, rather than from the framework alone. Critical scholarship on educational technology—including analyses of power relations in platform dependency, commercial data extraction and what Selwyn (2019) terms the political economy of educational technology—also informs the framework's normative stance. The framework draws primarily on OECD and European contexts, but the tensions it identifies between human-centred values and efficiency-driven adoption are not unique to high-income or Anglophone settings: scholarship on mobile and technology-mediated learning in diverse national contexts (e.g., Palalas & Ally, 2016) and systematic research across higher education systems beyond the Anglophone core (e.g., Zawacki-Richter et al., 2019) confirms that questions of access, agency and governance are pressing across a wide range of institutional and national conditions, including settings where infrastructure constraints make inclusion and equity particularly acute.

Table 1. ***Five Dimensions of the Human-Centred AI and Immersive Learning Design Framework***

Dimension	Core question	Design implication
Human-centred pedagogy	Does the technology genuinely support understanding, inquiry, reflection and meaningful participation?	Begin with learning outcomes; adopt AI and AR only when they strengthen disciplinary reasoning or provide defensible evidence of learning.
Immersive learning design	What becomes experientially, spatially, or contextually accessible through AR that would otherwise be inaccessible?	Design representations, interactions, sequencing and debriefing around epistemic access rather than novelty or engagement alone.
Learner and teacher agency	Who remains able to interpret, decide, question, revise and override technological mediation?	Keep students as active interpreters of knowledge and teachers as professional decision-makers with override capacity.
Inclusion and access	Who benefits, who is excluded and what equivalent alternatives are available?	Plan accessibility, device equity, linguistic support and alternative pathways from the beginning of design.
Governance and trust	Are risks, data practices, responsibilities and evidence standards transparent and institutionally governed?	Build privacy, safety, human oversight, auditability and accountability into design, procurement and evaluation.

5.1 Human-Centred Pedagogy

Human-centred pedagogy asks whether AI and AR are being used in ways that genuinely support understanding, inquiry, reflection and meaningful participation. Technology is subordinate to educational purpose. AI is not valuable because it produces rapid answers; it is valuable when it supports productive struggle, formative feedback, metacognitive reflection, disciplinary reasoning, or inclusive participation. AR is not valuable because it creates visually impressive experiences; it is valuable when it helps learners perceive relationships, test explanations, practise procedures, or connect abstract knowledge to meaningful contexts.

This dimension requires explicit alignment among learning outcomes, tasks, technological affordances and assessment evidence. Human-centred pedagogy is also attentive to cognitive load. Multimedia learning theory suggests that learners benefit when instructional materials manage essential processing, reduce extraneous processing and support generative processing (Mayer, 2021). AI and AR can support these goals by providing timely explanations, visualising otherwise hidden structures, or enabling interactive comparison. However, they can also increase extraneous load through excessive prompts, visual clutter, device friction, novelty effects, or conflicting representations. The framework therefore treats pedagogical restraint, clarity of sequencing and disciplinary purpose as design virtues. A human-centred pedagogical approach further requires that AI and AR support epistemic agency: learners should be positioned as questioners, interpreters, designers and evaluators rather than consumers of pre-scripted AI output or guided tourists in pre-designed immersive environments.

5.2 Immersive Learning Design

Immersive learning design refers to the deliberate use of AR and related technologies to make difficult, abstract, inaccessible, dangerous, or context-dependent phenomena more experientially available to learners. The term design is important: it shifts attention from immersion as a sensory condition to immersion as an instructional arrangement. Immersive learning design includes choices about representation, sequencing, interaction, collaboration, feedback, physical context, sensory load and debriefing. Slater (2009) distinguishes between place illusion—the presence experience—and plausibility, the sense that events are real and responsive; Makransky and Lilleholt (2018) demonstrate that emotional and cognitive value in immersive environments depends substantially on how content is designed and sequenced, not merely on the realism of the environment.

AR has particular value when learning depends on spatial, procedural, contextual, or embodied understanding. Bower et al. (2014) emphasise the pedagogical potential of AR, including student-generated AR experiences that support higher-order thinking. Radu's (2014) meta-review identifies educational benefits but also highlights negative effects and design factors that determine whether AR supports learning. Immersive learning design must therefore avoid representational realism as an unquestioned goal: sometimes simplified or abstracted representations better support learning by directing attention to conceptually relevant features. More recent empirical work has extended these foundational analyses into disciplinary contexts where AR's contribution to epistemic practice is particularly evident. In health sciences education, AR-supported anatomy and clinical simulation environments have demonstrated gains not simply in factual recall but in procedural competence and clinical reasoning, supporting learners in developing the perceptual discrimination and diagnostic judgement that are central to medical practice (Barteit et al., 2021). In engineering education, AR overlays on physical systems support the development of fault-finding and systems-thinking capacities that neither textbook instruction nor classroom-based explanation can replicate as effectively (Hamilton et al., 2021). In teacher education, AR-based classroom simulation and pedagogical event replay have been used to support the kind of reflective analysis that connects observation of practice to conceptual frameworks for professional judgement. Across these fields, what AR distinctively contributes is not primarily enhanced engagement or motivational benefit, but epistemic access: the capacity to perceive, manipulate and reason about phenomena that are otherwise invisible, procedurally inaccessible, hazardous, or remote from the learning environment. This epistemic access is educationally valuable only when immersive experience is explicitly connected to disciplinary questioning and knowledge-building processes; AR episodes that immerse learners without anchoring them in the epistemic practices of the discipline risk producing engagement without understanding. Table 2 provides disciplinary examples illustrating how AI and AR contributions can be combined for human-centred immersive learning across a range of higher education fields.

Table 2. ***Disciplinary Applications of Combined AI-AR Integration in Higher Education***

Discipline	AR application	AI contribution	Learning outcome focus
Health sciences	Anatomical layer visualisation; clinical procedure simulation in safe environment	Generates diagnostic reasoning prompts and misconception feedback	Clinical judgement, procedural competence and patient-safety reasoning
Engineering	AR inspection of mechanical systems, infrastructure, or circuit design in situ	Provides fault analysis feedback and explanatory scaffolding on errors	Structural reasoning, applied problem-solving and systems thinking
Teacher education	Classroom scenario simulation and pedagogical event replay in field placement	Supports reflective analysis and comparison with pedagogical principles	Professional reflection, instructional decision-making and adaptive practice

continued on following page

Table 2. Continued

Discipline	AR application	AI contribution	Learning outcome focus
Architecture and design	Spatial design prototype placed into physical environment for client review	Critiques design rationale and generates alternative propositions	Spatial reasoning, design argumentation and client communication
Environmental science	Ecological data layers overlaid on field site; species and climate data visualised	Enables scenario comparison and systems-level questioning	Field-based reasoning, environmental analysis and evidence-based argument
Mathematics and science education	Geometric, molecular, or physical structure visualised in three dimensions	Generates conceptual probes and guides hypothesis testing	Conceptual understanding, epistemic transfer and representational reasoning

Sources: Bower et al. (2014); Makransky & Lilleholt (2018); Radianti et al. (2020).

5.3 Learner and Teacher Agency

Agency is central to a human-centred learning ecosystem. Learner agency refers to the capacity to act intentionally, make choices, interpret information, monitor understanding, question technological outputs and participate meaningfully in learning. Teacher agency refers to professional judgement in designing tasks, selecting tools, interpreting evidence, supporting students and making ethical decisions. AI and AR integration becomes problematic when either form of agency is weakened.

AI systems can reduce learner agency when they provide answers so fluent that students accept them without verification, or when automated feedback is treated as authoritative rather than provisional. Assessment in AI-rich environments should therefore place greater emphasis on process evidence, oral defence, iterative drafts, reflective commentary and authentic performance rather than polished product alone. Teacher agency can also be compromised if institutions adopt AI systems primarily for efficiency, reducing educators to supervisors of automated workflows. OECD (2026b) emphasises the continuing importance of teachers' professional roles, judgement and capacity to adapt to changing learning conditions. Agency also involves transparency: students should know when AI is used, what data are collected, what assumptions guide automated recommendations and how outputs should be interpreted. Teachers should understand the limitations of the tools they are expected to use and retain the right to override, reinterpret, or reject technological mediation. Self-regulated learning theory provides a further basis for understanding agency in AI-rich environments. Zimmerman (2002) describes self-regulated learners as active participants who set goals, monitor their progress, adjust strategies and reflect on their own cognitive and motivational processes. AI tools that provide immediate corrective feedback, worked examples, or explanatory scaffolding can support self-regulation when they are designed to prompt metacognitive reflection rather than replace it. The risk is that AI-generated feedback structures cognitive effort in ways that diminish rather than develop learners' capacity to monitor and regulate their own understanding. Human-centred AI design in higher education should therefore prioritise the development of self-regulatory capacity as a goal alongside and sometimes above, task completion. A human-centred approach should also include student voice in the design, piloting and evaluation of AI-AR learning environments, particularly where accessibility, agency and trust are concerned: students should be positioned not only as users of these technologies but as co-designers, participants and evaluators whose experiential knowledge informs responsible integration. Equally, the framework recognises institutional agency as a third, often underacknowledged, dimension: universities themselves are active agents in this ecosystem, making consequential decisions about procurement, governance, faculty development and risk allocation that shape the conditions under which individual learner and teacher agency can meaningfully operate.

5.4 Inclusion and Access

AI and AR can expand educational opportunity, but they can also amplify inequality. Inclusion must therefore be treated as a constitutive design principle rather than a later implementation concern. AI tools may support multilingual learners, students with disabilities and students who benefit from flexible pacing, but these benefits depend on equitable access to devices, connectivity, institutional support, accessible design and culturally responsive pedagogy. Language models may reproduce linguistic, cultural, disciplinary, or geopolitical biases. AR tools may provide access to laboratories, field sites, or professional simulations that would otherwise be unavailable, but only where hardware costs, bandwidth requirements and physical accessibility have been adequately addressed.

Accessibility is not limited to disability accommodation, although that is essential. It includes linguistic access, device access, bandwidth access, cognitive accessibility, cultural relevance and assessment fairness (Radianti et al., 2020). At the institutional level, inclusion also concerns capacity: universities vary substantially in infrastructure, procurement expertise, staff development and data governance capacity. A responsible framework must therefore avoid assuming that all higher education institutions can implement AI and AR in identical ways. The framework treats inclusive redundancy as a non-negotiable design principle. Inclusive redundancy refers to the deliberate provision, from the earliest stages of curriculum design, of equivalent learning pathways and assessment alternatives that do not depend on access to any single technology, interface, or sensory modality. A learning environment designed with inclusive redundancy ensures that every student has a meaningful route to the intended learning outcomes regardless of whether they can access a particular device, tolerate an immersive environment, or use a given platform.

5.5 Governance and Trust

Governance and trust form the institutional layer of the framework. Trustworthy integration of AI and AR requires policy coherence, transparency, data protection, risk assessment, procurement standards, accountability mechanisms and alignment between educational aims and technological choices. In AI-supported education, governance issues include bias, explainability, reliability, intellectual property, academic integrity, automated decision-making and human oversight. When AI systems are used for grading, admission, progression, or high-stakes feedback, the risks increase substantially. The European AI Act's risk-based approach addresses precisely this: educational AI systems that influence access or evaluation must be auditable, contestable, transparent and subject to professional review (European Parliament and Council of the European Union, 2024). Selwyn's (2019) critical perspective on educational technology reminds us that governance failures are not merely technical oversights but expressions of political and institutional choices about whose interests technology adoption serves. Williamson (2017) identifies the growing role of big data in shaping educational policy and practice, raising concerns about who controls these data flows, what inferences are drawn from learner interactions and how algorithmic outputs influence institutional decisions that affect individual students. Perrotta and Selwyn (2020) extend this analysis by examining how algorithmic systems produce relational effects in educational settings, reshaping what counts as evidence of learning, who holds interpretive authority and how institutional power operates through automated recommendation systems. Taken together, these critical perspectives underscore why governance in AI-AR learning ecosystems cannot be reduced to regulatory compliance alone: it requires ongoing institutional deliberation about values, power and educational purpose.

In AR and immersive environments, governance issues include physical safety, psychological comfort, location data, biometric and behavioural data collection, digital security and the blurring of physical and digital boundaries (OECD, 2026c). The collection of spatial, gaze and behavioural data in immersive contexts raises particularly acute questions under the General Data Protection Regulation (GDPR), whose principles of data minimisation, purpose limitation, explicit consent and special-category data protection apply with full force to the biometric and sensitive personal data generated by AR platforms. Institutions operating in European jurisdictions must ensure that AI-AR data architectures are designed from the outset to respect these obligations and that learners are informed clearly about what data are collected, how they are processed and what rights they retain. Trust also depends on evidence: universities should not rely on vendor claims or novelty-driven adoption but should require evidence of pedagogical alignment, data protection standards, staff readiness, student experience and measurable learning outcomes. A trustworthy learning ecosystem is one in which technological innovation is continuously examined against educational purpose and human consequences.

6. DESIGN PRINCIPLES FOR AI-AR INTEGRATION IN HIGHER EDUCATION

The five dimensions presented in Section 5 provide the conceptual architecture of the framework: they identify what human-centred AI-AR integration must address and why each dimension matters. The design principles introduced in this section operationalise that architecture by translating each dimension into concrete instructional and institutional decisions. The principles do not derive from the dimensions independently; rather, each principle gives one or more dimensions a practical expression, making the framework actionable for curriculum designers, educators and institutional leaders. The move from dimensions to principles is therefore a move from analytical description to design prescription: from identifying what is at stake to specifying how those stakes can be addressed in practice.

The five-dimensional framework can be translated into six design principles for curriculum and assessment. The first principle is purpose before platform: AI or AR should be selected only after the learning problem has been clearly defined. Human-centred design resists technological escalation when simpler pedagogies are equally effective. The second principle is augmentation rather than substitution: AI should support learners in planning, questioning, explaining, revising and reflecting, rather than replacing those processes; AR should enrich perception and contextual interaction, rather than replacing disciplinary inquiry with passive experience. The third principle is visible learning processes: AI-rich environments require assessment practices that make reasoning, decision-making, revision and reflection visible; AR-rich environments require evidence that learners can transfer insights from immersive experience to conceptual explanation, professional judgement, or authentic performance.

The fourth principle is teacher-mediated flexibility: AI and AR should be embedded in designs that allow educators to adapt activities, interpret student responses and intervene when needed. Fully automated pathways may be efficient, but they are rarely adequate for the complex relational, ethical and disciplinary dimensions of higher education learning. The fifth principle is inclusive redundancy: learners should not be excluded because they cannot access a device, tolerate an immersive environment, afford a subscription, or use a particular interface. Alternative pathways and equivalent learning evidence should be planned from the beginning. The sixth principle is governance by design: data protection, transparency, accessibility, risk management and accountability should be built into curriculum design, procurement and evaluation rather than addressed after deployment. Figure 2 presents these principles as a cyclical design process.

Figure 2. Human-Centred AI-AR Learning Design Cycle

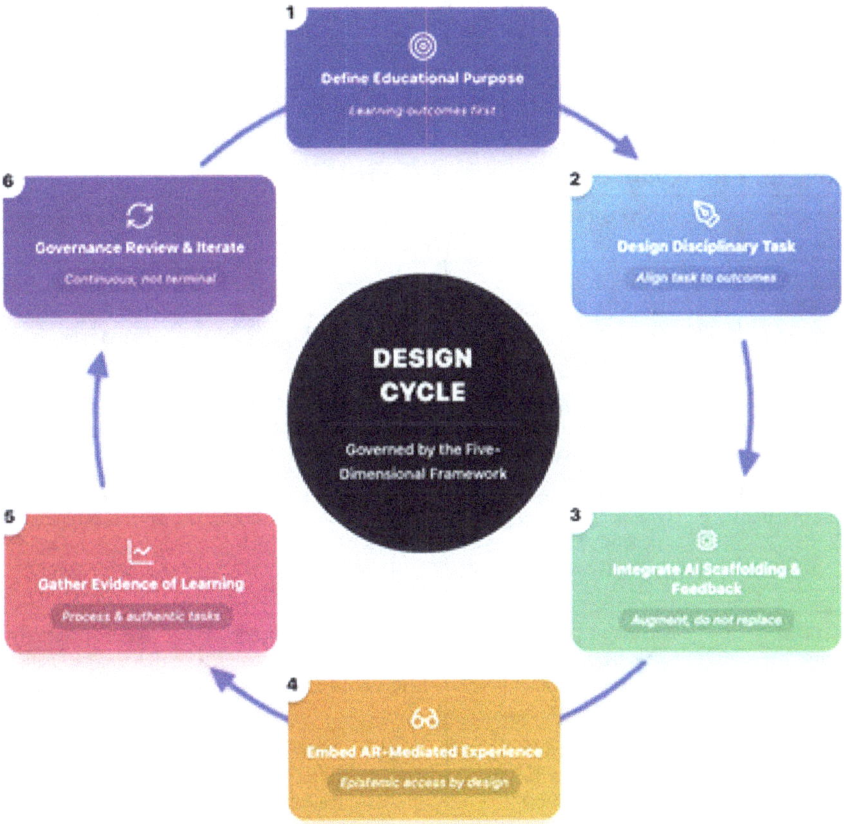

The design cycle presented in Figure 2 does not prescribe a rigid sequence but establishes a principled order of consideration. In practice, phases overlap and inform one another: a task designed in Phase 2 may reveal a gap in the learning purpose articulated in Phase 1; evidence gathered in Phase 5 may prompt refinement of the AR integration planned in Phase 4; and governance concerns identified at any point may require the entire cycle to pause and re-examine earlier decisions. This iterative character is not a limitation of the framework but a deliberate feature of human-centred design, which treats responsiveness to evidence as more valuable than procedural fidelity.

Applying the design cycle requires translating its abstract phases into concrete disciplinary decisions. The choice of learning challenge, the selection of AI scaffolding tools and the design of AR-mediated experience will differ substantially between, for example, a clinical simulation in medical education, a materials analysis task in engineering, or a source critique exercise in history. Table 3 operationalises the cycle across a range of such disciplinary contexts, mapping representative learning challenges to the specific contributions of AI and AR and identifying the human-centred safeguards that each integration requires.

Table 3. ***Design Matrix for Integrating AI and AR in Higher Education: Learning Challenges, Contributions and Human-Centred Safeguards***

Learning challenge	AI contribution	AR/Immersive contribution	Human-centred safeguard
Abstract or invisible phenomena	Generate prompts, analogies, formative questions and misconception checks.	Visualise structures, processes, or spatial relationships in context.	Require explanation, comparison and transfer beyond the visual experience.
Complex professional practice	Support scenario branching, reflective questioning and decision feedback.	Simulate authentic environments, equipment, or embodied procedures.	Keep expert debriefing and teacher judgement central; avoid over-scripted pathways.
Diverse learner needs	Offer language support, adaptive practice and alternative explanations.	Provide manipulable representations and situated experiences.	Avoid premium-only access; ensure equivalent assessment pathways for all learners.
Assessment integrity	Support formative feedback and iterative process documentation.	Generate performance traces and situational evidence of competence.	Assess reasoning, reflection and authentic performance rather than outputs alone.
Institutional accountability	Enable transparent, auditable analytics for improvement.	Provide simulation data for curriculum evaluation and accreditation.	Limit data collection, clarify consent, audit risks and maintain human oversight.

Sources: OECD (2026a, 2026c); Mayer (2021); European Parliament and Council of the European Union (2024).

7. IMPLICATIONS FOR CURRICULUM, ASSESSMENT, FACULTY DEVELOPMENT AND INSTITUTIONAL STRATEGY

7.1 Curriculum Design

In curriculum design, the proposed framework encourages programmes to identify where AI and AR provide distinctive educational value. AI may be most useful where students need frequent formative feedback, adaptive practice, language support, or opportunities to critique generated outputs. AR may be most useful where learning depends on spatial reasoning, embodied practice, contextual observation, or access to otherwise inaccessible phenomena. The strongest designs are those in which AI and AR are connected to disciplinary practices rather than treated as generic digital enhancements. A conventional assignment might become an AI-AR redesigned task in which students investigate an AR-based case, use AI to generate competing explanations, critique those explanations against disciplinary evidence and submit a reflective account of how their reasoning developed.

7.2 Assessment

Assessment policies must evolve in parallel. In AI-rich environments, prohibitive policies alone are insufficient because AI use may be pedagogically legitimate and technically difficult to detect. More robust approaches include transparent AI-use declarations, process portfolios, oral examinations, live problem-solving, peer critique and authentic tasks. In AR-rich environments, assessment should evaluate whether learners can explain represented phenomena, apply concepts beyond the simulated context and reflect on the representational limitations of the immersive experience. Crompton and Burke (2023) note that assessment reform in AI-integrated higher education requires sustained disciplinary community engagement rather than generic institutional policy alone. Table 4 summarises key assessment challenges alongside their AI/AR-related risks and the human-centred responses the framework supports.

Table 4. ***Assessment Challenges, AI/AR-Related Risks and Human-Centred Responses***

Assessment challenge	AI/AR-related risk	Human-centred response
Product-based essays	AI-generated outputs submitted as original work	Process portfolio combined with oral defence
AR simulation performance	Engagement mistaken for competence; novelty effects inflate perceived learning	Require conceptual explanation of represented phenomena plus near-transfer task
Automated AI feedback	Learner dependency on AI feedback; reduced self-regulatory capacity	Mandatory reflective feedback log requiring student interpretation and self-assessment
Learning analytics dashboards	Over-datafication; reductive metrics substituting for professional pedagogical judgement	Transparent evidence policy with educator oversight and learner access to own data

Sources: Crompton & Burke (2023); OECD (2026a); European Parliament and Council of the European Union (2024).

7.3 Faculty Development

Faculty development is indispensable. Educators need conceptual frameworks for evaluating AI's pedagogical role, critical capacity for assessing AI outputs and practical skills for designing AI-integrated learning environments that protect cognitive engagement and learner agency. UNESCO (2024) identifies AI pedagogy and ethics as core dimensions of teacher AI competency and OECD (2026b) argues that faculty development should position educators as active participants in shaping AI's role rather than passive recipients of mandated tools.

7.4 Institutional Strategy

Institutionally, AI and AR integration requires coordinated strategy across academic development, information technology, legal and governance and library and research support units. A human-centred institutional strategy should define success in terms of learning quality, inclusion, teacher capacity, student agency, assessment integrity and trustworthy governance—not merely deployment scale or platform access. Institutions also bear responsibility for managing the risks of vendor dependency and commercial platform lock-in: strategies that prioritise open-source tools, interoperability standards and institutional data sovereignty are more consistent with a human-centred approach than those that defer entirely to commercial AI providers. Leadership should invest in shared institutional infrastructure and equity impact assessment to ensure that AI-AR integration strengthens rather than stratifies educational opportunity across diverse student populations.

8. RISKS, MITIGATION STRATEGIES AND GOVERNANCE SAFEGUARDS

Section 5.5 established governance and trust as a conceptual dimension of the framework, addressing the institutional conditions, policy mechanisms and structural requirements for trustworthy AI-AR integration. This section moves from that conceptual level to the operational level: it identifies the specific categories of risk that materialise when AI and AR are deployed in practice, describes how those risks manifest in observable educational situations and specifies the mitigation strategies and governance safeguards that institutions and educators need to manage them. Where Section 5.5 asked what trustworthy governance should achieve, this section asks what can go wrong, how it appears in practice and what targeted responses are required. Three categories of risk can be identified: pedagogical, structural and governance.

Pedagogical risks arise from ways in which AI and AR can undermine rather than support learning. The most frequently cited is cognitive offloading: learners may use AI to complete tasks without engaging in the reasoning, argumentation, or disciplinary judgement that the task was intended to develop (OECD, 2026a). Contemporary generative AI accentuates this risk by producing sophisticated-sounding outputs that satisfy surface indicators of competence while leaving deeper understanding undeveloped. A related risk is assessment invalidity: if polished AI-generated outputs are submitted as evidence of learning, assessment judgements may no longer reliably represent what students understand or can independently do. In AR and immersive environments, representational distraction and cognitive overload (Mayer, 2021; Radianti et al., 2020) represent parallel pedagogical risks when immersive experiences are not carefully designed and sequenced.

Structural risks concern institutional and systemic conditions. Teacher deskilling arises when AI systems are adopted primarily for efficiency, gradually eroding educators' capacity to design and interpret learning. Inequitable access creates structural disadvantages when AI or AR integration assumes device availability, connectivity, or subscription access that is unevenly distributed. Vendor dependency—reliance on proprietary platforms—may limit institutional control over pedagogical design, data practices and system accountability. Governance risks arise from the data-intensive nature of AI and AR systems: granular interaction data, spatial tracking, gaze data and biometric markers raise privacy, consent and algorithmic transparency concerns of a kind that existing educational data governance frameworks were not designed to address (OECD, 2026c). Table 5 summarises principal risks and recommended mitigation and governance strategies.

Table 5. ***Risk Categories, Manifestations and Mitigation Strategies in AI-AR Learning Ecosystems***

Risk category and type	How it may appear in practice	Mitigation strategy and governance safeguard
Pedagogical — Cognitive offloading (AI)	Students use AI to complete tasks without engaging in disciplinary reasoning, argumentation, or reflective judgement.	Use process portfolios, oral examinations, AI-use declarations and tasks requiring critique of AI outputs; design assessment around reasoning, not product.
Pedagogical — Representational distraction (AR)	Learners focus on the visual or sensory richness of the immersive experience rather than engaging conceptual content.	Simplify AR representations, use structured guiding questions, provide mandatory debriefing and align AR episodes with explicit learning outcomes.
Pedagogical — Cognitive overload (AR)	Complex multi-sensory environments exceed learners' integration capacity, particularly for novices or learners with diverse sensory needs.	Apply multimedia learning principles (Mayer, 2021); reduce extraneous load; sequence immersive content from simple to complex.
Structural — Teacher deskilling	Educators become supervisors of automated workflows rather than designers of learning and professional decision-makers.	Invest in faculty development; preserve teacher override and redesign rights; involve educators in procurement, piloting and policy review.
Structural — Inequitable access	Students or institutions lack devices, subscriptions, bandwidth, accessible design, or technical support for meaningful participation.	Provide low-cost or open-source alternatives, shared institutional infrastructure and equivalent assessment pathways. Conduct equity impact assessments.
Governance — Data and privacy exposure	AI or AR systems collect sensitive behavioural, location, biometric, or performance data without adequate transparency or consent.	Implement data minimisation, privacy impact assessments, transparent consent procedures, security audits and institutional data governance policies aligned with the EU AI Act.

Sources: OECD (2026a, 2026c); Mayer (2021); European Parliament and Council of the European Union (2024).

9. FUTURE RESEARCH DIRECTIONS

The framework opens several directions for future empirical and theoretical research. First, empirical studies should examine how combined AI-AR environments influence learning processes—including analysis of student reasoning, attention, collaboration, metacognition and transfer—not only learning outcomes. Design-based research is especially suitable because it allows iterative refinement of tasks, technologies and pedagogical mediation. Second, research should examine teacher agency in AI-AR learning ecosystems. Many studies focus on student experience or system effectiveness, but educators' professional judgement is central to human-centred integration. Third, assessment validity requires sustained research attention: stronger methods are needed for determining what students have actually learned in AI-supported and immersive contexts, including process-based, multimodal and longitudinal evidence approaches.

Fourth, inclusion should be studied beyond access metrics: how AI and AR affect learners with different linguistic backgrounds, disabilities, socioeconomic conditions, disciplinary identities and digital confidence levels, as well as institutional disparities across higher education systems. Fifth, governance research should analyse how universities make procurement decisions, evaluate risks and build accountability systems, with particular attention to how European and international frameworks influence institutional practice. Finally, theoretical work should continue to extend the framework through emerging dimensions such as embodied cognition, affective dimensions of immersive experience (Makransky & Lilleholt, 2018), sustainability, student voice and discipline-specific epistemologies. Table 6 provides a structured overview of the proposed research agenda.

Table 6. ***Future Research Agenda for Human-Centred AI and Immersive Learning Design in Higher Education***

Research focus	Possible research question	Suitable designs
Learning processes	How do students reason, collaborate and revise understanding in combined AI-AR environments?	Design-based research; multimodal learning analytics; qualitative interaction analysis.
Teacher agency	How do academic staff exercise professional judgement when AI and AR mediate learning and assessment?	Case studies; semi-structured interviews; participatory design research.
Assessment validity	What forms of evidence best demonstrate learning in AI-supported and immersive contexts?	Mixed-methods validation; assessment design experiments; comparative validity studies.
Inclusion and equity	Which learners benefit from AI-AR integration and which encounter new barriers, particularly across institutional and national contexts?	Equity audits; accessibility studies; comparative institutional and cross-national research.
Governance and policy	How do universities translate regulatory frameworks into procurement decisions, risk management and professional practice?	Policy analysis; institutional ethnography; comparative European case studies.

10. LIMITATIONS

As a conceptual chapter, the framework does not claim empirical validation. Its dimensions are grounded in a synthesis of international policy documents, theoretical scholarship and empirical literature, but they have not been tested through implementation studies or evaluated against outcome data from specific institutional contexts. The synthesis draws primarily on OECD and European policy sources and English-language scholarship, which may not fully represent the diversity of higher education systems, pedagogical traditions and governance conditions in non-OECD or non-Anglophone contexts. Future research should therefore test the framework's dimensions through design-based research, institutional case studies, comparative policy analysis and discipline-specific implementation studies in varied higher education settings. Refinements to the framework's dimensions, indicators and governance implications are to be expected as empirical evidence accumulates.

11. CONCLUSION

AI and AR are powerful technologies, but their educational value depends on how they are designed, mediated, assessed and governed. Higher education does not need a technology-first model that treats AI and AR as symbols of innovation or competitive positioning. It needs a human-centred framework that asks what forms of learning are worth supporting, what human capacities should be strengthened, what risks must be governed and what evidence demonstrates genuine educational value.

This chapter has argued that AI and AR should be brought into a shared conceptual space. AI mediates feedback, language, prediction, adaptation and decision support. AR mediates perception, context, embodiment and experiential access. Together, they can enrich higher education when they support inquiry, reflection, disciplinary reasoning, inclusion and professional judgement. They can also weaken learning when they encourage dependency, spectacle, inequity, opacity, or uncritical automation. The proposed five-dimensional framework—human-centred pedagogy, immersive learning design, learner and teacher agency, inclusion and access and governance and trust—offers a language for responsible integration grounded in recent OECD and European policy frameworks and in established scholarship on educational technology, human-centred design and technology governance.

The framework invites universities to move beyond adoption narratives and toward educationally warranted, ethically defensible and institutionally accountable design. The future of AI and AR in higher education should be judged not by the sophistication of the technologies deployed, but by how effectively they serve human learning, human agency and public trust.

REFERENCES

Azuma, R. T. (1997). A survey of augmented reality. *Presence (Cambridge, Mass.)*, *6*(4), 355–385. DOI: 10.1162/pres.1997.6.4.355

Barteit, S., Lanfermann, L., Bärnighäusen, T., Neuhann, F., & Beiersmann, C. (2021). Augmented, mixed and virtual reality-based head-mounted devices for medical education: Systematic review. *JMIR Serious Games*, *9*(3), e29080. DOI: 10.2196/29080 PMID: 34255668

Bower, M., Howe, C., McCredie, N., Robinson, A., & Grover, D. (2014). Augmented reality in education: Cases, places and potentials. *Educational Media International*, *51*(1), 1–15. DOI: 10.1080/09523987.2014.889400

Crompton, H., & Burke, D. (2023). Artificial intelligence in higher education: The state of the field. *International Journal of Educational Technology in Higher Education*, *20*(1), 22. Advance online publication. DOI: 10.1186/s41239-023-00392-8

European Commission. (2020). Digital Education Action Plan 2021–2027: Resetting education and training for the digital age. Publications Office of the European Union. https://education.ec.europa.eu/focus-topics/digital-education/action-plan

European Parliament and Council of the European Union. (2024). Regulation (EU) 2024/1689 laying down harmonised rules on artificial intelligence (Artificial Intelligence Act). Official Journal of the European Union, L 2024/1689. https://eur-lex.europa.eu/legal-content/EN/TXT/?uri=OJ:L_202401689

Hamilton, D., McKechnie, J., Edgerton, E., & Wilson, C. (2021). Immersive virtual reality as a pedagogical tool in education: A systematic literature review of quantitative learning outcomes and experimental design. *Journal of Computers in Education*, *8*(1), 1–32. DOI: 10.1007/s40692-020-00169-2

Makransky, G., & Lilleholt, L. (2018). A structural equation modeling investigation of the emotional value of immersive virtual reality in education. *Educational Technology Research and Development*, *66*(5), 1141–1164. DOI: 10.1007/s11423-018-9581-2

Mayer, R. E. (2021). *Multimedia learning* (3rd ed.). Cambridge University Press., DOI: 10.1017/9781316941355

Milgram, P., & Kishino, F. (1994). A taxonomy of mixed reality visual displays. *IEICE Transactions on Information and Systems*, *E77-D*(12), 1321–1329.

OECD. (2023). OECD principles on artificial intelligence. https://oecd.ai/en/ai-principles

OECD. (2026a). *OECD Digital Education Outlook 2026: Exploring effective uses of generative AI in education.* OECD Publishing., DOI: 10.1787/062a7394-

OECD. (2026b). *Reimagining teaching in an accelerating world.* OECD Publishing., DOI: 10.1787/d0edfe8c-

OECD. (2026c). *An overview of national strategies and policies for immersive technologies. OECD Digital Economy Papers, No. 380.* OECD Publishing., DOI: 10.1787/2da1d7da-

Palalas, A., & Ally, M. (Eds.). (2016). *The international handbook of mobile-assisted language learning.* China Central Radio & TV University Press.

Perrotta, C., & Selwyn, N. (2020). Deep learning goes to school: Toward a relational understanding of AI in education. *Learning, Media and Technology, 45*(3), 251–269. DOI: 10.1080/17439884.2020.1686017

Radianti, J., Majchrzak, T. A., Fromm, J., & Wohlgenannt, I. (2020). A systematic review of immersive virtual reality applications for higher education: Design elements, lessons learned and research agenda. *Computers & Education, 147*, 103778. Advance online publication. DOI: 10.1016/j.compedu.2019.103778

Radu, I. (2014). Augmented reality in education: A meta-review and cross-media analysis. *Personal and Ubiquitous Computing, 18*(6), 1533–1543. DOI: 10.1007/s00779-013-0747-y

Schleicher, A. (2026, January 23). Designing safe AI systems for education. OECD Education and Skills Today. https://oecdedutoday.com/designing-safe-ai-systems-for-education/

Selwyn, N. (2019). *Should robots replace teachers? AI and the future of education.* Polity Press.

Shneiderman, B. (2022). *Human-centered AI.* Oxford University Press. DOI: 10.1093/oso/9780192845290.001.0001

Slater, M. (2009). Place illusion and plausibility can lead to realistic behaviour in immersive virtual environments. *Philosophical Transactions of the Royal Society of London. Series B, Biological Sciences, 364*(1535), 3549–3557. DOI: 10.1098/rstb.2009.0138 PMID: 19884149

UNESCO. (2023). Guidance for generative AI in education and research. UNESCO. https://unesdoc.unesco.org/ark:/48223/pf0000386693

UNESCO. (2024). AI competency framework for teachers. UNESCO. https://unesdoc.unesco.org/ark:/48223/pf0000391104

Williamson, B. (2017). *Big data in education: The digital future of learning, policy and practice*. SAGE Publications. DOI: 10.4135/9781529714920

Zawacki-Richter, O., Marín, V. I., Bond, M., & Gouverneur, F. (2019). Systematic review of research on artificial intelligence applications in higher education: Where are the educators? *International Journal of Educational Technology in Higher Education, 16*(1), 39. Advance online publication. DOI: 10.1186/s41239-019-0171-0

Zimmerman, B. J. (2002). Becoming a self-regulated learner: An overview. *Theory into Practice, 41*(2), 64–70. DOI: 10.1207/s15430421tip4102_2

Chapter 4
Artificial Intelligence in Architectural Education:
AI Pedagogy and Research Gaps

Hakan Tong
Istanbul Technical University, Turkey

Ayşegül Kıdık
http://orcid.org/0000-0002-1497-2455
Abdullah Gül University, Turkey

Sema Alaçam
http://orcid.org/0000-0002-5979-3282
Istanbul Technical University, Turkey

ABSTRACT

This chapter investigates the integration of artificial intelligence (AI) into architectural education between 2023 and 2025 through a systematic mapping review of fifteen peer-reviewed studies indexed in WoS and Scopus. Following a PRISMA-informed approach, the chapter examines the different ways AI tools are used across pedagogical frameworks. The findings suggest that while AI significantly accelerates idea generation and increases visual variety, its influence on deeper cognitive aspects, particularly design thinking and spatial reasoning, appears to be more uneven and less conclusive. The review identifies five key dimensions of transformation: ideation and representation, cognitive augmentation, pedagogical integration, student perception and ethics, and methodological constraints. It reveals persistent gaps, including the lack of longitudinal evidence, limited cross-cultural perspectives, and insufficient evaluation metrics. Overall, the chapter contributes a structured framework for understanding current trajectories and proposes directions for AI in architectural pedagogy.

DOI: 10.4018/979-8-3373-9883-9.ch004

1. INTRODUCTION

The rapid emergence of generative artificial intelligence (AI), particularly since 2023, has introduced a new epistemological condition within architectural education. Unlike previous digital technologies that primarily enhanced precision, simulation, or computational control, contemporary AI systems actively participate in visual and conceptual production processes. This shift is particularly visible within design studios, where architectural knowledge is traditionally constructed through iterative cycles of representation, critique, reflection, and reformulation. As text-to-image systems and large language models become increasingly embedded within studio culture, architectural education faces a critical question: whether AI merely accelerates representation or fundamentally reshapes the cognitive and pedagogical foundations of design learning.

Architectural education has historically been grounded in studio-based learning, where students construct knowledge through iterative processes of making, critique, reflection, and refinement. Within this pedagogical framework, drawing, modeling, and diagramming are not merely representational tools but essential mechanisms for the development of design thinking. As Schön (1984) argues, design knowledge emerges through reflective practice, where thinking and making are deeply intertwined. From this perspective, the integration of AI into the design studio extends beyond issues of efficiency or automation; it has the potential to reshape the processes through which architectural knowledge is produced and evaluated.

Previous digital transformations in architecture, such as Computer-Aided Design (CAD), Building Information Modeling (BIM), and parametric design, primarily enhanced the representational and computational capacities of designers. These tools enabled precision, simulation, and rule-based variation, yet they largely remained dependent on explicit human control and intentionality (Oxman, 2008; Oxman, 2017). In contrast, generative AI introduces a qualitatively different paradigm. Rather than functioning solely as a passive instrument, AI systems actively participate in the generation of visual and textual outputs, thereby influencing early-stage ideation and design exploration. This shift reconfigures the relationship between designer, tool, and process, repositioning AI from a passive representational instrument toward a semi-autonomous system that increasingly influences ideation, visualization, and exploratory decision-making processes.

Discussions on artificial intelligence in design are not entirely new within architectural and design research. Long before the emergence of contemporary generative AI systems, the Artificial Intelligence in Design (AID) conference series during the 1990s explored themes such as conceptual design, case-based reasoning, generative systems, design cognition, collaborative agents, creativity support, and computational representations of design knowledge. The proceedings repeatedly framed computers not merely as drafting instruments but as active participants capable of supporting exploration, reasoning, and conceptual development within design processes (Gero & Sudweeks, 1992; Gero & Sudweeks, 1994; Gero & Sudweeks, 1996; Gero & Sudweeks, 1998). Contemporary generative AI tools, therefore represent not a complete rupture, but rather a new technological phase within a longer trajectory of computational design research. However, unlike earlier expert systems and rule-based approaches, current large language and text-to-image models introduce unprecedented accessibility, conversational interaction, and real-time visual generation capacities into architectural education and creative practice.

Recent pedagogical experiments have also begun to position AI not only as a representational tool but also as an active participant in early-stage design thinking and visualization processes. Tong et al. (2023) investigated whether generative AI could function as a new mode of sketching within freshman architectural education by integrating AI-supported visualization workflows into a basic design studio. Their findings suggest that AI-assisted image generation can extend exploratory representation processes and support alternative modes of visual thinking, particularly during conceptual development and spatial imagination. This perspective reinforces the growing shift from understanding computers merely as instruments toward considering AI systems as collaborative design partners within studio pedagogy.

This transformation has generated both optimism and concern within architectural education. On one hand, recent studies on AI-assisted architectural and design education suggest that generative systems can support ideation by expanding the range of possible design alternatives and enabling rapid visual exploration (Çelik, 2024; Medel-Vera et al., 2025; Montenegro, 2024). Such capabilities may be particularly valuable in early design stages, where students often struggle with idea generation and representation. On the other hand, critical perspectives in design research emphasize that the production of multiple alternatives does not in itself constitute design expertise. Design thinking requires the ability to frame problems, evaluate competing constraints, and synthesize complex information into coherent proposals (Cross, 2011). In this context, AI-generated outputs are often argued to remain at the level of visual representation, with limited engagement in deeper spatial reasoning, tectonic logic, or contextual integration.

Despite the rapid adoption of AI tools in architectural studios, their pedagogical implications remain insufficiently understood. Existing literature on artificial intelligence in education highlights both the potential and the limitations of AI in supporting learning processes, emphasizing that technological affordances do not automatically translate into meaningful cognitive development (Holmes et al., 2019). Empirical evidence in this domain remains limited, often relying on short-term interventions, small samples, and exploratory methodologies. As a result, there is still no clear consensus on whether AI contributes to deeper learning outcomes in design education, particularly in relation to design thinking, critical judgment, and architectural synthesis.

A major challenge in the current literature lies in the distinction between perceived creativity and demonstrable cognitive transformation. Students frequently report that AI tools enhance their ability to generate ideas more efficiently and contribute to a heightened sense of creativity and engagement. However, research in educational psychology suggests that increases in perceived self-efficacy or engagement do not necessarily correspond to deeper cognitive change (Bandura, 1997). Similarly, within design research, the development of expertise is understood as a reflective and iterative process rather than a purely generative one (Schön, 1984; Cross, 2011). Therefore, the ability to produce a greater number of visually compelling alternatives does not automatically translate into improved problem framing, critical evaluation, or integrative reasoning.

This distinction is particularly critical in architectural education, where the primary aim extends beyond generating multiple design options to fostering higher-order cognitive abilities. These include the capacity to define and reframe design problems, negotiate environmental and contextual constraints, and develop spatially coherent and meaningful architectural proposals. Accordingly, the pedagogical value of AI should be evaluated not only in terms of efficiency or visual output, but also in relation to its contribution to design cognition and long-term learning processes (Holmes et al., 2019).

This chapter addresses these issues by presenting a systematic mapping review of fifteen peer-reviewed studies published between 2023 and 2025 and indexed in Web of Science and Scopus. Following a PRISMA-informed framework, the chapter critically examines how AI is operationalized within architectural education and evaluates its impact across multiple dimensions, including ideation, representation, cognition, pedagogy, student perception, ethics, and research methodology. Rather than treating AI as a singular or uniformly transformative technology, the chapter analyzes the different ways in which AI tools are positioned within architectural learning environments.

The primary aim of this chapter is threefold. First, it identifies emerging patterns in the integration of AI within architectural design education, particularly in relation to different stages of the design process. Second, it evaluates the extent to which AI contributes to or constrains cognitive development, especially in relation to design thinking, spatial reasoning, and critical judgment. Third, it highlights key methodological, theoretical, and ethical gaps in the current body of research and proposes directions for more rigorous and pedagogically grounded future studies.

By moving beyond descriptive accounts of technological adoption, this chapter contributes a structured and critical synthesis of recent developments in AI-assisted architectural education. It argues that while AI has the capacity to transform certain aspects of the design process, particularly ideation, visualization, and early-stage representation, it does not yet constitute a complete paradigm shift in architectural pedagogy. Instead, its current role is better understood as a powerful but unevenly integrated layer within existing educational frameworks. For AI to become pedagogically meaningful, its integration must be explicitly aligned with core architectural competencies, including spatial reasoning, design judgment, ethical awareness, contextual sensitivity, and critical evaluation.

2. BACKGROUND: THEORETICAL FOUNDATIONS OF AI IN ARCHITECTURAL EDUCATION

Architectural design education has historically been grounded in studio-based learning, where knowledge is constructed through iterative processes of making, testing, critique, and reflection. Unlike conventional lecture-based disciplines, architectural pedagogy is structured around open-ended design problems that rarely have predetermined solutions. Within this context, students are expected to develop the ability to frame problems, generate alternatives, test spatial ideas, respond to feedback, and progressively transform abstract intentions into architectural propositions. This pedagogical model is closely associated with the concept of reflective practice, in which design knowledge emerges through action, reflection-in-action, and reflection-on-action (Schön, 1984).

The introduction of artificial intelligence (AI) into architectural education should therefore be understood not merely as the adoption of a new technological tool, but as a development that potentially intervenes in the epistemological foundations of studio learning. Architectural education is not solely concerned with producing visually compelling outputs; it also aims to cultivate design judgment, spatial reasoning, critical thinking, and the ability to synthesize complex contextual, social, and technical information. For this reason, the pedagogical implications of AI must be examined not only in terms of efficiency or output quality, but also in relation to how design knowledge is generated, represented, evaluated, and internalized.

2.1. Architectural Design Education, Design Thinking, and Representation

Design thinking constitutes one of the central cognitive frameworks of architectural education. It is widely understood as a non-linear, iterative, and exploratory mode of reasoning in which designers actively construct and redefine problems throughout the design process rather than simply solving predefined ones (Dorst &

Cross, 2001; Cross, 2011). In architectural studios, problems and solutions co-evolve through cycles of exploration, testing, and evaluation.

This distinguishes design thinking from linear models of problem-solving. Instead of progressing in a fixed sequence, design processes involve continuous movement between divergent and convergent modes of reasoning. Divergent thinking supports the generation of alternatives and possibilities, whereas convergent thinking enables selection, refinement, and synthesis (Cross, 2011; Lawson, 2006). Effective design education must balance these modes; an overemphasis on generation without evaluation may lead to superficial outcomes, while premature convergence can constrain creativity.

Representation plays a fundamental role in this cognitive process. In architectural education, sketches, diagrams, models, and digital representations are not merely tools for communication but also thinking instruments. Goldschmidt (1991) demonstrated that sketching enables a form of visual reasoning in which designers discover new relationships through the act of drawing itself. Similarly, Schön and Wiggins (1992) described design as a reflective conversation with materials, where each representational act generates new possibilities for interpretation.

Recent pedagogical experiments also demonstrate how AI-supported workflows are beginning to reshape representational exploration, visual thinking, and creative interaction within architectural education. Tong et al. (2023) investigated the use of generative AI as a new mode of sketching in freshman design studios, suggesting that AI-assisted visualization can support conceptual exploration and spatial imagination. Similarly, Akçay Kavakoğlu et al. (2022) examined a first-year studio experiment integrating iterative sketching and AI-assisted image generation, emphasizing how AI can foster unexpected visual associations and exploratory design thinking. Expanding this discussion, Yaşar et al. (2025) explored prompt-based visual production processes through analog collage, digital collage, and AI-assisted image generation workflows. Their findings highlighted the growing importance of prompt literacy, iterative editing, and hybrid human-AI collaboration in creative design processes. Collectively, these studies indicate that AI is increasingly positioned not only as a representational aid but also as an active participant within contemporary design pedagogy.

This perspective is particularly important when considering the impact of AI-generated representations. Traditional representational practices require gradual externalization of ideas, supporting the development of spatial reasoning and design judgment. In contrast, generative AI systems can produce highly resolved visual outputs directly from textual prompts. While this capability may enhance early-stage exploration, it may also reduce engagement with intermediate representational processes that are essential for cognitive development.

2.2. From Digital Design Tools to Generative Artificial Intelligence

Architectural education has undergone several technological transformations before the emergence of generative AI. Computer-Aided Design (CAD) enhanced precision and efficiency in drawing production, while Building Information Modeling (BIM) introduced integrated systems that connect geometry with material, performance, and construction data. Parametric and algorithmic design tools further expanded the capacity to generate complex forms through rule-based processes (Kolarevic, 2003; Woodbury, 2010).

Despite these advancements, earlier digital tools remained largely dependent on explicit human input and control. Designers defined geometry, parameters, and relationships, and computational systems executed these instructions. Even when multiple variations were generated, they operated within frameworks established by the designer. In this sense, such tools extended human capability without fundamentally altering the locus of authorship.

Generative AI introduces a different condition. It refers to computational systems capable of producing new content, including text, images, and design concepts, based on patterns learned from large datasets (Goodfellow et al., 2016). In architectural contexts, this includes text-to-image systems and large language models that can generate visual concepts, narratives, and speculative design scenarios.

The key distinction lies in the degree of autonomy and interpretive agency. Rather than explicitly defining all parameters, designers provide prompts that describe intentions or qualities, which the system interprets to produce outputs. This shifts part of the design process from direct manipulation to mediated generation. As a result, prompt formulation becomes a form of design action, and the relationship between language, image, and spatial reasoning becomes increasingly significant.

Recent discussions on architectural curricula further indicate that the emergence of generative AI should be understood as part of a longer pedagogical transition from computer literacy toward algorithmic and machine learning literacy. Alaçam et al. (2025) argue that the integration of AI into architectural education extends earlier computational design paradigms by repositioning digital systems from representational tools toward intelligent and data-driven design partners. Their study highlights how AI-related courses, workshops, and experimental studios increasingly focus not only on technical proficiency but also on prompt literacy, data interpretation, and hybrid human-AI collaboration. This shift suggests that contemporary architectural education is gradually evolving toward new pedagogical models in which AI literacy becomes an essential component of design education.

However, while generative AI can accelerate visual exploration, it does not inherently ensure architectural coherence. AI-generated outputs are often discussed as visually persuasive but limited in terms of structural logic, contextual integration, spatial coherence, and functional resolution (Iranmanesh & Lotfabadi, 2025; Liu et al., 2025). This suggests that AI currently operates more effectively as a representational and exploratory tool than as a comprehensive system for architectural reasoning.

2.3. Creativity, Cognition, Ethics, and the Repositioning of AI in Design Pedagogy

Creativity is a central objective of architectural education, yet it remains a complex and contested concept. It is commonly defined as the production of ideas or outcomes that are both novel and appropriate (Runco & Jaeger, 2012). In architecture, however, creativity must also respond to spatial, environmental, and social constraints, meaning that originality alone is insufficient.

Generative AI is often associated with creativity because it can produce diverse and unexpected outputs. It supports divergent thinking by expanding the range of alternatives available to designers. However, the generation of multiple alternatives does not necessarily imply improved design quality. Creativity in architectural education also depends on the ability to evaluate, select, and synthesize ideas within specific contexts (Cross, 2011).

From a cognitive perspective, AI can be understood through the framework of extended cognition, which proposes that thinking is distributed across individuals, representations, tools, and environments (Clark & Chalmers, 1998). Architectural design has historically depended on such distributed cognitive systems through sketches, diagrams, models, and external representational media. Generative AI extends this condition by introducing systems that not only store or manipulate information, but also actively generate speculative visual and textual content. This transition potentially alters the balance between internal reasoning and externally mediated ideation within studio learning.

While this expansion offers new opportunities, it also introduces risks. One concern is cognitive offloading, where learners rely on external systems to perform tasks that would otherwise support cognitive development. Research in educational psychology suggests that increased engagement or perceived competence does not necessarily correspond to deeper learning or conceptual understanding (Bandura, 1997). This distinction is particularly relevant in AI-supported design processes, where efficiency gains may not translate into improved design thinking.

Ethical considerations further complicate the integration of AI into architectural education. Questions of authorship, originality, and accountability become more complex when design outputs are partially generated by AI systems. In addition, concerns about bias and representation have been widely discussed in AI research, as systems trained on large datasets may reproduce dominant cultural patterns while marginalizing others (Floridi et al., 2018).

For these reasons, AI should not be positioned as a replacement for architectural thinking but rather as a critical medium within design pedagogy. Its value depends not only on what it produces but also on how it is used to support reflection, evaluation, and critical inquiry. Effective integration requires both technical literacy and critical awareness, enabling students to engage with AI outputs reflectively and analytically.

In this sense, the future of AI in architectural education lies in the development of hybrid pedagogical models that combine the strengths of studio-based learning iteration, critique, and reflection with the exploratory capabilities of AI. Such models must ensure that technological augmentation does not replace core competencies such as spatial reasoning, design judgment, and contextual sensitivity, but instead supports their development.

3. SYSTEMATIC MAPPING REVIEW ANALYSIS (2023-2025)

This chapter adopts a systematic mapping review approach to examine recent research on the integration of generative artificial intelligence (AI) in architectural education. Rather than quantifying effects, the review aims to identify, categorize, and synthesize emerging patterns, methodological approaches, and research gaps within a rapidly evolving field. A systematic mapping review strategy was selected as it enables the structured classification of heterogeneous studies across themes, educational contexts, AI applications, and reported outcomes.

The literature search was conducted using the Web of Science and Scopus databases. The search was limited to peer-reviewed journal articles published in English between 2023 and 2025, reflecting the period during which generative AI tools-such as Midjourney, Stable Diffusion, DALL·E, and large language models-became widely adopted and discussed within architectural and design education. The following search query was applied:

("architectural education") AND ("artificial intelligence" OR "midjourney" OR "stable diffusion") AND ("design thinking" OR "pedagogy" OR "creative process" OR "cognitive")

The initial search yielded 34 records. After removing duplicate entries (n = 3), an additional three records were excluded due to clear irrelevance to the scope of the study (e.g., non-architectural contexts or absence of AI-related content). This resulted in 28 records for screening. Titles and abstracts were subsequently reviewed, leading to the exclusion of 13 studies that did not directly address AI integration in architectural education, design studio pedagogy, design cognition, creative processes, or pedagogical implications. Following this process, 15 studies were included in the final review.

The study selection process followed a PRISMA-guided logic consisting of identification, screening, and inclusion stages (Figure 1). To enhance transparency and reproducibility, the review protocol was designed to systematically document inclusion criteria, screening decisions, and thematic categorization. However, this study is positioned as a systematic mapping review rather than a meta-analysis, as the included studies are methodologically diverse and do not provide comparable quantitative outcome measures.

Figure 1. PRISMA-informed flow diagram showing the identification, screening, and inclusion process of studies on artificial intelligence in architectural education indexed in Web of Science and Scopus between 2023 and 2025.

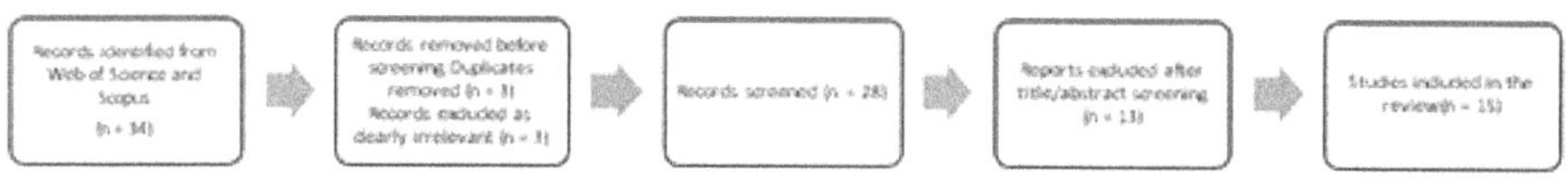

The included studies were analyzed based on their research aims, methodological approaches, educational contexts, AI tools employed, key findings, and reported limitations. Particular attention was given to how each study addresses AI in relation to ideation, representation, design cognition, pedagogical integration, student perception, ethical considerations, and methodological constraints.

Through this analysis, five major thematic areas were identified:

AI in ideation and representation, AI and design cognition, pedagogical integration, ethics and student perception, and methodological limitations.

Table 1. Characteristics of the Included Studies in the Systematic Mapping Review

No.	Author(s)	Year	Educational Context	AI Tool / Technology	Methodological Approach	Main Focus
1	Saritepeci & Durak	2024	Design-based learning	ChatGPT, Midjourney	Quasi-experimental	Design thinking, self-efficacy
2	Liu et al.	2025	Interior design education	Generative image models	Quantitative survey + expert review	Creativity and functionality
3	Alshahrani & Mostafa	2025	Architectural education	AI tools (general)	Survey-based	Awareness and adoption
4	Jin et al.	2024	Design course	LLMs and generative AI tools	Mixed-method case study	Workflow and decision-making

continued on following page

Table 1. Continued

No.	Author(s)	Year	Educational Context	AI Tool / Technology	Methodological Approach	Main Focus
5	Çelik	2024	Conceptual design	Midjourney, DALL·E	Experimental	AI-assisted form generation
6	Huh et al.	2025	Architecture education	Midjourney	Workshop survey	Perception and ethics
7	Wang et al.	2025	Design studio	LLMs and image-based AI	Case study + questionnaire	Curriculum and ethics
8	Fatima-tu-Zuhra & Iqbal	2025	Studio education	AI tools (general)	Mixed-method survey	Studio learning factors
9	Medel-Vera et al.	2025	Architectural learning	Midjourney v6	Mixed-method (CSI + semantic analysis)	Creativity and prompt literacy
10	Rana et al.	2025	Higher education	Generative AI tools	Mixed-method analysis	Creativity and critical thinking
11	Condorelli & Berti	2025	Heritage education	Text-to-image AI	Qualitative case study	Co-creation and ethics
12	Iranmanesh & Lotfabadi	2025	Design pedagogy	Text-to-image AI	Studio observation	Representation and bias
13	Montenegro	2024	Design education	Text-to-image AI	Workshop case study	Ideation and exploration
14	Almaz et al.	2024	Design education	Midjourney	Experimental	Efficiency and creativity
15	Cudzik et al.	2024	Design studio	Generative AI tools	Experimental studio study	Hybrid workflows

The final dataset reflects a diverse yet thematically convergent body of research on the integration of generative AI in architectural education. Despite variations in methodological approaches and educational contexts, the studies consistently engage with a shared set of concerns, including AI-supported ideation, shifts in representational practices, implications for design cognition, evolving pedagogical models, and emerging ethical challenges. This convergence provides a robust foundation for the thematic synthesis presented in the following sections.

3.1. AI in Ideation and Representation: From Visual Expansion to Representational Dependency

The most consistently reported function of generative artificial intelligence (AI) in architectural education is its role in early-stage ideation and visual representation. Across the reviewed studies, text-to-image systems such as Midjourney, Stable Diffusion, and DALL·E are widely employed to generate multiple design alternatives from textual prompts, significantly expanding the range of visual exploration available to students (Medel-Vera et al., 2025).

Empirical findings demonstrate that AI enhances ideation by enabling the rapid generation of diverse formal and stylistic variations. Experimental studies in conceptual design show that AI systems can produce multiple architectural alternatives by combining different conceptual frameworks, such as biomimetics and futurism, thereby extending conventional design processes (Çelik, 2024). In this sense, AI functions as a combinatorial system capable of synthesizing heterogeneous design logics into new visual configurations.

Research on AI-supported design workflows further indicates that generative tools facilitate rapid iteration and alternative testing within compressed timeframes. Studies report that tools such as Midjourney enable students to explore multiple design directions efficiently, shifting the emphasis of the design process from production toward selection (Çelik, 2024; Montenegro, 2024; Cudzik et al., 2024). This shift reconfigures the role of the designer, positioning students increasingly as curators of generated outputs rather than primary creators of form.

However, this transformation also alters the role of representation in architectural design. In conventional studio pedagogy, representation functions as a cognitive process through which ideas are iteratively developed and refined. Sketches, diagrams, and models serve as thinking tools that mediate between abstract concepts and spatial form. In contrast, AI-generated outputs often appear as highly resolved images at early stages of the design process, compressing iterative development into a single step. This condition constitutes a representational shortcut, in which intermediate stages of conceptual transformation are effectively bypassed. In such cases, visual resolution may precede conceptual maturation. This condition risks weakening the reflective dialogue traditionally established through iterative sketching, diagramming, and representational refinement, where ambiguity and incompleteness function as productive components of architectural thinking. As a result, opportunities for cognitive engagement through representational practices may be reduced.

Observational and studio-based studies indicate that engagement with multiple representational modes supports conceptual development and critical reflection (Jin et al., 2024; Cudzik et al., 2024). The reduction of these processes in AI-mediated workflows therefore, raises concerns regarding the depth of design thinking and spatial reasoning.

Another key dimension emerging from the literature is the increasing importance of prompt-based interaction. Studies show that the conceptual richness and divergence of textual prompts directly influence the creativity and variability of generated outputs (Medel-Vera et al., 2025). This suggests a shift in design practice toward linguistic articulation, where the ability to construct precise and conceptually rich prompts, often referred to as prompt literacy, becomes a critical design skill.

While this shift introduces new opportunities for conceptual exploration, it also raises concerns regarding the detachment of design from spatial and material engagement. Traditional design processes involve embodied interaction through drawing and modeling, whereas prompt-based design relies on abstract textual input. This transformation may reconfigure how students engage with spatial reasoning and architectural thinking.

Moreover, several studies indicate that AI-generated outputs, despite their visual richness, often lack architectural depth. Studio-based observations show that generated images tend to overlook critical considerations such as human scale, structural logic, and material feasibility (Iranmanesh & Lotfabadi, 2025). This suggests that AI currently operates primarily at the level of visual representation rather than integrated architectural design.

Student perception studies further reinforce this interpretation. AI tools are consistently reported as most useful during early design stages, particularly for inspiration and concept generation, while their perceived value decreases in later phases requiring originality, authorship, and critical judgment (Huh et al., 2025). This phase-dependent engagement highlights the uneven integration of AI across the design process.

In addition, empirical studies in design education indicate that while AI enhances creativity and efficiency, it may also encourage reliance on generated outputs, potentially limiting the development of independent design strategies (Liu et al., 2025). This suggests a shift toward externally supported design processes, where critical evaluation becomes more important than direct form generation.

From a broader theoretical perspective, the literature indicates that AI is not merely extending representation but restructuring its role within design processes. Representation, traditionally understood as a medium for developing ideas, increasingly becomes a primary driver of design exploration. This inversion challenges established pedagogical assumptions in architectural education.

Overall, the integration of AI into ideation and representation reveals a fundamental tension. On one hand, it expands the design space and enhances creative exploration. On the other hand, it risks reducing engagement with iterative design processes, leading to forms of creativity that are visually rich but architecturally shallow.

3.2. AI and Design Cognition

The relationship between generative artificial intelligence (AI) and design cognition represents one of the most debated dimensions in the current literature. While many studies report improvements in creativity, efficiency, and engagement, the extent to which AI contributes to deeper cognitive development remains limited and inconsistent.

Design cognition in architectural education involves processes such as problem framing, iterative exploration, evaluation, and synthesis. Within architectural education, these processes typically include problem framing, iterative reformulation, spatial abstraction, representational translation, contextual evaluation, and the synthesis of environmental, structural, and programmatic constraints. Accordingly, design cognition cannot be reduced to visual novelty alone, but must be understood as the ability to construct coherent relationships between ideas, representations, and spatial propositions. Empirical evidence suggests that AI supports certain aspects of these processes, particularly those related to ideation and reflective engagement. For example, Saritepeci and Durak (2024) demonstrate that AI-supported design-based learning improves creative self-efficacy and reflective thinking. However, their findings also indicate that these improvements do not translate into statistically significant changes in design thinking mindset. This distinction suggests that AI enhances perceived creativity without fundamentally transforming cognitive structures.

Further evidence highlights a shift in how students engage with the design process. Jin et al. (2024) observe that students using AI tools tend to rely on generated outputs as primary sources of inspiration. While this facilitates idea generation, it may reduce independent conceptual exploration, particularly when AI outputs are accepted without critical evaluation. Similarly, Liu et al. (2025) report that AI-assisted workflows improve efficiency and accelerate design processes, but may constrain the development of problem-solving strategies. Students are more likely to select from generated alternatives than to construct solutions through iterative reasoning.

The limitations of AI in supporting core architectural cognition are particularly evident in relation to spatial reasoning. According to Iranmanesh and Lotfabadi (2025), AI-generated images often lack spatial coherence, structural logic, and material feasibility. This suggests that while AI can produce visually convincing outputs, it does not adequately support the development of spatial thinking, which remains a central competency in architectural education.

At the same time, AI introduces new forms of cognitive engagement. Wang et al. (2025) show that students develop skills related to evaluating AI-generated outputs and making decisions within hybrid workflows. These findings indicate a shift toward distributed forms of cognition, where design thinking is partially externalized through interaction with AI systems.

Overall, the evidence suggests that AI functions primarily as a tool for cognitive augmentation rather than cognitive transformation. It enhances ideation, supports reflection, and improves efficiency, but does not consistently contribute to deeper processes such as design thinking, spatial reasoning, or conceptual synthesis. This distinction is critical for architectural education, where the goal is not only to generate ideas but to develop the capacity for critical evaluation and integrated design thinking.

3.3. Pedagogical Integration

The integration of generative artificial intelligence (AI) into architectural education is most commonly realized through hybrid pedagogical models that combine traditional studio practices with AI-supported workflows. Rather than replacing conventional design methods, the reviewed studies consistently position AI as a complementary tool embedded within existing educational structures.

Empirical evidence from studio-based research demonstrates that AI is typically introduced through experimental formats, workshops, or course modules. For example, Cudzik et al. (2024) identify multiple modes of AI use in design studios, including inspiration-based use, hybrid workflows, and interactive integration. These models suggest that AI functions most effectively when combined with conventional design practices, allowing students to alternate between manual and AI-assisted processes.

Similarly, Wang et al. (2025) show that AI-integrated courses contribute to the development of new competencies, particularly in evaluating generated outputs and making design decisions within hybrid workflows. However, their findings also emphasize that these benefits depend on structured pedagogical frameworks. Without clear guidance, AI use risks remaining superficial and focused primarily on visual production rather than conceptual development.

Student perception studies further reinforce the auxiliary role of AI in studio learning. According to Huh et al. (2025), students generally perceive AI tools as useful for early-stage ideation and visual exploration, but not as a replacement for traditional design processes. This indicates that AI is not yet fully integrated into the core of architectural pedagogy, but rather operates as a supportive layer within existing studio structures.

The reviewed literature also suggests that AI integration introduces a shift in the role of instructors. Instead of focusing solely on evaluating final design outcomes, educators increasingly act as facilitators who guide students in interpreting, selecting, and critically assessing AI-generated outputs. This reflects a broader transition toward process-oriented learning, where emphasis is placed on decision-making and critical evaluation rather than production alone.

Despite these developments, AI integration remains uneven and context-dependent. In many cases, its use is limited to specific courses or experimental settings rather than systematically embedded across curricula. This lack of standardization highlights the need for more coherent pedagogical models that align AI use with learning objectives, assessment criteria, and core architectural competencies.

A recurring issue across the reviewed studies is that AI integration often remains technologically driven rather than pedagogically structured. In many cases, AI tools are introduced because they are accessible or visually compelling, rather than because they align with clearly articulated learning objectives. This creates the risk of tool-centered pedagogy, where visual production begins to overshadow reflective inquiry, representational reasoning, and critical architectural development.

Overall, the evidence indicates that AI contributes to the emergence of hybrid pedagogical models, but does not yet constitute a fundamental transformation of architectural education. Its effectiveness depends on how it is structured, guided, and integrated within studio-based learning environments. Without such alignment, AI risks reinforcing surface-level engagement rather than supporting deeper design learning.

3.4. Ethics and Student Perception

The integration of generative artificial intelligence (AI) into architectural education introduces a range of ethical and perceptual challenges that extend beyond technical and pedagogical considerations. These challenges primarily relate to authorship, originality, bias, and the role of the designer in AI-mediated design processes.

One of the most significant concerns identified in the literature is the question of authorship. As design outputs are increasingly generated through interactions between human input and AI systems, the boundaries between designer and tool become less clearly defined. Wang et al. (2025) highlight that this ambiguity complicates traditional notions of intellectual ownership, raising questions about how authorship should be attributed in AI-assisted design work. Similarly, Condorelli and Berti (2025) emphasize the role of co-creation in AI-supported design processes, where design outcomes emerge through a collaborative interaction between human intention and algorithmic generation. This shift challenges established evaluation criteria in architectural education, which are traditionally based on individual authorship and originality.

Bias represents another critical ethical dimension. AI systems are trained on large datasets that inherently reflect existing cultural, aesthetic, and social patterns. As a result, generated outputs may reproduce dominant stylistic tendencies while limiting diversity in design exploration. Although not always explicitly measured, this issue is reflected in studies that highlight the tendency of AI-generated images to prioritize visually appealing but contextually shallow solutions (Iranmanesh & Lotfabadi, 2025). This raises concerns regarding the homogenization of design outcomes and the potential loss of contextual sensitivity.

Student perception studies provide further insight into how these ethical issues are experienced in practice. According to Huh et al. (2025), students generally perceive

AI tools as highly useful for enhancing creativity and efficiency, particularly in early design stages. However, this positive perception is accompanied by uncertainty regarding the reliability, originality, and authorship of AI-generated outputs. Students recognize the advantages of AI in generating ideas, but also express concerns about the extent to which these outputs can be considered their own work.

This dual perception reflects a broader tension between utility and authorship. On one hand, AI enables rapid exploration and supports creative processes; on the other hand, it introduces ambiguity regarding the origin and ownership of design ideas. This tension underscores the need for critical awareness in AI-assisted design practices.

More importantly, these discussions also concern disciplinary agency. If students increasingly rely on AI-generated imagery without critically transforming or spatially developing these outputs, architectural education risks shifting from design authorship toward aesthetic selection. Under such conditions, the role of the architect may gradually move from constructing spatial propositions toward curating visually persuasive alternatives.

Furthermore, the literature suggests that students may overestimate the capabilities of AI systems, particularly when outputs appear visually convincing. This can lead to reduced critical evaluation and increased reliance on generated results. Conversely, when guided appropriately, students can develop critical skills by comparing AI-generated outputs with their own design intentions and evaluating their limitations.

These findings highlight the importance of integrating ethical reflection into architectural education. Rather than treating ethics as a separate or supplementary topic, it should be embedded within studio practice, encouraging students to critically engage with issues of authorship, bias, and responsibility throughout the design process.

Overall, the reviewed studies indicate that ethical considerations are not peripheral but central to the integration of AI in architectural education. Addressing these issues requires not only awareness of the limitations of AI systems but also the development of pedagogical frameworks that support critical evaluation and responsible use of generative technologies.

3.5. Methodological Limitations

A recurring pattern across the reviewed studies is the presence of significant methodological limitations, which constrain the strength and generalizability of the reported findings. These limitations are particularly important given the rapid and exploratory nature of research on generative AI in architectural education.

One of the most common limitations concerns sample size and context. Many studies are conducted in single-studio settings or within specific course implementations, often involving a relatively small number of participants. For instance, studio-based and workshop-oriented studies such as those by Cudzik et al. (2024) and Huh et al. (2025) provide detailed insights into AI integration but remain context-specific, limiting the broader applicability of their findings.

A second major limitation is the short duration of most studies. The majority of the reviewed research focuses on short-term interventions, typically within a single course or workshop. For example, experimental and design-based studies such as Saritepeci and Durak (2024) assess immediate learning outcomes but do not capture long-term cognitive development or skill acquisition. As a result, there is limited evidence regarding how AI influences the development of design thinking and professional competencies over time.

Another important issue is the reliance on self-reported data. Several studies, particularly those examining student perception and creativity, depend on survey responses and subjective evaluations (Medel-Vera et al., 2025; Huh et al., 2025). While these approaches provide valuable insights into user experience, they do not necessarily reflect actual improvements in design performance or cognitive development.

Methodological heterogeneity also presents a significant challenge. The reviewed studies employ a wide range of research designs, including qualitative observations, experimental methods, mixed-method approaches, and survey-based analyses. While this diversity reflects the exploratory state of the field, it makes direct comparison between studies difficult and limits the possibility of cumulative knowledge building.

In addition, there is a lack of standardized evaluation criteria across studies. Measures of creativity, design quality, and cognitive development vary considerably, and in many cases are not clearly defined. This inconsistency complicates the interpretation of findings and makes it difficult to assess the actual impact of AI on learning outcomes.

Finally, there is a notable absence of longitudinal research. None of the reviewed studies systematically examines the long-term effects of AI use on design cognition, spatial reasoning, or professional skill development. This gap represents a critical limitation in understanding the sustained educational impact of generative AI.

Taken together, these limitations suggest that while current research provides valuable insights into the potential of AI in architectural education, it remains preliminary. More rigorous and longitudinal studies, supported by standardized evaluation frameworks and larger sample sizes, are necessary to establish a more robust evidence base.

3.6. Synthesis: Emerging Patterns and Contradictions

The reviewed studies do not support a simple narrative of technological transformation. Rather, they describe a field in transition: AI is becoming increasingly useful for rapid ideation, visual exploration, and student engagement, yet its contribution to deeper architectural learning remains uncertain. The central pattern emerging from the review is therefore not a complete pedagogical shift, but a partial and uneven transformation concentrated mainly in the early stages of design.

Across the reviewed studies, generative AI tools are consistently associated with faster ideation and expanded visual exploration. Students are able to generate multiple design alternatives within compressed timeframes, test different formal directions, and engage with broader stylistic possibilities than would typically be possible through manual production alone (Çelik, 2024; Jin et al., 2024; Medel-Vera et al., 2025; Montenegro, 2024). This acceleration can support divergent thinking, particularly when students use AI-generated outputs as prompts for comparison, critique, and further development.

However, this increase in visual productivity does not automatically correspond to deeper design cognition. The reviewed evidence indicates that AI-supported learning may improve creative self-efficacy, reflective engagement, and confidence, but it does not consistently strengthen design thinking mindset, spatial reasoning, or architectural synthesis (Saritepeci & Durak, 2024). This distinction is crucial. Architectural education does not aim only to produce more alternatives; it also aims to cultivate the ability to frame problems, evaluate constraints, develop spatial logic, and transform conceptual ideas into coherent architectural proposals.

A second pattern concerns the phase-dependent use of AI. The reviewed studies show that AI tools are most frequently used during early design stages, especially for inspiration, concept generation, and visual representation. Their role becomes less stable in later stages that require plan-section coherence, structural reasoning, material decisions, contextual response, and technical resolution (Huh et al., 2025; Iranmanesh & Lotfabadi, 2025; Jin et al., 2024). This suggests that AI is not yet integrated across the full design workflow. Instead, it often functions as an early-stage representational accelerator.

This uneven integration creates a pedagogical contradiction. On the one hand, AI expands the design space by allowing students to explore multiple possibilities quickly. On the other hand, it can compress or bypass the slow representational processes through which architectural judgment is normally developed. Drawing, modeling, diagramming, and critique require students to negotiate uncertainty step by step. AI-generated images, by contrast, may appear resolved before the project has passed through sufficient conceptual, spatial, or technical development. The risk is that students may mistake visual completeness for architectural resolution.

A third contradiction concerns creativity and standardization. AI is often associated with increased creativity because it produces diverse and unexpected outputs. Yet several studies also point to the danger of stylistic homogenization, particularly when students rely on similar platforms, datasets, aesthetic references, and prompt structures (Iranmanesh & Lotfabadi, 2025). In this sense, AI can simultaneously expand and narrow creative exploration. It expands creativity by multiplying alternatives, but it may narrow it when generated outputs reproduce dominant visual patterns or encourage students to select persuasive images without sufficient critical transformation.

Taken together, these findings indicate that the current role of AI in architectural education is best understood as augmentation without full transformation. AI enhances efficiency, expands representational capacity, and increases student engagement, but it does not yet fundamentally transform the cognitive or pedagogical foundations of architectural design education. Its educational value depends less on the sophistication of the tool itself and more on how it is embedded within studio culture, learning objectives, assessment criteria, and critical reflection.

The main implication is that the limitations of AI in architectural education are not only technological; they are pedagogical. More advanced tools may generate more refined outputs, but they will not automatically produce stronger design thinking. For AI to become educationally meaningful, it must be integrated into structured pedagogical frameworks that require students to document process, justify decisions, translate images into architectural drawings and models, evaluate spatial coherence, and reflect on authorship, bias, and responsibility. Without such frameworks, AI is likely to remain a powerful but fragmented layer within architectural education.

4. FUTURE RESEARCH DIRECTIONS

Future research on artificial intelligence in architectural education should move beyond short-term experimentation and focus on the long-term pedagogical effects of AI-supported design processes. Current studies provide valuable initial evidence regarding ideation, representation, and student perception; however, they offer limited insight into whether AI contributes to sustained development in design thinking, spatial reasoning, and architectural judgment. Longitudinal studies are therefore needed to examine how repeated engagement with AI tools affects students' cognitive development across multiple design studios, semesters, or curricular stages.

Another important direction concerns assessment. Future studies should develop more robust evaluation frameworks that distinguish between visual productivity and architectural learning. Rather than measuring AI's impact only through student satisfaction, perceived creativity, or the quantity of generated outputs, research should examine how AI-supported processes influence problem framing, spatial coherence, contextual integration, material logic, and design decision-making. Rubric-based assessment, expert evaluation, process documentation, and comparative analysis between AI-assisted and non-AI-assisted workflows may provide more reliable evidence.

Cross-cultural and institutional comparisons are also needed. The reviewed studies indicate that AI adoption is shaped by technological access, studio culture, institutional policy, and educational tradition. However, existing research remains concentrated in limited contexts. Comparative studies across different countries, schools, and pedagogical models could reveal how local educational cultures influence the use, acceptance, and ethical interpretation of AI in architectural education.

Finally, future research should address governance and ethical implementation. Clearer frameworks are needed for authorship, disclosure, academic integrity, bias awareness, and the acceptable use of AI-generated material in student work. These issues should not be treated as external policy concerns but as integral components of architectural pedagogy. Research that connects AI literacy with ethical design education would help define how students can use generative tools responsibly while maintaining critical agency and disciplinary accountability.

5. CONCLUSION

The integration of generative artificial intelligence into architectural education represents a significant but still partial transformation. The systematic review of fifteen peer-reviewed studies published between 2023 and 2025 shows that AI tools have rapidly entered design studios, design-related courses, and experimental pedagogical settings. Their strongest contribution lies in early-stage ideation and representation, where they enable students to generate diverse visual alternatives, accelerate exploratory processes, and engage with a broader range of formal and atmospheric possibilities.

At the same time, the findings show that AI's pedagogical impact remains uneven. While AI can increase visual productivity, creative confidence, and engagement, its contribution to deeper cognitive dimensions is less convincing. The reviewed studies do not provide sufficient evidence that AI consistently improves design thinking, spatial reasoning, critical judgment, or architectural synthesis. This distinction is important because architectural education is not only concerned with producing compelling images. It is fundamentally concerned with developing the capacity to think spatially, reason critically, synthesize constraints, and construct meaningful relationships between concept, context, program, materiality, and form.

A key conclusion of this chapter is that AI currently operates primarily as a representational and generative layer rather than as a fully integrated cognitive or pedagogical framework. Its use is most visible in the early phases of design, where image generation and prompt-based exploration are valuable. However, its role becomes less clear in later stages that require technical development, structural logic, material resolution, environmental response, and detailed spatial organization. This phase-dependent pattern shows that AI's potential in architectural education is not yet fully realized.

The review also highlights important ethical and methodological concerns. Questions of authorship, originality, transparency, bias, and academic integrity become increasingly significant when AI-generated images and texts enter student work. At the same time, current research remains limited by short-term interventions, small samples, single-course contexts, self-reported data, and the absence of longitudinal evidence. These limitations mean that claims about AI's transformative impact on architectural education should be made cautiously.

The future of AI in architectural education will therefore depend less on technological novelty and more on pedagogical design. AI should not be treated as a replacement for architectural thinking, nor should it be reduced to a tool for producing visually attractive outputs. Instead, it should be positioned as a critical medium that can support exploration, comparison, reflection, and decision-making when embedded within clear educational frameworks. Such frameworks should require students to move beyond prompt production and image selection toward interpretation, transformation, evaluation, and architectural translation.

Ultimately, the educational significance of AI in architecture does not lie solely in its capacity to generate images, accelerate workflows, or expand visual variation. Its deeper importance lies in how it repositions the relationship between thinking, representation, authorship, and architectural judgment within studio culture. The critical challenge for architectural education is therefore not whether AI should be integrated, but how it can be integrated without weakening the reflective, iterative, and spatially grounded nature of architectural thinking. Under such conditions, AI may evolve from a representational accelerator into a critically mediated component of contemporary design pedagogy.

AI Assistance Disclosure Statement

The author used AI-assisted tools to support language refinement, structural organization, and readability during the preparation of this chapter. The authors reviewed, revised, verified, and approved all content, arguments, citations, and references. No AI tool was used to generate the manuscript independently.

REFERENCES

Akçay Kavakoğlu, A., Almaç, B., Eser, B., & Alaçam, S. (2022). AI Driven Creativity in Early Design Education-A pedagogical approach in the age of Industry 5.0. In Pak, B., Wurzer, G., & Stouffs, R. (Eds.), *eCAADe 2022: Co-creating the Future - Inclusion in and through Design* (pp. 133–142)., DOI: 10.52842/conf.ecaade.2022.1.133

Alaçam, S., Güzelci, O. Z., Bacınoğlu, S. Z., Kızılyaprak, H. N., Uzun, C., Coşkun, E., & Karadağ, İ. (2025). Artificial intelligence 101 for architectural education. *Öneri Dergisi, 20 (MX Yaratıcı Endüstriler Çalıştayı 2024: Yapay Zeka Çağında Yaratıcı Endüstriler Özel Sayısı)*, 219-237.

Almaz, A. F., El-Agouz, E. A. E., Abdelfatah, M. T., & Mohamed, I. R. (2024). The future role of artificial intelligence design integration into architectural and interior design education: Improving efficiency, sustainability, and creativity. *Civil Engineering and Architecture*, *12*(3), 1749–1772. DOI: 10.13189/cea.2024.120336

Alshahrani, A., & Mostafa, A. M. (2025). Enhancing the use of artificial intelligence in architectural education: A case study of Saudi Arabia. *Frontiers in Built Environment*, *11*, 1610709. Advance online publication. DOI: 10.3389/fbuil.2025.1610709

Bandura, A. (1997). *Self-efficacy: The exercise of control.* W. H. Freeman.

Çelik, T. (2024). The effect of artificial intelligence on creativity in conceptual design in architectural education: The motion of biomimetics and futurism. *AI & Society*. Advance online publication. DOI: 10.1007/s00146-024-02042-7

Clark, A., & Chalmers, D. (1998). The extended mind. *Analysis*, *58*(1), 7–19. DOI: 10.1093/analys/58.1.7

Condorelli, F., & Berti, F. (2025). Creativity and awareness in co-creation of art using artificial intelligence-based systems in heritage education. *Heritage*, *8*(5), 157. Advance online publication. DOI: 10.3390/heritage8050157

Cross, N. (2011). *Design thinking: Understanding how designers think and work.* Berg. DOI: 10.5040/9781474293884

Cudzik, J., Nyka, L., & Szczepański, J. (2024). Artificial intelligence in architectural education: Green campus development research. *Global Journal of Engineering Education*, *26*(1), 20–25.

Dorst, K., & Cross, N. (2001). Creativity in the design process: Co-evolution of problem-solution. *Design Studies*, *22*(5), 425–437. DOI: 10.1016/S0142-694X(01)00009-6

Floridi, L., Cowls, J., Beltrametti, M., Chatila, R., Chazerand, P., Dignum, V., Luetge, C., Madelin, R., Pagallo, U., Rossi, F., Schafer, B., Valcke, P., & Vayena, E. (2018). AI4People An ethical framework for a good AI society: Opportunities, risks, principles, and recommendations. *Minds and Machines*, *28*(4), 689–707. DOI: 10.1007/s11023-018-9482-5 PMID: 30930541

Gero, J. S., & Sudweeks, F. (Eds.). (1992). *Artificial intelligence in design '92*. Springer., DOI: 10.1007/978-94-011-2787-5

Gero, J. S., & Sudweeks, F. (Eds.). (1994). *Artificial intelligence in design '94*. Springer., DOI: 10.1007/978-94-011-0928-4

Gero, J. S., & Sudweeks, F. (Eds.). (1996). *Artificial intelligence in design '96*. Kluwer Academic Publishers., DOI: 10.1007/978-94-009-0279-4

Gero, J. S., & Sudweeks, F. (Eds.). (1998). *Artificial intelligence in design '98*. Springer., DOI: 10.1007/978-94-011-5121-4

Goldschmidt, G. (1991). The dialectics of sketching. *Creativity Research Journal*, *4*(2), 123–143. DOI: 10.1080/10400419109534381

Goodfellow, I., Bengio, Y., & Courville, A. (2016). *Deep learning*. MIT Press.

Holmes, W., Bialik, M., & Fadel, C. (2019). *Artificial intelligence in education: Promises and implications for teaching and learning*. Center for Curriculum Redesign.

Huh, M. B., Miri, M., & Tracy, T. (2025). Students' perceptions of generative AI image tools in design education: Insights from architectural education. *Education Sciences*, *15*(9), 1160. Advance online publication. DOI: 10.3390/educsci15091160

Iranmanesh, A., & Lotfabadi, P. (2025). Critical questions on the emergence of text-to-image artificial intelligence in architectural design pedagogy. *AI & Society*, *40*(5), 3557–3571. DOI: 10.1007/s00146-024-02111-x

Jin, S., Tu, H., Li, J., Fang, Y., Qu, Z., Xu, F., Liu, K., & Lin, Y. (2024). Enhancing architectural education through artificial intelligence: A case study of an AI-assisted architectural programming and design course. *Buildings (Basel, Switzerland)*, *14*(6), 1613. Advance online publication. DOI: 10.3390/buildings14061613

Kolarevic, B. (Ed.). (2003). *Architecture in the digital age: Design and manufacturing*. Spon Press.

Lawson, B. (2006). *How designers think: The design process demystified* (4th ed.). Architectural Press. DOI: 10.4324/9780080454979

Liu, Y., Xu, B., Feng, J., & Wu, P. (2025). Analysis of the application of generative artificial intelligence in interior design education. *Ain Shams Engineering Journal*, *16*(12), 103757. Advance online publication. DOI: 10.1016/j.asej.2025.103757

Medel-Vera, C., Britton, S., & Gates, W. F. (2025). The role of generative AI in fostering creativity in architectural learning environments. *Computers and Education: Artificial Intelligence*, *9*, 100501. Advance online publication. DOI: 10.1016/j.caeai.2025.100501

Montenegro, N. (2024). Integrative analysis of text-to-image AI systems in architectural design education: Pedagogical innovations and creative design implications. *Journal of Architecture and Urbanism*, *48*(2), 109–124. DOI: 10.3846/jau.2024.20870

Oxman, R. (2008). Digital architecture as a challenge for design pedagogy: Theory, knowledge, models and medium. *Design Studies*, *29*(2), 99–120. DOI: 10.1016/j.destud.2007.12.003

Oxman, R. (2017). Thinking difference: Theories and models of parametric design thinking. *Design Studies*, *52*, 4–39. DOI: 10.1016/j.destud.2017.06.001

Rana, V., Verhoeven, B., & Sharma, M. (2025). Generative AI in design thinking pedagogy: Enhancing creativity, critical thinking, and ethical reasoning in higher education. *Journal of University Teaching & Learning Practice*, *22*(4). Advance online publication. DOI: 10.53761/tjse2f36

Runco, M. A., & Jaeger, G. J. (2012). The standard definition of creativity. *Creativity Research Journal*, *24*(1), 92–96. DOI: 10.1080/10400419.2012.650092

Saritepeci, M., & Durak, H. Y. (2024). Effectiveness of artificial intelligence integration in design-based learning on design thinking mindset, creative and reflective thinking skills: An experimental study. *Education and Information Technologies*, *29*(18), 25175–25209. DOI: 10.1007/s10639-024-12829-2

Schön, D. A. (1984). *The reflective practitioner: How professionals think in action*. Basic Books.

Schön, D. A., & Wiggins, G. (1992). Kinds of seeing and their functions in designing. *Design Studies*, *13*(2), 135–156. DOI: 10.1016/0142-694X(92)90268-F

Tong, H., Türel, A., Şenkal, H., Ergun, S. F. Y., Orkan, Z. G., & Alaçam, S. (2023). Can AI function as a new mode of sketching: A teaching experiment with freshman. *International Journal of Emerging Technologies in Learning (Online), 18*(18), 234. DOI: 10.3991/ijet.v18i18.42603

Wang, J., Shi, Y., Chen, X., Lan, Y., & Liu, S. (2025). Teaching with artificial intelligence in architecture: Embedding technical skills and ethical reflection in a core design studio. *Buildings (Basel, Switzerland), 15*(17), 3069. Advance online publication. DOI: 10.3390/buildings15173069

Woodbury, R. (2010). *Elements of parametric design*. Routledge.

Zuhra, F., & Iqbal, M.Fatima-tu-Zuhra. (2025). Exploration of the tangible and intangible aspects affecting students' learning in architectural studios: A case study of Lahore, Pakistan. *Nihon Kenchiku Gakkai Keikaku-Kei Rombunshu, 37*(3), 283–299. DOI: 10.33948/JAP-KSU-37-3-4

KEY TERMS AND DEFINITIONS

AI-Assisted Design: A design process in which artificial intelligence tools support human designers by generating alternatives, suggesting concepts, visualizing ideas, or helping organize design information. AI-assisted design does not replace the designer but changes the designer's role toward selecting, interpreting, evaluating, and transforming generated outputs.

Architectural Design Education: The pedagogical field concerned with teaching students how to think, represent, evaluate, and produce architectural ideas. It typically involves studio-based learning, iterative design development, critique, representation, contextual analysis, and the gradual formation of spatial and conceptual judgment.

Artificial Intelligence (AI): A broad field of computational systems capable of performing tasks that normally require human intelligence, such as recognizing patterns, generating content, interpreting language, or supporting decision-making. In architectural education, AI is increasingly used to support ideation, representation, analysis, and design process exploration.

Cognitive Augmentation: The use of external tools or systems to extend human cognitive processes such as memory, ideation, evaluation, and decision-making. In AI-assisted architectural education, cognitive augmentation refers to how AI may support exploration and reflection without necessarily replacing human judgment.

Design Cognition: The mental and reflective processes involved in designing, including problem framing, spatial reasoning, conceptual development, evaluation, decision-making, and synthesis. In AI-assisted design education, design cognition is important for distinguishing between visual productivity and deeper architectural learning.

Design Studio Pedagogy: A teaching model based on iterative project development, desk critiques, peer discussion, juries, and reflective practice. In this model, students learn by making, testing, receiving feedback, revising, and progressively transforming design ideas into architectural proposals.

Design Thinking: A non-linear and iterative mode of reasoning used in design fields. It involves framing and reframing problems, generating alternatives, testing possibilities, evaluating constraints, and synthesizing ideas into coherent solutions. In architecture, design thinking is closely related to spatial reasoning, representation, and judgment.

Generative Artificial Intelligence: A type of artificial intelligence that produces new content, including text, images, diagrams, scenarios, or design alternatives, based on patterns learned from large datasets. In design education, generative AI is commonly used to generate visual alternatives, conceptual prompts, and speculative architectural representations.

Human-AI Collaboration: A design relationship in which human designers and AI systems interact during the production of ideas, images, scenarios, or decisions. This collaboration requires the designer to remain responsible for interpretation, selection, ethical judgment, and architectural development.

Prompt Literacy: The ability to construct, refine, and evaluate textual or visual prompts used in generative AI systems. In architectural education, prompt literacy involves translating design intentions into precise instructions while critically assessing whether the generated outputs support architectural thinking.

Representation: The use of drawings, diagrams, models, images, digital visualizations, and other media to develop and communicate architectural ideas. In design education, representation is not only a communication tool but also a thinking process through which students discover, test, and refine design decisions.

Spatial Reasoning: The ability to understand, imagine, organize, and manipulate spatial relationships. In architectural education, spatial reasoning is essential for developing plans, sections, volumes, circulation systems, spatial sequences, and relationships between users, context, structure, and form.

Systematic Mapping Review: A structured review method used to identify, categorize, and synthesize research across a field. Unlike a meta-analysis, a systematic mapping review does not statistically combine findings but maps themes, methods, contexts, and gaps within a body of literature.

Chapter 5
AI and Augmented Reality for Teacher and Learner Support:
European Approaches to Adaptive and Inclusive Education

Doni Sugianto Sihotang
http://orcid.org/0009-0008-5222-4475
Universitas Negeri Jakarta, Indonesia

ABSTRACT

This chapter examines the role of augmented reality (AR) and artificial intelligence (AI) in promoting inclusive and adaptive education in European educational settings. This chapter's goal is to examine how new technologies can improve student engagement, teaching efficacy, and fair access to learning materials. The conversation examines pedagogical frameworks, European educational regulations, and technical advancements that influence the incorporation of AI and AR in educational settings. Accessibility, ethical issues, teacher digital competency, and institutional preparedness are among the major topics covered. Additionally, the chapter offers workable ways to incorporate AI and AR into professional development programs and pedagogical design. Lastly, future research possibilities are described, with a focus on immersive technologies, inclusive digital innovation, and adaptable learning ecosystems in modern educational systems.

DOI: 10.4018/979-8-3373-9883-9.ch005

INTRODUCTION

1. Digital Transformation in European Education

In modern European educational systems, digital transformation has emerged as a distinguishing phenomenon. In response to the changing needs of a knowledge-based, electronically mediated society, educational institutions throughout the European Union are increasingly incorporating digital technologies into teaching, learning, and administrative procedures. This change goes beyond the simple use of digital resources; it represents a more comprehensive shift in educational policies, institutional strategies, and pedagogical approaches to promote creativity, accessibility, and flexibility in learning environments. Digital transformation is recognized as a key strategy for enhancing educational quality and resilience in the European context as educational ecosystems become increasingly interconnected and technology-driven (Ivanova, 2025).

European policy frameworks have greatly influenced this change. The need to foster digital literacy, pedagogical innovation, and technological competence across all educational levels is underscored by strategic initiatives, including the Digital Education Action Plan and competency frameworks for educators and citizens. These frameworks emphasize the importance of equipping teachers with the tools they need to successfully integrate digital technology into teaching methods, while ensuring that students acquire the digital skills necessary for engagement in contemporary economies and communities. In this sense, digital transformation is both a technological change and a policy-driven educational reform that aims to align educational systems with broader societal and economic advancements (Ftacnik et al., 2020).

Higher education institutions around Europe are beginning to see digital transformation as a strategic necessity at the institutional level. To improve institutional performance and instructional delivery, colleges and universities are implementing digital infrastructures, learning management systems, and data-driven decision-making procedures. New learning methods, such as blended learning, online collaboration, and interactive digital environments that increase opportunities for student participation and knowledge production, have also been enabled by the digitization of education. Thus, in the context of global education, digital transformation is often linked to institutional competitiveness and long-term sustainability (Dimitrova, 2025; Pal'ová & Zoricaková, 2025).

The adoption of digital transformation in European education remains difficult and uneven, despite its potential advantages. Inadequate infrastructure, a lack of funding, and varying levels of digital competency among teachers and students are issues many institutions face. Additionally, traditional educational systems may resist the organizational and cultural changes often necessary to adopt digital technologies.

Therefore, in many European educational environments, the shift from policy vision to actual execution remains a crucial challenge (Ivanova, 2025).

Emerging technologies like augmented reality and artificial intelligence are receiving more attention as tools to improve inclusive and adaptive education amid this broader shift. These technologies provide new ways to improve teacher and learner assistance in European educational settings by facilitating individualized learning experiences, immersive simulations, and data-driven instructional tactics.

2. The Role of AI and AR in Teacher and Learner Support

In modern educational settings, artificial intelligence (AI) and augmented reality (AR) are increasingly recognized as revolutionary technologies. Their incorporation into educational institutions presents new opportunities to improve instructional strategies, accommodate a range of student needs, and promote more inclusive and flexible learning environments. AI and AR are not only technological advancements but also pedagogical tools that transform how educators design lessons and how students engage with information in rapidly changing digital education ecosystems. These technologies are increasingly essential parts of contemporary educational practices as educational institutions work to enhance learning outcomes and meet the needs of digital societies (Devi et al., 2025).

By facilitating individualized and flexible learning processes, artificial intelligence (AI) significantly benefits educators and students. AI systems can create personalized learning pathways by analyzing learners' activities, preferences, and progress using sophisticated data analytics and machine learning algorithms. These systems enable the dynamic modification of instructional materials to meet each learner's needs, increasing student engagement and learning efficacy. Additionally, AI-driven platforms include learning analytics, automated feedback systems, and intelligent tutoring systems that assist teachers in tracking student progress and more effectively identifying learning challenges (Yanjin et al., 2023). AI also reduces the administrative burden on teachers by automating repetitive tasks such as assessment, grading, and data management, freeing them to focus more on pedagogical innovation and student-centered instruction.

On the other hand, augmented reality primarily supports the development of interactive and immersive learning environments. AR enables students to visualize difficult ideas and engage with instructional material in more hands-on ways by superimposing digital objects on real-world environments. Because it turns abstract knowledge into concrete, interactive experiences, this technology is especially useful in courses that require spatial comprehension, simulation, or experiential learning. According to Zouhri and Mallahi (2024), augmented reality (AR) improves students' motivation, engagement, and information retention while also empowering educators to create innovative learning experiences that integrate digital and physical learning environments.

Innovation in education is made much more possible by the combination of AI and AR. Together, these technologies facilitate the creation of intelligent immersive learning systems that may modify learning scenarios in real time in response to student performance and interactions. By analyzing data produced by AR settings, AI can optimize learning experiences and personalize instructional content, enhancing student autonomy and instructor support (Lampropoulos, 2023). Particularly in European educational contexts that prioritize technology innovation and the development of digital competency, such integration offers a promising path for inclusive and adaptive education.

Notwithstanding these encouraging prospects, ethical, pedagogical, and infrastructure considerations must be carefully taken into account for the successful integration of AI and AR. To ensure the sustainable and appropriate use of these technologies in education, issues related to data privacy, algorithmic transparency, teacher readiness, and equal access to technology remain crucial obstacles.

3. Objectives and Scope of the Chapter

Artificial Intelligence (AI) and Augmented Reality (AR) are two examples of how the quick growth of digital technologies has drastically changed educational processes. These technologies present new opportunities to create inclusive, interactive, and adaptive educational systems that address the diverse needs of teachers and students. The integration of AI and AR has grown in importance in European education as institutions seek new ways to enhance pedagogical effectiveness, improve learning outcomes, and help teachers and students develop their digital competence. The potential of immersive and intelligent technologies to revolutionize educational practices necessitates critical thought and methodical analysis as these technologies continue to develop (Lampropoulos, 2023).

This chapter's main goal is to investigate how AI and AR technologies benefit educators and students in the context of inclusive and adaptable education in Europe. The chapter's specific goal is to investigate how new technologies might improve teaching methods, enable individualized learning, and produce more stimulating learning environments. While AR technologies provide immersive visualizations that make difficult topics more approachable and intelligible, AI-driven educational systems enable real-time analysis of learner data, which can be utilized to adapt instructional content and deliver tailored feedback. When taken as a whole, these technologies support learner-centered methods and pedagogical flexibility, marking a substantial advancement in educational innovation (Arrojula et al., 2025).

This chapter aims to examine the broader implications of AI and AR for educational inclusion, as well as their pedagogical advantages. Learning environments that support a range of cognitive, cultural, and accessibility needs are necessary for inclusive education. By offering customized learning paths, multimodal information representations, and adaptive instructional support, AI and AR offer intriguing solutions to these issues. For instance, interactive simulations in AR-based learning settings can enhance experiential understanding, and AI systems can help teachers identify learning gaps and offer tailored advice (Natarajan et al., 2025).

This chapter's aim extends beyond technology applications to include critical analyses of the challenges of incorporating AI and AR into educational settings. The effective adoption of these innovations depends on several crucial factors, including institutional readiness, technological accessibility, teacher training, and ethical considerations. How well modern technologies are incorporated into classroom practices largely depends on teachers' viewpoints and professional preparedness (Perifanou et al., 2022).

This chapter aims to give a thorough overview of how AI and AR might help educators and students in European educational settings. The chapter seeks to contribute to ongoing conversations about how intelligent and immersive technologies might support more flexible, inclusive, and forward-thinking educational systems by examining technological potential, pedagogical implications, and implementation obstacles.

BACKGROUND

1. Artificial Intelligence in Education (AIED)

To improve teaching, learning, and educational administration, the interdisciplinary field of Artificial Intelligence in Education (AIED) integrates artificial intelligence technologies with educational theory and practice. AI technologies are being used to provide more effective and responsive learning environments as educational systems progressively adjust to the digital transformation. Intelligent tutoring systems, learning analytics, automated assessment, and adaptive learning platforms are just a few of the many applications that fall under the umbrella of AIED. By analyzing vast amounts of student data and producing insights that enable individualized, data-driven instructional tactics, these technologies seek to maximize educational outcomes (Zawacki-Richter et al., 2019).

AIED's ability to support individualized learning is one of its most important advances. Standardized teaching methods are often used in traditional educational models, which may not adequately meet students' varied needs and learning preferences. To create personalized learning pathways, AI-driven systems can examine each learner's behavior, performance trends, and degree of engagement. These technologies allow educational systems to dynamically adapt assessment techniques, feedback, and learning materials to each learner's unique needs. Such adaptive learning environments have been shown to enhance student motivation, engagement, and academic outcomes by providing more relevant and individualized learning experiences (Tapalova & Zhiyenbayeva, 2022).

Beyond personalizing, AIED is crucial in helping teachers with their administrative and teaching duties. Teachers' administrative workload can be reduced by using AI to automate repetitive tasks such as data management, performance monitoring, and grading. AI-based learning analytics and intelligent tutoring systems provide teachers with important information about students' progress and learning challenges, enabling prompt pedagogical interventions. By offering real-time feedback and suggestions that guide students toward more effective learning techniques, these systems can also support formative assessment (Zawacki-Richter et al., 2019).

Even though AIED has significant potential, there are several institutional and technological obstacles to overcome. Adequate digital infrastructure, access to technology resources, and professional development for instructors are necessary for effective adoption. The lack of financing, inadequate training in digital capabilities, and technology readiness remain obstacles for many educational institutions. For AI technologies to be sustainably integrated into educational settings, these organizational and infrastructure limitations must be addressed (Vasou et al., 2025).

Moreover, ethical issues remain a major factor in the development and use of AIED. Fairness and accountability in educational settings are critically challenged by issues such as data privacy, algorithmic transparency, and potential biases in AI-driven systems. The importance of creating human-centered AI systems that prioritize inclusion, transparency, and ethical norms is increasingly emphasized by researchers and politicians. These strategies seek to preserve the crucial role that educators play in guiding meaningful learning experiences by ensuring that AI technologies enhance, rather than replace, human pedagogical skills (Fortuna et al., 2025).

Even if artificial intelligence is being more widely used in education, there are still a number of important questions about the institutional and pedagogical ramifications of AI-driven learning environments. Over-reliance on automated decision-making systems is one of the main concerns, as it may diminish teacher autonomy and professional judgment. Teachers may grow reliant on AI-generated insights when instructional recommendations are mostly produced by algorithms, which could restrict pedagogical innovation and contextual decision-making. AI-driven personalization systems may also inadvertently restrict learning routes by putting efficiency ahead of essential and exploratory learning opportunities. The balance between technological automation and human-centered pedagogy in adaptive learning environments is called into question by these restrictions (Fortuna et al., 2025).

Significant obstacles to AI-supported education also include algorithmic bias and data reliance. AI systems mainly rely on learner data from the past, which may represent socioeconomic and current inequality. Therefore, skewed datasets may result in misinterpretations of student abilities or unequal learning recommendations. Furthermore, instead of encouraging innovation, critical thinking, and learner autonomy, an over-reliance on AI-driven analytics may promote standardized learning optimization. These dangers emphasize how crucial it is to uphold ethical governance and human monitoring in order to guarantee that AI technologies support inclusive educational practices rather than impede them (Li & Huang, 2025; Vasou et al., 2025).

2. Augmented Reality in Learning Environments

In contemporary educational settings, augmented reality (AR) has become a major technological advancement, opening new avenues for immersive and interactive learning. By incorporating digital components such as three-dimensional models, animations, and multimedia content into real-world settings, augmented reality technology allows students to interact with virtual elements while maintaining a connection to their physical environment. Compared to traditional teaching approaches, this hybrid learning environment helps pupils visualize complicated events and abstract concepts. Because of this, educators and researchers who want to improve engagement, comprehension, and experiential learning across a variety of educational settings are paying increasing attention to AR (Ali et al., 2022).

AR's capacity to facilitate immersive and interactive learning is one of its most notable features in education. Through visualization, manipulation, and simulation, augmented reality (AR) allows students to engage with educational content by superimposing digital information onto real-world environments. By fusing academic knowledge with real-world observation, these interactive experiences help students gain a deeper conceptual understanding. AR-based apps, for instance, can show scientific procedures, architectural designs, or historical relics in ways that would be challenging to present in traditional classroom settings. As a result, AR helps turn passive learning into inquisitive and active learning opportunities (Ajao et al., 2024).

AR technologies have shown great promise for increasing student enthusiasm and engagement, as well as improving conceptual understanding. Gamified learning components, dynamic simulations, and interactive visualizations can pique students' interest and motivate them to take an active role in their education. Research has demonstrated that AR-based learning environments often lead to greater focus, enthusiasm, and information retention, especially when compared with conventional teaching methods. Learner motivation is further strengthened, and an engaging educational experience is fostered, through the use of game-like elements, such as prizes, challenges, and interactive tasks (Skraparli et al., 2025).

AR's role in pedagogical innovation and classroom change is another significant part of learning settings. Using augmented reality, educators can create innovative teaching activities that integrate digital and physical learning environments. To provide presentations, group problem-solving exercises, and practical learning scenarios that encourage greater student engagement, educators might use augmented reality applications. AR promotes more student-centered instructional approaches and active knowledge production in the classroom setting by enabling interactive and visual learning methodologies (Ugli et al., 2025).

Even with these encouraging prospects, there are several obstacles to overcome when implementing AR in educational settings. The broad adoption of AR technology may be hampered by financial and technical constraints, as well as the need for specialized instructional design. To successfully incorporate AR tools into their teaching practices, educators also need adequate training and pedagogical support. To guarantee that AR technologies can be applied in educational systems sustainably and equitably, several issues must be resolved (Ugli et al., 2025).

While augmented reality has prospects for immersive learning, there are a number of pedagogical and technological issues with its use. One major issue is cognitive overload, where too many interactive and visual components may divert students rather than improve comprehension. Even if they are captivating, immersive environments have the potential to divert attention from conceptual learning to technology innovation. This issue is especially pertinent when AR applications are used without robust instructional design frameworks, which could result in meaningless knowledge creation rather than surface-level engagement. To guarantee successful learning results, educators must carefully balance immersive elements with pedagogical goals (Ali et al., 2022).

Furthermore, infrastructure constraints and technological accessibility could lead to the emergence of new types of educational inequality. Advanced hardware, reliable connectivity, and technical assistance are frequently needed for AR technology, and these resources might not be equally accessible in all educational institutions. Contrary to the egalitarian objectives of technology-enhanced education, this digital gap may inadvertently exclude students from under-resourced areas. Additionally, an over-reliance on immersive technologies may diminish face-to-face pedagogical engagement and traditional collaborative learning interactions. These issues emphasize how crucial it is to include AR technology in methods that promote pedagogical efficacy while upholding inclusive learning environments and fair access (Ajao et al., 2024).

3. European Policy and Educational Frameworks

The integration of digital technology to enable inclusive, adaptable, and future-focused learning systems has become increasingly important in European educational policy. Frameworks developed by the European Union provide a strategic direction for integrating cutting-edge technologies such as augmented reality (AR) and artificial intelligence (AI) into learning environments. These frameworks seek to improve digital capabilities, ensure the ethical adoption of technology, and provide learning systems that adapt to the diverse needs of learners. European institutions aim to support inclusive and sustainable digital transformation in schools and higher education systems by coordinating technology innovation with educational policy (Skraparli et al., 2025).

The competence-based approach, supported by European policy frameworks, is one of the most significant initiatives shaping digital education in Europe. European educational approaches prioritize the development of critical thinking, creativity, problem-solving, and digital literacy over mere knowledge acquisition. These skills are seen as crucial for educating students in a rapidly changing digital society. By facilitating experiential learning, interactive simulations, and customized educational paths, AI-enabled learning systems and immersive technologies such as augmented reality (AR) promote this competence-oriented paradigm (Benvenuti et al., 2023).

Legislative frameworks and competency development now guide the ethical and appropriate application of AI technology in educational settings. To ensure that AI applications in education operate transparently and uphold fundamental rights, the European Union has established extensive legal frameworks. In this sense, the EU AI Act, which establishes standards for risk assessment, accountability, and ethical governance of AI systems, is a major turning point. These restrictions highlight the significance of openness, informed consent, and algorithmic accountability in educational environments, as educational technology may involve sensitive learner data and automated decision-making processes (Ivković et al., 2025).

Additionally, inclusion and fair access to education are highly valued in European educational frameworks. The goal of barrier-free education policies is to make learning opportunities available to students from diverse socioeconomic, cognitive, and physical backgrounds. These frameworks encourage educational institutions to create inclusive classrooms that meet a range of learning needs by using digital technologies. Educational institutions can offer individualized support mechanisms that enhance accessibility and engagement for a diverse variety of learners by utilizing AI-driven analytics and AR-based immersive learning tools (Deinega & Deineha, 2022).

To promote creative teaching and learning methods, European educational policy also encourages the integration of cutting-edge technologies such as AI,

AR, and intelligent tutoring systems. These technologies make it possible to create dynamic and immersive learning environments where students engage with virtual simulations and get real-time, tailored feedback. European legislative frameworks are increasingly encouraging the development of intelligent learning ecosystems that integrate pedagogical efficacy, ethical governance, and technological innovation as educational technologies advance (Lampropoulos, 2023).

The adoption of AI and AR technology frequently encounters institutional and practical obstacles, despite considerable policy backing for digital transformation in Europe. Although policy frameworks can offer strategic guidance, it is nevertheless difficult to implement these policies in the classroom. Adoption is inconsistent throughout European educational systems because to variations in institutional preparedness, finance capability, and teacher digital competency. Therefore, policy-driven digital transformation may inadvertently increase the disparity between institutions with little resources and those with superior technology. This variation emphasizes the necessity of consistent institutional investment and coordinated execution strategies (Ivković et al., 2025; Hul et al., 2025).

Furthermore, educational institutions may face new challenges as a result of legislative frameworks pertaining to ethical AI use. Many institutions lack the technological know-how and administrative capability needed to comply with privacy laws, transparency standards, and algorithm accountability. These difficulties could hinder the uptake of technology and make educators unsure about how to use AI-driven technologies responsibly. Furthermore, overly strict regulations may stifle exploration and innovation in the use of educational technology. Thus, a crucial issue in the transition of digital education in Europe continues to be striking a balance between innovation flexibility and regulatory oversight (Deinega & Deineha, 2022; Lampropoulos, 2023).

Table 1. Elements of European Educational Frameworks for AI and AR Integration

Aspect	Details
Competence Development	Emphasis on creativity, critical thinking, problem-solving, and computational thinking (Benvenuti et al., 2023).
Technological Tools	Integration of AI, AR, and intelligent tutoring systems to support immersive learning environments (Lampropoulos, 2023).
Regulatory Frameworks	EU AI Act promoting transparency, accountability, and the ethical implementation of AI in education (Ivković et al., 2025).
Inclusivity Policies	Barrier-free and inclusive education policies ensuring equal access to learning opportunities (Deinega & Deineha, 2022).
Strategic Goals	Development of adaptive, inclusive, and technology-driven education systems across Europe.

MAIN FOCUS OF THE CHAPTER

Issues, Controversies, Problems

To deepen understanding of how artificial intelligence and augmented reality integrate into education, a conceptual framework is proposed. It demonstrates how these technologies foster adaptive and inclusive learning environments. Artificial intelligence mainly supports personalized learning, teacher assistance, and data-driven strategies, while augmented reality boosts immersive experiences, student engagement, and experiential knowledge. Together, they create opportunities for educational ecosystems that are adaptable and inclusive, catering to diverse learner needs and enhancing outcomes (Tapalova & Zhiyenbayeva, 2022).

Figure 1 depicts the conceptual fusion of AI and AR in supporting teachers and learners. The framework features two parallel pathways: one for AI-driven adaptive learning and another for AR-based immersive environments. On the AI side, adaptive technologies aid teacher support and inclusive education by facilitating personalized strategies and data-based decisions (Zawacki-Richter et al., 2019). On the AR side, immersive environments improve engagement and outcomes via interactive visualization and experiential learning (Ali et al., 2022; Skraparli et al., 2025). These pathways merge into a digital education ecosystem that promotes equitable, flexible learning spaces (Lampropoulos, 2023; Chalkiadakis et al., 2024).

Figure 1. Conceptual Framework of AI and AR for Teacher and Learner Support

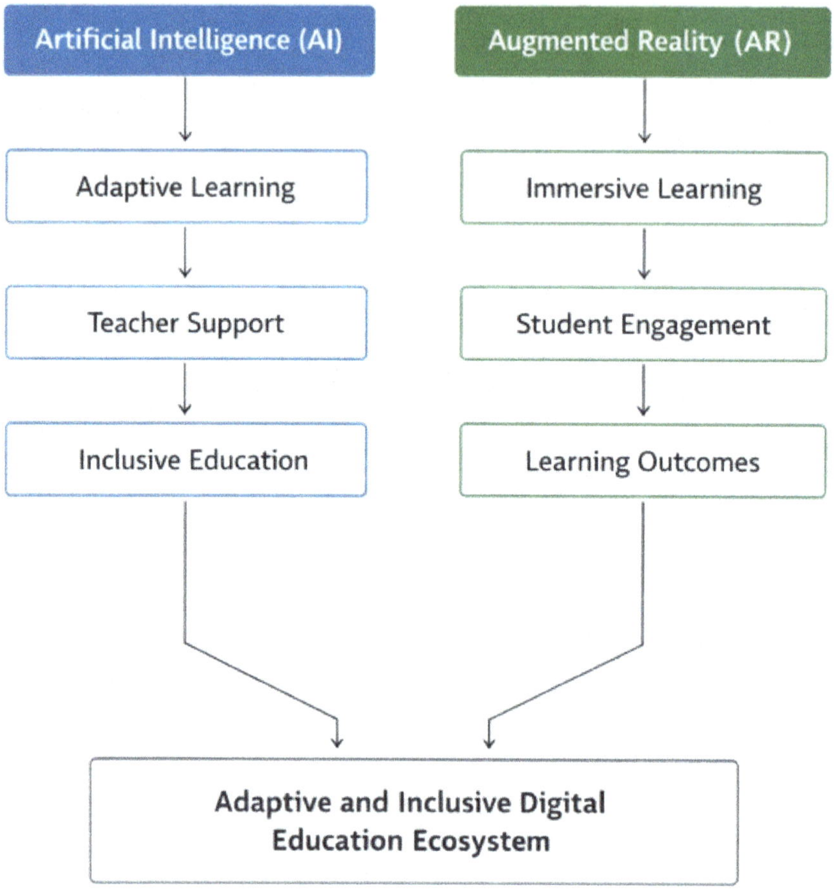

1. Adaptive Learning and Personalization Challenges

Personalization and adaptive learning have emerged as major issues in modern educational innovation, especially with the incorporation of augmented reality (AR) and artificial intelligence (AI) technologies. Using these technologies, educational systems can customize learning experiences based on each student's cognitive ability, learning speed, and engagement habits. Theoretically, educational platforms can automatically modify assessment, feedback, and instructional content depending on real-time data thanks to adaptive learning environments. In inclusive educational environments, these capabilities promise to boost student engagement, improve academic results, and accommodate a variety of learning needs. Nevertheless, many obstacles remain to the implementation of efficient adaptive learning systems, despite these encouraging prospects.

The difficulty of creating precise and trustworthy personalization processes is a major obstacle. Large volumes of learner data are crucial for AI-driven adaptive learning systems to generate insights into students' learning preferences and habits. To produce relevant educational recommendations, these data-driven systems require complex algorithms capable of interpreting cognitive, behavioral, and environmental aspects. However, inadequate information, computational limitations, and challenges in simulating intricate human learning processes can limit the precision and efficacy of such systems. As a result, adaptive systems may struggle to fully account for the variety of learners' experiences and learning preferences (Lampropoulos, 2023).

The pedagogical integration of adaptive learning systems is another significant difficulty. Although AI and AR systems can create customized learning paths, their successful application necessitates adherence to accepted pedagogical frameworks and instructional design principles. In technology-supported learning environments, educators must be able to interpret algorithmic recommendations, adapt teaching strategies accordingly, and sustain meaningful human connections. Adaptive technologies risk becoming merely technical instruments that cannot adequately support meaningful learning experiences without appropriate pedagogical guidance (Jaimes et al., 2026).

The creation of adaptive learning systems is also influenced by policy and regulatory factors. Emerging legal frameworks in Europe place a strong emphasis on the value of responsibility, openness, and the moral use of AI in education. The requirement to ensure that AI systems used in educational settings operate transparently and do not perpetuate biases or unfair learning opportunities is highlighted by laws such as the EU AI Act. Because of these regulations, educational institutions must carefully analyze the ethical implications of data-driven customization systems and make sure that students' privacy and rights are upheld (Ivković et al., 2025).

Lastly, broader concerns about equity and inclusivity are raised by the use of adaptive learning systems. Even while customization technologies are designed to accommodate a wide range of learners, their effectiveness across educational environments may be limited by unequal access to digital competencies and technological infrastructure. To ensure that adaptive learning technologies contribute to inclusive and equitable educational settings, addressing these gaps requires institutional investment, coordinated policies, and ongoing professional development for educators (Fachrurrazy et al., 2026).

2. Inclusivity and Accessibility Concerns

There are many opportunities to support inclusive and accessible learning systems when Artificial Intelligence (AI) and Augmented Reality (AR) are integrated into educational settings. By facilitating adaptable learning environments, assistive technology, and immersive educational experiences, these technologies are increasingly recognized for their ability to meet a variety of student needs. Accessibility and inclusion have become top priorities in European educational systems, especially as educational institutions work to ensure fair participation for students with diverse skills, backgrounds, and learning styles. Nevertheless, several institutional, social, and technological obstacles still exist despite the potential of AI and AR to promote inclusive education (Mitre & Zeneli, 2024).

The capacity of AI technology to customize educational experiences for pupils with a range of cognitive and physical needs is a significant contribution. AI-driven educational systems can analyze learner data to find unique learning patterns and offer customized instructional support. Because they allow for adaptive content delivery, real-time feedback, and intelligent tutoring support that can improve accessibility and engagement, these systems are especially beneficial for students with impairments. In a similar vein, augmented reality (AR) technologies offer immersive, interactive environments that help students visualize complex ideas and engage meaningfully with digital content. By providing multimodal information representations and chances for experiential learning, these immersive experiences can help individuals with learning difficulties (Chalkiadakis et al., 2024).

AI-driven assistive solutions are also essential for increasing accessibility in learning environments. Students with visual, hearing, or cognitive disabilities can engage with educational materials more effectively thanks to tools such as text-to-speech programs, speech recognition systems, and AI-based tutoring systems. By enabling students to access material through a variety of modalities and customized learning interfaces, these technologies enhance inclusive curricula. Because of this, AI technologies are now crucial components of contemporary inclusive education methods that aim to reduce learning barriers and increase academic engagement (Mitre & Zeneli, 2024).

Despite these developments, several obstacles still prevent the effective implementation of inclusive educational technologies. The digital gap, or unequal access to digital devices, infrastructure, and connectivity, is one of the most significant issues. Access to AI and AR tools may be restricted for students from underprivileged socioeconomic backgrounds, potentially exacerbating existing educational disparities. Additionally, to successfully integrate inclusive technologies into classroom settings, educators may need specialized training. Teachers may find it difficult to incorporate AI and AR tools into inclusive teaching practices in the absence of adequate professional development and institutional support (Odunga et al., 2025).

When talking about inclusive technology adoption, ethical issues are equally crucial. Algorithmic bias or privacy issues that disproportionately affect minority learners may be introduced unintentionally by AI-driven systems. As a result, when implementing new educational technologies, educational institutions need to adopt responsible AI procedures that emphasize ethical governance, transparency, and justice (Scott et al., 2025).

Table 2. Inclusivity and Accessibility Challenges and Opportunities in AI and AR-Based Education

Challenges	Opportunities
Digital divide and unequal access to technology	AI and AR enable personalized and immersive learning experiences
Limited teacher training in inclusive technologies	Professional development programs can improve digital pedagogical skills.
Ethical concerns such as data privacy and algorithmic bias	Responsible AI frameworks promote transparency and fairness
High costs of technological infrastructure	Scalable assistive technologies can expand accessibility.

3. Ethical, Privacy, and Pedagogical Implications

The use of Augmented Reality (AR) and Artificial Intelligence (AI) in education offers revolutionary possibilities for enhancing teaching and learning procedures. However, the use of these technologies also brings up significant privacy, ethical, and educational issues that need to be properly considered. Maintaining trust, justice, and openness in educational settings requires ethical governance and responsible implementation, as educational institutions increasingly rely on data-driven technologies to facilitate adaptive and personalized learning.

Algorithmic bias and fairness are two of the main ethical issues with AI in education. AI systems frequently use large datasets to produce forecasts and suggestions for students. AI systems may inadvertently perpetuate existing educational disparities if their datasets are biased or reflect only a narrow range of demographic viewpoints. Automated decision-making processes for learning evaluation, student monitoring, and customized recommendations may be affected by such biases. As a result, researchers emphasize the need for ethical AI design that promotes equity, responsibility, and openness in educational technology (Li & Huang, 2025).

In conversations about the application of AI and AR in educational settings, privacy considerations are also quite important. Large amounts of student data, such as study habits, academic achievement, and interaction patterns, are often gathered by AI-powered learning platforms. Although these data are necessary to enable tailored learning systems, there are hazards associated with data security and unauthorized access. Concerns over student surveillance and the improper use of private data may arise from the growing reliance on educational data analytics. Thus, to defend learners' rights and uphold ethical standards in digital education systems, robust privacy protection measures, open data governance policies, and responsible data management practices are required (Kaddouri et al., 2025).

The integration of AI and AR technology has important educational implications, as well as ethical and privacy concerns. By modifying instructional content based on learners' progress, preferences, and cognitive traits, these technologies allow for individualized learning experiences. While AI-driven analytics provide real-time feedback, enabling teachers to monitor student progress and adjust teaching strategies, AR-based settings can offer immersive learning experiences that enhance experiential and interactive learning. Thus, learner-centered educational approaches that encourage participation, teamwork, and knowledge creation are enabled by AI and AR technologies (Arrojula et al., 2025).

Despite these advantages, significant adjustments to teaching methods and teacher competencies are necessary for the successful pedagogical integration of AI and AR. Teachers need to acquire digital pedagogical abilities that enable them to create interactive learning environments, analyze the effects of developing technologies on student learning, and comprehend data-driven insights. The educational potential of AI and AR technologies may remain underused in the absence of suitable teacher training and institutional support. Therefore, to ensure that AI and AR technologies enable responsible and inclusive educational reform, it is imperative to integrate ethical principles, privacy protection systems, and pedagogical innovation (Sumbera, 2025).

SOLUTIONS AND RECOMMENDATIONS

The successful integration of AI and AR in education depends on a structured framework that aligns policy, institutional readiness, and pedagogical innovation. Implementing these emerging technologies requires more than just technological access; it needs institutional preparedness, skilled teachers, and supportive policies.

A systematic model guides educational institutions from initial experimentation to ongoing digital transformation (Aler Tubella et al., 2024).

Figure 2 illustrates this implementation framework, which follows a hierarchical, structured approach. It starts with policy frameworks providing regulations and ethical standards for technology use (Ivković et al., 2025). The second stage focuses on institutional readiness, emphasizing infrastructure, leadership, and strategic planning essential for successful adoption (Nisiforou & Kosmas, 2024).

Next, teacher training and digital skills are prioritized to enable educators to effectively incorporate AI and AR into their teaching (Nikou et al., 2024; Aimicheva et al., 2025). The integration phase involves embedding AI and AR tools into learning environments to create adaptive and immersive experiences (Lampropoulos, 2023; Garg et al., 2025). These innovations lead to personalized learning environments that boost student engagement (Tapalova & Zhiyenbayeva, 2022; Hariyanto et al., 2025).

The final stage aims at inclusive and accessible education, fostering equitable and flexible learning ecosystems that support sustainable digital transformation (Chalkiadakis et al., 2024; Domínguez et al., 2023).

Figure 2. Implementation Framework for AI and AR Integration in Education

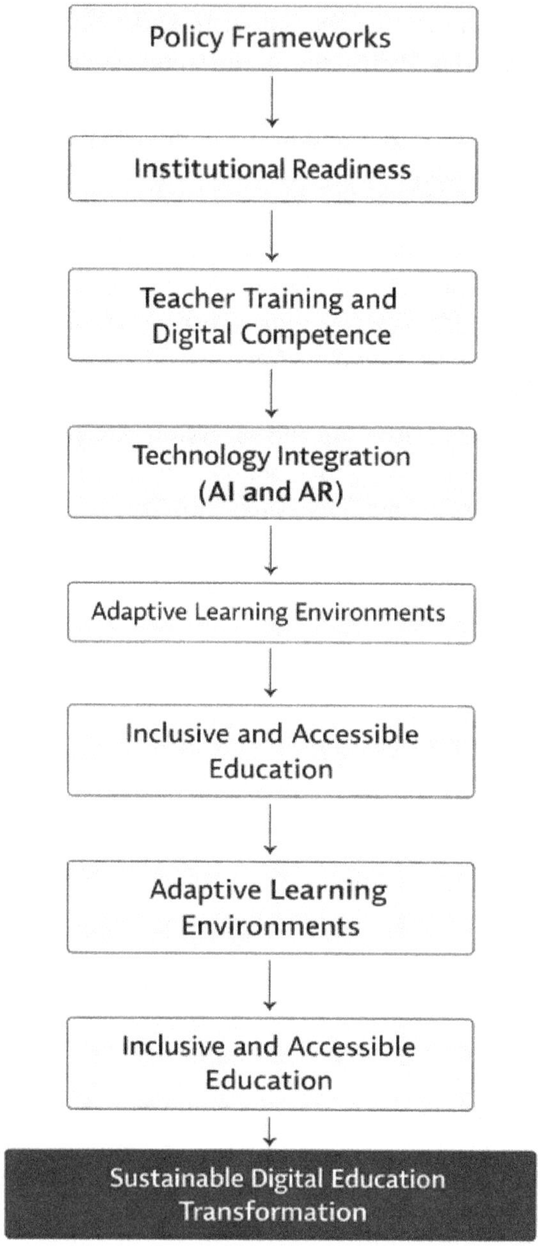

1. Integrating AI and AR into Pedagogical Design

To successfully incorporate Artificial Intelligence (AI) and Augmented Reality (AR) into pedagogical design, methodical approaches that balance technical innovation with strong educational principles are needed. By enabling individualized learning, immersive educational experiences, and data-driven instructional methodologies, AI and AR technologies have the potential to revolutionize conventional teaching approaches. However, creating pedagogically significant frameworks that guide teachers in integrating new technologies into curriculum design and learning activities is necessary for successful implementation.

Using AI-driven adaptive learning systems to provide individualized learning pathways is one of the most significant answers. To provide personalized learning recommendations, AI systems can analyze students' performance trends, engagement levels, and learning behaviors. By customizing instructional materials to each student's unique needs, these systems help teachers increase student engagement and learning efficacy. Additionally, learners can identify knowledge gaps and adjust their learning strategies using real-time feedback from adaptive AI systems (Yanjin et al., 2023).

Using augmented reality (AR) technologies to facilitate immersive learning environments is a crucial aspect of pedagogical integration. By enabling students to engage with virtual items and simulations in real-world settings, augmented reality (AR) applications improve conceptual understanding and encourage active learning. Students can explore intricate scientific, technical, or geographic concepts through AR-based simulations that are difficult to visualize with conventional teaching methods. In learning contexts, these interactive experiences promote deeper engagement and cooperative problem-solving (Garg et al., 2025).

Teachers must use instructional frameworks that integrate digital tools with pedagogical goals to benefit from AI and AR technologies fully. For example, the Technology, Pedagogy, and Content Knowledge (TPACK) framework highlights the importance of aligning instructional strategies and content knowledge with technology tools. While preserving significant instructor engagement in the learning process, AI-enabled learning activities created within such frameworks promote critical thinking, creativity, and reflective learning (Ravi, 2025).

Furthermore, ongoing institutional support and ongoing professional development for educators are necessary for the integration of AI and AR technology. To create technology-enhanced learning activities, analyze AI-generated insights, and lead immersive learning experiences, educators must acquire digital pedagogical competencies. The educational potential of AI and AR technologies may remain underutilized in educational institutions due to insufficient training and technological infrastructure (Yadav, 2025).

Table 3. Strategies for Integrating AI and AR into Pedagogical Design

Aspect	Pedagogical Solutions	Implementation Recommendations
Personalized Learning	AI-driven adaptive learning systems that tailor instruction to learner needs	Use learning analytics to monitor progress and adjust instructional strategies.
Immersive Learning	AR simulations and interactive visualizations for complex concepts	Integrate AR activities into collaborative and experiential learning tasks
Instructional Design	Alignment with pedagogical frameworks such as TPACK	Design technology-supported learning activities that foster critical thinking
Teacher Readiness	Development of digital pedagogical competencies	Provide continuous professional training and institutional support

2. Teacher Capacity Building and Digital Competence

Teachers' digital competency and capacity to integrate emerging technologies into pedagogical practices are critical to the successful application of AI and AR in educational contexts. Teachers need to acquire sophisticated digital skills to create technology-enhanced learning experiences, analyze digital data, and promote inclusive learning environments as AI and AR continue to transform educational settings. As a result, educational institutions seeking to deploy adaptive, technology-supported education systems have made teacher capacity building a strategic goal.

Establishing formal competence frameworks to help educators acquire the skills needed to integrate AI and AR is a crucial part of the solution. For instance, the Teachers' Augmented Reality Competences (TARC) framework outlines the fundamental skills teachers must possess to develop, oversee, and use AR-based learning materials successfully. Digital literacy, technical innovation, and the capacity to integrate augmented reality tools into teaching methods are among these competencies. According to research, teachers' willingness and ability to implement AR-based teaching methods are strongly influenced by their attitudes toward innovation and their degree of digital competency (Nikou et al., 2024).

Additionally, professional development programs are essential for enhancing teachers' digital competency. Teachers can participate in interactive, practice-based learning activities that mimic actual classroom settings thanks to AI-supported training environments. Teachers can gain expertise in technology-supported instructional design, the interpretation of learning analytics, and digital content development through these programs. These programs increase instructors' confidence in utilizing digital technologies in classroom settings and prepare them to use AI-driven learning systems and interactive augmented reality tools (Aimicheva et al., 2025).

Using adaptable and ongoing professional training models is another crucial tactic. Based on instructional design methods such as ADDIE and ASSURE, micro-course approaches offer modular training options that enable teachers to enhance their digital competencies progressively. Teachers can learn technology skills and apply them in their professional practice through brief, focused learning modules delivered in blended or online learning environments. According to Abuhassna et al. (20245), this gradual approach facilitates instructors' adaptation to quickly emerging instructional technologies and encourages sustainable professional development.

Strengthening teachers' ability for digital education also heavily depends on institutional support and policy frameworks. Strategic initiatives that support educators' digital readiness and give them access to the right technology infrastructure and training materials must be developed by universities and educational institutions. Educators' ability to use AI and AR tools in classroom practice can be greatly enhanced by institutional programs that combine technical training with pedagogical innovation. Additionally, these programs foster cooperative learning communities in which educators exchange experiences, develop cutting-edge instructional strategies, and enhance their collective digital competencies (Stare et al., 2023).

Table 4. Strategies for Teacher Capacity Building and Digital Competence Development

Area	Strategies	Expected Outcomes
AR Competence Development	Implementation of the TARC framework to guide teachers in creating and managing AR learning resources	Improved ability to integrate AR technologies into instructional practices
Professional Development	AI-supported training environments and digital teaching workshops	Increased teacher confidence and technological readiness
Continuous Learning	Micro-courses based on instructional design models such as ADDIE and ASSURE	Gradual and sustainable development of digital competencies
Institutional Support	Institutional policies promoting digital readiness and collaborative teacher learning communities	Enhanced long-term adoption of AI and AR in education

3. Policy and Institutional Support in European Education

Strong institutional support and policy frameworks that match technological innovation with educational goals are necessary for the effective integration of artificial intelligence (AI) and augmented reality (AR) in education. Policymakers and educational institutions across Europe are increasingly recognizing that sustained investments, legal frameworks, and coherent policies are necessary to enable the digital transformation of education. The potential advantages of AI and AR technologies for inclusive and adaptable learning environments may remain restricted in the absence of coordinated legislative actions and institutional preparedness.

European initiatives at the policy level stress the significance of implementing AI in educational environments ethically and responsibly. It is recommended that policymakers translate high-level regulatory frameworks into workable plans that guide the integration of new technology into educational institutions. Transparency, accountability, and human-centered technology design are essential components of ethical standards for reliable AI. In educational settings where AI-driven systems affect learning pathways, assessment procedures, and instructional support, these concepts are especially crucial. Incorporating ethical issues into teacher training programs and digital literacy curricula is also necessary to promote responsible AI teaching (Aler Tubella et al., 2024).

Strengthening coordinated initiatives across European education systems is another important policy recommendation. Countries can set shared standards, exchange resources, and advance inclusive digital education practices through collaborative policy creation. Coordinated investment in digital infrastructure, research projects, and teacher training programs greatly enhances institutional preparedness for technological transformation, according to comparative assessments of AI integration across European educational systems. These cooperative methods guarantee that AI-driven innovations uphold high ethical and pedagogical standards while benefiting a variety of educational contexts (Hul et al., 2025).

Effective technology adoption requires institutional backing as well. Strategic frameworks for integrating AI and AR into teaching, research, and administrative procedures must be developed by educational institutions. The availability of digital infrastructure, technology resources, and support services that help teachers adopt cutting-edge teaching techniques is a component of institutional readiness. Aligning digital transformation activities with institutional missions and learning objectives also requires strategic planning and a commitment to leadership (Nisiforou & Kosmas, 2024).

Institutions could also promote experimentation by conducting research and pilot projects to investigate the educational potential of AI and AR technologies. Prior to widespread use, pilot programs enable institutions to assess the efficacy of immersive learning resources, pinpoint implementation issues, and improve teaching methods. When integrated into carefully designed pedagogical frameworks, AR-based learning environments can significantly increase student engagement and enable personalized learning, according to evidence from European pilot studies (Domínguez et al., 2023).

Lastly, a major legislative challenge remains ensuring fair access to AI and AR technologies. To stop new types of digital inequality, educational institutions need to address concerns about data governance, technology affordability, and digital infrastructure. European school systems can establish sustainable environments where AI and AR technologies support inclusive, adaptive, and morally sound teaching by combining institutional leadership, collaborative innovation, and regulatory frameworks.

FUTURE RESEARCH DIRECTIONS

1. Emerging Trends in AI-Driven Adaptive Learning

By providing individualized learning pathways and data-driven teaching methodologies, artificial intelligence (AI)-driven adaptive learning is quickly revolutionizing educational institutions. Future research will concentrate more on improving the flexibility, responsiveness, and inclusivity of digital learning environments as AI technologies develop. For European educational institutions seeking to integrate intelligent technologies that support a range of student needs while upholding pedagogical efficacy and ethical governance, these advancements are especially pertinent.

The creation of sophisticated personalization techniques in adaptive learning systems is one important new trend. Learners' performance data, including test scores and interaction patterns, is the primary source of information for traditional adaptive learning platforms. However, more sophisticated variables, such as behavioral indications, cognitive profiles, and emotional responses, can be incorporated into evolving AI models. These systems enable the real-time modification of instructional tactics, pacing, and learning content according to the unique qualities of each student. By matching educational materials to students' unique skills and preferences, research indicates that these adaptive mechanisms can greatly improve student engagement and learning results (Akavova, 2023).

The incorporation of cutting-edge machine learning models—specifically, deep learning and transformer-based architectures—into educational systems is another significant area of research. Intelligent tutoring systems and instructional chatbots are increasingly using these models to enhance their natural language comprehension and conversational skills. These technologies can facilitate automatic feedback, contextual explanations, and ongoing learning support by enabling more advanced human-machine interaction. The future generation of AI-powered educational systems is anticipated to be significantly shaped by these developments (Subramanian et al., 2025).

Another exciting area of research is the integration of adaptive AI systems with immersive technologies such as virtual reality (VR) and augmented reality (AR). Students can engage with simulated scenarios that mimic real-world settings in immersive learning environments, thereby improving conceptual understanding and experiential learning. These immersive environments may dynamically modify learning experiences based on user interactions and performance data when paired with AI-driven analytics. In a variety of fields, such as science, engineering, and medical education, these integrated systems offer chances for individualized experience learning (Rani et al., 2025).

Future studies must address important ethical and practical issues related to AI-driven adaptive learning amid these technological developments. Concerns about algorithmic bias, data privacy, and the transparency of AI decision-making processes remain significant issues in educational settings. The significance of explainable AI models, which allow educators and students to understand how adaptive suggestions are generated, is increasingly emphasized by researchers. Systems that are understandable and transparent can foster responsible educational innovation and increase confidence in AI-driven learning environments (Hariyanto et al., 2025).

2. Integration of AR with Immersive Learning Ecosystems

The rapid advancement of immersive technologies has created new avenues for transforming the educational environment. Among these developments, Augmented Reality (AR) is essential for creating immersive learning environments that combine online and offline learning. To provide flexible, dynamic, and inclusive learning environments, future research will increasingly focus on investigating how augmented reality (AR) can be systematically integrated with artificial intelligence (AI), virtual reality (VR), and other immersive technologies. By facilitating experiential learning, contextual understanding, and individualized educational routes, these ecosystems have the potential to transform how students engage with knowledge completely.

Integrating AR with adaptive learning technologies and intelligent tutoring systems is a significant area of research. AR environments may dynamically modify learning experiences based on learners' behaviors, performance patterns, and engagement levels when paired with AI-driven analytics. These systems enable the creation of adaptive learning environments, allowing instructional tactics, feedback mechanisms, and educational content to adapt to individual students' needs. This integration supports personalized and student-centered learning strategies that encourage greater engagement and more efficient knowledge acquisition (Lampropoulos, 2025).

Multisensory and experiential learning in immersive environments is the subject of another new field of study. Through augmented reality (AR) technologies, students can engage with three-dimensional digital objects integrated into real-world settings, providing an opportunity to investigate complex ideas in practice. AR-based systems can provide fully immersive learning environments that mimic real-world situations when paired with VR and Mixed Reality (MR). These experiences are especially beneficial in domains such as science, engineering, and healthcare, where gaining practical competencies requires experiential learning and the ability to visualize complex systems (Crogman et al., 2025).

The significance of emotional computing in AR-based learning environments will also be highlighted in future studies. Through physiological signals, behavioral patterns, and interaction data, affective computing technologies allow educational systems to identify students' emotional and cognitive states. Learning systems can respond dynamically to students' emotional engagement, motivation, and cognitive load by incorporating these factors into AR settings. Immersion learning ecosystems can improve learner engagement and facilitate more responsive educational experiences by modifying instructional content based on affective reactions (Lampropoulos et al., 2024).

Notwithstanding these technological advantages, using augmented reality in immersive learning environments poses significant research obstacles. To ensure that immersive learning technologies are usable across a variety of educational settings, issues related to technological infrastructure, accessibility, and scalability must be addressed. To develop robust pedagogical frameworks that enable the successful application of immersive learning technologies, researchers also emphasize the need for multidisciplinary collaboration among educators, computer scientists, and cognitive scientists (Lee et al., 2024).

3. Research Opportunities in Inclusive AI Education

The rapid proliferation of Artificial Intelligence (AI) in educational settings has created substantial opportunities for advancing inclusive education. However, more research is needed to make sure AI-driven learning systems actually advance accessibility and equity. Future directions for inclusive AI education research should focus on addressing ethical issues, enhancing accessibility, refining adaptive learning tools, and creating legislative frameworks that promote equitable educational innovation.

Addressing algorithmic prejudice and ethical issues in AI-based educational systems is a crucial subject for future research. Large datasets that may contain biases are frequently used by AI systems, which could exacerbate already-existing social and educational disparities. Therefore, research should focus on developing explainable AI models, fairness-aware algorithms, and bias-mitigation strategies to improve accountability and transparency in educational decision-making systems (Murari & Parmar, 2025). To ensure that AI-driven educational technologies promote inclusive learning rather than perpetuate structural gaps, such activities are crucial.

User-centered design and accessibility are important areas of study. Participatory design methods that actively involve a range of stakeholders, including educators, students with disabilities, and marginalized communities, are necessary for inclusive AI education. AI systems can better meet a range of cognitive, sensory, and sociocultural needs by integrating user perspectives into the development process. Research shows that inclusive design techniques can greatly enhance the usability and accessibility of AI-powered educational resources, especially for students with special needs or impairments (El Morr et al., 2024).

The development of AI-driven adaptive learning tools for inclusive classrooms should be a focus of future study. By offering customized educational materials and flexible feedback systems, intelligent tutoring programs, and personalized learning platforms have great promise for serving students with a range of skill levels. To assess the long-term efficacy and scalability of these technologies across various educational settings, more research is needed. Research should specifically examine how AI-based learning environments can be tailored to support students with neurodiverse learning profiles, learning challenges, or sensory impairments (Kumari & Patra, 2025).

Assessing the long-term effects of inclusive AI technology on student engagement and academic achievement is another exciting field of study. There is still no long-term data on the educational benefits of AI-driven learning tools, despite several pilot studies showing their potential. To evaluate how inclusive AI systems affect student motivation, learning outcomes, and educational equity over time, future research should conduct long-term empirical studies (Al-Zahrani, 2025).

In general, multidisciplinary techniques that integrate knowledge from education, computer science, ethics, and the social sciences should be used in future research on inclusive AI education. Developing AI technologies that are not only technologically sophisticated but also socially conscious and pedagogically successful requires such cooperation. Researchers can help create inclusive AI-driven educational environments that promote fair learning opportunities for all students by placing a high priority on ethical design, accessibility, and long-term effect assessment.

CONCLUSION

1. Summary of Key Arguments

This chapter examined the transformative potential of augmented reality (AR) and artificial intelligence (AI) in promoting inclusive and adaptive education within European educational contexts. The conversation focused on how these technologies may transform education by enabling data-driven teaching, immersive learning environments, and customized learning pathways. By analyzing learner behaviors, progress, and preferences, AI-driven adaptive learning systems enable educational platforms to customize content and feedback to meet each learner's needs. By superimposing digital data on real-world settings, augmented reality (AR) also improves conceptual understanding by facilitating interactive study of challenging topics. The chapter also emphasized the importance of digital fairness, accessibility, and ethical considerations when integrating new technologies into educational ecosystems. It takes careful pedagogical design, accountable data administration, and methodical professional development for teachers to ensure inclusivity. Additionally, the European policy environment, characterized by robust regulatory frameworks and human-centered technical governance, provides a crucial foundation for integrating AI and AR into education that prioritizes social responsibility, accountability, and transparency.

2. Implications for Educators and Policymakers

There are important ramifications for educators and legislators when AI and AR are incorporated into educational practices. These technologies provide instructors with effective tools to assess student progress, improve instructional design, and create more engaging learning environments. However, the development of advanced digital competences, pedagogical innovation, and ongoing professional growth is necessary for the successful deployment of these technologies. To become facilitators of technology-enhanced learning environments, educators must transcend their traditional classroom duties. The quick development of educational technologies requires policymakers to provide frameworks that encourage responsible innovation while upholding moral principles. Ensuring equitable access to emerging technologies requires strategic investments in research projects, teacher training, and digital infrastructure. To stop the perpetuation of educational disparities, officials must also address issues with data privacy, algorithmic accountability, and the digital divide. Building inclusive and sustainable digital learning environments thus requires coordinated cooperation between academic institutions, IT companies, and governmental organizations.

3. Final Reflections on AI and AR in Future Education

In the future, AI and AR will likely be essential components of educational institutions, radically changing how knowledge is created, disseminated, and experienced. As these technologies advance, their incorporation into immersive learning environments may enable more comprehensive educational models that integrate collaborative, experiential, and cognitive learning processes. However, technological progress by itself cannot ensure that education will change. A balanced strategy that places a high priority on social inclusion, ethical responsibility, and human-centered learning will be necessary for the future success of AI and AR in education. Educational systems may leverage the promise of AI and AR to provide more flexible, inclusive, and resilient learning environments for diverse learners across Europe and beyond by coordinating technological breakthroughs with pedagogical concepts and equitable legislative frameworks.

ACKNOWLEDGMENT

The authors acknowledge financial support from the Indonesian Ministry of Higher Education, Science, and Technology (Kemendiktisaintek) through the PMDSU (Pendidikan Magister menuju Doktor untuk Sarjana Unggul) program under Grant Numbers 0419/C3/DT.05.00/2025 and 083/C3/DT.05.00/PL/2025.

REFERENCES

Abuhassna, H., Alnawajha, S., Awae, F., Adnan, M. A. B. M., & Edwards, B. I. (2024). Synthesizing technology integration within the Addie model for instructional design: A comprehensive systematic literature review. *Journal of Autonomous Intelligence*, *7*(5), 1–28. DOI: 10.32629/jai.v7i5.1546

Aimicheva, G., Shaikhanova, A., Iklassova, K., Tazabekova, P., Nazyrova, A., & Kadyr, Y. (2025). Fostering Teachers' Digital Competence in AI-Supported Learning Environments: Implications for Interactive Teaching and Student Achievement. *Applied Sciences (Basel, Switzerland)*, *15*(23), 12597. DOI: 10.3390/app152312597

Ajao, S. O., Aworinde, H. O., Falola, P. B., Adeniyi, A. E., & Sakpere, A. B. (2024). Augmented Reality in Experiential Learning: An Overview. In *2024 IEEE 5th International Conference on Electro-Computing Technologies for Humanity (NIGERCON)* (pp. 1-8). IEEE.

Akavova, A., Temirkhanova, Z., & Lorsanova, Z. (2023). Adaptive learning and artificial intelligence in the educational space. In *E3S web of conferences* (Vol. 451, p. 06011). EDP Sciences. DOI: 10.1051/e3sconf/202345106011

Al-Zahrani, A. M. (2025). Evaluating the impact of inclusive and accessible learning technologies on student engagement and academic performance in higher education. *International Journal of Inclusive Education*, •••, 1–29. DOI: 10.1080/13603116.2025.2593563

Aler Tubella, A., Mora-Cantallops, M., & Nieves, J. C. (2024). How to teach responsible AI in Higher Education: Challenges and opportunities. *Ethics and Information Technology*, *26*(1), 3. DOI: 10.1007/s10676-023-09733-7

Ali, N. A., Sadiq, M. H., Albabawat, A. A., & Salah, R. M. (2022). Methods and applications of augmented reality in education: a review. In *2022 international conference on computer science and software engineering (CSASE)* (pp. 175-181). IEEE. DOI: 10.1109/CSASE51777.2022.9759807

Arrojula, S. P., Bhaskaran, D., Lekkala, S., & Gurijala, P. (2025). Bridging Augmented Reality and Ai for Secure and Personalized Educational Experiences. In *2025 IEEE International Conference on AI and Data Analytics (ICAD)* (pp. 1-7). IEEE. DOI: 10.1109/ICAD65464.2025.11114028

Benvenuti, M., Cangelosi, A., Weinberger, A., Mazzoni, E., Benassi, M., Barbaresi, M., & Orsoni, M. (2023). Artificial intelligence and human behavioral development: A perspective on new skills and competences acquisition for the educational context. *Computers in Human Behavior*, *148*, 107903. DOI: 10.1016/j.chb.2023.107903

Chalkiadakis, A., Seremetaki, A., Kanellou, A., Kallishi, M., Morfopoulou, A., Moraitaki, M., & Mastrokoukou, S. (2024). Impact of artificial intelligence and virtual reality on educational inclusion: A systematic review of technologies supporting students with disabilities. *Education Sciences*, *14*(11), 1223. DOI: 10.3390/educsci14111223

Crogman, H. T., Cano, V. D., Pacheco, E., Sonawane, R. B., & Boroon, R. (2025). Virtual reality, augmented reality, and mixed reality in experiential learning: Transforming educational paradigms. *Education Sciences*, *15*(3), 303. DOI: 10.3390/educsci15030303

Deinega, I. I., & Deineha, M. A. (2022). Implementation of the Right of Access to Higher Education: Barrier-Free and Inclusive Education Policy in International Documents and Acts of National Legislation. *education*, *3*, 135.

Devi, C. M., Gobinath, A., & Ilango, D. (2025). Artificial Intelligence in Training and Education. In *AI Insights on Nuclear Medicine* (pp. 143–162). IGI Global Scientific Publishing. DOI: 10.4018/979-8-3373-1275-0.ch007

Dimitrova, V. (2025). Analysis of the Main Factors for the Digitalization of Higher Education. In *ENVIRONMENT. TECHNOLOGY. RESOURCES. Proceedings of the International Scientific and Practical Conference* (Vol. 3, pp. 83-89). DOI: 10.17770/etr2025vol3.8539

Domínguez, A., Pacho, G., Bowers, L., Wild, F., Alcock, S., Chiazzese, G., Farella, M., Arrigo, M., Ross, D., Treacy, R., Yegorina, D., Mangina, E., & Masneri, S. (2023). Dataset of user interactions across four large pilots on the use of augmented reality in learning experiences. *Scientific Data*, *10*(1), 823. DOI: 10.1038/s41597-023-02743-6 PMID: 38001128

El Morr, C., Singh, D., Sawhney, V., Fernandes, S., El-Lahib, Y., & Gorman, R. (2024). Exploring the intersection of AI and inclusive design for people with disabilities. *Digital Health and Informatics Innovations for Sustainable Health Care Systems*, 556-559.

Fachrurrazy, M., Beddu, R., Efendi, E., Firmansyah, F., Jamaluddin, F., & SIliwadi, D. N. (2026). AI policy framework in education for advancing society 5.0 with safe AI implementation. In *AI, Policy, and the Future of Human-Centered Education* (pp. 165-196). IGI Global Scientific Publishing.

Fortuna, A., Prasetya, F., Samala, A. D., Rawas, S., Criollo-C, S., Kaya, D., Raihan, M., Andriani, W., Safitri, D., & Nabawi, R. A. (2025). Artificial intelligence in personalized learning: A global systematic review of current advancements and shaping future opportunities. *Social Sciences & Humanities Open*, *12*, 102114. DOI: 10.1016/j.ssaho.2025.102114

Garg, N., Kaur, A., Ahmad, F., & Dutta, R. (2025). Augmenting education: The transformative power of AR, AI, and emerging technologies. *Human Behavior and Emerging Technologies*, *2025*(1), 5681184. DOI: 10.1155/hbe2/5681184

Hariyanto, K., Kristianingsih, F. X. D., & Maharani, R. (2025). Artificial intelligence in adaptive education: A systematic review of techniques for personalized learning. *Discover Education*, *4*(1), 458. DOI: 10.1007/s44217-025-00908-6

Hul, T., Matviichuk, N., & Hodzhal, S. (2025). Integration of AI into learning and education: A comparative analysis of European and Ukrainian experiences. *Journal of Learning for Development*, *12*(3), 599–614. DOI: 10.56059/jl4d.v12i3.1675

Ivanova, A. (2025). The Digital Transformation of Education-From Vision to Reality. In *2025 10th International Conference on Energy Efficiency and Agricultural Engineering (EE&AE)* (pp. 1-5). IEEE. DOI: 10.1109/EEAE65901.2025.11273760

Ivković, R., Vučković, D., Ječmenić, M., Ananieva, D., Stanković, M., Petković, M., & Janković, N. (2025). The EU AI act and its contractual and educational implications: AI, education, and the law of obligations. *International Journal of Cognitive Research in Science. Engineering and Education*, *13*(2), 551–562.

Jaimes, M. Á. R., Navarro, Y. T., Castillo, Á. I. D., Morales, T. H. V., Cortes, A. L. B., & Vanoye, J. A. R. (2026). Applications of Artificial Intelligence in Instructional Design and Educational Strategies. In *AI Applications in Instructional Education Strategies* (pp. 189–222). IGI Global Scientific Publishing.

Kaddouri, M., Mhamdi, K., Chniete, I., Marhraoui, M., Khaldi, M., & Jmad, S. (2025). Adopting AI in education: Technical challenges and ethical constraints. In *Fostering Inclusive Education With AI and Emerging Technologies* (pp. 25–72). IGI Global Scientific Publishing.

Kumari, N., & Patra, B. C. (2025). AI and Inclusive Education: Enhancing Equity, Engagement and Excellence. In *AI Based Solutions for Inclusive Quality Education* (pp. 27-44). CRC Press.

Lampropoulos, G. (2023). Augmented reality and artificial intelligence in education: Toward immersive intelligent tutoring systems. In *Augmented reality and artificial intelligence: The fusion of advanced technologies* (pp. 137–146). Springer Nature Switzerland. DOI: 10.1007/978-3-031-27166-3_8

Lampropoulos, G., Fernández-Arias, P., Antón-Sancho, Á., & Vergara, D. (2024). Affective computing in augmented reality, virtual reality, and immersive learning environments. *Electronics (Basel), 13*(15), 2917. DOI: 10.3390/electronics13152917

Lee, L. K., Wei, X., Chui, K. T., Cheung, S. K., Wang, F. L., Fung, Y. C., Lu, A., Hui, Y. K., Hao, T., U, L. H., & Wu, N. I. (2024). A systematic review of the design of serious games for innovative learning: Augmented reality, virtual reality, or mixed reality? *Electronics (Basel), 13*(5), 890. DOI: 10.3390/electronics13050890

Li, J., & Huang, Q. (2025). Navigating ethical dilemmas in AI-enhanced education: A critical bibliometric analysis of global research trends and collaboration networks. [IJKM]. *International Journal of Knowledge Management, 21*(1), 1–21. DOI: 10.4018/IJKM.382384

Mitre, X., & Zeneli, M. (2024). Using AI to improve accessibility and inclusivity in higher education for students with disabilities. In *2024 21st International Conference on Information Technology Based Higher Education and Training (ITHET)* (pp. 1-8). IEEE. DOI: 10.1109/ITHET61869.2024.10837607

Murari, U. K., & Parmar, H. (2025). Ethical Integration of Artificial Intelligence in Inclusive Education: Addressing Challenges and Advancing Opportunities for Equitable Learning. In *Ethics and AI Integration Into Modern Classrooms* (pp. 439-470). IGI Global Scientific Publishing.

Natarajan, G., Raja, S. R., Elango, E., & Soman, S. (2025). Augmented Reality and Virtual Reality: Transforming the Learning Experience with AI Tools. *Virtual Reality and Augmented Reality with 6G Communication*, 217-243.

Nikou, S. A., Perifanou, M., & Economides, A. A. (2024). Development and validation of the teachers' augmented reality competences (TARC) scale. *Journal of Computers in Education, 11*(4), 1041–1060. DOI: 10.1007/s40692-023-00288-6

Nisiforou, E., & Kosmas, P. (2024). Assessing institutional readiness for emerging technologies integration in higher education. *Journal of Interactive Learning Research, 35*(4), 425–450. DOI: 10.70725/441907jrwrsw

Odunga, J. O., Musuva, P. M., & Ndiege, J. R. A. (2025, May). Exploring Emerging Technologies for Inclusive Education in Students with Learning Disabilities: A Systematic Literature Review. In *2025 IST-Africa Conference (IST-Africa)* (pp. 1-13). IEEE. DOI: 10.23919/IST-Africa67297.2025.11060558

Pal'ová, D., & Zoričaková, J. (2025). Digital Transformation of Higher Education Institutions. In *2025 MIPRO 48th ICT and Electronics Convention* (pp. 559-564). IEEE. DOI: 10.1109/MIPRO65660.2025.11132039

Perifanou, M., Economides, A. A., & Nikou, S. A. (2022). Teachers' views on integrating augmented reality in education: Needs, opportunities, challenges and recommendations. *Future Internet*, *15*(1), 20. DOI: 10.3390/fi15010020

Rani, J., Guru, R., Santhanam, S., Molla, W. T., Singh, J., & Dutt, S. (2025). AI Revolutionizing Education: Exploring Trends, Technologies, and Ethical Considerations for Future Learning Environments. *Implementing AI Tools for Language Teaching and Learning*, 1-24.

Ravi, M. (2025). Using the TPACK Framework for Gen-AI Enabled Learning Activities: Design, Delivery and Evaluation. *Journal of Engineering Education Transformations*, 175-181.

Scott, L. M., Wilder, T., Zaugg, T., & Romualdo, A. (2025). Enhancing special education using AI: The intersection of personalized learning and inclusivity. In *Transforming special education through artificial intelligence* (pp. 45–78). IGI Global Scientific Publishing.

Skraparli, G., Stefanidis, T., & Tsiatsos, T. (2025, April). Evaluating the Impact of Gamification in ePhos AR: A Comparison of Usability, Engagement, and Motivation. In *2025 IEEE Global Engineering Education Conference (EDUCON)* (pp. 1-9). IEEE. DOI: 10.1109/EDUCON62633.2025.11016547

Stare, J., Klun, M., & Dečman, M. (2023). A case study on the development of digital competences of teachers at the University of Ljubljana. *NISPAcee Journal of Public Administration and Policy*, *16*(1), 138–166. DOI: 10.2478/nispa-2023-0006

Subramanian, S. R. S., Anurekha, G., Gomathi, C., Saha, S., Rajalakshmi, A., Elavarasi, J., & Ezhilvendan, M. (2026). Deep Learning and Transformer Models for Educational Chatbots: Enhancing Intelligent Tutoring Systems. In *Educational Applications of Natural Language Processing, Chatbots, and AI* (pp. 117-146). IGI Global Scientific Publishing.

Sumbera, B. G. (2025). The Ethical Use of AI in Education. In *Integrating AI Into Pedagogical Education* (pp. 175–210). IGI Global Scientific Publishing.

Tapalova, O., & Zhiyenbayeva, N. (2022). Artificial intelligence in education: AIEd for personalised learning pathways. *Electronic Journal of e-Learning*, *20*(5), 639–653. DOI: 10.34190/ejel.20.5.2597

Ugli, E. B. S., Vincy, V. B. S., Lakshmikantham, B., & Kizi, M. N. T. (2025). Enhancing pedagogical practice through immersive technology with the transformation of classrooms with AR. In. AIP Conference Proceedings: Vol. 3306. *No. 1* (p. 030076). AIP Publishing LLC. DOI: 10.1063/5.0275886

Vasou, M., Kyprianou, G., Amanatiadis, A., & Chatzichristofis, S. A. (2024). Transforming Education with AI and Robotics: Potential, Perceptions, and Infrastructure Needs. In *European, Mediterranean, and Middle Eastern Conference on Information Systems* (pp. 3-18). Cham: Springer Nature Switzerland.

Yadav, S. (2025). Revolutionizing Classroom Learning With Advanced Technology: Harnessing Augmented Reality (AR) and Virtual Reality (VR) for Immersive Education. In *Blending Human Intelligence With Technology in the Classroom* (pp. 223-246). IGI Global Scientific Publishing.

Yanjin, S., Qian, L., Kun, Z., & Ruirui, Z. (2023). The application of artificial intelligence technology in personalized teaching of vocational education. In *2023 13th International Conference on Information Technology in Medicine and Education (ITME)* (pp. 846-850). IEEE. DOI: 10.1109/ITME60234.2023.00172

Zawacki-Richter, O., Marín, V. I., Bond, M., & Gouverneur, F. (2019). Systematic review of research on artificial intelligence applications in higher education–where are the educators? *International Journal of Educational Technology in Higher Education*, *16*(1), 39. DOI: 10.1186/s41239-019-0171-0

Zouhri, A., & El Mallahi, M. (2024). Improving teaching using artificial intelligence and augmented reality. *Journal of Automation, Mobile Robotics and Intelligent Systems*, 57-61.

KEY TERMS AND DEFINITIONS

Adaptive Learning: Adaptive learning is a personalized teaching method that leverages artificial intelligence and learning analytics to customize content, pacing, and assessments according to each learner's traits. These systems examine student performance and engagement data to design customized learning paths, addressing diverse needs and enhancing academic results. This strategy fosters learner-centered education and inclusive environments by catering to various learning styles and cognitive skills (Tapalova & Zhiyenbayeva, 2022; Akavova, 2024; Hariyanto et al., 2025).

Artificial Intelligence in Education (AIED): Artificial Intelligence in Education refers to the application of artificial intelligence technologies, including machine learning, learning analytics, and intelligent tutoring systems, to support teaching, learning, and educational management. AIED enables personalized learning experiences by analyzing learner behavior, performance, and engagement patterns to adapt instructional content and provide real-time feedback. These systems also assist educators by automating administrative tasks and generating data-driven insights that enhance pedagogical decision-making and instructional effectiveness (Zawacki-Richter et al., 2019; Tapalova & Zhiyenbayeva, 2022; Fortuna et al., 2025).

Augmented Reality (AR): Augmented Reality (AR) is technology that superimposes digital content, like 3D objects, animations, and multimedia, onto real-world settings. In the educational field, AR facilitates more interactive and hands-on learning by helping students visualize complex ideas and participate in immersive experiences. These AR tools boost student engagement, motivation, and understanding, especially in disciplines that depend on spatial awareness and experiential learning methods (Ali et al., 2022; Ajao et al., 2024; Skraparli et al., 2025).

Digital Competence: Digital competence encompasses educators and learners' ability to use digital technologies effectively for teaching, learning, communication, and problem-solving. It involves technical skills, pedagogical understanding, and ethical awareness needed to incorporate emerging tools like AI and AR into education. Building this competence is crucial for fostering innovation and supporting environments enhanced by technology (Nikou et al., 2024; Stare et al., 2023; Aimicheva et al., 2025).

Ethical AI in Education: Ethical AI in education involves designing and implementing AI technologies responsibly, focusing on fairness, transparency, accountability, and data privacy. Ethical frameworks help ensure AI systems promote inclusive learning and do not perpetuate biases or inequalities. These factors are vital for building trust and encouraging responsible innovation in digital education systems (Li & Huang, 2025; Kaddouri et al., 2024).

Immersive Learning Environments: Immersive learning environments are educational settings enriched with technology, blending digital and physical components to foster interactive experiences. They frequently utilize AI, AR, and virtual reality to boost engagement, hands-on learning, and deeper understanding of concepts. These immersive tools also promote learner independence and teamwork within contemporary educational systems (Lampropoulos, 2023; Crogman et al., 2025).

Inclusive Education: Inclusive education encompasses teaching practices that provide equal learning opportunities for all students, regardless of their cognitive, physical, socioeconomic, or cultural backgrounds. AI and AR technologies enhance inclusive education by supporting multimodal content, assistive tools, and adaptable learning settings that meet diverse needs. These innovations help break down learning barriers and foster fair participation in digital learning environments (Chalkiadakis et al., 2024; Mitre & Zeneli, 2024; Odunga et al., 2025).

Learning Analytics: Learning analytics involves collecting, analyzing, and interpreting student data to enhance teaching methods and educational results. AI-powered systems assist educators in identifying gaps in learning, tracking student progress, and offering personalized feedback. These analytics enable adaptive learning and support data-driven decisions within educational settings (Zawacki-Richter et al., 2019; Hariyanto et al., 2025).

Teacher Digital Competence: Teacher digital competence encompasses educators' skills in incorporating emerging technologies into their teaching methods and classroom activities. It involves instructional design, technological literacy, and the capacity to analyze AI-generated learning insights. This competence is essential for the effective integration of AI and AR in education (Nikou et al., 2024; Yadav, 2025).

Chapter 6

AI and Augmented Reality for Enhancing Teacher and Learner Support in the UK Educational System

Deepak Gupta
http://orcid.org/0000-0003-3929-1362
Institute of Technology and Management, Gwalior, India

Shaturaev Jakhongir
Termez University of Economics and Service, Uzbekistan

Ismailov Azizbek
Alfraganus University, Tashkent, Uzbekistan

Tulaganova Dilfuza Abdukabilovna
Tashkent State University of Economics, Uzbekistan

Mirzaev Abdullajon Topilovich
Fergana State University, Uzbekistan

Tadjieva Nargiza
Mamun University, Uzbekistan

Abdujabbarova Feruza Abdunazarovna
http://orcid.org/0000-0002-9348-8484
Oriental University, Tashkent, Uzbekistan

ABSTRACT

Schools, colleges, and universities across the United Kingdom are now confronted with a convergence of pressures—deepening attainment inequalities, overstretched SEND provision, and a persistent recruitment crisis among teaching staff—that has sharpened the professional and policy interest in Artificial Intelligence (AI) and Augmented Reality (AR) as instructional technologies. This chapter provides a

DOI: 10.4018/979-8-3373-9883-9.ch006

critical and evidence-grounded examination of how AI and AR function within UK educational settings, drawing on published evaluations, case studies, and policy analyses from primary, secondary, further, and higher education. The discussion spans adaptive learning systems and intelligent tutoring, AR-mediated immersive environments, teacher-facing analytics and assessment tools, and the deployment of simulation for professional development. Equity, data governance, and the risk of teacher de-professionalisation receive sustained attention. The chapter closes by advancing a four-phase implementation framework and identifying productive directions for further empirical inquiry.

1. INTRODUCTION

Few developments in recent educational history have attracted quite the mixture of enthusiasm, scepticism, and practical urgency that currently surrounds AI and AR in UK schools. Institutions at every phase are operating under sustained pressure: the attainment gaps that widened during the pandemic have proved stubborn, the number of pupils with Education, Health and Care Plans has grown year-on-year, teacher vacancies remain at historically elevated levels, and the inspection regime rewards data-informed practice without always providing the infrastructure to support it (Luckin et al., 2016; Holmes et al., 2019; DfE, 2023). Advocates of educational technology argue that AI-powered personalisation and AR-enabled immersive environments offer meaningful partial responses to each of these pressures. Critics, rightly, point to an implementation record littered with expensive initiatives that failed to survive contact with underfunded classrooms and undertrained staff (Selwyn, 2019; Williamson, 2019).

Government policy has, for the most part, framed technology optimistically. The DfE's Realising the Potential of Technology in Education (2019) presented a vision of reduced teacher workload and improved learner outcomes; the National AI Strategy (HM Government, 2021) positioned education as a priority sector for AI-generated public benefit; and the AI Opportunities Action Plan (2024) directed attention towards responsible procurement, teacher AI literacy, and the development of public data infrastructure for classroom applications. What these documents have not consistently produced is the investment in technical infrastructure, professional development, and independent evaluation that would be needed to translate that vision into durable practice—a gap that this chapter treats as a central analytical problem rather than a peripheral qualification.

The chapter is organised around a progression from context and theory to practice and ethics. Section 2 surveys the UK and European policy environment and the structure of the EdTech market. Section 3 develops the theoretical foundations that make AI and AR educationally significant, including constructivist, multimodal, and situated learning frameworks, as well as the Technology Acceptance Model and TPACK. Sections 4 and 5 examine applications for learners and teachers respectively, and Section 6 presents four UK case studies spanning primary, secondary, FE, and vocational contexts. Sections 7 and 8 address ethics and equity, and propose a phased deployment framework. The chapter concludes with Section 9 on future research and Section 10 with synthesising observations.

Throughout, a distinction is maintained between what these technologies can do in optimal conditions and what they typically do when introduced into resource-constrained institutions without adequate preparation. That distinction matters because the evidence base for AI and AR in education remains thin in the UK context, geographically concentrated in better-resourced schools and universities, and often produced under conditions—dedicated research staff, vendor involvement, enthusiastic early adopters—that do not generalise to the majority of settings. Honest appraisal of that limitation is not defeatism; it is a precondition for building practice that actually works.

2. POLICY CONTEXT: AI AND AR IN UK EDUCATION

2.1 National Policy Frameworks

Since 2019, successive DfE publications have constructed AI and AR as solutions to long-standing challenges in English education rather than as technologies requiring careful contextualisation. The EdTech Strategy of that year identified five priority use cases: reducing teacher workload, supporting pupils with SEND, improving assessment feedback, enabling distance learning, and informing school improvement planning. Each of these use cases has attracted subsequent policy attention, but implementation support has been fragmented and unevenly distributed. Oak National Academy's move towards AI-enhanced resources and the JISC National Centre for AI in Tertiary Education represent meaningful institutional investments; the Pupil Premium regime, however, has not been systematically aligned with EdTech procurement guidance, meaning that the schools most in need of technology-enabled differentiation are often those least equipped to deploy it effectively.

Ofsted's Education Inspection Framework (2022) merits particular attention in this policy landscape. By placing sustained emphasis on the quality of curriculum intent, implementation, and impact—and by treating the use of data to track pupil progress as a marker of professional competence—the framework has created powerful indirect incentives for AI adoption without specifying what responsible adoption looks like. Head teachers navigating Ofsted preparation sometimes purchase analytics platforms primarily as audit trail generators rather than as instructional tools, a pattern that instrumentalises AI in ways that serve compliance rather than pedagogy. Policy coherence would require that inspection criteria, procurement guidance, and CPD frameworks be developed in explicit alignment with one another.The Sutton Trust's (2021) research on digital access documented that reliable broadband, functional devices, and technical support staff remain distributed highly unequally between schools serving affluent and deprived communities. Under these conditions, policies that accelerate EdTech adoption without addressing the underlying infrastructure deficit risk producing a technology divide that maps precisely onto the existing attainment divide—an outcome that is both educationally damaging and politically indefensible.

2.2 European Context and Comparative Perspectives

Post-Brexit, UK education policy is no longer formally subject to European frameworks, but the EU's Digital Education Action Plan (2021–2027) and the Ethics Guidelines for Trustworthy AI (European Commission, 2019) continue to influence UK practice through research collaborations, the operations of multinational EdTech vendors, and the voluntary alignment of UK institutions with European procurement and governance standards. The EU AI Act (European Commission, 2021), which classifies certain educational AI applications as high-risk and subjects them to mandatory conformity assessment, will affect UK-based companies selling into European markets and may, over time, set a de facto standard that UK regulators find it expedient to match.Comparative evidence from Finland, Estonia, and the Netherlands suggests that sustainable EdTech integration is less a function of technology access than of teacher professional culture (Voogt & Roblin, 2012; Ertmer et al., 2012). Finland's success, documented in multiple cross-national studies, rests on a policy tradition that treats teachers as expert professionals capable of making principled pedagogical choices—including choices about when and whether to use digital tools. Mandating specific technologies within tightly controlled curricula, as some UK academy trust chains have done with particular adaptive platforms, runs against this grain and risks producing surface compliance rather than genuine pedagogical integration.

2.3 Funding, Governance, and the EdTech Market

Britain's EdTech market, valued at upwards of £3.5 billion annually, is among the largest in Europe and encompasses several hundred companies targeting every phase of education (Nesta, 2020). Venture capital investment in UK EdTech reached record levels during and after the pandemic, funding a wave of platform development that has considerably outpaced the evidence base. Many of the products currently marketed to schools make claims about learning outcomes that rest on vendor-conducted evaluations, pre-post designs without control groups, or studies conducted in contexts very different from the UK maintained sector. Schools making procurement decisions typically lack the time, expertise, or independent evaluation data to assess these claims critically.

The EdTech Demonstrator Programme has worked to build a more trustworthy evidence base by funding independent evaluations and supporting school-to-school knowledge transfer, but its reach remains limited relative to the scale of the market. Dedicated EdTech leadership roles—whether at school, multi-academy trust, or local authority level—are far more common in the independent and well-resourced maintained sectors than in under-resourced primaries and secondaries. Addressing this asymmetry, through regional EdTech networks or a strengthened national accreditation scheme, constitutes a policy gap that the DfE has not yet adequately filled.

3. THEORETICAL FOUNDATIONS

3.1 Learning Theories Underpinning AI in Education

The most durable theoretical justification for AI-driven personalisation draws on Vygotsky's (1978) concept of the Zone of Proximal Development. Where traditional classroom instruction necessarily pitches challenge at a level that suits some learners and misses others, adaptive AI systems can, in principle, maintain each learner within their productive challenge zone by continuously adjusting difficulty, modality, and scaffolding in response to performance data. Bloom's revised taxonomy (Anderson & Krathwohl, 2001) provides a complementary framework for assessment design: by mapping learner responses to cognitive levels—from recall through to synthesis and evaluation—AI tools can direct subsequent instruction to the level at which each learner is ready to work, rather than processing all pupils through the same sequence at the same pace.

Self-Determination Theory (Deci & Ryan, 1985) adds a motivational dimension that purely cognitive accounts of AI tutoring tend to underweight. Learners who perceive themselves as autonomous agents—making meaningful choices about how and what they learn, experiencing growth in competence, and operating in environments that feel relationally supportive—demonstrate more durable engagement and deeper conceptual processing than those whose learning is externally controlled. Adaptive platforms that build in genuine learner agency, rather than merely varying the difficulty of a predetermined sequence, are therefore more theoretically well-founded than those that maximise efficiency of curriculum coverage at the expense of learner ownership.

Siemens' (2005) connectivist framework, while contested as a stand-alone learning theory, illuminates the relational dimension of AI in networked educational environments. When AI recommendation engines connect learners with peers, resources, and expertise at the moment of need—rather than following a fixed course structure—they enact a model of learning as participation in evolving knowledge networks that suits both the pedagogical ambitions of progressive educators and the institutional realities of large FE colleges and universities with diverse, time-pressured student bodies.

3.2 Theoretical Basis for Augmented Reality in Education

AR's educational significance is most precisely captured through the lens of embodied cognition (Wilson, 2002), which holds that understanding is shaped not only by abstract mental operations but by the physical relationship between body and environment. Screen-based learning, however interactive, cannot fully replicate the spatial and kinaesthetic dimensions of direct physical engagement with the material world. AR narrows this gap by anchoring digital information to real physical contexts—the laboratory bench, the school building, the local landscape—in ways that activate spatial reasoning capacities associated with superior performance in mathematics, science, and engineering (Uttal et al., 2013).

Mayer's (2009) Cognitive Theory of Multimedia Learning provides a complementary account of why AR environments tend to support conceptual learning more effectively than single-modality instruction. When visual, auditory, and kinaesthetic channels are engaged simultaneously in ways that are semantically coherent, learners can build richer and more integrated mental models than those constructed from verbal instruction alone. The meta-analytic review by Akçayır and Akçayır (2017), covering 68 empirical studies across multiple educational levels, found motivation and engagement to be the most consistently reported benefits of AR, with spatial reasoning and conceptual understanding also well evidenced—though with substantial variation attributable to design, discipline, and implementation quality.

Lave and Wenger's (1991) situated learning theory offers a third theoretical lens, particularly relevant to AR applications in vocational and field-based learning. Learning that is anchored to the contexts in which knowledge will ultimately be applied—whether a construction site, a hospital ward, or a chemical laboratory—produces more robust transfer than decontextualised classroom instruction. AR enables this contextual anchoring without requiring learners to be physically present in environments that may be inaccessible, dangerous, or prohibitively expensive to reproduce for training purposes.

3.3 Technology Acceptance and the TPACK Framework

Teachers' decisions about whether and how to use AI and AR tools are shaped not only by the technical quality of those tools but by professional and contextual factors that technology designers and school leaders frequently underestimate. Davis's (1989) Technology Acceptance Model identifies perceived usefulness and perceived ease of use as the principal antecedents of adoption intention. For classroom teachers, perceived usefulness is primarily a function of whether a tool demonstrably reduces workload or improves outcomes for their specific pupils in their specific subject—generic claims about learning gains in large-scale studies are insufficient to generate confident classroom uptake. Perceived ease of use is often the decisive variable: a platform requiring significant configuration time, generating dashboards that are difficult to read quickly, or disrupting established lesson routines is unlikely to survive long past the initial training period, regardless of its underlying pedagogical logic.

Mishra and Koehler's (2006) TPACK framework offers a more granular account of what genuine technology integration requires of teachers. Effective technology use in the classroom is not merely the co-presence of technological, pedagogical, and content knowledge—it is the development of integrated understanding at their intersections. Teachers who know their subject well and have sound pedagogical instincts but lack specific knowledge of how AR visualisation enhances the teaching of molecular geometry, or how learning analytics platforms interpret phonics error data, cannot deploy these tools in ways that genuinely serve their pupils. Subject-specific, contextually grounded, and sustained professional development is not a luxury enhancement to EdTech programmes but their structural prerequisite.

4. AI APPLICATIONS FOR LEARNER SUPPORT

4.1 Personalised and Adaptive Learning Systems

Adaptive learning platforms—among them Century Tech, Sparx Reader, and DoodleLearning—now occupy a significant share of the UK EdTech market and are deployed in thousands of schools across all phases. These systems use machine learning algorithms to maintain continuously updated profiles of individual learner performance, distinguishing between random errors, habitual misconceptions, and areas of developing mastery, and using these profiles to sequence content, adjust challenge level, and determine when to introduce new material. The pedagogical logic is sound and well-supported theoretically; the empirical record is more varied, reflecting the substantial differences in implementation quality that characterise real-world deployments (Holmes et al., 2019).

The most rigorous UK evaluation to date—a two-year randomised controlled trial across twelve secondary schools by Pearce (2022)—found that pupils using Century Tech for three or more hours per week made statistically significantly greater gains in mathematics and English than matched controls, with the effect concentrated among Pupil Premium-eligible pupils. The finding that adaptive AI may be particularly beneficial for disadvantaged learners is theoretically plausible: these are precisely the pupils most likely to receive undifferentiated instruction in under-resourced classrooms, and for whom individually calibrated challenge and non-judgmental feedback may represent a qualitative improvement over their typical learning experience. Whether this finding generalises across platforms, subjects, and year groups is, however, not yet established.

Beyond raw attainment, EEF evaluations of AI-enhanced mathematics platforms have documented improvements in learners' metacognitive awareness—their capacity to identify their own knowledge gaps, monitor comprehension, and adjust study strategies accordingly (EEF, 2021). Metacognitive skills are among the strongest predictors of long-term academic achievement identified in the educational psychology literature, and their development through AI-mediated practice—via structured self-assessment prompts and progress visualisation—represents a potentially significant secondary benefit of adaptive platform use that deserves more systematic measurement in future evaluation designs.

4.2 Support for Learners with Special Educational Needs and Disabilities

With approximately 1.5 million pupils in England carrying identified special educational needs (DfE, 2023), and high-needs budgets in many local authorities effectively exhausted, the question of how AI can extend SEND support without proportional increases in specialist staffing is not merely an efficiency question but one of educational justice. NLP tools such as Microsoft's Immersive Reader and TextHelp's Read&Write deliver real-time text-to-speech, predictive text, reading simplification, and vocabulary support in ways that can meaningfully reduce the literacy barriers that prevent pupils with dyslexia or EAL from accessing subject content. Speech recognition tools support learners with motor impairments in producing written work without physical typing. Emotion-recognition AI systems—currently at pilot stage in a small number of UK schools—seek to identify affective states associated with anxiety or disengagement, enabling pastoral intervention before difficulties escalate.

AR's contribution to SEND provision is most clearly evidenced in the domain of social communication skills for autistic learners. Freina and Ott (2015), along with subsequent UK practitioner research, document that rehearsing social scenarios in AR environments—where responses can be repeated without social consequence, pacing can be adjusted, and sensory input can be controlled—reduces the anxiety that renders direct social practice inaccessible for many autistic young people. Several UK schools have also used AR motion-feedback overlays to support pupils with Developmental Coordination Disorder in Physical Education, providing real-time visual guidance on movement quality that verbal instruction alone cannot replicate.A qualifying consideration warrants attention here. Technology designed specifically for SEND learners risks reinforcing the categorical thinking that Universal Design for Learning (UDL) principles seek to move beyond. UDL holds that educational environments should be flexibly designed from the outset to accommodate the full range of learner variability, rather than adapting a standard environment for those who fall outside assumed norms. Features developed for SEND learners—text simplification, audio support, visual scaffolding—frequently benefit the whole class, and procurement decisions that treat these as SEND-specific add-ons rather than universal instructional tools may inadvertently limit their reach and reinforce stigma.

4.3 AR-Enhanced Immersive Learning Environments

Across Biology, History, Geography, and Chemistry, AR applications have moved from research prototypes to regularly used classroom tools in a growing number of UK schools, driven partly by the declining cost of tablet devices and partly by the development of curriculum-aligned content libraries. AR dissection tools enable pupils to examine detailed three-dimensional anatomical structures at their own pace and from any angle, without the animal welfare implications and logistical complexity of physical dissection. Geography departments have used AR globe applications to make topographic, climate, and demographic data spatially navigable in ways that build the geospatial literacy increasingly demanded by both university admissions and employers. History teachers have partnered with English Heritage and the British Museum to develop location-based AR resources that anchor curriculum content to specific physical sites—a direct application of situated learning principles that transforms the school trip from passive observation into active historical investigation.

In UK higher education, institutions including UCL and the University of Birmingham have trialled AR pre-laboratory simulations in which students practise experimental procedures virtually before handling real apparatus. Studies in this genre consistently find reduced procedural error rates and improved laboratory safety awareness following simulated preparation (Mikropoulos & Natsis, 2011). The mechanism appears to be the development of procedural schemas in a context where errors carry no real-world consequence, allowing cognitive resources to be directed towards understanding rather than anxiety management when the real laboratory encounter occurs.

Figure 1. AI and AR Adoption Rates Across UK Education Sectors (2023–2024).

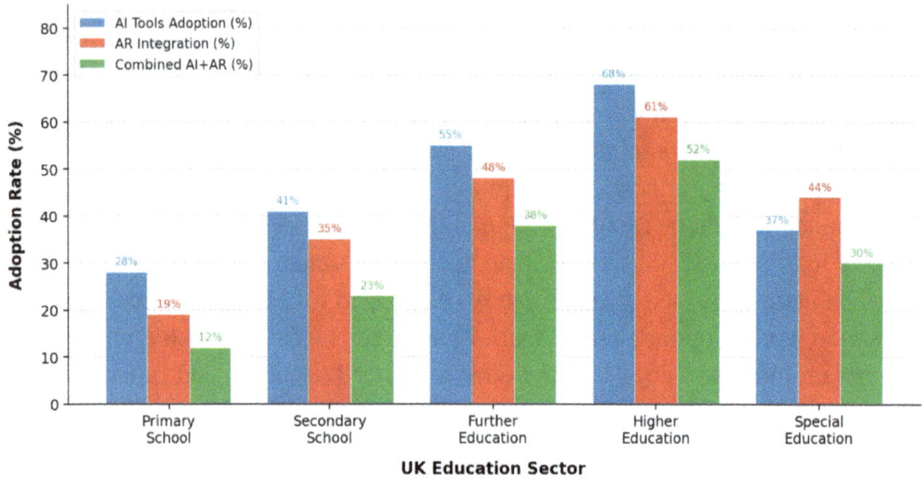

Figure 1 shows 'Combined AI+AR' denotes institutions reporting integrated use of both technologies within the same curriculum programmes.

5. AI AND AR APPLICATIONS FOR TEACHER SUPPORT

5.1 Learning Analytics and Teacher Dashboards

Learning analytics platforms—Arbor, Bromcom, and Pupil Progress being among the most widely used in UK maintained schools—aggregate data from assessments, attendance logs, behavioural records, and VLE engagement to generate dashboards that support class-level and whole-school monitoring. Their value lies less in the novelty of the data they present than in the speed and granularity with which they surface patterns that would otherwise emerge only slowly through teacher observation. Early-warning algorithms that flag pupils at elevated risk of disengagement or attainment decline before those trends become visible through conventional monitoring are particularly valuable in secondary schools, where teachers routinely carry pupil loads of 200 or more and cannot maintain detailed real-time knowledge of every individual's trajectory (Long & Siemens, 2011).

EEF evaluations have, however, established a consistent pattern: analytics platforms generate better pupil outcomes when teachers receive structured data literacy training alongside platform access, compared with platform access alone (EEF, 2021). Without training, teachers often either ignore dashboard outputs they cannot readily interpret or, conversely, defer to algorithmic flags in ways that override contextual knowledge about individual pupils. Neither response is desirable. Selwyn's (2019) concept of 'data fundamentalism'—an unreflective privileging of quantitative algorithmic outputs over qualitative professional understanding—captures the second failure mode precisely. Sustainable analytics deployment requires school cultures in which data is treated as one source of professional evidence among several, subject to critical interpretation and capable of being overridden when circumstances warrant.

5.2 AI-Supported Assessment and Feedback

Formative assessment is the highest-leverage teaching practice identified in the research literature (Black & Wiliam, 1998), but it is also among the most time-demanding. Teachers in England regularly report that marking and feedback preparation consume a disproportionate share of their working time, contributing to workload-related attrition. AI tools capable of generating draft feedback on written work—identifying recurring errors, flagging gaps relative to assessment criteria, and suggesting revision priorities—offer a meaningful partial response to this problem, provided they are positioned as tools that augment teacher feedback rather than replace it. Lee and Sidhu's (2023) finding that AI-generated feedback supports greater revision depth than no feedback but less than teacher feedback establishes a clear role: AI can hold the position when teacher capacity is stretched, particularly for lower-stakes formative tasks, without displacing the higher-quality feedback that experienced teachers provide.

Automated marking of extended writing remains contentious in the UK context. Platforms such as Pearson's Intelligent Essay Assessor are being evaluated primarily for formative use, with human moderation required before any AI-generated assessment informs high-stakes decisions. The core technical challenge is cross-population reliability: systems trained predominantly on writing from native English speakers produce systematically less reliable judgements on writing from EAL learners, students with dyslexia, or students from rhetorical traditions that differ from those dominant in the training data. Addressing this requires not only diversified training sets but regular disaggregated fairness auditing by protected characteristics—a practice that few current platforms have institutionalised and that procurement guidance does not yet routinely require.Oral assessment presents an underexplored frontier for AI support in UK schools. Speech recognition systems capable of analysing learner talk for accuracy, vocabulary range, and syntactic complexity are at an early stage of development but show promise for supporting speaking and listening assessment in MFL and English, as well as for monitoring the quality of classroom discussion more broadly. The ethical dimensions of continuous voice recording in classrooms require careful governance design, but the pedagogical potential—particularly for learners whose writing skills underrepresent their thinking—is considerable.

5.3 Continuing Professional Development and AR Simulation

The use of AI-driven virtual classroom simulations for teacher training is among the more innovative developments in UK ITT, drawing on a long tradition of simulation-based professional development in medicine, aviation, and the military. Platforms such as TeachLivE and its successors allow trainee teachers to interact with AI-controlled virtual pupils that can be programmed to exhibit specific behaviours—persistent distraction, underlying misconceptions, anxiety-driven withdrawal, or social communication difficulties consistent with autism spectrum conditions—enabling deliberate practice of differentiated responses without placing real children in the role of training subjects (Dieker et al., 2014). The theoretical grounding in Schön's (1983) notion of reflection-in-action is sound: the value of simulation lies not in its fidelity to the full complexity of real classrooms, which no simulation can match, but in its provision of a protected space for rehearsing difficult decisions at a pace and with a repeatability that live teaching cannot offer.

Early qualitative evidence from UK SCITT providers piloting AI simulation platforms suggests improvements in trainee confidence around behaviour management and responsive differentiation, consistent with findings from larger-scale US studies (Darling-Hammond et al., 2017). The most productive integration models appear to be those in which simulation is embedded within mentored reflective conversations rather than used as a standalone activity—where mentors and trainees jointly review simulation recordings, identify decision points, and consider alternative responses in the light of pupil needs and curriculum objectives.

5.4 AI-Assisted Curriculum Planning and Resource Generation

By the end of the 2022–23 academic year, approximately one in four secondary teachers in England reported regular use of generative AI tools to support lesson preparation, according to survey data from the Chartered College of Teaching (2023). Tools including Microsoft Copilot, Eduaide.Ai, and a growing range of subject-specific content generators are being used to draft lesson plans, produce differentiated worksheets at varying reading levels, generate assessment rubrics, and create explanatory resources for pupils who missed lessons. The productivity gains are real: tasks that might previously have required an hour of preparation time can often be completed in minutes, freeing teacher time for the planning decisions that genuinely require professional expertise and contextual knowledge.

Whether this productivity gain is educationally neutral is less clear. Subject knowledge deepens through the process of translating it into accessible explanations and well-designed tasks; teachers who routinely delegate this translation work to AI tools may find, over time, that their own subject expertise develops less than it would under conditions of more active curriculum authorship. The risk is not hypothetical—similar concerns were raised about excessive reliance on commercially produced worksheets in the 1990s—and it warrants attention from ITT providers and CPD designers. Professional norms that position AI-generated resources as starting points requiring critical evaluation and adaptation, rather than as finished products, represent a constructive institutional response to this tension.

Figure 2. AI-Enhanced Personalised Learning Ecosystem

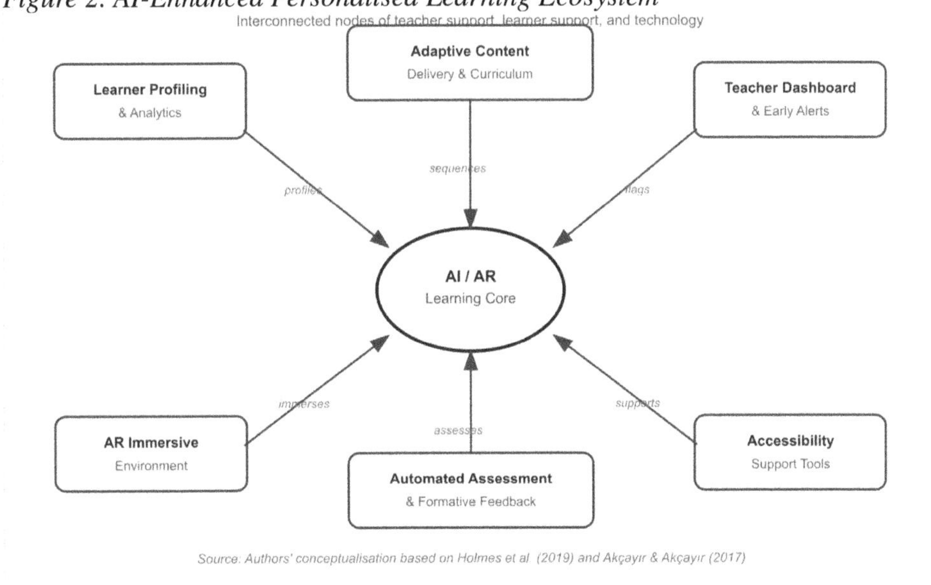

Figure 2 showing the interconnected relationship between adaptive content, learner profiling, teacher dashboards, AR environments, automated assessment, and accessibility tools.

Table 1. Summary of AI and AR Technologies, Applications, Target Users, Benefits, and Challenges in UK Education

Technology	Application Domain	Target Users	Key Benefits	Challenges & Limitations
Intelligent Tutoring Systems (ITS)	Mathematics, Science, Literacy	Primary & Secondary learners	Personalised pacing; real-time corrective feedback; automated identification of misconceptions; reduced marking load for teachers	High initial cost; reliance on robust ICT infrastructure; risk of reductionist view of learning
NLP Chatbots & Virtual Assistants	SEND support, language acquisition, revision	SEN pupils, EAL learners, HE students	24/7 accessible support; multilingual scaffolding; removes stigma in help-seeking; scalable across large cohorts	Accuracy concerns for niche queries; over-reliance risk; safeguarding governance required
Marker-Based AR	Biology, History, Geography, Chemistry	KS2–KS4 pupils	Contextual 3D visualisation; heightened curiosity; improved retention of spatial concepts; low device prerequisites	Requires printed markers; limited spontaneous use contexts; teacher setup burden
Markerless (SLAM) AR	Engineering, Architecture, Art & Design	FE & HE students	Real-world overlay without markers; spatial reasoning development; project-based and problem-based learning integration	Device compatibility and processing demands; motion calibration errors
AI-Driven Learning Analytics	Cross-subject monitoring, pastoral care	Teachers, tutors, school leaders	Early identification of at-risk learners; data-informed CPD planning; Ofsted inspection readiness; attendance pattern analysis	Data privacy and UK GDPR obligations; staff training requirements; risk of over-surveillance
Wearable AR / Head-Mounted Displays	STEM laboratories, vocational, apprenticeships	FE colleges, HE, apprentices	Hands-free immersive simulation of complex or high-risk environments; supports kinaesthetic learning styles	High equipment cost; hygiene concerns in shared environments; motion sickness in some users
Generative AI Writing & Feedback Tools	English, Humanities, Academic Writing, EAL	Secondary, FE, HE students	Scaffolded writing support; differentiation at scale; formative draft feedback; language modelling for EAL students	Academic integrity concerns; algorithmic bias in feedback; requires explicit guidance on appropriate use

6. EMPIRICAL EVIDENCE AND CASE STUDIES FROM THE UK

6.1 Primary Education: AI-Driven Literacy Intervention

Yorkshire and the Humber provided the setting for a two-year randomised controlled trial across 42 primary schools examining an AI-powered literacy platform targeting phonics and reading comprehension at Key Stage 1 (Pearce, 2022). Pupils in intervention schools who used the platform for 90 or more minutes weekly recorded an average gain of 4.3 months of reading progress over the year, compared to 2.8 months among matched controls. Disaggregated analysis showed that EAL pupils and those receiving Free School Meals benefited most, suggesting that the platform's adaptive, linguistically flexible, and low-stakes design was especially well-suited to learners for whom reading aloud in class carries social risk.

Teacher responses were instructive. Marking time fell by roughly 35 per cent, and practitioners reported greater confidence in identifying specific phonological difficulties. Several teachers were also candid about a less welcome dynamic: the platform's data could identify which phoneme a child was struggling with, but offered no explanation of why—whether the cause was a processing difference, limited English exposure, low confidence, or an auditory issue undetected by school screening. That diagnostic reasoning, they emphasised, remained a professional task that no platform could currently discharge. The observation points to a general principle: AI that narrows the search space for teacher attention is genuinely useful; AI that is relied upon to replace the interpretive work that follows is not.

6.2 Secondary Education: AR in Science Education

Marker-based AR was the focus of a mixed-methods investigation across six London and West Midlands secondary schools in KS4 Chemistry (Johnson et al., 2016). Pupils used tablet-based AR to manipulate three-dimensional molecular models overlaid on their laboratory workbenches, with end-of-unit assessments then disaggregated by question type. The AR group outperformed controls on spatial reasoning and molecular geometry items (Cohen's d = 0.58) but showed no significant advantage on procedural chemistry tasks. Student focus groups described the AR visualisations as the first time molecular concepts such as polarity and orbital geometry had felt genuinely intuitive rather than abstractly symbolic—a response consistent with embodied cognition theory's prediction that spatially grounded representations support more durable conceptual understanding than verbal description alone.

The implementation lessons were as informative as the outcomes data. Inconsistent tablet availability, the preparation time required to print and position AR markers, and the absence of dedicated technical support meant that the pedagogical benefits described by pupils coexisted with substantial teacher stress and logistical friction. The study's authors are explicit that AR deployment in secondary schools should be treated as a whole-school infrastructure project rather than an individual teacher initiative—a recommendation that aligns with the broader literature and that has significant resource and planning implications for school leaders.

6.3 Further and Higher Education: Learning Analytics in Practice

Edinburgh is home to one of the most thoroughly documented learning analytics deployments in UK higher education (Sclater et al., 2016). The university integrated VLE engagement data, library usage, attendance records, and prior attainment into predictive models flagging first-year students at elevated risk of withdrawal, with personal tutors receiving AI-generated alerts that prompted structured outreach. Over three years, first-year withdrawal rates fell by 12 per cent among students who received tutor contact prompted by analytics alerts, compared with historical baselines. In a university of Edinburgh's size—approximately 35,000 enrolled students—that percentage reduction represents several hundred individuals per cohort whose trajectories were measurably altered.

What distinguished Edinburgh's approach from many HE analytics deployments was the quality of its ethical governance architecture. Rather than treating data use as an internal operational matter, the university published its algorithmic logic, developed an explicit student consent framework, and produced a student data rights charter co-designed with the Students' Association. This transparency did not inhibit analytical ambition; it created the institutional trust that made student and staff engagement with analytics outputs constructive rather than defensive. The model has since been adapted by multiple other UK universities and is broadly consistent with JISC's (2015) Code of Practice for Learning Analytics—a framework that should, in the authors' view, be treated as a baseline standard rather than an aspirational benchmark.

6.4 Vocational and Further Education: AR in Apprenticeship Training

A North West FE college's use of HMD-based AR to deliver working-at-height training for construction apprentices offers a clear illustration of AR's comparative advantage in vocational contexts (Bacca et al., 2014). Authentic experience of working at height—essential for developing the situational awareness and procedural competence that safe site work requires—cannot be economically or safely replicated in a training facility. AR simulation provides a sufficiently immersive approximation that activates relevant perceptual and cognitive responses while removing the physical risk. Apprentices completing ten hours of AR simulation prior to on-site assessment made significantly fewer procedural errors than historical cohorts trained through classroom instruction alone, a finding the college attributes primarily to the development of spatial orientation skills and decision routines that transfer effectively to real working conditions.

Industry partner involvement in content development proved essential to simulation fidelity. Apprentices and assessors both reported that early prototype simulations lacked sufficient environmental detail to feel authentic—surface textures, wind effects, and the peripheral visual cues that experienced workers use for orientation were absent in ways that broke immersion and reduced transfer. Iterative co-design with site supervisors and Health and Safety professionals produced a markedly more credible simulation environment. This collaborative development model has cost and time implications that colleges should factor explicitly into procurement and implementation planning.

7. ETHICAL, EQUITY, AND SAFEGUARDING CONSIDERATIONS

7.1 Data Privacy and UK GDPR Compliance

The personalisation that makes AI educationally valuable rests on continuous collection and analysis of learner data—performance records, engagement logs, biometric responses, and in some cases emotional states. UK GDPR, as enacted through the Data Protection Act 2018, imposes substantial obligations on the handling of children's personal data: lawful basis must be established for each data processing activity, data must be minimised and used only for specified purposes, and processing that is likely to result in high risk to individuals requires a Data Protection Impact Assessment. The ICO's Children's Code (2021) adds further requirements for online services directed at or likely to be accessed by children, including privacy-by-default settings and prohibitions on profiling children for commercial purposes.

Williamson's (2019) empirical research and Digital Futures Commission investigations have documented persistent gaps between these legal requirements and the actual data governance practices of many UK schools, particularly smaller primaries. Terms of service agreements for EdTech platforms are frequently lengthy, technically complex, and signed without adequate scrutiny—in some cases permitting secondary commercial use of pupil data that the school's own privacy notice does not mention. The DfE's EdTech Accreditation Scheme attempts to address this by providing schools with independently assessed assurance about the data practices of accredited vendors, but take-up remains limited and accreditation is voluntary. Strengthening procurement requirements to mandate accreditation for any platform processing pupil personal data at scale would represent a meaningful policy advance.

7.2 Algorithmic Bias and Equity

The 2020 A-level grades crisis—in which a statistical moderation algorithm systematically disadvantaged students from state schools and deprived communities relative to their peers from independent schools—demonstrated, with unusual clarity and public visibility, that algorithmic systems in education can encode and amplify structural inequalities rather than correcting them (Luckin, 2018; Hardt & Barocas, 2017). The same risk attaches to adaptive learning platforms trained on data from predominantly advantaged learner populations: if the training data underrepresents the error patterns, prior knowledge structures, and learning preferences of disadvantaged groups, the platform's recommendations will be less well calibrated for those groups—potentially routing them towards lower-challenge content and constructing a digital ceiling rather than a ladder.

Schools and colleges operating under the Equality Act 2010 have existing legal obligations to promote equality of opportunity for pupils and students sharing protected characteristics. These obligations extend to technology procurement: an EdTech tool that produces demonstrably worse outcomes for girls, Black British pupils, or students with disabilities than for other groups is not merely a pedagogical disappointment but potentially a source of institutional liability. Procurement frameworks that require vendors to supply disaggregated outcome data by protected characteristic, and that include algorithmic bias auditing as a pre-condition of contract renewal, would create market incentives for vendors to address these issues rather than obscure them.

7.3 Teacher Autonomy and the De-professionalisation Risk

Critical scholarship on EdTech has identified a structural tension between AI deployment and teacher professional autonomy that requires direct acknowledgement. When analytics platforms are used as the primary basis for teacher performance reviews—when line managers treat AI-generated pupil progress flags as definitive evidence of teaching quality, or when adaptive platforms reduce teacher planning responsibilities in ways that are not accompanied by equivalent increases in teacher agency elsewhere—the de-professionalisation risk described by Selwyn (2019) and Williamson (2019) becomes concrete. Teachers who experience AI tools as instruments of surveillance and managerial control are unlikely to engage with them productively, and institutions that deploy AI in this spirit are unlikely to realise the pedagogical benefits that motivate the investment.

A practical response to this risk involves three institutional commitments: positioning AI outputs explicitly as tools for professional inquiry rather than performance metrics; building teacher capacity to interrogate, contextualise, and override algorithmic recommendations; and protecting spaces of teacher professional judgement that are not subject to algorithmic mediation. The Chartered College of Teaching's emerging work on AI literacy for teachers, and several subject associations' development of subject-specific AI guidance, represent constructive steps in this direction. Their integration into Initial Teacher Training curricula, as a standard rather than optional component, would signal a sector-wide commitment to professional agency that currently exists only in pockets.

8. PROPOSED FRAMEWORK FOR ETHICAL AI AND AR DEPLOYMENT IN UK SCHOOLS

8.1 Framework Overview

The Ethical EdTech Deployment Framework proposed here draws directly on the empirical patterns and practical lessons documented in previous sections. Four interdependent phases—Infrastructure and Policy Readiness, Pilot Implementation and Professional Development, Scaled Deployment, and Evaluation and Iteration—are designed to be mutually reinforcing and continuously refined as evidence accumulates. The framework's organising principle is that AI and AR deployment is most likely to improve learner outcomes and teacher working conditions when it is slow, well-supported, and governed by equity criteria rather than efficiency metrics alone. The phased structure is intended to prevent the premature scaling that has characterised many previous EdTech initiatives—where enthusiasm and vendor pressure produced institution-wide rollouts before pilot evidence was available, with predictably disappointing results.

Figure 3. Phased AI and AR Deployment Framework for UK Educational Institutions.

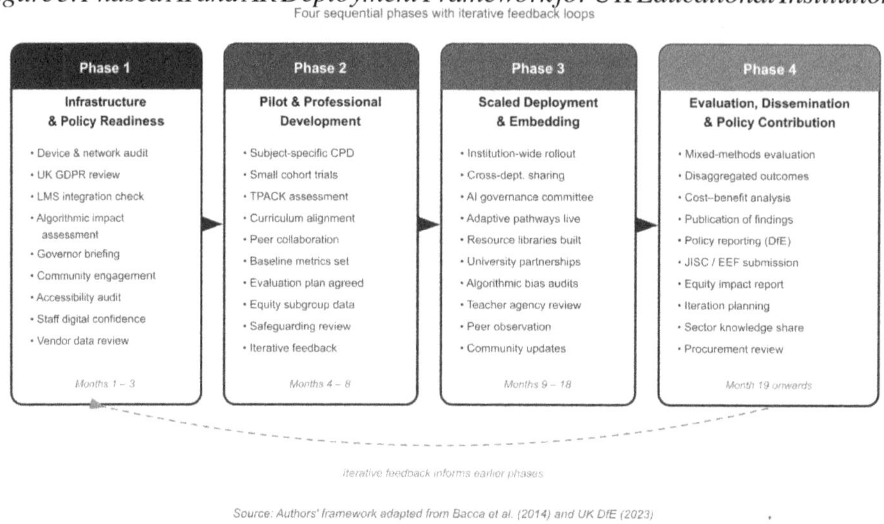

Figure 3 Arrows indicate sequential progression with iterative feedback loops between phases.

8.2 Phase 1: Infrastructure and Policy Readiness

Before any AI or AR platform is introduced, institutions should conduct a systematic audit covering four domains: technical infrastructure (device availability, network capacity, accessibility provisions, and technical support capacity); data governance (UK GDPR compliance, ICO Children's Code obligations, and vendor data practice review); professional readiness (staff digital confidence, existing TPACK profile, and senior leadership commitment); and community engagement (parent and carer communication plans, pupil data rights education, and governor oversight mechanisms). Each domain presents potential failure points that are more costly to address after deployment than before. Governing bodies should be briefed on their oversight responsibilities in relation to AI procurement, and algorithmic impact assessments from vendors should be reviewed and shared in accessible form with all stakeholders before contracts are signed.

8.3 Phase 2: Pilot Implementation and Professional Development

Pilot programmes should be time-limited, subject-specific, and accompanied by structured CPD that extends throughout the pilot period rather than front-loading training into a single preparatory session. The EEF and Teacher Development Trust evidence is unambiguous: technology-focused professional development produces lasting changes in classroom practice only when it is sustained over time, grounded in collaborative professional inquiry, and explicitly linked to curriculum and learner outcomes (EEF, 2021; Darling-Hammond et al., 2017). Pilot design should include a clear evaluation plan from the outset—defining the outcomes to be measured, the comparison group or baseline to be used, and the protected characteristic disaggregations to be reported—so that the evidence generated is usable in decisions about broader rollout.

8.4 Phase 3: Scaled Implementation and Institutional Embedding

Scaling from successful pilot to institution-wide deployment is a change management challenge as much as a technical one. Cross-departmental knowledge-sharing structures—communities of practice, structured peer observation, and subject-specific resource libraries—help ensure that early adopters' hard-won implementation wisdom reaches colleagues who were not part of the pilot. AI governance committees, with representation from teachers, pupils, parents, and governors, provide the institutional legitimacy and diverse perspective needed to ensure that deployment decisions remain aligned with the school's educational values and responsive to emerging equity concerns. Partnerships with universities, regional school improvement alliances, and JISC's National Centre for AI in Tertiary Education can supply the external technical and evaluative expertise that most individual schools cannot independently sustain.

8.5 Phase 4: Evaluation, Dissemination, and Policy Contribution

Longitudinal evaluation using mixed methods—combining quantitative attainment and engagement data with qualitative accounts of teacher and learner experience—should be treated as a standard institutional practice rather than a research luxury. The sector's evidence base on AI and AR in education is genuinely weak by comparison with other high-income countries, partly because too few institutions have invested in rigorous self-evaluation and publication of findings. Reciprocal accountability logic suggests that institutions benefiting from publicly funded educational infrastructure have an obligation to contribute to the knowledge commons. Standardised evaluation templates, developed collaboratively by the DfE, JISC, and research universities, would enable aggregation of findings across institutions and provide the sector-level evidence that policy and regulatory decisions require.

9. FUTURE RESEARCH DIRECTIONS

Several empirical gaps in the literature on AI and AR in UK education stand out as priority areas for sustained research investment. Longitudinal studies tracking the effects of adaptive learning platforms on attainment and wellbeing over three or more years are almost entirely absent in the UK context; the few that exist derive from US or Australian higher education and may not generalise to the maintained school sector (VanLehn, 2011; Sclater et al., 2016). UKRI's Trustworthy Autonomous Systems programme and the ESRC's EdTech research strand both offer relevant funding mechanisms, but commissioning priorities have not yet been systematically aligned with the most significant empirical gaps.

Intersectional equity questions—how AI and AR tools perform for pupils carrying multiple overlapping disadvantages, rather than for single protected characteristic groups in isolation—require both better data and better research designs than the field currently employs. Participatory methodologies that position pupils as co-investigators in EdTech evaluation, rather than as subjects of adult-designed research protocols, would address the democratic accountability deficit that Selwyn (2019) identifies and generate more contextually valid evidence about the pupil experience of AI-mediated learning. Article 12 of the UN Convention on the Rights of the Child provides normative support for this approach that national policy frameworks have not yet translated into research funding criteria.

Generative AI and large language models present the most rapidly evolving and least well-understood research frontier in current EdTech. The development of a nationally agreed framework for the use of generative AI in educational assessment—one that distinguishes between legitimate pedagogical applications and academic integrity violations, and that is workable across the full diversity of UK assessment contexts—is an urgent priority that neither government nor sector bodies have yet adequately addressed. The integration of findings from educational neuroscience, particularly neuroimaging research on attention regulation and cognitive load, with empirical studies of AR and AI in classroom settings represents a productive inter-disciplinary agenda that could significantly strengthen the theoretical foundations of both fields (Mayer, 2009; Wilson, 2002).

Teacher experience of AI and AR deployment demands considerably more empirical attention than it currently receives. Most published studies treat teacher experience as implementation context rather than as a primary outcome variable. Research that takes seriously the professional identity implications of AI deployment for teachers—the renegotiation of expertise, the emotional labour of working alongside algorithmic systems, and the practical strategies that experienced practitioners develop for maintaining professional agency within increasingly data-saturated environments—would provide the sector with understanding it needs to design deployment conditions that genuinely serve teachers rather than merely instrumentalise them.

10. CONCLUSION

The evidence examined in this chapter supports a cautiously affirmative assessment of AI and AR as educational technologies, qualified by substantial concerns about equity, governance, and professional culture. Adaptive learning platforms, when well-implemented and accompanied by structured teacher development, can produce meaningful attainment gains—particularly for disadvantaged learners who are most likely to benefit from individually calibrated instruction and non-judgmental feedback. AR environments can deepen spatial reasoning, enhance motivation, and extend learning into contexts that classroom instruction cannot reach, from molecular scale to construction site height. Learning analytics platforms can direct teacher attention to at-risk learners more efficiently than manual monitoring. AI-driven simulation can create protected rehearsal spaces for teacher professional development. These benefits are real and educationally significant.

They are not, however, automatic. The same evidence base that documents these benefits also documents the conditions under which they fail to materialise: inadequate infrastructure, one-off training without sustained follow-up, procurement driven by vendor marketing rather than independent evaluation, analytics deployed as surveillance tools, and AI recommendations treated as authoritative rather than as professional aids. The gap between the optimal conditions documented in published evaluations and the typical conditions prevailing in most UK schools is wide, and bridging it requires investment in teacher professional development, technical infrastructure, and independent evaluation that current policy frameworks do not consistently provide.

Equity must be foregrounded throughout. Technologies that raise average outcomes while widening the gap between advantaged and disadvantaged learners are not educational goods; they are redistributive mechanisms that benefit those already most likely to succeed. Procurement frameworks, evaluation designs, and regulatory oversight all need to be explicitly oriented towards equity as a primary criterion—not as a secondary consideration added after efficiency and scalability have been addressed. The 2020 A-level algorithm controversy demonstrated the political as well as the educational consequences of failing to think carefully about algorithmic equity in advance. The sector should not need another such demonstration.

The Ethical EdTech Deployment Framework advanced in Section 8 is offered not as a prescriptive blueprint but as a structured starting point for institutional deliberation. Its value lies not in its specific phases but in its insistence that deployment be slow enough, and evaluation rigorous enough, that schools accumulate genuine knowledge about what works in their specific contexts before committing to institution-wide rollout. UK education's tradition of teacher professionalism, independent scrutiny, and evidence-informed practice provides the cultural foundations for an approach to AI and AR integration that is genuinely principled. Building upon those foundations, rather than displacing them in the rush to technological innovation, is the central argument this chapter has sought to make.

REFERENCES

Bacca, J., Baldiris, S., Fabregat, R., Graf, S., & Kinshuk, K. (2014). Augmented reality trends in education: A systematic review of research and applications. *Journal of Educational Technology & Society*, *17*(4), 133–149.

Black, P., & Wiliam, D. (1998). Assessment and classroom learning. *Assessment in Education: Principles, Policy & Practice*, *5*(1), 7–74. DOI: 10.1080/0969595980050102

Darling-Hammond, L., Hyler, M. E., & Gardner, M. (2017). Effective teacher professional development. *Learning policy institute.*

Deci, E. L., & Ryan, R. M. (1985). The general causality orientations scale: Self-determination in personality. *Journal of Research in Personality*, *19*(2), 109–134. DOI: 10.1016/0092-6566(85)90023-6

Dieker, L. A., & Rodriguez, J. A., Lignugaris/Kraft, B., Hynes, M. C., & Hughes, C. E. (2014). The potential of simulated environments in teacher education: Current and future possibilities. *Teacher Education and Special Education*, *37*(1), 21–33. DOI: 10.1177/0888406413512683

Ertmer, P. A., Ottenbreit-Leftwich, A. T., Sadik, O., Sendurur, E., & Sendurur, P. (2012). Teacher beliefs and technology integration practices: A critical relationship. *Computers & Education*, *59*(2), 423–435. DOI: 10.1016/j.compedu.2012.02.001

European Commission. (2019). Ethics guidelines for trustworthy AI. https://digital-strategy.ec.europa.eu/en/library/ethics-guidelines-trustworthy-artificial-intelligence

Hardt, M., & Barocas, S. (2017, December). Fairness in machine learning. In *Neural Information Processing Symposium, Tutorials Track.*

Holmes, W., Bialik, M., & Fadel, C. (2019). *Artificial intelligence in education promises and implications for teaching and learning*. Center for Curriculum Redesign.

Long, P., & Siemens, G. (2011). Penetrating the fog: Analytics in learning and education. *EDUCAUSE Review (Online).*

Luckin, R. (2018). *Machine Learning and Human Intelligence. The future of education for the 21st century*. UCL institute of education press.

Luckin, R., Holmes, W., Griffiths, M., & Forcier, L. B. (2016). *Intelligence unleashed: An argument for AI in education*. Pearson. https://discovery.ucl.ac.uk/1475756/

Mikropoulos, T. A., & Natsis, A. (2011). Educational virtual environments: A ten-year review of empirical research (1999–2009). *Computers & Education*, *56*(3), 769–780. DOI: 10.1016/j.compedu.2010.10.020

Sclater, N., Peasgood, A., & Mullan, J. (2016). Learning analytics in higher education. *London: Jisc. Accessed February*, *8*(2017), 176.

Selwyn, N. (2019). *Should robots replace teachers?: AI and the future of education*. John Wiley & Sons.

Uttal, D. H., Miller, D. I., & Newcombe, N. S. (2013). Exploring and enhancing spatial thinking: Links to achievement in science, technology, engineering, and mathematics? *Current Directions in Psychological Science*, *22*(5), 367–373. DOI: 10.1177/0963721413484756

VanLehn, K. (2011). The relative effectiveness of human tutoring, intelligent tutoring systems, and other tutoring systems. *Educational Psychologist*, *46*(4), 197–221. DOI: 10.1080/00461520.2011.611369

Voogt, J., & Roblin, N. P. (2012). A comparative analysis of international frameworks for 21st century competences: Implications for national curriculum policies. *Journal of Curriculum Studies*, *44*(3), 299–321. DOI: 10.1080/00220272.2012.668938

Williamson, B. (2019). Datafication of education: A critical approach to emerging analytics technologies and practices. In *Rethinking pedagogy for a digital age* (pp. 212–226). Routledge. DOI: 10.4324/9781351252805-14

KEY TERMS AND DEFINITIONS

Artificial Intelligence in Education: The application of machine learning algorithms, natural language processing, and predictive modelling within educational settings to automate administrative tasks, personalise content delivery, generate adaptive assessments, and provide real-time feedback that enhances both teaching effectiveness and student learning outcomes.

Augmented Reality: A technology that superimposes digitally generated content—including three-dimensional models, annotations, and interactive simulations—onto the physical learning environment, enabling students to engage with abstract or complex concepts through immersive, contextually situated experiences that enhance comprehension and knowledge retention.

Intelligent Tutoring Systems: Computer-based educational platforms that use artificial intelligence to model individual learner knowledge states, diagnose misconceptions, and deliver dynamically adapted instructional guidance and feedback—approximating the responsiveness of one-to-one human tutoring without requiring constant direct teacher intervention.

Learning Analytics: The systematic measurement, collection, analysis, and interpretation of data generated by learners and educational environments, used to understand learning patterns, predict at-risk student behaviour, evaluate programme effectiveness, and inform evidence-based decisions by educators and institutional administrators.

Personalised Learning: An instructional approach that tailors the pace, content, sequence, and format of educational experiences to each learner's individual needs, prior knowledge, learning preferences, and performance data, thereby maximising engagement and achievement outcomes across diverse student populations.

Teacher Professional Development: Structured, ongoing training and learning opportunities designed to expand educators' subject knowledge, pedagogical repertoires, and technological competencies, enabling teachers to respond effectively to evolving curriculum demands, integrate emerging instructional technologies, and sustain high-quality student learning experiences.

Chapter 7
Teacher and Learner Support:
European Perspectives on AI and AR in Learning

Ashish Gupta
http://orcid.org/0009-0002-4460-6605
Institute of Technology and Management, Gwalior, India

Abdurakhmanova Mukaddas
National University of Uzbekistan, Tashkent, Uzbekistan

Kadirova Buzulayho
Andijan State Pedagogical Institute, Uzbekistan

Xaydarova Mahliyo
Termez University of Economics and Service, Termez, Uzbekistan

Nozim Muminov Gaffarovich
Alfraganus University, Tashkent, Uzbekistan

D. Y. Putheara
http://orcid.org/0009-0005-8474-7957
Royal University of Law and Economics, Cambodia

P. O. K. Phearak
http://orcid.org/0009-0008-9159-521X
Royal University of Law and Economics, Cambodia

Filipe Moreira
http://orcid.org/0000-0002-3461-9827
inED, Escola Superior de Educação, Instituto Politécnico do Porto, Portugal

ABSTRACT

Over the past decade, debates on effective teaching have shifted, especially with the rise of Artificial Intelligence (AI) and Augmented Reality (AR) in education. This chapter examines these technologies not as standalone solutions but as resources shaped by institutional, pedagogical, and ethical conditions. It highlights their role in supporting teacher professional development and personalising student learning

DOI: 10.4018/979-8-3373-9883-9.ch007

across diverse contexts. The discussion draws on recent empirical and theoretical scholarship, covering generative AI tools, intelligent tutoring systems, adaptive learning architectures, immersive VR-based teacher preparation, and AR-enhanced classroom environments. A European perspective frames the analysis, influenced by regulatory frameworks such as the EU AI Act and GDPR, which impose governance obligations not present in many other regions. The chapter concludes that neither optimism nor scepticism is sufficient; instead, a critical, evidence-informed engagement with the practical realities and limitations of these technologies is essential.

1. INTRODUCTION

When teachers in Finnish secondary schools began experimenting with AI-generated lesson materials in 2023, they were doing something that would have seemed implausible five years earlier. Not because the concept of AI was unfamiliar — researchers had been writing about intelligent tutoring systems since the 1980s — but because the tools had, quite suddenly, become genuinely usable by ordinary practitioners without specialist technical knowledge. That shift in accessibility is one of the defining features of the current moment in educational technology, and it distinguishes the present wave of AI and AR adoption from all the previous ones that preceded it.

European education systems are navigating this moment within a specific set of institutional and regulatory constraints. The EU's Artificial Intelligence Act, the Digital Education Action Plan, the GDPR, and a cluster of competence frameworks including DigComp 2.2 and DigCompEdu create what might be described as a governed technology environment — one in which the deployment of AI in schools is not merely encouraged but conditionally licensed, subject to transparency requirements, human oversight obligations, and data protection rules that have no parallel in, say, the United States or parts of South-East Asia (Holmes & Tuomi, 2022). This regulatory scaffolding does not make European adoption of AI in education straightforward, but it does make it distinctive, and that distinctiveness is one reason why a specifically European perspective on these technologies carries genuine scholarly interest.

This chapter works with a deliberate dual focus: the teacher as professional who requires support and development, and the learner as the beneficiary of technologies designed to personalise and improve educational experience. These two roles are sometimes treated as analytically separate in the literature on educational technology, but they are in practice deeply entangled. A teacher who does not understand how an adaptive learning system works cannot interpret its outputs, cannot respond intelligently when the system's recommendations miss the mark, and cannot protect students from the risks embedded in algorithmic decision-making. The technologies addressed here — AI-driven tools, AR environments, VR simulations — demand sophisticated professional judgment from the educators who deploy them, and any account of their educational value that sidesteps this demand is incomplete.

The chapter proceeds through nine sections. Section 2 establishes a conceptual framework grounded in constructivist and socio-cultural learning theory and attentive to the European policy landscape. Sections 3 and 4 examine AI as a resource for teacher professional development and for personalised learner support. Sections 5 and 6 address augmented and virtual reality in teacher education and classroom practice, with a dedicated discussion of inclusive applications for learners with special educational needs. Section 7 takes up the ethical and governance dimensions of AI in education, which cannot, on the evidence, be treated as secondary considerations. Section 8 synthesises the evidence through comparative figures, a graph, and a structured overview table. Section 9 offers conclusions and recommendations directed at practitioners, institutional leaders, and educational researchers.

Figure 1. Conceptual Framework: AI and AR as Dual Supports in Education

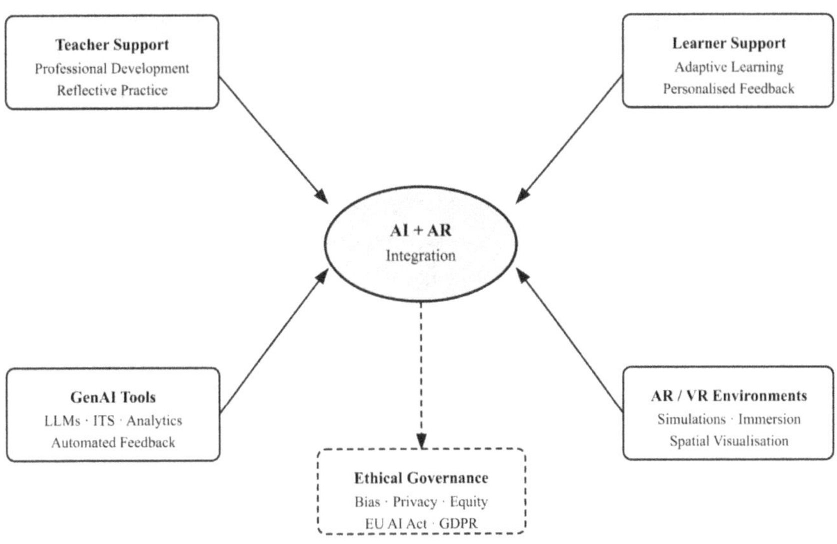

Figure 1 illustrates a conceptual map showing the relationship between AI and AR tools, teacher support, learner support, and the ethical governance layer that conditions their use in European educational contexts.

2. CONCEPTUAL FRAMEWORK: AI AND AR AS DUAL SUPPORTS IN EDUCATION

2.1 Theoretical Foundations

There is a risk, in discussions of AI and AR in education, of treating the technologies as the object of analysis in isolation from the learning processes they are meant to serve. Doing so tends to produce either advocacy or critique but rarely the kind of principled assessment that practitioners can actually use. A more productive starting point is to ask what we already know about how learning happens and then consider how these technologies relate to that knowledge.

Vygotskian socio-cultural theory has remained one of the most generative frameworks in educational psychology precisely because it insists on the mediational character of learning: human cognition develops not in isolation but through interaction with social environments and through the use of cultural tools that extend and restructure mental activity. Viewed through this lens, AI and AR are not merely delivery mechanisms for content but potential cognitive tools — instruments that can reorganise the cognitive space available to learners in ways that affect what thinking is possible. An intelligent tutoring system that monitors a student's performance, identifies persistent misconceptions, and adjusts the difficulty of subsequent tasks is, in Vygotskian terms, operating in the zone of proximal development: supporting the learner to accomplish what they could not yet manage alone. The analogy is imperfect, of course — the ITS is not a 'more knowledgeable other' in any rich sense of that phrase — but it is close enough to suggest that the learning-science warrant for these tools is not merely rhetorical (Creed et al., 2024).

AR's relationship to learning theory is different but equally interesting. Bruner's account of representation modes — enactive, iconic, and symbolic — locates the development of abstract understanding in a movement from bodily engagement with physical objects to diagrammatic depiction and finally to symbolic manipulation. AR sits somewhere between the iconic and the enactive: it provides visual representations but makes them interactively manipulable, allowing learners to physically reorient a three-dimensional model, walk around a simulated organism, or observe the dynamic behaviour of a molecular structure overlaid on their own workbench. Whether this specifically supports the movement toward symbolic reasoning, or whether it more often creates a kind of engaging but shallow interactivity, is a question that the empirical literature has not yet answered definitively — but it is the right question to be asking.

The critical dimension of this theoretical grounding lies in the sociology of education. AI systems trained on historical data bring with them the assumptions encoded in that data, and those assumptions are rarely neutral. Baker and Hawn

(2022) provided extensive documentation of the ways in which educational AI systems reproduce structural inequalities: systems trained predominantly on data from high-achieving, English-speaking, or socio-economically privileged student populations tend to make recommendations that are poorly calibrated for students who fall outside that profile. A conceptual framework for AI and AR in education that attends only to the technologies' affordances, without accounting for the social relations that shape how those affordances are distributed, is not merely incomplete — it is likely to mislead.

2.2 The European Policy Environment

What makes the European context distinctive for AI and AR in education is not simply the existence of regulatory frameworks, but the density and coherence of those frameworks and the degree to which they are binding rather than aspirational. The EU AI Act, provisionally agreed in 2024, classifies AI systems used in education as high-risk applications, placing them in the same regulatory tier as systems used in critical infrastructure and law enforcement. The practical implication is that educational AI tools must undergo conformity assessment before deployment, must be accompanied by technical documentation sufficient for regulatory scrutiny, and must include mechanisms for human oversight and for learner redress. These are not requirements that most commercially developed educational AI tools currently meet, which means that the Act, when fully enforced, will reshape the educational technology market in ways that are still difficult to anticipate (Ofusu-Asare, 2025).

GDPR already imposes conditions on the use of learner data that constrain the design of adaptive learning systems in ways not present in many other jurisdictions. The granular interaction data generated by adaptive platforms — keystroke patterns, time-on-task, error sequences — constitutes personal data under GDPR, and its use for profiling or prediction requires a legal basis that many institutions have not yet carefully established. Alongside these hard law instruments, the DigComp 2.2 and DigCompEdu frameworks provide softer structuring: they define what digital competence means for citizens and for educators, respectively, and are increasingly incorporated into national teacher education requirements and school quality assessment systems across EU member states.

Europe's internal diversity complicates any generalised account of how these frameworks operate in practice. The digital infrastructure available to schools in Denmark or the Netherlands is materially different from that available in rural Romania or parts of southern Italy, and teachers' pre-existing digital competences vary accordingly. Holmes and Tuomi's (2022) review of AI in European education was notably candid about this heterogeneity, noting that policy ambitions which appear coherent at the EU level often encounter conditions at the national and institutional level that make their realisation uneven. Any honest discussion of what AI and AR can offer European education must hold this variation in view.

3. AI-ENHANCED TEACHER PROFESSIONAL DEVELOPMENT

3.1 Generative AI and Self-Directed Professional Learning

It is worth pausing on what exactly it means to say that AI tools support teacher professional development, because the phrase can cover a wide range of quite different activities. At one end of the spectrum, there is something quite modest: a teacher uses ChatGPT to generate a draft lesson plan, edits it, and teaches from it. Whether this constitutes professional development in any meaningful sense — or whether it is simply a time-saving device — depends on what happens to the teacher's professional knowledge and judgment in the process. At the other end of the spectrum, there are teachers who engage with AI tools in a genuinely exploratory way: asking the tool to present alternative approaches to a concept they have always taught the same way, generating student misconceptions they can use for diagnostic discussion, or comparing AI-produced assessment feedback with their own to identify gaps in their thinking. The second kind of use develops professional knowledge in ways the first does not.

Li, Wang, and Bonk (2025) found, through mixed-methods research spanning several national contexts, that a significant minority of their teacher participants were using generative AI in precisely this more exploratory, professionally developmental way — though they were often doing so independently, without institutional support or recognition. What their study also showed, however, was that the pattern of self-directed AI use was not randomly distributed: teachers with stronger prior digital competence, more professional learning time, and supportive school cultures were more likely to engage with AI tools in ways that deepened professional knowledge. This is an important finding because it suggests that the oft-cited democratising potential of AI tools for teacher learning — the idea that any teacher with a smartphone and a free account can access professional development on demand — needs to be qualified by attention to the prior conditions that make such access productive.

Jeon and Lee (2023) addressed the question of what kind of professional relationship between teachers and AI tools is educationally sustainable, arguing against both utopian and dystopian readings. Their framework of complementarity is grounded in an analysis of what AI systems can and cannot yet do well: they are good at drafting, generating options, identifying relevant resources, and providing rapid initial feedback, but they lack the contextual knowledge of a particular student's history, family situation, and motivational profile that shapes a skilled teacher's decision-making. Distributing tasks according to this analysis — AI handles the cognitively routinisable, teacher handles the contextually embedded — does not diminish teacher professional identity; it clarifies what is genuinely irreplaceable about it.

Adiguzel, Kaya, and Cansu (2023) were among the first to examine teachers' experiences of generative AI integration in their classrooms, and their findings pointed to a consistent pattern: the teachers who reported most satisfaction with AI tools were those who had been supported to think critically about their use, rather than those who had simply been given access and left to determine their own practice. This finding has practical implications for how professional development programmes should be designed — not as tool-familiarisation sessions, but as opportunities for critical professional inquiry into the assumptions and affordances of AI tools in specific subject and institutional contexts.

3.2 Institutional Dimensions and the Problem of Equity

Individual teacher agency and initiative, however genuine and significant, operate within institutional structures that either amplify or constrain what is possible. The school that provides structured professional learning time, that has a digital leadership strategy, that actively supports peer learning communities around technology integration — that school will generate different outcomes from AI-supported professional development than one in which digital technology is left to individual enthusiasts without institutional backing. Díaz and Nussbaum's (2024) concept of 'pedagogical intelligence' names something important here: it is not the technology that generates educational value, but the organisational capacity to align technological affordances with clear educational purposes. Without that organisational capacity, AI tools in schools tend to produce uneven, fragmented, and often superficial patterns of adoption.

The equity dimension of AI-supported teacher development is one that European education researchers have begun to examine with some rigour, though much of the most important work remains to be done. Holmes and Tuomi's (2022) mapping of AI in European education documented substantial variations in access, competence, and institutional readiness that correspond, broadly, to existing regional and socio-economic inequalities. Teachers in under-resourced schools, in rural areas with poor connectivity, in systems that have faced years of budget constraint — these teachers are less likely to have access to the high-quality AI tools available to their colleagues in better-resourced settings, less likely to have professional learning time to develop competence with them, and less likely to work in institutions with the capacity to support evidence-based adoption.

Collaborative professional development, in which AI tools serve as shared objects of inquiry for groups of teachers rather than as individual productivity tools, has been proposed as one way of combining AI's personalisation affordances with the relational and institutional benefits of collective professional learning (Ouyang et al., 2023). When teachers examine AI-generated materials together — interrogating what assumptions the tool has made, what it has missed, how its outputs would need to be adapted for their specific students — the professional learning is richer than anything achievable in individual use, and the institutional knowledge base that results has value beyond the development of any one practitioner.

4. PERSONALISED LEARNING AND AI-SUPPORTED LEARNER DEVELOPMENT

4.1 Intelligent Tutoring Systems and Adaptive Learning Platforms

Personalisation has been a recurring aspiration in educational thought at least since the mid-twentieth century, and the persistence of that aspiration is testimony to how thoroughly ordinary schooling fails to achieve it. A student who already knows the material a teacher is explaining must sit through the explanation anyway; a student who has not yet grasped a prerequisite concept must keep pace with a class that has moved on. These mismatches between instruction and individual readiness are not incidental features of mass schooling — they are structural consequences of the fundamental organising principle of teaching groups of students at the same time. Intelligent tutoring systems and adaptive learning platforms address this structural problem directly, and their educational warrant is, at root, a response to one of the deepest tensions in organised education.

Lin, Huang, and Lu's (2023) systematic review of ITS applications in STEM education found strong evidence of positive learning effects, particularly in contexts involving well-defined procedural skills — mathematical problem-solving, coding tasks, science reasoning chains — where the system's ability to diagnose error patterns and provide targeted corrective feedback at the moment of difficulty closely mirrors the kind of one-to-one tutoring that Bloom's 'two sigma problem' identified as the gold standard for learning outcomes. Du Plooy, Casteleijn, and Franzsen's (2024) scoping review of personalised adaptive learning in higher education added important nuance: the platforms that produced the strongest effects were those designed with modular content structures, genuine learner agency over pacing and pathway, and integration with human instructional support. The worst-performing platforms were those that treated personalisation as synonymous with automation — replacing the teacher rather than augmenting teacher capacity.

This distinction between augmentation and replacement matters considerably for how institutions approach adaptive learning procurement and deployment. Platforms that are marketed on the promise of replacing expensive teaching time with cheaper algorithmic instruction tend to produce disappointing learning outcomes precisely because they misunderstand what effective teaching actually consists of. Teachers do more than deliver information; they read the room, respond to the emotional state of individual students, notice when a student's confusion has its source in something other than the immediately preceding lesson, and make dozens of micro-decisions in every class that no current AI system can replicate. Adaptive platforms work best when they take the task of information practice and corrective feedback off the teacher's hands, freeing teacher attention for the relational and contextual dimensions of instruction that are genuinely irreplaceable.

4.2 AI-Generated Feedback, Learning Analytics, and Their Limits

Feedback is — on the evidence of several decades of educational research — one of the strongest levers available for improving learning outcomes, and AI's capacity to provide immediate, detailed, and differentiated feedback at a scale impossible for human teachers represents one of its most compelling educational applications. The relevant question is not whether AI can provide feedback but what kind of feedback it can provide and for what kinds of learning tasks that feedback is adequate.

Stamper, Xiao, and Hou (2024) drew on the ITS research tradition and the learning sciences to analyse where LLM-based feedback currently falls short. Their framework distinguishes between feedback that identifies surface-level errors — spelling, grammatical form, procedural mistakes — and feedback that diagnoses the underlying conceptual or reasoning failure that produced the error. Current LLMs are substantially better at the former than the latter, and their capacity to generate plausible-sounding diagnostic commentary does not guarantee that the diagnosis is accurate for a particular student's particular difficulty. The pedagogical risks of overconfident automated feedback — students accepting incorrect diagnoses, losing trust in their own reasoning, developing learned helplessness in relation to their errors — are not widely discussed in the literature but deserve attention.

Jin et al. (2025) gave students direct voice in this discussion, finding that learners valued the immediacy of AI-generated feedback but were frustrated by its inability to engage with the specific situation of their work. A student who receives feedback telling them that their argument lacks sufficient evidence is not helped very much if that feedback was generated without reference to the particular claim they were trying to make or the particular sources available to them. The generic nature of AI feedback — its tendency to produce responses that are technically accurate but contextually thin — is a fundamental limitation that hybrid feedback models, in which AI-generated commentary is reviewed and personalised by a teacher, may partially address without eliminating entirely.

Perhaps the most practically significant application of AI in learner support that the literature documents is not feedback generation but predictive analytics. Ouyang et al. (2023) demonstrated, in the context of an online engineering course at a research university, that machine learning models applied to interaction data — login frequency, video watch time, assessment submission patterns, forum participation — could identify at-risk students several weeks before they would otherwise have come to instructor attention, enabling targeted outreach and support that reduced failure rates measurably. In the context of large online or hybrid courses where the physical co-presence cues that alert classroom teachers to student difficulty are absent, this kind of early warning system has genuine value. Its responsible use requires, however, that students be fully informed about the data being collected and the purposes for which it is being used — a requirement whose practical implementation is less straightforward than it might appear.

5. AUGMENTED AND VIRTUAL REALITY IN TEACHER EDUCATION AND CLASSROOM PRACTICE

5.1 VR Simulation in Pre-Service Teacher Preparation

Teaching is one of the few professional preparation contexts in which the most important learning — learning to manage a classroom, to read student affect, to improvise when a lesson's momentum collapses, to sustain the simultaneous attention to content, individual, and group that skilled teaching requires — can really only be acquired through direct practice. University-based pedagogy courses can develop candidates' theoretical understanding and repertoire of approaches, but the knowledge involved in knowing what to do with thirty particular students at a particular moment in a particular school is ineliminably experiential. This creates the enduring problem of teacher preparation: the most important learning happens in schools, but schools are not unconditionally available as learning laboratories, because the students in them are not experimental subjects.

Virtual reality addresses this problem with a directness that no previous technology has matched. The capacity to simulate classroom environments in which trainee teachers can respond to student behaviour, practice instructional sequences, and make the errors that novice teachers inevitably make — without those errors having consequences for real learners — is not a marginal convenience. It is a solution to a genuine structural difficulty in professional preparation. Han, Luo, Wang, and

Zhang's (2025) meta-analysis, drawing on a decade of empirical research on VR use in teacher education across multiple national contexts, found significant positive effects on self-efficacy, reflective practice, and classroom management competence, with the strongest results in studies that combined VR simulation with structured post-simulation debriefing. The debriefing component is not incidental — it is where much of the professional learning actually occurs, as trainees analyse their own decisions with the support of a mentor who can direct attention to what they noticed, what they missed, and what alternative responses might have been available.

Hong and colleagues (2025) pushed this work in an especially interesting direction by examining what happens when the simulated students in a VR training environment are controlled not by predetermined scripts but by a generative AI system capable of responding dynamically to whatever the trainee teacher says and does. Earlier VR systems for teacher training relied on branching scripts: the simulated student would respond in one of a finite set of pre-authored ways depending on what the trainee said, which limited the ecological validity of the simulation to situations that the authors had anticipated. With generative AI, the simulation's behavioural space is, in principle, unlimited: the system produces contextually plausible student responses to any teacher action, creating a training environment that more closely resembles the genuine unpredictability of real classrooms. Their mixed-methods analysis found significantly stronger outcomes on measures of pedagogical reasoning and reflective practice in the AI-enhanced condition, and — perhaps most tellingly — trainees in the AI-enhanced condition reported a higher sense of readiness to enter real classrooms. The implications for pre-service teacher education are considerable, as are the questions the approach raises about what it means for teacher preparation when simulated students are themselves AI.

5.2 AR in Classroom Practice: Subject Learning and Teacher Competence

The literature on AR in classroom teaching is, at this point, substantial enough to draw reasonably confident conclusions about when and how the technology adds educational value, even if many important questions remain open. Ironsi and Tian's (2025) controlled experiment in secondary science, which found significant improvements in content knowledge and spatial reasoning among students in AR-integrated conditions, is representative of a broader pattern that Koumpouros (2024) documented across a comprehensive review of over a decade of AR research in education: positive effects on motivation, concept comprehension, and collaborative engagement, particularly in subjects with a strong spatial or three-dimensional conceptual component.

The mechanism is not difficult to understand in principle. When a student studying cellular biology can observe a three-dimensional model of a mitochondrion overlaid on their own laboratory bench, rotating it, examining its internal structures from different angles, watching the movement of molecules across its membranes — the learning experience differs not merely in degree but in kind from reading a textbook diagram or watching a video. The student is doing something more akin to examination than to observation; the encounter with the concept involves a degree of agency and physical involvement that passive media cannot provide. This aligns with embodied cognition perspectives in cognitive science, which suggest that the body's involvement in a task shapes the nature of the resulting knowledge in ways that purely symbolic processing does not.

What the literature also makes clear, however, is that the pedagogical value of AR depends heavily on teachers knowing how to use it. Nikou, Perifanou, and Economides' (2024) international survey of teacher competences for AR integration found substantial gaps between teachers' positive attitudes toward the technology — most of their respondents thought AR had genuine educational potential — and their actual readiness to deploy it: knowledge of specific AR tools, ability to design lesson activities that exploit AR's affordances, and confidence in handling the technical difficulties that real classroom AR deployment routinely involves were all significantly underdeveloped. This gap between enthusiasm and capability is a pattern familiar from previous waves of educational technology adoption, and it suggests that access to tools is a much weaker predictor of effective use than the professional development investment needed to build genuine pedagogical competence.

Figure 2. AR Integration Pathway in Learner-Centred Educational Practice: Benefits and Challenges

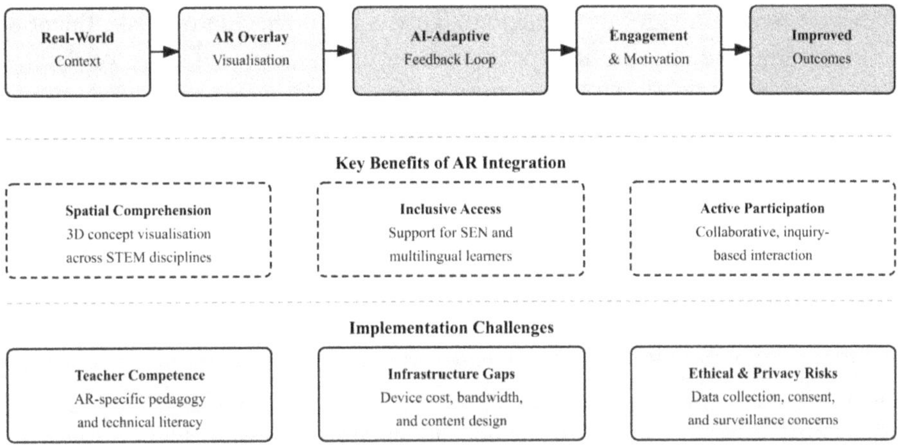

Figure 2 illustrates a diagrammatic overview of the AR integration pathway and associated benefits and implementation challenges discussed in Sections 5 and 6.

6. INCLUSIVE APPLICATIONS OF AI AND AR IN EDUCATION

6.1 AI, Personalisation, and the Reproduction of Inequality

The claim that AI makes education more equitable through personalisation has a surface plausibility that deserves scrutiny. Personalisation means giving each student something closer to the instruction that matches their individual level, pace, and style — and on that understanding, a system that genuinely personalised instruction for every student would be more equitable than one that teaches all students the same way at the same pace, because it would be more responsive to the full range of learners rather than optimised for the notional average. The problem, documented with considerable care by Baker and Hawn (2022), is that real AI systems do not personalise instruction on the basis of some neutral assessment of each student's individual characteristics; they do so on the basis of data, and the patterns in that data carry the fingerprints of the systems in which it was collected.

An AI system trained on data from a school system in which socio-economically advantaged students have historically outperformed their less advantaged peers will learn to associate certain interaction patterns — quick response times, specific vocabulary in free-text responses, particular patterns of help-seeking — with high performance. When it uses those patterns to make predictions about new students, it will tend to produce predictions that disadvantage students whose interaction styles reflect different cultural norms, different language backgrounds, or the effects of material poverty on learning behaviour. This is not a speculative risk; Baker and Hawn documented specific instances of these effects across a range of deployed educational AI systems. Addressing them requires more than algorithmic tinkering — it requires rethinking whose data shapes the system and who has a voice in determining what the system is for.

There is also a more straightforward equity problem that sits upstream of algorithmic bias: differential access to the technologies in the first place. Students from lower-income households are less likely to have reliable home internet access, less likely to have access to a dedicated study device, and less likely to be in schools with the funding to deploy high-quality adaptive learning platforms. AI tools designed to promote equity can, in a school system with these structural features, actually widen existing gaps — by providing additional enrichment and support to students who are already relatively advantaged, while the students most likely to benefit from adaptive support remain outside the circle of access (Holmes & Tuomi, 2022).

6.2 AR for Special Educational Needs: Possibilities and Research Priorities

The case for AR in SEN and inclusive education rests on a somewhat different foundation than its case in mainstream subject learning. In mainstream contexts, the argument is primarily one of enhancement: AR makes certain kinds of concept visualisation more effective, more engaging, and more interactively available than conventional media. In SEN contexts, the argument is often one of access: AR can make curriculum content accessible to students for whom conventional presentation modes create barriers that cannot be fully addressed by other means. Piqueras, Díaz-Noguera, and Hervás-Gómez's (2022) systematic review covered the literature from 2016 to 2021 and found positive outcomes across a range of conditions and applications — social communication development in autism spectrum conditions, motor skill support in developmental coordination disorder, alternative communication systems for students with severe physical disabilities — suggesting a breadth of applicability that warrants continued investment in research and practice.

Creed and colleagues (2024) set out a research agenda for inclusive AR and VR that is notable for its practical precision. They identified accessible interface design — the question of whether the AR application itself creates new barriers for users with sensory, motor, or cognitive differences — as a foundational issue that commercial AR development consistently underweights in favour of technical novelty. An AR application that requires fine motor control to operate accurately will be inaccessible to students with motor disabilities; an application that presents dense text overlays will create barriers for students with visual processing difficulties. These are not edge cases in inclusive contexts — they are central design challenges, and addressing them requires not merely technical expertise but the genuine involvement of disabled learners in the design and evaluation process.

The research base for AR in SEN, despite its genuine promise, has significant limitations that should temper enthusiasm. Most published studies are small-scale, short-term, and conducted in conditions that differ substantially from everyday inclusive classroom practice. Longitudinal studies that could establish whether AR interventions produce sustained learning gains for specific SEN populations, rather than short-term engagement effects, are rare and often methodologically constrained. This remains an important research priority, and institutions considering investment in AR for inclusive purposes should do so with realistic expectations about what the current evidence can and cannot support.

7. ETHICAL DIMENSIONS AND GOVERNANCE IMPERATIVES

7.1 The Ethical Terrain of AI in Education

Ethics discussions in educational AI have multiplied rapidly since 2022, partly in response to the public availability of capable generative AI tools and partly as a result of growing policy attention to AI governance. Not all of this discussion has been equally rigorous. Some contributions have addressed the topic at a level of generality that provides little traction for institutional decision-making; others have focused so narrowly on particular risks — academic dishonesty, most frequently — that the broader ethical landscape remains obscured. Zhu, Sun, and Yang's (2025) systematic review is one of the more comprehensive attempts to map the full terrain, identifying five primary categories of ethical risk in educational AI: data privacy and security, algorithmic bias and fairness, transparency and explainability, autonomy and human oversight, and cognitive dependency. Each of these is a genuine concern in its own right, and their practical significance differs across educational levels and institutional contexts.

The academic integrity concern has attracted disproportionate attention, arguably at the expense of other more structurally significant issues. Crompton and Burke's (2024) review of the educational literature on ChatGPT found that academic integrity dominated the published discourse in a way that reveals something important about what educators most immediately fear — the erosion of their capacity to assess what students know — but that obscures the more fundamental question of what assessed writing is actually for. If the purpose of a written assignment is to demonstrate mastery of content, then AI-generated text represents a straightforward evasion of that purpose. But if the purpose is to develop the student's capacity for argument, synthesis, and critical reasoning through the disciplined practice of writing, then the appropriate response to AI availability is not detection and prohibition but curriculum redesign: creating assessment tasks in which the process of thinking is itself visible and assessable, and in which AI-generated content cannot substitute for demonstrated reasoning.

Akgun and Greenhow (2022) made the prescient observation, before ChatGPT's public arrival made the issue impossible to avoid, that effective ethical guidance in K-12 settings needed to do much more than establish rules about tool use. Building the capacity among students to engage with AI critically — to understand what these systems do, what they cannot do, what assumptions they encode, and how their outputs should be evaluated rather than accepted — is itself an educational goal of considerable importance, and one that belongs in the curriculum rather than being relegated to a series of policy prohibitions.

7.2 Governance Frameworks for Responsible AI Use

Ofusu-Asare's (2025) ethical framework for generative AI in education, developed through extended international consultation, operationalises a set of principles whose value lies less in their novelty than in their systematic application to a specific and often underspecified domain. Transparency, accountability, beneficence, non-maleficence, justice, and respect for human dignity are not new principles in applied ethics, but their translation into concrete institutional obligations for schools and universities — what does transparency mean in the context of an adaptive platform that makes recommendations about student learning pathways? what does accountability mean when a predictive analytics system contributes to a decision about student support? — requires exactly the kind of careful specification that Ofusu-Asare's work attempts.

Chiu's (2023) analysis of how educational institutions have actually responded to the governance challenges posed by rapid AI deployment is less optimistic. His account of a widespread pattern of reactive rather than proactive institutional response — policies drafted in haste after tools have already been deployed, guidance that addresses last year's problem while this year's developments continue unchecked — is recognisable to anyone who has worked in educational administration during the period since 2022. The appropriate remedy is not primarily regulatory: it requires institutions to invest in the human and organisational capacity to anticipate change rather than merely react to it. This means supporting the development of in-house expertise, building sustained professional learning communities around AI governance, and creating structures for ongoing dialogue between academic staff, professional staff, students, and technical developers about the purposes and limits of AI in educational settings.

8. SYNTHESIS OF EVIDENCE: COMPARATIVE ANALYSIS AND KEY FINDINGS

8.1 A Structured Overview

Table 1 draws together the principal technologies, their application domains, their documented benefits, their key challenges, and representative references. The table is intended as a reference point for educators and policymakers working within specific institutional contexts, and as a basis for identifying where the evidence is strongest and where research gaps remain.

Table 1. Comparative Overview of AI and AR Technologies in Teacher and Learner Support

Technology	Application Domain	Benefit	Principal Challenge	Reference(s)
ChatGPT / LLMs	Writing & Assessment	Personalised feedback at scale	Academic integrity risks	Kasneci et al., 2023; Jeon & Lee, 2023
ITS Platforms	STEM Learning	Adaptive scaffolding	Algorithmic bias	Lin et al., 2023; Baker & Hawn, 2022
GenAI (Teacher Use)	CPD & Planning	Self-directed upskilling	Digital equity gaps	Li et al., 2025; Baidoo-Anu & Ansah, 2023
AR (School Subject)	Science Visualisation	Spatial concept gains	Teacher readiness	Ironsi & Tian, 2025; Nikou et al., 2024
VR Simulation	Pre-Service Teacher Ed.	Safe classroom rehearsal	Cost and access barriers	Han et al., 2025; Hong et al., 2025
AR for SEN	Inclusive Classrooms	Motor & social skill gains	Limited evidence base	Piqueras et al., 2022; Creed et al., 2024
Learning Analytics	Online/Hybrid HE	Early at-risk detection	Student data ethics	Ouyang et al., 2023; Jin et al., 2025
Adaptive Platforms	Higher Education	GPA and engagement gains	Implementation fidelity	du Plooy et al., 2024

8.2 Technology Adoption Trajectories, 2020–2024

Figure 3 presents composite estimates, synthesised from published surveys and empirical reports, of the institutional adoption rates for generative AI tools and AR/VR technologies in education over the period from 2020 to 2024. The two trajectories tell quite different stories about how these technologies have entered educational settings. Generative AI adoption was relatively modest in 2020, concentrated in higher education and in technology-forward school systems, but accelerated sharply from late 2022 onwards with the public availability of capable consumer-accessible LLMs. By 2023 and 2024, surveys were reporting majorities of institutions — particularly in higher education — reporting at least some institutional engagement with generative AI tools, even where formal policies for their use remained underdeveloped.

Figure 3. Institutional Adoption of Generative AI and AR/VR in Education, 2020–2024

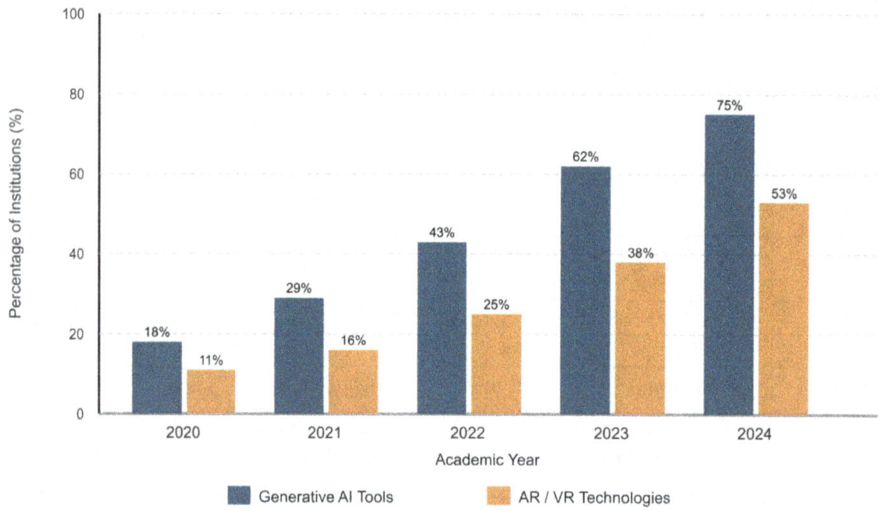

Figure 3 illustrates the coloured bar chart below comparing annual adoption rates of Generative AI tools versus AR/VR technologies across educational institutions, 2020–2024. Note the accelerating divergence from 2022 onwards.

AR and VR adoption followed a slower and more linear trajectory over the same period. The infrastructure requirements — dedicated devices, content creation investment, reliable connectivity, teacher training — are substantially more demanding than those associated with generative AI tools, which typically require nothing more than an internet browser. The pedagogical competence required to deploy AR and VR effectively is also more specialised, and the professional development provision needed to build that competence is time-consuming and costly. By 2024, AR and VR remained minority technologies in terms of institutional adoption, despite consistent positive research findings and growing commercial interest.

What this divergence implies for educational policy is worth spelling out carefully. The rapid adoption of generative AI in educational institutions has, as Chiu (2023) observed, generally outrun the governance and professional development frameworks needed to support responsible and pedagogically effective use. Institutions that adopt tools before they have developed the policy, pedagogical, and ethical infrastructure to manage them create risks for learners and for institutional reputation that are not trivial. The slower AR and VR adoption trajectory, while it reflects genuine barriers, also represents an opportunity: institutions moving into this space now have the benefit of a richer evidence base and more time to develop integrated strategies than those that adopted generative AI tools in the reactive conditions of 2022 and 2023.

The relationship between these two technology categories is also likely to evolve significantly over the next several years. The convergence of generative AI and immersive VR — in which AI generates dynamic, contextually responsive simulation content rather than relying on pre-authored scripts — is already visible in research contexts, as Hong et al.'s (2025) work illustrates. As these convergent technologies become more widely available, the analytical distinction between AI tools and AR/VR environments may become less useful than a more integrated framework that treats AI-driven adaptation and immersive embodied experience as complementary dimensions of a single technological approach.

9. CONCLUSIONS AND RECOMMENDATIONS

9.1 What the Evidence Supports

Three broad conclusions emerge from the evidence reviewed in this chapter, and they point in somewhat different directions. The first is straightforwardly positive: AI and AR technologies have produced well-documented and replicable educational benefits across a range of contexts, populations, and subject areas. AI-driven feedback, adaptive scaffolding, predictive analytics, and generative AI-supported professional development have all generated measurable positive effects in conditions that are sufficiently varied to rule out simple artefacts of research design or context-specificity. AR-enhanced concept visualisation, VR-based teacher preparation, and AR applications for SEN learners similarly rest on a substantial empirical base. Institutions that ignore these findings on the grounds of generalised scepticism about educational technology are not serving their students or their teachers well.

The second conclusion qualifies the first significantly: the documented benefits are conditional, not automatic. They depend on quality pedagogical design, adequate teacher preparation, institutional commitment to evidence-based adoption, and governance frameworks that manage the risks as seriously as they pursue the benefits. Where any of these conditions is absent, the research record offers numerous examples of AI and AR deployments that failed to produce the outcomes their advocates predicted — and in some cases created new problems, from the entrenchment of existing inequalities to the erosion of student engagement with forms of learning that do not offer the stimulation of interactive digital media.

The third conclusion is perhaps the most important for the long run: the ethical dimensions of AI in education are not peripheral features that can be addressed through policy addenda. They are central to the question of what these technologies are being asked to do and in whose interests they are being deployed. The documented risks of algorithmic bias, privacy violation, academic integrity erosion, and cognitive dependency are serious enough that institutions proceeding without robust ethical frameworks are not simply making an oversight — they are taking risks with learner welfare that cannot be justified by the promise of efficiency or the attractions of novelty.

9.2 Practical Recommendations

For teachers, the most important recommendation is also the most difficult to implement in schools under significant time pressure: take the time to understand the tools, not just to use them. Teachers who invest in understanding how an adaptive platform decides what to show a student, or what assumptions underlie the feedback generated by an LLM, are in a position to deploy these tools intelligently and to protect their students from their limitations. Professional learning communities focused specifically on critical AI and AR pedagogy, supported by institutions that recognise professional learning time as a core resource, represent one of the most productive vehicles for this kind of development. The work of Nikou et al. (2024) is a pointed reminder that access to tools and competence to use them well are very different things.

For institutional leaders, the priority is integration: developing AI and AR strategies that treat professional development, infrastructure, ethical governance, and quality assurance as mutually dependent rather than separately manageable concerns. Adopting European frameworks — DigComp 2.2, DigCompEdu, the EU AI Act compliance framework — provides structural grounding, but compliance is a floor. What institutions committed to genuinely equitable and educationally effective AI and AR adoption need is not merely the minimum required by regulation but a coherent pedagogical vision of what these technologies are for in their specific institutional context, connected to the evidence base and revisable as that evidence develops (Wang et al., 2024).

For researchers, the current evidence base has gaps that matter practically. Longitudinal studies of AI and AR adoption — following schools or cohorts over multiple years rather than measuring short-term outcomes in controlled conditions — are needed to understand whether the benefits documented in published research persist, fade, or deepen as the novelty of the technology settles. Studies conducted in languages other than English, in educational traditions outside the North Atlantic, and with populations that have historically been marginalised in educational technology research are a priority for any field that aspires to produce knowledge with genuine generalisability. And the ethical dimensions of educational AI research itself — the governance of the interaction data that AI research routinely generates, the consent frameworks appropriate for minors, the obligations of researchers to the communities their tools affect — deserve considerably more methodological attention than they have yet received.

AI and AR are not going to resolve the fundamental difficulties of education — the difficulties of motivating students whose lives outside school make engagement hard, of teaching subjects to students whose prerequisites are shaky, of preparing teachers for professional work that is endlessly contextually specific. But they can, with the right institutional conditions, the right professional preparation, and the right ethical governance, make some of those difficulties a little more tractable. That is, on balance, a more honest and more useful conclusion than either the techno-optimist's promise of transformation or the sceptic's dismissal of tools that the evidence shows can genuinely help.

REFERENCES

Adiguzel, T., Kaya, M. H., & Cansu, F. K. (2023). Revolutionizing education with AI: Exploring the transformative potential of ChatGPT. *Contemporary Educational Technology*, *15*(3), ep429. DOI: 10.30935/cedtech/13152

Akgun, S., & Greenhow, C. (2022). Artificial intelligence in education: Addressing ethical challenges in K-12 settings. *AI and Ethics*, *2*(3), 431–440. DOI: 10.1007/s43681-021-00096-7 PMID: 34790956

Baidoo-Anu, D., & Owusu Ansah, L. (2023). Education in the era of generative artificial intelligence (AI): Understanding the potential benefits of ChatGPT in promoting teaching and learning. *Journal of AI*, *7*(1), 52–62. DOI: 10.61969/jai.1337500

Baker, R. S., & Hawn, A. (2022). Algorithmic bias in education. *International Journal of Artificial Intelligence in Education*, *32*(4), 1052–1092. DOI: 10.1007/s40593-021-00285-9

Chiu, T. K. F. (2023). The impact of generative AI (GenAI) on practices, policies and research direction in education: A case of ChatGPT and Midjourney. *Interactive Learning Environments*. Advance online publication. DOI: 10.1080/10494820.2023.2253861

Creed, C., Al-Kalbani, M., Theil, A., Sarcar, S., & Williams, I. (2024). Inclusive augmented and virtual reality: A research agenda. *International Journal of Human-Computer Interaction*, *40*(20), 6200–6219. DOI: 10.1080/10447318.2023.2247614

Crompton, H., & Burke, D. (2024). The educational affordances and challenges of ChatGPT: State of the field. *TechTrends*, *68*(3), 380–392. DOI: 10.1007/s11528-024-00939-0

Díaz, B., & Nussbaum, M. (2024). Artificial intelligence for teaching and learning in schools: The need for pedagogical intelligence. *Computers & Education*, *217*, 105071. DOI: 10.1016/j.compedu.2024.105071

du Plooy, E., Casteleijn, D., & Franzsen, D. (2024). Personalized adaptive learning in higher education: A scoping review of key characteristics and impact on academic performance and engagement. *Heliyon*, *10*(22), e39630. DOI: 10.1016/j.heliyon.2024.e39630 PMID: 39524879

Han, X., Luo, H., Wang, Z., & Zhang, D. (2025). Using virtual reality for teacher education: A systematic review and meta-analysis of literature from 2014 to 2024. *Frontiers in Virtual Reality*, *6*, 1620905. DOI: 10.3389/frvir.2025.1620905

Holmes, W., & Tuomi, I. (2022). State of the art and practice in AI in education. *European Journal of Education*, *57*(4), 542–570. DOI: 10.1111/ejed.12533

Hong, S., Moon, J., Eom, T., Awoyemi, I. D., & Hwang, J. (2025). Generative AI-enhanced virtual reality simulation for pre-service teacher education: A mixed-methods analysis. *Education Sciences*, *15*(8), 997. DOI: 10.3390/educsci15080997

Ironsi, C. S., & Tian, X. (2025). Examining the impact of augmented reality on students' learning outcomes. *Scientific Reports*, *15*(1), 7213. DOI: 10.1038/s41598-025-20833-w PMID: 41125660

Jeon, J., & Lee, S. (2023). Large language models in education: A focus on the complementary relationship between human teachers and ChatGPT. *Education and Information Technologies*, *28*(12), 15873–15892. DOI: 10.1007/s10639-023-11834-1

Jin, F. J.-Y., Maheshi, B., Lia, W., & Li, W. (2025). Students' perceptions of generative AI-powered learning analytics in the feedback process. *Journal of Learning Analytics*, *12*(1), 152–168. Advance online publication. DOI: 10.18608/jla.2025.8609

Kasneci, E., Sessler, K., Küchemann, S., Bannert, M., Dementieva, D., Fischer, F., & Kasneci, G. (2023). ChatGPT for good? On opportunities and challenges of large language models for education. *Learning and Individual Differences*, *103*, 102274. DOI: 10.1016/j.lindif.2023.102274

Koumpouros, Y. (2024). Revealing the true potential and prospects of augmented reality in education. *Smart Learning Environments*, *11*(1), 5. DOI: 10.1186/s40561-023-00288-0

Li, Z., Wang, C., & Bonk, C. J. (2025). Generative AI for teachers' self-directed professional development: A mixed-methods study. *TechTrends*. Advance online publication. DOI: 10.1007/s11528-025-01123-8

Lin, C. C., Huang, A. Y. Q., & Lu, O. H. T. (2023). Artificial intelligence in intelligent tutoring systems toward sustainable education: A systematic review. *Smart Learning Environments*, *10*(1), 41. DOI: 10.1186/s40561-023-00260-y

Nikou, S. A., Perifanou, M., & Economides, A. A. (2024). Exploring teachers' competences to integrate augmented reality in education: Results from an international study. *TechTrends*, *68*(6), 1024–1037. DOI: 10.1007/s11528-024-01014-4

Ofusu-Asare, Y. (2025). *Guiding the future: Developing an ethical framework for generative AI use in education*. International Journal of Information and Learning Technology., DOI: 10.1108/IJILT-06-2024-0113

Ouyang, F., Wu, M., Zheng, L., Zhang, L., & Jiao, P. (2023). Integration of artificial intelligence performance prediction and learning analytics to improve student learning in online engineering course. *International Journal of Educational Technology in Higher Education, 20*(1), 4. DOI: 10.1186/s41239-022-00372-4 PMID: 36683653

Piqueras, C., Díaz-Noguera, M., & Hervás-Gómez, C. (2022). Use of augmented reality for students with educational needs: A systematic review (2016–2021). *Societies (Basel, Switzerland), 12*(2), 36. DOI: 10.3390/soc12020036

Stamper, J., Xiao, R., & Hou, X. (2024). Enhancing LLM-based feedback: Insights from intelligent tutoring systems and the learning sciences. arXiv. /arXiv.2405. 04645DOI: 10.1007/978-3-031-64315-6_3

Wang, S., Wang, F., Zhu, Z., Wang, J., Tran, T., & Du, Z. (2024). Artificial intelligence in education: A systematic literature review. *Expert Systems with Applications, 252*, 124167. DOI: 10.1016/j.eswa.2024.124167

Zhu, H., Sun, Y., & Yang, J. (2025). Towards responsible artificial intelligence in education: A systematic review on identifying and mitigating ethical risks. *Humanities & Social Sciences Communications, 12*(1), 456. DOI: 10.1057/s41599-025-05252-6

KEY TERMS AND DEFINITIONS

Artificial Intelligence in Education: Artificial Intelligence in Education refers to the use of AI technologies to support teaching and learning processes. It includes intelligent tutoring systems, automated assessment, learning analytics, and adaptive platforms that help educators personalize instruction, monitor student progress, and improve educational outcomes through data-driven insights.

Augmented Reality: Augmented Reality (AR) is a technology that overlays digital information—such as images, animations, or text—onto the real-world environment through devices like smartphones, tablets, or AR glasses. In education, AR enhances interactive learning by visualizing complex concepts and creating immersive learning experiences.

Generative AI: Generative AI refers to artificial intelligence systems capable of creating new content such as text, images, audio, or code based on learned patterns from large datasets. In education, it can assist with content creation, tutoring support, lesson planning, and generating personalized learning materials.

Teacher Professional Development: Teacher Professional Development involves continuous learning opportunities that help educators improve their teaching skills, pedagogical knowledge, and subject expertise. It includes workshops, training programs, mentoring, and collaborative learning activities that enable teachers to adapt to new technologies and educational practices.

Personalised Learning: Personalised Learning is an educational approach that tailors instruction, learning pace, and learning pathways to the individual needs, interests, and abilities of each student. It often uses technology and data analytics to provide customized resources, feedback, and support for improved learning outcomes.

Chapter 8
Teacher and Learner Support for Artificial Intelligence Augmented Reality Applications in Education

Bülent Gürsel Gürsel Emiroğlu
http://orcid.org/0000-0002-1656-6450
Engineering and Natural Sciences Faculty, Kırıkkale University, Turkey

ABSTRACT

The rapid integration of Artificial Intelligence (AI) and Augmented Reality (AR) into European educational landscapes has created a profound shift in pedagogical structures. While these technologies offer unprecedented opportunities for immersive and personalized learning, their success is contingent upon the robust support systems provided to both teachers and learners. This chapter explores the multifaceted dimensions of support required to effectively implement AI and AR in educational settings. Drawing on European frameworks such as DigCompEdu and the Digital Education Action Plan (2021-2027), the chapter analyzes the technical, pedagogical and emotional support mechanisms necessary for stakeholders. Through a synthesis of literature and case studies, the chapter outlines how AI-driven tutoring systems and AR-enhanced visualizations can be scaffolded to prevent cognitive overload in students and professional burnout in educators. A strategic roadmap for European higher education institutions and K-12 schools to foster a sustainable ecosystem for emerging technologies is provided.

DOI: 10.4018/979-8-3373-9883-9.ch008

1. INTRODUCTION

The European education sector is currently navigating a pivotal digital crossroads, shaped by the rapid convergence of data-driven intelligence and immersive visualization. Across Europe, the European Commission's emphasis on high-quality, inclusive, and accessible digital education has accelerated the adoption of advanced technologies such as Artificial Intelligence (AI) and Augmented Reality (AR) (European Commission, 2020). From primary classrooms in Scandinavia to higher education lecture halls in Southern Europe, the integration of these technologies is no longer a futuristic vision but a present-day reality. Yet this transformation is complex: adoption frequently progresses faster than pedagogical adaptation, professional capacity building, and governance mechanisms that ensure educational legitimacy and human accountability can fully catch up.

A recurring problem highlighted in scholarship and implementation experience is that "technological push"—driven by rapid innovation, vendor availability, and institutional urgency—often outpaces "pedagogical pull," leaving teachers and learners navigating tools and learning experiences that are not sufficiently aligned to classroom realities (Haleem et al., 2022). AI, through predictive analytics, generative capabilities, and adaptive algorithms, and AR, through the overlay of digital information onto physical environments, represent a powerful vanguard for this change (Ouyang & Jiao, 2021). However, the presence of these technologies does not automatically produce improved learning. When AI and AR are treated as add-ons, isolated pilots, or replacements for established instructional practices, they can generate new barriers: cognitive overload, professional uncertainty, ethical ambiguity, and inequitable access. For this reason, this chapter argues that success in AI and AR integration in European education depends on a robust "Human Infrastructure"—an integrated support ecosystem that addresses technical, pedagogical, ethical, and socio-emotional needs of all stakeholders.

The chapter therefore frames the core challenge as socio-technical enactment: how digital systems are embedded into learning design, teacher practice, and institutional governance so that AI and AR empower educators and build learner agency. Teachers are not merely users of digital systems; they become orchestrators of learning processes supported by AI and enhanced through AR. Learners, in turn, require scaffolding to engage actively, interpret feedback responsibly, and maintain a critical stance toward algorithmic guidance and spatial representations.

1.1 Methodological Framework: Narrative Review with Transparent Policy-Embedded Analysis

This chapter uses a narrative review approach designed for interpretive synthesis and conceptual clarity. The analysis is grounded in a structured search and selection strategy across major academic databases—including Scopus, Web of Science, and ERIC—combined with a critical evaluation of relevant European Union policy frameworks and regulatory guidance. The intent is to integrate empirical insights with policy-critical reasoning about what must be built to enable sustainable implementation in European educational contexts.

The selection criteria prioritize peer-reviewed research published between 2016 and 2024 that addresses the intersection of AI in Education (AIEd), Augmented Reality, and educational support structures. Particular attention is given to studies that clarify how support mitigates cognitive overload and split-attention effects in AR-enhanced learning environments; how AI can be integrated into teacher practice through appropriate scaffolding and human oversight; how learning analytics and personalization relate to privacy, transparency, and learner agency; and how professional and institutional supports—such as professional learning networks and governance practices—shape long-term adoption.

In addition, the review explicitly embeds a European policy lens. That is, the chapter does not treat classroom adoption as independent from regulatory and ethical constraints. Instead, it evaluates how European human-centric requirements translate into operational support responsibilities at institutional and classroom levels. This framing aligns with reviewer requests for methodological transparency and an emphasis on the conditions under which technology becomes educationally legitimate and socially sustainable.

The chapter also addresses a key gap: while the literature often emphasizes AI and AR capabilities, novelty effects, and measurable learning outcomes, it under-specifies integrated human-infrastructure models that reconcile technological opportunity with classroom accountability, teacher agency, and learner rights. To address this, the review develops a conceptual shift from technology-centric adoption to human-centric orchestration supported by a structured and ethically governed framework for teacher and learner support.

1.2 The Technological Landscape: AI and AR in the European Context

AI in Education (AIEd) has evolved beyond basic automation toward systems that support adaptive learning, real-time feedback, and instructionally responsive pathways. Intelligent Tutoring Systems (ITS) and AI-driven personalization tools can provide individualized feedback and dynamically adjust learning trajectories (Luckin & Holmes, 2016). Yet, as European implementation challenges demonstrate, capability does not automatically translate into classroom effectiveness. AI outputs must be interpretable by teachers, meaningful to learners, and accountable within regulatory constraints.

In Europe, AI adoption is strongly shaped by a human-centric regulatory and ethical framework grounded in the General Data Protection Regulation (GDPR) (European Commission, 2022). This environment implies specific support needs. Institutions must enable AI literacy and ethical discernment so that educators and learners understand what systems do, what data they use, and what limitations apply to algorithmic guidance (Chiu et al., 2023). Importantly, support must operationalize compliance: it should inform procurement governance, vendor accountability expectations, transparency procedures, and classroom workflows that maintain human responsibility.

Parallel to AI, AR has become increasingly relevant in European learning contexts. AR overlays digital content onto the physical world, enabling learners to visualize molecular structures, historical sites, and complex engineering components in three-dimensional space (Ibáñez & Delgado-Kloos, 2018). Unlike Virtual Reality (VR), AR maintains the learner's connection to the physical classroom and can support collaborative learning (Radianti et al., 2020). However, AR introduces cognitive demands inherent in dual-environment interaction. Learners must integrate digital overlays with physical context, instructional prompts, and peer activity. When this integration is insufficiently scaffolded, the "split-attention effect" can occur, reducing learning efficiency and increasing cognitive overload (Akçayır & Akçayır, 2017). Thus, AR's educational potential depends on more than content quality; it depends on instructional design and support mechanisms that coordinate attention and meaning-making.

1.3 The Teacher's Evolution: From Instructor to Orchestrator (Teacher-in-the-Loop)

For teachers, AI and AR integration requires professional transformation rather than simple tool adoption. Educators must develop AI-readiness and AR-fluency—competencies that allow them to orchestrate learning environments while sustaining pedagogical authority. This transition redefines teaching roles within a mediated classroom ecosystem where human judgement remains central.

A key mechanism is the "Teacher-in-the-loop" (HITL) model. HITL positions AI as an assistant that can delegate administrative burdens—such as grading support and routine monitoring—so that teachers can focus on mentorship, socio-emotional support, and pedagogical intervention (Selwyn, 2019). However, HITL cannot succeed through delegation alone. It requires trust, interpretability, and actionable integration. Teachers need support to understand how AI makes decisions and how to respond when recommendations are uncertain or incomplete. Nazaretsky et al. (2022) emphasize that teacher trust is contingent and must be cultivated through transparency and meaningful interpretive structures.

This is where explainable AI (XAI) becomes operationally important. Rather than treating AI outputs as opaque signals, XAI-oriented support helps teachers access interpretable, pedagogically relevant insights that can guide intervention at appropriate moments (Molenaar, 2022). In this chapter, "Actionable Insights" are understood as outputs translated into pedagogical options a teacher can evaluate and implement based on curricular goals, classroom context, and learner needs. Such a model also aligns with the need for "context-aware" just-in-time support in dynamic learning environments (Ouyang & Jiao, 2021).

For AR, teachers need spatial orchestration skills—abilities that support classroom logistics and learner attention when students view different overlays and interpret 3D representations. This includes managing pacing, ensuring collaborative meaning-making, and coordinating guidance so that immersion enhances conceptual understanding rather than generating disorientation. Professional Learning Networks (PLNs) can support these capabilities; European collaboration platforms such as eTwinning can help teachers share implementation strategies, lesson designs, and practical troubleshooting approaches (Caena & Redecker, 2019; Karasavvidis, 2022).

1.4 The Learner's Journey: Agency and Cognitive Scaffolding

For learners, support requirements in AI-AR environments are primarily about agency and cognitive scaffolding. When AI provides constant feedback and adaptive pathways, learners risk becoming passive recipients of algorithmic decisions. Support must therefore foster self-regulated learning and critical engagement with AI-mediated feedback. Students should learn how to interpret AI guidance, recognize when outputs may be biased or inaccurate, and validate learning through appropriate verification strategies. UNESCO (2021) highlights that AI literacy includes understanding system limitations and developing judgement that preserves human agency.

Immersive AR adds a second layer: learners must acquire spatial literacy. AR can enhance STEM learning by making invisible phenomena visible; nonetheless, it can also introduce emotional and cognitive dissonance if experiences are not structured. Learners require cues that orient attention, guided discovery activities that sequence exploration, and collaborative smart learning arrangements that reduce isolation and distribute cognitive load (Ruiz-Ariza et al., 2018; Pellas et al., 2020). These supports ensure that AR functions as a scaffold for meaning-making rather than as a source of distraction.

In Europe, the learner journey is further shaped by multilingualism and diverse cultural contexts, especially in the European Higher Education Area (EHEA). Learners interpret digital information through linguistic and cultural frameworks; therefore, scaffolding must be accessible and pedagogically interpretable across contexts (Parmaxi & Demetriou, 2020). The chapter thus treats learner support as both cognitive and ethical: cognitive scaffolding manages attention and processing, while ethical scaffolding preserves agency in the face of algorithmic guidance.

1.5 Situating Support within European and Global Policy: GDPR, AI Governance, and Comparative Needs

European education technology adoption is inseparable from policy. The Digital Education Action Plan (2021–2027) calls for a high-performing digital education ecosystem that supports quality, accessibility, and inclusion (European Commission, 2020). This chapter situates AI and AR implementation within that broader commitment, emphasizing that European governance prioritizes equity, data sovereignty, and accountability rather than market efficiency alone (Köhler & Münster, 2021).

A central policy tension concerns learning analytics and personalization: the "personalization–privacy paradox." Adaptive learning often requires data to function effectively, yet learners' rights to privacy and data protection must be preserved. European institutions therefore need privacy-preserving support tools that allow adaptive learning while protecting learner identity and complying with GDPR principles (Ifenthaler & Schumacher, 2023). In addition, European compliance expectations differ from global paradigms such as FERPA or COPPA, which structure consent and rights in different ways. This comparative perspective matters for support design because institutions must implement specific governance and procurement structures—particularly when third-party vendors operate across jurisdictions (Köhler & Münster, 2021; European Commission, 2022).

Therefore, policy is treated here as a design constraint and a support blueprint: European human-centric governance generates operational support requirements for teachers and institutions, including transparency procedures, accountability pathways, and procurement governance that ensure AI and AR are used responsibly.

1.6 Technostress and Emotional Support: Making Implementation Sustainable

Beyond cognitive and technical dimensions, AI and AR integration requires emotional and social support. "Technostress"—anxiety linked to rapid technological change and concerns about replacement or obsolescence—can undermine adoption and lead to superficial implementation (Karasavvidis, 2022). Support systems must therefore address psychological and social dimensions alongside training.

For teachers, one practical solution is enabling Communities of Practice that allow educators to share implementation experiences and normalize challenges associated with transitioning to AI-mediated teaching. For learners, emotional sustainability also depends on whether AR enhances collaboration or intensifies isolation. Collaborative smart learning designs can reduce isolation by embedding interaction, shared tasks, and peer-to-peer meaning-making within AR settings (Radianti et al., 2020). This ensures that immersive learning strengthens social learning rather than replacing it.

1.7 Objectives and Scope of the Chapter

This chapter addresses a critical gap by focusing on support structures rather than only technological features. Its objectives are:

- Evaluate AI and AR support needs within European educational policy frameworks, particularly the Digital Education Action Plan and AI governance expectations.
- Identify pedagogical scaffolds required for learners to engage with AR-enhanced immersive environments without cognitive overload.
- Analyze professional development needs for teachers transitioning to AI-integrated classrooms, focusing on HITL and the evolution of TPACK toward AI-readiness.
- Examine the role of Intelligent Tutoring Systems (ITS) in providing personalized support while reducing administrative burden and workload pressure.
- Discuss ethical and psychological support requirements addressing AI bias, data privacy concerns, and potential digital isolation in AR settings.
- Provide actionable recommendations for European policymakers and institutional leaders to build resilient support ecosystems for emerging XR and learning technologies.

1.8 Conclusion of the Introduction

The integration of AI and AR in European education is evolutionary and demands a revolution in support rather than a revolution in hardware. Institutions that move from experimental pilots to mainstream practice must invest in pedagogical scaffolding, teacher orchestration capacities, privacy-preserving governance, and socio-emotional infrastructure. The goal is not only to adopt advanced technologies, but to build "Resilient Education" systems in which AI and AR function as catalysts for human potential, preserving learner agency and maintaining teacher authority.

Grounded in European frameworks and synthesized evidence, this chapter offers a strategic, human-centric roadmap for developing an inclusive and sustainable digital educational ecosystem. The subsequent sections develop conceptual scaffolding frameworks, examine mechanisms of support for teachers and learners, and show how European governance expectations connect to classroom-level implementation.

2. OBJECTIVES OF THE CHAPTER

The rapid infusion of disruptive technologies into education—particularly Artificial Intelligence (AI), Learning Analytics (LA), and Augmented Reality (AR)—requires more than descriptive discussion of tool capabilities. It demands a clear, multi-dimensional roadmap for research, design, and implementation that addresses the human infrastructure required for sustained educational value. The reviewers of this chapter repeatedly emphasized that the work's unique contribution should be sharper: the chapter should not only explain what AI and AR can do, but also clarify what must be built—pedagogically, professionally, ethically, and emotionally—so that these tools function responsibly and effectively within European learning contexts. In response, this section presents six objectives that collectively operationalize the chapter's central thesis: the success of AI and AR depends on robust teacher–learner support systems and policy-embedded governance mechanisms that reconcile technological opportunity with classroom legitimacy.

A further refinement motivated by the reviewers concerns the chapter's conceptual structure. Multiple "scaffolding" constructs (hybrid, spatial, ethical, professional, and affective) appear across different sections. To prevent fragmentation and redundancy, the objectives below are framed as interdependent components of a single integrated support logic. This provides an early alignment of terms and later enables the chapter to instantiate the framework in case studies and policy discussions. The objectives also address the reviewers' request for clearer operationalization: each objective specifies what practitioners and policymakers should look for, decide, or implement, rather than only describing general tendencies in the literature.

Accordingly, the objectives are structured along three axes: (1) policy and regulatory translation into institutional support; (2) pedagogical scaffolding that makes immersive AR and AI personalization cognitively sustainable; and (3) professional, ethical, and socio-emotional support mechanisms that sustain adoption and protect learner agency.

2.1 Critical Evaluation of European (and Comparative) Policy Frameworks

The first objective is to critically evaluate how European policy frameworks shape the implementation conditions for AI and AR in education. European digital education governance does not treat technology adoption as purely technical or market-driven; it embeds human-centric expectations regarding inclusion, accountability, and data sovereignty. This chapter therefore examines how the Digital Education Action Plan (2021–2027) frames system-level responsibilities for quality and accessibility (European Commission, 2020) and how governance approaches translate into practical institutional support.

Crucially, this objective includes a comparative regulatory lens. Reviewers asked for a "comparative regulatory framework" and for the references to align with in-text citations. In response, the objective contrasts European requirements grounded in GDPR principles with global privacy and rights regimes frequently discussed in the education technology literature (e.g., FERPA/COPPA). The purpose is not to provide legal commentary, but to identify why European institutions must build distinct support capacities for privacy-preserving personalization, transparency, and cross-border vendor accountability. In practice, this objective asks: What must institutions be able to do so that procurement, deployment, teacher use, and student experience remain compliant and ethically defensible?

In doing so, this objective also helps clarify what is "genuinely new" in the chapter's approach. Rather than presenting policy as background context, the chapter treats policy as a design and support constraint that determines how teachers can legitimately use AI outputs, how learning analytics can be governed, and how learners can retain agency and rights. The policy evaluation thus becomes a foundation for the chapter's later operational recommendations.

2.2 Identification of Taxonomy-Based Pedagogical Scaffolds for AR

The second objective is to identify taxonomy-based pedagogical scaffolds required for learners to engage effectively with AR-enhanced learning environments. AR's educational value is often framed in terms of immersion and visualization; however, immersion does not automatically produce learning. Learners may experience cognitive overload, confusion, or reduced comprehension when they must process simultaneous streams of information—physical context and digital overlays. The chapter therefore focuses on scaffolding mechanisms that manage attention, reduce extraneous cognitive load, and structure meaning-making.

This objective explicitly operationalizes "spatial scaffolding" and aligns it with other scaffolding constructs. Rather than treating scaffolding as an abstract metaphor, this objective defines it in practical design terms. The taxonomy is expected to cover, at minimum:

- Interface cues and visual guidance that orient learners to relevant elements in 3D overlays.
- Sequenced guided inquiry that structures exploration to avoid split-attention effects.
- Collaborative task structures that distribute attention across learners and reduce isolation.
- Progressive complexity that gradually increases the cognitive demands of the AR experience.

This objective also reflects the reviewers' request for earlier definitions of key terms. Concepts such as "spatial scaffolding" should therefore be anchored to concrete design functions—what the system displays, how learners move through the activity, and how teachers can adapt tasks when cognitive overload emerges. Later sections will instantiate this taxonomy in cases (e.g., STEM lab visualizations and structured immersive environments for learners with special needs).

2.3 Analysis of Professional Development Needs Through Teacher-in-the-Loop and AI-Readiness

The third objective centers on the educator and the professional development required for sustainable AI–AR classroom integration. Reviewers emphasized the chapter's central theme—Teacher-in-the-loop—and asked for operational clarity regarding what teachers need and why the approach matters. This objective addresses that requirement.

The objective is to analyze how teacher development must evolve to include AI-readiness and AR orchestration skills. In particular, it examines the HITL philosophy: AI should augment rather than replace human pedagogical authority. Teachers need support to interpret AI-generated outputs, understand system limitations, and decide how to intervene within learners' Zone of Proximal Development. This objective revisits and expands the TPACK framework toward the AI era by identifying what teachers require to integrate AI tools into lesson design, assessment practices, and learner support routines.

Importantly, this objective does not treat HITL as a slogan. It investigates what "human oversight" means in classroom workflow terms. For example, support must help teachers move from raw or automated signals toward actionable pedagogical decisions—what to do when a learner struggles, when a system's recommendation is uncertain, and how to document and justify intervention. It also examines the role of trust and explainability in fostering sustainable adoption (i.e., moving from black-box uncertainty toward transparent, teacher-interpretable insights).

Finally, the objective integrates the emotional dimension of professional development: technostress is a barrier to deeper integration. Teacher development must therefore include Communities of Practice and peer learning mechanisms that support teachers not only technically but psychologically.

2.4 Examination of Intelligent Tutoring Systems as Dual-Layer Support Tools

The fourth objective is to examine the role of Intelligent Tutoring Systems (ITS) as dual-layer support for learners and teachers. Reviewers requested practical operationalization and clearer linkage between system outputs and teacher action. This objective therefore assesses ITS effectiveness not merely as adaptive technology, but as a support mechanism that should accomplish two tasks simultaneously:

- Learner support: providing personalized explanations, feedback, and adaptive learning pathways that respond to learner progress.
- Teacher relief: reducing administrative burden (e.g., grading support, routine feedback generation, and progress monitoring) so that teachers can focus on mentorship and pedagogy.

This objective explicitly evaluates whether ITS produces "Actionable Insights"—information that teachers can translate into classroom action rather than data overload. It also examines how ITS can support learner agency by encouraging reflection and critical evaluation instead of creating passivity. In the European context, ITS adoption must also align with privacy expectations and transparency requirements, which reinforces the need for institutional support systems.

By connecting ITS to teacher workload and learner agency at the same time, this objective addresses the dual-stakeholder contribution repeatedly requested by reviewers.

2.5 Addressing Ethical, Psychological, and Social Support Requirements

The fifth objective addresses ethical and psychological support requirements that protect learners and sustain adoption. The European governance context makes this objective non-optional: ethical use is central to the legitimacy of AI and the safety of data-driven personalization.

This objective focuses on the "personalization–privacy paradox," where data is needed for adaptation but privacy rights must be preserved. It examines support requirements for privacy-preserving AI tools and how institutions can provide governance structures that ensure data minimization, transparency, and accountability when third-party vendors are used. It also addresses bias and the risk of incorrect outputs (including "hallucinations" or unreliable guidance), emphasizing AI literacy as a learner support function.

However, ethical support is not only legal or technical. Reviewers requested stronger emphasis on the human and emotional dimensions of implementation. Therefore, this objective includes socio-emotional risks such as technostress, digital isolation in immersive contexts, and the erosion of trust. It evaluates support mechanisms such as collaborative smart learning designs and Communities of Practice for teachers. It treats emotional wellbeing as an implementation variable that affects sustainability, equity, and the long-term effectiveness of AI–AR interventions.

2.6 Strategic Recommendations for Building a Resilient Support Ecosystem

The final objective is to provide actionable, evidence-based recommendations for policymakers and institutional leaders. Reviewers requested a practitioner-oriented orientation—design and implementation guidelines that convert analysis into concrete steps. This objective therefore synthesizes the preceding objectives into a strategic roadmap for building resilient support ecosystems.

These recommendations should cover the transition from pilots to mainstream adoption, including:

- Institutional governance pathways for ethical procurement, cross-border vendor accountability, and transparent deployment.
- Design and implementation requirements for AR spatial scaffolding that reduces cognitive overload and supports meaningful exploration.
- Professional development structures that support HITL practices, including AI-readiness training and Communities of Practice.

- Privacy-preserving learning analytics principles that allow adaptation without undermining learner rights.
- Wellbeing and inclusion strategies that mitigate technostress and promote collaborative smart learning.

This objective ensures that the chapter's contribution is not only conceptual but also practical: it clarifies what institutional leaders should fund, develop, standardize, and monitor to ensure that AI and AR integration is sustainable, inclusive, and pedagogically defensible.

2.7 Synthesis: Interdependence of Objectives and the Integrated Support Logic

The objectives above are intentionally interdependent. Pedagogical scaffolding for AR (Objective 2.2) cannot be achieved without teacher professional development and orchestration capacity (Objective 2.3). Ethical and privacy governance (Objective 2.5) influences what AI-based personalization and learning analytics can do and how teachers can interpret outputs responsibly (Objectives 2.4 and 2.1). ITS and AI personalization systems (Objective 2.4) must be supported by regulatory translation and procurement governance (Objective 2.1). Emotional sustainability and social learning structures (Objective 2.5) reinforce adoption by reducing technostress and supporting learners' collaborative meaning-making.

By addressing these objectives together, the chapter fulfills the reviewers' core request: it moves beyond technological fascination toward a unified model of human-centric support. The dual-stakeholder lens—teachers and learners—becomes the organizing principle of the chapter's conceptual contribution and its strategic roadmap for European education.

3. CONTENT

The following sections detail the core thematic pillars of the chapter, moving from macro-level governance and regulatory constraints to micro-level pedagogical interactions and operational classroom support. In response to reviewer requests for consolidation, clarity, and a reduction of conceptual overlap, this section establishes an integrated Hybrid Scaffolding Model early and treats later sub-sections as instantiations of that model across (1) policy and procurement, (2) learner cognition and agency, (3) teacher orchestration and professional capacity, and (4) ethical and emotional governance.

To avoid fragmentation among multiple "scaffolding" constructs, the chapter groups scaffolding into a single framework that can be expressed in different forms depending on context:

- Pedagogical Scaffolding (Hybrid): combining algorithmic support (AI/ITS) with teacher-led instructional judgement.
- Spatial Scaffolding (AR): managing attention, comprehension, and cognitive load in 3D environments.
- Ethical Scaffolding (AI governance): ensuring transparency, privacy-preserving design, and responsible use.
- Professional Scaffolding (HITL competence): enabling teachers to interpret system outputs and intervene at the right moments.
- Affective/Emotional Scaffolding (wellbeing): mitigating technostress and digital isolation through social and psychological supports.

These components are interdependent: algorithmic personalization can only be pedagogically meaningful if teachers can orchestrate interventions; spatial scaffolding can only work if learners are prepared to interpret overlays; ethical scaffolding is only operational if institutional support translates policy into classroom routines; and affective scaffolding sustains adoption over time.

3.1 The European Landscape: Policy, Infrastructure, and Regulatory Governance

The implementation of Artificial Intelligence (AI) and Augmented Reality (AR) in European classrooms is not occurring in a policy vacuum. It is steered by the European Commission's vision for a human-centric, sovereign digital future. The Digital Education Action Plan (2021–2027) functions as an overarching roadmap for building high-performing digital education ecosystems (European Commission, 2020). In parallel, AI governance initiatives and data protection requirements establish additional constraints for educational use of algorithmic systems (European Commission, 2022).

A key implication for this chapter is that "support" is not optional—support is the mechanism through which policy values become enforceable classroom practices. Institutions must be able to demonstrate that adopted tools meet human-centric expectations, that learner data is governed responsibly, and that teachers retain meaningful oversight.

3.1.1 Comparative Regulatory Framework: GDPR-Centered Support vs. Global Contexts

European implementation is distinctive due to GDPR-centered principles such as privacy by design, data minimization, and accountability. To clarify why European support systems require specific capabilities, this chapter contrasts European expectations with global approaches frequently referenced in the broader education technology debate. In the United States context, privacy frameworks often emphasize consent processes and restrictions on certain disclosure pathways (e.g., FERPA/COPPA, as commonly discussed in AIEd literature). In contrast, GDPR emphasizes data sovereignty, stronger rights protections, and structured accountability.

This comparative view matters for operational support. When third-party vendors operate across jurisdictions, European institutions must build procurement and governance support capacities that ensure cross-border data handling remains compliant and ethically defensible. Therefore, the chapter treats regulatory differences as drivers of institutional scaffolding requirements: procurement guidelines, transparency procedures, and educator-facing explainability routines are not administrative burdens; they are the foundations for legitimate educational use.

3.2 Conceptualizing Support: The Hybrid Scaffolding Model

To move beyond descriptive technology adoption, the chapter establishes a Hybrid Scaffolding Model integrating human expertise with algorithmic precision.

3.2.1 Scaffolding and the ZPD Through Algorithmic Mediation

Traditionally, the teacher manages learning within Vygotsky's Zone of Proximal Development (ZPD) through prompts, feedback, and adaptive guidance. In the AI era, Algorithmic Scaffolding can identify learning patterns in real time and offer "just-in-time" hints (Luckin & Holmes, 2016; Ouyang & Jiao, 2021). Yet, algorithmic mediation must be constrained by pedagogical judgement. The Hybrid Scaffolding Model therefore treats AI outputs as provisional scaffolds: they must be validated, interpreted, and adjusted by the teacher at moments where human instruction is pedagogically necessary.

Practically, this means that the model requires:

- evidence-based teacher interpretability of AI outputs,
- workflow structures that enable timely intervention, and
- pedagogical protocols defining when AI support should yield to teacher-led guidance.

3.2.2 Revisiting TPACK Toward AI-Readiness and Orchestration Support

Professional scaffolding in the model requires teachers to extend Technological Pedagogical Content Knowledge (TPACK) toward AI-readiness and AR orchestration capacity. Teachers need to understand how AI systems support learning tasks, where their limits are, and how AI and AR affordances influence instructional design. This professional scaffolding does not replace content or pedagogy; it extends them to a socio-technical classroom ecology (Redecker, 2017; Saltan & Arslan, 2017).

Within the Hybrid Scaffolding Model, teacher support focuses on orchestration: ensuring that routine administrative processes can be delegated through HITL while learning-critical judgement remains human-led (Selwyn, 2019; Molenaar, 2022). This sets the foundation for later sections addressing dashboards, learning analytics interpretation, and classroom management routines.

3.3 Support Mechanisms for Learners: Cognitive Load, Spatial Literacy, and Agency

Learner support in AI-AR settings requires both cognitive management and agency development. The chapter consolidates learner scaffolding under two operational themes: (i) cognitive sustainability in spatial environments and (ii) agency preservation under algorithmic guidance.

3.3.1 Spatial Scaffolding in AR: Reducing Split-Attention and Overload

AR can lead to split-attention effects where attention is divided between physical context and digital overlays (Akçayır & Akçayır, 2017). Without spatial scaffolding, learners may experience cognitive overload—interpreting novelty rather than learning concepts. Within the Hybrid Scaffolding Model, spatial scaffolding is treated as a design system that includes:

- visual cues that highlight relevant elements in the overlay,
- progressive disclosure that sequences complexity rather than presenting all information at once,
- guided discovery structures that help learners follow meaningful exploration trajectories, and
- interface constraints that minimize extraneous information.

AR instructional design therefore becomes a form of cognitive scaffolding that protects learning goals from the distractive potential of immersion. The chapter also emphasizes that spatial scaffolding must be teacher-orchestrated: teachers need routines for distributing attention, checking comprehension, and adjusting tasks if learners become disoriented or overloaded.

3.3.2 AI-Driven Personalization and Agency Support

Learning analytics and AI personalization can provide adaptive pathways (Ifenthaler & Schumacher, 2023). However, algorithmic personalization risks transforming learners into passive recipients of recommendations. The Hybrid Scaffolding Model therefore includes Agency Support as a deliberate design requirement.

Agency support includes mechanisms such as:

- teaching students how to interpret AI feedback and learning suggestions,
- encouraging verification habits (e.g., checking outputs for inconsistency), and
- supporting critical literacy to recognize bias and unreliable outputs.

UNESCO (2021) frames AI literacy as essential for developing responsible engagement with algorithmic content. In this chapter, agency support becomes the ethical and pedagogical bridge between personalization and autonomy: learners are scaffolded not only to learn, but to learn with judgement.

3.3.3 Multilingual and Sociocultural Interpretability

European classrooms include multilingual learners and diverse cultural contexts. AR overlays and AI feedback interact with language interpretation and cultural sense-making. Therefore, learner scaffolding must ensure that both the linguistic interface and the interpretive meaning of digital feedback are accessible and pedagogically valid across contexts (Parmaxi & Demetriou, 2020). This inclusion principle guides how educational content is localized, how explanations are scaffolded, and how teachers mediate meaning where algorithmic language support is insufficient.

3.4 Support Mechanisms for Teachers: HITL Orchestration, Dashboards, and Wellbeing

Teacher support mechanisms are the engine that makes hybrid scaffolding sustainable. Without teacher readiness and wellbeing, AI and AR tools may be underused, misinterpreted, or implemented in ways that conflict with learning intentions.

3.4.1 The Teacher-in-the-Loop Dashboard as an Orchestration Instrument

Reviewers requested operational clarity about what teacher-facing tools should display. In the Hybrid Scaffolding Model, an effective teacher dashboard (or orchestration tool) should provide Actionable Insights rather than raw telemetry. Operationally, it should display:

- learning-state summaries tied to curriculum-relevant objectives (e.g., readiness indicators, misconception flags),
- AR interaction evidence (e.g., engagement markers linked to learning tasks rather than device metrics),
- explainable recommendation rationales (what signals led to a suggestion and what uncertainty exists),
- recommended next interventions (suggested teacher actions mapped to lesson design options), and
- privacy-preserving controls that clarify what data is used and how it is governed.

Holstein et al. (2019) supports the broader idea that real-time orchestration tools must be co-designed with teachers to support action, not simply information presentation. In this chapter, orchestration dashboards function as professional scaffolding by enabling teachers to interpret system outputs and decide pedagogical responses within the ZPD.

3.4.2 Orchestration and Professional Learning Networks

Teachers also need professional scaffolding beyond tools. European PLNs such as eTwinning can enable shared practice around AR lesson design and AI integration (Caena & Redecker, 2019; Karasavvidis, 2022). This peer support mechanism is essential for normalization and long-term sustainability because it reduces isolation and improves collective interpretability of system limits and best practices.

3.4.3 Technostress Mitigation as an Implementation Requirement

Technostress is a barrier to adoption and sustainable integration (Karasavvidis, 2022). Therefore, emotional scaffolding for teachers is treated as part of institutional support: communities of practice, supportive leadership routines, and training pathways that validate teacher agency reduce fear and strengthen confidence. In HITL terms, teachers are supported to remain responsible pedagogical agents rather than anxiety-driven tool users.

3.5 Ethical Support and Third-Party Accountability: Operationalizing Privacy and Explainability

Ethical scaffolding is a central design requirement in European contexts. It bridges GDPR obligations with practical classroom use. This section consolidates ethical support into three operational requirements:

- privacy-preserving design for learning analytics and personalization (Ifenthaler & Schumacher, 2023),
- teacher interpretability through explainability-oriented practices (Molenaar, 2022; Nazaretsky et al., 2022), and
- vendor accountability through procurement governance aligned with human-centric expectations (European Commission, 2020; European Commission, 2022).

Ethical scaffolding also addresses algorithmic profiling risks and discriminatory outcomes. The chapter emphasizes that ethical support is not only a compliance activity; it is a pedagogical condition for maintaining learner agency. When privacy and transparency are integrated into operational support systems, teachers can better justify how AI and AR are used and learners can understand their role in algorithmically mediated learning.

3.6 Case Instantiations: From Framework to Operational Classroom Support

The integrated scaffolding framework becomes meaningful when instantiated in specific educational contexts. The chapter therefore provides case-based demonstrations (conceptual examples) showing how hybrid scaffolding works in practice:

- *Case 1 (AR in STEM – Germany/Scandinavia)*: spatial scaffolding reduces split-attention by projecting task cues directly onto the learner's field of vision, anchoring digital information to physical procedures (Radianti et al., 2020). Teacher routines coordinate pacing and confirm comprehension, ensuring immersion remains pedagogically directed rather than cognitively distracting.
- *Case 2 (AI in Language Learning – Spain/France)*: contextual scaffolding supports learner agency by integrating low-stakes practice with feedback

that respects regional linguistic variations. The teacher mediates meaning and verifies relevance when AI outputs are uncertain, preserving responsible learning (Parmaxi & Demetriou, 2020).

- *Case 3 (Inclusive Education – Italy)*: affective and structured immersive scaffolding supports neurodivergent learners by simplifying AR navigation and using AI-mediated signals to detect overload triggers, prompting micro-interventions guided by teacher judgement. Ethical governance ensures that data use remains justified and privacy-preserving (Ruiz-Ariza et al., 2018; Pellas et al., 2020).

These cases exemplify how the same Hybrid Scaffolding logic adapts across pedagogical domains while preserving its integrated structure: cognitive sustainability, teacher orchestration, privacy-preserving governance, and socio-emotional support.

3.7 Conclusion and Future Directions for Content Synthesis

This chapter synthesis concludes by positioning integrated support as the foundation of resilient education. As Europe moves toward Extended Reality (XR) and increasingly capable generative AI, the educational value of technology will depend on the scaffolding ecosystem that enables legitimate interpretation, ethical governance, and pedagogical sustainability. The future roadmap is therefore not limited to broader deployment of AI and AR tools; it requires coordinated development of teacher capacity, learner agency supports, privacy-preserving institutional infrastructure, and socio-emotional learning design.

In this integrated view, AR and AI are not ends. They are mediators—whose educational impact is determined by human infrastructure. The next section will deepen this synthesis through discussion of the interdependence among teacher orchestration, spatial scaffolding, ethical governance, and emotional wellbeing, reinforcing the chapter's strategic roadmap for institutional leadership and policy-aligned implementation.

4. CONTENT DISCUSSION

The integration of Artificial Intelligence (AI) and Augmented Reality (AR) into the European educational fabric requires a granular examination of how technologies interact with pedagogy and—most importantly—how human agents are supported to make responsible decisions. This discussion section therefore expands the chapter's argument around four interlocking pillars: (1) teacher orchestration through the Teacher-in-the-loop (HITL) philosophy, (2) spatial and cognitive scaffolding for

AR-mediated learning, (3) ethical support that operationalizes the personalization–privacy paradox and learner AI literacy, and (4) emotional and social scaffolding that mitigates technostress and digital isolation.

Responding to reviewer requests, this section also clarifies what the "new" contribution is: the chapter does not treat scaffolding as separate metaphors scattered across sections. Instead, it frames them as instantiations of one integrated support logic—Hybrid Scaffolding—where AI offers algorithmic assistance, AR provides spatial visualization, teachers orchestrate meaning and intervention, and institutions ensure ethical governance and wellbeing conditions. The discussion translates these pillars into practical design implications for classrooms and institutional implementation priorities.

4.1 The Teacher-in-the-Loop Philosophy: Beyond Automation Toward Actionable Oversight

A central theme of this chapter is that AI and AR should not replace teachers but empower them. In the HITL model, AI systems are designed to augment human decision-making rather than automate it entirely. Delegation is targeted at administrative and routine burdens—such as grading assistance, scheduling support, and preliminary learning progress monitoring—so teachers can concentrate on mentorship, emotional support, and pedagogical judgement (Selwyn, 2019).

However, HITL succeeds only when teacher oversight is supported by tools and training. Otherwise, teachers are forced into "supervision without meaning," where they receive alerts but lack interpretive capacity or confidence to act. For this reason, support must shift from raw data provision toward interpretability and actionable guidance. Reviewers requested clearer operationalization of the "orchestration dashboard" concept. In practical terms, a teacher-facing dashboard should present:

- learning-state summaries connected to curricular objectives,
- evidence of learner interactions with AR modules and AI-supported tasks,
- explainable recommendation rationales (including what the system used and what uncertainty exists), and
- suggested intervention pathways that teachers can evaluate and adapt in context.

In this discussion, "Actionable Insights" mean that system output is translated into pedagogical options that respect classroom constraints and human responsibility. This aligns with the broader need to move away from black-box signals toward explainable AI that supports appropriate student and teacher agency (Molenaar,

2022). Teacher trust also matters; as Nazaretsky et al. (2022) suggest, trust must be cultivated through transparency and institutional support, not assumed.

Finally, HITL is not only a cognitive or technical issue—it is an emotional one. Teachers can experience technostress when adoption is rushed or when they fear losing pedagogical authority (Karasavvidis, 2022). Therefore, professional scaffolding must include Communities of Practice and supportive training pathways that validate teacher agency while building AI-readiness.

4.2 AR and Spatial Scaffolding: Managing Cognitive Load and Meaning-Making

AR introduces a spatial dimension to learning that requires entirely new support mechanisms. Unlike flat-screen instructional media, AR requires learners to integrate digital overlays with physical context and task goals. Without scaffolding, this integration can produce split-attention effects, where learners expend cognitive resources coordinating attention rather than constructing conceptual understanding (Akçayır & Akçayır, 2017). This is where spatial scaffolding becomes essential.

Within the Hybrid Scaffolding Model, spatial scaffolding is treated as a design principle that manages cognitive load through three operational strategies:

- Visual orientation: cues that highlight relevant elements and reduce search effort inside complex 3D environments.
- Sequenced information: progressive disclosure that prevents overload by introducing complexity step-by-step.
- Guided interaction: structured exploration pathways where teachers and activities coordinate learner movement, attention, and reflection.

AR's benefits—such as making abstract phenomena visible—are therefore realized when scaffolding protects learning goals from novelty-driven distraction (Ibáñez & Delgado-Kloos, 2018). Cognitive sustainability must be paired with teacher orchestration because teachers determine timing, pacing, group configuration, and troubleshooting routines when learners become confused or overwhelmed (Karasavvidis, 2022).

Moreover, spatial scaffolding is not only cognitive; it is social. Immersive tasks can isolate learners if they are structured as solitary visualization. Collaborative smart learning designs mitigate this by requiring peer interaction within the augmented environment (Radianti et al., 2020). This ensures AR strengthens community learning rather than replacing it.

4.3 AI Personalization and the Personalization–Privacy Paradox: European Ethical Support

In the European context, AI support is inseparable from ethical governance. Learning analytics and personalization can improve responsiveness, but they also require data, which raises privacy and rights concerns. The personalization–privacy paradox refers to the tension between data-driven adaptation and learners' right to privacy and data protection. In practical terms, support systems must allow adaptive learning while ensuring privacy-preserving design and GDPR-aligned governance (Ifenthaler & Schumacher, 2023; European Commission, 2022).

This ethical support must be operational for classrooms, not merely theoretical for policy. It involves at least three support layers:

- Institutional governance scaffolding: procurement guidelines and vendor accountability structures that ensure data minimization, transparency, and cross-border compliance.
- Teacher interpretability scaffolding: explainability support that allows teachers to understand AI outputs and respond responsibly.
- Learner AI literacy scaffolding: training and interface design that teach students how to interpret AI feedback, recognize limitations, and verify outputs when needed (UNESCO, 2021).

A key implication is that ethical support also sustains pedagogical legitimacy. When learners understand that systems have limitations and when teachers can justify interventions, trust increases and the risk of harmful reliance decreases. Thus, ethics becomes a condition for learning effectiveness, not a separate compliance task.

4.4 Emotional and Social Support: Addressing Technostress and Digital Isolation

A frequently overlooked barrier to sustainable AI and AR integration is emotional sustainability. Technostress can undermine teachers' willingness to adopt and persist with technologies (Karasavvidis, 2022). For learners, immersion can unintentionally generate isolation, especially when headset-based or device-centered experiences reduce peer interaction. This can harm motivation and belonging, which are prerequisites for productive learning.

Therefore, emotional and social scaffolding must be built into implementation. For teachers, Communities of Practice and peer support structures provide a mechanism to normalize learning curves, share strategies, and reduce anxiety. For learners, collaborative smart learning arrangements ensure that AR experiences remain social and interactive (Radianti et al., 2020). In this way, emotional support becomes part of the scaffolding ecosystem that sustains both adoption and learning outcomes.

4.5 Synthesis: Interdependence of the Support Pillars

The four pillars—teacher orchestration, spatial scaffolding, ethical governance, and emotional support—are not isolated components. They form a single socio-technical support system. AI personalization is only pedagogically meaningful when teachers can interpret outputs within HITL routines (4.1). AR benefits depend on cognitive scaffolding and on teacher orchestration to coordinate attention and meaning-making (4.2). Ethical and privacy governance shapes what data can be used and how learners can trust and engage with feedback (4.3). Emotional support and social learning design stabilize adoption and reduce the psychological risks of immersive, technology-mediated education (4.4).

This interdependence is the chapter's strategic contribution to European education discourse. It reframes the "integration question" from "How powerful are AI and AR?" to "What human infrastructure makes them legitimate, effective, and sustainable in practice?" The following conclusion will translate this integrated support logic into a roadmap for institutional leaders and policymakers, emphasizing resilient adoption rather than short-term pilot enthusiasm.

5. SIGNIFICANCE AND CONTRIBUTION TO THE FIELD

The rapid integration of Artificial Intelligence (AI) and Augmented Reality (AR) into educational settings has often been characterized by a technology-first narrative. In much of the literature and in early implementation efforts, emphasis tends to fall on tool capabilities, novelty effects, and performance outcomes measured within limited contexts. While such work is valuable, it can obscure a central educational question: what human infrastructure is required for AI and AR to produce sustained learning benefits that are ethically legitimate, pedagogically coherent, and socially inclusive. This chapter addresses that gap by shifting the analytical focus from the "wow factor" and technical potential of tools toward the support systems that make their use educationally meaningful.

Responding to reviewer feedback, the chapter's significance can be articulated through five intertwined contributions to the field: theoretical innovation, dual-stakeholder integration, comparative policy grounding, operational reframing of scaffolding constructs, and practical value for institutional resilience. Together, these contributions position the chapter as both a conceptual and actionable reference for European education stakeholders.

5.1 Addressing the Pedagogical Pull Gap Through Human Infrastructure

A key significance of this work is its response to the imbalance between "technological push" and "pedagogical pull." Many studies document how AI algorithms personalize or how AR enhances visualization, but fewer address the human infrastructure that enables educators and learners to use these tools responsibly over time. This chapter contributes by introducing the Human Infrastructure perspective as a guiding framework: success is not a technical certainty; it is a pedagogical achievement made possible by support structures spanning teacher orchestration, learner scaffolding, ethical governance, and wellbeing conditions.

In this sense, the chapter advances a conceptual argument that is distinct from capability-focused analyses. It reframes educational integration as a socio-technical process in which the primary determinant of educational value is whether institutions can translate policy and design principles into classroom enactment. This reframing directly supports the chapter's European human-centric lens by emphasizing accountability, inclusion, and agency rather than efficiency alone.

5.2 A Dual-Stakeholder Contribution: Linking Teacher and Learner Support

Another central contribution is the chapter's dual-stakeholder approach. Existing research often treats support for teachers and support for learners as separate domains—professional development on one side, student scaffolding on the other. This chapter argues that such separation is analytically limiting because the effectiveness of learner support is contingent on teacher orchestration capacity, and teacher capacity is contingent on ethical governance and implementation sustainability.

For example, AR's spatial scaffolding is not simply an interface design problem; it depends on teachers coordinating attention, pacing, and interpretation tasks during classroom activities. Similarly, AI personalization does not function as intended without HITL practices that enable teachers to interpret system outputs and intervene pedagogically rather than accepting recommendations passively. By integrating teacher and learner needs into one support ecosystem, the chapter presents a more accurate model of classroom implementation dynamics.

This dual lens also strengthens the chapter's alignment with European digital competence expectations, which emphasize educator competence as a facilitator of student agency rather than a narrow set of technical skills. Consequently, the chapter provides a coherent conceptual bridge between teacher practice and learner experience—an integration that reviewers highlighted as a strength but requested to be further operationalized across sections.

5.3 Comparative Policy Grounding: Turning Governance Into Classroom Support Requirements

A third contribution lies in comparative policy grounding. The European context is distinctive because governance frameworks—particularly GDPR-centered expectations and human-centric AI commitments—create specific support requirements. This chapter does not treat policy as background context; it treats policy as a design constraint that determines what institutions must build.

The chapter's comparative regulatory reasoning (contrasting GDPR-centered expectations with other global privacy paradigms commonly discussed in the literature) clarifies why European institutions need distinct support mechanisms. It connects governance to operational responsibilities such as procurement accountability, transparency routines, privacy-preserving learning analytics, and teacher-facing interpretability supports. The significance here is that the chapter offers an explanation of why support ecosystems differ across regions, thereby helping institutional leaders avoid "copy-paste" implementations that fail under European compliance and ethics requirements.

In field terms, this contributes a more actionable policy-to-practice pathway: institutional adoption is supported not only by funding and tools, but by governance-aware instructional infrastructure.

5.4 Operational and Theoretical Integration of Scaffolding Constructs

Reviewers asked for consolidation and clearer definitions of scaffolding constructs. In response, the chapter's significance includes the establishment of an integrated conceptual logic: scaffolding constructs are treated as instantiations of a unified Hybrid Scaffolding Model. This model links algorithmic mediation (AI/ITS), spatial cognition management (AR), ethical governance (privacy and explainability), and professional capacity (HITL orchestration) with emotional and social wellbeing.

The chapter's theoretical contribution is therefore both integrative and explanatory. It offers a structured way for researchers and practitioners to understand how different scaffolding types relate rather than compete. This reduces conceptual redundancy and improves the chapter's ability to support future research design: investigators can examine specific components (e.g., spatial scaffolding effectiveness) while preserving awareness of required dependencies (e.g., teacher orchestration capacity and governance constraints).

5.5 Practical Impact: Roadmap for Institutional Resilience and Sustainable Adoption

Beyond theory, the chapter has practical significance. It provides a strategic roadmap for European policymakers and institutional leaders to move from pilot excitement toward sustainable adoption. The chapter's recommendations focus on resilient implementation rather than short-term deployment. In particular, it emphasizes:

- institutional ethical procurement and vendor accountability,
- teacher support structures that enable HITL and AI-readiness,
- pedagogical design requirements for AR spatial scaffolding that prevents cognitive overload,
- privacy-preserving learning analytics aligned with GDPR principles, and
- wellbeing and social learning designs that mitigate technostress and digital isolation.

This practical contribution directly responds to reviewer requests for actionable design and implementation guidelines for practitioners. By translating the integrated support logic into implementation priorities, the chapter supports institutional decision-making in ways that enhance legitimacy, inclusion, and long-term effectiveness.

5.6 Summary of Contribution to the Field

In summary, this chapter contributes to the field of educational technology and learning sciences by:

- Reframing integration success as a human-infrastructure problem rather than a technical capability problem.
- Offering a dual-stakeholder model that connects teacher orchestration with learner scaffolding and agency.
- Grounding support requirements in European governance while using comparative reasoning to clarify regulatory drivers.
- Integrating scaffolding constructs into a coherent Hybrid Scaffolding logic that reduces fragmentation across the literature.
- Providing practical resilience-oriented recommendations for policymakers and institutional leaders to support sustainable AI and AR adoption.

By prioritizing human judgement, ethical governance, and socio-emotional sustainability, this chapter strengthens the discourse around European AI and AR applications in learning. It supports a future in which technology amplifies human teaching and learner agency—rather than replacing them or creating fragile, compliance-sensitive classroom practices.

6. CONCLUSION

The integration of Artificial Intelligence (AI) and Augmented Reality (AR) into the European educational landscape represents one of the most significant pedagogical shifts of the 21st century. Yet, this shift cannot be reduced to procurement decisions, hardware availability, or the novelty of immersive interfaces. As this chapter has argued throughout its sections, the decisive factor for meaningful educational impact is the support infrastructure that enables teachers and learners to use AI and AR effectively, ethically, and sustainably. In European contexts—where governance, data sovereignty, inclusion, and human oversight are central values—the question is not only whether learning technologies are capable, but whether institutions can build the Human Infrastructure that makes their use legitimate and resilient.

This chapter has examined how AI and AR integration can succeed when the classroom is treated as a socio-technical ecosystem rather than a purely technical environment. The core thesis is that successful adoption depends on interdependent support mechanisms spanning pedagogical design, teacher orchestration, learner scaffolding, privacy-preserving governance, and emotional wellbeing. Technology can catalyze learning—but only if it is coordinated through robust human-centered systems.

Synthesis of Support Mechanisms and Theoretical Contributions: Across the chapter, four interlocking pillars have emerged as the practical logic of resilient adoption: teacher orchestration, spatial and cognitive scaffolding, ethical support and privacy-preserving governance, and emotional/social support:

- *First,* teacher orchestration through the Teacher-in-the-loop (HITL) philosophy reframes AI from replacement to augmentation. AI should support teachers by delegating routine administrative burdens while enabling teachers to retain responsibility for learning-critical judgement. However, HITL is not sustainable without interpretability, trust cultivation, and professional learning structures. Teachers need dashboards and workflow designs that provide explainable, actionable insights rather than opaque data streams. They also need training and Communities of Practice that reduce technostress and strengthen AI-readiness. In this sense, HITL is both a pedagogical model and a professional support requirement.

- *Second,* AR's educational promise depends on scaffolding that manages cognitive load. AR's spatial overlays can produce split-attention effects when learners must coordinate attention between physical tasks and digital information. Therefore, spatial scaffolding must be treated as instructional design: cues, progressive disclosure, guided exploration structures, and collaborative arrangements. The goal is to ensure that AR supports meaning-making rather than driving novelty-driven cognitive overload. Importantly, spatial scaffolding is not only the design of the AR interface; it requires teacher orchestration routines that coordinate pacing, attention distribution, and comprehension checks.
- *Third,* ethical support is not an "add-on" to implementation; it is a condition for legitimate learning. European frameworks and GDPR-centered governance create concrete requirements: privacy-preserving design for learning analytics, accountability in vendor procurement, transparency practices, and explainability-oriented integration. The chapter has highlighted the personalization–privacy paradox: systems require data to support adaptive learning, but learners' rights require data minimization and responsible processing. Ethical scaffolding therefore includes institutional governance and classroom-level routines that protect learner agency and enable teachers to justify AI use pedagogically rather than procedurally.
- *Fourth,* emotional and social support determines sustainability. Technostress affects teachers' willingness to adopt and persist with new practices, while AR immersion can unintentionally generate digital isolation. Resilient adoption thus requires wellbeing-aware professional development and social learning designs—such as collaborative smart learning tasks embedded into AR activities. When emotional and social needs are addressed, technology becomes a supportive medium rather than a stressor.

Together, these pillars form an integrated support ecosystem. The chapter's conceptual contribution is that these scaffolds should not be treated as unrelated constructs. Instead, they are best understood as instantiations of one integrated support logic: Hybrid Scaffolding, where algorithmic support is mediated by teacher judgement, cognitive sustainability is protected through spatial design, ethical governance constrains and legitimizes use, and emotional wellbeing stabilizes adoption over time.

The European Strategic Roadmap: From Pilots to Resilient Adoption

To foster a sustainable ecosystem for AI and AR, European higher education institutions and K–12 schools must shift from short-term pilots to resilient, policy-aligned implementation. The transition requires a strategic roadmap that prioritizes support capacity rather than novelty. Based on the chapter's synthesis, the roadmap includes the following priorities:

Ethical Procurement and Cross-Border Governance

Institutions must establish procurement and vendor accountability practices that ensure GDPR-aligned data handling and human-centric expectations. This includes clear documentation of what data systems use, how insights are produced, what transparency exists, and how teachers and learners can understand system limitations.

Hybrid Scaffolding Implementation in Classroom Design

Instructional design must combine algorithmic assistance with teacher-led pedagogical intervention. For AR, this means implementing spatial scaffolding strategies that prevent split-attention effects. For AI, it means aligning personalization and feedback with curricular goals and supporting learner agency rather than passive dependence.

Teacher Capacity Building through HITL and AI-Readiness

Professional development must support teachers to interpret AI-driven recommendations, understand explainability elements, and intervene when system outputs are uncertain or pedagogically insufficient. Training should be ongoing, context-aware, and supported by Communities of Practice to reduce technostress.

Privacy-Preserving Learning Analytics and Learner AI Literacy

Institutions must implement support tools that allow adaptive learning without compromising learner rights. At the same time, learners must receive AI literacy scaffolding so that they can interpret feedback critically and verify outputs when required.

Collaborative Smart Learning and Emotional Sustainability

AR experiences should be designed to support collaboration and shared meaning-making, reducing isolation risks. Teacher and learner wellbeing must be treated as implementation requirements, supported through social learning structures and supportive professional environments.

This roadmap reframes adoption as resilience-building. The most important "upgrade" is not a new interface or model—it is the development of human infrastructure that makes responsible, inclusive educational use possible.

Toward a Resilient and Sustainable Future

The ultimate goal is the creation of Resilient Education systems capable of adapting to rapid technological evolution without sacrificing human agency, ethical legitimacy, or learning quality. The cases and arguments presented in this chapter—from AR-enhanced STEM experiences to AI-mediated language learning and inclusive support contexts—demonstrate that technology can catalyze inclusion and excellence when support is prioritized. Yet the journey from experimental pilots to mainstream practice remains incomplete. Continued progress requires sustained investment in teacher preparation, institutional governance, learner agency scaffolding, and emotional/social learning design.

As Europe looks ahead, it is essential to remember that the value of AI and AR is mediated by human coordination. The algorithm or headset is not the educational outcome; rather, it is the structured orchestration of learning meaning, interpretation, accountability, and wellbeing that determines outcomes. If institutions maintain this focus, they can ensure that the technological push leads to inclusive and sustainable pedagogical progress rather than fragile or ethically problematic adoption.

Future Research Agenda: To advance the field beyond synthesis and conceptual modeling, future research should prioritize:

- Longitudinal impact studies evaluating how AI personalization affects motivation, critical thinking, and learner autonomy over time.
- Comparative regulatory implementation research examining how GDPR-centered governance and global regulatory differences shape classroom adoption and vendor responsibility.
- Teacher wellbeing and technostress measurement investigating whether HITL-supported professional development reduces burnout and improves sustainable practice.

- Student perspectives and agency outcomes incorporating learner voices to measure trust, reliance, and interpretive competence regarding AI-mediated feedback.

These directions align with the chapter's core premise: educational transformation requires evidence not only of technological effectiveness, but of support ecosystem efficacy.

Final Reflections

In conclusion, the integration of AI and AR in European education demands a holistic, dual-stakeholder approach anchored in resilient support systems. By focusing on the scaffolding ecosystem—teacher orchestration, spatial and cognitive support, ethical governance, and emotional sustainability—this chapter provides both conceptual and strategic grounding for how to build a sustainable digital future. As the education horizon extends toward 2030, success will depend on whether institutions empower teachers and learners to navigate AI-mediated and AR-enhanced learning environments with confidence, agency, and ethical discernment. The catalysts for change are already present in classrooms; it is the responsibility of educational systems to provide the support they need to thrive.

7. REFERENCES

Akçayır, M., & Akçayır, G. (2017). Advantages and challenges associated with augmented reality for education: A systematic review of the literature. *Educational Research Review*, *20*, 1–11. DOI: 10.1016/j.edurev.2016.11.002

Caena, F., & Redecker, C. (2019). Aligning teacher competence frameworks to 21st century challenges: The case for the European Digital Competence Framework for Educators (DigCompEdu). *European Journal of Education*, *54*(3), 356–369. DOI: 10.1111/ejed.12345

Chiu, T. K. F., Xia, Q., Zhou, X., Chai, C. S., & Cheng, M. (2023). Systematic literature review on opportunities, challenges, and future research directions of artificial intelligence in education. *Computers and Education: Artificial Intelligence*, *4*, 100118. DOI: 10.1016/j.caeai.2023.100118

European Commission. (2020). Digital Education Action Plan 2021–2027: Resetting education and training for the digital age. European Union. https://education.ec.europa.eu/focus-topics/digital-education/action-plan

European Commission. (2022). *Ethical guidelines on the use of artificial intelligence and data in teaching and learning for educators.* Publications Office of the European Union., DOI: 10.2766/153756

European Commission. (2024). The AI Act: First regulation on AI. European Parliament. https://www.europarl.europa.eu/news/en/headlines/society/20230601STO93804/eu-ai-act-first-regulation-on-artificial-intelligence

Haleem, A., Javaid, M., Qadri, M. A., & Suman, R. (2022). Understanding the role of digital technologies in education: A review. *Sustainable Operations and Computers*, *3*, 275–285. DOI: 10.1016/j.susoc.2022.05.004

Holstein, K., McLaren, B. M., & Aleven, V. (2019). Co-designing a real-time classroom orchestration tool for teachers. In *Proceedings of the 2019 CHI Conference on Human Factors in Computing Systems* (pp. 1–12). DOI: 10.1145/3290605.3300828

Ibáñez, M. B., & Delgado-Kloos, C. (2018). Augmented reality for STEM learning: A systematic review. *Computers & Education*, *123*, 109–123. DOI: 10.1016/j.compedu.2018.05.002

Ifenthaler, D., & Schumacher, C. (2023). Reciprocal relationship between learning analytics and personalized learning. *Journal of Computing in Higher Education*, *35*(1), 1–15. DOI: 10.1007/s12528-022-09343-w PMID: 36714821

Karasavvidis, I. (2022). Augmented reality in the classroom: A study of teacher adoption and implementation barriers. *Journal of Educational Computing Research, 60*(3), 720–745. DOI: 10.1177/07356331211045231

Köhler, T., & Münster, S. (2021). Digital transformation of higher education in Europe: A review of current strategies and practices. European Journal of Higher Education, 11(Sup1), 211–228. https://doi.org/DOI: 10.1080/21568235.2021.1944410

Luckin, R., & Holmes, W. (2016). *Intelligence unleased: An argument for AI in education*. Pearson Education.

Molenaar, I. (2022). Towards hybrid human-AI learning: Technologies to support appropriate student and teacher agency. *Computers and Education: Artificial Intelligence, 3*, 100054. DOI: 10.1016/j.caeai.2022.100054

Nazaretsky, T., Ariely, M., Itzhak, H., & Alexandron, G. (2022). Exploring teacher trust in AI-based educational technology. *Scientific Reports, 12*(1), 18567. DOI: 10.1038/s41598-022-22611-z PMID: 36329160

Ouyang, F., & Jiao, P. (2021). Artificial intelligence in education: The three paradigms. *Computers and Education: Artificial Intelligence, 2*, 100020. DOI: 10.1016/j.caeai.2021.100020

Parmaxi, A., & Demetriou, A. A. (2020). Augmented reality in language learning: A state-of-the-art review of 2014–2019. *Interactive Learning Environments, 28*(6), 686–700. DOI: 10.1080/10494820.2020.1712429

Pellas, N., Kazanidis, I., & Palaigeorgiou, G. (2020). A systematic literature review of mixed reality in K-12 education: A 10-year complementary study of benefits, challenges, and instructional strategies. *IEEE Access : Practical Innovations, Open Solutions, 8*, 37385–37405. DOI: 10.1109/ACCESS.2020.2975608

Radianti, J., Majchrzak, T. A., Fromm, J., & Wohlgenannt, I. (2020). A systematic review of immersive virtual reality applications for higher education: Design elements, challenges, and future avenues. *Information & Management, 57*(1), 103183. DOI: 10.1016/j.im.2019.103183

Redecker, C. (2017). European Framework for the Digital Competence of Educators: DigCompEdu (Pun. Y., Ed.). Publications Office of the European Union. DOI: 10.2760/159770

Ruiz-Ariza, A., Casuso, R. A., Suarez-Manzano, S., & Martínez-López, E. J. (2018). Effect of augmented reality game Pokémon GO on cognitive performance and emotional intelligence in adolescent students. *Computers & Education, 116*, 49–63. DOI: 10.1016/j.compedu.2017.09.002

Saltan, F., & Arslan, Ö. (2017). A comparison of in-service and pre-service teachers' technological pedagogical content knowledge regarding self-efficacy for using augmented reality in education. *Contemporary Educational Technology*, *8*(3), 203–217. DOI: 10.30935/cedtech/6198

Selwyn, N. (2019). *Should robots replace teachers? AI and the future of education*. Polity Press.

UNESCO. (2021). AI and education: Guidance for policy-makers. United Nations Educational, Scientific and Cultural Organization. https://unesdoc.unesco.org/ark:/48223/pf0000376709

UNESCO. (2023). Guidance for generative AI in education and research. United Nations Educational, Scientific and Cultural Organization. https://unesdoc.unesco.org/ark:/48223/pf0000386693

Zawacki-Richter, O., Marín, V. I., Bond, M., & Gouverneur, F. (2019). Systematic review of research on artificial intelligence applications in higher education – where are the educators? *International Journal of Educational Technology in Higher Education*, *16*(1), 39. DOI: 10.1186/s41239-019-0171-0

Chapter 9

Personalized Learning and Teacher Assistance Using AI and AR: A European Perspective

Deepak Gupta
http://orcid.org/0000-0003-3929-1362
Institute of Technology and Management, Gwalior, India

ABSTRACT

This chapter examines how artificial intelligence and augmented reality are reshaping classrooms and teaching practices across Europe. Drawing on peer-reviewed studies published between 2018 and 2026, it analyses applications including personalised learning systems, learning analytics, AI chatbots, generative tools, and AR-enhanced environments, along with the professional development required for effective use. A four-layer convergent framework—data collection, AI processing, AR environment, and personalised output—is presented to explain how these technologies interact. The chapter also addresses unresolved challenges, including digital equity, uneven GDPR compliance, limited teacher preparation, and assessment practices disrupted by generative AI. It concludes with recommendations for institutional leaders, educators, curriculum designers, and policy makers.

1. INTRODUCTION

Walk into a classroom in Warsaw, in Seville, or in Turku, and you will find teachers wrestling with a version of the same fundamental tension: the tools available to them are, in many respects, more powerful than anything their professional

DOI: 10.4018/979-8-3373-9883-9.ch009

training prepared them for, yet the conditions in which they work—the class sizes, the timetables, the accountability structures—haven't changed nearly as much as the rhetoric surrounding digital education would suggest. Artificial intelligence and augmented reality sit squarely in the middle of this tension. Both technologies have been the subject of substantial investment, considerable hype, and genuinely impressive research findings over the past decade. Neither has become routine in European schools and universities in the way that, say, the interactive whiteboard once threatened to. Understanding why—and what it would take to change that—is one of the motivating questions behind this chapter.

The European Commission's Digital Education Action Plan (2021–2027) provides the formal policy frame. Its language about harnessing digital technologies for learning is unambiguous, and its commitments to equity and inclusion are well-intentioned. Holmes and Tuomi (2022) place this ambition in historical context, noting that the lineage of intelligent tutoring systems extends back to the 1970s—long before 'AI in education' became a funding priority—but that something genuinely different happened when mobile devices, cloud infrastructure, and modern machine learning converged in the 2010s. For the first time, adaptive and personalised learning tools became feasible at institutional scale, not just in research laboratories. Molenaar (2022) draws out the pedagogical implications of this shift with particular clarity, arguing that the teacher's role is being repositioned—not eliminated, but substantially transformed—from someone who transmits knowledge to someone who orchestrates learning environments that happen to include intelligent systems.

That repositioning is not painless. Nguyen et al. (2023) document several of the ethical fracture lines that run through this transformation: algorithmic bias that reproduces existing inequalities, privacy erosion when learner data is collected without meaningful consent, and the risk that automation amplifies rather than corrects the structural disadvantages facing learners from less privileged backgrounds. Christ-Brendemühl (2025) captures the confusion that large language models specifically have created in European universities, where institutional responses range from blanket prohibition to cautious embrace, and where the pedagogical reasoning behind either stance is often underdeveloped. Meanwhile, Kasinidou et al. (2025) found—surveying teachers in Cyprus, whose situation reflects broader European patterns—that the gap is not primarily about motivation. Most teachers want to engage with AI. The problem is that their initial training didn't give them the conceptual vocabulary to do so critically, and continuing professional development has rarely picked up the slack.

This chapter is organised into nine sections. Section 2 addresses the theoretical grounding of personalised learning and its relationship to AI. Section 3 examines what the evidence actually shows about AR in European educational contexts. Section 4 looks at AI tools from the teacher's perspective—both as learning subject and as professional support. Section 5 presents the four-layer convergent framework. Section 6 surveys the AI and AR technology landscape comparatively, supported by Table 1 and Figure 3. Sections 7 and 8 tackle the harder questions about ethics, equity, governance, and what policy and practice changes are genuinely needed. Section 9 concludes.

2. PERSONALISED LEARNING AND ARTIFICIAL INTELLIGENCE: THEORETICAL FOUNDATIONS

2.1 What Personalised Learning Actually Means—and Doesn't Mean

Few phrases in contemporary education policy carry more weight while meaning less precisely than 'personalised learning.' It functions, often, as an all-purpose endorsement of learner-centredness—a signal that whoever is speaking takes individual differences seriously. When pressed for operational definition, however, the concept requires more careful handling. Personalised learning refers, at minimum, to instructional arrangements in which the content, pace, sequencing, and support offered to a learner are determined by that learner's own characteristics and history rather than by the assumed needs of an average pupil. The intellectual roots of that aspiration reach back through Bloom's mastery learning studies of the 1960s and 1970s, through Vygotsky's insistence that learning is most productive at the edge of a learner's current competence, and through decades of work on self-regulated learning that has consistently shown how much learners vary in their metacognitive capacity and their strategies for managing difficulty.

What AI brings to this old aspiration is computational scale. Bayly-Castaneda et al. (2024), in a systematic review of AI-powered personalised learning specifically for lifelong learning contexts, identify three interlocking mechanisms: learner modelling, which builds a dynamic computational representation of what an individual knows and can do; curriculum sequencing, which determines how content should be ordered and paced for that individual; and feedback generation, which closes the loop between learner action and instructional response. Fernandes et al. (2023) add a caveat that deserves emphasis: every one of these mechanisms is only as good as the data that feeds it and the design assumptions embedded in the algorithm. There is no magic here—a learner model built on log data from a particular platform will reflect the implicit theory of learning built into that platform, and if that theory is narrow, the personalisation will be narrow too.

The European policy frame adds specific urgency to this conversation. Both the European Pillar of Social Rights and the Pact for Skills treat continuous learning throughout working life not as an optional add-on but as an economic and social necessity in an era when technological change is rendering skill sets obsolete faster than traditional qualification cycles can accommodate. Bayly-Castaneda et al. (2024) argue that AI-powered personalisation is probably the only mechanism capable of delivering genuinely individualised continuing education at the scale that European labour market transformation demands. That is a strong claim, and one worth scrutinising—but it also reflects an honest assessment of the limits of what human tutoring can achieve when the learner population runs to tens of millions and the timeline is urgent.

2.2 The Range of AI in European Classrooms

European schools and universities aren't deploying one type of AI—they're encountering a heterogeneous cluster of technologies that share a label but differ substantially in how they work and what they can do. At one end sit relatively simple rule-based systems: decision trees that route learners through branching content depending on their quiz performance, or keyword-matching chatbots that handle frequently asked administrative questions. At the other end sit deep learning architectures capable of modelling nuanced patterns in learner behaviour over time, and large language models that can generate extended explanatory text, translate across European languages, and sustain open-ended academic conversation. The practical implications of these differences are considerable. A rule-based chatbot will handle a question it was designed for well and fail transparently when it encounters something unexpected; an LLM will handle unexpected questions fluently and may fail in ways that are much harder to detect.

Generative AI—meaning tools built on large language models—has moved to the centre of this conversation with remarkable speed. Jauhiainen and Garagorry Guerra (2024) demonstrated that ChatGPT-based systems can produce school learning materials that are linguistically appropriate, conceptually scaffolded to individual pupil profiles, and available at a speed and cost that individual teachers cannot replicate. Consider what that means practically: a teacher in a Slovak school managing a class that includes native Czech, Hungarian, and Slovak speakers at different curricular attainment levels can, in principle, produce differentiated materials in all three languages within the time it previously took to photocopy a single worksheet. This is a qualitative shift in what personalised instruction is practically possible—not merely an efficiency gain, though it is certainly that too.

The empirical record is more cautious than the promotional literature. Copur-Gencturk et al. (2024) ran a randomised controlled trial of a personalised computer-based professional development programme and found measurable improvements in both teacher competence and downstream student performance—solid, controlled evidence for the cascade effect of AI-supported teacher learning. Arztmann et al. (2024), examining in-game learning performance in an AR context, found that socio-economic status and self-efficacy moderated outcomes significantly even when device access was equalised. That second finding matters because it complicates the first: AI personalisation can shift average outcomes, but without attention to the conditions that shape how learners engage with technology in the first place, it tends to benefit those who were already better positioned.

2.3 Learning Analytics: Evidence-Rich Pedagogy and Its Complications

Learning analytics has become one of the most discussed applications of data science in European higher education—and one of the most contentious. Aldowah et al. (2019) surveyed the landscape comprehensively, identifying five application clusters: predicting student performance, analysing learning behaviour, personalising feedback, optimising curriculum design, and allocating institutional resources. The breadth of that list hints at both the promise and the problem: learning analytics is being asked to do a great many different things simultaneously, and the quality of the evidence supporting each application varies considerably.

Early alert and dropout prediction have attracted the most sustained policy attention, for understandable reasons. Widening participation agendas across European higher education have expanded access substantially, bringing into universities student populations whose engagement patterns and support needs differ from the traditional cohort. When a dashboard flags a student who has stopped logging in, stopped submitting work, and stopped attending contact sessions, it creates the possibility of intervention at a point when something can still be done—rather than at the point of withdrawal or failure, when it's too late. The challenge Aldowah et al. (2019) identify is that 'early alert' systems are only useful if they are accurate enough that the alerts mean something, transparent enough that staff trust them, and embedded in workflows that make acting on them practically feasible.

There's a subtler problem with learning analytics that doesn't get discussed enough: the gap between what these systems can measure and what actually matters in education. Time on task, click frequency, submission timestamps, quiz scores—these are recordable because they happen in the platform. Intellectual curiosity, productive confusion, the capacity to sit with a genuinely hard problem without giving up prematurely—these are not recordable in the same way, and systems that optimise for proxy measures risk gradually reshaping what teachers and institutions treat as evidence of learning. Tammets and Ley (2023) are careful about this in their model of AI tools for teacher professional learning: the value of the data depends entirely on the quality of the human interpretation brought to it. A dashboard that flags risk is not a decision; it is an input to a decision that a teacher makes.

Learning analytics also creates knowledge asymmetries worth taking seriously. Institutions accumulate detailed behavioural portraits of their students; students rarely know what picture is being built, on what basis, or how it is being used. Addressing this imbalance—through learner-facing dashboards, meaningful explanation of how flags are generated, and genuine mechanisms for students to query or contest automated recommendations—is both ethically necessary and, under Article 22 of the GDPR, increasingly a legal obligation. European institutions that approach data transparency as a genuine value rather than a compliance nuisance will find it easier to build the kind of trust that makes learning analytics worth doing in the first place.

3. AUGMENTED REALITY IN EUROPEAN EDUCATIONAL SETTINGS: APPLICATIONS AND EVIDENCE

3.1 What AR Does That Other Technologies Don't

The distinction between augmented reality and virtual reality is not merely technical—it has real pedagogical consequences. Virtual reality immerses learners in a digitally constructed world and, in doing so, severs them from their immediate physical and social context. AR does the opposite: it layers digital content onto the physical world without replacing it. That sounds like a small difference, but in practice it means that AR can be used in shared classrooms without requiring learners to disappear into private headsets. Two students examining the same AR molecular model overlaid on a laboratory bench can talk to each other, point at what they see, argue about it, and build shared understanding in ways that are much harder to arrange when each learner is isolated in their own virtual environment. Zekeik et al. (2025) make this point explicitly in their systematic review, concluding that AR's compatibility with collaborative and situated learning tasks is one of its most significant advantages over fully immersive VR—particularly in the social learning environments that characterise European primary and secondary education.

The research literature has documented three main typologies of educational AR. Marker-based systems are the most common: a smartphone or tablet camera recognises a visual trigger—a QR code, an image, a printed symbol—and overlays digital content on whatever the device is pointed at. These systems are cheap to deploy, require no specialist hardware, and work on devices many learners already own. Location-based AR uses GPS to connect digital content to specific physical places—useful for outdoor learning, heritage education, and geography fieldwork in contexts ranging from archaeology sites in Greece to urban ecology studies in

Rotterdam. Projection-based AR maps digital content onto physical surfaces and objects using depth sensors, and while more expensive, enables whole-class engagement with shared augmented environments. Singh et al. (2024), analysing a decade of AR research bibliometrically, confirmed that STEM education, language learning, and special education dominate the application literature, with European institutions—particularly in Spain, Germany, the UK, and the Netherlands—contributing a substantial share of the published evidence base.

3.2 Engagement, Digital Literacy, and the Limits of What We Know

Across the European AR literature, findings on learner engagement are remarkably consistent: AR-enhanced lessons tend to produce higher reported motivation and stronger situational interest than their conventional equivalents. Nevrelova et al. (2024) documented this in a Slovak primary school digital literacy programme, where the shift to AR-based instruction reduced the technology anxiety that many younger pupils brought to computing tasks and produced measurable improvements in their capacity to interact critically with digital information and create their own content. What was particularly striking in their findings was that attainment level didn't predict who benefited—the engagement gains appeared across the ability range, suggesting that AR's motivational effects aren't just a phenomenon for high-achieving pupils who would engage with almost anything.

The three-dimensional visualisation that AR affords matters especially in science and mathematics, where so many foundational concepts resist adequate representation in two dimensions. A chemistry student in Bratislava who can pick up and rotate a representation of a covalent bond overlaid on her bench encounters the concept quite differently from a student reading about it in a textbook or watching an animation on a screen. A civil engineering student in Madrid who can walk through a scaled structural model overlaid on an empty building site develops spatial reasoning that no drawing exercise produces with equivalent depth. These aren't peripheral benefits—they address a real limitation of traditional science and mathematics teaching. Arztmann et al. (2024) found that AR game-based learning produced significantly higher situational interest than conventional instruction, though their equally important finding—that socio-economic background moderated how much students benefited—will be taken up again in Section 7.

AR also offers something that tends to get underplayed in individual cognition-focused studies: genuine support for collaborative learning. Because AR operates in shared physical space rather than inside individual screens, it enables groups of learners to interact simultaneously with the same overlaid content—pointing, debating, co-constructing meaning around a shared augmented object. This fits well with the sociocultural learning traditions that have long emphasised knowledge as a social achievement rather than an individual accumulation. European classrooms that bring together learners from different language backgrounds, different levels of prior knowledge, and different cultural reference points have particular reason to value technologies that create shared objects for joint attention and collaborative interpretation.

That said—and this needs saying honestly—the evidence on whether AR-produced engagement translates into durable learning and genuine skill transfer is thinner than the engagement data alone would suggest. Singh et al. (2024) noted that bibliometric analysis of AR in education reveals a heavy concentration on short-term engagement and immediate recall measures rather than on retention over weeks or months, or on the transfer of understanding to novel problems. This doesn't invalidate AR's educational value, but it does counsel against overclaiming. Deploying AR purposefully, measuring whether it actually produces the learning gains it's expected to produce in a given context, and reporting findings honestly—including when AR doesn't outperform well-designed conventional instruction—is what responsible adoption looks like.

Figure 1. Four-Layer Convergent Framework for AI-Powered Personalised Learning.

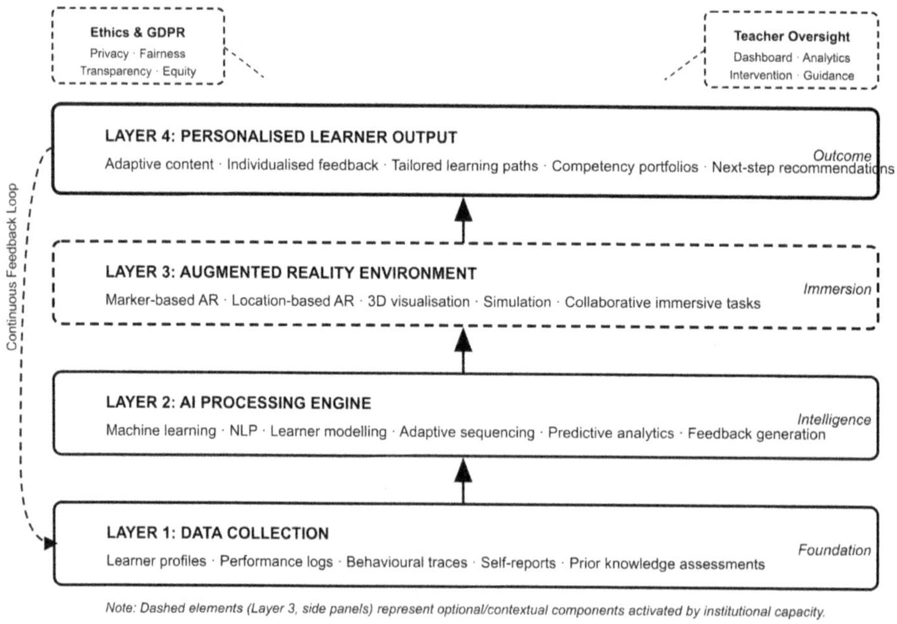

Figure 1 shows the sequential relationship between data collection (Layer 1), AI processing (Layer 2), the AR learning environment (Layer 3), and personalised learner output (Layer 4), with continuous feedback loops and ethical governance overlays spanning all layers.

3.3 AR, Special Educational Needs, and the Inclusion Imperative

Perhaps the most compelling strand of European AR research concerns learners with special educational needs—and it is also the strand where the gap between research evidence and routine practice is most glaring. Kultan et al. (2025) examined AR-based digital literacy instruction for primary school children with SEN in Slovakia and found not only higher engagement but improved knowledge retention and greater task persistence compared to conventional instruction. The explanation that emerges from their analysis is intuitive once stated: AR's simultaneous engagement of visual, auditory, and kinaesthetic channels provides natural scaffolding for learners whose cognitive profiles don't fit the assumptions of text-heavy, print-centred pedagogy. A learner with dyslexia who struggles with printed instructions may navigate an AR task fluently; a learner with an autism spectrum condition who finds unstructured social interaction difficult may engage with a shared AR object as a productive mediator of peer collaboration.

The accessibility barriers that Creed et al. (2023) identify in their review are, however, real and not trivial. Six categories of challenge—visual impairment, hearing impairment, motor impairment, elevated cognitive load, socio-economic constraints, and technical complexity—remind us that AR is not universally accessible by default, and that designing it to be so requires deliberate effort. Their core argument, which deserves to be taken seriously by European EdTech developers, is that accessibility shouldn't be retrofitted: it needs to be designed in from the beginning. When a development team assumes that its default user is a non-disabled young adult with a modern smartphone and reliable home broadband, accessibility features will always come too late, cost too much, and work imperfectly. The inversion of that assumption—starting from the most constrained user and designing outward—tends to produce experiences that work better for everyone.

The teacher dimension of SEN-inclusive AR is also worth attention. Even well-designed accessible AR tools will underserve learners with disabilities if the teachers deploying them haven't been prepared to use them with pedagogical intentionality. Configuring accessibility features appropriately for a specific learner's profile, adapting tasks on the fly as a session unfolds, evaluating honestly whether AR is genuinely helping a particular pupil or just occupying them differently—these capacities require sustained professional development, specialist mentoring, and ongoing reflective practice. They cannot be acquired in a single training session. The five-stage professional development model illustrated in Figure 2 offers a framework within which this kind of embedded, iterative competence development can be organised and sustained.

4. ARTIFICIAL INTELLIGENCE TOOLS FOR TEACHER ASSISTANCE AND PROFESSIONAL DEVELOPMENT

4.1 The Teacher Anxiety That Nobody's Naming Directly

There's an anxiety circulating among European teachers that doesn't often surface in official discourse, because naming it too directly tends to seem defensive or technophobic. It goes something like this: if an AI can answer students' questions, adapt content to their needs, monitor their progress, and flag risks to their engagement—what exactly is left for me to do? The research literature is fairly clear that this anxiety misreads what the technology can and cannot accomplish. But dismissing the anxiety doesn't help. It reflects something real about how AI is sometimes presented by enthusiasts—as a solution to problems that teachers are implicitly part of—and addressing it honestly is a precondition for the kind of professional engagement with AI tools that productive adoption requires.

Molenaar (2022) offers probably the most useful reframing: the teacher is not being replaced but repositioned, from the person who holds and transmits knowledge to the person who orchestrates an intelligent learning environment. That repositioning is not a diminishment—it may actually require more sophisticated professional judgement than conventional didactic teaching, because it demands the capacity to interpret algorithmic outputs critically, to identify where the AI is wrong or where its recommendation doesn't fit the particular learner in front of you, and to make relational and ethical decisions that no algorithm is structured to make. Mikeladze et al. (2024) reviewed AI competence frameworks for educators across EU member states and found emerging consensus around five core competency domains: understanding how AI systems work at a conceptual level; evaluating AI outputs sceptically rather than accepting them at face value; integrating AI tools within coherent pedagogical frameworks; protecting learner data and maintaining privacy; and developing students' own capacity to use and critique AI. None of those competencies is trivial, and none of them is currently well-served by most European teacher education programmes.

Sperling et al. (2024), whose scoping review of AI literacy in teacher education is probably the most thorough currently available for the European context, found exactly what one might expect given the above: a persistent and uncomfortable gap between the ambitious AI literacy objectives that policy documents articulate and the concrete, practice-oriented training models that teacher educators can actually access and deliver. Kasinidou et al. (2025) found that the problem isn't primarily attitudinal—most Cypriot teachers surveyed held positive orientations towards AI in education, reflecting patterns documented elsewhere in Europe. The problem is structural: teacher education systems have not been redesigned around the competencies that AI integration actually requires, and continuing professional development has not scaled to fill the gap.

4.2 AI as Both the Subject and the Instrument of Professional Learning

There's something genuinely interesting about AI's dual role in teacher professional development—interesting, and also somewhat vertiginous if you think about it too carefully. Teachers need to learn about AI; and AI can be one of the means by which they learn. Tammets and Ley (2023) work through this dual role carefully in their conceptual model, drawing on an illustrative case to show how AI tools can support personalised professional learning trajectories for educators: surfacing patterns in teaching practice through classroom observation data, generating targeted developmental resources matched to individual teachers' identified needs, and facilitating structured reflection through visualised analytics. Their crucial point is that the AI assistance in this model is situated within a broader human ecology—peer collaboration, mentoring relationships, engagement with research—rather than substituting for it. AI that generates professional development recommendations is only as useful as the human conversation it stimulates.

Khalid et al. (2026), whose systematic review of AI-integrated professional development for pre-service teachers represents the most recent and methodologically rigorous synthesis in this area, found that well-designed AI-integrated PD programmes did meaningfully improve pre-service teachers' technological self-efficacy and expanded their pedagogical strategy repertoire. The qualification is important, though: effects were strongest when AI tools were embedded in reflective practice frameworks rather than used as standalone information delivery systems. Data about teaching practice generated by AI is most valuable when it becomes the starting point for a conversation between a teacher and a mentor—when it opens a reflective space—rather than when it produces an automated performance rating that the teacher receives passively. This distinction has direct implications for how professional development programmes are designed, and for how institutions should think about what AI tools are for in the CPD context.

Figure 2. AR-Enhanced Teacher Professional Development: A Five-Stage Progression Model

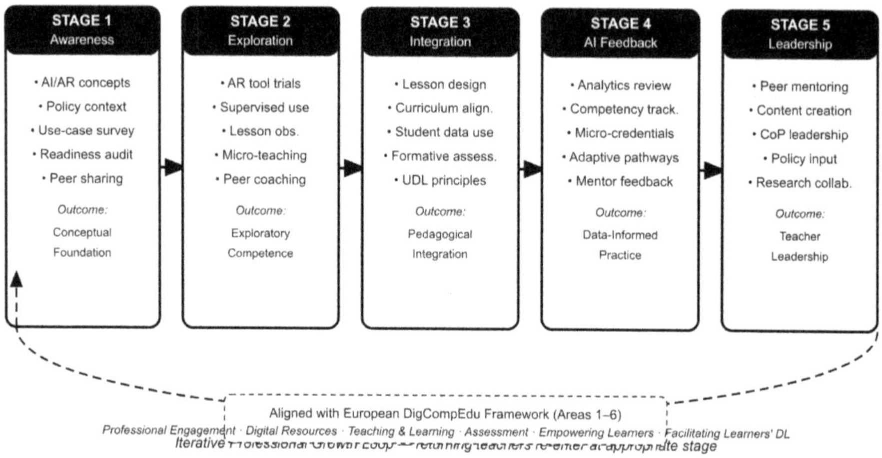

Figure 2 maps the five-stage AR-enhanced teacher professional development model proposed in this chapter. The model runs from Awareness through Exploration, Integration, AI Feedback, and Leadership, and includes an iterative re-entry loop aligned with the European DigCompEdu framework.

4.3 Chatbots, LLMs, and the Learner-Facing AI Dimension

Institutional discourse on AI in education tends to concentrate on what happens at the level of the system—analytics dashboards, adaptive curricula, strategic data use—rather than on what learners themselves encounter directly. That's an odd blind spot, given that the AI tools most European students interact with most often are chatbots and, increasingly, large language model-based conversational systems. Okonkwo and Ade-Ibijola (2021) documented the range of chatbot applications in education across tutoring, administrative support, emotional scaffolding, and student services, noting that the quality of these deployments varies enormously: from genuinely useful tools that handle common queries competently and free staff time for more complex work, to frustrating dead ends that send students in circles and ultimately make them more likely to email a person.

Winkler and Söllner (2018) made an early and still relevant case for chatbots as equity tools—as a way of extending educational support access to learners who, for financial or logistical reasons, can't readily access a human tutor. Part-time students managing work and family alongside study. Distance learners in rural areas where institutional support services are a long drive away. First-generation university students who don't yet have the cultural capital to know when and how to seek help from a lecturer. For these learners, a competently designed chatbot that can answer a question at eleven o'clock on a Sunday night is not a diminished substitute for human support—it's support that would otherwise simply not have been available. The issue, as both Winkler and Söllner and Okonkwo and Ade-Ibijola note, is that 'competently designed' is doing a lot of work in that sentence. Poorly designed chatbots are not neutral—they waste learner time and erode trust.

European contexts present a specific challenge that has received insufficient attention: linguistic diversity. The commercial educational chatbots that dominate the market were built primarily for English-language interaction. Their performance in Polish, Greek, Estonian, or Catalan tends to be noticeably weaker—slower, less accurate, less sensitive to disciplinary conventions and rhetorical norms that differ across language communities. This is not a trivial quality issue; it's an equity issue. Learners whose home language is not English are being offered systematically inferior AI support tools, which is precisely the opposite of what personalised learning is supposed to accomplish. Building genuinely multilingual educational AI—not translation-layer solutions, but tools trained on high-quality pedagogical corpora in multiple European languages—is an urgent research and infrastructure priority that European institutions and the European Commission should be taking far more seriously.

Large language models have added both capability and complication to this picture. Jauhiainen and Garagorry Guerra (2024) showed that GPT-based systems can produce differentiated learning materials at a speed and specificity that individual teachers cannot replicate, and that these materials are sufficiently well-calibrated to learner profiles to be genuinely pedagogically useful. The same systems, however, confabulate—generating fluent, confident text that is factually wrong—with a consistency that is particularly alarming in educational contexts where learners may not have the domain knowledge to identify the error. European institutions deploying LLM chatbots in any capacity that involves substantive academic content bear a responsibility to build learner education about these limitations into their deployment, to maintain human review processes for high-stakes content, and to monitor accuracy actively rather than assuming competence.

5. A FOUR-LAYER CONVERGENT AI-AR FRAMEWORK FOR EUROPEAN EDUCATION

The preceding sections have treated AI and AR mostly as distinct topics, which is how the research literature tends to organise them. In practice, their real educational power lies in what happens when they work together—when AI's capacity for data-driven, individualised adaptation is combined with AR's capacity for spatially situated, immersive experience. This section proposes a four-layer convergent framework as a model for thinking through and implementing that integration in a principled way. The framework is illustrated in Figure 1 (see above, Section 3).

Layer 1 is data collection—the foundation on which everything else depends. AI personalisation systems need learner data: performance records, engagement patterns, prior knowledge assessments, self-reported preferences and goals. The quality and granularity of this data layer sets the ceiling on what any AI processing system built on top of it can accomplish. European institutions approaching this layer responsibly must design their data collection architectures in compliance with GDPR from the outset—not retrofitting compliance after the system is built. That means minimum necessary collection, clear and specific purpose limitation, meaningful consent processes that learners can actually understand, robust anonymisation, and retention periods that are justified rather than indefinite.

Layer 2 is AI processing—the algorithmic engine that transforms data into actionable pedagogical intelligence. Machine learning models build and update learner profiles; recommendation systems generate content sequencing proposals; NLP systems power the conversational interfaces through which many learners experience AI directly. The human teacher is not peripheral to this layer—the teacher is the essential interpreter and quality-control mechanism for everything it produces. An AI flag indicating that a student is at risk of disengagement is a prompt for human attention, not a directive. A content recommendation is a suggestion, not a prescription. Systems that obscure this distinction—that present algorithmic outputs as conclusions rather than inputs—undermine the professional judgement that responsible AI-assisted teaching requires.

Layer 3 is the AR environment—the experiential dimension of the framework. When institutional capacity, pedagogical intent, and content characteristics align, AR transforms the personalised content generated by the AI layer into spatially situated, interactive learning experiences that deepen conceptual understanding and sustain motivation in ways that screen-based delivery cannot. A student whose AI-generated learning profile has identified a persistent gap in spatial geometry reasoning engages with an AR visualisation that makes three-dimensional relationships literally manipulable. A student whose profile indicates high kinaesthetic learning preference and low print literacy receives content primarily through AR-mediated physical interaction rather than text. This layer is marked as optional in the framework—not because it's unimportant, but because not all content or all institutional contexts warrant or can support AR deployment. Pedagogical judgement about when AR adds genuine value matters more than consistent AR use.

Layer 4 is personalised learner output—the concrete educational outcomes that the integrated system produces: adaptive content, individualised feedback, tailored learning paths, competency portfolios, and the communications to teachers, parents, and institutional administrators that make progress visible across the full stakeholder ecosystem. Two cross-cutting elements complete the framework. A continuous feedback loop uses outcome data from Layer 4 to refine the learner models in Layer 1 and improve the quality of AI processing in Layer 2—making the system progressively more useful as it accumulates evidence about what works for whom. And an ethics and governance overlay spans all four layers, encompassing GDPR compliance, algorithmic transparency, equity monitoring, and the institutional commitment to human oversight that both good pedagogy and European law require.

6. COMPARATIVE OVERVIEW OF AI AND AR TOOLS IN EUROPEAN EDUCATIONAL CONTEXTS

Table 1 organises the principal AI and AR technologies discussed in previous sections by application domain, the key evidence supporting each, and the European institutional contexts in which each has been deployed or studied. It is offered as a practical reference point rather than an exhaustive catalogue—the technology landscape is moving fast enough that any catalogue would be partial before it was finished.

Table 1. Summary of AI and AR Educational Technologies: Applications, Evidence, and European Implementation Contexts

Technology	Primary Application	Key Evidence / Study	European Implementation Notes
Adaptive Learning Systems (AI-ML)	Personalised content sequencing; mastery-based progression	Copur-Gencturk et al. (2024) – RCT on personalised teacher PD; positive student performance gains	Netherlands, Germany, Finland HEIs; Moodle-integrated adaptive plugins
AI Chatbots & NLP Tutors	24/7 learner support; formative Q&A; administrative queries	Okonkwo & Ade-Ibijola (2021); Winkler & Söllner (2018) – systematic reviews	Deployed in language learning programmes across UK, Spain, and Portugal universities
Generative AI (LLMs/ChatGPT)	Dynamic creation of differentiated learning materials and assessments	Jauhiainen & Garagorry Guerra (2024) – personalised pupil materials via ChatGPT	University guidelines vary widely: prohibition to full integration (Christ-Brendemühl, 2025)
Learning Analytics Platforms	Early warning systems; dropout prediction; cohort-level monitoring	Aldowah et al. (2019) – comprehensive higher education EDM review	Bologna Process aligned analytics dashboards in Nordic and Baltic HEIs

continued on following page

Table 1. Continued

Technology	Primary Application	Key Evidence / Study	European Implementation Notes
Marker-Based AR (Mobile)	STEM visualisation; vocabulary acquisition; historical reconstruction	Nevrelova et al. (2024) – Slovak primary digital literacy study	Primary schools in Slovakia, Czech Republic; secondary STEM in Netherlands
Location-Based AR	Outdoor/field learning; geography; cultural heritage education	Singh et al. (2024) – bibliometric analysis confirming STEM dominance	Heritage and museum-based AR trails in France, Italy, and Greece
AR for Special Educational Needs	Multisensory scaffolding for learners with dyslexia, ASD, ADHD	Kultan et al. (2025) – AR digital literacy for SEN primary pupils in Slovakia	SEN schools in Slovakia; accessibility-centred AR prototypes (Creed et al., 2023)
AI-Integrated Teacher PD	Personalised CPD pathways; reflective analytics; micro-credentials	Khalid et al. (2026); Tammets & Ley (2023) – conceptual model and case study	DigCompEdu-aligned PD programmes across Erasmus+ participating institutions

Figure 3. Comparative Institutional Adoption Rates of AI and AR Technologies: European Higher Education vs Global Average (2019–2024)

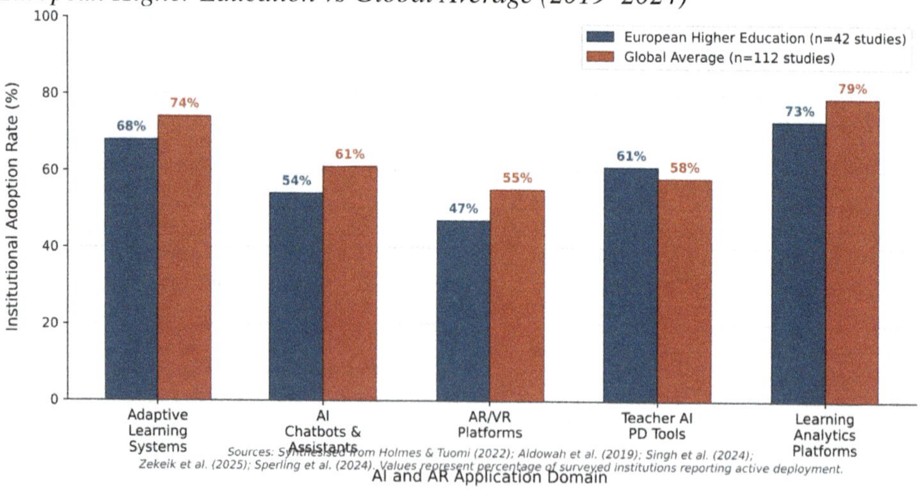

Figure 3 presents comparative data on institutional adoption rates across five AI and AR application domains, contrasting European higher education with global averages synthesised from Holmes & Tuomi (2022), Aldowah et al. (2019), Singh et al. (2024), and Zekeik et al. (2025). Note that European institutions report higher adoption of learning analytics platforms than the global average, while AR/VR platform adoption lags behind—a gap with direct implications for the strategic investment priorities discussed in Sections 7 and 8.

7. ETHICAL, EQUITY, AND GOVERNANCE CONSIDERATIONS

7.1 Why Ethics Isn't a Section You Can Leave to the End

There is a tendency in technology-in-education writing to treat ethics as the responsible concluding gesture—the section that acknowledges concerns before returning to enthusiastic description of what the technology can do. This chapter is trying to resist that tendency, because the ethical questions aren't separate from the technical and pedagogical ones; they're woven through them. Nguyen et al. (2023) offer the most systematic treatment of AI ethics in education in the European-relevant literature, organising their framework around five principles: transparency, accountability, fairness, non-maleficence, and human oversight. Each principle has concrete implications that bear on design choices, institutional governance, and pedagogical practice.

Transparency means that learners and teachers need to be able to understand, in terms that make sense to them, how an AI system has reached a particular recommendation or output. Not the source code—but a meaningful explanation of the kind of evidence and reasoning the system used. Accountability means that someone—a person, not an algorithm—is responsible for what AI outputs lead to in educational practice. The phrase 'the algorithm decided' cannot be an acceptable account of why a student was streamed into a particular curriculum pathway or given a particular risk classification. Fairness means ongoing empirical monitoring of whether AI systems are producing systematically different outcomes for different groups of learners—by gender, by ethnicity, by socio-economic background, by first language. Non-maleficence means that institutions conduct genuine risk assessment before deploying AI in high-stakes educational contexts rather than assuming that well-intentioned deployment is risk-free. And human oversight means that educators retain genuine decision-making authority rather than becoming the human interface through which algorithmic outputs are implemented without scrutiny.

The European regulatory environment provides some structural support for these principles, though implementation remains uneven. The GDPR established foundational data protection requirements. The EU AI Act, which came into force in 2024, classifies AI systems used in educational and vocational training contexts as high-risk, imposing additional requirements for transparency, robustness, and human oversight. Christ-Brendemühl (2025) found that many European university guidelines on generative AI were developed in apparent unawareness of these legal requirements—not maliciously, but because the pace of technology adoption has consistently outrun institutional legal awareness. Closing that gap will require systematic legal literacy development for institutional leaders, not just for technology officers.

7.2 The Equity Problem Is Bigger Than the Access Problem

Digital equity in European education tends to get discussed primarily as a hardware and connectivity problem—schools in rural Romania don't have the same device-to-student ratios as schools in urban Finland, and this disparity maps onto learning outcomes in ways that are ethically troubling and practically important. But Arztmann et al. (2024) identified something that should complicate this picture: in their study, socio-economic background moderated AR learning game outcomes even after device access was controlled for. That is, students from lower-SES backgrounds engaged with the same AR content on equivalent devices and still showed smaller learning gains than their higher-SES peers. The explanation probably lies in what are sometimes called learner capital differences: prior technology familiarity, the confidence to take risks in digital environments, parental educational background, and access to informal learning support outside school hours.

This matters because it suggests that simply providing AI and AR tools to under-resourced schools will not, by itself, produce equitable learning outcomes. The technology is not a neutral pipe through which equal education flows to all who receive it. It arrives in social and cultural contexts that shape how it is used, by whom, and to what effect. Addressing this requires investment that goes beyond hardware provision: culturally responsive design processes that involve underserved communities in creating the tools that will be used in their schools; multilingual content provision that doesn't treat English as the default language of intelligent educational technology; pedagogical support for teachers in low-resource institutions that helps them deploy AI and AR tools with the intentionality that maximises benefit for their specific learner communities. Da Costa et al. (2025) make a related point about the alignment between graduate outcomes and labour market needs—the skills gap their analysis identifies is sharpest for learners from communities where formal education has historically delivered less, and technology that doesn't address this specifically may widen it.

7.3 Data Privacy in Practice: GDPR Is Necessary but Not Sufficient

The GDPR is genuinely important. The principle that learners—many of them children—have rights over their own data, that institutions must be able to justify what they collect and demonstrate what they do with it, and that the right not to be subject to solely automated decisions with significant effects on one's life applies in educational as much as in other contexts: these are substantial protections. Article 22 specifically has direct relevance for any educational AI system that automatically classifies learners, streams them into differentiated pathways, or generates performance ratings without meaningful human review. But GDPR compliance is a floor, not a ceiling, and treating it as sufficient—as long as the privacy notice was sent and the consent box was ticked—misses what the regulation is actually for.

Genuine data stewardship in educational AI requires technical and organisational capacity that many European institutions are still developing. Data protection impact assessments should be conducted for every AI system that processes learner data in ways that could produce significant effects—not selectively, not only when a compliance officer flags a problem. Pseudonymisation and anonymisation protocols need to be implemented with technical rigour rather than nominal gesture. And learner rights need to be operationalised in accessible, usable ways—not buried in forty-page privacy policies but explained in language that learners can actually act on. Teacher data literacy is part of this: educators who don't understand what data AI systems collect, how that data influences recommendations about their students, and what recourse students have are not in a position to exercise the oversight that GDPR and good pedagogy both require.

Algorithmic transparency deserves particular emphasis here. Systems that generate recommendations without explainable rationale create at least three compounding problems. They make it impossible for teachers to exercise genuine professional judgement rather than algorithmic implementation. They prevent learners from understanding and developing their own metacognitive awareness of how they are being assessed. And they make bias detection essentially impossible, since you can't identify where the algorithm is wrong if you can't see what the algorithm is doing. The EU AI Act's transparency requirements for high-risk AI systems are a step in the right direction, but they will only make a practical difference if European educational institutions invest in the technical infrastructure and professional capacity to implement them meaningfully.

7.4 Generative AI and the Assessment Crisis It Has Exposed

When a university lecturer sets an essay question in 2024 that a large language model can answer competently in four minutes, something has been revealed—not invented. The assessment design was already insufficient; the LLM just made the insufficiency unmistakable. Christ-Brendemühl (2025) documents the spectrum of European institutional responses, ranging from outright prohibition backed by AI detection software to essentially permissive frameworks that require disclosure but little else. Neither extreme is satisfying. Prohibition is practically unenforceable and—more importantly—trains students to see AI avoidance as the point of assessment, which is not a useful professional skill for any labour market they will enter. Uncritical permissiveness, on the other hand, risks producing credentials that represent AI performance rather than learner competence, which is a more serious problem than it sometimes appears to institutional leaders who are primarily worried about short-term reputational risk.

The more honest and pedagogically productive response treats the LLM disruption as a belated prompt to redesign assessment around things that actually matter and that AI cannot straightforwardly replicate. If an essay prompt is answerable by a language model, the prompt is probably measuring information retrieval or structural argumentation—tasks that, frankly, are not the highest-order capabilities that higher education is supposed to develop. Viva voce examinations, portfolio assessment that requires evidence of iterative thinking over time, collaborative projects with individually assessed contributions and process documentation, reflective accounts that require the integration of specific personal experience and disciplinary learning—these formats are harder to complete by AI proxy precisely because they require dimensions of human cognition and life history that AI cannot authentically provide. This is not a comfortable conclusion for institutions that have built their assessment systems around efficient, scalable written formats. But it is the intellectually defensible one, and the European universities that engage with it seriously will be better prepared for whatever the next generation of AI capability produces.

8. IMPLICATIONS FOR POLICY AND PRACTICE

8.1 Teacher Education Cannot Keep Treating AI as an Add-On

The single most consequential structural change that would improve the prospects of beneficial AI and AR integration in European education is the systematic redesign of teacher education—both pre-service and in-service—around the competencies that working with intelligent systems actually requires. This is not a modest proposal. It means revising curriculum content, redesigning assessed learning outcomes, retraining teacher educators themselves, and rethinking the relationship between university-based professional preparation and school-based practice. It also means resisting the temptation to treat AI as a separate module—something added to an unchanged programme—rather than as a cross-cutting consideration that changes how subject knowledge, pedagogical knowledge, and professional identity are all understood.

Sperling et al. (2024) and Khalid et al. (2026) converge on the same diagnosis: the bottleneck is not teacher motivation, it's structural. Mikeladze et al. (2024) add that the proliferation of AI competency frameworks without coherent alignment between them has produced confusion rather than clarity—each member state producing its own framework, often with different underlying assumptions about what AI literacy for educators means in practice. The DigCompEdu framework developed by the European Commission's Joint Research Centre provides a useful shared reference point, but it needs to be supplemented by practical, tool-specific training that develops not just conceptual familiarity but genuine applied competence in authentic pedagogical contexts.

For in-service professional development, the five-stage model illustrated in Figure 2 (above) provides a structured developmental pathway. Crucially, the model is iterative rather than linear: teachers who have reached Stage 5 in relation to one generation of tools may appropriately re-enter at Stage 2 when substantially new tools emerge. Institutional support systems that treat CPD as a one-off event rather than an ongoing developmental relationship will not sustain the kind of progressive professional learning that AI and AR integration requires. Mentoring, peer observation, communities of practice, and access to current research—these are the human scaffolding within which tool-specific training becomes genuinely transformative.

8.2 Curriculum Needs Rethinking, Not Just Supplementing

Adding AI and AR tools to curricula that were designed without them tends to produce awkward results—tools deployed for their novelty value in contexts where they don't add much, or where they add motivation without adding understanding. The more fundamental challenge is to use the affordances of AI and AR as an occasion for rethinking what curriculum is for and how learning should be organised. Fernandes et al. (2023) and Nevrelova et al. (2024) both conclude that AI and AR are most educationally productive when embedded within constructivist, inquiry-based learning designs that leverage the technologies' adaptive and immersive affordances while genuinely preserving learner agency. That combination—adaptive technology within inquiry-based pedagogy—is harder to design than either element alone, and it requires teacher preparation that addresses both.

Capogna et al. (2025) tackle the higher education dimension directly, arguing that AI is reshaping the competency profiles that graduates need to the point that universities cannot simply add AI modules to otherwise unchanged degree programmes. The capacities that AI cannot replace—critical evaluation of AI-generated outputs, creative synthesis that draws on personal experience and disciplinary depth, ethical reasoning in technologically mediated professional contexts, collaborative intelligence that negotiates meaning across different knowledge frameworks—are precisely the capacities that higher education should be developing most deliberately. Refocusing degree programmes around these higher-order capabilities is not a concession to AI; it is the most coherent educational response to a world in which AI exists.

8.3 Pan-European Collaboration Is Practical Necessity, Not Aspirational Rhetoric

The infrastructure investments required for sustainable, equitable AI and AR integration across European education are not ones that individual institutions or small member states can sustain in isolation. The development of multilingual AI personalisation systems trained on high-quality European pedagogical corpora; the creation of open-source AR content libraries that schools can access regardless of institutional budget; the establishment of pan-European longitudinal research programmes capable of generating the evidence base that policy needs to be grounded in—these require coordination at European level. The mechanisms exist: the European Education Area, the Digital Education Action Plan, Erasmus+, and Horizon Europe all provide institutional scaffolding for the collaborative research and resource development that the scale of transformation demands.

Capogna et al. (2025) highlight the potential of European universities specifically to lead in developing AI-integrated approaches to student professionalisation—career coaching, employability support, and lifelong learning facilitation that leverages AI-AR tools rather than treating them as peripheral to the core educational mission. Realising that potential at scale requires institutional strategies that go beyond individual pioneering projects, and it requires the interdisciplinary collaboration—between computer scientists, educational researchers, domain specialists, and practitioners—that major European research programmes are well-positioned to support when the governance structures are right.

8.4 The Evidence Problem: What Counts as Good Enough Reason to Adopt?

Too many AI and AR adoption decisions in European schools and universities are being made on the basis of commercial promotion, conference presentations by enthusiastic early adopters, or the anxiety of not being seen to be behind. Holmes and Tuomi (2022) identify this as a systemic problem: the evidence standards applied to educational technology adoption are routinely lower than those applied to curriculum design, assessment reform, or teaching method change. This disparity is not sustainable if the sector is serious about responsible stewardship of public resources and learner welfare.

A minimum evidential standard for institutional AI and AR adoption should include: a clearly specified educational problem that the technology is expected to address; baseline measurement of relevant outcomes before deployment; an evaluation design capable of attributing changes to the intervention rather than to confounded factors; and systematic reporting of findings in forms that other practitioners can access and learn from. This is not unrealistic—it is what professionally responsible adoption looks like, and it is no more demanding than what would be expected of a pharmacist introducing a new treatment protocol. Institutions that cannot meet this standard should be honest about the fact that their adoption is exploratory rather than evidence-based, and should design their monitoring accordingly.

Finally: the teachers who use these tools every day are an underutilised source of design intelligence. Their observations about what works for their specific learner communities, their frustrations with tool limitations, their creative adaptations of intended use cases—this knowledge is valuable to developers, policy makers, and researchers, but it is rarely systematically collected or acted upon. Pan-European practitioner knowledge-exchange platforms, built on existing communities of practice, could change this. The accumulated experiential wisdom of a continent's worth of teachers is not a marginal resource—it is the most ecologically valid evidence base available for iterative improvement of AI and AR tools in authentic educational contexts.

9. CONCLUSION

European education is not at the beginning of its encounter with AI and augmented reality; it's somewhere in the difficult middle. The technologies exist, they are in use, and the evidence base—imperfect and uneven as it is—confirms that they can produce genuine educational value under the right conditions. The technologies are also being deployed carelessly in too many contexts, by institutions without adequate teacher preparation, without coherent ethical governance, and without the equity commitments that would ensure their benefits are distributed rather than concentrated. Both of these things are true simultaneously, and writing honestly about AI and AR in European education requires holding both.

The four-layer convergent framework proposed here—data collection, AI processing, AR environment, personalised output—offers a way of thinking about integration that keeps the human dimensions of teaching and learning central rather than peripheral. The framework is only useful, though, if the conditions for its responsible implementation are in place: teachers who have been genuinely prepared to work with intelligent systems; institutions that take GDPR compliance seriously as a practice rather than as a paperwork exercise; equity monitoring that goes beyond hardware provision to the deeper dimensions of learner capital that shape how technology benefits are distributed; and assessment practices that have been honest enough to ask what they are actually measuring and whether AI has exposed their inadequacies.

The research gaps that remain are substantial. Longitudinal studies examining sustained effects on learning, identity, and competence are rare. Comparative analyses of how different European national regulatory frameworks are shaping AI adoption in practice are almost nonexistent. Participatory research that centres the experiences of marginalised learners—those with SEN, those from economically disadvantaged communities, those studying in their second or third language—in the design of tools that are supposed to serve all European learners is urgently needed and underfunded. These gaps will not close on their own. They will close if European researchers, institutions, and funders treat them as priorities, and if the policy frameworks that govern AI in education are built on evidence gathered in the institutions where that education actually happens, by the teachers and learners who are actually living with the consequences of these choices.

REFERENCES

Aldowah, H., Al-Samarraie, H., & Fauzy, W. M. (2019). Educational data mining and learning analytics for 21st century higher education: A review and synthesis. *Telematics and Informatics*, *37*, 13–49. DOI: 10.1016/j.tele.2019.01.007

Arztmann, M., Domínguez Alfaro, J. L., Hornstra, L., Jeuring, J., & Kester, L. (2024). In-game performance: The role of students' socio-economic status, self-efficacy and situational interest in an augmented reality game. *British Journal of Educational Technology*, *55*(2), 484–498. DOI: 10.1111/bjet.13395

Bayly-Castaneda, K., Ramirez-Montoya, M.-S., & Morita-Alexander, A. (2024). Crafting personalized learning paths with AI for lifelong learning: A systematic literature review. *Frontiers in Education*, *9*, 1424386. DOI: 10.3389/feduc.2024.1424386

Capogna, S., Pellegrini, S., & Sebastiani, R. (2025). Transition and artificial intelligence: The case of student professionalisation. *European Journal of Education*, *60*(1), e12866. DOI: 10.1111/ejed.12866

Christ-Brendemühl, S. (2025). Leveraging generative AI in higher education: An analysis of opportunities and challenges addressed in university guidelines. *European Journal of Education*, *60*(1), e12891. DOI: 10.1111/ejed.12891

Copur-Gencturk, Y., Li, J., Cohen, A. S., & Orrill, C. H. (2024). The impact of an interactive, personalized computer-based teacher professional development program on student performance: A randomized controlled trial. *Computers & Education*, *210*, 104963. DOI: 10.1016/j.compedu.2023.104963

Creed, C., Al-Kalbani, M., Theil, A., Sarcar, S., & Williams, I. (2023). Inclusive AR/VR: Accessibility barriers and research agenda. *International Journal of Human-Computer Interaction*, *40*(19), 6200–6219. DOI: 10.1080/10447318.2023.2247614

da Costa, T., Aranda Lopez, L. I., Perussello, C., Quinn, F., Crowley, Q. G., McMahon, H., & Holden, N. M. (2025). Addressing the demand for green skills: Bridging the gap between university outcomes and industry requirements. *Sustainability (Basel)*, *17*(6), 2732. DOI: 10.3390/su17062732

Fernandes, C. W., Rafatirad, S., & Sayadi, H. (2023). Advancing personalized and adaptive learning experience in education with artificial intelligence. *Proceedings of the 2023 32nd Annual Conference of the European Association for Education in Electrical and Information Engineering (EAEEIE)*, 1–6. DOI: 10.23919/EAEEIE55804.2023.10181336

Holmes, W., & Tuomi, I. (2022). State of the art and practice in AI in education. *European Journal of Education*, *57*(4), 542–570. DOI: 10.1111/ejed.12533

Jauhiainen, J. S., & Garagorry Guerra, A. (2024). Generative AI and education: Dynamic personalization of pupils' school learning material with ChatGPT. *Frontiers in Education*, *9*, 1288723. DOI: 10.3389/feduc.2024.1288723

Kasinidou, M., Kleanthous, S., & Otterbacher, J. (2025). Cypriot teachers' digital skills and attitudes towards AI. *Discover Education*, *4*(1), 6. DOI: 10.1007/s44217-024-00390-6

Khalid, S., Tadesse, E., Abdellahi, M. L., Jiali, Y., & Dainkun, J. (2026). AI-integrated professional development for pre-service teachers: A systematic review of impacts on pedagogical strategies and technological self-efficacy. *European Journal of Education*, *61*(2), e70547. DOI: 10.1111/ejed.70547

Kultan, J., Baimuldina, N., Rakhimzhanova, L., Issabayeva, D., Issabayeva, Z., & Aituganova, Z. (2025). Using augmented reality to teach digital literacy course to primary school children with special educational needs. *European Journal of Educational Research*, *14*(1), 55–71. DOI: 10.12973/eu-jer.14.1.55

Mikeladze, T., Meijer, P. C., & Verhoeff, R. P. (2024). A comprehensive exploration of artificial intelligence competence frameworks for educators: A critical review. *European Journal of Education*, *59*(3), e12663. DOI: 10.1111/ejed.12663

Molenaar, I. (2022). Towards hybrid human-AI learning technologies. *European Journal of Education*, *57*(4), 632–645. DOI: 10.1111/ejed.12527

Nevrelova, N., Korenova, L., Lavicza, Z., Bruzkova, N., & Schmid, A. (2024). Enhancing digital literacy in primary education through augmented reality. *Frontiers in Education*, *9*, 1390491. DOI: 10.3389/feduc.2024.1390491

Nguyen, A., Ngo, H. N., Hong, Y., Dang, B., & Nguyen, B. P. T. (2023). Ethical principles for artificial intelligence in education. *Education and Information Technologies*, *28*(4), 4221–4241. DOI: 10.1007/s10639-022-11316-w PMID: 36254344

Okonkwo, C. W., & Ade-Ibijola, A. (2021). Chatbots applications in education: A systematic review. *Computers and Education: Artificial Intelligence*, *2*, 100033. DOI: 10.1016/j.caeai.2021.100033

Singh, S., Kaur, A., & Gulzar, Y. (2024). The impact of augmented reality on education: A bibliometric analysis. *Frontiers in Education*, *9*, 1458695. DOI: 10.3389/feduc.2024.1458695

Sperling, K., Stenberg, C.-J., McGrath, C., Åkerfeldt, A., Heintz, F., & Stenliden, L. (2024). In search of artificial intelligence (AI) literacy in teacher education: A scoping review. *Computers and Education Open*, *6*, 100169. DOI: 10.1016/j.caeo.2024.100169

Tammets, K., & Ley, T. (2023). Integrating AI tools in teacher professional learning: A conceptual model and illustrative case. *Frontiers in Artificial Intelligence*, *6*, 1255089. DOI: 10.3389/frai.2023.1255089 PMID: 38130325

Winkler, R., & Söllner, M. (2018). Unleashing the potential of chatbots in education: A state-of-the-art analysis. Academy of Management Annual Meeting Proceedings. DOI: 10.5465/AMBPP.2018.15903abstract

Zekeik, H., Chahbi, M., Sefian, M. L., & Bakkali, I. (2025). Augmented reality and virtual reality in education: A systematic narrative review on benefits, challenges, and applications. *Eurasia Journal of Mathematics, Science and Technology Education*, *21*(6), em2616. Advance online publication. DOI: 10.29333/ejmste/16830

KEY TERMS AND DEFINITIONS

Adaptive Learning Systems: Technology-driven educational platforms that continuously analyse individual learner performance data to dynamically adjust content difficulty, sequencing, and format in real time, providing personalised instructional pathways that respond to each student's demonstrated mastery, engagement patterns, and identified areas of weakness.

Artificial Intelligence in Education: The application of machine learning algorithms, natural language processing, and intelligent tutoring systems within educational contexts to automate administrative tasks, generate adaptive content, provide real-time student feedback, and support data-driven instructional decisions by educators and institutional administrators.

Augmented Reality: A technology that overlays digitally generated information—images, annotations, simulations, or interactive models—onto the physical learning environment through devices such as smartphones or headsets, enabling students to engage with abstract or complex concepts through immersive, contextually enriched experiential learning.

Personalised Learning: An educational approach that tailors content, pace, and instructional methods to each learner's individual needs, prior knowledge, and learning preferences, enabling students to progress through curriculum at their own rate while receiving targeted support aligned with specific competency gaps.

Teacher Professional Development: Continuous, structured learning opportunities designed to enhance educators' subject knowledge, pedagogical skills, and technological competencies beyond initial qualification, encompassing workshops, coaching, peer collaboration, and formal programmes that ultimately improve instructional quality and student learning outcomes.

Chapter 10

Pre-Service Teachers' Perceptions of Developing Educational Materials Using Generative Artificial Intelligence Tools

Erman Yukselturk
http://orcid.org/0000-0003-0690-0010
Kırıkkale University, Turkey

Osman Aslan
Kırıkkale University, Turkey

ABSTRACT

The rapid expansion of generative artificial intelligence (GAI) tools is transforming educational material development processes. This study examines the anxiety and acceptance levels of Special Education and Turkish pre-service teachers regarding the pedagogical use of GAI. Employing a mixed-methods, single-group pre-test/post-test design, 82 participants completed an eight-week structured GAI training. Data were collected through validated anxiety and acceptance scales and semi-structured interviews. Quantitative findings revealed no statistically significant change in overall anxiety or acceptance levels. However, a significant decrease was observed in job replacement anxiety, while effort expectancy showed a meaningful shift after training. Qualitative results indicated that participants adopted a cautiously optimistic

DOI: 10.4018/979-8-3373-9883-9.ch010

stance, recognizing efficiency and productivity benefits while expressing ethical and professional concerns. Overall, pre-service teachers positioned GAI as a supportive instructional tool rather than a substitute for the human-centered nature of teaching.

INTRODUCTION

In recent years, with the rapid acceleration of digital transformation, artificial intelligence (AI) technologies have become a major driver of change in education, as in many other areas of social life. The use of AI in educational settings offers a wide range of opportunities, including the personalization of learning processes, continuous monitoring of student performance, provision of data-driven feedback to teachers, and diversification of instructional materials (Chen, Xie & Hwang, 2020). These developments contribute to making teaching and learning processes more flexible, accessible, and learner-centered. The increasing visibility of AI-supported digital tools, in particular, has strengthened the role of technology in supporting teachers' pedagogical decision-making processes.

As a subfield of AI, generative artificial intelligence (GAI) introduces a new dimension to educational material development through its ability to produce original content such as text, images, video, and music (Kohnke & Zou, 2025). GAI tools can support teachers in various instructional tasks, including lesson planning, assessment design, development of individualized learning materials, and creation of creative learning activities. In this respect, GAI should be viewed not merely as a technological tool that reduces teachers' workload, but also as a pedagogical support mechanism with the potential to enrich and diversify students' learning experiences. However, the effective realization of this potential largely depends on teachers' and pre-service teachers' perceptions, attitudes, and emotional responses toward these technologies.

Despite the increasing interest in GAI, the existing literature shows that empirical studies specifically targeting pre-service teachers are still limited (Oruç, Yeşilyurt & Kurt, 2024). In Turkey, the Ministry of National Education has released an Artificial Intelligence Applications Curriculum. This curriculum offers a general guide for students to understand AI ideas, study its history, and learn about where it is used. (MEB, 2023) However, these efforts give little information about how teachers or those who want to become teachers will use GAI tools in their teaching, how much they trust these technologies, and how they might see GAI in their job roles. Suluk (2025) emphasized that future research should be designed with experimental designs to fill the existing gap in the literature. Accordingly, the present research, designed with a single-group pretest-posttest quasi-experimental design, will help to address this need in the literature.

The integration of GAI into educational processes is a complex process that goes beyond simply acquiring technical skills. Many studies show that the integration of GAI into teacher training should be evaluated not only in a technological context but also in its pedagogical and ethical dimensions (Kelley and Wenzel, 2025). Similarly, Kohnke and Zou (2025) emphasize that GAI contributes to pedagogical decision-making processes by providing prospective teachers with a critical perspective in the context of TESOL (Teaching English to Speakers of Other Languages) teacher training. Vartiainen et al. (2025) share in their study that teacher trainers created different situations to think about how GAI should fit into future learning environments. These results suggest that GAI can help support teachers in their work.

Despite the possible advantages of GAI, many pre-service teachers have significant worries about it. The literature shows that ethical risks, reliability problems, false information, privacy concerns, copying others' work, and the feeling that AI lacks a human element are all reasons why people are careful or not willing to use AI technologies (AlAli & Wardat, 2024). Specific worries, especially the fear of losing a job, are seen as one of the main mental factors that make new teachers hesitant to use technology. Overcoming these anxieties is possible not only by gaining technical skills but also by embracing the supportive role of technology in professional settings.

Research conducted in Turkey shows that prospective teachers generally have low or moderate levels of AI literacy and that concerns about artificial intelligence are widespread (Demir & Çelebi, 2025). In particular, empirical research focusing on the use of GAI in Education remains scarce (Karagöl & Yıldırım, 2025; Azizoğlu & Çakır, 2025). This gap is noteworthy, given that GAI tools offer significant advantages in these fields such as facilitating the preparation of individualized education programs (IE in Special Education and supporting creative writing and content production in Turkish language instruction. At the same time, the distinct pedagogical sensitivities of these disciplines may shape pre-service teachers' acceptance of and anxiety toward GAI in different ways.

BACKGROUND

The main objective of this study is to examine the views, acceptance levels, and anxiety levels of prospective teachers in the fields of Special Education and Turkish Language Education regarding the use of GAI tools such as text-based tools, image generation, video generation, music generation, and lesson planning in the educational material development processes. In today's educational context, pre-service teachers' ability to adapt to technological innovations and to design instructional materials in line with the requirements of the digital age has become critically important (Azizoğlu & Çakır, 2025). Therefore, identifying how pre-service teachers perceive GAI tools within a pedagogical framework, as well as their emotional (anxiety-related), technological acceptance, and behavioral (use and acceptance) tendencies toward these tools, provides valuable data for both teacher education programs and the strategic integration of technological innovations into the education system.

This study aims not only to describe the current situation but also to evaluate the impact of an eight-week structured GAI training intervention on pre-service teachers' acceptance and anxiety levels towards GAI, and the changes in these levels over time. The study looks into how pre-service teachers' understanding, willingness to use, and feelings of worry about GAI tools change as they go through their training. This part of the research is likely to give valuable information about how GAI can be used in the training and growth of future teachers.

The study also looks at whether personal traits of future teachers, like their gender and the field they study in, make a difference in how much they accept and use GAI tools. It also checks if anxiety levels change depending on the subject area they are studying. The results from this analysis should help leaders make changes to teacher training programs so they better suit the different needs of various groups of students.

This study serves as a means to address the following research questions:

- Does the implemented GAI training have a statistically significant effect on pre-service teachers' levels of anxiety, both in terms of overall scores and sub-dimensions?
- Does the implemented GAI training have a statistically significant effect on pre-service teachers' levels of acceptance, considering both overall scores and sub-dimensions?
- Do the changes observed in pre-service teachers' levels of GAI acceptance and anxiety differ significantly according to department and gender?
- What are pre-service teachers' views regarding the use of GAI in educational material development processes?

By addressing these questions, the study aims not only to describe the current situation but also to develop effective strategies for integrating artificial intelligence into teacher education. In this situation, the study wants to create results that will help make teacher education programs better match the changes in technology both within the country and around the world. Therefore, the findings from this study on teacher education should help give a wider understanding of how artificial intelligence can be used in education and act as a useful guide for those who make education policies, plan educational programs, and work in teaching settings.

MAIN FOCUS OF THE CHAPTER

Issues, Controversies, Problems

This study uses a mixed-methods approach, combining both quantitative and qualitative research methods in a sequence. This mixed-methods approach aims to address the research problem more comprehensively by integrating the collection, analysis, and interpretation of both quantitative and qualitative data (Creswell, 2008).

The study's numerical part was created to look at how the anxiety and acceptance levels of future teachers change when it comes to using GAI tools. To achieve this, a pre-test and post-test quasi-experimental design was employed. Before the test, data was gathered to find out what people thought about AI tools, how nervous they were about them, and how open they were to using them. After that, an eight-week structured AI training program was started, and data from a test were gathered after the program to see how things changed over time. This method serves to evaluate the effects of an experimental intervention and enables comparison of responses between two measurement points of participants within the same group (Creswell & Plano Clark, 2018).

The qualitative component of the study aimed to delve deeper into pre-service teachers' experiences, perceptions, and suggestions regarding the use of GAI tools. For this purpose, data was collected through a semi-structured interview form administered to the participants. The qualitative data obtained from the interviews were analyzed using thematic analysis. These qualitative findings were used to support and explain the quantitative results by providing insight into the underlying reasons for the observed statistical patterns. In this context, the study was structured according to an explanatory sequential mixed methods design (Creswell & Plano Clark, 2018).

Accordingly, the quantitative and qualitative data used in this study are complementary and integrated to provide a holistic understanding of pre-service teachers' attitudes, anxiety levels, and acceptance levels towards generative artificial intelligence tools.

Participants

The study group consisted of 82 pre-service teachers studying at Kırıkkale University, Faculty of Education, Turkey during the 2024–2025 academic year. 42 of the participants were enrolled in the Special Education Teaching program, and 40 were enrolled in the Turkish Language Teaching program. 52 of the participants were female and 30 were male. Participants were included in the study on a voluntary basis.

Table 1. Participant Properties

Variable	Category	N	%
Department	Special Education Teaching	42	51.2
	Turkish Language Teaching	40	48.8
Gender	Female	52	63.4
	Male	30	36.6

Data Collection Tools

Both quantitative and qualitative data collection tools were used in the research. Quantitative data analysis was performed using SPSS 26.0 program. In this context, a Paired-Samples T-Test was applied to determine the effect of the training by comparing the anxiety and acceptance scores of pre-service teachers before and after the training (pre-test and post-test). In addition, a One-Sample T-Test was performed to determine whether the GAI acceptance and anxiety levels of the participants showed a significant difference from the scale midpoint of 3.00, i.e., to determine their general trends. Before the analyses, the Shapiro-Wilk test was used to check whether the data exhibited a normal distribution; significant deviations were observed in some dimensions, and the skewness and kurtosis values of the variables were examined. In the analyses performed, it was determined that the skewness and kurtosis values of all variables ranged from -1 to +1. Therefore, the data were considered to be normally distributed, and it was decided to use the Related Samples t-test as a parametric test in the analyses.

Data obtained from semi-structured interviews were subjected to Thematic Analysis using the steps suggested by Braun and Clarke (2006). The analysis resulted in the identification of four main themes ('General Attitudes toward Artificial Intelligence', 'The Future of the Professional Role', 'Perceived Benefit and Practical Use', 'Social Environment Impact') and sub-themes related to these main themes.

GAI Anxiety Scale: In this study, the GAI Anxiety Scale was used to determine the anxiety levels of pre-service teachers regarding artificial intelligence. The scale was developed by Wang and Wang (2019); it was adapted into Turkish by Akkaya, Özkan, and Özkan (2021), and validity and reliability studies were conducted. Permission for use of the scale was obtained, and the scale items are presented in the appendices of the thesis. It consists of a total of 16 items and 4 factors: learning anxiety (5 items), job change anxiety (4 items), sociotechnical blindness (4 items), and artificial intelligence configuration (3 items). The scale is structured as a 5-point Likert type (1 = Strongly disagree, 5 = Strongly agree). In the adaptation study, the overall Cronbach α coefficient of the scale was reported as 0.937.

GAI Acceptance Scale: In this study, the GAI Acceptance Scale developed by Karaoğlan Yılmaz, Yılmaz, and Ceylan (2024) was also used to measure the acceptance levels of generative artificial intelligence tools among pre-service teachers. The scale is structured based on the Unified Theory of Technology Acceptance and Use (UTAUT). Consisting of 20 items and four sub-dimensions, the scale includes performance expectation (7 items), effort expectation (5 items), facilitating situations (3 items), and social influence (5 items) factors. The scale has a 5-point Likert-type rating scale (1 = Strongly disagree, 5 = Strongly agree). In the development study, the overall Cronbach α coefficient of the scale was 0.97; the reliability coefficients of the sub-dimensions were reported between 0.89 and .95. The construct validity of the scale was proven by exploratory and confirmatory factor analyses, and it was determined that it explained 82.42% of the total variance.

Semi-Structured Interview: In the qualitative dimension of the research, a semi-structured interview form was applied to reveal the opinions, concerns, and suggestions of pre-service teachers regarding GAI. The form contains a total of 10 questions, which were prepared and finalized in line with expert opinions. The questions focus on anxieties and fears related to artificial intelligence, perception of professional threat, opinions on the use of AI in daily life and in developing educational materials, the encouraging effect of the social environment, its contribution to productivity, and thoughts on the future of the teaching profession. Participants were given the opportunity to support their answers with examples and justifications. The interviews were conducted by audio recording, then transcribed and analyzed.

Data Collection Procedure

This study was approved by the Kırıkkale University Social and Human Sciences Research Ethics Committee, ensuring all research procedures adhered to ethical research principles, including informed consent, confidentiality, and the right to withdraw from the study at any time. The research collected data in three stages: first, a pre-test was done, then there was a training process, followed by a post-test, and finally interviews were conducted.

This method serves as an initial stage (pre-test): Pre-service teachers who voluntarily agreed to participate in the study were first provided with comprehensive information regarding the purpose, scope, and significance of the research, as well as the principles of confidentiality, anonymity, and their right to withdraw at any stage without any consequences. Once everyone agreed to take part willingly and understood what they were agreeing to, they were given two questionnaires: one had 16 questions to measure their anxiety about generative AI, and the other had 20 questions to check their level of acceptance toward these technologies. The administration of the scales was conducted in organized sessions during off-class periods to minimize any disruption to regular academic activities. Each session lasted approximately 20 minutes, during which participants completed the scales independently under the supervision of the researcher to ensure consistency and to provide clarification if needed.

Second stage (training process): Participants were included in an eight-week training program. This program was organized with 2 class hours once a week. During the training, participants were introduced to various generative artificial intelligence tools (text generation, visual generation, video and music production, translation, presentation preparation, etc.), and sample applications were performed and practiced. The training discussed and debated how these tools could be used in developing educational and instructional materials. Participants had the opportunity to experience these tools practically through weekly assignments.

Third stage (post-test and interviews): Once the training was done, the same scales were used again, and data from the post-test were gathered. After gathering the numerical data, the study moved on to the qualitative part. For this, interviews were carried out with 5 people who were chosen from the group of participants using a random method. These interviews were done with a prepared semi-structured form. This method serves as an interview conducted for approximately 5–35 minutes. Each interview was planned and conducted. Audio recordings were made and later transcribed. This method let us gather both numerical information, like the scores from before and after tests, and non-numerical information, like the themes found in interviews, which meets the needs of a mixed methods approach.

Generative Artificial Intelligence Training Process: The eight-week GAI training program was designed and put into action based on the research goals and the teaching needs of future teachers in Special Education and Turkish Language Education. The tools were chosen on purpose, not just by chance. They were picked based on things like how well they fit into teaching, how easy they are to use, how accessible they are, their ability to create different types of content, and how they match modern teaching methods. The main goal of the training was to give participants more than just technical skills—they also gained meaningful educational insights, a strong ethical foundation, and the ability to think critically about how to use GAI tools when creating teaching materials.

In this setup, tools like ChatGPT, Gamma, and Ideogram were chosen because they can create both text and images easily, and they have simple interfaces that make it quick to develop teaching materials. This method serves as a tool for pre-service teachers to perform tasks such as lesson plan development, instructional text creation, concept visualization and presentation design are still waiting for the concrete blocks. This method also serves to enhance participants' prompt-writing abilities and their critical assessment of the generated outputs. Their command-based interaction structures have contributed to improving participants' prompt-writing skills and critical evaluation of generated outputs. To highlight the importance of hearing and using materials that engage multiple senses—especially in special education and language teaching—tools like Suno and ElevenLabs were included in the program. This method serves as a tool for participants to create differentiated audio materials, produce texts in various accents and tones, and design background music tailored to instructional contexts. The ciment and the gravier. There is a shortage, and it's really a problem. This method serves to enhance accessibility, learner engagement, and inclusive educational practices.

To enhance the effectiveness of visual and video-based instruction, Runway and HeyGen were used. These platforms let participants create short instructional videos, turn text into engaging visual content, and build digital avatars that mimic a teacher's presence. Pre-service teachers used these tools to discover how AI-powered multimedia environments can be used in teaching and thought about how using virtual representations in lessons affects teaching methods. This method serves as a tool to elicit and organize content systematically, promoting academic rigor. Additionally, research-oriented tools such as Elicit and NotebookLM were integrated to support structured content organization and academic rigor. This method serves as a tool for literature exploration, document summarization, idea synthesis, and the creation of organized knowledge repositories. By using these platforms, participants learned how to carefully check AI-made information and make sure it's trustworthy for academic work.

This method serves as a structured approach, progressing from conceptual foundations and ethical discussions to more complex multimodal production tasks. Overall, the training program is structured progressively, moving from conceptual foundations and ethical discussions to increasingly complex multimodal production tasks. Every week, the program includes teaching the theory, hands-on practice with guidance, time to apply what's learned on your own, and group discussions to think about what's been learned. Participants were asked to try out different tools, figure out what works well and what doesn't, and think about the results from teaching, ethical, and career viewpoints. In this way, the training was designed not just to improve technical skills, but also to help people develop the ability to think critically, understand different contexts, and use AI in a more informed and thoughtful way. The general timeline and content of the 8-week training program are summarized in Table 2.

Table 2. 8-weeks Generative AI Training Program and Its Content

Weeks	Subject Heading	Content and Tools Used
Week 1	Pre-Test Application, Introduction, Artificial Intelligence, Ethics, and Digital Portfolio Creation	Artificial intelligence, generative artificial intelligence (GAI) concepts, its role in education, and an introduction to ethical debates (plagiarism, accuracy). Creating a personal portfolio.
Week 2	Text-Based AI and Translation	Idea generation, lesson plan design, and text editing. Tools: ChatGPT, DeepL
Week 3	Information Management and Research	Creating a personal AI assistant for resource analysis, document summarization, and research. Tools: NotebookLM, Elicit
Week 4	Presentation Tools	Design interactive lesson presentations from scratch using only commands. Tool: Gamma
Week 5	Visual Production and Creativity	Creating original visuals (concept cards, story scenes, etc.) for lesson materials. Tool: Ideogram
Week 6	Sound and Music Production	Recording texts in different languages and accents, creating original background music for lessons. Tools: ElevenLabs, Suno.ai
Week 7	Video Production and Avatars	Generating short video clips from text or images, creating digital avatars (digital teachers) for teaching lessons. Tools: Runway, HeyGen
Week 8	Project Presentations and Evaluation	A general evaluation session where participants present the materials and blogs they developed over the past 8 weeks.

Data Analysis

Quantitative data were analyzed using the SPSS 26.0 software package. Before proceeding with the analysis results, the dataset was checked for erroneous entries, missing data, and outliers; the security of data configuration was ensured. The normality of the data distribution was primarily determined through the Shapiro-Wilk test, histogram graphs, and skewness-kurtosis coefficients. The differences in participants' scores on the GAI Anxiety Scale and the GAI Acceptance Scale (total and sub-dimensions) before and after training were analyzed using a paired samples t-test for the entire study group, departments (Special Education and Turkish Language Teaching) and gender. The significance level was set at $p < .05$. Qualitative data were obtained from semi-structured interviews. The interviews were audio-recorded, transcribed, and then analyzed using thematic analysis. The analysis process followed the six stages suggested by Braun and Clarke (2006): Familiarization with the data, Creation of initial codes, Combining codes to form candidate themes, Review of themes, Naming and defining themes, and Reporting findings.

Findings

This section presents the results of the analysis of both quantitative and qualitative data obtained from the research. This method serves as a function for the analysis. The goal is to check how the GAI training program affects people's anxiety and how willing they are to accept GAI technologies.

The Impact of the GAI Training on All Participants: To check if the GAI training made a big difference for the participants, the scores from the pre-test and post-test on the GAI Anxiety and Acceptance Scale were looked at. This method was used to compare the scores before and after the intervention. The paired samples t-test was conducted. This test was selected because it works well for looking at changes in the same group as time passes, which helps us see the direct effect of the training.

Table 3. Pre-test and Post-test Results of the Anxiety and Acceptance Scale for Pre-service Teachers

Scale	Group	N		S	t	p
Anxiety	Pre-test	82	2.88	0.77	1.52	.132
	Post-test		2.73	0.66		
Acceptance	Pre-test	82	3.72	0.52	-1.11	.267
	Post-test		3.81	0.56		
**p<.05*						

According to the analysis results, the pre-test mean of GAI anxiety among the participants was ($\bar{X}$ = 2.88, S = 0.77), while the post-test mean was ($\bar{X}$ = 2.73, S = 0.66). There was no statistically significant difference between the pre-test and post-test mean (t(81) = 1.52, p = .132). This finding shows that the training given did not create a statistically significant change in the total score of the general anxiety levels of pre-service teachers. When the GAI acceptance scale scores were examined, the pre-test mean was ($\bar{X}$ = 3.72, S = 0.52), while the post-test mean was ($\bar{X}$ = 3.81, S = 0.56). No statistically significant difference was found between the pre-test and post-test means (t(81) = -1.11, p = .267). Although an arithmetic increase was observed in the acceptance levels of artificial intelligence among pre-service teachers, it was seen that this increase did not reach the level of statistical significance.

In table 4, descriptive statistics on the sub-dimensions of the GAI Anxiety Scale for pre-service teachers and the changes within these dimensions are presented. The analyses, conducted based on the four core dimensions of artificial intelligence anxiety, aim to comparatively reveal the anxiety levels of the participants before (pre-test) and after (post-test) the 8-week training intervention. According to the analysis results, an only statistically significant difference was found between the pre-test mean ($\bar{X}$ = 3.24) and post-test mean ($\bar{X}$ = 2.93) in the sub-dimension of Job Change Anxiety, t(81) = 2.39, p = .019. This finding shows that the training provided significantly reduced the anxiety levels of pre-service teachers stemming from the thought that "artificial intelligence will replace professional roles".

Table 4. Comparison of Pre-test and Post-test Anxiety Levels of Pre-service Teachers Regarding Artificial Intelligence, Based on Dimensions.

Dimensions	**Group**	**N**	**$\bar{X}$**	**S**	**t**	**p**
Learning	Pre-test	82	2.07	0.90	0.533	.595
	Post-test		2.02	0.75		
Job Change	Pre-test	82	3.24	1.02	2.398	.019*
	Post-test		2.93	0.90		
Sociotechnical Blindness	Pre-test	82	3.40	0.86	1.834	.070
	Post-test		3.19	0.82		
Restructuring	Pre-test	82	3.05	1.19	0.073	.942
	Post-test		3.04	1.12		
$*p<.05$						

In table 5, descriptive statistics on the sub-dimensions of the GAI Acceptance Scale for pre-service teachers and the process of change in these dimensions are presented. Similarly, the analyses, conducted based on the four fundamental dimensions that determine technology acceptance, aim to comparatively reveal the acceptance levels of the participants before (pre-test) and after (post-test) the 8-week training intervention. According to the analysis results, an only statistically significant difference was found between the pre-test mean ($\bar{X}$ = 3.47) and post-test mean ($\bar{X}$ = 3.19) in the Effort Expectation sub-dimension, t(81) = 2.37, p = .020. This finding shows that the training given significantly changed the effort expectations (perception of ease of use) of pre-service teachers towards the use of artificial intelligence.

Table 5. Pre-test and Post-test Distribution of Generative Artificial Intelligence Acceptance Levels of Teacher Candidates by Dimension

Dimensions	Group	N	X	S	t	p
Performance Expectation	Pre-test	82	3.98	0.66	-0.551	.583
	Post-test		4.03	0.65		
Effort Expectation	Pre-test	82	3.47	0.77	2.374	.020*
	Post-test		3.19	0.82		
Facilitating Circumstances	Pre-test	82	3.83	0.60	-0.459	.647
	Post-test		3.87	0.66		
Social Impact	Pre-test	82	3.57	0.73	0.253	.801
	Post-test		3.54	0.82		
**p<.05*						

In addition, the pre-test and post-test results of the anxiety and acceptance scale for pre-service special education teachers and pre-service Turkish language teachers were analyzed using dependent samples t-tests separately for each department to understand whether the effect of the training differed between departments. The findings reveal that the 8-week training alone did not have a statistically significant effect on either reducing anxiety or increasing acceptance levels at the total score level in either department ($p < .05$). Also, whether the effect of the training differed according to gender was examined using a paired samples t-test conducted separately for each gender group. When anxiety and acceptance scores were examined, no statistically significant difference was found between the pre-test and post-test scores in either gender group at the $p < .05$ level.

Qualitative Findings: The qualitative dimension of the research aims to deeply examine the opinions, concerns, and perceptions of pre-service teachers regarding GAI tools after an 8-week training. Thematic analysis of the data obtained from the semi-structured interview form revealed four main themes: (1) Anxiety and Trust Towards Artificial Intelligence, (2) The Future of the Professional Role, (3) Perceived Benefit and Practical Use, and (4) Social Environment Influence. Table 6 presents the findings related to these themes and sub-themes in detail.

Table 6. Theme, Sub-theme, and Frequency Distribution Obtained from Interview Data

Main Themes	Sub-Themes	Codes	f
General Attitudes Towards Artificial Intelligence	Anxiety about Learning Technology	Opportunity for growth and excitement	5
		Desire and curiosity to learn	5
	Fear	Concerns about uncontrolled growth	3
	Confidence	Professional perception	2
The Future of the Professional Role	Job Security for the Teaching Profession	The need for human touch and emotional connection	5
		AI remaining a supporting tool	5
	Perceived Risks for Other Occupations	Professions performing routine tasks (Translation, etc.)	3
		Engineering and service sector	2
Perceived Benefit and Practical Use	Increased Daily Life and Productivity	Time saving and speed	5
		Ease of idea generation and research	4
	Use in Educational Material Development	Lesson plan and content creation support	5
		Individualized question/material preparation	3
Social Environment Influence	Environmental Incentives and Motivation	Attention from friends and family	3
		Teacher incentives and academic guidance	2

Participants' views on the use of artificial intelligence tools were generally positive. All participants stated that learning a new technology did not worry them; on the contrary, they saw the process as an opportunity for development and an exciting innovation. For example, one participant stated: "*I'm not worried. On the contrary, I think it improves us. People can solve their problems by asking artificial intelligence.*" When asked whether artificial intelligence was generally "frightening" the majority of participants stated that they did not have a personal fear, but the possibility of uncontrolled growth or misuse of the technology was a cause for concern. For example, one participant stated: "*It doesn't scare me, but its uncontrolled growth and misuse are worrying. I think there should be some kind of oversight.*" One of the clearest findings of the research is that all participants agreed that artificial intelligence cannot replace the teaching profession. They emphasized the "human touch," "emotional connection," and "conscientious" aspects of teaching as the main reasons for this assurance. For example, one participant stated: "*I don't think AI will replace teachers because teaching requires not only the transfer of knowledge but also a human touch. Emotion and conscience are absent in AI.*"

Other opinions of the participants concern how useful they find GAI tools in daily life and especially in educational processes, and how they use them. All participants stated that they actively use these tools and find them very useful, especially in terms of "saving time" and "increasing productivity." For example, one participant stated: "*I find it useful. It saves time, especially in my research and assignments. It increases my productivity.*"

The role of their social environment (teachers, friends, family) in pre-service teachers' initiation and continued use of GAI tools is mentioned. The findings show that the social environment is an encouraging source of motivation. For example, one participant stated: "*My friends and family are very curious about this and encourage me. This increases my motivation.*"

SOLUTIONS AND RECOMMENDATIONS

In this study, the anxiety and acceptance levels of pre-service teachers towards GAI tools were evaluated considering quantitative and qualitative data following an eight-week training intervention. The overall quantitative findings of the study show that structured GAI training did not create a statistically significant change in the total GAI anxiety scores of the participants ($t(81)=1.52$; $p = 0.132$). This result is consistent with the literature indicating that established attitudes and anxieties toward technology do not show a rapid transformation with short-term training interventions. However, unlike the overall total score, a significant decrease occurred in the "Job Change Anxiety" subscale of the anxiety scale ($p = 0.019$). It was found that the pre-service teachers at first saw GAI tools as a threat to their jobs, but as they used these tools and made teaching materials during their training, this worry decreased. Previous research has shown that this method serves as an instructional intervention that does not always result in statistically significant changes regarding general artificial intelligence or technology-related anxiety. However, when people become more familiar with AI tools and use them directly, some worries tend to go away, especially worries about changing jobs or moving to different roles (Brougham & Haar, 2018; Schepman & Rodway, 2020).

After the training program, there was no noticeable increase in how much participants accepted the GAI, and this result wasn't statistically significant ($p = 0.267$). This finding shows that accepting technology involves more than just feeling less anxious and suggests that changing people's attitudes might happen in other ways besides just reducing their anxiety. TAM says that whether people adopt a system depends not just on how easy they think it is to use, but also on factors like how useful they believe it is and their intention to use it (Davis, 1989). When looking at the sub-dimension analyses of the acceptance scale, the significant drop in the "Expectation of Effort" dimension ($p = 0.020$) stands out as one of the most noticeable findings of the study. This method has served as a tool for pre-service teachers who initially thought using GAI tools would require minimal effort, but after eight weeks of hands-on training, they realized that effectively using these tools (such as writing correct commands, checking content, etc.) demands more mental effort and technical skill than anticipated. In the qualitative results, the theme of "Perceived Benefit and Practical Use" showed that even though participants thought these tools helped them work more efficiently, their overall acceptance levels did not change much. This happens because when technology moves quickly, it also brings more responsibility for thinking and decision-making. This situation fits with the growing trend of people accepting new technologies, as Ünsal Serim (2019) pointed out, but it also shows that people need to really put in the effort and time to use the technology before they fully accept it. This method serves as a tool for pre-service teachers who have some reservations about the use of artificial intelligence in the educational process. It was concluded that pre-service teachers have some reservations about the use of artificial intelligence in the educational process. According to Demir Dülger's (2023) study, the main concerns about using artificial intelligence in education focus on issues like reliability, ethical concerns, and a lack of oversight. This situation is similar to the theme of "The Future of the Professional Role" that came up in the qualitative part of the research. This method serves as an instrument for addressing issues such as data security and the accuracy of information. The participants' awareness shows that their approach to artificial intelligence is not merely about acceptance or rejection, but rather a process of questioning acceptance. The eight-week training program helped participants improve their technical skills, but it didn't directly turn them into people who adopt new technology. Also, it enabled pre-service teachers to evaluate technology from an educational and ethical perspective, aligning with the principle of "conscious technology integration" a fundamental aim of teacher education programs (Ertmer and Ottenbreit-Leftwich, 2010).

Qualitative analysis was done to find out why these results happened, and when combined with numerical data, it shows that pre-service teachers' views on artificial intelligence come from various angles. The analysis of the data, which used Braun and Clarke's (2006) thematic analysis approach, showed that the pre-service teachers' views fell into four main themes: their general attitude towards artificial intelligence, what they think the future holds for their professional role, the benefits they see and how they plan to use AI in practice, and how their social environment affects their motivation. This structure helps explain why the "General Acceptance" scores didn't go up much in the numbers; it's because even though people are focusing on the useful parts of the technology like how fast it works and how efficient it is, they are also being careful about problems like ethical concerns and losing the original idea. According to the study by Nyaaba et al. (2024), the careful attitude shown by future teachers, even though they see artificial intelligence as a useful tool, comes from them thinking carefully and questioning things on purpose. On the other hand, when pre-service teachers experienced technology as a tool they could control to help them, their overall worries went down. This was especially true for the "Job

Change Anxiety" part, which showed a significant drop ($p = 0.019$). This shows that AI tools don't take away jobs, but instead help people with their work. The important finding in the "Effort Expectation" part of the acceptance scale ($p = 0.020$) shows that the pre-service teachers now see AI tools as needing more mental effort than they first believed. When looking at the effect sizes of the significant differences in the sub-dimensions (Job Change Anxiety and Effort Expectation), it was found that Cohen's d coefficients ($d = 0.26$) indicated a small effect size. This shows that the eight-week training didn't change the attitudes of the future teachers much.

FUTURE RESEARCH DIRECTIONS

Based on the results from both numerical and descriptive studies, there are several suggestions that can be made for teacher training programs, government decision-makers, and future research projects. These recommendations are designed to help educators systematically, ethically, and in a pedagogically sound way incorporate GAI tools into educational settings.

Recommendations for Implementation: Firstly, teacher training programs should emphasize how to use AI tools in teaching, and practical courses should be made more thorough and detailed. Programs should not just focus on technical skills when incorporating AI, but instead present technological knowledge in a broader way that includes teaching methods and the ability to think critically about technology. Pre-service teachers need chances to find new teaching ideas with AI tools, think about what they learn, and carefully consider both what these tools can do and what they can't.

Secondly, ethics and digital citizenship education should be classified as visibility into AI connectivity as a fundamental tool. The dissemination of this information highlights pre-service teachers' concerns about misinformation, data privacy, and the potential erosion of the "human touch" in education. Therefore, teacher planning plans should systematically address issues such as algorithmic priorities, intellectual richness, academic integrity, data protection, and responsible AI use. Integrating ethical literacy into AI education can promote stored and portable technology integration rather than uncritical transfer.

Third, domain-specific pedagogical practices should be developed to ensure that GAI tools are adapted to different disciplines individually. For example, the pedagogical applications of GAI in Special Education (such as individualized material preparation) may differ significantly from its use in Turkish Language Education, where creative writing and content production are more prominent. Designing discipline-sensitive application models will increase both the suitability and ease of use of AI-assisted instruction.

Finally, continuous professional development programs should be structured to maintain long-term competence in AI computing. Considering the rapid evolution of AI technologies, short-term interventions may not be sufficient to ensure lasting competence. Continuous workshops, teamwork-based learning groups, and one-on-one mentoring can help keep knowledge current and support the ability to adapt to new developments.

Recommendations for Policymakers: At the policy level, it is important to create national standards and practice guidelines for the ethical and educational use of generative AI in schools. Clear rules and regulations can lower confusion and help organizations follow shared standards for keeping data safe, being responsible, and maintaining good teaching standards. Policymakers should also promote teamwork between universities, schools, and tech creators to make sure that plans for using AI are thoughtful and fit with what education stands for.

Recommendations for Future Research: Future research should aim to include a more diverse range of participants and compare findings across different fields to produce results that can be applied more broadly. Studying more about how teachers are trained in different programs, at various schools, and in different cultures can help us better understand how people from different fields and backgrounds see the use of generative AI.

Longitudinal studies are particularly recommended to examine how pre-service teachers' perceptions of acceptance, anxiety, and professional identity evolve over time, especially after entering the teaching profession. These studies will help understand better how long the effects of education last over time.

This method serves as a tool for experimental designs, incorporating control groups and random sampling techniques are needed to enhance causal inferences about the effectiveness of AI training interventions. Future studies should employ more robust experimental designs, including control groups and random sampling methods, to strengthen causal inferences regarding the effectiveness of AI training interventions. Finally, an in-depth examination of gender-related and other demographic dynamics can contribute to a more nuanced understanding of how sociocultural factors shape attitudes toward generative AI in educational settings.

Discuss future and emerging trends. Provide insight about the future of the book's theme from the perspective of the chapter focus. Viability of a paradigm, model, implementation issues of proposed programs, etc., may be included in this section. If appropriate, suggest future research opportunities within the domain of the topic.

CONCLUSION

This study examined the effects of an eight-week GAI training program on pre-service teachers' anxiety and acceptance levels toward GAI tools through a mixed-methods approach. The findings revealed that while the training did not produce a statistically significant change in overall anxiety or acceptance levels, it contributed to a significant reduction in job change anxiety and increased participants' awareness of the competencies required for effective GAI use. Qualitative findings further demonstrated that pre-service teachers perceive GAI as a beneficial instructional tool that can enhance efficiency and support teaching practices; however, they also expressed concerns related to ethics, reliability, data security, originality, and the future of the teaching profession. These results suggest that short-term training interventions may be effective in reducing specific concerns and fostering critical awareness, but may not be sufficient to substantially transform broader attitudes and acceptance of emerging technologies. Therefore, teacher education programs should focus not only on developing technical competencies related to GAI tools but also on promoting critical, ethical, and pedagogically informed technology integration.

ACKNOWLEDGMENT

This research received no specific grant from any funding agency in the public, commercial, or not-for-profit sectors.

REFERENCES

Akkaya, B., Özkan, A., & Özkan, H. (2021). Yapay zeka kaygı (YZK) ölçeği: Türkçeye uyarlama, geçerlik ve güvenirlik çalışması. *Alanya Akademik Bakış*, *5*(2), 1125–1146. DOI: 10.29023/alanyaakademik.833668

AlAli, R., & Wardat, Y. (2024). Opportunities and challenges of integrating generative artificial intelligence in education. *International Journal of Religion*, *5*(7), 784–793. Retrieved May 30, 2026, from. DOI: 10.61707/8y29gv34

Azizoğlu, B., & Çakır, R. (2025). Özel eğitim öğretmenlerinin BİT tutumları, dijital materyal tasarımı yeterlikleri ve üretken yapay zekâ okuryazarlıklarının incelenmesi. *Necmettin Erbakan Üniversitesi Ereğli Eğitim Fakültesi Dergisi*, *7*(1), 231–257. Retrieved May 30, 2026, from. DOI: 10.51119/ereegf.2025.129

Braun, V., & Clarke, V. (2006). Using thematic analysis in psychology. *Qualitative Research in Psychology*, *3*(2), 77–101. DOI: 10.1191/1478088706qp063oa

Brougham, D., & Haar, J. (2018). Smart technology, artificial intelligence, robotics, and algorithms (STARA): Employees' perceptions of our future workplace. *Journal of Management & Organization*, *24*(2), 239–257. DOI: 10.1017/jmo.2016.55

Chen, X., Xie, H., & Hwang, G. J. (2020). A multi-perspective study on artificial intelligence in education: Grants, conferences, journals, and patents. *Journal of Educational Technology & Society*, *23*(4), 1–18.

Creswell, J. W. (2008). *Educational research: Planning, conducting, and evaluating quantitative and qualitative research* (3rd ed.). Pearson Education.

Creswell, J. W., & Plano Clark, V. L. (2018). *Designing and conducting mixed methods research* (3rd ed.). SAGE Publications.

Davis, F. D. (1989). Perceived usefulness, perceived ease of use, and user acceptance of information technology. *Management Information Systems Quarterly*, *13*(3), 319–340. DOI: 10.2307/249008

Demir, U., & Çelebi, C. (2025). Sınıf Öğretmeni Adaylarının Yapay Zekâ Okuryazarlık Düzeylerinin Çeşitli Değişkenler Açısından İncelenmesi. *Necmettin Erbakan Üniversitesi Ereğli Eğitim Fakültesi Dergisi, 7(Özel Sayı), 142-166.*

Demir Dülger, S. (2023). Lise müdürlerinin ve öğretmenlerinin yapay zekânın eğitimde kullanımına ilişkin görüşleri. *Milli Eğitim Dergisi, 52*(237), 1–20.

Ertmer, P. A., & Ottenbreit-Leftwich, A. T. (2010). Teacher technology change: How knowledge, confidence, beliefs, and culture intersect. *Journal of Research on Technology in Education, 42*(3), 255–284. DOI: 10.1080/15391523.2010.10782551

Karagöl, E., & Yıldırım, D. (2025). Türkçe eğitiminde yapay zekâ kullanımı: Türkçe eğitimcileri yapay zekâ hakkında ne düşünüyor? *Ana Dili Eğitimi Dergisi, 13*(2), 356–374. DOI: 10.16916/aded.1611540

Kelley, M., & Wenzel, T. (2025). Advancing Artificial Intelligence Literacy in Teacher Education Through Professional Partnership Inquiry. *Education Sciences, 15*(6), 659. DOI: 10.3390/educsci15060659

Kohnke, L., & Zou, D. (2025). Artificial Intelligence Integration in TESOL Teacher Education: Promoting a Critical Lens Guided by TPACK and SAMR. *TESOL Quarterly, 59*(S3). Advance online publication. Retrieved May 30, 2026, from. DOI: 10.1002/tesq.3396

Ministry of National Education. (2023). Yapay zekâ uygulamaları dersi öğretim programı (I-II) (*Ortaokul ve imam hatip ortaokulu 7 ve 8. sınıflar*) [Artificial intelligence applications course curriculum (I-II) (*Middle school and imam hatip middle school 7th and 8th grades*)]. MoNE Publications.

Nyaaba, A., Mensah, M., & Amponsah, K. D. (2024). Pre-service teachers' perceptions and readiness for integrating generative artificial intelligence in teaching and learning in Ghana. *Cogent Education, 11*(1), 1–17.

Oruç, T., Yeşilyurt, M., & Kurt, M. (2024). Eğitimde Yapay Zekâ Konulu Çalışmaların Betimsel Analizi. *Temel Eğitim, 6*(24), 44–60.

Schepman, A., & Rodway, P. (2020). Initial validation of the general attitudes towards Artificial Intelligence Scale. *Computers in Human Behavior Reports, 1*, 100014. DOI: 10.1016/j.chbr.2020.100014 PMID: 34235291

Suluk, B. (2025). İlkokul Eğitiminde Yapay Zekâ: Türkiye'de Öğrenci ve Öğretmen Odaklı Çalışmaların Sistematik İncelemesi. *Temel Eğitim Araştırmaları Dergisi, 5*(2), 205–222. Retrieved May 30, 2026, from. DOI: 10.55008/te-ad.1757856

Ünsal Serim, H. (2019). The effect of gamification on the acceptance of coding education. *Journal of Educational Technology & Society*, *22*(3), 116–128.

Vartiainen, H., Valtonen, T., Kahila, J., & Tedre, M. (2025). ChatGPT and imaginaries of the future of education: Insights of Finnish teacher educators. *Information and Learning Science*, *126*(1/2), 75–90. DOI: 10.1108/ILS-10-2023-0146

Wang, W., & Wang, Y. (2019). Factors influencing students' behavioral intentions to use the artificial intelligence-powered chatbot. *Computers & Education*, *134*, 113–124.

Yilmaz, F. G. K., Yilmaz, R., & Ceylan, M. (2024). Generative Artificial Intelligence Acceptance Scale: A Validity and Reliability Study. *International Journal of Human-Computer Interaction*, *40*(24), 8703–8715. DOI: 10.1080/10447318.2023.2288730

KEY TERMS AND DEFINITIONS

Artificial Intelligence (AI): Artificial intelligence refers to computer systems designed to perform tasks that typically require human intelligence, such as learning, reasoning, problem-solving, and decision-making.

Generative Artificial Intelligence (GAI): Generative artificial intelligence is a branch of AI that can create new content, including text, images, audio, and videos, based on patterns learned from existing data.

Generative Artificial Intelligence Tools: Generative AI tools are software applications that use generative AI technologies to assist users in producing, editing, or enhancing content and completing various tasks.

Pre-Service Teachers: Pre-service teachers are individuals enrolled in teacher education programs who are preparing to become professional teachers but have not yet entered full-time teaching practice.

Teacher Education: Teacher education is the process of preparing prospective teachers with the knowledge, skills, values, and competencies required for effective teaching and professional practice.

Technology Acceptance: Technology acceptance refers to an individual's willingness and intention to adopt and use a technological system based on perceptions of its usefulness and ease of use.

Technology Anxiety: Technology anxiety is the feeling of worry, discomfort, or apprehension that individuals may experience when interacting with or anticipating the use of technological systems.

Chapter 11

Between Promise and Uncertainty: Portuguese Primary Teachers Navigating Generative AI in Education

Filipe T. Moreira
http://orcid.org/0000-0002-3461-9827
inED, Escola Superior de Educação, Instituto Politécnico do Porto, Portugal

Sara Martins
http://orcid.org/0009-0001-5335-6241
DECA, Universidade de Aveiro, Portugal

Alexandre M. Pereira Figueiredo
http://orcid.org/0000-0002-6021-8779
Instituto Politécnico de Portalegre, Portugal

ABSTRACT

This chapter explores how Portuguese primary school teachers perceive the integration of generative artificial intelligence in educational contexts. Set against the rapid expansion of AI in society, it discusses both the opportunities these technologies offer and the challenges they raise for teaching and learning in early schooling. Drawing on an exploratory mixed-methods case study with teachers following a professional development workshop, the chapter examines their views on AI's potential to support personalised learning, feedback, and the creation of teaching materials. At the same time, it highlights key concerns related to teacher preparedness, ethical use, data protection, and the impact on students' cognitive development. The findings reveal a stance of cautious optimism, where interest in innovation coexists with uncertainty

DOI: 10.4018/979-8-3373-9883-9.ch011

and the need for guidance. The chapter argues that meaningful integration of AI depends on continuous teacher training, clear policy frameworks, and thoughtful pedagogical mediation, offering reflections and recommendations for educators.

INTRODUCTION

Educational systems worldwide are currently experiencing significant transformation driven by the rapid development of Artificial Intelligence (AI). Over the past decade, advances in machine learning, deep learning, and natural language processing have accelerated the integration of intelligent technologies into everyday life, influencing sectors such as healthcare, industry, public administration, and education. Schools increasingly encounter digital tools capable of generating content, providing automated feedback, supporting decision-making processes, and personalising learning experiences. While these developments open new possibilities for teaching and learning, they also raise complex pedagogical, ethical, and organisational questions for educational institutions, teachers, and administrators. Understanding how educators interpret and respond to these technological changes has therefore become an important topic of international research.

These questions acquire particular relevance in primary education. At this stage of schooling, teachers play a central role in supporting foundational learning while also safeguarding the development of young learners who are still building essential cognitive, social, and digital competencies. Decisions regarding the adoption of emerging technologies must therefore be approached with careful consideration. Teachers' perceptions of AI tools, as well as their confidence in using them, may strongly influence how such technologies shape classroom practices, learning environments, and students' engagement with knowledge.

Recent developments in generative artificial intelligence have intensified these discussions. Ideas that were once associated mainly with science fiction—machines capable of generating coherent text, engaging in dialogue, or assisting with complex reasoning—are increasingly part of everyday reality. Although AI as a scientific field dates back to the mid-twentieth century, its presence in daily life has expanded considerably in recent years due to advances in machine learning, deep learning, and natural language processing (Russell & Norvig, 2021; Mitchell, 2019). Many digital systems have incorporated AI functionalities for some time, often without users being fully aware of it. What distinguishes the current moment is the emergence of large language models (LLMs), such as ChatGPT, which have significantly expanded the accessibility and visibility of AI technologies. These systems can generate coherent text, sustain conversational interaction, and assist with complex reasoning tasks in ways that differ markedly from earlier rule-based or narrowly specialised systems (OpenAI, 2023; Floridi & Chiriatti, 2020).

Educational systems across the world were largely unprepared for the speed with which these technologies became accessible to the general public. International reports suggest that schools, teachers, and policy frameworks had limited time to reflect on the pedagogical, ethical, and organisational implications of generative AI before such tools became widely available (UNESCO, 2023; OECD, 2023). In Portugal, as in many other countries, educators have suddenly encountered systems capable of producing explanations, lesson plans, assessment tasks, personalised feedback, and even creative outputs. However, most teachers have received little specialised training regarding how these technologies might be integrated meaningfully into classroom practice (Dias-Trindade & Moreira, 2022).

As a result, many professionals have begun experimenting with AI tools, sometimes even within classroom environments, without fully considering questions related to ethical safeguards or data protection. These concerns become particularly relevant when the users are underage students. Interestingly, this situation contrasts with the careful selection of digital platforms that occurred during the Covid-19 pandemic, when educational institutions paid considerable attention to issues of digital security and privacy. At the same time, resistance to the use of AI in education has also begun to emerge. Some educators remain hesitant because they are unfamiliar with these technologies or uncertain about their pedagogical value, while others raise concerns about delegating certain cognitive or instructional tasks to automated systems. In the Portuguese context, this cautious attitude appears particularly visible in the early years of schooling, where questions related to children's cognitive development, ethical safeguards, and the preservation of fundamental learning processes are often emphasised. Despite these debates within professional communities, empirical evidence capable of clarifying whether such reservations represent the dominant perspective among education professionals remains limited. This lack of systematic evidence reinforces the need for research examining how teachers perceive and interpret the integration of AI tools in primary education.

It is also important to recognise that the relationship between artificial intelligence and education is not entirely new. Experiments involving intelligent systems in educational contexts can be traced back to the 1960s, including the well-known ELIZA chatbot (Rajaraman, 2023) and early attempts to analyse student interactions within computer-assisted learning environments. However, AI has never been integrated into educational practices with the level of accessibility and visibility observed today. Generative AI systems introduce the possibility of creating new educational content rather than simply analysing existing data or automating predefined tasks. Recent literature therefore highlights their potential to support differentiated instruction, provide adaptive feedback, automate administrative tasks, and strengthen formative assessment practices (Holmes et al., 2019; Luckin et al., 2016; Baker, 2016; Teles & Moreira, 2025). In primary education, these tools may also help teachers adapt learning materials to different developmental levels, support early literacy and numeracy development, and encourage creative exploration through multimodal learning activities (Kasneci et al., 2023).

At the same time, these opportunities coexist with significant challenges. Researchers have drawn attention to concerns related to ethical responsibility, algorithmic bias, transparency, and the protection of students' personal data (Williamson & Eynon, 2020; Kizilcec & Lee, 2022). As Norris (2001) and Hargittai (2002) have long argued, unequal access to technology does not disappear with its proliferation—it evolves and deepens, manifesting in successive layers of exclusion that extend from connectivity gaps to disparities in digital skills and, more recently, in the capacity to navigate algorithmically curated environments. In educational contexts, this means that access to devices, connectivity, and technological support continues to vary considerably across schools and communities, with the risk that AI-powered tools may widen rather than narrow existing inequalities. Moreover, meaningful learning processes require time, reflection, and practice that cannot simply be replaced by technological efficiency. The integration of AI into education therefore requires careful consideration of how technology can support, rather than undermine, pedagogical processes.

Within this context, teachers occupy a particularly important position. Their perceptions, beliefs, and levels of digital competence strongly influence whether technological innovations translate into genuine pedagogical improvement or merely reproduce existing limitations within educational systems. Previous research consistently shows that teachers' attitudes toward technology play a decisive role in determining whether digital tools are adopted and how they are used in classroom practice (Ifenthaler & Yau, 2020; Zawacki-Richter et al., 2019). In primary education, this issue becomes especially relevant because teachers are responsible for guiding foundational learning processes while supporting students who are still developing the ability to critically evaluate digital information. Despite growing international attention to AI in education, empirical studies focusing specifically on primary school teachers' perceptions of generative AI—particularly within the Portuguese context—remain relatively scarce.

Against this background, examining how Portuguese primary teachers perceive the opportunities and risks associated with tools such as ChatGPT becomes both timely and necessary. Teachers' perspectives can provide valuable insights into levels of acceptance, perceived usefulness, ethical awareness, and professional readiness, while also revealing structural needs related to professional development, technological infrastructure, and policy guidance. Analysing these perceptions also contributes to the broader international discussion about the role of AI in compulsory education by offering evidence from a national context that has not yet been widely explored in the literature.

With this chapter we want to analyse the perceptions of Portuguese primary teachers regarding the potential of ChatGPT to enhance personalised learning and student engagement, as well as the ethical, pedagogical, and organisational challenges associated with its use. Drawing on data collected from teachers with experience in educational technologies, the study seeks to deepen understanding of both the opportunities and limitations associated with generative AI in early schooling. Based on these insights, the chapter also proposes recommendations for policymakers, teacher education institutions, and schools seeking to integrate AI into educational practice in a responsible and pedagogically meaningful way. Ultimately, the chapter argues that the effective and equitable integration of AI in education depends on sustained investment in teacher training, clear governance frameworks, and ongoing reflection on the pedagogical purposes that should guide the adoption of emerging technologies.

This chapter is organised as follows. The next section presents the theoretical framework, defining key concepts related to artificial intelligence, generative models, and ChatGPT, and discussing their potential and limitations in primary education. The following section describes the methodological design of the study, including the research paradigm, participants, data collection instruments, and procedures for data analysis. The empirical findings are then presented and discussed, situating Portuguese primary teachers' perceptions within the broader international literature on AI in education. The chapter concludes by summarising the main findings, outlining practical implications for schools and educators, presenting policy recommendations aligned with current international guidelines on AI in education, and identifying directions for future research aimed at supporting the responsible and evidence-informed integration of AI in primary schooling.

THEORETICAL FRAMEWORK

The field of AI has undergone profound conceptual and technological evolution since its emergence as a scientific discipline in the mid-twentieth century. Early research in AI was largely centred on symbolic reasoning and rule-based systems designed to replicate logical decision-making processes. These systems relied on explicit programming and predefined rules, reflecting the dominant computational paradigms of the time. Over the last decades, however, the field has shifted significantly toward data-driven approaches based on statistical learning, deep neural networks, and large-scale data processing (Russell & Norvig, 2021; Mitchell, 2019).

In broad terms, Artificial Intelligence can be understood as the capacity of computational systems to perform tasks that traditionally require human intelligence. These tasks may include perception, learning from experience, reasoning, problem solving, decision-making, and language comprehension (Luckin et al., 2016; European Commission, 2019). Within this perspective, AI is not limited to a single technology but encompasses a wide range of algorithms and computational models capable of analysing information, identifying patterns, and generating responses or decisions based on accumulated data and prior interactions.

Sub-Areas of AI and the Emergence of Generative AI

Artificial intelligence should not be understood as a single technology, but rather as a broad interdisciplinary field encompassing several complementary subdomains. Among the most prominent are machine learning (ML), natural language processing (NLP), computer vision, robotics, and expert systems. These areas often interact with one another, forming complex technological ecosystems in which data processing, perception, and decision-making capabilities are combined. Over the last decade, machine learning has become the dominant paradigm within AI development, largely due to the availability of large datasets and increased computational power. ML approaches rely on data-driven models capable of identifying patterns and generating predictions or classifications without the need for explicitly programmed rules (European Commission, 2019; Jordan & Mitchell, 2015).

Within this domain, deep learning has played a particularly important role in expanding the capabilities of AI systems. Deep learning architectures use multi-layered neural networks that allow models to learn increasingly complex representations of data. These architectures have enabled major advances in fields such as image recognition, speech processing, and language modelling. Convolutional neural networks (CNNs), for example, have been widely applied in computer vision tasks, while transformer-based architectures have significantly improved the performance of natural language processing systems (Goodfellow et al., 2016).

In recent years, the emergence of generative AI has marked a new phase in the evolution of artificial intelligence. Unlike earlier systems primarily designed to classify or analyse existing data, generative models are capable of producing new content based on patterns learned from large-scale datasets. These systems can generate a wide range of outputs, including text, images, audio, video, and computer code, often combining several modalities within the same interaction. Technologies such as generative adversarial networks (GANs) and transformer-based models exemplify this paradigm and have significantly expanded the creative and productive capacities of AI systems.

A particularly influential development within generative AI has been the rise of large language models (LLMs). Models belonging to the GPT family, including GPT-3 and GPT-4, illustrate how transformer architectures can generate coherent and contextually appropriate text based on relatively simple prompts (Brown et al., 2020; OpenAI, 2023). More recent systems have further extended these capabilities by incorporating multimodal functionalities, allowing AI models to process and generate combinations of text, images, and other forms of data within the same interaction.

Since the early 2020s, the public availability of these models has accelerated their adoption across a wide range of sectors, including business, healthcare, scientific research, media production, and education. Their growing accessibility through user-friendly interfaces and digital platforms has contributed to a rapid diffusion of AI-assisted practices, bringing generative technologies into everyday professional and educational activities.

AI in Education and the Role of Generative Models

Although generative AI has only recently captured widespread public attention, the use of artificial intelligence in educational contexts has a considerably longer history than is often assumed. Early experiments in computer-assisted instruction began in the late 1950s and early 1960s, when researchers started exploring how computers could support learning processes by simulating instructional dialogue or providing step-by-step guidance to students (Suppes & Atkinson, 1967). These early initiatives reflected a broader interest in understanding whether computational systems could assist or partially replicate certain instructional functions traditionally performed by teachers.

ELIZA is, maybe, the most frequently cited examples from this early period, developed by Joseph Weizenbaum in 1966. ELIZA is widely recognised as one of the first conversational computer programs capable of interacting with users through natural-language text. Using relatively simple pattern-matching techniques, the program simulated a Rogerian psychotherapist by reformulating user statements as reflective questions (Weizenbaum, 1966). Although the system lacked genuine semantic understanding, its ability to sustain structured interaction revealed an important insight: users often attributed meaning and intentionality to computer-generated responses, even when these responses were produced through relatively simple computational mechanisms.

The significance of ELIZA extended beyond its technical simplicity. The program illustrated the potential for computers to participate in forms of educational dialogue and influenced subsequent developments in intelligent tutoring systems

(ITS), natural-language interfaces, and adaptive learning environments (Carbonell, 1970; Woolf, 2010). From this perspective, contemporary generative AI tools such as ChatGPT should not be interpreted as a complete rupture with earlier educational technologies. Rather, they represent the most recent stage in a long trajectory of research exploring how computational systems can support, mediate, and potentially enhance learning processes.

Over the past decades, AI has gradually been incorporated into a wide range of educational technologies. Early applications included intelligent tutoring systems, adaptive learning platforms, automated assessment tools, and recommendation systems designed to personalise educational content according to students' progress or performance (Holmes et al., 2019; Baker, 2016). What distinguishes generative AI from many of these earlier systems is its ability to produce new content dynamically rather than relying solely on predefined instructional structures or rule-based feedback mechanisms.

In practical terms, generative AI tools can support both teachers and students in multiple ways. These systems are capable of generating explanatory texts, summarising information, translating content between languages, assisting with problem-solving processes, and providing formative feedback on student work (Kasneci et al., 2023). In educational contexts, such functionalities open new possibilities for supporting teaching preparation, facilitating access to information, and enriching learning activities through interactive dialogue.

In primary education, these possibilities may be particularly relevant. Classrooms at this level often include students with diverse learning rhythms, linguistic backgrounds, and levels of prior knowledge. Generative AI tools can potentially support instructional differentiation by helping teachers adapt materials to different developmental stages or specific learning difficulties (OECD, 2023). Teachers may use systems such as ChatGPT to generate reading passages, exercises, or explanatory examples aligned with curricular goals. Furthermore, these technologies may contribute to inclusive education by supporting the creation of adapted learning materials for students with special educational needs, such as simplified texts, scaffolded explanations, or multimodal learning resources (Holmes et al., 2019; UNESCO, 2023).

Moreover, the growing presence of generative AI in education has also generated important debates regarding its potential impact on students' cognitive engagement. Some scholars have raised concerns that excessive reliance on AI-generated responses may lead to forms of cognitive offloading, where learners delegate intellectual tasks to technological systems instead of actively engaging in problem solving and reflection. This phenomenon has sometimes been described as "automation bias" or, more informally, as a form of "brain laziness," referring to situations in which learners may accept AI-generated information without critically evaluating its accuracy or meaning (Selwyn, 2019; Kasneci et al., 2023).

These concerns are particularly relevant in primary education, where students are still developing fundamental cognitive skills such as critical thinking, reasoning, and independent problem solving. For this reason, the integration of generative AI into educational practice requires careful pedagogical mediation. Rather than replacing students' intellectual effort, AI tools should ideally be used to scaffold learning processes, stimulate inquiry, and encourage reflection. Understanding how teachers perceive these opportunities and challenges therefore becomes essential for evaluating the role that AI may play in contemporary educational environments.

Potential Benefits of AI Integration in Primary Education

The growing presence of artificial intelligence in educational environments has stimulated considerable discussion regarding its potential contributions to teaching and learning. Although many of these discussions remain exploratory, several recurring themes can be identified in the literature. Researchers frequently emphasise the capacity of AI systems to support more personalised learning processes, improve feedback mechanisms, assist teachers in managing complex classroom dynamics, and facilitate the creation of educational resources adapted to diverse learning contexts.

These possibilities may also be interpreted through the concept of hypersituation in educational environments. According to Moreira, Vairinhos, and Ramos (2021), hypersituations emerge when digital technologies allow individuals to access multiple layers of contextual information simultaneously, expanding their capacity to interpret and engage with a given situation. In educational contexts, such environments can combine physical experiences with digitally mediated data, creating richer and more complex learning scenarios. Artificial intelligence technologies may contribute to the development of these hypersituated environments by dynamically generating explanations, feedback, and learning materials that interact with existing pedagogical resources. When explored through appropriate pedagogical strategies, such environments may offer meaningful opportunities for students to engage with knowledge from multiple perspectives and through diverse forms of interaction.

Also related to this, one potentiality that is more referred is the possibility of personalised instruction. Traditional classroom environments often require teachers to address groups of students with different learning needs, prior knowledge, and learning rhythms. AI-supported systems may assist teachers in responding to this diversity by generating materials or suggestions adapted to individual learning trajectories. According to Luckin et al. (2016), AI has the potential to support forms of "intelligent tutoring" in which systems analyse student interactions and provide tailored guidance or learning pathways. Similar arguments appear in the work of

Holmes, Bialik, and Fadel (2019), who argue that AI technologies may contribute to more learner-centred pedagogical approaches by enabling differentiated instruction and adaptive learning strategies. More recent studies also highlight the growing role of generative AI in creating personalised learning experiences, particularly through adaptive explanations and content generation tailored to individual students' needs.

A related benefit concerns the development of educational resources, including resources specifically designed for particular learning contexts or individual students. Generative AI tools can support teachers in producing teaching materials such as reading passages, worksheets, quizzes, summaries, or explanatory examples. In some cases, these materials may be adapted to different levels of complexity or linguistic accessibility, allowing teachers to respond more effectively to classroom diversity. This capacity to generate customised educational content is increasingly recognised as one of the most practical applications of generative AI in everyday teaching practice, particularly in contexts where teachers face significant time constraints.

Another area where AI systems may offer meaningful support is formative assessment. Timely feedback is widely recognised as one of the most powerful factors influencing student learning, yet providing detailed feedback to large groups of students can be challenging. Research on intelligent tutoring systems has already demonstrated that AI-supported feedback mechanisms can contribute significantly to students' conceptual understanding (VanLehn, 2011). With the emergence of generative AI, new possibilities are being explored for supporting formative assessment practices. For example, AI systems may help teachers analyse student responses, generate suggestions for feedback, or propose follow-up questions that encourage deeper reflection.

Recent work examining AI-supported assessment within Universal Design for Learning (UDL) frameworks also highlights the potential of these technologies to support inclusive formative assessment practices. In particular, AI can assist educators in identifying students' learning needs, providing differentiated feedback, and adapting assessment activities to diverse learning profiles (Teles & Moreira, 2025). The integration of AI-driven tools within formative assessment processes may therefore contribute to more flexible and inclusive evaluation practices that emphasise learning progression rather than simply measuring performance.

AI may also support teachers in managing some of the practical and organisational demands associated with teaching. Preparing instructional materials, designing exercises, or drafting assessment tasks can require considerable time and effort. Generative AI tools can assist with these preparatory tasks by quickly producing draft materials that teachers may later adapt to their pedagogical objectives. While such systems cannot replace professional judgement, they may help reduce routine workload and allow teachers to dedicate more time to direct interaction with students (Baker, 2016).

Some authors also suggest that AI-based tools may contribute to creative and exploratory learning activities. Because generative systems can produce multiple alternative responses to the same prompt, they may encourage students to experiment with different ideas, perspectives, or forms of expression. In this sense, AI tools may function not only as sources of information but also as interactive partners capable of stimulating inquiry and reflection (Kasneci et al., 2023).

For primary education in particular, these possibilities may be especially relevant. Early schooling involves supporting the development of foundational skills such as reading, writing, and numeracy while simultaneously addressing significant variability in students' learning pace and comprehension. AI tools may assist teachers in designing scaffolded learning materials, simplifying complex explanations, and providing additional practice activities adapted to students' needs (OECD, 2023). In addition, generative AI can support inclusive education by facilitating the creation of adapted resources for learners with diverse linguistic, cognitive, or socio-educational backgrounds (Holmes et al., 2019).

Taken together, these potential benefits suggest that AI should not be understood simply as a technological novelty entering educational environments. Rather, its value lies in the ways it can complement human teaching practices. As several authors have argued, the most productive role of AI in education is likely to be one of augmentation rather than substitution, where technological systems support teachers in designing richer and more responsive learning experiences while pedagogical decision-making remains firmly grounded in human expertise (Luckin et al., 2016; Holmes et al., 2019; Zawacki-Richter et al., 2019).

Challenges and Risks of AI Implementation in Primary Education

Despite the opportunities discussed in the previous section, the integration of artificial intelligence in educational environments also raises a number of important challenges. Researchers increasingly stress that the educational value of AI does not reside solely in the technological capabilities of these systems, but in the ways they are implemented, interpreted, and mediated within pedagogical contexts. For this reason, the discussion around AI in education has progressively shifted from technological enthusiasm toward a more critical examination of its pedagogical, ethical, and social implications.

One of the most frequently mentioned concerns relates to teacher preparedness and professional development. Many educators report feeling insufficiently equipped to understand how AI systems operate or how they might be integrated meaningfully into teaching practice. This challenge has been documented in several studies examining digital competence and technology adoption among teachers

(Ifenthaler & Yau, 2020; Zawacki-Richter et al., 2019). Without adequate training, there is a risk that AI tools may either be used superficially or avoided altogether due to uncertainty about their pedagogical value. Effective professional development therefore needs to go beyond technical familiarity and include critical AI literacy, pedagogical applications, and ethical considerations.

Another major concern relates to data protection and privacy, particularly when AI systems are used by younger learners. Many generative AI platforms process and store user interactions on remote servers, and the exact ways in which prompts, responses, and user data are stored or reused are not always fully transparent to educators or institutions. In school contexts, this raises significant questions about where student data are stored, how long they remain accessible, and whether such information may be used for further training of AI systems. Scholars have described this phenomenon as part of a broader process of "datafication" in education, where increasing amounts of student data are collected and analysed by digital platforms (Williamson & Eynon, 2020). For primary school students, these concerns are particularly sensitive, given their age and the need for strong safeguards regarding the use and storage of personal data (UNESCO, 2023).

Strictly connected to these issues are concerns about algorithmic bias and fairness. AI systems learn patterns from the data on which they are trained, and these datasets may contain social, cultural, or linguistic biases. As a consequence, AI-generated responses may inadvertently reproduce or amplify existing inequalities. Research examining bias in machine learning systems has demonstrated how such biases can influence the information users receive or how certain perspectives are prioritised (Bender & Gebru, 2021; Mehrabi et al., 2021). In educational environments, where the credibility and neutrality of information sources are essential, these risks highlight the importance of maintaining a critical stance toward AI-generated content.

A further challenge concerns digital inequalities and infrastructural limitations. The integration of AI technologies presupposes access to digital devices, reliable connectivity, and institutional support structures capable of sustaining technological innovation. However, these conditions are not equally distributed across educational systems. OECD reports have repeatedly highlighted persistent disparities in digital access between schools and socioeconomic groups (OECD, 2021). If not carefully addressed, the increasing presence of AI tools in education may therefore risk reinforcing existing inequalities between learners and institutions.

Recent debates have also raised questions about the potential impact of generative AI on students' cognitive engagement and learning processes. Some scholars argue that excessive reliance on AI-generated answers may encourage forms of cognitive offloading, where learners delegate intellectual tasks to technological systems instead of actively engaging with the learning process. This phenomenon is sometimes associated with what has been described as automation bias, where users tend to accept automated outputs without critically evaluating their reliability (Selwyn, 2019; Kasneci et al., 2023). In school contexts, such tendencies may reduce opportunities for reflection, reasoning, and independent problem-solving if AI tools are used primarily as shortcuts rather than as supports for learning.

Related to this issue is the phenomenon commonly referred to as AI hallucinations. Large language models may generate responses that appear coherent and convincing but are factually inaccurate or unsupported by reliable evidence. Because these outputs are often expressed with high linguistic confidence, students may interpret them as authoritative information. This presents a pedagogical challenge, particularly in primary education, where learners are still developing the ability to evaluate the credibility of digital information sources (Kasneci et al., 2023).

The advent of generative AI has also raised concerns regarding assessment practices and academic integrity. AI systems are capable of producing essays, problem solutions, and other forms of written output that may resemble student work. As access to these tools becomes more widespread, educators have begun to question how traditional forms of assessment can ensure that students' work reflects their own learning processes. While this debate has been particularly visible in higher education, similar concerns are gradually emerging in earlier stages of schooling (Cotton et al., 2023).

In this respect, some scholars have warned about the possibility of overdependence on technological systems. If teachers or students rely excessively on automated tools for generating explanations, feedback, or learning materials, there is a risk that certain cognitive or professional skills may gradually weaken. Selwyn (2019) cautions that educational technologies should be approached critically, recognising that innovation does not automatically translate into educational improvement.

An additional challenge for researchers concerns the limited empirical evidence currently available, particularly in primary education. While interest in AI in education has increased rapidly in recent years, many studies remain exploratory, small-scale, or short-term. Comprehensive longitudinal studies involving large numbers of primary school students are still relatively scarce. As a result, it remains difficult to draw fully consensual conclusions about the long-term pedagogical effects of generative AI at this educational level. In contrast, research in secondary and higher education contexts has already produced a somewhat broader evidence base, partly because students in these settings have earlier access to digital tools and are more frequently involved in technology-based learning environments (Zawacki-Richter et al., 2019; Kasneci et al., 2023).

Simultaneously, these challenges highlight the importance of approaching AI integration in education with careful reflection rather than technological enthusiasm alone. While AI systems offer significant opportunities for supporting teaching and learning, their effective and responsible use requires robust governance frameworks, clear ethical guidelines, and sustained investment in teacher training. In primary education in particular, where students are still developing fundamental cognitive and social skills, the role of teachers as mediators of technology remains central in ensuring that AI tools contribute positively to learning processes.

The Crucial Role of Teachers and the Importance of Continuous Training

While technological innovation often attracts most of the attention in discussions about artificial intelligence, the success of AI integration in education ultimately depends on how these tools are interpreted and used by teachers. Technology alone does not transform educational practice; rather, it is the pedagogical decisions of educators that determine whether new tools contribute meaningfully to learning processes or simply add another layer of complexity to classroom environments. For this reason, the role of teachers has become a central theme in research examining the adoption of AI in education.

A substantial body of literature indicates that teachers' beliefs, attitudes toward technology, and levels of digital self-efficacy strongly influence whether educational technologies are adopted and how they are used in practice. Studies examining technology integration have consistently shown that teachers who perceive digital tools as useful and manageable are more likely to incorporate them into their pedagogical strategies (Ifenthaler & Yau, 2020; Zawacki-Richter et al., 2019). Conversely, when educators feel uncertain about the functioning or implications of emerging technologies, adoption tends to remain limited or purely experimental.

The introduction of generative AI tools has intensified this discussion. Unlike many previous educational technologies, generative systems are capable of producing explanations, exercises, or textual content that resemble human-generated outputs. This characteristic has raised new questions regarding the evolving role of teachers as mediators of knowledge, facilitators of learning, and guides for critical thinking. Recent research suggests that teachers are increasingly required to develop new forms of AI literacy, enabling them not only to use these tools but also to evaluate their reliability, limitations, and ethical implications (Holmes et al., 2022; UNESCO, 2023).

In primary education, the role of teachers becomes even more significant. Young learners are still developing the cognitive and metacognitive abilities necessary to interpret digital information critically. As a result, teachers must play an active role in guiding students' interactions with AI systems, helping them understand that AI-generated responses should be examined, questioned, and contextualised rather than accepted uncritically. Several authors have therefore emphasised that AI integration should be understood as a pedagogically mediated process, where teachers remain responsible for framing technological tools within meaningful learning activities (Selwyn, 2019; Kasneci et al., 2023).

Given these challenges, continuous professional development becomes essential. Traditional forms of digital training often focus on technical aspects of using educational technologies. However, the complexity of AI systems requires broader forms of professional learning that include pedagogical, ethical, and critical dimensions. Teachers need opportunities to explore how AI tools function, how they can be integrated into classroom practice, and how potential risks—such as bias, misinformation, or overreliance—can be addressed responsibly.

Recent policy discussions also highlight the importance of developing AI literacy frameworks for educators. International organisations such as UNESCO and the European Commission have stressed that teachers must be supported in developing competencies that combine technological understanding with ethical awareness and pedagogical reflection (European Commission, 2022; UNESCO, 2023). Such frameworks aim to ensure that educators are not merely users of AI technologies but informed professionals capable of critically evaluating their educational implications.

Another important dimension of teacher development concerns collaborative professional learning environments. Research in educational innovation has shown that teachers often learn most effectively when they can exchange experiences, reflect collectively on classroom practices, and experiment with new approaches in supportive professional communities (Schleicher, 2018; Koper, 2020). Communities of practice, peer mentoring initiatives, and collaborative workshops can therefore play a crucial role in supporting teachers as they navigate the rapidly evolving landscape of AI in education.

In this sense, the integration of AI in schools should not be approached simply as a technical challenge but as a broader process of pedagogical transformation. Supporting teachers in this transition requires sustained institutional investment, opportunities for reflective professional learning, and clear ethical guidelines that help educators navigate the opportunities and risks associated with AI technologies. Ultimately, the effectiveness of AI in education will depend less on the sophistication of the algorithms involved and more on the capacity of teachers to integrate these tools thoughtfully into their pedagogical practice.

METHODOLOGY

This study adopts an interpretative case study approach combining qualitative and quantitative elements in order to explore primary school teachers' perceptions regarding the pedagogical potential of artificial intelligence tools—particularly generative systems such as ChatGPT—in educational practice. The study was designed as an exploratory investigation aimed at understanding how teachers interpret the opportunities and challenges associated with AI integration in primary education.

Rather than seeking statistical generalisation, the research focuses on developing a contextualised understanding of teachers' experiences, beliefs, and concerns. Such an approach is particularly appropriate in emerging research areas where empirical evidence is still limited and where exploratory insights can contribute to identifying relevant patterns and issues for further investigation (Cohen et al., 2018; Creswell & Creswell, 2022).

The study was guided by the following research question: What are the perceptions of primary school teachers regarding the potential of AI tools to enhance personalised teaching and student engagement?

In order to address this question, two specific objectives were defined:

- To identify teachers' perceptions regarding the relevance and potential uses of AI tools in primary education.
- To analyse teachers' views about the contribution of AI tools to students' learning processes after participating in a specialised workshop on AI in education.

These objectives align with existing literature highlighting the importance of examining educators' perceptions when analysing the integration of emerging technologies in educational contexts (Ifenthaler & Yau, 2020; Zawacki-Richter et al., 2019).

Research Design

The study follows a case study design focusing on a specific group of primary school teachers who participated in a professional development workshop dedicated to artificial intelligence in education. Case studies are widely used in educational research when the aim is to explore complex phenomena within their real-life contexts (Stake, 2005; Yin, 2018).

Given the exploratory nature of the study, a mixed-methods approach was adopted. Quantitative data were collected through closed-ended questionnaire items in order to provide an overview of participants' responses, while qualitative data obtained through open-ended questions allowed a deeper examination of teachers' perspectives and experiences.

Combining qualitative and quantitative approaches allowed for a more comprehensive understanding of the phenomenon under investigation. Mixed-methods designs are particularly valuable in educational technology research because they allow researchers to complement numerical trends with contextual interpretations derived from participants' narratives (Creswell & Plano Clark, 2018).

Participants

The study involved 22 primary school teachers working in Portuguese public schools. Participants were recruited through their participation in a national conference on educational technologies that included a workshop specifically dedicated to the pedagogical use of AI tools.

This sampling strategy can be described as purposeful sampling, as participants were selected because they had a demonstrated interest in educational technology and had voluntarily attended a professional development session on AI integration in education. Such an approach is common in exploratory studies where the aim is to gather informed perspectives from participants who have some familiarity with the topic under investigation (Cohen et al., 2018).

Demographic data collected through the questionnaire indicate the following distribution:

Gender: 11 female and 11 male teachers

Teaching experience:

- 11 teachers with more than 30 years of experience
- 10 teachers with between 21 and 30 years of experience
- 1 teacher with between 5 and 10 years of experience

Institutional context: all participants were currently working in Portuguese public schools.

Although the number of participants is relatively small, the sample includes experienced educators with substantial professional backgrounds in primary education. As the objective of the study is exploratory rather than representative, the findings should be interpreted as indicative insights rather than statistically generalisable results.

Instrument

Data were collected using a structured questionnaire designed to capture both quantitative and qualitative information about teachers' perceptions of AI in education.

The questionnaire included three types of items:

- Likert-scale items, designed to measure the degree of agreement with statements related to the pedagogical potential of AI tools.

- Multiple-choice questions, focusing on teachers' experiences and uses of AI technologies.
- Open-ended questions, allowing participants to describe perceived benefits, concerns, and challenges associated with AI use in educational contexts.

The questionnaire was reviewed by experts in educational technology and by experienced teachers of Portuguese in order to ensure clarity of wording and conceptual coherence. This review process contributed to improving the instrument's content validity.

The design of the questionnaire was informed by previous research examining teacher perceptions of emerging educational technologies and digital competence development (Hallowell, 2023; Santos et al., 2021).

Data Collection Procedures and Analysis

The questionnaire was administered immediately after the AI-focused workshop. This timing allowed teachers to reflect on both prior experiences and new insights gained during the event, following recommendations for technology acceptance studies.

Participation was voluntary, and informed consent was obtained. No identifying personal data were collected.

The analysis combined descriptive statistical techniques for the quantitative data and thematic analysis for the qualitative responses.

Quantitative data obtained from Likert-scale and multiple-choice questions were analysed using descriptive statistics, including frequencies and percentages. Given the exploratory nature of the study and the relatively small sample size, descriptive statistics were considered the most appropriate method for generalizat participants' responses without attempting statistical generalization.

Qualitative responses were analysed using thematic analysis, following the methodological framework proposed by Braun and Clarke (2021). This approach allows researchers to identify recurring patterns and themes within qualitative datasets while maintaining flexibility in interpretation.

The thematic analysis followed six main stages:

- Familiarisation with the data – All responses were read multiple times in order to gain an overall understanding of the participants' perspectives.
- Initial coding – Key ideas and recurring expressions were identified and labelled through initial codes.
- Theme identification – Codes were grouped into broader thematic categories reflecting common perceptions among participants.

- Theme review – Emerging themes were examined and refined in order to ensure conceptual coherence and internal consistency.
- Theme definition – Each theme was clearly defined and linked to the research objectives.
- Interpretation and reporting – The themes were interpreted in relation to existing literature on AI in education.

The integration of quantitative and qualitative data allowed for triangulation, strengthening the interpretative validity of the findings by examining teachers' perceptions from multiple analytical perspectives (Creswell & Creswell, 2022).

RESULTS AND DISCUSSION

This section presents a deeper interpretation of the results by situating Portuguese teachers' perceptions within the broader international research landscape on AI in education. By comparing local findings with studies conducted in Europe, North America, and Asia, it becomes possible to contextualise the attitudes of Portuguese primary teachers and identify convergences, divergences, and unique trends.

Adoption of AI Tools in Educational Contexts: A Global Comparison

The study revealed that 72.7% of teachers had already used AI in educational contexts, indicating relatively high early adoption (see Figure 1).

Figure 1. Teachers who have already used AI tools in educational contexts

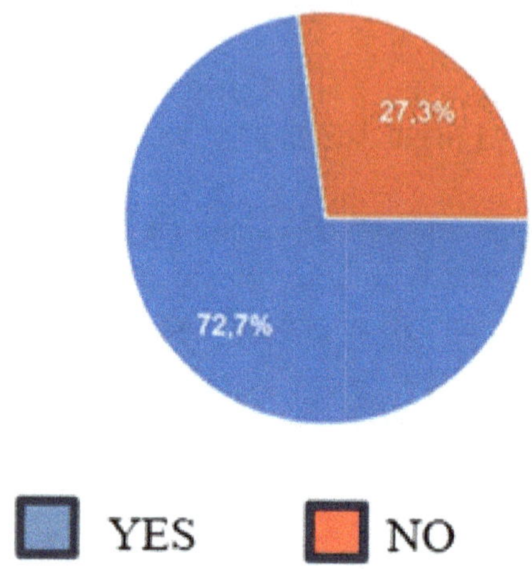

When compared with international data, this adoption rate is notably higher than figures observed internationally. For instance, Hallowell (2023) noted that only 51% of US educators had experimented with these tools by late 2023, while 60% in the UK. To quantify the magnitude of these differences, Cohen's h was calculated for each pairwise comparison: the gap between the Portuguese sample and US educators yields h = 0.45, approaching a medium effect, while the comparison with UK educators yields h = 0.27, a small-to-medium effect. These values indicate that the higher adoption rate observed in this study is not a marginal fluctuation but a substantively meaningful difference, most plausibly attributable to the purposeful sampling of teachers who had voluntarily engaged in technology-focused professional development.

This early adoption reflects broader global enthusiasm where educators rapidly experiment with AI tools despite limited training, as documented in multiple cross-national analyses (OECD, 2023; UNESCO, 2023).

Perceived Potential for Personalisation: Alignment with Global Trends

The finding that most teachers believe AI can personalise teaching is strongly aligned with international literature.

In the group of these teachers, only 12.5% considered that this use was not productive. These teachers did not consider that their use of AI in educational contexts had added anything to the teaching and learning process. However, we cannot ignore the fact that the type of use made was not questioned.

When asked to respond to the question "AI has the potential to personalize teaching and meet students' individual needs?", the majority of respondents answered affirmative, as shown in Figure 2. It should be noted that 1 corresponded to "Strongly Disagree" and 5 to "Strongly Agree" with the statement.

Figure 2. Teachers' responses to the statement "AI has the potential to personalize teaching and meet students' individual needs".

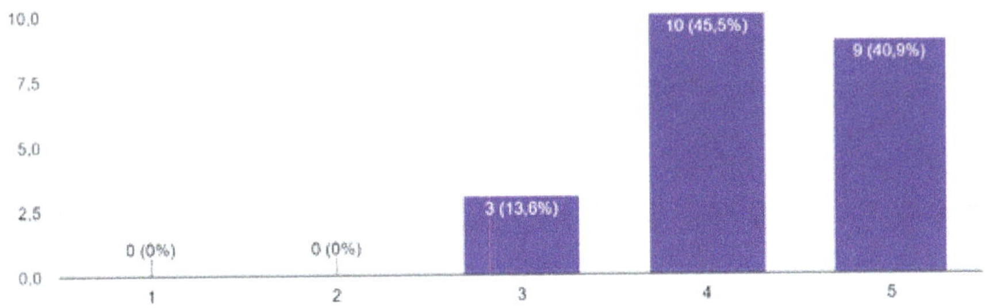

Personalisation is consistently identified in the literature as one of the most promising applications of AI in education. Comprehensive reviews by Holmes et al. (2019), Luckin et al. (2016), as well as Baker and Hawn (2022) and Zawacki-Richter et al. (2019), argue that AI's capacity to process vast amounts of data allows for the dynamic adaptation of content to individual needs. This capability is particularly critical in primary education, where the heterogeneity of learning paces is most pronounced.

This perspective is not limited to Western contexts; research in Asian nations, particularly China and South Korea, similarly indicates high confidence in adaptive learning systems which are already widely deployed. In this light, the optimism expressed by the Portuguese teachers in our study is not an isolated phenomenon, but rather reflects a globally shared consensus regarding AI's potential to address long-standing challenges in differentiation.

Feedback and Teaching Effectiveness: Convergence with ITS Research

The strong consensus (81%) that AI can improve feedback reflects established findings from research on Intelligent Tutoring Systems (ITS). Decades of studies demonstrate that AI-driven feedback can approximate the effectiveness of human tutoring, sometimes achieving learning gains of one standard deviation (VanLehn, 2011).

This perception is also consistent with more recent literature on LLM-based personalised feedback:

- Kasneci et al. (2023) and Teles & Moreira (2025) note that ChatGPT can generate high-quality, formative feedback in literacy and mathematics.
- Kasneci et al. (2023) highlight its potential for real-time conversational scaffolding.
- Akgun & Greenhow (2024) found that AI-enhanced feedback accelerates revision cycles in writing.

Thus, Portuguese teachers' views align with the international evidence base suggesting that AI can significantly enhance formative assessment processes.

Teacher Preparedness: A Worldwide Challenge

Perhaps one of the most critical findings is the fact that a significant majority, 86.4% of teachers, report feeling unprepared to integrate AI effectively into their professional practice. This concern is not unique to the Portuguese context; rather, it echoes a pervasive global pattern where large-scale studies consistently identify teacher readiness as the primary barrier to meaningful AI integration.

For instance, the UNESCO (2023) highlights a profound global training gap, noting that fewer than 10% of countries possess formal AI guidelines for educators. Furthermore, the OECD (2021, 2023) has repeatedly underscored a widespread lack of AI literacy among educators across European nations, a trend similarly reflected in research from Spain and Italy. In the US, for example, only 20% of teachers feel adequately trained (Hallowell, 2023), implying that 80% report insufficient preparedness — a figure comparable to the 86.4% observed in this study. A Cohen's h calculation confirms this convergence: the difference between the two proportions yields $h = 0.17$, a negligible effect falling below the conventional threshold for a small effect (h = 0.20). This result provides quantitative support for the interpretation that Portuguese primary teachers' sense of unpreparedness is not an idiosyncratic national phenomenon but part of a consistent global pattern. These findings align particularly closely with those from Southern Europe, where digital transformation policies are often unevenly distributed and pedagogical integration is still an emerging process.

ETHICAL CONCERNS AND DATA PRIVACY: A GLOBAL PRIORITY

The significant level of concern regarding ethics and data privacy observed among these teachers closely mirrors prevailing global trends. Across Europe, legislative efforts—most notably the EU AI Act—have placed a strong emphasis on transparency, data protection, and bias mitigation, reflecting a broad institutional move toward safeguarding digital environments. This teacher apprehension is well-supported by current literature: Williamson and Eynon (2020) have highlighted the profound risks of 'datafication' in primary schooling, while Kizilcec and Lee (2022) document persistent uncertainties regarding the fairness and accountability of AI-driven tools. Furthermore, the synthesis of evidence by Mehrabi et al. (2021) underscores the reality of algorithmic bias within large datasets. In this context, the fact that 72.7% of the participants in this study expressed anxiety over student data security is not an isolated finding; rather, it reflects a justified international unease. These concerns are grounded in tangible risks, particularly as generative systems often store or repurpose user prompts for model training (Bender & Gebru, 2021). Ultimately, the ethical reservations voiced by these Portuguese teachers align with a growing global movement advocating for a more responsible and ethically-grounded adoption of AI in education.

Benefits and Challenges: Convergence with Global Reviews

Benefits - The advantages highlighted by the participants—namely speed, efficiency, tutoring support, and enhanced creativity—find strong resonance in recent international research. For instance, the efficiency gains noted by the teachers are consistent with the findings of Fowler (2023), while the perceived value of AI as a tutoring agent aligns with decades of established research into Intelligent Tutoring Systems (Woolf, 2010; VanLehn, 2011). Furthermore, the potential for creativity enhancement, which several teachers mentioned, is a recurring theme in studies exploring multimodal generative AI, such as those by Akgun and Greenhow (2024).

Challenges - Conversely, the challenges identified by the teachers are deeply reflective of broader global concerns. Issues surrounding security and privacy remain at the forefront of the debate, as emphasized by both UNESCO (2023) and the OECD (2023). Similarly, the ethical risks and the potential for plagiarism correspond to the growing body of literature on academic integrity in the age of LLMs (Cotton et al., 2024). Perhaps most significantly, the fear of an over-dependence on AI echoes the critical perspective of Selwyn (2019) regarding 'automation bias' in educational settings.

Ultimately, the close alignment between these local perceptions and global trends suggests that Portuguese teachers are navigating the same complex tensions as their peers worldwide: a genuine enthusiasm for pedagogical innovation, tempered by a necessary caution regarding ethics, privacy, and readiness.

A Cautious Optimism Consistent with International Trends

Lastly, the finding that 59.1% of teachers consider the potential benefits of AI to outweigh its challenges aligns with a broader pattern of cautious and informed optimism identified in international research. Studies conducted in contexts such as the United States, the United Kingdom, Australia, and South Korea consistently report teacher attitudes that are neither uncritically enthusiastic nor predominantly resistant but rather recognised by an appreciation of AI's pedagogical possibilities alongside persistent concerns. While teachers tend to recognise the potential of AI to support teaching and learning, this optimism is tempered by uncertainty surrounding ethical implications and by pronounced concerns regarding their own preparedness to work with these technologies. The Portuguese data presented in this study therefore reflect an emerging global consensus in which AI is increasingly viewed as a transformative yet inherently ambivalent tool—one that demands careful governance frameworks, sustained investment in teacher education, and deliberate attention to equity in implementation.

CONCLUSIONS

The rapid expansion of generative AI has introduced new possibilities and challenges for educational systems worldwide. As these technologies become increasingly accessible, teachers are beginning to explore their potential to support teaching and learning processes, while simultaneously confronting new pedagogical, ethical, and organisational questions. This chapter sought to examine how a group of Portuguese primary school teachers perceive the opportunities and challenges associated with the use of AI tools in educational contexts.

The findings suggest that teachers generally recognise the potential of AI to support pedagogical practice. Participants highlighted several possible benefits, including the generation of teaching materials, support for personalised learning, and assistance in providing feedback to students. These perceptions are consistent with recent literature suggesting that generative AI can contribute to more flexible and adaptive forms of instruction when used as a complement to teacher-led learning activities.

However, the study also revealed important challenges. A large majority of participants reported feeling insufficiently prepared to integrate AI tools effectively into their professional practice. This finding highlights the existence of a significant gap between the rapid technological development of AI systems and the training opportunities available to teachers. Without adequate support and professional development, the pedagogical potential of these tools may remain underutilised.

Ethical and governance issues also emerged as relevant concerns among the participants. Teachers expressed uncertainty about the reliability of AI-generated information and about how data entered into AI platforms may be stored or used. Such concerns reflect broader debates in the literature regarding data protection, algorithmic transparency, and responsible AI adoption in educational environments.

A different point of reflection relates to the possible impact of AI on students' cognitive engagement. While AI tools may facilitate access to information and assist in learning tasks, there is also a risk that excessive reliance on automated responses could reduce opportunities for independent thinking and problem solving. In primary education in particular, where students are still developing foundational cognitive and critical thinking skills, careful pedagogical mediation is therefore essential.

Despite these concerns, the overall perception among participants can be described as one of cautious optimism. Teachers appear willing to explore the potential of AI technologies, provided that appropriate guidance, training, and ethical safeguards are in place. Rather than viewing AI as a substitute for teachers, participants tend to perceive it as a tool that may support teaching practices when integrated thoughtfully into classroom activities.

Lastly, this study also highlights the need for further empirical research in this field. Although interest in AI in education has grown rapidly, there are still relatively few longitudinal and large-scale studies focusing specifically on primary education contexts. Expanding the evidence base will therefore be essential for developing informed educational policies and pedagogical strategies that allow schools to benefit from AI technologies while addressing the risks associated with their use.

PRACTICAL IMPLICATIONS

The findings of this study suggest several practical implications for schools, teachers, and educational leaders seeking to integrate artificial intelligence into primary education. Rather than focusing solely on the technical adoption of AI tools, the results highlight the importance of careful pedagogical integration, institutional guidance, and sustained professional development. In this sense, the effective use of AI in schools depends not only on technological availability but also on the capacity of educational institutions to create supportive environments that enable responsible and meaningful use of these technologies (UNESCO, 2023; OECD, 2023).

Implications for Schools

For schools, one of the main challenges lies in integrating AI tools within existing pedagogical frameworks. Artificial intelligence should not be treated as an isolated technological solution, but rather as a resource that can support curriculum development and teaching practices. Schools therefore need to evaluate how AI tools can complement specific learning objectives and contribute to students' development.

Creating supportive technological environments is also essential. This includes ensuring reliable digital infrastructure, access to appropriate devices, and the availability of secure platforms that comply with data protection requirements. As generative AI systems often process user interactions on external servers, schools must pay particular attention to issues related to student data protection and responsible platform use.

In addition, schools should develop clear institutional guidelines regarding the pedagogical use of AI. Such policies can help clarify expectations regarding responsible use, academic integrity, and ethical considerations when interacting with AI-generated content. International policy frameworks increasingly emphasise the importance of governance structures that help schools navigate the opportunities and risks associated with emerging AI technologies (European Commission, 2022; UNESCO, 2023).

Implications for Teachers

For teachers, the increasing presence of AI in education highlights the need to strengthen AI literacy as part of professional competence. This involves more than simply learning how to operate new digital tools. Teachers need to understand how

AI systems generate responses, recognise their limitations, and critically evaluate the information produced by these technologies.

In classroom practice, teachers remain essential mediators between technological tools and students' learning processes. Rather than replacing traditional pedagogical strategies, AI tools should ideally support learning activities that encourage reflection, inquiry, and problem-solving. Teachers therefore need to design tasks that prompt students to analyse and question AI-generated information rather than simply accepting automated responses.

At the same time, educators have an important role in fostering critical digital literacy among students. As generative AI becomes increasingly present in everyday life, learners must develop the capacity to evaluate the credibility of digital information, recognise potential biases, and understand the limitations of automated systems. These competencies are increasingly recognised as essential components of contemporary digital education (OECD, 2023).

Implications for Leadership and Administration

Educational leadership plays a crucial role in shaping how AI technologies are introduced and used within schools. School leaders and administrators are responsible for establishing a shared vision regarding the pedagogical role of AI in education. This includes supporting teachers in exploring new tools while ensuring that technological innovation remains aligned with educational goals and ethical standards.

Leadership also has an important role in providing the conditions necessary for responsible experimentation. Allocating time for professional development, supporting collaborative learning among teachers, and ensuring access to appropriate technological infrastructure are all essential factors in facilitating sustainable innovation in schools.

Ultimately, school leadership should encourage systematic evaluation of how AI technologies affect educational practices. Monitoring their impact on teaching, student engagement, and teacher workload can help institutions identify both the benefits and potential challenges associated with AI integration. Such evidence-informed approaches are increasingly recommended in international policy discussions regarding the responsible use of AI in education (UNESCO, 2023; OECD, 2023).

POLICY RECOMMENDATIONS

While technological innovation often progresses faster than institutional regulation, the growing presence of generative AI tools in schools makes it increasingly necessary for policymakers to establish clear frameworks that guide their responsible and pedagogically meaningful use. The findings of this study reinforce the idea that effective AI integration requires coordinated action involving educational authorities, schools, teacher education institutions, and technology developers.

An important development in this area is the approval of the European Union Artificial Intelligence Act (EU AI Act) in 2024, which represents the first comprehensive legal framework aimed at regulating the development and use of AI systems. The regulation adopts a risk-based approach that classifies AI systems according to the potential risks they pose to fundamental rights and social systems. Within this framework, several educational applications—particularly those related to student evaluation, admission processes, or decisions that may significantly affect learners' educational trajectories—are considered high-risk systems and are therefore subject to strict requirements regarding transparency, accountability, human oversight, and data protection (European Commission, 2024). Although the regulation focuses primarily on the governance of AI systems rather than on specific pedagogical practices, it establishes an important legal foundation that educational institutions must take into account when adopting AI technologies.

A significant immediate policy priorities concerns the development of institutional and national guidelines for the pedagogical use of AI in schools. Teachers participating in this study expressed uncertainty about how AI tools should be used in classroom contexts, particularly with regard to ethical considerations and responsible use by students. Clear policy frameworks can help reduce this uncertainty by providing guidance on acceptable uses of AI in learning activities, the role of AI in assessment processes, and the responsibilities of educational institutions when adopting AI technologies. International organisations have also emphasised the need for educational systems to develop governance frameworks capable of balancing innovation with ethical safeguards (UNESCO, 2023; OECD, 2023).

Another key policy dimension concerns data protection and platform governance. Many generative AI tools operate through cloud-based infrastructures in which user interactions may be stored and analysed by external service providers. In educational contexts—especially when the users are minors—this raises significant concerns regarding where student data are stored, how long they are retained, and how they may be used. Policymakers therefore need to ensure that schools have access to secure and compliant digital platforms, as well as clear protocols regarding the responsible management of student data. In this regard, the principles established by the EU AI Act, together with existing European data protection frameworks, highlight the importance of transparency, accountability, and strong safeguards for the use of AI technologies in sensitive environments such as education (European Commission, 2024).

Teacher education policies also represent a crucial area of action. The results of this study confirm that many teachers feel insufficiently prepared to work with AI technologies in pedagogical contexts, with 86.4% of participants reporting insufficient readiness to integrate AI effectively into their professional practice. This finding is consistent with international evidence indicating that the gap between technological availability and teacher preparedness constitutes one of the most significant structural barriers to meaningful AI integration in schools (UNESCO, 2023; OECD, 2023; Hallowell, 2023). Addressing this gap requires more than isolated training sessions or voluntary participation in professional development workshops. It demands the design and sustained implementation of national training programmes that are systematically embedded within teacher education structures, adequately resourced, and aligned with pedagogical rather than merely technical objectives.

In practical terms, national training programmes for AI in primary education should be organised around three interconnected dimensions. The first is technological literacy, which involves equipping teachers with a sufficiently robust understanding of how AI systems — and generative models in particular — produce outputs, what data they rely on, and what their inherent limitations are. This dimension should not be reduced to the ability to operate a specific tool; rather, it should develop a conceptual understanding transferable across different platforms and contexts. The second dimension is pedagogical integration, which concerns the capacity to design learning activities in which AI tools support rather than replace intellectual effort, promote inquiry and critical thinking, and remain anchored in clearly defined curricular goals. The third dimension is ethical and critical awareness, encompassing the ability to recognise algorithmic bias, evaluate the reliability of AI-generated content, protect student data, and navigate questions of academic integrity responsibly. Competency frameworks such as UNESCO's AI Competency Framework for Teachers (UNESCO, 2023) and the European DigComp and DigCompEdu frameworks (European Commission, 2022) offer useful reference points for structuring this type of integrated professional development. National educational authorities should draw on these frameworks to define minimum competency standards for the use of AI in schools and ensure that training programmes are designed to meet them across all career stages, from initial teacher preparation to mid-career and late-career continuing education.

Equity considerations must also be addressed at the policy level. Access to digital technologies, infrastructure, and training opportunities varies considerably across educational systems and institutions. Without targeted policy measures, the increasing adoption of AI tools may risk reinforcing existing educational inequalities. Ensuring equitable access to digital resources, as well as providing support for schools with limited technological capacity, should therefore form part of broader national strategies for AI in education.

That said, policymakers should encourage collaboration between education systems, research institutions, and technology developers. The complexity of AI integration in education requires multidisciplinary expertise that combines pedagogical knowledge, technological development, ethical reflection, and policy analysis. Establishing collaborative networks and research–practice partnerships can help ensure that AI tools designed for educational purposes are aligned with real classroom needs and pedagogical objectives.

Taken together, these policy considerations suggest that the integration of AI in education should not be understood simply as a technological shift, but as a broader process of educational transformation. The existence of emerging regulatory frameworks such as the EU AI Act provides an important foundation, but their effective implementation will depend on how educational systems translate these principles into concrete policies, professional development initiatives, and responsible practices within schools.

DIRECTIONS FOR FUTURE RESEARCH

As both UNESCO (2023) and the OECD (2023) have observed, the integration of artificial intelligence in education is still at an early stage. Consequently, further research is not merely beneficial but essential for moving beyond conceptual debates and toward evidence-informed educational practice. While a growing body of literature has examined AI in higher education contexts, important gaps remain regarding its implications for primary schooling. Building on the tensions and opportunities identified in this study, several research directions emerge as particularly relevant for advancing knowledge in this field.

Longitudinal and Intervention-Based Approaches

An important pressing need concerns the development of longitudinal research examining how teachers' perceptions and practices evolve over time. Teachers' attitudes toward technology are not static; rather, they tend to develop as educators gain experience, confidence, and access to professional support structures (Ifenthaler & Yau, 2020). Future studies should therefore investigate how AI becomes— or fails to become—embedded in everyday pedagogical routines over extended periods.

In addition to longitudinal approaches, there is also a need for classroom-based intervention studies. Earlier research on intelligent tutoring systems demonstrated significant improvements in learning outcomes in certain contexts (VanLehn, 2011), yet the impact of contemporary generative AI tools, particularly large language models, on foundational learning areas such as literacy and numeracy remains largely unexplored in primary education. Design-Based Research methodologies may prove particularly valuable in this regard, as they allow for iterative refinement of pedagogical interventions through close collaboration between researchers and practitioners.

Exploring Student Agency and Ethical Practice

Other important research direction concerns the perspectives and experiences of students themselves. Much of the current research on AI in education has focused primarily on teachers, educational leaders, and policy discussions. However, primary-aged learners actively interpret and engage with digital technologies in ways that are shaped by their developmental stage and prior technological experiences (Selwyn, 2019).

Future research should therefore explore how children conceptualise AI systems, how they distinguish between human and machine expertise, and how interactions with AI tools influence their autonomy, creativity, and help-seeking behaviours. At the same time, more empirical work is needed to understand how ethical challenges related to AI emerge in real educational contexts. While policy discussions frequently emphasise concerns such as algorithmic bias and data privacy (Bender & Gebru, 2021), there is still limited evidence on how schools operationalise these safeguards in practice. Understanding how teachers mediate AI-generated content and address issues such as authorship, originality, and responsibility will be particularly important in primary education contexts (Kizilcec & Lee, 2022).

Comparative Perspectives and Professional Development

Comparative international research also offers promising opportunities for understanding how different educational systems approach AI integration. Adoption patterns vary significantly across countries, influenced by factors such as technological infrastructure, cultural values, educational traditions, and policy priorities. For instance, education systems in East Asia have explored large-scale implementation of AI-driven adaptive learning technologies (Chen et al., 2020; UNESCO, 2021), while several European countries have emphasised digital ethics, teacher autonomy, and responsible innovation.

Comparative studies examining these different approaches may help identify transferable practices while highlighting contextual constraints that influence implementation. Such research could also contribute to a better understanding of how national policy frameworks shape teachers' readiness, institutional support structures, and classroom practices.

At the same time, future research should continue to explore effective models of teacher professional development for AI integration. Moving beyond technical training, studies should examine how professional learning initiatives - such as communities of practice, peer mentoring, and collaborative experimentation - support teachers in developing critical awareness, ethical judgement, and pedagogical confidence when working with AI technologies.

Taken together, these research directions highlight the need for a sustained and multidisciplinary research agenda capable of addressing the pedagogical, ethical, and organisational implications of AI in primary education. Expanding the empirical evidence base will be essential for ensuring that educational systems are able to harness the potential of AI technologies while safeguarding the values of equity, responsibility, and meaningful learning.

REFERENCES

Baker, R. S. (2016). Stupid tutoring systems, intelligent humans. *International Journal of Artificial Intelligence in Education, 26*(2), 600–614. DOI: 10.1007/s40593-016-0105-0

Baker, R. S., & Hawn, A. (2022). Algorithmic bias in education. *International Journal of Artificial Intelligence in Education, 32*(4), 1052–1092. DOI: 10.1007/s40593-021-00285-9

Bender, E. M., & Gebru, T. (2021). On the dangers of stochastic parrots: Can language models be too big? *Proceedings of the 2021 ACM Conference on Fairness, Accountability, and Transparency*, 610–623. https://doi.org/DOI: 10.1145/3442188.3445922

Braun, V., & Clarke, V. (2021). Thematic analysis: A practical guide. *Sage (Atlanta, Ga.).*

Brown, T. B., Mann, B., Ryder, N., Subbiah, M., Kaplan, J. D., Dhariwal, P., . . . Amodei, D. (2020). Language models are few-shot learners. *arXiv preprint arXiv:2005.14165*. https://arxiv.org/abs/2005.14165

Carbonell, J. R. (1970). AI in CAI: An artificial-intelligence approach to computer-assisted instruction. *IEEE Transactions on Man-Machine Systems, 11*(4), 190–202. DOI: 10.1109/TMMS.1970.299942

Chen, X., Xie, H., Zou, D., & Hwang, G.-J.CHEN. (2020). Application and theory gaps during the rise of Artificial Intelligence in Education. *Computers and Education: Artificial Intelligence, 1*, 100002. Advance online publication. DOI: 10.1016/j.caeai.2020.100002

Cohen, L., Manion, L., & Morrison, K. (2018). *Research methods in education* (8th ed.). Routledge.

Cotton, D. R. E., Cotton, P. A., & Shipway, J. R. (2024). Chatting and cheating: Ensuring academic integrity in the era of ChatGPT. *Innovations in Education and Teaching International, 61*(2), 228–239. DOI: 10.1080/14703297.2023.2190148

Creswell, J. W., & Creswell, J. D. (2022). *Research design: Qualitative, quantitative, and mixed methods approaches* (6th ed.). SAGE.

Creswell, J. W., & Plano Clark, V. L. (2018). *Designing and conducting mixed methods research* (3rd ed.). SAGE.

Dias-Trindade, S., & Moreira, A. (2022). Digital competence in Portuguese education: A national perspective. *Education Sciences*, *12*(3), 184. DOI: 10.3390/educsci12030184

European Commission. (2019). *A definition of AI: Main capabilities and disciplines.* Publications Office of the European Union. https://data.europa.eu/doi/10.2759/177365

European Commission. (2022).Ethical guidelines on the use of artificial intelligence (AI) and data in teaching and learning for educators. Publications Office of the European Union. https://education.ec.europa.eu/news/ethical-guidelines-on-the-use-of-ai-and-data-in-teaching-and-learning-for-educators

Floridi, L., & Chiriatti, M. (2020). GPT-3: Its nature, scope, limits, and consequences. *Minds and Machines*, *30*(4), 681–694. DOI: 10.1007/s11023-020-09548-1

Goodfellow, I., Bengio, Y., & Courville, A. (2016). *Deep learning*. MIT Press.

Hallowell, M. (2023). *Educator AI Report: Perceptions, practices, and potential.* Imagine Learning.

Hargittai, E. (2002). Second-level digital divide: Differences in people's online skills. *First Monday*, *7*(4). Advance online publication. DOI: 10.5210/fm.v7i4.942

Holmes, W., Bialik, M., & Fadel, C. (2019). *Artificial intelligence in education: Promises and implications for teaching and learning*. Center for Curriculum Redesign.

Ifenthaler, D., & Yau, J. Y.-K. (2020). Utilising learning analytics to support study success in higher education: A systematic review. *Educational Technology Research and Development*, *68*(4), 1961–1990. DOI: 10.1007/s11423-020-09788-z

Jordan, M. I., & Mitchell, T. M. (2015). Machine learning: Trends, perspectives, and prospects. *Science*, *349*(6245), 255–260. DOI: 10.1126/science.aaa8415 PMID: 26185243

Kasneci, E., Sessler, K., Küchemann, S., Bannert, M., Janson, A., Sailer, M., & Kasneci, G. (2023). ChatGPT for good? On opportunities and challenges of large language models for education. *Learning and Individual Differences*, *5*, 100128. DOI: 10.1016/j.lindif.2023.102274

Kizilcec, R. F., & Lee, H. (2022). Algorithmic fairness in education. In Holmes, W., & Porayska-Pomsta, K. (Eds.), *Ethics in Artificial Intelligence in Education.* Routledge. DOI: 10.4324/9780429329067-10

Koper, R. (2020). How do students want to learn in online distance education? Profiling student preferences. *International Review of Research in Open and Distance Learning, 35*(3), 263–283. DOI: 10.19173/irrodl.v16i1.2000

Luckin, R., Holmes, W., Griffiths, M., & Forcier, L. B. (2016). *Intelligence unleashed: An argument for AI in education.* Pearson., DOI: 10.1063/5.0129803

Mehrabi, N., Morstatter, F., Saxena, N., Lerman, K., & Galstyan, A. (2021). A survey on bias and fairness in machine learning. *ACM Computing Surveys, 54*(6), 1–35. DOI: 10.1145/3457607

Mitchell, M. (2019). *Artificial intelligence: A guide for thinking humans.* Penguin.

Moreira, F. T., Vairinhos, M., & Ramos, F. (2021). Conceptualization of Hypersituation as Result of IoT in Education. In Mealha, Ó., Rehm, M., & Rebedea, T. (Eds.), *Ludic, Co-design and Tools Supporting Smart Learning Ecosystems and Smart Education. Smart Innovation, Systems and Technologies* (Vol. 197). Springer., DOI: 10.1007/978-981-15-7383-5_6

Norris, P. (2001). *Digital divide. Civic engagement, information poverty and the internet world-wide.* Cambridge University Press., DOI: 10.1108/146366903322008287

OECD. (2021). *21st-century readers: Developing literacy skills in a digital world.* OECD Publishing., DOI: 10.1787/a83d84eb-

OECD. (2023). *AI and the future of skills.* OECD Publishing., DOI: 10.1787/5e031222-

Open, A. I. (2023). *GPT-4 technical report.* https://doi.org//arXiv.2303.08774DOI: 10.48550

Rajaraman, V. (2023). From ELIZA to ChatGPT. *Reson, 28*(6), 889–905. DOI: 10.1007/s12045-023-1620-6

Russell, S., & Norvig, P. (2021). *Artificial intelligence: A modern approach* (4th ed.). Pearson.

Santos, J. M., Almeida, M., & Celina, A. A. (2021). Computational thinking in elementary school in the age of artificial intelligence: Where is the teacher? *Review of Education, 14*(2), 55–71. DOI: 10.33947/1980-6469-v14n2-3

Schleicher, A. (2018). *Valuing our teachers and raising their status: How communities can help.* OECD Publishing. DOI: 10.1787/9789264292697-en

Selwyn, N. (2019). *Should robots replace teachers? AI and the future of education.* Polity Press.

Stake, R. E. (2005). Qualitative case studies. In Denzin, N. K., & Lincoln, Y. S. (Eds.), *The SAGE handbook of qualitative research* (3rd ed., pp. 443–466). SAGE.

Suppes, P., & Atkinson, R. C. (1967). *Computer-assisted instruction: Methods and results*. Academic Press.

Teles, R. O., & Moreira, F. T. (2025). Integrating AI in Formative Assessment Under UDL Principles in Diverse Learning Environments. In Moreira, F., & Teles, R. (Eds.), *Improving Student Assessment With Emerging AI Tools* (pp. 95–122). IGI Global Scientific Publishing., DOI: 10.4018/979-8-3693-6170-2.ch004

UNESCO. (2021). *AI and education: Guidance for policy-makers*. UNESCO Publishing. https://unesdoc.unesco.org/ark:/48223/pf0000376709

UNESCO. (2023). *Guidance for generative AI in education and research*. UNESCO Publishing. https://unesdoc.unesco.org/ark:/48223/pf0000386693

VanLehn, K. (2011). The relative effectiveness of human tutoring, intelligent tutoring systems, and other tutoring systems. *Educational Psychologist*, *46*(4), 197–221. DOI: 10.1080/00461520.2011.611369

Weizenbaum, J. (1966). ELIZA—A computer program for the study of natural language communication between man and machine. *Communications of the ACM*, *9*(1), 36–45. DOI: 10.1145/365153.365168

Williamson, B., & Eynon, R. (2020). Historical threads, missing strands, and future directions: A sociotechnical perspective on AI in education. *Learning, Media and Technology*, *45*(3), 223–235. DOI: 10.1080/17439884.2020.1798995

Woolf, B. P. (2010). *Building intelligent interactive tutors: Student-centered strategies for revolutionizing e-learning*. Morgan Kaufmann.

Yin, R. K. (2018). *Case study research and applications: Design and methods* (6th ed.). SAGE.

Zawacki-Richter, O., Marín, V., Bond, M., & Gouverneur, F. (2019). Systematic review of research on artificial intelligence applications in higher education. *International Journal of Educational Technology in Higher Education*, *16*(1), 39. DOI: 10.1186/s41239-019-0171-0

Chapter 12
Bibliometric Analysis of the Use of Artificial Intelligence in Chemistry Education With VOSviewer

Buket Koçak
http://orcid.org/0009-0009-3564-4870
Hacettepe University, Turkey

Fatma Alkan
http://orcid.org/0000-0003-2784-875X
Hacettepe University, Turkey

Ayşem Seda Yücel
http://orcid.org/0000-0002-7654-582X
Hacettepe University, Turkey

ABSTRACT

The aim of this study is to present a general map of the studies on the use of artificial intelligence in chemistry education to date. The articles were analyzed with Scopus database using bibliometric analysis method. The studies were examined with various keywords and maps of citations were created according to the results of the analysis. Bibliometric analysis results were visualized with VOSviewer program. In this study, 1,538 results were found. The research results were limited to the last ten years between 2014 and 2024, various publication names, subject areas and language options were used, and analysis studies were carried out on 772 research

DOI: 10.4018/979-8-3373-9883-9.ch012

results. As a result of the analysis, they were classified according to keywords, countries, publications, authors and citations. According to this classification; it was determined that the most studies on the concept of artificial intelligence in chemistry education were conducted in the USA. This research covers the results of studies on the use of artificial intelligence in chemistry education.

INTRODUCTION

Today, technological advances are the most striking element of a country's level of development. Like every field, education has taken its share from these advances and directly affected education (Akbaba & Kılıç, 2022). Bibliometric methods are used to draw a big picture of these developments and provide us with an idea about the studies. In a period when we live in the age of technology, the use of technology in the educational environment has emerged as a result of students' interest in technology and the use of technology in every aspect of their lives (Erdoğan & Yıldırım, 2023). The use of technology in educational activities; It is understood that technology affects education from the studies that include the results of the effect of computer-aided, simulation, animation or artificial intelligence use on some variables that attract attention in education such as academic achievement, attitude, etc. (Alkan & Mustafaoğlu 2023; Altundağ & Koçer, 2023; Akbaba & Ertaş, 2022; Uyulgan & Akkuzu Güven, 2022; Karyağdı & Aydın, 2023). It is very important to adapt students to technology-supported online teaching environments (Bezen, 2023). As a result, teachers, who are the most important element of education, are expected to have both field knowledge and to adapt technology with field knowledge in a professional sense (Sağlam-Kaya, 2019). It is necessary to survey the latest advancements in artificial intelligence and examine their integration into the educational frameworks.

Artificial intelligence is a digital technology. This technology is a computer-managed system that compiles data transmitted by humans, performs tasks, and combines and processes human experience by imitating human intelligence (Tamer & Övgün, 2020; Meço & Çoştu, 2022). With the development of technology, artificial intelligence spreads on the World. The use of artificial intelligence in education provides various benefits for teachers, students or each individual learner. It is seen that the use of artificial intelligence applications in the field of education has an impact in many areas such as the planning of educational programs, the organization of course materials, and the development of teaching techniques in the work and functioning of individuals in the education and training process (Meço & Çoştu, 2022). Artificial intelligence is a field that has been developing recently due to the development of technology. It has been developed with the development of an interdisciplinary approach by various fields such as computer science, mathematics, philosophy, neuroscience and psychology (Jia et al., 2023; Kok et al., 2009; Simmons & Chappell, 1988; Wang, 2019). For instance, Artificial Intelligence (AI) and the Internet of Things (IoT) are now key components in the Philippines' technological development framework, with a profound impact across sectors like education, healthcare, finance, disaster management, and public administration. These technological advancements are fostering innovations in quality management systems within higher education institutions and are regarded as strategic instruments for automation and sustainability. The Philippines, as a developing nation, is slowly embracing these technologies not only in urban areas but also in rural locations, indicating a concerted nationwide effort to keep abreast of the demands of the Fourth Industrial Revolution. Notably, Filipino professionals tend to view AI favorably as a mechanism to augment productivity and efficiency, demonstrating a willingness to engage in training and integrate AI into their professional endeavors. This indicates an increasing societal receptiveness to AI and IoT as tools for sustainable development and equity within the Philippine context (Asio & Soriano, 2025). Furthermore, artificial intelligence is being used across various levels of education in Europe. In recent years, European education policies have focused more on the integration of digital technologies and artificial intelligence into teaching and learning solutions. Accordingly, various strategies and action plans exist within the framework of the European approach to artificial intelligence. The Digital Education Action Plan (2021–2027) provided by the European Commission emphasizes the importance of digital transformation, technologically supported learning environments and digital competencies in education.

In other words, AI supports teachers in organizing and planning their lessons. Teachers, structure their lessons in advance, carry them out in the classroom, and reflect on outcomes to enhance their teaching methods. A lesson plan plays a crucial role in helping educators organize and demonstrate effective instructional strategies (Lee & Zhai, 2024; Lee et al., et al., 2022). The use of AI in education, especially in chemistry education, contributes to the comprehensive expansion of lesson planning, laboratory activities, technologically supported simulations, animations and videos supported by artificial intelligence.

Rapid developments and advances in the application of machine learning have brought about a trend towards the use of artificial intelligence in the assessment of students' learning situations. This has paved the way for students to identify themselves in the field of artificial intelligence and how they can be trained in this field. Bower et al., (2014) stated that augmented reality applications offer interactive and visualization-supported learning environments in educational processes. This study examines the applications and pedagogical potential of augmented reality in education. It specifically highlights the importance of AR applications in terms of visualization, interaction, and supporting students' higher-order thinking skills. The use of artificial intelligence is seen as an aid that can increase teaching efficiency in the educational environment. An example of this is the use of Scratch to instruct students to learn and practice grouping and simple neural network structure (Estevez et al., 2019). When teaching AI, it is not only about giving students the basics of deep learning technology. It is also necessary to apply AI methods in practical education to help students fully understand the concepts involved. For example, different types of AI assistants for foreign language teaching have been organized and their effects have been studied (Pokrivčáková, 2019). Another example is the visualized neural network interface application. Using this artificial intelligence application, students can create neural network models by changing the structure and parameters of different models. This feature offers students the opportunity to develop a more intuitive understanding (Choo & Liu, 2018). Learning attitudes have a positive impact on everyone's performance. It has been determined that the use of artificial intelligence in teaching positively affects students' interest in learning and learning attitudes. Also, the study which is about the students' attitudes toward AI, the level of AI literacy, and AI self-efficacy reveals that students' attitudes toward artificial intelligence significantly influences their learning processes across cognitive, affective, and behavioral dimensions. Additionally, AI literacy and AI self-efficacy emerge as significant predictors of these attitudes (Asio & Gadia, 2024). With a model based on multiple theories and an AI learning platform, the learning status of students was effectively revealed. Artificial intelligence applications should be included when planning a student-centered learning environment, so that students' attitudes towards learning will be increased and their concerns about artificial intelligence will be reduced (Chang et al., 2024). The use of productive artificial intelligence in chemistry education; in addition to these, the use of laboratories in virtual environment, the use of animation, simulation in education with the use of technology and artificial intelligence, modeling of abstract concepts, increasing or improving the mental, affective, psychological and academic development of students have important contributions. There are also various analysis methods for investigating the use of artificial intelligence in chemistry education. Previous studies have highlighted that students generally perceive chemistry as an abstract and challenging subject, which leads to reduced motivation and participation in chemistry learning environments. To address these challenges, researchers emphasize the importance of laboratory-based, student-centered, and technology-enhanced learning environments that support conceptual understanding, self-efficacy, and meaningful learning experiences (Mustafaoğlu & Alkan, 2024).

Recently, bibliometric methods are often used to track developments in a subject. Bibliometrics is a widely used method to draw big pictures in literature review. Bibliometrics can be performed with various parameters depending on the purpose of the research or the topic of interest of the researcher. Bibliometrics is a tool that collects data from published works such as books, journals, proceedings, etc. from the conceptual, social and intellectual aspects of disciplines; analyzes a large number of studies by applying basic or advanced statistical techniques and using statistical tools, thus revealing trends and citations and/or co-citations on a particular topic by year, country, author, journal, method, theory and research problem (Toker, 2022). In recent years, advances in computer technology have made bibliometric analysis more widespread and effective. Researchers use bibliometrics in areas such as resource allocation, policy development, and performance evaluation. This method contributes to research and decision-making processes by revealing trends and gaps in the literature (Duran & Aydın, 2024).

Bibliometric methods are based on obtaining bibliographic datas from databases to obtain an image of the field of science of interest (Zupic, 2015) and are generally done for two purposes. Descriptive and evaluative bibliometrics aim to measure productivity and literature use (Demir & Erigüç, 2018). Based on this, the aim of this study is to examine the use of artificial intelligence in chemistry education with bibliometric analysis method and to contribute to the field with research findings. In this article, the use of artificial intelligence in chemistry education was investigated through bibliometric analysis.

This study aims to reveal general trends in the field by examining research on the use of artificial intelligence in chemistry education using bibliometric analysis. In recent years, artificial intelligence applications have become increasingly widespread in education, and are becoming more visible, especially in areas with a high concentration of abstract concepts, such as chemistry education. AI-supported applications make significant contributions in terms of visualizing abstract chemical processes, creating personalized learning environments, and supporting laboratory practices. It is thought that augmented reality, virtual reality, and AI-supported applications can support the learning process, especially in schools with limited laboratory facilities.

Although there are various bibliometric studies in the literature on artificial intelligence and education, it is observed that the majority of existing studies focus on general education or science education. It is noteworthy that bibliometric studies examining artificial intelligence applications specifically in chemistry education are limited. The importance of artificial intelligence in chemistry education is not limited only to technological advancements; it is also significant in terms of teaching abstract concepts, supporting laboratory practices, and making learning processes more effective. It is believed that AI-assisted applications can contribute to the teaching of topics that are difficult for students to understand, especially atomic models, chemical bonds, and reaction mechanisms.

In this study, publication trends, prominent concepts, countries, institutions, and research relationships regarding the use of artificial intelligence in chemistry education were examined using bibliometric analysis. It is thought that this study will provide a general framework for current research trends in the field, guide researchers, and contribute to future studies. The introduction of artificial intelligence into chemistry education has contributed to the development of student-centered and interactive learning environments. AI-powered simulations, particularly those used in teaching abstract chemistry topics such as atomic models, support conceptual learning by providing students with individualized feedback and encourage active participation in the lesson (Köfter et al., 2026).

Although there are various bibliometric studies in the literature on artificial intelligence and education, studies specifically focused on chemistry education appear to be limited. Jia et al. (2024) examined general trends in the use of artificial intelligence in science education. However, it is observed that while the existing abundance of science education fields focuses generally, the bibliometric series specifically on educational chemistry are limited. Zawacki-Richter et al. (2019) examined the applications of artificial intelligence in higher education by conducting a systematic review. Nonetheless, research concentrating explicitly on the use of artificial intelligence in chemistry education remain limited. To give another example, Chen et al. (2020) examined the use of artificial intelligence in education from multifaceted perspectives and highlighted the growing interest in AI-assisted learning environments. However, discipline-specific analyses focusing on chemistry education are still limited in the literature. In addition, Virtual reality-supported learning environments have come to the forefront more in higher education and technology-supported learning research in recent years. Existing systematic reviews mainly focused on virtual reality environments and distance learning in general higher education contexts. However, bibliometric investigations examining artificial intelligence-supported technologies such as virtual reality, augmented reality, and immersive learning specifically within chemistry education are still scarce (Mystakidis et al., 2021).

RESEARCH METHOD

Bibliometrics is broadly defined as a set of methods that examines scientific publications such as journals, books, and articles according to many features such as subject, year, contributing institution, keywords used, number of authors, citations, and co-citations, and provides clues to the relevant discipline, field, subject, institutions, countries, authors, and collaboration between authors (Al & Tonta, 2004; Ukşul, 2016). Bibliometric analysis is related to informetric. Here, different aspects of information are examined quantitatively (Wolfram, 2003). Bibliometric analysis method has recently been highly preferred by researchers as it helps to understand the nature and dynamics of a research field (Ellegaard & Wallin, 2015; Mejia et al., 2021). The databases used internationally in bibliometric analysis are Web of Science (WoS), Scopus, Google Scholar, ProQuest databases, while databases such as ULAKBIM and YÖK Thesis Center are preferred in Turkey.

One of the main focuses of this study was to obtain data for comprehensive bibliometric analysis of research publications on AI and chemistry education from 1984 to 2024. The traces of AI and chemistry education research in the Scopus database emerged in 1984. In the present study, the researchers divided the research methodology into three main phases. First, data was collected from the Scopus database. The search results were then examined to generate the results of the citation analysis, which formed the second part of the research. In the third stage, the citation analysis which includes co-occurrence – keywords, citation – sources, citation – organization, co-citations – cited references, was performed using VOSviewer. The co-citation analysis helped to identify emerging clusters that provide a framework for further research in ethics and higher education.

Document scanning method was used in this research. 1,538 results were reached and 772 data results were bibliometrically analyzed with various limitations and network maps were created with the VOSviewer program showing the results of the studies. The studies between the years 2014-2024 were examined and current data were obtained. Document analysis is the process of collecting, examining, and interpreting documents for research. This method is often used as a complement to other methods, but it can also be used alone (Sak, R. et al., 2021; Bowen, 2009; Saldana 2011).

Figure 1. Bibliometric Analysis Approach

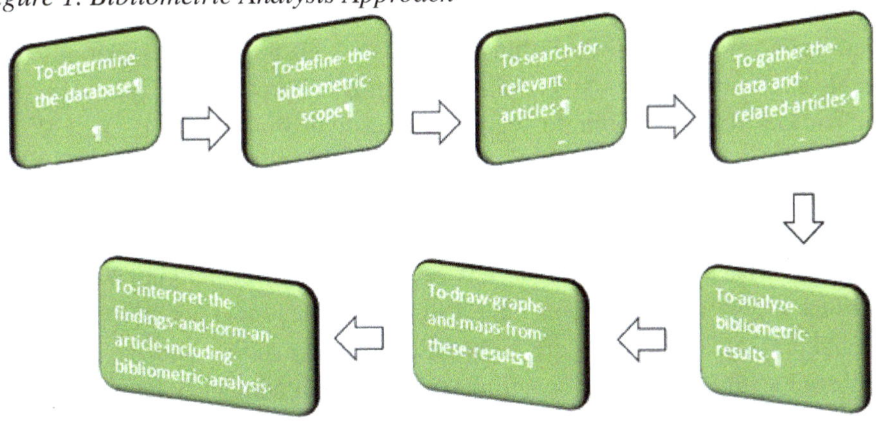

In the literature, studies on the use of artificial intelligence in chemistry education were examined with the keywords "chemistry education" and "artificial intelligence" and 1,533 results were found. One way of using technology in education is the application of artificial intelligence (AI). According to the Merriam-Webster dictionary, AI is the ability of a machine to imitate intelligent human behavior. It is used for computer programs to perform tasks that require human intelligence (Becker, 2017; Luckin et al., 2016). Popenici and Kerr (2017) define AI systems as systems that deal with complex human actions such as learning, analyzing, synthesizing and adapting (Hopcan et al., 2023). With the development of technology, it is seen that artificial intelligence has changed and developed for the needs of artificial intelligence, and the effect of artificial intelligence is seen in fields such as medicine, engineering, industry as well as computer technology (Doğan, 2002; Arslan, 2020). When the studies that artificial intelligence provides to education are examined, different approaches with knowledge, logic and data-based applications are seen (Holmes et al., 2019).

The use of artificial intelligence in chemistry education contributes to chemists and chemistry educators in areas such as laboratory work, experiments and measuring students' performance. It is also important for chemistry teachers to receive the necessary training to use AI ethically and effectively and to implement it in chemistry teaching practices, courses, laboratories, and assessment stages. In other words, chemistry educators should also focus on the ethical aspects of using generative AI in order to promote its responsible integration into teaching practices. AI studies the creation of systems that can perform activities that normally require human intelligence, such as making choices, learning, and adapting to new environments (Blonder, R. & Feldman-Maggor, Y.,2024; Samoili et al., 2020). In this context, it is important for both educators and learners in chemistry education to integrate AI use ethically and efficiently. All things considered, even though AI chatbots offer valuable support in solving and explaining chemistry problems, it should be used by human knowledge, meaningful learning and critical thinking (Clark, T.M.,2023).

In addition to the use of artificial intelligence in chemistry education, generative artificial intelligence literacy has become important not only in chemistry but also in many other fields. This is because AI literacy includes different skills such as understanding what artificial intelligence is, being able to use it, applying it in different situations, evaluating the outputs, and also having awareness about ethical issues (Ng et al., 2021). These skills are highlighted in many studies and are considered necessary for students in today's digital world. The four competencies suggested by Ng and colleagues are also used in different university contexts. For example, some universities in Hong Kong have already included AI literacy into their curriculum in order to improve students' skills in this area (Ng et al., 2024; Ng et al., 2023a; Kong et al., 2023). This shows that AI literacy is not only theoretical but also applied in real educational settings. According to Ng and O'Dea (2024), generative artificial intelligence literacy has a multidimensional structure and is affected by different individual and contextual factors. In their study, it is emphasized that factors such as the country context and previous learning about artificial intelligence play an important role in developing AI literacy. However, factors like age and education level do not have a significant effect. In addition, it is stated that although students are able to use AI tools, they are not always able to evaluate the results critically. On the other hand, students who receive training about artificial intelligence become more aware and use these tools in a more critical and conscious way. This situation shows that teaching AI literacy is important for developing not only technical skills but also critical thinking skills.

RESULTS AND DISCUSSION

On 01/06/2024, a bibliometric analysis of the use of generative artificial intelligence in chemistry education was made and 1,538 results were reached, and the research results were summarized by using VOSviewer program with 772 data results and graphs and network maps in 9 different subheadings by making various limitations. These 1,538 results were found in the search conducted by selecting "all fields" with the keywords "Artificial Intelligence" and "Chemistry Education". According to the years, 885 articles, 414 conference papers,

112 reviews, 27 books, 85 book chapters, 6 editorials, 4 retracted articles, 3 notes and 2 conference reviews were found. The data were analyzed by author - citation - journal - country - institution - keyword and abstract. Scopus indexed contents and criteria were used as database. For the bibliometric analysis of the use of artificial intelligence in chemistry education, English was selected as the language option, document type as article, keywords as "artificial intelligence", "chemistry education" and "bibliometric analysis", 12 fields as social sciences, computer sciences, engineering, chemistry, psychology, chemical engineering, material science, environmental science, arts and humanities, energy, multidisciplinary and decision science were selected as subject areas of the 1,538 results obtained. The last 10 years were limited to 2014 – 2024 in order to obtain current data and to follow the latest developments in the use of artificial intelligence in chemistry education. After all limitations, 772 data results were obtained, and network maps were created using the scientific mapping techniques and 9 different sub-headings and network maps were created with the Visualizing of scientific landscapes (VOSviewer) program.

Figure 2. Steps of article search

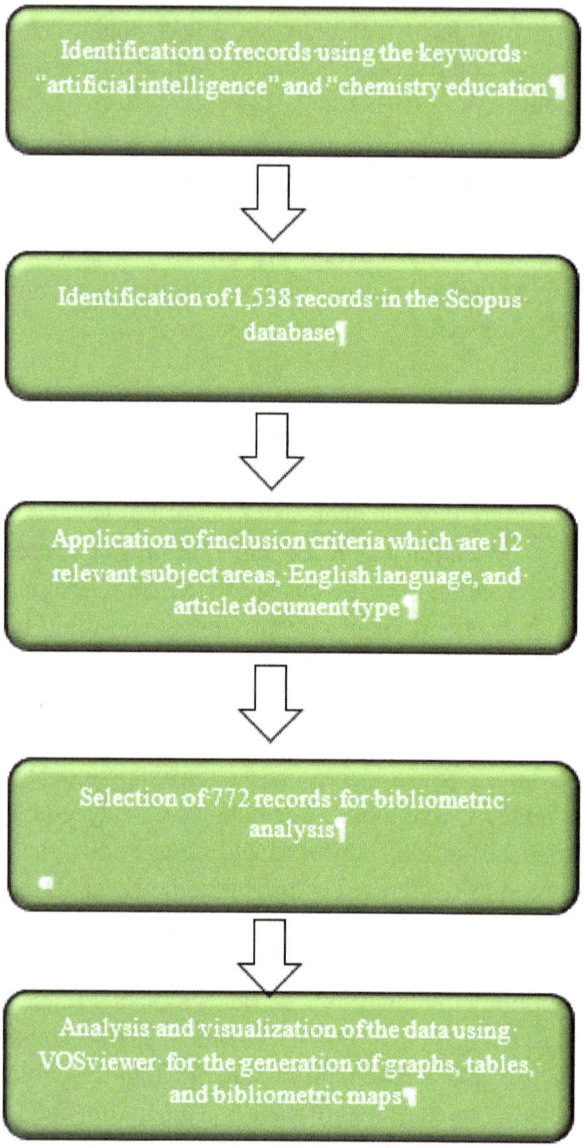

Graphs and tables are given below according to the 772 results obtained.

Figure 3. Documents by subject area

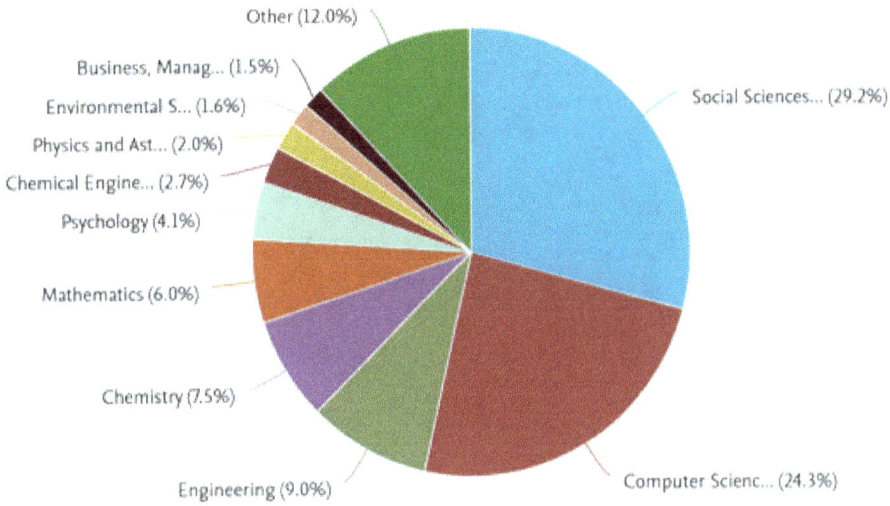

The distribution of documents by subject area in Figure 3. In the study, the abbreviation "f" refers to frequency, indicating the number of publications identified within each category. The findings show that the top five fields with the most documents are social sciences (f=566), computer science (f=274), chemistry (f=138), engineering (f=131) and psychology (f=82). The fact that chemistry ranks shows that both chemistry and chemistry education have an important place in artificial intelligence studies. The fact that the subject-area distribution is highest in the social sciences and computer science suggests that research on artificial intelligence in chemistry education focuses not only on technological developments but also on pedagogical and educational perspectives regarding artificial intelligence's role in learning, instructional design and educational practice. The high number of documents in computer science indicates that chemistry education research is linked to topics such as machine learning, data analysis, and scientific problem-solving.

The presence of other subject areas, although at lower proportions, highlights the interdisciplinary nature of the fields. The five fields with the least number of documents are Earth and Planetary Sciences (f=3), Economics, Econometrics and Finance (f=2), Pharmacology, Toxicology and Pharmaceutics (f=2), Immunology and Microbiology (f=1), and Nursing (f=1). This distribution implies that research in this field is highly concentrated in specific subject areas, while others remain relatively unexplored. The scarcity of documents in these areas within chemistry education suggests that the applications of artificial intelligence in cognitive, emotional, sustainability, and environmental fields have not been sufficiently researched.

Figure 4. Documents by year

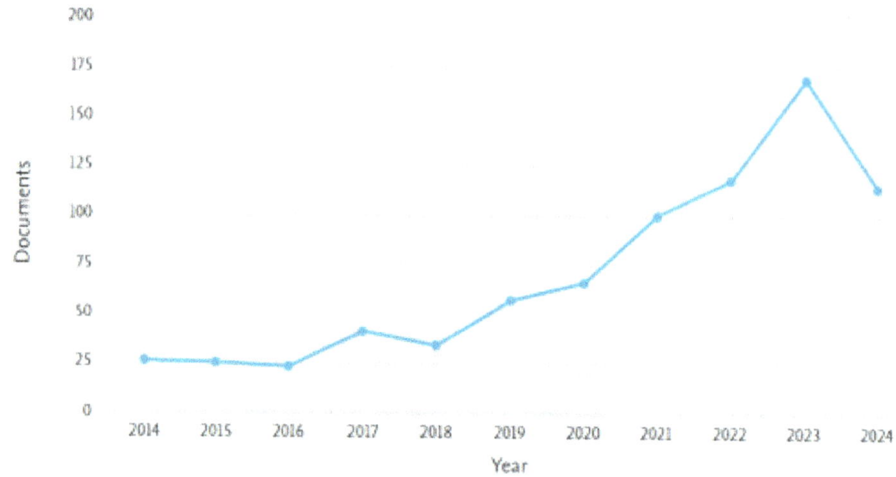

Figure 4 shows the number of publications by year between 2014 and 2024. The graph derived from the number of documents by year shows a general upward trend in the number of studies over the years, and that academic interest in this research area is increasing. Since it was obtained using various filters such as the last decade, the values of the five documents closest to the present day are 2024 (f=114), 2023 (f=169), 2022 (f=118), 2021 (f=100) and 2020 (66), respectively. It was observed that the highest number of documents was in 2023 and the lowest number of documents was in 2016 (f=23). As seen in the graph, the number of documents remained relatively low and stable between 2014 and 2016, showing only minor changes. A significant increase was observed in 2017, followed by a slight decrease in 2018. The number of publications began to increase more significantly from 2019 onwards, showing a general upward trend. This indicates that artificial intelligence technologies are increasingly being incorporated into chemistry education research. This increase continued steadily until 2022. The highest number of publications was reached in 2023, marking a peak in research activity. However, the number of publications decreased in 2024 compared to the previous year. This decrease may be due to the fact that the 2024 data is not yet complete. Overall, the findings in the graph show that studies on the use of artificial intelligence in chemistry education have become a rapidly developing research area over time.

Figure 5. Documents per year by source

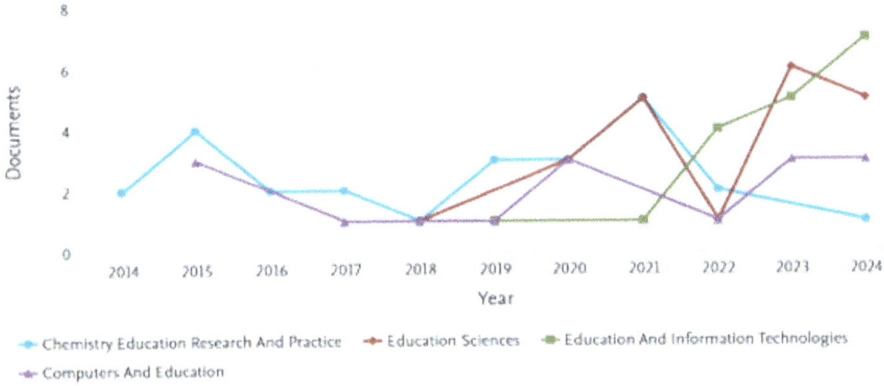

Figure 5 shows the distribution of studies in the field of artificial intelligence and chemistry education across different journals over the years. Examining the findings, it is seen that the highest number of publications appeared in the Journal of Chemical Education (f = 67). This journal is followed by Chemistry Education Research and Practice (f = 25), Education Sciences (f = 21), Education and Information Technologies (f = 18), and Computers and Education (f = 16). This indicates that studies on artificial intelligence and chemistry education are not limited to the field of chemistry education alone, but are also included within educational technologies and interdisciplinary educational research. When the graph is evaluated generally, it is noteworthy that there have been significant increases in the number of publications in some journals, especially after 2020. The increase in Education Sciences and Education and Information Technologies, in particular, shows that artificial intelligence applications are increasingly being addressed in conjunction with digital learning environments and educational technologies. Similarly, studies in Computers and Education reveal an increasing interest in technology-supported learning processes. On the other hand, while there have been some year-to-year variations in the number of publications in the journal Chemistry Education Research and Practice, it can be said that the journal maintains its importance within the field. The fact that the Journal of Chemical Education has the highest publication frequency throughout the period suggests that artificial intelligence applications are being intensively studied, particularly in the context of chemistry teaching, instructional design, and classroom applications. Overall, the findings reveal that the field of artificial intelligence and chemistry education has an interdisciplinary structure and has become more visible in recent years, especially with research focused on educational technologies.

Figure 6. Documents by country or territory

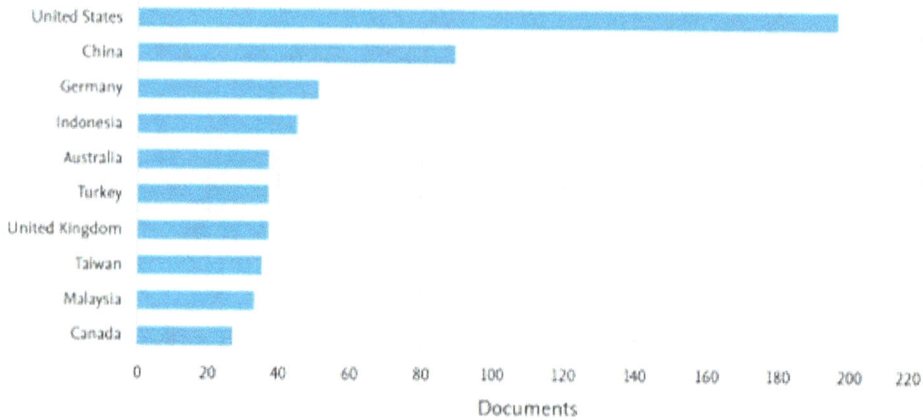

Figure 6 shows the distribution of publications. The findings are organized, and it is observed that the highest number of publications belong to the United States (f = 196). The United States is followed by China (f=89), Germany (f=51), Indonesia (f=45), and Australia and Turkey (f=37). The results indicate that artificial intelligence and chemistry education programs are being implemented more intensively and without interruption. When the graphs are evaluated generally, it is noted that the United States and China have higher publication interruptions compared to others. In addition, Germany ranks highly among European countries. Indonesia's high publication duration is also noteworthy. Turkey's ranking among the countries with the most publications suggests that families are increasingly being influenced by the use of artificial intelligence in chemistry education.Overall, it is observed that artificial intelligence and chemistry education programs are becoming more widespread, but publication production is concentrated at certain intervals.

Figure 7. Documents by affiliation

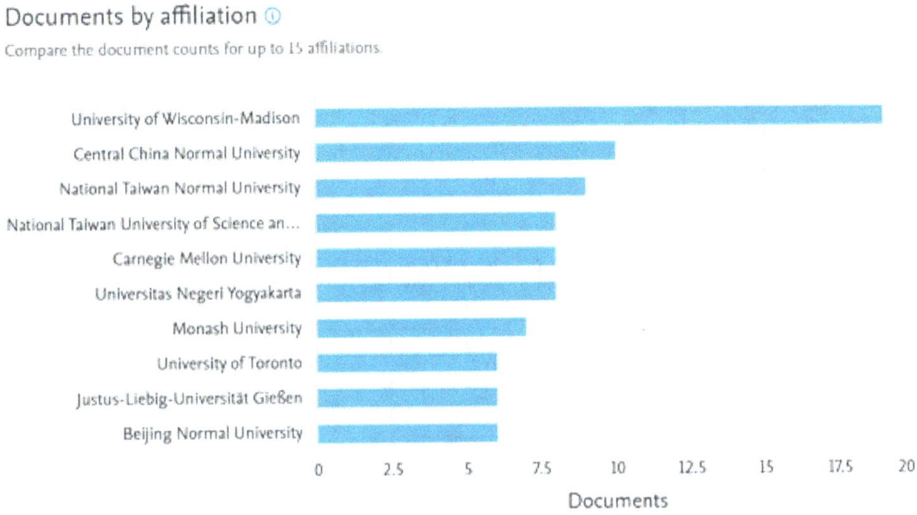

Figure 7 illustrates the distribution of publications by institutional affiliation. When the number of certificates is analyzed by institutions, it is seen that the institutions with the highest number of certificates are University of Wisconsin-Madison (f=19), Central China Normal University (f=10), National Taiwan Normal University (f=9), National Taiwan University of Science and Technology (f=8) and Carnegie Mellon University (f=8). When the number of certificates is analyzed by institutions, it is seen that the institutions with the highest number of certificates are University of Wisconsin-Madison (f=19), Central China Normal University (f=10), National Taiwan Normal University (f=9), National Taiwan University of Science and Technology (f=8), and Carnegie Mellon University (f=8). When the graph is evaluated as a whole, it is noteworthy that universities in the United States, China, and Taiwan have higher publication numbers. In addition, the inclusion of universities from different countries in the list indicates that research in artificial intelligence and chemistry education is being conducted in different countries. The findings show that certain institutions are playing an important role in this field, with some universities producing more publications in artificial intelligence and chemistry education than other institutions.

According to the documents, some keywords are used. These are "Student (f =128), Virtual Reality (f =75), E-learning (f =72), Education (f =70), Augmented Reality (f=62), Artificial Intelligence (f= 51), Teaching (f =50), Learning System (f =46), Computer Aided Instruction (f =38), Engineering Education (f =37), Science Education (f =36), Learning (f=32), Human (f=31), Higher Education (f = 31),

Education Computing (f =31), Chemistry (f=30), Motivation (f =27), First - Year Undergraduate/General (f =23), Curricula (f =23), Article (f=23).

They allow us to understand the frequency of keywords in bibliometric studies and to see the overall framework of our research. Keyword frequency analysis is crucial for identifying fundamental themes in the field of bibliometrics. In this study, the limitations are chosen as English language and article as a source type. The network maps of the 772 data obtained are given below.

Figure 8. The network map of the co-occurrence relationship of keywords

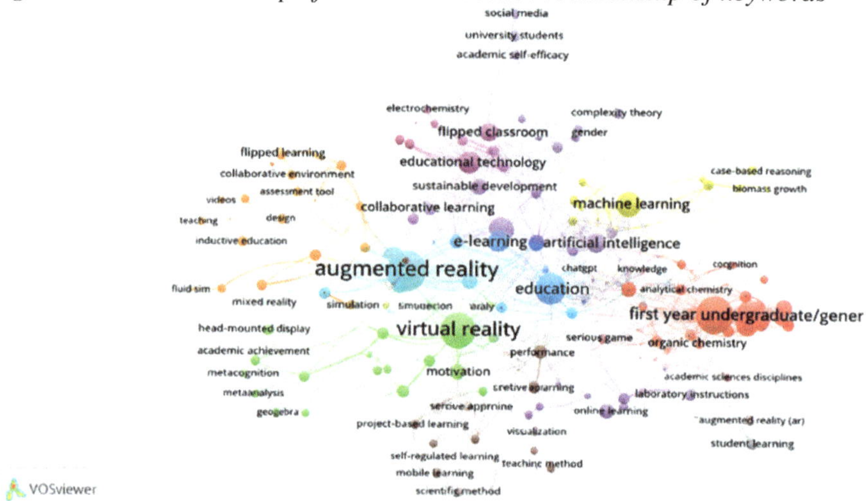

Figure 8 displays the network map of the co-occurrence relationship of keywords generated using VOSviewer. When the association of keywords is analyzed, the 20 most frequently used keywords are: "Augmented Reality (52), Virtual Reality (49), Education (31), Science Education (31), Higher Education (29), Chemistry (25), First Year Undergraduate/General (24), Computer Based Learning (23), Postgraduate (18), Internet/Web Based Learning (17), High School / Introductory Chemistry (16), Artificial Intelligence (16), Chemistry Education (16), Organic Chemistry (15), E-learning (15), Gamification (15), Online Learning (14), STEM (14), Learning (14) and Multiple representations (14)" and a network map was drawn. Examining the findings, it is seen that the most central concepts are "augmented reality" and "virtual reality." It is noteworthy that these concepts form strong connections with keywords such as "education," "e-learning," "artificial intelligence," and "machine learning."

This indicates that studies in the fields of artificial intelligence and chemistry education largely focus on technology-supported learning environments.

Examining the clusters in the network map, it is seen that some keywords are concentrated around specific research topics. In particular, concepts such as "first year undergraduate/general," "organic chemistry," and "analytical chemistry," located in the red cluster, indicate that a significant portion of the studies are directed towards undergraduate-level chemistry courses. The prominence of these chemistry disciplines suggests that AI-supported applications are studied more frequently, especially in specific areas of chemistry.

Concepts such as "motivation," "academic achievement," and "metacognition," which are included in the green cluster, indicate that studies related to students' learning processes are attracting attention. This reveals that research focuses not only on technological applications but also on student success, motivation, and learning experiences. Concepts such as "flipped classroom," "educational technology," "collaborative learning," and "e-learning," which are included in the purple and pink clusters, show that active learning methods and digital learning environments are widely addressed within the field. Furthermore, the proximity of "artificial intelligence" and "machine learning" concepts to the center of the network reveals that AI-based applications have become more visible in chemistry education research in recent years. Overall, the findings show that artificial intelligence, augmented reality, and virtual reality applications are increasingly being used in chemistry education; and that studies are focusing on both technology-based learning environments and student learning processes.

Figure 9. The network map of the relationship of sources and citations

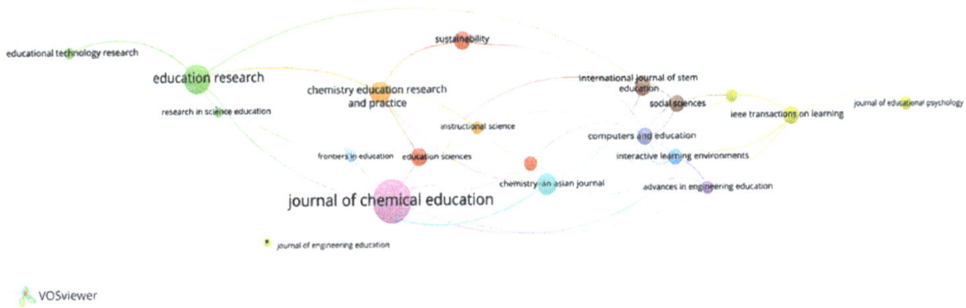

The network map of the relationship of sources and citations is illustrated in Figure 9. When the relationships between citations and references were examined, 14 clusters of 72 items were evaluated. The most 5 of the documents, citations and sources were evaluated as Journal of Chemical Education (documents:67 / citations:624), Chemistry Education Research and Practice (documents:25 / citations:338), Education Sciences (documents:21 / citations:333), Education and Information Technologies (documents:18 / citations:173), and Computer and Education (documents:16 / citations:607), and a network map was drawn. An overview of the network map suggests that the Journal of Chemical Education and Chemistry Education Research and Practice, in particular, have more intense interactions with other sources. Therefore, it can be stated that research on artificial intelligence and chemistry education tends to cluster around journals that publish research on the subject of chemistry education. Additionally, the visibility of the journals Education Sciences and Computers and Education within the network demonstrates that research is not only connected with the subject of chemistry education but also associated with the sphere of educational technology. In summary, based on the analysis of citations and references, it can be argued that artificial intelligence and chemistry education studies demonstrate an interdisciplinary nature, and some journals have a dominant position in the field.

Figure 10. The network map of the relationship of organizations and citation

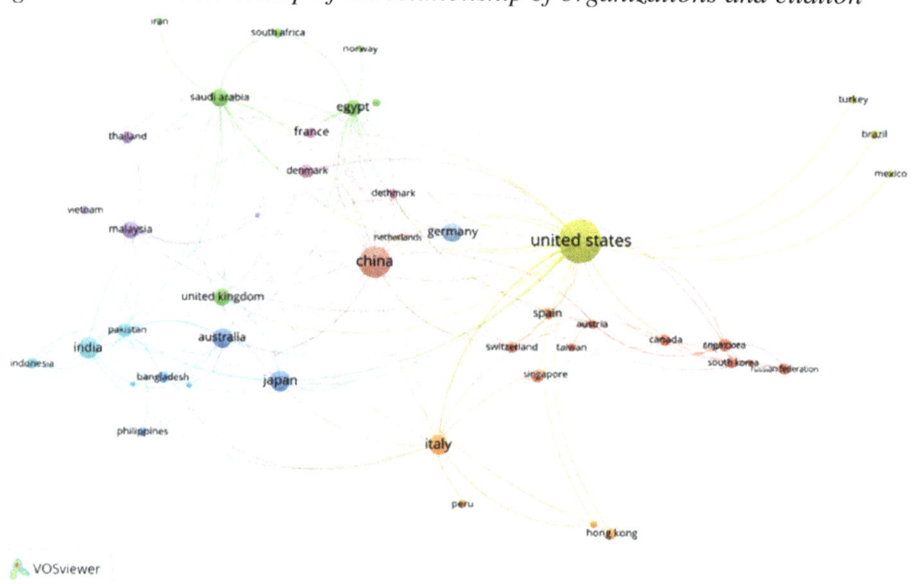

The network map of the relationship of organizations and citations is presented in Figure 10. The citations relationship of countries; 48 items were classified into 12 clusters, and network maps were drawn. The five most cited countries are United States (documents: 194 / citations: 3595), Turkey (documents: 37 / citations: 1038), China (documents: 89 / citations: 854), Australia (documents: 37 / citations: 773) and Denmark (documents: 7 / citations: 758). When the network map is evaluated as a whole, it is noteworthy that the United States is at the center of the network in terms of both publication and citation count. This indicates that a significant portion of the research in artificial intelligence and chemistry education originates from the United States. In addition, China and Australia also appear to have strong connections within the network. The fact that Turkey has a high number of citations compared to its publication count is among the striking findings. Similarly, Denmark's high citation value despite a low number of publications shows that the studies published in these countries have gained visibility within the field and demonstrate the depth of meaning of the research. Overall, the citation relationships between countries reveal that research in artificial intelligence and chemistry education has international connections and that some countries hold a more visible position within the field.

Figure 11. The network map of the relationship of cited references and co- citations

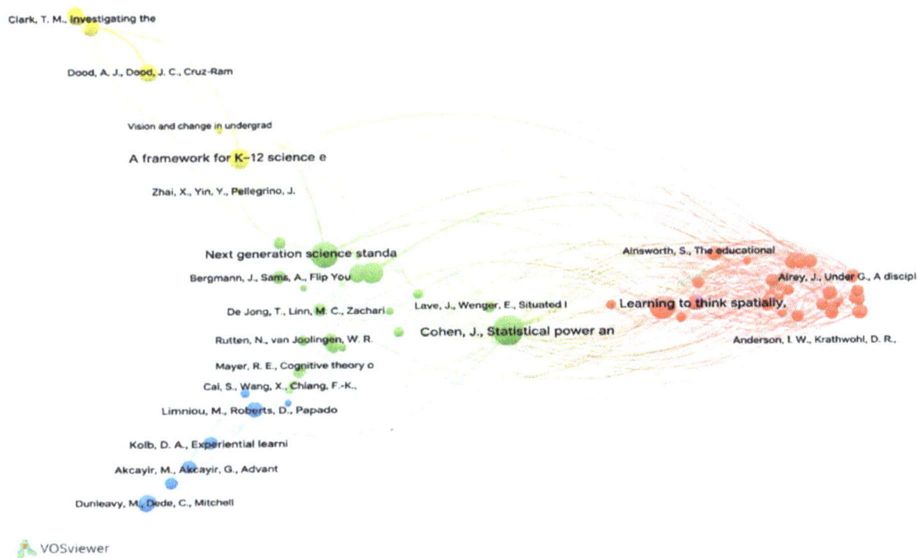

Figure 11 shows the distribution of the network map of the relationship between cited references and co-citations. Co-citations and cited references are grouped into 5 clusters of 113 items, each containing at least 5 co-citations, from a total of 49,693 sources, and the groups are shown in the network map in different colors. Examining the network map, it is seen from the clusters and colors that some sources have more connections than other studies. In addition, studies related to science education, learning processes, and teaching methods are seen to be among the co-citations.

This study focuses on the use of artificial intelligence in chemistry education literature in the last decade. A big picture was drawn about the conflicts conducted using the bibliometric analysis method and general information was provided about the studies. While conducting the research, the results were obtained by making limitations such as language, year, publication, keywords, citations, and databases. With this research, general information and quantitative results were seen about the use of artificial intelligence in chemistry education, and from this perspective, it is thought that it will contribute to future studies by guiding researchers in terms of contextual information, ethical use, students' pedagogical development, and effects on education quality.

The results mentioned above were generated based on the filters specified in the Scopus database worldwide. Results generated using the same filters but selecting only European countries for the years 2014-2024 are shown in the table below.

Table 1. European countries Scopus database

COUNTRY	DOCUMENTS	CITATIONS	COUNTRY	DOCUMENTS	CITATIONS
Austria	8	51	Montenegro	1	57
Belgium	3	11	Netherlands	14	137
Czech Republic	5	69	Norway	3	11
Denmark	7	758	Poland	4	147
Finland	7	87	Portugal	9	78
France	12	116	Romania	2	36
Germany	51	633	Serbia	4	20
Greece	15	172	Slovakia	3	27
Hungary	1	6	Slovenia	3	16
Luxembourg	2	9	Spain	25	688
Sweden	8	123	Turkey	37	1038
Switzerland	10	130	Ukraine	2	15
United Kingdom	37	628			

Figure 12. The network mapping the documents and citations for European countries

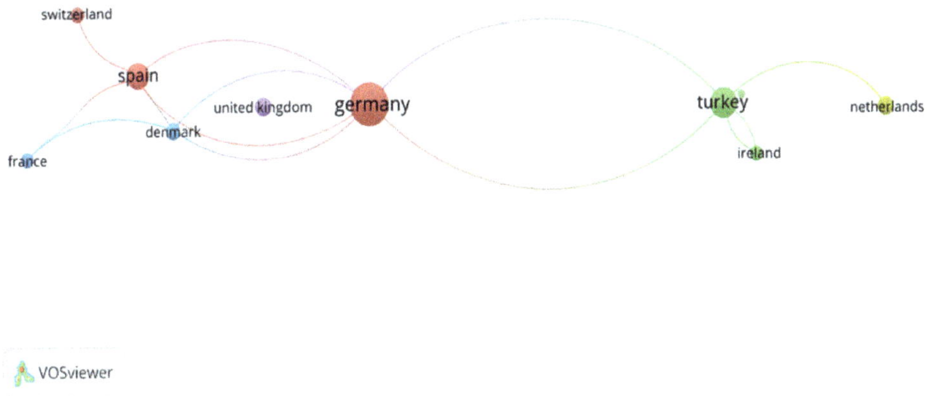

As these results show, the top five countries with the most documents are, in order: Germany (f=51), Turkey (f=37), the United Kingdom (f=37), Spain (f=25), and Greece (f=15). Similarly, the top five countries with the most citations are respectively Turkey (f=1038), Denmark (f=758), Spain (f=688), Germany (f=633), and the United Kingdom (f=628).

According to the findings, Turkey's ranking first with 1038 citations and its presence among the top five countries with the most documents indicates that high-volume research is being conducted in this field; this is important in terms of depth of meaning, visibility, and acceptance of the studies. Furthermore, Denmark's ranking second with 758 citations compared to only 7 documents shows that the studies are relevant to the field and that rigorous research is being conducted. High citation numbers in Spain, Germany, and the United Kingdom, and high citation rates in European countries in general, demonstrate the growing interest in artificial intelligence in chemistry education.

In addition to these research, when the keywords "augmented reality", "virtual reality", "chemistry education", and "artificial intelligence" are used, 16 results are found on the Scopus database with the same limitations.

Figure 13. The network map of the occurrence some limited keywords

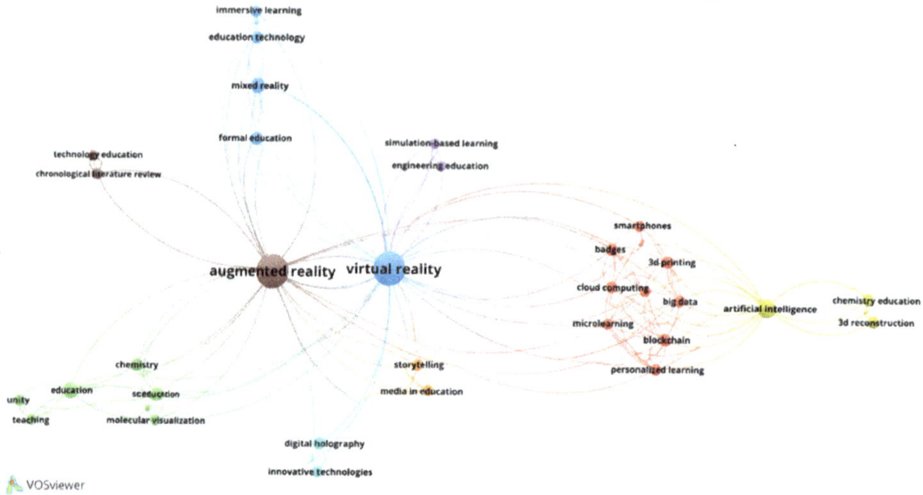

As seen in the network map showing the frequency of the keywords in Figure 8, the keywords augmented reality, virtual reality, artificial intelligence and chemistry education are directly important for this study and were therefore evaluated within the scope of bibliometric analysis with an additional mapping. According to the results shown in Figure 13, which illustrates the network map of co-occurrence relationships of keywords, the concepts of "augmented reality" and "virtual reality" are at the center of the network and are linked to many other concepts. Particularly significant are the concepts of "education technology," "immersive learning," "formal education," and "simulation-based learning." Furthermore, the concept of "artificial intelligence" is seen alongside concepts such as "big data," "cloud computing," "block chain," and "personalized learning." This indicates that artificial intelligence studies are considered in conjunction with digital learning technologies. The concepts of "chemistry," "molecular visualization," and "education," located in the green cluster, show that augmented reality and virtual reality applications are used in studies related to chemistry education. Additionally, the connection between the concept of "chemistry education" and artificial intelligence indicates that artificial intelligence applications have become more visible in the field of chemistry education in recent years.

In recent years, two articles have drawn attention to the use of artificial intelligence in chemistry education. The first of these articles; In the article titled "Virtual Special Issue Call for Papers: Exploring the Uses and Impacts of Generative Artificial Intelligence in Chemistry Education" by Yuriev, Wink and Holme in 2023, the effects on the use of artificial intelligence in chemistry education are sought with various questions such as "What level of detail should be provided about an assignment in order to provide chemistry students with productive prompts for using generative artificial intelligence software? Can the application of generative artificial intelligence be used to help students develop specific writing skills related to chemistry or science more broadly? How do students interact with generative artificial intelligence when solving chemistry problems? What effective support can be provided to students to use generative artificial intelligence productively and ethically in the context of laboratory learning? How are ethical issues related to the use of generative artificial intelligence addressed in chemistry classroom environments? How can generative artificial intelligence be used in pre-university, teacher education and introductory settings?" Yuriev, Wink, and Holme say these questions will increase the popularity of research on the use of AI in today's chemistry education. The second article is "Students' Experience of a ChatGPT-Enabled Final Exam Non-Major Chemistry Course," published in 2024 by Clark, Reynders, and Holme. This article describes the comparison of the science and sustainability articles on the final exam with the article written by the AI application ChatGPT and their evaluation of this computational activity.

Based on a bibliometric analysis of the use of artificial intelligence in chemistry education, it is believed that AI applications can play a significant role in concretizing abstract concepts in high school chemistry education. In chemistry, topics that cannot be directly observed, such as atomic structure, intermolecular interactions, chemical bonds, and reactions, can be challenging for students. Therefore, visualizing and making these concepts more understandable through AI-supported tools is seen as a crucial element supporting the learning process.

It is believed that artificial intelligence-supported applications can be used in teaching many abstract topics and concepts included in the high school chemistry curriculum in Turkey. Artificial intelligence is expected to support students' learning processes in many areas such as atomic models, periodic properties, interactions between chemical species, states of matter, chemical calculations, acids and bases, rate, equilibrium and energy in chemical reactions, chemistry and electricity, organic chemistry, nanotechnology, and macro and micro-scale experiments. It is considered that these topics, which are particularly rich in abstract concepts, can be made more understandable through artificial intelligence-supported applications, and that this can increase students' interest in the subject. The prominence of augmented reality, virtual reality, simulation, and visualization themes in the bibliometric analysis results indicates that artificial intelligence-supported applications have become an important research area, especially in the teaching of abstract chemistry topics. Furthermore, Turkey's ranking among the leading countries in terms of publication volume shows the increasing interest in artificial intelligence-supported applications in chemistry education. This situation is thought to support the use of technology-supported applications in teaching abstract topics in the high school chemistry curriculum.

Accordingly, it is predicted that visualizing content through artificial intelligence applications; AI-supported activities, videos, animations, and simulations can contribute to students learning subjects more effectively and meaningfully. Furthermore, the opportunity for students to experience laboratory experiments in a virtual environment whenever they want, to repeat experiments, and to observe the processes better provides a significant advantage. This is thought to play an important role in developing students' cognitive, affective, and psychomotor skills and supporting the learning process. However, using these technologies alone is not considered sufficient for the effective use of artificial intelligence in education. It is also important for students to possess AI literacy skills. AI literacy encompasses students' ability to understand AI, use it correctly, question and evaluate the information obtained. In particular, students need to be aware that the information generated by AI may not always be accurate and to be able to evaluate this information from a critical perspective. Similarly, studies examining pre-service teachers' attitudes and perceptions towards artificial intelligence show that AI is considered a supportive tool, particularly in lesson planning, material development, visualization, and individual learning processes.

However, there are also various concerns regarding ethical use, data security, misinformation generation, and potential impacts on students' critical thinking skills. Mustafaoğlu and Alkan (2025) stated that developing pre-service teachers' AI literacy skills is important for the effective use of AI applications in educational settings.

At the same time, the ethical dimension is an important issue that should not be overlooked. When using artificial intelligence tools, issues such as information accuracy, referencing, academic integrity, and data security must be considered. Students' conscious, responsible, and ethical use of artificial intelligence both improves the quality of the learning process and supports the correct use of these technologies. Therefore, it is believed that artificial intelligence applications have significant potential in chemistry education. These applications are particularly important in contributing to students' better understanding of abstract concepts and supporting the learning process. However, in order for these opportunities offered by artificial intelligence to be used effectively, more prominence in educational environments needs to be given and applications in this field need to be developed.

CONCLUSION

This article presents a bibliometric analysis of the use of artificial intelligence (AI) in chemistry education and examines general research trends in the field. The analysis results show a significant increase in studies on the use of AI in chemistry education in recent years, making this area an increasingly prominent research topic. Themes such as visualization, simulation, augmented reality, virtual reality, and technology-supported learning environments are particularly prominent in chemistry education research. This indicates that AI-supported applications are becoming more widely used, especially in the teaching of abstract chemistry concepts.

When the findings are evaluated by country, the United States, China, Germany, Indonesia, Australia, and Turkey stand out in terms of publication productivity. Turkey's prominence in the analysis suggests an increased interest in AI-supported applications in chemistry education in recent years. Furthermore, it is noteworthy that studies on AI-supported learning environments are also becoming increasingly widespread in European countries. The Digital Education Action Plan (2021–2027), published by the European Commission, emphasizes the importance of digital transformation, digital competencies, and technology integration in education. This is thought to have contributed to the increasing use of AI-assisted educational applications in Europe.

Based on the bibliometric findings of this study, it is believed that AI-assisted applications can make significant contributions to the teaching of chemistry topics that students perceive as abstract and difficult. In particular, it is predicted that AI-assisted visualization applications can support students' conceptual understanding in topics such as atomic models, chemical bonds, molecular structures, and reaction mechanisms. Furthermore, it is thought that simulation-supported virtual laboratory environments can enable students to repeat experiments, observe processes in more detail, and access laboratory experiences independently of time and place.

Alongside the increasing use of AI in chemistry education, issues such as ethical use, AI literacy, data reliability, and equal access to educational technologies are also gaining increasing importance. Therefore, it is recommended that future studies focus not only on technological advancements but also more thoroughly on the pedagogical, cognitive, affective, and ethical dimensions of AI-supported chemistry education. Furthermore, although there are various bibliometric studies in the literature on AI and education, studies specifically focused on chemistry education are still limited. In this respect, it is believed that this study will contribute to the literature by offering a field-focused bibliometric perspective on the use of AI in chemistry education.

The prominence of concepts related to augmented reality, virtual reality, STEM education, simulation, and AI-supported learning environments in the bibliometric analysis results indicates that these areas are gaining increasing importance in chemistry education research. In particular, it is thought that augmented reality and virtual reality-supported applications can contribute to students' better understanding of abstract chemistry concepts and their interactive learning experiences. It is recommended that future studies focus more thoroughly on the long-term pedagogical impacts of these technologies on chemistry education, student achievement, motivation, AI literacy, and ethical usage dimensions.

However, the research was limited to the Scopus database, specific year ranges, document types, and filtering criteria. Therefore, using different databases and larger datasets in future research could contribute to obtaining more comprehensive results regarding the use of artificial intelligence in chemistry education.

AUTHOR CONTRIBUTIONS

All three authors have conceptualized the work. B. Koçak worked on methodology and biblometric analyse. F. Alkan worked on introduction and results. A.S. Yücel reviewed and edited by supervising the work. All authors provided critical feedback and helped shape the research, analysis and manuscript.

CONFLICTS OF INTEREST

"The authors declare no conflict of interest."

ACKNOWLEDGMENTS

The authors are thankful to Hacettepe University Graduate School of Educational Sciences for this research.

REFERENCES

Akbaba, K., & Ertaş Kılıç, H. (2022). Web 2.0 uygulamalarinin öğrencilerin fene ve teknoloji kullanimina yönelik tutumlarina etkisi. *Erzincan Üniversitesi Eğitim Fakültesi Dergisi*, *24*(1), 130–139. DOI: 10.17556/erziefd.880542

Al, U., & Tonta, Y. (2004). Atıf analizi: Hacettepe Üniversitesi Kütüphanecilik Bölümü tezlerinde atıf yapılan kaynaklar. *Bilgi Dünyası*, *5*(1), 19–47. DOI: 10.15612/BD.2004.497

Alkan, F., & Mustafaoğlu, F. M. (2023). Using web tools in lecture: example of micro teaching lesson. In Queirós, R. (Eds.), *Fostering Pedagogy Through Micro and Adaptive Learning in Higher Education: Trends, Tools, and Applications* (pp. 261–286). IGI Global., DOI: 10.4018/978-1-6684-8656-6.ch012

Altundağ, C. K., & Koçer, M. Y. (2023). Web 2.0 tools supported innovative applications in science education based on the context-based learning approach. In Braun, J., & Trajkovski, G. (Eds.), *Designing Context-Rich Learning by Extending Reality* (pp. 179–204). IGI Global., DOI: 10.4018/978-1-6684-7644-4.ch010

Arslan, K. (2020). Eğitimde yapay zeka ve uygulamalari. *Batı Anadolu Eğitim Bilimleri Dergisi*, *11*(1), *71-88*. https://dergipark.org.tr/en/pub/baebd/issue/55426/690058

Asio, J. M., & Soriano, I. D. (2025). The State of Artificial Intelligence (AI) Use in Higher Education Institutions (HEIs) in the Philippines. In Mobo, F. (Ed.), *Impacts of AI on Students and Teachers in Education 5.0* (pp. 523–552). IGI Global Scientific Publishing., DOI: 10.4018/979-8-3693-8191-5.ch01

Asio, J. M. R., & Gadia, E. D. (2024). Predictors of student attitudes towards artificial intelligence: Implications and relevance to the higher education institutions. *International Journal of Didactical Studies*, *5*(2), 27763. DOI: 10.33902/IJODS.202427763

Becker, B. (2017). Artificial intelligence in education: What is it, where is it now, where is it going? In Mooney, B. (Ed.), *Ireland's yearbook of education 2017-2018* (pp. 42–46). Education Matters.

Bezen, S. (2023). Challenges of motivating students in online learning platforms: an analysis through the eyes of teachers. In Bilodeau, J., & Hughes, L. (Eds.), *Handbook of Research on Creating Motivational Online Environments for Students* (pp. 59–81). IGI Global., DOI: 10.4018/978-1-6684-4533-4.ch004

Blonder, R., & Feldman-Maggor, Y. (2024). AI for chemistry teaching: Responsible AI and ethical considerations. *Chemistry Teacher International : Best Practices in Chemistry Education*, *6*(4), 385–395. DOI: 10.1515/cti-2024-0014

Bowen, G. A. (2009). Document analysis as a qualitative research method. *Qualitative Research Journal*, *9*(2), 27–40. DOI: 10.3316/QRJ0902027

Bower, M., Howe, C., McCredie, N., Robinson, A., & Grover, D. (2014). Augmented reality in education: Cases, places and potentials. *Educational Media International*, *51*(1), 1–15. DOI: 10.1080/09523987.2014.889400

Chang, J. H., Wang, C. J., Zhong, H. X., Weng, H. C., Zhou, Y. K., Ong, H. Y., & Lai, C. F. (2024). Artificial intelligence learning platform in a visual programming environment: Exploring an artificial intelligence learning model. *Educational Technology Research and Development*, *72*(2), 997–1024. DOI: 10.1007/s11423-023-10323-z

Chen, X., Xie, H., & Hwang, G.-J. (2020). A multi-perspective study on artificial intelligence in education. *Education and Information Technologies*, *25*(3), 1819–1842. DOI: 10.1007/s10639-019-10069-9

Choo, J., & Liu, S. (2018). Visual analytics for explainable deep learning. *IEEE Computer Graphics and Applications*, *38*(4), 84–92. DOI: 10.1109/MCG.2018.042731661

Clark, M. J., Reynders, M., & Holme, T. A. (2024). Students' experience of a ChatGPT-enabled final exam in a non-majors chemistry course. *Journal of Chemical Education*, *101*(5), 1983–1991. DOI: 10.1021/acs.jchemed.4c00161

Clark, T. M. (2023). Investigating the Use of an Artificial Intelligence Chatbot with General Chemistry Exam Questions. *Journal of Chemical Education*, *100*(5), 1905–1916. DOI: 10.1021/acs.jchemed.3c00027

Demir, H., Erigüç, G. (2018). Bibliyometrik bir analiz ile yönetim düşünce sisteminin incelenmesi. *İş ve İnsan Dergisi*, *5*(2), 91-114. https://doi.org/DOI: 10.18394/iid.395214

Doğan, A. (2002). *Yapay zeka*. Kariyer Yayıncılık.

Duran, V., & Aydın, E. (2024). Eğitimde yapay zekanın kapsamlı incelenmesi: Web of Science veri tabanı üzerinden bir AI destekli bibliyometrik analiz. *Zenodo*. https://doi.org/DOI: 10.5281/zenodo.10737254

Ellegaard, O., & Wallin, J. A. (2015). The bibliometric analysis of scholarly production: How great is the impact? *Scientometrics, 105*(3), 1809–1831. DOI: 10.1007/s11192-015-1645-z

Estevez, J., Garate, G., Guede, J., & Graña, M. (2019). *Using Scratch to teach undergraduate students' skills on artificial intelligence* (arXiv No. 1904.00296). arXiv. https://arxiv.org/abs/1904.00296

European Commission. (2021). *Digital Education Action Plan (2021–2027)*. European Commission. https://education.ec.europa.eu/focus-topics/digital-education/action-plan

Holmes, W., Bialik, M., & Fadel, C. (2019). *Artificial intelligence in education promises and implications for teaching and learning*. The Center for Curriculum Redesign. https://curriculumredesign.org/our-work/artificial-intelligence-in-education/

Hopcan, S., Polat, E., Ozturk, M. E., & Ozturk, L. (2023). Artificial intelligence in special education: A systematic review. *Interactive Learning Environments, 31*(10), 7335–7353. DOI: 10.1080/10494820.2022.2067186

Jia, F., Sun, D., & Looi, C.-K. (2024). Artificial intelligence in science education (2013–2023): Research trends in ten years. *Journal of Science Education and Technology, 33*(1), 94–117. DOI: 10.1007/s10956-023-10077-6

Karyağdı, M., & Aydın, G. (2023). Fen bilgisi öğretmen adaylarıyla gerçekleştirilen teknoloji destekli kavramsal değişim etkinliklerinin etkileri. *Mehmet Akif Ersoy Üniversitesi Eğitim Fakültesi Dergisi, 68*(68), 156–184. DOI: 10.21764/maeuefd.1346077

Köfter, B., Alkan, F., & Yücel, A. S. (2026). AI-based interactive simulation for atomic models: Pilot study. *Periódico Tchê Química, 23*(52), 1–14. DOI: 10.52571/PTQ.v23.n52.2026_01_BILLUR_pgs_01_14.pdf

Kok, J. N., Boers, E. J., Kosters, W. A., Van der Putten, P., & Poel, M. (2009). Artificial intelligence: Definition, trends, techniques, and cases. *Artificial Intelligence, 1*, 270–299.

Kong, S. C., Cheung, W. M. Y., & Zhang, G. (2023). Evaluating an artificial intelligence literacy programme for developing university students' conceptual understanding, literacy, empowerment and ethical awareness. *Journal of Educational Technology & Society, 26*(1), 16–30. DOI: 10.30191/ETS.202301_26(1).0002

Lee, G.-G., & Zhai, X. (2024). Using ChatGPT for science learning: A study on pre-service teachers' lesson planning. *IEEE Transactions on Learning Technologies, 17*, 1643–1660. DOI: 10.1109/TLT.2024.3401457

Lee, I., Park, J., & Yoon, H.-G. (2022). Science teachers' theory-based teaching: Connecting a learning cycle model to a lesson plan. *Journal of Baltic Science Education, 21*(3), 462–480. DOI: 10.33225/jbse/22.21.462

Luckin, R., Holmes, W., Griffiths, M., & Forcier, L. B. (2016). *Intelligence unleashed: An argument for AI in education*. Pearson. https://discovery.ucl.ac.uk/1475756/

Meço, G., & Coştu, F. (2022). Eğitimde yapay zekânin kullanilmasi: betimsel içerik analizi çalişmasi. *Karadeniz Teknik Üniversitesi Sosyal Bilimler Enstitüsü Sosyal Bilimler Dergisi, 12*(23). https://dergipark.org.tr/en/pub/sbed/issue/70445/1092727

Mejia, C., Wu, M., Zhang, Y., & Kajikawa, Y. (2021). Exploring topics in bibliometric research through citation networks and semantic analysis. *Frontiers in Research Metrics and Analytics, 6*, 742311. DOI: 10.3389/frma.2021.742311

Mustafaoğlu, F. M., & Alkan, F. (2024). An analysis of high school students' laboratory self-efficacy beliefs and perceptions of laboratory applications. *Periódico Tchê Química, 21*(48), 16–31. DOI: 10.52571/PTQ.v21.n48.2024_02_FATMA_pgs_16_48.pdf

Mustafaoğlu, F. M., & Alkan, F. (2025). Artificial intelligence in education: Attitudes and perceptions of pre-service teachers. *Information Technologies and Learning Tools, 110*(6), 120–134. DOI: 10.33407/itlt.v110i6.6341

Mystakidis, S., Berki, E., & Valtanen, J. P. (2021). Deep and meaningful e-learning with social virtual reality environments in higher education: A systematic literature review. *Applied Sciences (Basel, Switzerland), 11*(2), 694. DOI: 10.3390/app11052412

Ng, D. T. K., Lee, M., Tan, R. J. Y., Hu, X., Downie, J. S., & Chu, S. K. W. (2023a). A review of AI teaching and learning from 2000 to 2020. *Education and Information Technologies, 28*(7), 8445–8501. DOI: 10.1007/s10639-022-11491-w

Ng, D. T. K., Leung, J. K. L., Chu, S. K. W., & Qiao, M. S. (2021). Conceptualizing AI literacy: An exploratory review. *Computers and Education: Artificial Intelligence, 2*, 100041. DOI: 10.1016/j.caeai.2021.100041

O'Dea, X. (2024). Generative AI: Is it a paradigm shift for higher education? *Studies in Higher Education, 49*(5), 811–816. DOI: 10.1080/03075079.2024.2332944

Pokrivčáková, S. (2019). Preparing teachers for the application of AI-powered technologies in foreign language education. *Journal of Language and Cultural Education*, *7*(3), 135–153. DOI: 10.2478/jolace-2019-0025

Popenici, S. A. D., & Kerr, S. (2017). Exploring the impact of artificial intelligence on teaching and learning in higher education. *Research and Practice in Technology Enhanced Learning*, *12*(1), 22. DOI: 10.1186/s41039-017-0062-8

Sağlam-Kaya, Y. (2019). Öğretmen adaylarının teknopedagojik eğitim yeterliklerinin çeşitli değişkenler ve öğretmen öz yeterlikleri bağlamında incelenmesi. *Journal of Theoretical Educational Science*, *12*(1), 185–204. DOI: 10.30831/akukeg.420909

Sak, R., Şahin Sak, İ. T., Öneren Şendil, Ç., & Nas, E. (2021). Bir araştırma yöntemi olarak doküman analizi. *Kocaeli Üniversitesi Eğitim Dergisi*, *4*(1), 227–250. DOI: 10.33400/kuje.843306

Saldana, J. (2011). *Fundamentals of qualitative research.* Oxford University Press.

Samoili, S., Cobo, M. L., Gómez, E., De Prato, G., Martínez-Plumed, F., & Delipetrev, B. (2020). *AI Watch. Defining Artificial Intelligence. Towards an operational definition and taxonomy of artificial intelligence.* Luxembourg: Publications Office of the European Union. EUR 30117 EN. https://eprints.ugd.edu.mk/id/eprint/28047

Simmons, A. B., & Chappell, S. G. (1988). Artificial intelligence: Definition and practice. *IEEE Journal of Oceanic Engineering*, *13*(2), 14–42. DOI: 10.1109/48.551

Tamer, H. Y., & Övgün, B. (2020). Yapay zekâ bağlaminda dijital dönüşüm ofisi. *Ankara Üniversitesi SBF Dergisi*, *75*(2), 775–803. DOI: 10.33630/ausbf.691119

Toker, A. (2022). Bir araştırma metodolojisi olarak sistematik literatür incelemesi: Meta-sentez yöntemi. *Anadolu Üniversitesi Sosyal Bilimler Dergisi, 22*(Özel Sayı 2), 313–340. https://doi.org/DOI: 10.18037/ausbd.1227360

Ukşul, Ş. (2016). *Türkiye'de eğitimde ölçme ve değerlendirme alanında yapılmış bilimsel yayınların sosyal ağ analizi ile değerlendirilmesi: Bir bibliyometrik çalışma* (Yüksek Lisans Tezi). Akdeniz Üniversitesi Eğitim Bilimleri Enstitüsü, Antalya

Uyulgan, M. A., & Akkuzu Güven, N. (2022). Web 2.0 Tools in Chemistry Teaching: An Analysis of Pre-Service Chemistry Teachers' Competencies and Views. *Instructional Technology and Lifelong Learning*, *3*(1), 88–114. DOI: 10.52911/itall.1127618

Wang, P. (2019). On defining artificial intelligence. *Journal of Artificial General Intelligence*, *10*(2), 1–37. DOI: 10.2478/jagi-2019-0002

Wolfram, D. (2003). *Applied informetrics for information retrieval research* (New Directions in Information Management, No. 36). Greenwood Publishing Group.

Yücel, A. S., & Koçak, C. (2010). Evaluation of the basic technology competency of the teachers' candidate according to the various variables. *Procedia: Social and Behavioral Sciences*, *2*(2), 1310–1315. DOI: 10.1016/j.sbspro.2010.03.192

Yuriev, E., Wink, D. J., & Holme, T. A. (2023). Virtual Special Issue Call for Papers: Investigating the Uses and Impacts of Generative Artificial Intelligence in Chemistry Education. *Journal of Chemical Education*, *100*(9), 3168–3170. DOI: 10.1021/acs.jchemed.3c00829

Zawacki-Richter, O., Marín, V. I., Bond, M., & Gouverneur, F. (2019). A systematic review of research on artificial intelligence applications in higher education. *International Journal of Educational Technology in Higher Education*, *16*(1), 39. DOI: 10.1186/s41239-019-0171-0

Zupic, I., & Čater, T. (2015). Bibliometric methods in management and organization. *Organizational Research Methods*, *18*(3), 429–472. DOI: 10.1177/1094428114562629

KEY TERMS AND DEFINITIONS

Artificial Intelligence (AI): Artificial Intelligence refers to computer systems designed to perform tasks that typically require human intelligence, such as learning, reasoning, problem-solving, and decision-making.

Bibliometric Analysis: Bibliometric Analysis is a research method that uses quantitative techniques to evaluate academic literature, such as publications and citations, to identify trends, patterns, and the impact of research within a field.

Chemistry Education: Chemistry Education is a field that focuses on teaching and learning chemistry, including the development of instructional methods, curricula, and tools to improve students' understanding of chemical concepts.

Chapter 13

AI in Education:
Compliance With FERPA, GDPR, COPPA, and Intellectual Property in Academic Environments

Devanshi Soni
Ajeenkya D.Y. Patil University, India

Sunil Sankathala
http://orcid.org/0009-0004-7809-7647
Ajeenkya D.Y. Patil University, India

Krutika Patre
http://orcid.org/0009-0001-7969-4409
Ajeenkya D.Y. Patil University, India

Kritikka Kunte
http://orcid.org/0009-0002-4820-8831
Ajeenkya D.Y. Patil University, India

Susanta Das
http://orcid.org/0000-0002-9314-3988
Ajeenkya D.Y. Patil University, India

ABSTRACT

Artificial Intelligence (AI) application in education is changing the teaching, learning, and institutional management by providing personalized learning systems, automated assessment, and intelligent analytics. Nevertheless, this fast-paced adoption comes with alarming issues regarding the privacy of data, legal conformance, copyright, and ethical governance. The FERPA, GDPR, and COPPA frameworks have stringent

DOI: 10.4018/979-8-3373-9883-9.ch013

conditions on the manner in which student data is gathered, processed, and stored, and adherence to these standards has become a major concern among educational institutions. Also, AI tools create complications in upholding academic integrity and ownership of intellectual work. To solve these dilemmas, it is necessary to take a middle ground so that technological innovation and ethical responsibility and legal obligation can be closely linked. The chapter addresses the use of AI in education, regulatory measures, intellectual property issues, ethical issues, and responsible AI implementing approaches.

1. INTRODUCTION

The advent and increasing use of artificial intelligence (AI) in the learning setting have redefined the old teaching paradigm by introducing AI-based learning environments, intelligent tutoring system (ITS), and automated academic analytics. During the last ten years, AI technologies have been spreading in schools and universities across the globe, providing the means of personalization at scale and making informed decisions in pedagogy based on data (Mousavinasab et al., 2018). In the latest scoping reviews, there has been an increase in the number of AIEd applications between 2019 and 2023 that are registered in Scopus, which indicates that they are becoming part of various educational settings. Such systems such as adaptive platforms such as the ones at Georgia Tech use machine learning to aid mass instruction (Chan, 2023; Mousavinasab et al., 2018).

Significant opportunities of AI in education include personalized learning, where individual needs are considered and materials are modified to meet the needs of the student, adaptive learning assessments, which adjust difficulty to the individual requirements of the student in real-time, and improved learning analytics, which predicts student performance. The systematic reviews support that AI-based ITS is very effective regarding learning outcomes in K-12 classes as it can model the behavior of learners and offer tailored feedback. Individualized learning through AI algorithms, Bayesian networks and deep learning, is more effective than the conventional approaches, and it enhances engagement and retention throughout higher education. In addition, adaptive systems, which are based on reinforcement learning, are more accurate in assessment and skill-gap analysis as opposed to conventional LMS (Holmes et al., 2021).

Nevertheless, AI based learning technologies present significant threats and risks, such as privacy of student data due to mass data gathering, and bias in the algorithms leading to inequalities and abuse of sensitive information to non-educational ends. Disparities in AI educational platforms are caused by biased training data in 73% of the platforms, including 23% reduced accuracy of students of color on recognition systems. Trust is destroyed by privacy breaches and surveillance concerns, which teachers provide as obstacles to adoption. Data breaches and bias are found to be common issues in AIEd platforms through systematic literature reviews (Alasadi & Baiz, 2023; Holmes et al., 2021).

Compliance with laws and ethics are most crucial in AI-based education, especially considering the data protection legislation such as FERPA and GDPR, laws on child privacy such as COPPA, and intellectual property in academic contexts where AI-generated texts erase the boundary between authors and the written text. Encoding, permission, and auditing are the key components of the compliance schemes that will bring AI in line with the student record privacy safeguards of FERPA and data minimization of GDPR (Isukapalli & Srirama, 2024). In the case of AI-generated educational contents, the IPR frameworks present licensing and watermarking to address ownership issues in human-AI partnerships. These rules guarantee fair use and protect the information of minors according to COPPA (a variety of compliance guides).

The review article frames compliance of AI in education according to FERPA, GDPR, COPPA, and intellectual property regulations in the academic setting and synthesizes recent peer-reviewed research (2018-2025) to analyze areas of intersection between innovation and regulation. Its aims include to critically analyze the existing models of governance, define the gaps in the agreements, and suggest models of responsible AI stewardship in institutions (Harry & Sayudin, 2023). Serving as solutions to such, the paper highlights the necessity of implementing ethical AI governance as soon as possible to gain benefits and reduce risks in the educational context.

2. ARTIFICIAL INTELLIGENCE IN EDUCATION: TECHNOLOGIES AND APPLICATIONS

AI has become a revolutionary initiative in the educational setting, driving the use of technologies, including learning management system (LMS), intelligent tutoring system (ITS), adaptive learning platform, automated assessment system, and academic analytics system, that dynamically redefine the process of teaching and learning (Chen et al., 2019). Using machine learning algorithms and natural language processing, these AI-based systems can use large amounts of student interaction data to customize educational content and pacing in real-time, which has been demonstrated to be more engaging and effective at retention than the traditional one-size-fits-all model of education delivery. Importantly, although LMS such as Moodle with the use of AI plugins will help provide smooth delivery of content and cooperative learning, their effectiveness will depend on the effective integration of data, which will frequently expose their inability to scale to a variety of institutional settings (Chih-Ming & Ying-You, 2020).

Intelligent tutoring systems are one of the most important AI applications that can replicate the human-like pedagogical experience via cognitive modeling and reinforcement learning to offer scaffolded support in the specific learner profile. The new developments have also expanded the scope of ITS to include multimodal inputs, which use speech recognition and affective computing to perceive a student feeling frustrated or disengaged, and thus modify the teaching methods and enhance learning outcomes in the classroom in mathematics and language arts. Nonetheless, weaknesses continue to exist such as excessive use of historical data that can further tend to perpetuate biases in underrepresented groups of learners hence the need to design algorithms in an equitable way that draws on learning sciences.

Adaptive and personalized learning systems create another example of using AI, relying on the recommender systems and knowledge tracing to make the curriculum change to fit the learner, as were the case with Duolingo and Knewton, which dynamically adjust the difficulty to predictive analytics of the learner performance. AI-driven, automated grading and evaluation systems, like the BERT essay grading model, provide increased efficiency to a teacher in the feedback loop, with a highly detailed view of the student mastery, but tend to be insensitive when it comes to sophisticated creative work and cultural background. Analytics academic tools combine the data on these tools to predict at-risk students and make strategic plans at the institutional level, improving decisions but posing challenges to the interpretive validity of data aggregation and privacy (Kajamaa et al., 2019).

Teachers and learners are becoming increasingly active users of AI, not only in the creation of content with the aid of artificial intelligence programs such as generative AI assistants in lesson development but also in the research process with the help of automated literature synthesis, transforming classroom teaching and self-studying. The advantages are increased teaching performance, since AI will allow more time to the instructor to engage in high-value interactions, and enhanced learning results, as meta-analyses have proven 0.5 standard deviations of effect sizes. However, these benefits come with critical constraints: the lack of algorithmic transparency, biased data that increases inequalities, and reduced critical thinking due to over-reliance, which, according to the research on digital pedagogy, is associated with the risk of deskilling educators and standardizing the experiences of learners (Alatrash et al., 2024).

3. DATA PRIVACY AND REGULATORY FRAMEWORKS IN AI-DRIVEN EDUCATION

The advent of AI in learning settings has heightened the concern of student data management and privacy where huge amounts of personal, behavioral, and academic data are being collected, analyzed, and stored on online learning platforms. Online systems enabled by AI like adaptive learning systems, predictive analytics tools, and automated assessment tools are progressively being made dependent on minute traces of student activity, keystrokes, response times, biometric indicators, and interaction logs, which are both very sensitive education data that can be reidentified or used against them in case of poor security safeguards.

Some of the regulatory requirements that put different, yet similar, responsibility on both educational institutions and EdTech vendors mandate explicit consent, purpose limitation, and robust security protection when processing information of students, include the Family Educational Rights and Privacy Act (FERPA), the General Data Protection Regulation (GDPR), and the Children Online Privacy Protection Act (COPPA). The FERPA provides educational agencies with the responsibility to make sure that personally identifiable information in education records is not disclosed without parental or eligible student consent, making the utilization of AI tools based on the third party processing and data sharing in the clouds complicated. In the same way, GDPR requires data minimization, lawful basis testing, and data protection impact assessment of high-risk AI applications, which force the institution to carry out stringent audits of AI driven analytics and profiling systems on the school and higher education settings (Wang & Piper, 2018).

Regardless of such regulatory signals, institutions implementing AI based educational technologies face significant compliance issues especially when they act in more than one jurisdiction, where FERPA, GDPR, and COPPA all apply at the same time. As an illustration, the explicit consent and the right to be forgotten provision of GDPR clashes with the standard long-term storage and reutilizing of student data in most predictive analytics systems, where many of them train and optimize their models using previous data. COPPA enhances the level of scrutiny of the data collection of children.

4. INTELLECTUAL PROPERTY AND ACADEMIC INTEGRITY IN AI-ENABLED EDUCATION

The introduction of AI-generated content to the educational process has fundamentally broken the usual concept of intellectual property (IP) ownership, especially when it comes to the authorship of content created by generative technology. Existing laws, including those in the U.S. copyright laws, do not protect works that are purely AI-generated, unless they are significantly contributed to by humans, in which case they would be owned by the human member, not by the machine (Rowley, 2023). Such a position provides ambiguity in educational settings where learners and professors use AI to work on assignments, lesson plans, and research manuscripts because the line between the human-AI collaboration and machine autonomy is debated. As a result, institutions face the risk of losing the IP protected over AI assisted instructional materials, making it more difficult to license and commercialize AI guided educational resources and placing users at the risk of receiving a derivative infringement notice, in which training data includes copyrighted materials.

These issues are enhanced by the presence of copyright implications, where AI tools that are trained with large amounts of safeguarded content might be able to reproduce or remix the elements in the resulting product, or the outcomes of such processing may harm fair use defenses and encourage infringement. The question whether model training using copyrighted texts counts as transformative use has bedevilled the courts, but the results of writing based on a model of original styles or phrases compromise the originality of scholarly input to AI-assisted writing and research. To teachers using automated creativity generators, that creates liability to unattributed derivatives, especially on online learning systems where AI is synthesizing syllabi or multimedia and it is difficult to distinguish what had been licensed versus what is new. This is criticized in the literature of digital ethics which attempts to disclose artificial intelligence provenance as it is seen to be eroding the public domain, requiring disclosure requirements to follow the harmonization of national laws in the evolving EU directives.

The same process of academic integrity has been paralleled by plagiarism and ambiguity in authorship as generative AI allows submitting an essay or a piece of code made through algorithms to be graded without detection, going against the culture of evaluation. Research draws attention to the role of such instruments as large language models in promoting so-called ghost-writing that cannot be traced, which has been difficult to detect using anti-plagiarism software and has fuelled fears that the issue is a matter of ethical integrity in scholarship. Misuse is furthered to the research outputs, with AI imagining references or creating data to affect the peer review and publication abilities in the higher education sector (Graham, 2023). This creates a crisis of credit assignment as the hybrid human-AI authorship is against traditional requirements of human agency, and the use of AI laundering is suggested to redefine the issue of plagiarism.

5. ETHICAL AND GOVERNANCE CHALLENGES

The ethical environment is further complicated by data security and conscientious implementation of AI, particularly with the sensitivity of the records of academic history, behavioral evidence, and biometric data gathered using AI supported systems. Cloud based learning analytics and AI based tutoring systems tend to concentrate large volumes of student data, which present a appealing target to cyberattacks and rogue surveillance as well as put institutions at risk of FERPA and GDPR compliance liability. Recent studies point to the fact that the traditional security architecture is not well equipped to cope with AI-related threats, such as data poisoning, model inversion, and adversarial manipulations, that may jeopardize both privacy and integrity of the educational assessment. Therefore, it is necessary not only technical protection, including encryption, federated learning, and differential privacy, but also a strict administration of data life cycle management, contract of sharing with EdTech vendors, and ever-present risk evaluation in accordance with the law (Siddiqui & Bergquist, 2021).

The institutional governance structures and codes of conduct and policy formulation are thus constitutive in mitigating the tension between innovation and equity in the AI inspired academic setting. Universities are being pressured to establish AI ethics boards, algorithmic impact evaluation, and coding of conduct that are explicitly biased, consent and transparency in AI aided teaching and research. These governance frameworks should be based on both legal requirements, including the introduction of data protection impact assessment by GDPR and limitations on handling data of children imposed by COPPA, and the larger normative obligations to educational justice, student autonomy, and democratic engagement (Steegh et al., 2021). Practically, this would require the joint effort and collaboration of legal counsel, academic leadership, IT departments and faculty to make sure that AI systems are purchased, configured and assessed via participatory, iterative, and evidence-based methods and not top-down technical directives (Siddiqui & Bergquist, 2021).

6. STRATEGIES FOR RESPONSIBLE AI IMPLEMENTATION IN EDUCATION

The application of AI responsibly in education requires an intentional adoption of privacy by design principles into the structure of educational technologies, the data handling, and the algorithms of educational technologies. Privacy by design does not approach privacy as a post deployment requirement, but instead moves data protection requirements to the upstream stages of system development, and requires educational AI tools to restrict data collection, process only to well-specified pedagogical goals, and provide technical protection measures, such as anonymization, pseudonymization, and differential privacy, at the protocol layer. Examples of these approaches include federated learning and edge-based processing, which enable AI systems to derive insights based on student interactions without consolidating sensitive learning records, meaning that the surface area to regulatory non-compliance in addition to data breaches is minimized (Thelwall, 2020).

These technical designs should be aligned with the jurisdictional patchwork of laws that mandate severe conditions on data minimization, consent, and transparency in educational institutions, including FERPA, GDPR, and COPPA (Thelwall, 2020). These legal requirements can be operationalized on a manner that is both auditable and scalable by the universities and school districts that implement integrated compliance architectures which include institutional data protection impact assessments (DPIAs), standardized data flow mapping, and role-based access controls. Meanwhile, the dependency on third party AI vendors will require a contractual relationship, such as clarified provisions on data ownership, data used to train models, and timelines on data retention, meaning that institutions still have control over student data even when the computation is sub-contracted (Thelwall, 2020).

Technology providers are not the only ones who need to be held responsible on AI but educators, administrators, and policymakers should also come up with governance ecosystems that prioritize pedagogical, ethical, and legal priorities (Ng et al., 2021). Faculty and instructional designers, such as will need to be prepared to assess AI tools, not only based on accuracy, but also based on their effects on learner autonomy, bias, and surveillance and school and university leaders will need to invest in ongoing professional education in digital ethics and data protection literacy. Policymakers, in their turn, can have a beneficial impact on equalizing regulatory demands across jurisdictions and explaining the position of AI-developed educational material in intellectual property regimes, such that institutions can continue to inadvertently infringe copyright and licensing terms (Thelwall, 2020; Ng et al., 2021).

The current best practice in the field of responsible AI adoption in academic settings can thus be summarized as multi layered governance structures in which both technical protection, legal and ethical governance are combined into a cohesive institutional policy. Risk assessment procedures, including rights impact assessments and algorithmic audits, must become standard procedures, instead of being a one-time compliance activity, which would allow universities to identify bias, drift, as well as unforeseen misuse of AI generated analytics.

7. BIBLIOMETRIC ANALYSIS

In this section, a comprehensive bibliometric analysis is carried out on the application of AI in Education specifically about compliance to Family Educational Rights and Privacy Act (FERPA), General Data Protection Regulation (GDPR), and Children's Online Privacy Protection Act (COPPA) and the problem of Intellectual Property in the Academia. The study uses publication information from Lens.org to conduct this bibliometric analysis of the field and the investigation of intellectual structure and theme progression of the research. It applies VOSviewer to construct the bibliometric network where it maps the relationship between keywords, significant themes and time trend.

7.1. AI in Education

Figure 1 shows the network visualization of keyword co-occurrence in the research field of AI in Education. This visualization was created using VOSviewer software and data from the Lens.org database. The diagram provides a view of the field by mapping connections among the most commonly used keywords. Each node represents a keyword, and the lines between nodes indicate how closely related pairs are; the thicker the line, the stronger the connection. The size of the nodes shows their importance in the overall research network, with larger nodes indicating higher activity and significance. Different colors represent various thematic areas within the research field. The graph highlights the central role of the term 'artificial intelligence,' which has the broadest reach and serves as a key element across different research fields and themes. This prominence emphasizes the foundational role of AI in today's educational research and innovation.

The central node is connected to several keywords, including "humans," "curriculum," "education," "higher education," "learning," and "deep learning." These terms reflect a focus on improving educational practices, learning outcomes, and curriculum development. The presence of "humans" in the cluster emphasizes a human-centered approach to AI applications, especially in education, where the use of AI varies between the education system and students. This cluster is linked to phrases like "students," "education, medical," "educational status," and "empathy," showing a trend toward exploring how AI systems influence students and their educational experiences.

A significant number of keywords highlighted in green include: learning, teaching strategy, academic performance, deep learning, and delivery of healthcare. This cluster represents research on intelligent learning environments, adaptive learning systems, and AI-supported teaching methods. Medical education terms are increasingly included, indicating that AI's role in the medical field is growing, particularly for education and training purposes.

Another important cluster focuses on ethics, technology, responsible AI, and educational technology. There is an increasing interest in the ethical aspects of AI in education, as seen in terms like "ethics," "AI ethics," "responsible AI," "technology," and "bibliometric analysis." These terms reflect scholarly interest in the ethical and societal implications of AI, including issues of transparency, fairness, and governance. Current research concerns privacy, bias, accountability, and the responsible implementation of AI.

Figure 1. Network Visualization on AI in Education

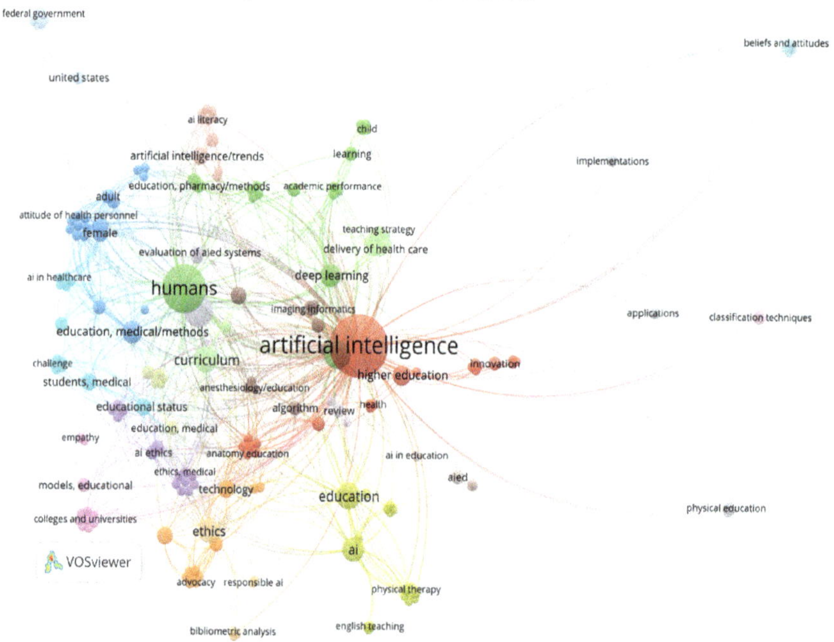

Source: Lens.Org Database; generated by using VOSviewer (Data may vary slightly).

The network also highlights popular and emerging topics such as "AI literacy," "artificial intelligence trends," "classification techniques," "applications," and "beliefs and attitudes." These topics point to a trend of preparing students and educators for the future with AI technologies, while also exploring perceptions and acceptance of these technologies. Additionally, terms like federal government, policy implementation, and educational institutions indicate a policy perspective and institutional practices that shape how AI is implemented.

Overall, Figure 1 depicts a multidisciplinary and well-connected area of research around AI in education. There are strong links between technology innovation, pedagogy, ethics, healthcare education, policy, and human-centered learning. The richness and dynamism of the thematic clusters suggest that AI is moving from purely technological research to a broader examination of its applications in education, society, and ethics. This interconnected research landscape shows the influence of AI on reshaping the future of learning, both globally and within education systems.

Figure 2 is an overlay visualization showing trends over time with VOSviewer on the research themes of the domain AI in Education over time, based on data from Lens.org. The overlay visualization is a modified version of a network map that represents an extra dimension of time; where the darker blue & purple represent early topics (around 2021-2022), green represents intermediate topics (around 2023-2024) and the yellow represent current & future topics (around 2025). In addition to explaining current trends, the visualization presents an overview of the evolution of this research field over time and outlines some emerging and existent topics.

The main largest and most dominant node on the network map is 'AI', representing the strongest link with most of the others. This keyword is at the heart of the network as a strong link to the largest number of keywords related to education, technology, ethics and healthcare. It is interesting to see how closely linked 'AI' is to important keywords such as 'humans', 'education', 'curriculum', 'higher education', 'deep learning', 'technology' and this can demonstrate how the application of AI within the field is interdisciplinary. Notably, these keywords retain a high importance value across a recent period of research shown by the “green” color.

The map illustrates a large grouping of topics surrounding 'humans' including 'female', 'adult', 'students, medical', 'education, medical', 'educational status', 'health personnel'. The grouping of this cluster in yellowish-green colors indicates a substantial amount of focus in research at this moment toward learning and education with the focus on humans and healthcare through AI. This may imply growing attention to use of AI in healthcare for medical education, training, evaluation of students, and personal learning.

One striking feature in the map are the newer topics in “shiny yellow” nodes. Current areas of interest appear to be related to education implementation and/or AI literacy, beliefs and attitudes and physical education. 'AI literacy' suggests a growing emphasis on both the educators' and students' competence and understanding when it comes to AI. The existence of 'beliefs', 'attitudes' and 'perceptions' indicates a growing importance given to the social fit and the ethical aspects of integrating AI into education.

Figure 2. Overlay Visualization on AI in Education

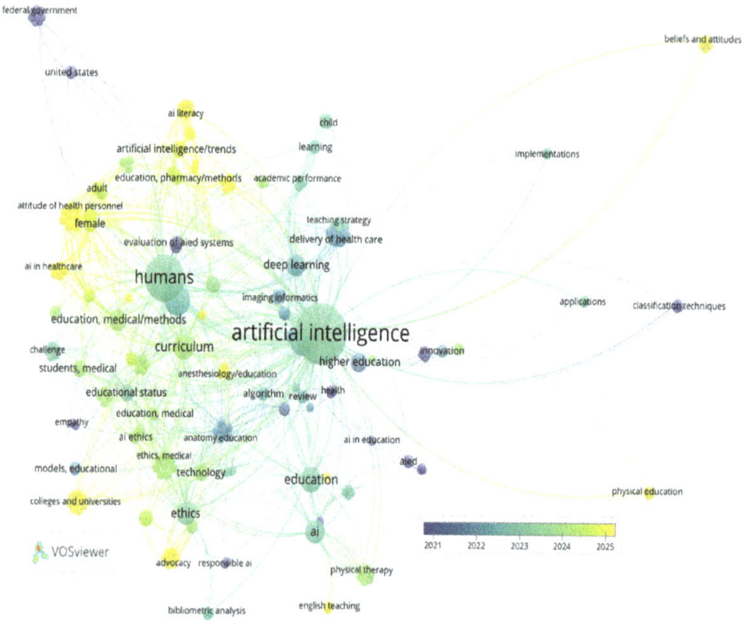

Source: Lens.Org Database; generated by using VOSviewer (Data may vary slightly).

A prevalent trend throughout the network is the use of technology in a research capacity. Previous topics in darker blue color include 'classification techniques' and 'responsible AI'. However, the most recent topics tend to be linked to the application of AI, innovation of AI as well as implementation of the new technology within education institutions. Words such as 'applications', 'innovation', and 'implementations' illustrate a research tendency that has gradually moved away from theory and toward practical use of AI in the school and education systems.

Another obvious trend visible is the increasing relevance of ethics and Governance related issues. For instance, while the topics of 'ethics' or 'AI ethics' are linked to other recent education areas, 'responsible AI' also remained a central theme, and can be interpreted as issues about Fairness, transparency, accountability and the responsible application of AI in education is of interest. Such topics are expected to become more prominent as more schools begin integrating AI within the curriculum.

Overall, the research trends associated with the field of AI in education appear to be rapidly becoming both more far-reaching and interdisciplinary, from pedagogy, healthcare education, ethics, policy and innovation to the learning about humans. The distinctive use of color scale signifies the move from the early approaches in the field towards subjects such as AI literacy, implementation strategies for AI, beliefs and attitudes on the topic, and real-world applications of AI in education. Overall the figure demonstrates how the research field has evolved, and studies in this topic are anticipated to remain focused on using AI in a responsible and innovative way for teaching and learning, involving the learner and creating the most effective and human-centric learning environment.

In contrast to network and overlay visualization, density visualization (Figure 3) emphasizes the proportion, density and strength of occurrence of the keywords within a certain research area. This research area is illustrated by color intensity. A high density is displayed by yellow and a low density is colored with blue, with green representing medium or median density. The visualization provides an overview of the knowledge base that has been established at the time of creation.

The most prevalent and highest density area (bright yellow) on the graph is the word 'artificial intelligence'. The location at the top of the graph indicates that the overall concept of AI is the most common and foundational keyword within the research field and will likely encompass most of the work done to date with the context being the creation, application and results of the technologies within education. This central idea closely links with other keywords including 'humans', 'curriculum', 'higher education', 'education', 'deep learning', 'technology' which also belong in the yellow and green density area. These words link AI research closely with education in terms of teaching, the curriculum and overall educational principles and processes.

Other strong connections to the topmost research clusters involve 'humans', this suggests that the researcher's intent and focus for this research area and its keywords heavily focus on the people involved, be they the student, teacher or other stakeholders in AI. With terms like "education, medical" "students, medical", "adult" "educational status", "health personnel" appear, the context is clearly a wider sphere of education and links in healthcare and medicine and will further highlight how AI is impacting these areas through education and learning.

The next section has keywords with moderate densities "learning", "academic performance", "teaching strategy" "delivery of health care" and "evaluation of aided systems" which indicate higher levels of research efforts, these are looking into whether educational strategies employing intelligent technologies actually impact a student's learning outcome, performance, achievement. With this is also the mention of 'deep learning', an indication of higher-level computations within AI education research.

Figure 3. Density Visualization on AI in Education

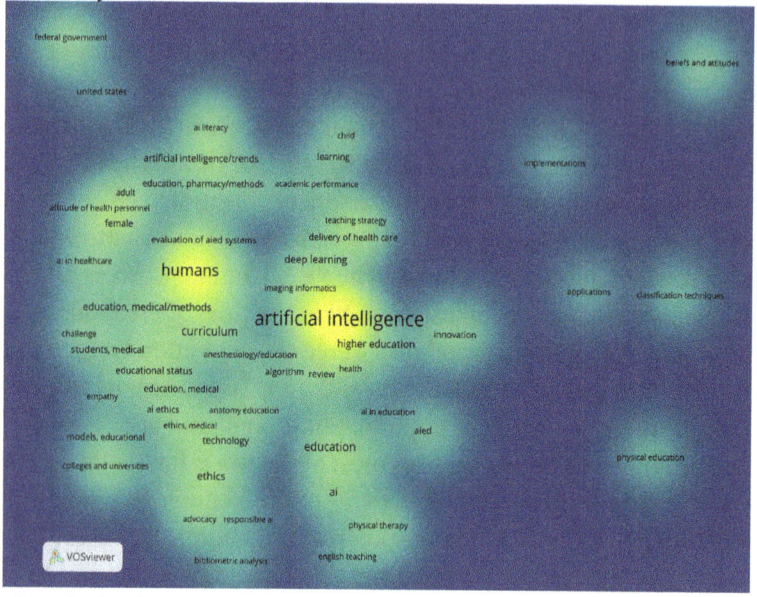

Source: Lens.Org Database; generated by using VOSviewer (Data may vary slightly).

There are also strong connections related to ethical issues involving "ethics" and "AI ethics" "responsible AI" and "technology" which show the growing importance of how the technologies used are fair, accountable and trustworthy, especially within education.

Lower density research topics appear on the sides of the visualization, here keywords such as "beliefs and attitudes" "classification techniques" "applications" "implementations" "physical education", and "federal government" appears within isolated sections highlighted inbeige and blue colors. These represent the stand-alone smaller fields or emerging areas of research. The distance away from the central cluster indicates that it may be a newer less widely researched area but could potentially be significant in the future.

In general, Figure 3 is an effective tool used for understanding and interpreting the intellectual domain concerning AI within education. It depicts how low concentration areas can transition to high concentration areas within education as intelligent technologies become prevalent in the classroom. AI, humans, curriculum, education and higher education have shown up and are the strong connecting pieces within the research as the central driving forces of AI in education. As well as an illustration of the role AI has in multiple research spheres such as pedagogy, medicine, ethics, technology and government, the results presented open up avenues of research such as implementation strategies of AI tools into classrooms and how the ethics within AI can contribute to educational practices, promoting AI literacy in the education system.

7.2. Children Online Privacy Protection Act (COPPA)

Figure 4 is a network visualization of COPPA researches by VOSviewer. The visualization displays keyword co-occurrence relationships extracted from the literature where nodes represent keywords, and edges represent co-occurrence strength. The larger the size of the node, the more common the term, while different colors distinguish thematic clusters. The mapping indicates that this research field is tight-knit and interdisciplinary; ranging from privacy to cyber security, children protection to social media, AI to education, health care to digital governance.

The most significant term present in the network is 'privacy,' acting as a pivotal node that centralizes numerous research topics. 'Privacy' has a notably large node size which signals that it remains a central concern in the body of COPPA research. Many keywords co-occurring with 'privacy' often implicitly or explicitly entail concerns about children's data protection such as “data protection”, “security”, “Internet”, “Internet of things” and “children's privacy”. These relationships between keywords clearly reflect children's online data security being an important policy and technical issue.

Another dominant cluster involves keywords such as “humans”, “children”, “adolescent”, and “social media”. The humanistic aspects of COPPA research are covered here, specifically how children and adolescents utilize the internet and online environments. “Communication”, “social networks”, “digital media”, “YouTube”, “marketing” keywords demonstrate the considerable scholarly research examining children's interaction with platforms and children's use of social media. Children's use of the Internet to access on-line material, children's behavior tracking and the collection of commercial data is evidenced by the appearance of these keywords.

An additional cluster includes “Artificial Intelligence”, “Machine Learning”, “Computer Security” and “Educational Technology”. Many researchers agree that current technologies both pose problems and offer solutions to children's online privacy. Keywords such as AI monitoring, automated content management systems, privacy-preserving technology, and cybersecurity are examples of AI technologies used to increase child safety online. The appearance of “Educational Technology” within this cluster signifies that researchers are focusing on developing innovative teaching and learning materials aimed at increasing the digital literacy and awareness of privacy risks amongst young people.

The network also maps a “healthcare and digital health cluster,” with terms such as “telemedicine”, “mobile health”, “mHealth”, “health equity”, and “mobile applications”. This highlights the increasing attention paid to the protection of children's sensitive health data online and the emerging importance of secure systems in digital health services delivery. The increased utilization of remote online systems for health service delivery makes adherence to privacy regulations like COPPA increasingly central for research and development.

Another important cluster includes keywords representing "governance", "ethics" and "policy" such as "regulation", "law", "policy", "accountability", "surveillance studies", and "research ethics". This Cluster reflects the ongoing debates around current and proposed policy frameworks, regulatory responsibilities, and corresponding levels of accountability and monitoring that seek to protect minors in the digital age. The presence of "schema new*papers" is potentially an indicator of increased scrutiny of children's data collection and algorithmic monitoring, and the subsequent obligation for firms serving online child platforms.

The visualization also indicates the trend toward the mainstreaming of the importance of children's privacy protections and education in interdisciplinary contexts. Terms like "teacher education" and "education" along with "educational technology" and "contextual integrity" demonstrate an emphasis on the study of educational approaches to children's awareness of online privacy and respectful technology usage, and the promotion of children's and adolescent's digital citizenship.

Figure 4. Network Visualization on Children Online Privacy Protection Act (COPPA)

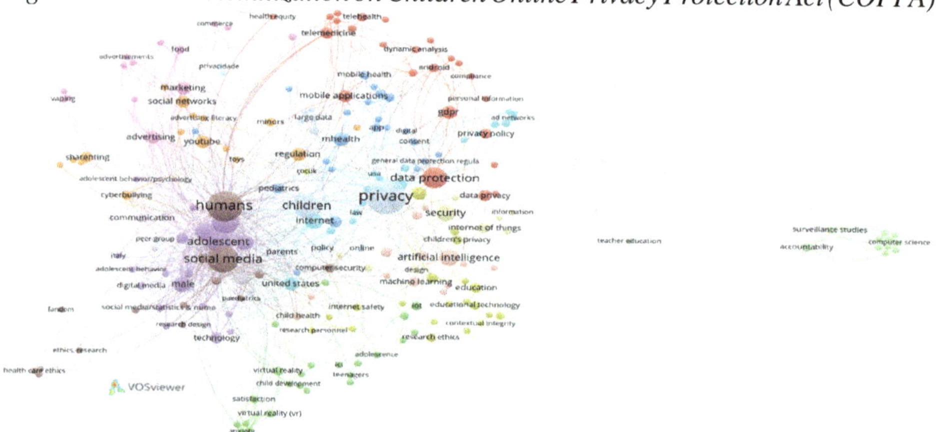

Source: Lens.Org Database; generated by using VOSviewer (Data may vary slightly).

In summary, the visualization presented in Figure 4 highlights that the research on COPPA is multidisciplinary and extends beyond simple regulatory compliance to encompassing a diverse array of fields such as computer science, cybersecurity, social sciences, public policy, teaching and learning, health care, and ethics. The strong representation of privacy-related results underscores the critical importance of protecting children's personal information online, while the interlinking of various clusters showcases the expanding and dynamic nature of the field. Overall, it is apparent from this visualization that the ongoing and future research agendas will increasingly incorporate comprehensive policy development, responsible data practices, healthcare security, governance of social media, and privacy-by-design solutions based on artificial intelligence.

Figure 5 illustrates an overlay visualization as part of the analysis of keywords co-occurrence derived from data on Lens.org database of research concerning Children's Online Privacy Protection Act (COPPA). Created by VOSviewer, time was added to the overlay with a colour spectrum. In Map, dark blue- and purple-colored topics signify previous topics of research (approx. 2016-2018); green colored topics are topics of research with more prominent features since 2019 to 2022 and yellow-colored topics symbolize recent and emergent topics of research from 2023 to 2024. Through this they are able to identify changes in their areas of interests within the topics of child online privacy and digital protection in different timeframes.

In the center of the network, "privacy" is the central and most connected term, suggesting its relevance across all periods of study. Throughout the 2016-2018 timeframe, research concentrated on basic terms such as Data Privacy, Computer Security, Internet Safety, Research Ethics, Law, Regulation and Digital Governance, indicated mostly with blue and purple nodes which represents early areas of research focused on compliance challenges and setting legal standards for the protection of children's privacy online.

The field of research has expanded dramatically and became more interdisciplinary between 2019 and 2022. Keywords like "children" and "humans" appear in a significant amount of results and are therefore green. In this time, attention has shifted from exclusively focusing on legal and regulatory matters towards the broader impact of digital technologies and social networking sites, health care technology and online services on children. Research papers concerning the effect of digital technologies on the well-being of children and their safety in the real world and their online behaviors have increased.

In the newest period (yellow keywords 2023 - 2024), we can distinguish new research topics such as "accountability" along with "computer science", "surveillance studies", "teacher education", "artificial intelligence", "machine learning" and new advances within the context of privacy governance. These topics all relate to algorithmic decision-making, AI powered data collection, automated surveillance and platform accountability. Researchers are now focusing on the detrimental and helpful effects that new technologies might have on the privacy of children.

Out of these new research interests, one particularly stands out: artificial intelligence and machine learning have become important areas of research. The inclusion of privacy, security and educational technologies is a rising area where researchers leverage AI to identify threats to privacy, trace online behaviors, and improve child protection standards. Moreover, a growing emphasis on surveillance and accountability studies highlights the increase in scholarly interests about the ethical aspects of digital surveillance and on the level of responsibility of tech companies regarding children's personal data.

The overall overlay visualization represents a continuation and increase in progress from legal and regulatory research in 2016-2018, general children online privacy and social media research in 2019-2022 to AI related privacy protection, accountability and governance research in 2023-2024. This evolution reflects the growing complexity of issues surrounding children online privacy. Future research should aim at advancing child-centered, child-friendly, ethically responsible and safe online environments that are compatible with technological innovations.

Figure 5. Overlay Visualization on Children Online Privacy Protection Act (COPPA)

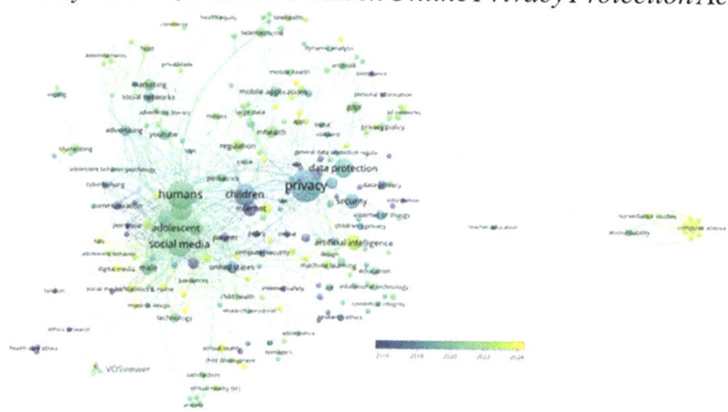

Source: Lens.Org Database; generated by using VOSviewer (Data may vary slightly).

Figure 6 displays a density visualization (by using VOSviewer) for the most dominant and dense research topics revealed by the data from Lens.org on Children's Online Privacy Protection Act (COPPA) research field. As colors: they are varying from dark blue, representing low density, low commonness of keywords, up to the green color, representing middle density, and the highest is bright yellow for high density, most interconnected topics (keywords). Yellow parts of the figure represent research issues that frequently appear together and are highly related to other topics, while blue parts are unexplored or emerging issues of research. Visualization that provides an overview of the entire intellectual structure and key research foci within a certain discipline like "Children's Online Privacy and Protection".

The most bright, dense part of the map is dominated by the term "privacy" in yellow. Privacy is the most central notion that is at the core of the COPPA research field, as clearly represented on the map through its central position on the map and its highest density. The strong focus of research within this keyword reveals that the concern of researchers is focused onchildren's 'privacy' and 'privacy practices', in the context of safe online environment and safe collection of personal data, among others by "data protection", "security", "children's privacy", "internet of things", and "law".

The next highest density of themes focuses on words like "humans", "children", "adolescent" and "social media". These topics can be seen in the yellow and green area indicating broad research interest concerning the use of digital environment and devices by children and adolescents. The high occurrence of the keywords like "communication", "digital media", "internet", "YouTube", "marketing", "social networks", reveals that the researchers' interests are greatly concerned about children's and adolescents' interaction with the digital environment, how personal data is collected and used. The presence of terms related to the issue shows the growing concern with the increase of online advertising, behavioral profiling, the widespread use of social media and the perceived risks concerning children online.

We can see a moderate density visualization, relating to the technologies-related clustered terms: "artificial intelligence", "machine learning", "computer security", "educational technology" and "internet safety". Theme 1, Theme 3 and Theme 4 show the growing interest in developing innovative technologically-based solutions for children's privacy and safety. AI supported monitoring systems, automated privacy management solutions, cybersecurity frameworks as well as educational programs and workshops on digital literacy and responsible behavior online represent key areas within this field of research.

There is an important concentration of words associated with healthcare and digital health, such as "telehealth", "telemedicine", "mobile health", "mHealth", "mobile applications", "health equity", which represents a certain level of meaningful relationship, however the discourse around these terms shows a growing interest for studyingchildren's health information during the use of digital platforms. Since technology is progressively turning into a central component of medical assistance, and as the medical system continuously moving to remote and mobile locations has opened new challenges concerning compliance with legal standards and data protection.

Figure 6. Density Visualization on Children Online Privacy Protection Act (COPPA)

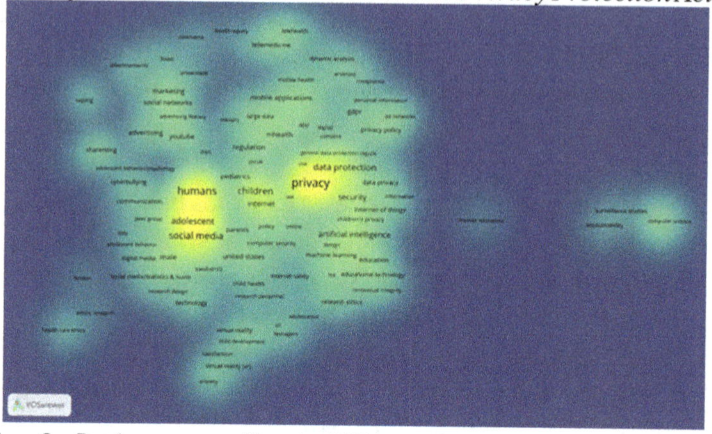

Source: Lens.Org Database; generated by using VOSviewer (Data may vary slightly).

Several marginal parts in our visualization can be detected as green and blue indicating that the research in the following terms has not been performed to a large extent yet. Such terms may be located further away from the center, and perhaps can be clustered around "teacher education", "computer sciences", "surveillance studies", "accountability", "virtual reality" and "research ethics". As they show low density, they indicate the novelty or niche research fields about which a lower number of scientific publications can be found. Nevertheless, they are likely to contribute to the emerging research areas in the future, as advanced digital technologies and their uses develop and influence more domains and ethical principles.

In summary, it can be identified from Figure 6 that "privacy", "data protection", "children", "adolescent" and "social media" are the main research areas under the COPPA topic of study. The visualization clearly represents the interdisciplinary nature of the research field, integrating input from law, cyber security, health care, education, computer sciences and social sciences. The strong centrality of "privacy" reflects its position as a core element within the field and the fundamental research interest in protection it has throughout time. Meanwhile, novel research directions, like those based on artificial intelligence, accountability, surveillance studies and digital health, show the development of the field towards addressing more complex privacy issues arising from rapidly evolving technologies and digital ecosystems.

7.3. Family Educational Rights and Privacy Act (FERPA)

Figure 7 illustrates a VOSviewer network visualization of the landscape of FERPA research within education, privacy, policy, technology, and public health. Built using the Lens.org database of research terms and their frequencies of co-occurrence (nodes represent words; links represent the strength of the relationship between two nodes), it is understood that larger nodes signify more frequent terms and different clusters are associated with colors. This visualization clearly depicts the intersectionality of and the growth of FERPA research across different fields.

The most prominent node is the “human” keyword that is centrally located, acting as a connecting piece between various themes of research. Its size indicates the predominant theme and suggests that FERPA research focuses mainly on humans' roles in implementation, education, and in regards to privacy and healthcare as well as the application of policy. Following “human” on both sides are traditional terms of child protection, such as “child”, “female”, “young adult”, and “public health.” These terms suggest child and demographic information is a main consideration in terms of FERPA and privacy issues.

Highlighted as a cluster on the upper-right and center of the network is a focus on education and higher education. A high concentration of terms are related to education and higher education, such as “higher education”, “education”, “curriculum”, “online learning”, “educational technology”, and “assessment”. These terms signify the strong and continuous impact of FERPA on student data in current educational practices, specifically with the increasing development of online learning and digitization being a prime area of FERPA implementation.

Another notable cluster focuses on data privacy and ethics, consisting of words such as “privacy”, “ethics”, “data privacy”, “data protection”, “confidentiality”, and “machine learning”. With more technology being implemented in education, data privacy and protection is becoming crucial, particularly with increasing concern for the responsible usage of data. The involvement of machine learning and AI signals new and advanced research in the field.

The network also outlines a cluster focused on information security at the right edge of the diagram; key terms here are “information security”, “security regulation”, and “big data”. It highlights the growing importance and necessity for cybersecurity measures in educational settings.

Further illustrating the breadth of FERPA's scope, clusters focused on public health, epidemiology, health policy and coronavirus research are apparent in the diagram, showing how the rules around education and privacy also extends to areas of health. With an integration of health and education data, there are numerous considerations to be addressed in terms of policy, privacy, and compliance.

Figure 7. Network Visualization on Family Educational Rights and Privacy Act (FERPA)

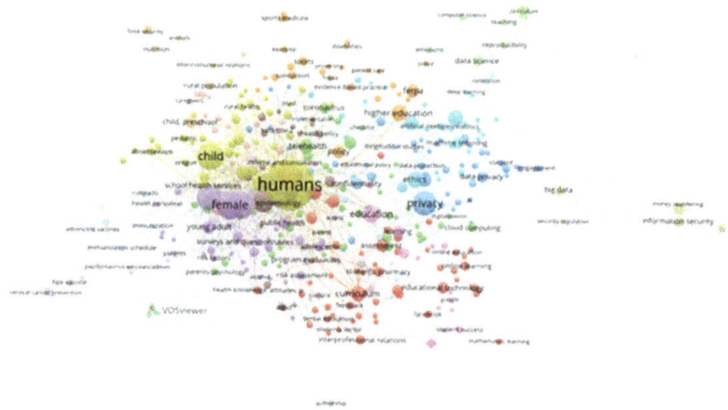

Source: Lens.Org Database; generated by using VOSviewer (Data may vary slightly).

In conclusion, Figure 7 visually confirms that research around FERPA has become an extensive field in regards to education, technology, data privacy and security, public policy, and public health. The intersectionality of these clusters demonstrates how the rules and guidelines around FERPA are a constantly developing aspect of today's education systems.

Figure 8 plots the merging of scores of relevant keyword co-occurrences gathered from the Lens.org database, about FERPA. Similar to a typical network visualization but with a time element, the overlay map displays the average year of publication of the keywords with different colors. Older topics are shown in darker blues/purples, intermediate research activity in green, and more recent and emerging research topics in yellow. With this method, both older research trends and new research trends and gaps of FERPA and educational data privacy could be identified.

The center is the most connected and largest node of the network and the keywords related to humanities arts subject are connected to it. The keyword "humans" is the largest and most connected node in the network, which represents its importance and central role across different kinds of research subjects related to humanities arts. The highly connected nature between "female", "child" and "education", "public health", and "privacy" signifies the interdisciplinary nature of FERPA research related to educational, healthcare, and social science research. Such keywords clearly signify the humane side of privacy laws and its role in managing educational data.

It is quite an interesting finding from the reading of overlay visualization, that topics of privacy, data privacy, ethics, machine learning, and artificial intelligence are recent research fields, shown as green-yellow colors. This clearly shows the current focus in research activities being on technologies and topics regarding to digital learning, data learning, data-driven decision making, and role of AI in educational institutions. When such keywords becoming omnipresent, they reflect the ever-increasing concern for issues of student privacy, transparency and ethics related to use of technology in education.

Newer research topics like higher education, online learning, learning technology, educational technology and digitalization can also be easily noticed in the visualization. The inclusion of their account in articles indicates that the rapid spread of online learning platform and digital learning tools is contributing a large amount to the debate about FERPA compliance and student privacy. The increasing need to protect educational records, whilst offering access and promoting innovation, also accompanied the rapid rise in the digital learning ecosystem.

Another emerging region of information security-security regulation-big data is in the right side of the network, which related to more recent research activities and represents the emerging requirement for sound information security system and regulation to protect private information. This strong connectivity between information security and privacy related keywords indicate the rise in the convergence of educational policy research and cybersecurity research.

On the other hand, the dark colors for immunization schedule, vaccination programs, public health services and etc., shows the history research activities that had preceded the current times. These were predominantly studies on educational and healthcare record management, now followed by digital privacy and technology related studies under FERPA.

Figure 8. Overlay Visualization on Family Educational Rights and Privacy Act (FERPA)

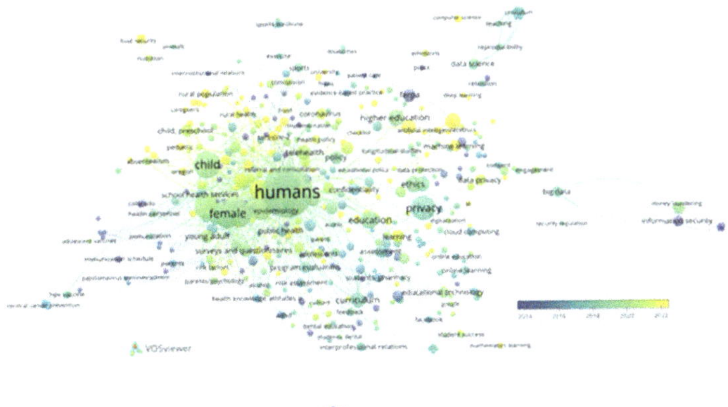

Source: Lens.Org Database; generated by using VOSviewer (Data may vary slightly).

Overall, the Figure 8 clearly illustrates the evolution of FERPA research, from classical consideration of confidentiality in educational and healthcare records to current studies focusing on digital learning, AI, machine learning, data privacy and information security. The overlay visualization shows it is clearly a contemporary issue on FERPA due to transformation of information to digital world, and increasing focus on the ethical, technical and regulatory dilemma around managing and safeguarding students' information in academic institutions nowadays. This result demonstrates that need of privacy preserving technologies and data management practices is more and more important for religious information community to address it in future research and information security activities. The conclusion highlights growing relevance of data governance and privacy preserving technologies to future information security practice and need of religious information community.

Figure 9 provides a VOSviewer density map of keyword co-occurrences for the FERPA using a database extracted from Lens.org. Unlike the courses network overlay visualization, the density map emphasizes where research effort and concentration appears in the diagram, through color representation. Dark yellow areas represent where research clusters are highest in density and keywords are common and closely related. Areas in shades of green and blue represent lower densities of research work or nascent topics. This representation of keywords quickly visualizes the most discussed and most studied aspects of FERPA research.

"humans" are one of the brightest and densest keywords and indicates that research in the area of human-centered studies is an important aspect of FERPA research. It's high density can be related to people like pupils, educators, as well as teachers, school staff, and school administrators. It can help educators and students remain private and secure when dealing with their information. High-density keywords are near education related topics such as "female," which can be seen as strongly associated with education, and other health related concepts such as "child," "young adult," "epidemiology," and "public health." Such closely related terms such as "female" or "public health" and "child" or "young adult" and "epidemiology" are found in the areas related to education at a high density as well, suggesting demographic and health related concerns are often intertwined and analyzed along with investigations of education issues.

Another strong topic of study was "privacy," "education," "ethics," "confidentiality," and "assessment" and appear in the middle of the density map. These are of crucial concern for FERPA studies and reveal the emphasis on securing students' data, proper ethics in education, and using information appropriately in the classroom. These terms are closely clustered in order to demonstrate how much they have become embedded in educational policies and practices.

One more cluster that appear is education, machine learning, data privacy, and education technology are are at a medium-dense level of study. This implies that the increasing number of studies examining the application of new technology in an educational setting has begun to increase in relevance as they appear together. The prevalence of terms such as artificial intelligence, machine learning, cloud computing, and online learning in research proposals clearly demonstrates a shift in the field as education continues to incorporate technology-rich environments. In this day and age of increasingly integrated technology use, compliance, transparency, and appropriate data usage will increasingly be examined.

Information security and security regulation appear on the right side of the density map as distinct clusters of related terms; however, these were not quite as dense as the core clusters but they are nevertheless represented and indicate an increasing area of study that impacts teachers and students alike. These terms emphasize the importance of robust security protocols for educational data.

Areas in lower density clusters colored blue include topics such as sports medicine, food security, public health intervention, and vaccination programmes. While these areas do not appear as dense and dominant as others, they are representative of the interdisciplinary nature of FERPA studies and show its relevance to various areas such as healthcare, public policy and social services.

Figure 9. Density Visualization on FERPA

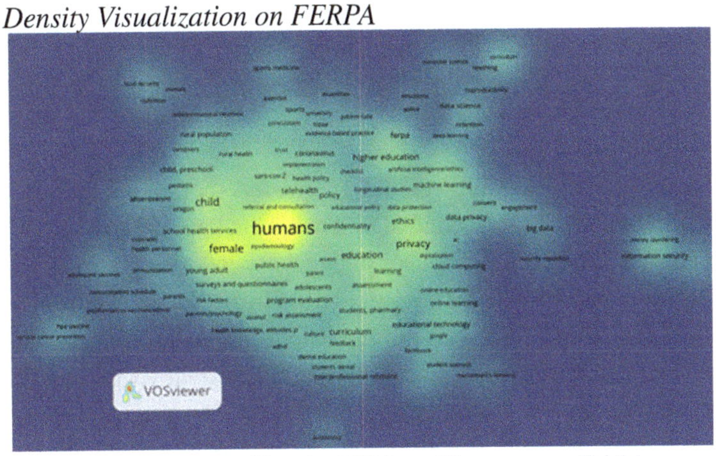

Source: Lens.Org Database; generated by using VOSviewer (Data may vary slightly).

Overall, the main clusters of FERPA related research in this map concern human-centered studies, the protection of privacy, the field of education and a greater understanding of how to handle sensitive data. The density of the various research areas indicates that while privacy and confidentiality is the most central theme, an increasing concern has begun to develop regarding technology and security in an educational setting, demonstrated through the presence of terms relating to artificial intelligence, machine learning and information security.

7.4. General Data Protection Regulation (GDPR)

As presented below in Figure 10, this network visualization on the co-occurrence of the research information of the GDPR which produced by the VOSviewer by using the search information form the database which called the Lens.org display the frame of intellectual framework and topic relations of GDPR. In the network diagram, each node represents a keyword and edges between nodes represent their co-occurrence relationships. Keywords that appear more frequently are bigger and each colour indicates the different clusters. It clearly displays the major research themes, Topical area of the research and its interdisciplinary areas in the area of data protection and privacy.

GDPR is visually the largest keyword as well as the central point of all the networks that relates to privacy, governance, security, legal compliance and digital rights. From the central position, the keywords associated with it closely are those of privacy, personal data, data protection, compliance and security that are at the core of the Regulation on data privacy and its ethical usage.

GDPR has become a cornerstone with regard to privacy and personal data protection. The keyword correspondence between personal data and data protection, data sharing and privacy, and data sharing and confidentiality are found to be very high. Privacy rights and data governance have become central focus of GDPR research. There is extensive research interest on how personal data is collected, shared and how organizations are regulated to achieve the goals of data privacy and effective data management practices.

In addition to this, legal and regulatory related themes including legislation, regulations, fundamental rights, controller, processor, applicable law can be grouped together in another cluster. This focuses on legal aspects related to the GDPR; organizations are expected to abide by the Regulation to ensure legal compliance. These results suggest that there are diverse engagement in legal and operational aspects, implementation policy, and legal liability regarding privacy rules and provisions.

This can be interpreted as "technological" theme that groups keywords such as Information security, Cloud computing, Cyber security, data processing and risk analysis. This reflects the convergence of the IT discipline with GDPR research, digital infrastructure is also under growing research interest since companies' shift to the cloud, and larger amounts of data analytics were used. Risk management, as the other research topic is concerned about the security to guard information from cyber threat or any kind of access by intruders.

Apart from the legal and the IT aspects of the GDPR, a secondary geographical and policy-specific area including European Union, United Kingdom that includes relevant policy structures and implications can be observed in the network diagram. This is related to the nature that the GDPR is an EU regulation and its global impact on the international law for privacy; it is proved by the network that it will become a worldwide precedent for all data protection policies relating to privacy outside EU.

Figure 10. Network Visualization on General Data Protection Regulation (GDPR)

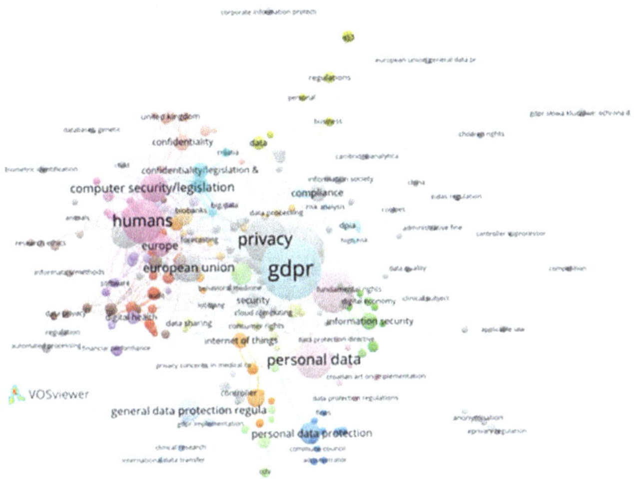

Source: Lens.Org Database; generated by using VOSviewer (Data may vary slightly).

Additionally, there were numerous smaller clusters relating to ethics, digital economy, consumer rights, healthcare, and biometrics, showing expanding area of research about GDPR. This implies the data protection topic also extends to healthcare industry, commercial sector, finance sector and new technology sector.

In conclusion, the network of the GDPR related studies shown above in Figure 10 demonstrated its multidisciplinary aspects by blending areas of legal, IT, cybersecurity, ethics, governance and policy areas. The research on GDPR focused primarily on privacy and personal data protection along with increasing convergence with legal compliance, information security and digital transformation. The network indicated that GDPR has become a significant and emerging trend and have global relevance to the research field, policies and technological developments, as a guiding standard for the protection of individual privacy in this fast-changing data driven world.

Figure 11 is an overlay visualization showing keyword co-occurrence in research about the General Data Protection Regulation (GDPR). Through coloring the nodes with hues ranging from dark blue (earliest research in ~2018) to yellow (latest research in ~2022), this overlaid visualization represents a time dimension to a network graph of research trends, providing insight into the evolving nature of GDPR-related research and suggesting key themes and more recent topics within data protection and privacy research. The central node is "GDPR," which is the largest and most significant node as it has been incorporated into numerous research topics. Similar themes, like “privacy” and “personal data,” “compliance,” “data protection” and “information security” cluster together, depicting key concepts that were among the first addressed after the enactment of the GDPR and demonstrating that they represent core areas within GDPR-related research. It is easy to note that these central nodes appear colored in a range of dark blue and green colors in the diagram. With regard to the colors of the nodes in the illustrated visualization, those with blue and green tones represent that key concepts like confidentiality, computer security, and legislation were early concerns after GDPR was introduced in 2018.

Therefore, early research trends have included a focus on understanding legal obligations, an organization's approach to compliance, data governance procedures, and how data protection provisions influence computer security systems. The newest research trends are highlighted in yellow on the graph and show that an increasing interest in topics such as artificial intelligence, digital health, and internet of things, risk analysis, data sharing, and consumer rights are more recent research focus. These findings demonstrate an emerging interest in how the GDPR relates to current innovations in information technology. Given the emergence of new concepts, there is a focus on how the GDPR can address the risks associated with AI and the development of technology such as artificial intelligence and machine-driven tools. It has become apparent that there is a greater interest in topics in the domain of digital health and computer security. New research in areas such as data transfers, data sharing, the internet of things, and consumer protection has risen as GDPR, has had to meet the requirements and demands of the European organizations and businesses worldwide.

It is clear that in research about the GDPR the original legal and security aspects are gradually being replaced by studies concerning artificial intelligence, digital health, the development of new technologies, data transfers, consumer protection, and internet security. It appears that research on data protection, security, legislation and information systems has shifted and evolved over time and is expected to evolve even further into new topics such as AI, digital health, computer security and the use of the internet.

Figure 11. Overlay Visualization on General Data Protection Regulation (GDPR)

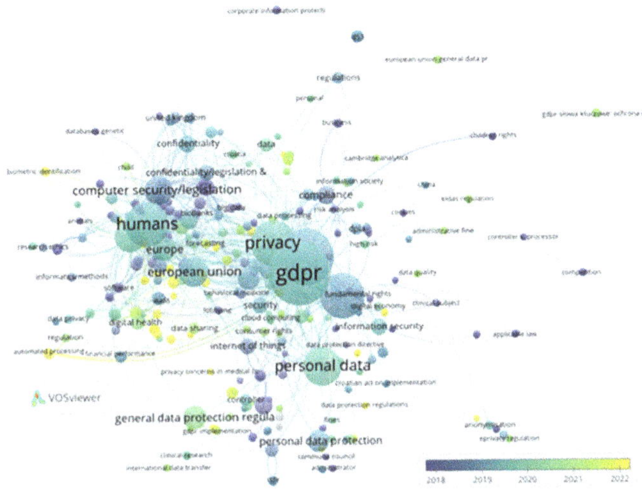

Source: Lens.Org Database; generated by using VOSviewer (Data may vary slightly).

The color scale (Figure 11) illustrates an increasing trend over time in research that applies to areas like artificial intelligence, internet safety, digital health, risk analysis and consumer rights which indicates an increased researcher awareness about applying GDPR regulations across emerging information technology. One of the emerging topics which seems to have gained high attention is in the field of digital health/healthcare in combination with privacy concerns and it seems that new research studies are being conducted, in these areas of privacy and data protection. As research is continuously developing in these and similar areas and with the help of this visualization, it is clear that GDPR has turned out to be an interdisciplinary topic including a variety of domains that include legal matters, information technology, computer security, healthcare, management sciences and ethics. The temporal analysis on the visualization seems to be suggesting that future studies of the GDPR shall explore how the development of new information technology aspects can be maintained to be regulated by data protection legislation, without compromising privacy rights of individuals and customers worldwide.

In Figure 12 there is shown the VOSviewer density visualization of co-occurrence keywords concerning researches on the General Data Protection Regulation (GDPR), using as base of researches the Lens.org data-base. In a density map use of a color gradient in order to recognize a cluster and concentration in field of the research; whereas the light yellow is high density level of the research/relevance, green shows a medium density level of the research/relevance and blue shows a low-density level of the research/relevance or emergent areas of study. The visualization provides clear picture of the mainstream ideas and conceptual networks within GDPR studies.

It seems to appear that highest visibility and highest frequency region on the map is represented by the keywords centered on "GDPR", with the colored yellow clusters that make-up the strongest representation on the map; it implies that the keyword "GDPR" is at the heart of researches about privacy, data governance, legal implications and data security. With the keyword "privacy" on below, there are found many words around it that are also very dense such as personal data, EU and humans; all the latter keywords show great interest research-wise to investigate the implication of GDPR in digital era on an individual, organizational and Governmental level.

The keywords privacy, personal data, European Union and humans represent a collection of related terms around GDPR and are found in dense area; which means privacy protection and management of personal data is an important research topic in research. The high density of keyword demonstrates that many are similar and they confirm general interest to enhance individual's privacy right over personal data and to guarantee the transparency of processing operations, the legal concept in reference is therefore the privacy right.

Information security, security, compliance, data sharing and Internet of Things must be monitored and carefully analyzed because they can be observed with average and high density value, that suggest their rising relevance in the field; all this implies a greater concern towards cybersecurity, secured data handling, and regulation compliance for those systems driven by technological applications. The dependence on data systems driven by the Cloud systems and IoT technology are therefore drawing researchers' attention over their development against the risk for privacy rights.

In the visualization density also shows up a concentrated cluster about law of computer security, legislative law, confidentiality and data protection laws that refers to aspects that are linked among themselves and show legal and technical considerations in implementing GDPR; all these concerns about law, regulation and technology guarantee data protection.

We find several niche fields that are not very dense such as biometric identification, digital health, clinical research, anonymisation, child's right, international data transfer and consumer right; that show up on the map with very low density but do not mean that they are less important but just less explored areas of research concerning GDPR and their evolution and rise may suggest what would be the main research areas about this regulation in the future; moreover these niche areas represent application of GDPR in health, education, administration and business sector.

The map also displays the role and the density of EU (European Union) about the GDPR researches. The high density is correlated to EU's role as origin of the regulation and to its globalization; it should be pointed out how the GDPR became a strong example for data protection regime transfer to other states and regions.

Figure 12. Density Visualization on General Data Protection Regulation (GDPR)

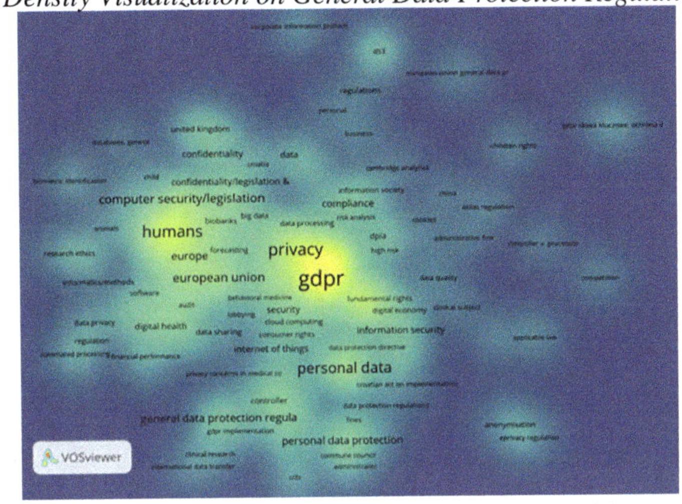

Source: Lens.Org Database; generated by using VOSviewer (Data may vary slightly).

8. CONCLUSION

AI is rapidly changing the educational landscape. The latest technologies such as machine learning, generative AI, chatbots, and large language models allow for more intelligent, responsive, and customized learning experiences. With the rising use of AI in education, the area of education faces more challenges on how to protect users from the misuse of data, violations of regulatory standards, child abuse, and protection of intellectual property rights. Data privacy, adherence to regulatory standards, child protection and protection of intellectual property rights are among some of the main topics of interest and concern in the field of education. We described the research domain of AI in Education: Compliance with Family Educational Rights and Privacy Act (FERPA), General Data Protection Regulation (GDPR), Children Online Privacy Protection Act (COPPA), and Intellectual Property in Academic Environments. Bibliometric analyses were conducted to understand research trends and themes, networks of keywords, evolution and interdisciplinary character of the area using publication data extracted from 'Lens.org' data base and illustrated using VOSviewer software. It highlighted awareness on the current research trend, emerging issues, and increased focus on privacy, security, ethical and legal considerations of use, and IP when dealing with AI in learning environments. It revealed valuable information on trends and research perspectives for the ethical, secure, and compliant development and implementation of AI in education. Finally, the implementation of AI requires a harmonious synthesis in which the interdisciplinary knowledge of education technology and learning sciences informs ethical applications to achieve the greatest pedagogical value and reduce the systemic disadvantages.

REFERENCES

Alasadi, E. A., & Baiz, C. R. (2023). Generative AI in Education and Research: Opportunities, concerns, and solutions. *Journal of Chemical Education, 100*(8), 2965–2971. DOI: 10.1021/acs.jchemed.3c00323

Alatrash, R., Chatti, M. A., Ain, Q. U., Fang, Y., Joarder, S., & Siepmann, C. (2024). "ConceptGCN: Knowledge concept recommendation in MOOCs based on knowledge graph convolutional networks and SBERT" *Computers and Education Artificial Intelligence*, *6*, 100235. DOI: 10.1016/j.caeai.2024.100235

Chan, C. K. Y. (2023). A comprehensive AI policy education framework for university teaching and learning. *International Journal of Educational Technology in Higher Education*, *20*(1), 38. Advance online publication. DOI: 10.1186/s41239-023-00408-3

Chen, M. A., Hwang, G., & Chang, Y. (2019). A reflective thinking-promoting approach to enhancing graduate students' flipped learning engagement, participation behaviors, reflective thinking and project learning outcomes. *British Journal of Educational Technology*, *50*(5), 2288–2307. DOI: 10.1111/bjet.12823

Chih-Ming, C., & Ying-You, L. (2020). Developing a computer-mediated communication competence forecasting model based on learning behavior features. *Computers and Education Artificial Intelligence*, *1*, 100004. DOI: 10.1016/j.caeai.2020.100004

Graham, F. (2023). Daily briefing: AI detects risk of Parkinson's from retinal images. *Nature*. Advance online publication. DOI: 10.1038/d41586-023-02903-z PMID: 37773285

Harry, A., & Sayudin, S. (2023). Role of AI in Education. [INJURITY]. *Interdiciplinary Journal and Hummanity*, 2(3), 260–268. DOI: 10.58631/injurity.v2i3.52

Holmes, W., Porayska-Pomsta, K., Holstein, K., Sutherland, E., Baker, T., Shum, S. B., Santos, O. C., Rodrigo, M. T., Cukurova, M., Bittencourt, I. I., & Koedinger, K. R. (2021). Ethics of AI in Education: Towards a Community-Wide framework. *International Journal of Artificial Intelligence in Education*, *32*(3), 504–526. DOI: 10.1007/s40593-021-00239-1

Isukapalli, S., & Srirama, S. N. (2024). A systematic survey on fault-tolerant solutions for distributed data analytics: Taxonomy, comparison, and future directions. *Computer Science Review*, *53*, 100660. DOI: 10.1016/j.cosrev.2024.100660

Kajamaa, A., Kumpulainen, K., & Olkinuora, H. (2019). Teacher interventions in students' collaborative work in a technology-rich educational makerspace. *British Journal of Educational Technology, 51*(2), 371–386. DOI: 10.1111/bjet.12837

Lens. (2025). *Scholar search: AI in Education.* https://www.lens.org/lens/search/scholar/list?q=AI%20in%20Education

Lens. (2025). *Scholar search: Children Online Privacy Protection Act.* https://www.lens.org/lens/search/scholar/list?q=Children%20Online%20Privacy%20Protection%20Act&p=0&n=10&s=_score&d=%2B&f=false&e=false&l=en&authorField=author&dateFilterField=publishedYear&orderBy=%2B_score&presentation=false&preview=true&stemmed=true&useAuthorId=false

Lens. (2025). *Scholar search: evolving role of AI in higher education.* Family Educational Rights and Privacy. https://www.lens.org/lens/search/scholar/list?q=Family%20Educational%20Rights%20and%20Privacy&p=0&n=10&s=_score&d=%2B&f=false&e=false&l=en&authorField=author&dateFilterField=publishedYear&orderBy=%2B_score&presentation=false&preview=true&stemmed=true&useAuthorId=false

Lens. (2025). *Scholar search: General Data Protection Regulation.*https://www.lens.org/lens/search/scholar/list?q=General%20Data%20Protection%20Regulation&p=0&n=10&s=_score&d=%2B&f=false&e=false&l=en&authorField=author&dateFilterField=publishedYear&orderBy=%2B_score&presentation=false&preview=true&stemmed=true&useAuthorId=false

Mousavinasab, E., Zarifsanaiey, N., Kalhori, S. R. N., Rakhshan, M., Keikha, L., & Saeedi, M. G. (2018). Intelligent tutoring systems: A systematic review of characteristics, applications, and evaluation methods. *Interactive Learning Environments, 29*(1), 142–163. DOI: 10.1080/10494820.2018.1558257

Ng, C., Graham, S., Lau, K., Liu, X., & Tang, K. (2021). Writing motives and writing self-efficacy of Chinese students in Shanghai and Hong Kong: Measurement invariance and multigroup structural equation analyses. *International Journal of Educational Research, 107*, 101751. DOI: 10.1016/j.ijer.2021.101751

Post, D. G. (2017). How the Internet is making jurisdiction sexy (again). *International Journal of Law and Information Technology, 25*(4), 249–258. DOI: 10.1093/ijlit/eax019

Rowley, J. (2023). E. H. Carr: Imperialism, war and lessons for post-colonial IR. *International Affairs, 99*(2), 840–841. DOI: 10.1093/ia/iiad045

Siddiqui, S., & Bergquist, E. P. (2021). Family characteristics of female-headed households in Pakistan in the context of health promotion. *Health Promotion International*, *37*(1), daab111. Advance online publication. DOI: 10.1093/heapro/daab111 PMID: 34259864

Steegh, A., Höffler, T., Höft, L., & Parchmann, I. (2021). Exploring science competition participants' expectancy-value perceptions and identification: A latent profile analysis. *Learning and Instruction*, *74*, 101455. DOI: 10.1016/j.learninstruc.2021.101455

Thelwall, M. (2020). Measuring societal impacts of research with altmetrics? common problems and mistakes. *Journal of Economic Surveys*, *35*(5), 1302–1314. DOI: 10.1111/joes.12381

Wang, E. Q., & Piper, A. M. (2018). Accessibility in action. *Proceedings of the ACM on Human-Computer Interaction, 2*(CSCW), 1–25. https://doi.org/DOI: 10.1145/3274449

Chapter 14
Ethical Frictions in AI-Enhanced Learning Environments:
A Comparative European Analysis

Enrico Moch
http://orcid.org/0009-0005-4722-0961
GrandEdu Research School, Germany

Jan Vrba
http://orcid.org/0000-0002-8404-5091
Akademia Jagiellońska w Toruniu, Poland

Tobias Oberdieck
http://orcid.org/0009-0002-2017-4991
GrandEdu Research School, Germany

ABSTRACT

The integration of artificial intelligence in education is often framed as a technical implementation problem, overlooking the institutional decision-making processes in which its effects emerge. This article analyses how these structures change under conditions of technological uncertainty. Drawing on institutional and governance theory, it develops a mechanism-based model that conceptualises transformation as a sequence: technological triggers (T) generate conflicts (K), which are processed through institutional mechanisms (M) and stabilised in governance structures (G). Three core mechanisms are identified: diffusion of responsibility, coordination tension, and legitimacy reconstruction. Based on a theory-driven reconstruction of empirical studies and comparative analysis, the findings show a stable mechanism sequence

DOI: 10.4018/979-8-3373-9883-9.ch014

across contexts, while variation in outcomes depends on governance configurations. The study shifts the focus from technological effects to institutional mechanisms and highlights conflict processing as the key condition for successful integration.

1 INTRODUCTION

The integration of artificial intelligence into learning environments is not primarily changing technical processes, but rather institutional decision-making systems (Scott, 2014; Hinings et al., 2018). Digital systems are increasingly taking on the functions of performance assessment, learning control and individual support (Ifenthaler & Yau, 2020; Holmes et al., 2019). As a result, responsibility structures, interpretation logics and forms of legitimate decision-making are shifting (Bovens & Zouridis, 2002; March & Olsen, 2006). Educational practice is not supplanted by technological systems, but undergoes a structural reconfiguration (Williamson et al., 2020).

Although global university rankings are now a primary benchmark for higher institutions to enhance their reputation and recruit top-tier candidates (Vrba & Huynh, 2026), the increasing integration of AI algorithms requires a rigorous ethical examination of their dependability.

Within the European context, this transformation unfolds under legally binding regulatory frameworks (European Commission, 2019; Regulation (EU) 2024/1689), while simultaneously being intensified by competitive pressures that prioritise performance visibility and institutional reputation. Requirements such as transparency, traceability, data protection, and human oversight function as operative structuring principles of this reconfiguration. They not only control the introduction of technological systems, but also define how decisions can be reviewed and responsibility assigned (Jobin et al., 2019; Smuha, 2021).

This results in a structural conflict. Data-based optimisation increases the pressure to innovate and accelerates adaptation processes. At the same time, institutions need stable and controllable responsibility architectures. These two requirements follow different logics and remain permanently tense (Janssen & Kuk, 2016). Both logics operate simultaneously and generate conflicts in implementation (Ansell & Torfing, 2016).

Research to date has mainly focussed on the effects, acceptance and functional fields of application of artificial intelligence in the education sector (Zawacki-Richter et al., 2019; Holmes et al., 2022). Questions of institutional embedding, governance and conflict management remain underdeveloped (Selwyn, 2019; Prinsloo & Slade, 2017). Although existing studies show the potential of personalised learning systems, they also point to risks such as algorithmic bias, a lack of transparency and growing dependencies on platform infrastructures (Kasneci et al., 2023; Kitchin, 2017; Van Dijck et al., 2018). These problems do not affect individual technologies, but the institutional organisation of digitalised education as a whole (Williamson, 2017).

Current developments in the field of generative artificial intelligence mark a qualitative break (Mollick, 2024; Kasneci et al., 2023). Systems no longer only generate the basis for decisions, but also content, evaluations and suggestions (Tlili et al., 2023). Knowledge production is partly outsourced to technical systems (Beer, 2017). This changes the epistemic basis of institutional decisions (Kitchin, 2017). Responsibility becomes situational, authorship becomes unclear and evaluation practices lose stability (Raji et al., 2020). Institutions must legitimise decisions whose knowledge base can only be verified to a limited extent (Floridi et al., 2018).

A purely technology-centred perspective falls short under these conditions. Institutional and governance theory approaches show that technological innovation only becomes effective in conjunction with organisational routines, professional norms and legitimising expectations (Scott, 2014; Ansell & Torfing, 2016). Artificial intelligence in the educational context must therefore be analysed as a process of institutional reorganisation under uncertainty (Hinings et al., 2018). Analysing these dynamics requires a shift in focus from evaluating technological effects to reconstructing institutional decision-making processes.

The research question is thus: How do ethical conflicts emerge and evolve in the institutional implementation of AI-supported learning systems in European educational contexts, and which governance configurations explain divergent integration trajectories?

This question is answered by reconstructing concrete decision-making sequences in which conflicts become visible and institutional adjustments are triggered (Beach & Pedersen, 2019). A comparative qualitative research design with mechanism-centred process tracing is used for implementation (Beach & Pedersen, 2019; Seawright et al., 2008). Cases from different educational contexts are analysed in order to identify recurring patterns of responsibility attribution, coordination and legitimacy production (Ansell & Torfing, 2016).

The contribution of this work lies in an explanation-oriented analysis of institutional transformation processes. Ethical tensions are not interpreted as implementation problems, but as mechanisms that trigger organisational adaptation (Madaio et al., 2020). Different combinations of regulatory requirements, organisational autonomy and technological infrastructure lead to divergent integration paths (Yoo et al., 2010).

The analytical added value consists of three shifts. Firstly, the focus is shifted from evaluating technological effects to analysing causal mechanisms. Secondly, decision-making processes are reconstructed instead of describing technologies. Thirdly, different development paths are explained by configuration-dependent governance structures. This makes it clear why comparable technologies lead to different results in different institutional contexts.

2 THEORETICAL BACKGROUND

The integration of artificial intelligence into educational contexts should not be understood as an isolated technological innovation, but as an institutional transformation process. Organisations do not change their decision-making logics through new technologies alone, but by embedding them in existing normative, regulatory and cognitive orders. Institutions stabilise expectations, structure responsibilities and define which forms of knowledge are considered legitimate (Scott, 2014). Technological systems intervene in these orders by shifting the basis for decision-making and creating new forms of action coordination.

Institutional theory approaches show that organisational decisions are not primarily determined by efficiency, but by situational appropriateness. Actions are orientated towards established rules, roles and expectations (March & Olsen, 2006). This logic comes under pressure when data-based systems support or partially replace decision-making processes. Organisations must then decide to what extent algorithmically generated evidence is weighted against professional judgement. This decision is not purely technical, but institutional in nature.

Digital innovation is also changing the structure of organisational processes. Data is becoming a central resource, modular systems enable flexible combinations of functions, and platform architectures structure interactions between actors (Yoo et al., 2010; Van Dijck et al., 2018). This development leads to a partial decoupling of decision-making processes and their institutional anchoring. Technical infrastructures are increasingly defining what information is available and what actions are possible. Organisational control over the basis for decision-making is thus relativised (Williamson, 2017).

Algorithmic systems are not neutral tools. They organise information, set priorities and thus shape possible courses of action (Kitchin, 2017; Beer, 2017). At the same time, their functional logic is often only visible to a limited extent. Effectiveness and a lack of transparency occur together. Organisations make decisions under conditions of incomplete control. This results in structural uncertainty.

These effects are intensified in the educational context. Learning processes are continuously recorded and analysed on the basis of data. Adaptive systems enable differentiated learning paths. At the same time, they shift assessment standards and change pedagogical decision-making routines. Empirical studies point to an ambivalent result: efficiency gains are offset by new forms of inequality (Zawacki-

Richter et al., 2019; Selwyn, 2019). The evaluation of these systems can therefore not be reduced to their efficiency. The decisive factor is their institutional integration.

A governance-theoretical perspective makes it possible to analyse these relationships. It does not focus on the technology itself, but on the structures in which decisions are made. Governance describes the coordination of different actors under conditions of distributed decision-making powers (Ansell & Torfing, 2016). Regulatory requirements, organisational strategies, professional norms and technological structures act simultaneously and are not necessarily consistent. Organisations must make decisions that are legally permissible, organisationally feasible and normatively legitimate (Janssen & Kuk, 2016).

Under these conditions, legitimacy becomes a central resource. Decisions must not only be functional, but must also be perceived as appropriate and comprehensible. Requirements such as transparency, accountability and human oversight therefore not only structure regulatory frameworks, but also intervene directly in organisational decision-making processes (European Commission, 2019; Floridi et al., 2018). A lack of traceability or perceived unfairness can significantly impair the acceptance of technological systems.

At the same time, new challenges arise at the level of responsibility. Digital systems shift decision-making responsibilities between human and technical actors. As a result, responsibility becomes fragmented and difficult to assign. Organisations need to clarify who is responsible for decisions based on algorithmic processes. This shift in responsibility is a central feature of digitalised administration and decision-making (Bovens & Zouridis, 2002).

Coordination problems arise from the diversity of actors and perspectives involved. Teachers, students, administrative units and external technology providers pursue different goals and interpret requirements differently. Decisions are made under conditions in which there is no standardised evaluation logic. Organisations must develop mechanisms to coordinate these divergences and remain capable of acting.

Current developments in the field of generative artificial intelligence are exacerbating these fundamental tensions. Generative systems generate content, evaluations and suggestions for action independently. This changes the role of technical systems from supporting tools to active players in knowledge and decision-making processes (Kasneci et al., 2023; Mollick, 2024). Organisations are increasingly confronted with the question of the extent to which generated content can be used as a valid basis for decisions.

This development leads to a further destabilisation of existing institutional orders. Authorship becomes unclear as content cannot be clearly assigned. The epistemic basis of decisions becomes fragile. Generated content appears very convincing because it is linguistically coherent. However, their substantive correctness is not assured (Tlili et al., 2023). This results in a structural verification problem. Plausibility partially replaces verification. Assessment practices come under pressure as a result, especially where performance and knowledge must be clearly demonstrated. Organisations must determine how they deal with this uncertainty. They decide whether to regulate, specifically integrate or deliberately limit utilisation.

In the European context, regulatory approaches respond to precisely this problem. Risk-based models categorise systems according to their hazard potential. They derive graduated requirements from this. These primarily concern transparency obligations, control options and accountability structures (Regulation (EU) 2024/1689; Veale & Zuiderveen Borgesius, 2021). At the same time, the concrete implementation of these requirements in organisational practice remains open. Institutions must develop their own solutions that combine regulatory requirements with operational requirements.

The theoretical background of this article makes it clear that the integration of artificial intelligence cannot be understood as a technical implementation problem. Rather, it is a process of institutional reorganisation in which existing decision-making logics, responsibility structures and legitimacy requirements are renegotiated.

3 CONCEPTUAL FRAMEWORK

The following conceptualisation is based on an empirically observable case that illustrates the emergence of institutional decision-making sequences under conditions of uncertainty (Scott, 2014; Ansell & Torfing, 2016). The regulation of generative artificial intelligence such as ChatGPT in European universities since 2023 represents a particularly clearly observable case of institutional decision-making under conditions of high uncertainty (Kasneci et al., 2023; Mollick, 2024). In contrast to gradual implementations of data-based systems, the pressure to act arises abruptly here. With the widespread availability of generative systems, universities will soon be faced with the question of whether and to what extent these technologies may be used in examinations, coursework and learning processes (Cotton et al., 2024; Tlili et al., 2023). Teachers report texts whose origin can no longer be clearly determined. At the same time, it remains unclear whether the use of such systems should be regarded as cheating, as legitimate support or as a new form of academic practice (Cotton et al., 2024). Existing examination regulations do not offer any clear guidance in this regard. The problem thus immediately becomes visible as an institutional challenge that affects the foundations of performance assessment (Kasneci et al., 2023; Cotton et al., 2024).

In an initial reaction phase, universities are faced with the decision of whether to prohibit, tolerate or actively integrate the use of generative systems into existing processes (Ansell & Torfing, 2016). These decisions are made under time pressure and without established decision-making rules (March & Olsen, 2006). Some institutions issue short-term bans, particularly in examination-relevant contexts, in order to safeguard the integrity of existing assessment procedures (Cotton et al., 2024). Others refrain from immediate intervention and treat its use as part of individual learning practice (Kasneci et al., 2023). Others are starting to develop guidelines at an early stage to enable controlled and transparent use (European Commission, 2019).

For example, initial institutional guidelines from European universities from 2023 show that numerous institutions initially introduced restrictive regulations and either prohibited the use of generative AI in examination-relevant contexts or only permitted it with explicit disclosure, before these positions were gradually differentiated in later versions of the guidelines (Cotton et al., 2024; Kasneci et al., 2023). In this phase, diffusion of responsibility becomes clearly visible (Bovens & Zouridis, 2002). Generative systems are used by students, assessed by teachers and rules are set by institutional management levels, while at the same time it remains unclear to what extent responsibility also lies with the providers of the systems (Raji et al., 2020). Decisions are made without responsibility being clearly assigned, which leads to inconsistent regulations and rapid adjustments (Ansell & Torfing, 2016).

With increasing experience, the conflict shifts from an immediate reaction to a structural confrontation with the consequences of generative AI (Kasneci et al., 2023). A general ban is proving difficult to enforce, as it is almost impossible to reliably demonstrate its use and at the same time, didactic potential is becoming apparent (Cotton et al., 2024; Tlili et al., 2023). Universities are caught between the conflicting priorities of examination integrity and innovation requirements (Janssen & Kuk, 2016). Strict control can ensure the comparability of performance, but limits new forms of learning and working (Holmes et al., 2019). Open utilisation enables experimental approaches, but undermines established assessment logics (Selwyn, 2019). This situation creates pronounced coordination tensions between different stakeholder groups (Ansell & Torfing, 2016). Teachers demand clear rules to ensure academic standards, while institutional management levels often adopt a strategically more open attitude towards technological innovation (Hinings et al., 2018). Students, on the other hand, use generative systems pragmatically and question existing expectations of personal achievement and authorship (Kasneci et al., 2023). Decisions are made under conditions of divergent objectives that cannot be fully harmonised (March & Olsen, 2006).

As time goes on, many universities begin to structure these tensions through formalised regulations (Scott, 2014). Guidelines emerge that do not prohibit the use of generative systems in principle, but rather attach conditions to them (European Commission, 2019; Regulation (EU) 2024/1689). Disclosure of use is often required, examination formats are adapted and more strongly focussed on processes, oral performance or individual reflection (Cotton et al., 2024). At the same time, requirements for documentation and traceability are increased (Jobin et al., 2019). In this phase, legitimacy reconstruction becomes the central mechanism. Decisions must not only be coordinated internally, but must also be made comprehensible to students and teachers (Floridi et al., 2018). Transparency becomes the central strategy for ensuring trust in changed assessment practices (Jobin et al., 2019). Legitimacy does not arise from the technology itself, but from institutional procedures of justification, control and communication (Floridi et al., 2018; Ansell & Torfing, 2016).

As the practice stabilises, hybrid governance models are developing that mediate between prohibition and unrestricted use (Ansell & Torfing, 2016). Generative AI is authorised in certain contexts and restricted or excluded in others (Regulation (EU) 2024/1689). Institutions define areas of application, develop testing mechanisms and establish new forms of quality assurance (Raji et al., 2020). This development changes the original mechanisms without dissolving them. Diffusion of responsibility is partially limited by formal regulations, but remains, as the allocation of responsibility between human and technical actors remains unclear (Bovens & Zouridis, 2002). Coordination tensions are structured by institutional guidelines, but do not disappear as different groups of actors continue to pursue divergent interests (Janssen & Kuk, 2016). Legitimacy reconstruction becomes a permanent process as technological developments progress faster than institutional adaptations (Smuha, 2021).

The regulation of generative AI in European universities is thus an example of how institutional decision-making processes take place under conditions of radical uncertainty (Scott, 2014). Decisions are not made in a linear fashion, but in a sequence of problem perception, short-term reaction, intensification of conflict and gradual stabilisation (Beach & Pedersen, 2019). It is precisely this process that makes it clear that ethical tensions do not arise as downstream problems, but form the core of institutional transformation and act as mechanisms through which organisational structures change (Madaio et al., 2020).

4 METHODOLOGY

The study follows a comparative qualitative research design that is geared towards analysing institutional decision-making processes under conditions of uncertainty (Ansell & Torfing, 2016; Scott, 2014). The aim is not to measure effects, but to reconstruct causal mechanisms through which ethical conflicts arise, are processed and trigger institutional adjustments (Beach & Pedersen, 2019).

Methodologically, a mechanism-centred approach of process tracing is used (Beach & Pedersen, 2019). This approach makes it possible to systematically reconstruct complex causal relationships within individual cases and to analyse the sequence of events, decisions and reactions (Beach & Pedersen, 2019; Seawright et al., 2008). The focus is on the question of how specific mechanisms become effective in specific contexts and lead to different results (Beach & Pedersen, 2019).

Process tracing is based on the assumption that social processes are structured by sequential causality (Beach & Pedersen, 2019). Decisions are not made in isolation, but as part of chains of events in which earlier decisions influence later options (March & Olsen, 2006). The analysis therefore focuses on the identification of decision sequences in which conflicts become visible and institutional reactions take place (Beach & Pedersen, 2019).

The selection of cases is theory-driven and aims to maximise variation along key contextual dimensions (Seawright et al., 2008). Differences in regulatory density, organisational autonomy and technological infrastructure are taken into account (Scott, 2014; Janssen & Kuk, 2016). These dimensions are crucial as they influence the characteristics of the identified mechanisms and enable different integration paths (Yoo et al., 2010). The selection of cases therefore does not pursue the goal of statistical representativeness, but rather analytical comparability (Seawright et al., 2008).

Each case is analysed according to a uniform analytical structure. Firstly, the institutional context in which the implementation takes place is described (Scott, 2014). Specific decision-making situations in which ethical conflicts arise are then identified (Ansell & Torfing, 2016). The focus is on the reconstruction of these situations as sequences of problem perception, decision-making and organisational reaction (Beach & Pedersen, 2019). This involves analysing which mechanisms are effective in these sequences and how they influence each other (Beach & Pedersen, 2019).

The data basis includes documented implementation processes, institutional guidelines, publicly available reports and empirical studies on comparable contexts (Zawacki-Richter et al., 2019; Holmes et al., 2022). In addition, secondary analyses of existing research are used to validate the reconstruction of the cases (Selwyn, 2019). The aim is to integrate different perspectives and increase the plausibility of the identified mechanisms (Prinsloo & Slade, 2017).

The analysis is carried out in several steps. Firstly, causal sequences are reconstructed within the individual cases (Beach & Pedersen, 2019). This involves analysing how problems are defined, decisions are made and measures are implemented (March & Olsen, 2006). In the second step, the identified mechanisms are systematically coded and assigned along the three central categories - diffusion of responsibility, coordination tension and legitimacy reconstruction (Bovens & Zouridis, 2002; Ansell & Torfing, 2016). The third step involves a cross-case comparison in order to identify patterns and differences in the manifestation of these mechanisms (Seawright et al., 2008).

Particular attention is paid to the identification of critical decision points. These arise where organisations have to choose between competing options for action (March & Olsen, 2006). Such situations are particularly relevant from an analytical point of view, as they make the underlying mechanisms visible (Beach & Pedersen, 2019). The analysis therefore focuses specifically on these decision moments and their consequences (Beach & Pedersen, 2019).

The integration of generative artificial intelligence is explicitly taken into account in the analysis (Kasneci et al., 2023; Mollick, 2024). Generative systems change the structure of decision-making processes by generating content and evaluations independently (Tlili et al., 2023). In the cases examined, we therefore analyse how organisations react to these changed conditions, what additional uncertainties arise and what governance measures are developed (Floridi et al., 2018).

Several strategies are used to ensure validity. The reconstruction of the cases is based on triangulated data sources in order to avoid one-sided interpretations (Beach & Pedersen, 2019). The identification of mechanisms is theory-driven, but is verified by empirical evidence within the cases (Seawright et al., 2008). The cross-case comparison serves to distinguish random observations from systematic patterns (Beach & Pedersen, 2019).

The limits of the approach lie in the limited generalisability in the statistical sense. However, the aim of the analysis is not to derive universal laws, but to develop explanatory mechanisms that can be transferred to comparable contexts (Beach & Pedersen, 2019). The strength of the approach lies in the depth of the analysis and the ability to make complex institutional processes comprehensible (Seawright et al., 2008).

By combining mechanism-centred process tracing with a configuration-oriented comparison, the methodology enables a differentiated analysis of institutional transformation processes (Beach & Pedersen, 2019; Yoo et al., 2010). It creates the basis not only for describing differences in the integration of AI, but also for explaining how and why these differences arise (Ansell & Torfing, 2016).

5 CASE STUDIES

5.1 Implementation of Learning Analytics in a European University

Learning analytics systems are typically introduced in European universities with the aim of improving student success, identifying dropout risks at an early stage and managing learning processes based on data (Ifenthaler & Yau, 2020; Zawacki-Richter et al., 2019). These systems are based on the systematic collection and analysis of learning data and promise more efficient management of institutional decisions (Ifenthaler & Yau, 2020). However, implementation is not a purely technical process, but generates fundamental institutional decision-making situations (Scott, 2014; Williamson et al., 2020).

A first central decision-making situation concerns the scope of data collection and processing. Universities must decide whether to use comprehensive data sets to maximise analytical accuracy or to strictly prioritise data protection restrictions (Janssen & Kuk, 2016). This decision is made under regulatory pressure and normative expectations regarding informational self-determination (Regulation (EU) 2024/1689; European Commission, 2019). Studies show that data-intensive systems enable more precise predictions on the one hand, but on the other hand trigger considerable concerns regarding monitoring and control (Prinsloo & Slade, 2017; Selwyn, 2019).

In this situation, diffusion of responsibility becomes visible (Bovens & Zouridis, 2002). Algorithmic systems generate assessments without bearing responsibility themselves, while decisions are made simultaneously by organisations and individual actors (Beer, 2017). The distribution of responsibility is a feature of digitalised decision-making processes (Bovens & Zouridis, 2002; Beer, 2017). Different actors and technical systems share responsibility for decisions. This makes a clear allocation difficult.

Universities respond to this uncertainty with formal regulations. These include data protection guidelines, authorisation procedures and restrictions on automated decisions (Jobin et al., 2019). Responsibility in critical cases usually remains unclear. In the case of incorrect classifications or biased analyses, responsibility often cannot be clearly assigned (Raji et al., 2020).

A second decision-making situation arises when using the generated analyses in an educational context. Teachers are faced with the question of the extent to which algorithmic recommendations should be integrated into their decisions (Ifenthaler & Yau, 2020). While data-based advice can provide additional information, there is a risk that professional judgement will be pushed back in favour of standardised decision-making logic (Williamson, 2017; Williamson et al., 2020). Organisations must decide whether to make the use of such systems mandatory, optional or completely decentralised (Ansell & Torfing, 2016).

This is where coordination tension arises (Ansell & Torfing, 2016). Different stakeholders interpret the function of the systems differently. University management and central administrative bodies emphasise efficiency and scalability. IT departments prioritise technical feasibility and system security. In contrast, teachers prioritise independent pedagogical decisions, while students expect comprehensible and fair evaluation processes (Selwyn, 2019; Janssen & Kuk, 2016). These divergent requirements are in tension with each other and hinder the establishment of uniform decision-making standards (March & Olsen, 2006). Organisations react with different approaches. Some rely on centralised guidelines from university management or ministries. Others open up room for manoeuvre at faculty and lecturer level (Scott, 2014). Both solutions create new tensions between standardisation and flexibility (Janssen & Kuk, 2016).

Another decision-making situation arises when dealing with analysis results. If students are classified as at risk, teachers, student counsellors and the administration decide on suitable measures and how to communicate them (Prinsloo & Slade, 2017). Transparency can promote trust. At the same time, there is a risk of negative self-attributions or strategic adjustments in behaviour (Selwyn, 2019). At the same time, the question arises as to what extent students can contest decisions (Raji et al., 2020).

In this phase, legitimacy reconstruction becomes central (Floridi et al., 2018). Decisions based on algorithmic assessments must be actively justified (Jobin et al., 2019). Organisations develop strategies to establish trust, for example through transparency measures, documentation or the integration of human control (European Commission, 2019). Legitimacy is not created through technology itself, but through institutional practices of justification (Floridi et al., 2018; Ansell & Torfing, 2016).

The increasing integration of generative artificial intelligence exacerbates these dynamics considerably (Kasneci et al., 2023; Mollick, 2024). Generative systems extend learning analytics with the ability to generate automated feedback, evaluations or recommendations for action (Tlili et al., 2023). This shifts the role of the systems from analytical tools to active producers of decision bases (Beer, 2017). Studies show that these systems can generate plausible but potentially erroneous content, creating new forms of epistemic uncertainty (Tlili et al., 2023).

This development increases diffusion of responsibility, as generated content cannot be clearly assigned (Bovens & Zouridis, 2002). Universities must decide whether such content may be used as a basis for interventions or whether additional review mechanisms are required (Raji et al., 2020). At the same time, coordination problems are increasing as different stakeholders use and evaluate generative systems differently (Ansell & Torfing, 2016). Legitimacy requirements are increasing as decisions are increasingly based on probabilistic and not fully verifiable foundations (Floridi et al., 2018; Cotton et al., 2024).

The specific nature of these mechanisms depends on the institutional framework (Scott, 2014). Universities are subject to regulatory requirements, especially in the European context, which define requirements for transparency, control and accountability (Regulation (EU) 2024/1689; Veale & Zuiderveen Borgesius, 2021). At the same time, organisational autonomy and technological dependency vary considerably (Hinings et al., 2018). Platform-based infrastructures can limit control over data and decision-making processes and create new dependencies (Van Dijck et al., 2018; Ritter et al., 2025).

The analysis shows that the implementation of learning analytics is not primarily a technical problem, but a process of institutional negotiation under uncertainty (Ansell & Torfing, 2016). Decisions are made in sequences in which competing requirements have to be weighed up (Beach & Pedersen, 2019). Responsibility diffusion, coordination tension and legitimacy reconstruction structure these processes and explain why comparable systems in different contexts lead to different results (Bovens & Zouridis, 2002; Ansell & Torfing, 2016).

5.2 Use of AI-Supported Assessment Systems in School Education

AI-supported assessment systems are used in the school context with the aim of standardising performance assessment, reducing the workload and enabling more objective decisions (Zawacki-Richter et al., 2019; Holmes et al., 2019). Systems for the automated assessment of texts, tasks or examination performance promise efficiency gains and comparability, but intervene directly in central pedagogical decision-making processes (Williamson et al., 2020).

An initial key decision-making situation arises when it comes to the question of the extent to which automated assessment systems should be used. School institutions must decide whether AI-based assessments should be used as a support tool or established as a binding basis for performance decisions (Holmes et al., 2019). This decision is made under the pressure of increasing demands for efficiency as well as normative expectations regarding fairness and individualised support (European Commission, 2019; Jobin et al., 2019).

In this phase, diffusion of responsibility becomes clear (Bovens & Zouridis, 2002). Assessments are generated by algorithmic systems, while responsibility formally remains with teachers and institutions (Beer, 2017). Studies show that automated assessment systems can contain systematic biases, particularly with regard to linguistic, cultural or socio-economic differences (Kitchin, 2017; Beer, 2017). Schools are faced with the decision of whether to utilise these systems despite potential biases or to limit their use (Raji et al., 2020). Responses often include the introduction of hybrid models in which algorithmic assessments are supplemented by human control (Holmes et al., 2022).

A second decision situation concerns the integration of these systems into existing pedagogical practices. Teachers must decide whether to adopt, correct or ignore algorithmic assessments (Holmes et al., 2019). The issue is not limited to technical aspects, but also encroaches on the areas of professional autonomy and pedagogical responsibility (Scott, 2014). At the same time, administrative actors aim to standardise assessment processes and ensure their comparability (Williamson et al., 2020).

In this context, there are pronounced coordination problems (Ansell & Torfing, 2016). The stakeholder groups involved evaluate automated assessment systems differently. Management levels focus on efficiency and standardisation, while teachers see risks for the quality of teaching and individual support (Holmes et al., 2019). Students particularly question the fairness and traceability of the results (Selwyn, 2019).

Organisations are therefore faced with a fundamental directional decision: centralised guidelines or decentralised freedom of design (Janssen & Kuk, 2016). Both options create structural tensions between standardisation and pedagogical flexibility (March & Olsen, 2006).A third decision situation arises when dealing with incorrect or disputed assessments. When algorithmic systems lead to obviously problematic results, organisations must decide how to correct them and what role human control plays (Raji et al., 2020). At the same time, the question arises as to whether and how evaluation processes can be made transparent (Jobin et al., 2019). Transparency can strengthen trust, but presupposes that evaluation logics can be explained (Floridi et al., 2018).

In this phase, legitimacy reconstruction becomes central (Floridi et al., 2018). Decisions based on algorithmic evaluations must be actively justified (Jobin et al., 2019). Organisations develop strategies to ensure trust, for example by introducing complaints mechanisms, disclosing evaluation criteria or committing to human review (European Commission, 2019). Legitimacy is not created by the technical quality of the systems alone, but by institutional practices of safeguarding and communication (Ansell & Torfing, 2016).

The integration of generative artificial intelligence exacerbates these dynamics considerably (Kasneci et al., 2023; Mollick, 2024). Generative systems enable the automatic creation of feedback, assessments or even examination content (Tlili et al., 2023). This fundamentally changes the structure of assessment processes. Decisions are no longer based solely on algorithmic analyses, but on generated content whose epistemic basis is uncertain (Beer, 2017).

This development increases the diffusion of responsibility, as it is no longer clear whether assessments are based on human judgement or generated content (Bovens & Zouridis, 2002). Schools must decide whether generative systems may be integrated into assessment processes or whether their use must be restricted (Cotton et al., 2024). Coordination problems increase as different stakeholders use and evaluate generative systems differently (Ansell & Torfing, 2016). Legitimacy requirements increase as decisions are based on potentially flawed or incomprehensible foundations (Tlili et al., 2023; Cotton et al., 2024).

The specific nature of these mechanisms is influenced by institutional framework conditions (Scott, 2014). School systems are often subject to more centralised regulatory requirements than universities. Requirements for equal treatment, transparency and traceability are correspondingly high (European Commission, 2019; Regulation (EU) 2024/1689). At the same time, individual schools only have limited autonomy in the design of assessment systems (Scott, 2014). This combination favours formally structured governance approaches, but can limit adaptability (Ansell & Torfing, 2016).

The analysis shows that the use of AI-supported assessment systems is not a purely technical instrument, but intervenes deeply in institutional decision-making processes (Williamson et al., 2020). Decisions are made in sequences in which efficiency, fairness and pedagogical quality have to be weighed up against each other (March & Olsen, 2006). Responsibility diffusion, coordination tension and legitimacy reconstruction structure these processes and explain why similar systems lead to different results in different school contexts (Bovens & Zouridis, 2002; Ansell & Torfing, 2016).

5.3 Regulation of Generative AI in European Universities

The regulation of generative artificial intelligence such as ChatGPT in European universities since 2023 represents a particularly clearly observable case of institutional decision-making under conditions of high uncertainty (Kasneci et al., 2023; Mollick, 2024). In contrast to the gradual implementation of data-based systems, the pressure to act arises abruptly here (Hinings et al., 2018). With the widespread availability of generative systems, universities are confronted in the short term with the question of whether and to what extent these technologies may be used in examinations, assignments and learning processes (Cotton et al., 2024; Tlili et al., 2023). Teachers report texts whose origin can no longer be clearly determined, while at the same time it remains unclear whether the use of such systems is to be seen as cheating, as legitimate support or as a new form of academic practice (Cotton et al., 2024). Existing examination regulations do not provide clear guidance for this situation, so that the problem immediately becomes visible as an institutional challenge that affects the basis of performance assessment (Kasneci et al., 2023; Cotton et al., 2024).

In an initial reaction phase, universities are faced with the decision of whether to prohibit, tolerate or integrate the use of generative systems in a controlled manner (Ansell & Torfing, 2016). These decisions are made under time pressure and without established decision-making rules (March & Olsen, 2006). Many institutions initially react restrictively, particularly in examination-relevant contexts, in order to safeguard the integrity of existing assessment procedures (Cotton et al., 2024). At the same time, the limited enforceability of such measures quickly becomes apparent, as it is virtually impossible to provide reliable technical evidence of their use (Kasneci et al., 2023). Other institutions refrain from intervening directly or start developing guidelines for transparent utilisation at an early stage (European Commission, 2019). Decisions are thus made under conditions of incomplete information and diverging expectations (Janssen & Kuk, 2016).

A specific decision case illustrates this dynamic. At a European university, a seminar paper is submitted in spring 2023 whose linguistic quality differs significantly from the students' previous work (Cotton et al., 2024). The teacher is faced with the decision of whether the work should be assessed as normal or questioned as potentially AI-generated. As there is no reliable method for clearly identifying generative content, this decision cannot be based on technical evidence (Kasneci et al., 2023).

The teacher initially decides not to reject the work immediately, but to schedule a supplementary oral examination to check the student's own performance (Holmes et al., 2019). This shifts the decision from the text-based assessment to a situational examination interaction. At the same time, institutional uncertainty arises as it remains unclear whether this procedure is covered by existing examination regulations (Scott, 2014).

The case is then forwarded to the examination board. There, divergent assessment logics come to light (Ansell & Torfing, 2016). While one position aims for strict control and possible sanctions, another argues in favour of adapting existing assessment practices under the condition of transparent use (European Commission, 2019). The Commission ultimately decides against a sanction and in favour of introducing a disclosure obligation for the use of generative systems (Jobin et al., 2019).

This decision stabilises the situation in the short term, but creates new consequential problems. Students have to declare the use of generative systems without it being clearly defined which forms of support are to be recorded (Cotton et al., 2024). Teachers are confronted with the task of integrating this information into assessment decisions (Holmes et al., 2019). At the same time, the handling of undisclosed but presumed use remains unclear (Kasneci et al., 2023). The original decision-making situation is therefore not resolved, but rather transferred into new decision-making requirements (March & Olsen, 2006).

With increasing experience, the institutional focus shifts from short-term reactions to the structural handling of the resulting tensions (Hinings et al., 2018). A general ban proves to be impractical, while unregulated use undermines established assessment regulations (Cotton et al., 2024). Universities are responding by developing formalised regulations that do not prohibit use in principle, but instead attach conditions to it (Regulation (EU) 2024/1689; European Commission, 2019). Disclosure requirements, adapted examination formats and new forms of performance assessment are emerging in response to the changed framework conditions (Holmes et al., 2019).

This development reveals three central mechanisms. Firstly, diffusion of responsibility can be seen in the fact that decisions are based on the use of generative systems without responsibility being clearly assigned (Bovens & Zouridis, 2002). Secondly, coordination tension becomes visible as different groups of actors formulate diverging expectations regarding the use of generative AI and decisions have to be made under these conditions (Ansell & Torfing, 2016). Thirdly, legitimacy reconstruction becomes central, as institutional decisions must be actively justified and made comprehensible to different groups of actors (Floridi et al., 2018; Jobin et al., 2019).

With increasing consolidation, control is shifting towards hybrid governance arrangements that provide for neither a complete ban nor unrestricted use (Ansell & Torfing, 2016). The use of generative AI is regulated in a differentiated manner depending on the situation: permitted, restricted or excluded (Regulation (EU) 2024/1689). As part of this process, institutions define specific areas of application, develop procedures for review and ensure the traceability of decisions through appropriate structures (Raji et al., 2020).

These adaptations change the nature of the mechanisms without resolving them. Questions of responsibility remain partially unresolved, coordination problems persist and legitimacy must be continually re-established (Smuha, 2021).

The case thus exemplifies that institutional decision-making processes under conditions of generative AI are not linear, but are organised as sequences of problem perception, situational decision-making and subsequent adaptation (Beach & Pedersen, 2019). Ethical tensions do not occur as marginal phenomena, but structure these processes and act as mechanisms of institutional transformation (Madaio et al., 2020).

6 CROSS-CASE ANALYSE

The three cases analysed - learning analytics in universities, AI-supported assessment in the school context and the regulation of generative AI (ChatGPT) in European universities - show that the integration of artificial intelligence is not a uniform process, but rather a sequence of institutional decision-making sequences under different contextual conditions (Scott, 2014; Ansell & Torfing, 2016). While the first two cases are characterised by planned implementations, the third case is characterised by an abrupt external impulse that forces immediate decisions (Hinings et al., 2018; Kasneci et al., 2023).

In the case of ChatGPT regulation, the process does not begin with strategic planning, but with an acute disruption of existing assessment regulations (Cotton et al., 2024). Universities are confronted at short notice with the situation that written work can no longer be clearly assigned to individual authors (Kasneci et al., 2023). This results in an initial decision: should the use of generative systems be prohibited, even though their use can hardly be reliably proven, or should it be tolerated, even though this undermines existing assessment logics? This decision is often made without a stable information base and under time pressure, which leads to widely divergent institutional reactions (Janssen & Kuk, 2016; March & Olsen, 2006).

In comparison, the introduction of learning analytics is much more structured. Here, the decision on data use and scope of analysis is at the centre of the process (Ifenthaler & Yau, 2020). Universities decide whether to use existing data sets for predictive purposes and how to take regulatory requirements into account (European Commission, 2019; Regulation (EU) 2024/1689). The conflict does not arise abruptly, but develops along the question of how far data-based control may extend (Selwyn, 2019). In the school context, on the other hand, the process begins with the decision as to whether automated assessment systems should be used at all (Holmes et al., 2019). Here, the starting point is more normative, as questions of fairness and equal treatment are central from the outset (Jobin et al., 2019).

These different starting points lead to varying characteristics of the central mechanisms.

Diffusion of responsibility is evident in all three cases, but with varying intensity and structure (Bovens & Zouridis, 2002). In the learning analytics case, responsibility is distributed between data analysis, organisational decision-making and pedagogical implementation (Beer, 2017). In the school context, the question of responsibility is more closely linked to specific assessment decisions, which creates institutional pressure to define clear responsibilities (Williamson et al., 2020). In the case of generative AI, diffusion of responsibility takes on a new quality (Kasneci et al., 2023). When students submit generated texts, teachers evaluate them and institutions define rules, it remains unclear who is responsible for the epistemic quality of the output (Raji et al., 2020). This situation initially leads to restrictive measures such as bans, but these are often revised as soon as their limited enforceability becomes apparent (Cotton et al., 2024).

Coordination tension also varies systematically (Ansell & Torfing, 2016). In learning analytics systems, it arises primarily between administrative units and teachers who have different ideas about the use of data-based control (Janssen & Kuk, 2016). In the school context, coordination shifts more towards the implementation of centralised guidelines by teachers (Scott, 2014). In the ChatGPT case, on the other hand, coordination tensions arise simultaneously on several levels. Teachers adapt examination formats individually, while institutional management attempts to establish standardised guidelines (Holmes et al., 2019). Students use generative systems independently of institutional regulations, which creates a discrepancy between formal guidelines and actual practice (Kasneci et al., 2023). This multi-level coordination means that regulations have to be adapted iteratively (Ansell & Torfing, 2016).

Legitimacy reconstruction plays a central role in all cases, but shows different dynamics (Floridi et al., 2018). In the case of learning analytics, legitimisation is primarily achieved through transparency in data use and decision-making processes (European Commission, 2019). In the school assessment context, the traceability of assessments takes centre stage (Jobin et al., 2019). In the case of generative AI, legitimacy shifts to a more fundamental level (Smuha, 2021). Universities not only have to justify individual decisions, but also re-justify the validity of their entire assessment system (Cotton et al., 2024). The introduction of disclosure requirements, adapted examination formats and new assessment practices is an expression of this process (Holmes et al., 2019). Legitimacy is not established here in a stable manner, but must be continuously generated anew (Floridi et al., 2018).

The three cases also differ along the configuration dimensions of regulatory density, organisational autonomy and technological infrastructure (Scott, 2014). In the school context, high regulatory density leads to more standardised decision-making processes (European Commission, 2019; Regulation (EU) 2024/1689). Universities have greater autonomy, which enables both experimental solutions and inconsistent practices (Hinings et al., 2018). The ChatGPT case shows that high organisational autonomy in combination with low initial regulation leads to particularly dynamic and sometimes contradictory decision-making processes (Kasneci et al., 2023). More stable regulations only emerge over time (Smuha, 2021).

Technological infrastructure acts as a structuring factor in all cases, but to varying degrees (Yoo et al., 2010). Learning analytics is based on institutionally controlled data systems, while generative AI is typically based on external platforms (Van Dijck et al., 2018). This dependency reduces direct controllability and increases uncertainty in decision-making processes (Plantin et al., 2018). Universities cannot fully control the use of generative systems, but can only regulate their institutional embedding (Janssen & Kuk, 2016).

The comparative analysis thus shows three different modes of institutional transformation. Firstly, a planning-driven mode, as in the case of learning analytics, in which decisions are made sequentially and in a relatively controlled manner (Beach & Pedersen, 2019). Secondly, a normatively regulated mode, as in the school assessment context, in which decisions are strongly structured by external guidelines (Scott, 2014). Thirdly, a shock-driven mode, as in the case of generative AI, in which decisions are made under time pressure, high uncertainty and a lack of rules and only stabilise afterwards (Kasneci et al., 2023; March & Olsen, 2006).

The decisive factor is that the same mechanisms are effective in all three modes, but their specific characteristics depend on the respective contextual conditions (Ansell & Torfing, 2016). Institutional transformation does not result from technological characteristics alone, but from the way in which organisations react to the conflicts triggered by technology (Hinings et al., 2018). The combination of diffusion of responsibility, coordination tension and legitimacy reconstruction forms the central analytical approach to explaining these processes (Bovens & Zouridis, 2002; Floridi et al., 2018; Ansell & Torfing, 2016). These patterns indicate that institutional mechanisms not only explain different developments, but also require a structured implementation in operational decision-making architectures (Madaio et al., 2020).

7 OPERATIONAL GOVERNANCE LAYER: TRANSLATION OF INSTITUTIONAL MECHANISMS INTO DECISION-MAKING STRUCTURES

The comparative analysis shows that the integration of artificial intelligence does not fail due to a lack of knowledge about risks, but rather due to the lack of translation of analytical mechanisms into operational decision-making structures (Ansell & Torfing, 2016; Hinings et al., 2018). Responsibility diffusion, coordination tension and legitimacy reconstruction explain institutional dynamics, but remain ineffective without a concrete implementation logic (Bovens & Zouridis, 2002; Floridi et al., 2018). It is therefore crucial to transform them into structured decision-making architectures (Madaio et al., 2020).

A first central dimension concerns the organisation of responsibility. In all the cases analysed, uncertainty does not arise from the lack of responsibilities, but from their overlapping (Bovens & Zouridis, 2002). Algorithmic systems generate decision bases without bearing responsibility themselves, while human actors make decisions whose epistemic basis they only have limited control over (Beer, 2017; Kitchin, 2017). This constellation requires an explicit differentiation of types of responsibility. Institutions must distinguish between system responsibility, decision-making responsibility and accountability (Raji et al., 2020). System responsibility encompasses the selection, configuration and operation of technical systems. Decision-making responsibility lies with those actors who translate algorithmic results into concrete actions. Accountability, on the other hand, refers to the institutional level at which decisions can be reviewed, challenged and corrected (Jobin et al., 2019). This differentiation does not reduce diffusion of responsibility, but it does make it manageable (Bovens & Zouridis, 2002).

A second dimension concerns the structure of coordination. The analysis shows that conflicts do not arise from a lack of coordination, but from the simultaneity of incompatible evaluation logics (Ansell & Torfing, 2016). Educational, administrative and regulatory requirements cannot be fully harmonised (Janssen & Kuk, 2016). Organisations often respond by either centralising or decentralising without resolving the underlying tension (Scott, 2014). A more stable solution is to formalise decision-making sequences (Beach & Pedersen, 2019). The use of AI-supported systems should be linked to standardised coordination processes that separate problem definition, risk assessment and institutional decision-making (Ansell & Torfing, 2016). Decisions are then not made as selective acts, but as sequential processes in which different perspectives are systematically integrated (March & Olsen, 2006).

The third dimension concerns the establishment of legitimacy. In all cases, it can be seen that legitimacy does not result from the performance of technical systems, but from the comprehensibility of institutional procedures (Floridi et al., 2018; Jobin et al., 2019). It must be possible to justify decisions, especially if they are based on algorithmic or generative processes (Smuha, 2021). This requires the establishment of justification structures in which the role of technical systems is explicitly recognised (European Commission, 2019). Institutions must disclose what function a system fulfils in the decision-making process, to what extent human control is envisaged and what possibilities exist for correction (Raji et al., 2020). Legitimacy thus does not arise as a property of technology, but as a result of institutional transparency (Floridi et al., 2018).

These three dimensions are concretised in recurring decision-making situations. Situations of introduction, application and conflict management are particularly relevant (Beach & Pedersen, 2019). During implementation, organisations must decide whether and under what conditions a system will be used (Janssen & Kuk, 2016). In the application phase, the question arises as to the extent to which algorithmic results will guide actions (Ifenthaler & Yau, 2020). In conflict situations, decisions must be reviewed, corrected or revised (Raji et al., 2020). These decision points structure institutional processes and make the underlying mechanisms empirically observable (Beach & Pedersen, 2019).

A minimal set of governance instruments is sufficient to stabilise these processes (Ansell & Torfing, 2016). Firstly, structured risk analyses prior to implementation enable the early identification of critical areas of application (OECD, 2022). Secondly, the mandatory integration of human control ensures that algorithmic decisions remain verifiable (European Commission, 2019). Thirdly, defined testing mechanisms make it possible to address systematic errors or conflicts (Raji et al., 2020). Fourthly, comprehensive documentation ensures the traceability of decisions (Jobin et al., 2019). These instruments do not work in isolation, but in combination and form the operational basis of institutional management (Ansell & Torfing, 2016).

The specific design of these instruments leads to different governance configurations (Ansell & Torfing, 2016). In formal-stabilising arrangements, clear rules and responsibilities are defined in order to reduce uncertainty (Scott, 2014). Reflexive-legitimising approaches rely more on transparency and iterative adaptation to ensure acceptance (Floridi et al., 2018). Adaptive-experimental configurations, on the other hand, prioritise flexibility and enable organisational learning processes under uncertain conditions (Hinings et al., 2018). The decisive factor is that these configurations are not determined by technological characteristics, but are the result of institutional decisions on how to deal with uncertainty (Yoo et al., 2010).

The key gain in knowledge therefore lies in the shift from analysing institutional tensions to dealing with them in a structured way (Ansell & Torfing, 2016). The integration of artificial intelligence does not require the complete resolution of uncertainty, but rather the establishment of decision-making processes that remain stable under conditions of limited control (March & Olsen, 2006). Institutional capacity to act does not arise through the elimination of conflicts, but through their systematic organisation (Scott, 2014).

8 IMPLICATIONS AND GOVERNANCE TOOLKIT

The preceding analysis shows that the integration of artificial intelligence in educational contexts cannot be understood primarily as a technical implementation problem, but rather as a process of institutional decision-making under conditions of structural uncertainty (Scott, 2014; Hinings et al., 2018). Organisations are confronted with recurring tensions resulting from diffusion of responsibility, coordination problems and demands for legitimacy (Bovens & Zouridis, 2002; Ansell & Torfing, 2016; Floridi et al., 2018). These tensions cannot be completely resolved, but require systematic ways of dealing with them in order to maintain the ability to act (March & Olsen, 2006).

The central challenge is to translate the identified mechanisms into concrete governance structures (Ansell & Torfing, 2016). Institutions must be able to make decisions under uncertainty without losing transparency, accountability or legitimacy (Jobin et al., 2019; Smuha, 2021). In this context, governance means structuring decision-making processes in such a way that they remain stable despite limited control (Ansell & Torfing, 2016). Responsibility must be clearly assigned, even if technical systems are involved (Raji et al., 2020). Coordination must integrate divergent perspectives without blocking the ability to make decisions (Janssen & Kuk, 2016). Legitimacy must be actively established, as it no longer emerges automatically from established procedures (Floridi et al., 2018).

This perspective results in an operationalisable governance approach that is based on the systematic processing of the identified mechanisms (Madaio et al., 2020). An initial central component is the early assessment of risks using structured analysis procedures (OECD, 2022). Before implementing AI-supported systems, organisations must clarify in which areas decisions are particularly sensitive, which uncertainties exist and which regulatory requirements apply (European Commission, 2019). Such analyses make it possible to identify potential conflicts at an early stage and define responsibilities (Jobin et al., 2019).

Building on this, a clear responsibility architecture is required (Bovens & Zouridis, 2002). Decisions must remain clearly assignable, even if algorithmic systems are involved (Raji et al., 2020). Organisations must define who is responsible for certain decision-making areas, how escalation processes are designed and how the basis for decisions is documented (Jobin et al., 2019). Without such structures, there is a diffusion of responsibility that makes both internal control and external accountability more difficult (Bovens & Zouridis, 2002).

At the same time, the integration of artificial intelligence requires the systematic integration of human control (European Commission, 2019). In critical decision-making situations, it must be ensured that algorithmic results can be checked, corrected or rejected (Raji et al., 2020). These forms of integration should not be seen as a step backwards compared to automation, but rather as a necessary prerequisite for stable decision-making processes under uncertainty (Floridi et al., 2018). Human control acts as a corrective that addresses both the susceptibility to error and the epistemic uncertainty of technical systems (Kitchin, 2017).

Another key component of effective governance is ensuring traceability (Jobin et al., 2019). Decisions must be documented and justified, especially if they are based on algorithmic or generative systems (Smuha, 2021). Organisations must make transparent which data is used, which models are used and how decisions are reached (European Commission, 2019). This form of documentation not only enables accountability, but also forms the basis for trust (Floridi et al., 2018; Ritter et al., 2025).

Coordination is another key challenge. Different stakeholders pursue different goals and interpret technological possibilities and regulatory requirements differently (Ansell & Torfing, 2016; Janssen & Kuk, 2016). Institutions must therefore develop mechanisms that systematically integrate these perspectives (Scott, 2014). Interdisciplinary coordination processes, regular feedback loops and the involvement of different stakeholder groups help to reduce coordination problems without restricting the necessary flexibility (Prinsloo & Slade, 2017).

Closely linked to this is the active creation of transparency and communication. Decisions must not only be comprehensible internally, but must also be explained to those affected (Floridi et al., 2018). This includes both the disclosure of decision-making logic and the communication of uncertainties (Jobin et al., 2019). Particularly in the context of artificial intelligence, it is crucial not only to present results, but also to make their limitations visible (Kitchin, 2017). Trust is not created through perfection, but through comprehensible and accountable decision-making processes (Floridi et al., 2018).

As institutional transformation is a dynamic process, governance must be continuously adapted (Hinings et al., 2018). Organisations need mechanisms to continuously monitor and evaluate their systems (OECD, 2022). Indicators such as fairness, accuracy or acceptance can help to recognise problems at an early stage and make adjustments (Raji et al., 2020). Governance itself thus becomes an iterative process based on feedback and continuous improvement (Ansell & Torfing, 2016).

The integration of generative artificial intelligence significantly intensifies the requirements described above (Kasneci et al., 2023; Mollick, 2024). Generative systems produce content and assessments whose epistemic basis is uncertain (Tlili et al., 2023). Organisations must therefore decide in which contexts such systems may be used and where their use should be restricted (Cotton et al., 2024). Additional review mechanisms are needed, especially in areas where decisions have a direct impact on performance evaluation or individual development (Raji et al., 2020). The challenge is to utilise the benefits of generative systems without losing control over the basis for decision-making (Floridi et al., 2018).

The existing governance approaches do not resolve the fundamental tensions. Efficiency is pitted against fairness, automation against control, standardisation against context sensitivity (Janssen & Kuk, 2016; Selwyn, 2019). These opposites are structural. They cannot be cancelled out, they can only be worked on (March & Olsen, 2006). This is precisely the real task of governance: not to create stability, but to organise decision-making processes in such a way that they remain capable of acting under permanent instability (Ansell & Torfing, 2016).This study shows that ethical conflicts must not be understood as marginal phenomena, but as structuring elements of institutional transformation (Madaio et al., 2020). By identifying central mechanisms, it becomes clear how decisions arise under conditions of technological uncertainty and how organisations react to them (Beach & Pedersen, 2019). At the same time, a governance approach is developed that makes it possible to actively shape these processes and ensure institutional capacity to act (Scott, 2014).

Future research should examine the identified mechanisms in other contexts and analyse their long-term effects (Seawright et al., 2008). In particular, the role of generative artificial intelligence should be empirically investigated in greater depth, as its importance for institutional decision-making processes continues to grow (Kasneci et al., 2023; Mollick, 2024). At the same time, lifelong learning perspectives suggest that the integration of artificial intelligence will increasingly extend beyond formal educational institutions and could characterise continuous, adaptive learning processes throughout the life course (Oberdieck & Moch, 2024).

REFERENCES

Ansell, C., & Torfing, J. (2016). *Handbook on theories of governance*. Edward Elgar Publishing. DOI: 10.4337/9781782548508

Beach, D., & Pedersen, R. B. (2019). *Process-tracing methods: Foundations and guidelines* (2nd ed.). University of Michigan Press., DOI: 10.3998/mpub.10072208

Beer, D. (2017). The social power of algorithms. *Information Communication and Society*, *20*(1), 1–13. DOI: 10.1080/1369118X.2016.1216147

Bovens, M., & Zouridis, S. (2002). From street-level to system-level bureaucracies: How information and communication technology is transforming administrative discretion and constitutional control. *Public Administration Review*, *62*(2), 174–184. DOI: 10.1111/0033-3352.00168

Cotton, D. R. E., Cotton, P. A., & Shipway, J. R. (2024). Chatting and cheating: Ensuring academic integrity in the era of ChatGPT. *Innovations in Education and Teaching International*, *61*(2), 228–239. DOI: 10.1080/14703297.2023.2190148

European Commission. (2019). Ethics guidelines for trustworthy AI.: https://digital-strategy.ec.europa.eu/en/library/ethics-guidelines-trustworthy-ai

Floridi, L., Cowls, J., Beltrametti, M., Chatila, R., Chazerand, P., Dignum, V., Luetge, C., Madelin, R., Pagallo, U., Rossi, F., Schafer, B., Valcke, P., & Vayena, E. (2018). AI4People-An ethical framework for a good AI society: Opportunities, risks, principles, and recommendations. *Minds and Machines*, *28*(4), 689–707. DOI: 10.1007/s11023-018-9482-5

Hinings, B., Gegenhuber, T., & Greenwood, R. (2018). Digital innovation and transformation: An institutional perspective. *Information and Organization*, *28*(1), 52–61. DOI: 10.1016/j.infoandorg.2018.02.004

Holmes, W., Bialik, M., & Fadel, C. (2019). *Artificial Intelligence in Education: Promises and Implications for Teaching and Learning*. Center for Curriculum Redesign.

Holmes, W., Porayska-Pomsta, K., Holstein, K., Sutherland, E., Baker, T., Shum, S. B., Santos, O. C., Rodrigo, M. T., Cukurova, M., Bittencourt, I. I., & Koedinger, K. R. (2022). Ethics of AI in education: Towards a community-wide framework. *International Journal of Artificial Intelligence in Education*, *32*(3), 504–526. DOI: 10.1007/s40593-021-00239-1

Ifenthaler, D., & Yau, J. Y. K. (2020). Utilising learning analytics to support study success in higher education: A systematic review. *Educational Technology Research and Development*, *68*(4), 1961–1990. DOI: 10.1007/s11423-020-09788-z

Janssen, M., & Kuk, G. (2016). The challenges and limits of big data algorithms in technocratic governance. *Government Information Quarterly*, *33*(3), 371–377. DOI: 10.1016/j.giq.2016.08.011

Jobin, A., Ienca, M., & Vayena, E. (2019). The global landscape of AI ethics guidelines. *Nature Machine Intelligence*, *1*(9), 389–399. DOI: 10.1038/s42256-019-0088-2

Kasneci, E., Sessler, K., Küchemann, S., Bannert, M., Dementieva, D., Fischer, F., Gasser, U., Groh, G., Günnemann, S., Hüllermeier, E., Krusche, S., Kutyniok, G., Michaeli, T., Nerdel, C., Pfeffer, J., Poquet, O., Sailer, M., Schmidt, A., Seidel, T., & Kasneci, G. (2023). ChatGPT for good? On opportunities and challenges of large language models for education. *Learning and Individual Differences*, *103*, 102274. DOI: 10.1016/j.lindif.2023.102274

Kitchin, R. (2017). Thinking critically about and researching algorithms. *Information Communication and Society*, *20*(1), 14–29. DOI: 10.1080/1369118X.2016.1154087

Madaio, M. A., Stark, L., Wortman Vaughan, J., & Wallach, H. (2020). Co-designing checklists to understand organizational challenges and opportunities around fairness in AI. In *Proceedings of the 2020 CHI Conference on Human Factors in Computing Systems* (pp. 1–14). Association for Computing Machinery. DOI: 10.1145/3313831.3376445

March, J. G., & Olsen, J. P. (2006). The logic of appropriateness. In Moran, M., Rein, M., & Goodin, R. E. (Eds.), *The oxford handbook of public policy* (pp. 689–708). Oxford University Press.

Mollick, E. (2024). *Co-intelligence: Living and working with AI.* Portfolio.

Oberdieck, T., & Moch, E. (2024). Lifelong Learning with Artificial Intelligence: Potentials, Challenges, and Future Perspectives. *International Journal of Advanced Research*, *12*(06), 545–555. DOI: 10.21474/IJAR01/18915

OECD. (2022). OECD Framework for the Classification of AI systems. In *OECD Digital Economy Papers, No. 323*. OECD Publishing., DOI: 10.1787/cb6d9eca-

Plantin, J.-C., Lagoze, C., Edwards, P. N., & Sandvig, C. (2018). Infrastructure studies meet platform studies in the age of Google and Facebook. *New Media & Society*, *20*(1), 293–310. DOI: 10.1177/1461444816661553

Prinsloo, P., & Slade, S. (2017). An elephant in the learning analytics room: The obligation to act. In *Proceedings of the Seventh International Learning Analytics & Knowledge Conference (LAK '17)* (pp. 46-55). Association for Computing Machinery. DOI: 10.1145/3027385.3027406

Raji, I. D., Smart, A., White, R. N., Mitchell, M., Gebru, T., Hutchinson, B., Smith-Loud, J., Theron, D., & Barnes, P. (2020). Closing the AI accountability gap: Defining an end-to-end framework for internal algorithmic auditing. In Proceedings of the 2020 Conference on Fairness, Accountability, and Transparency (pp. 33–44). Association for Computing Machinery. Regulation (EU) 2024/1689 of the European Parliament and of the Council of 13 June 2024 laying down harmonised rules on artificial intelligence (Artificial Intelligence Act). Official Journal of the European Union. https://eur-lex.europa.eu/eli/reg/2024/1689/ojDOI: 10.1145/3351095.3372873

Ritter, L. A., Barenkamp, M., & Moch, E. (2025). Plattform und Kontrolle: Technischer Datenschutz in digitalen Lernsystemen. *Wirtsch Inform Manag*, *17*(5-6), 251–258. DOI: 10.1365/s35764-025-00571-4

Scott, W. R. (2014). *Institutions and Organizations: Ideas, Interests, and Identities* (4th ed.). Sage Publishing.

Seawright, J., George, A., & Bennett, A. (2008). *Case Studies and Theory Development in the Social Sciences.* By Alexander George and Andrew Bennett. (MIT Press, 2005.). *The Journal of Politics*, *70*(1), 276–278. DOI: 10.1017/S0022381607080231

Selwyn, N. (2019). What's the Problem with Learning Analytics? *Journal of Learning Analytics*, *6*(3), 11–19. DOI: 10.18608/jla.2019.63.3

Smuha, N. A. (2021). From a 'race to AI' to a 'race to AI regulation': Regulatory competition for artificial intelligence. *Law, Innovation and Technology*, *13*(1), 57–84. DOI: 10.1080/17579961.2021.1898300

Tlili, A., Shehata, B., Adarkwah, M. A., Bozkurt, A., Hickey, D. T., Huang, R., & Agyemang, B. (2023). What if the devil is my guardian angel: ChatGPT as a case study of using chatbots in education. *Smart Learning Environments*, *10*(1), 15. DOI: 10.1186/s40561-023-00237-x

Van Dijck, J., Poell, T., & De Waal, M. (2018). *The Platform Society: Public Values in a Connective World.* Oxford University Press. DOI: 10.1093/oso/9780190889760.001.0001

Veale, M., & Zuiderveen Borgesius, F. J. (2021). Demystifying the draft EU Artificial Intelligence Act-Analysing the good, the bad, and the unclear elements of the proposed approach. *Computer Law Review International*, *22*(4), 97–112. DOI: 10.9785/cri-2021-220402

Vrba, J., & Huynh, T. N. Q. (2026). *The impact of universities rankings on academic research.* In Academic Research Challenges for Modern Society., DOI: 10.4018/979-8-3373-0897-5.ch004

Williamson, B. (2017). *Big data in education.* SAGE Publications Ltd., DOI: 10.4135/9781529714920

Williamson, B., Bayne, S., & Shay, S. (2020). The datafication of teaching in Higher Education: Critical issues and perspectives. *Teaching in Higher Education*, *25*(4), 351–365. DOI: 10.1080/13562517.2020.1748811

Yoo, Y., Henfridsson, O., & Lyytinen, K. (2010). Research Commentary: The New Organizing Logic of Digital Innovation: An Agenda for Information Systems Research. *Information Systems Research*, *21*(4), 724–735. https://www.jstor.org/stable/23015640. DOI: 10.1287/isre.1100.0322

Zawacki-Richter, O., Marín, V. I., Bond, M., & Gouverneur, F. (2019). Systematic Review of Research on Artificial Intelligence Applications in Higher Education-Where Are the Educators? *International Journal of Educational Technology in Higher Education*, *16*(1), 1–27. DOI: 10.1186/s41239-019-0171-0

Compilation of References

Abuhassna, H., Alnawajha, S., Awae, F., Adnan, M. A. B. M., & Edwards, B. I. (2024). Synthesizing technology integration within the Addie model for instructional design: A comprehensive systematic literature review. *Journal of Autonomous Intelligence*, *7*(5), 1–28. DOI: 10.32629/jai.v7i5.1546

Achuthan, K.. (2025). Artificial intelligence and learner autonomy: A meta-analysis of self-regulated and self-directed learning. *Frontiers in Education*, *10*, 1738751. DOI: 10.3389/feduc.2025.1738751

Adiguzel, T., Kaya, M. H., & Cansu, F. K. (2023). Revolutionizing education with AI: Exploring the transformative potential of ChatGPT. *Contemporary Educational Technology*, *15*(3), ep429. DOI: 10.30935/cedtech/13152

AI HLEG. (2019). Ethics guidelines for trustworthy AI. European Commission, High-Level Expert Group on Artificial Intelligence. https://digital-strategy.ec.europa.eu/en/library/ethics-guidelines-trustworthy-ai

Aimicheva, G., Shaikhanova, A., Iklassova, K., Tazabekova, P., Nazyrova, A., & Kadyr, Y. (2025). Fostering Teachers' Digital Competence in AI-Supported Learning Environments: Implications for Interactive Teaching and Student Achievement. *Applied Sciences (Basel, Switzerland)*, *15*(23), 12597. DOI: 10.3390/app152312597

Ajao, S. O., Aworinde, H. O., Falola, P. B., Adeniyi, A. E., & Sakpere, A. B. (2024). Augmented Reality in Experiential Learning: An Overview. In *2024 IEEE 5th International Conference on Electro-Computing Technologies for Humanity (NIGERCON)* (pp. 1-8). IEEE.

Akavova, A., Temirkhanova, Z., & Lorsanova, Z. (2023). Adaptive learning and artificial intelligence in the educational space. In *E3S web of conferences* (Vol. 451, p. 06011). EDP Sciences. DOI: 10.1051/e3sconf/202345106011

Akbaba, K., & Ertaş Kılıç, H. (2022). Web 2.0 uygulamalarinin öğrencilerin fene ve teknoloji kullanimina yönelik tutumlarina etkisi. *Erzincan Üniversitesi Eğitim Fakültesi Dergisi*, *24*(1), 130–139. DOI: 10.17556/erziefd.880542

Akçay Kavakoğlu, A., Almaç, B., Eser, B., & Alaçam, S. (2022). AI Driven Creativity in Early Design Education-A pedagogical approach in the age of Industry 5.0. In Pak, B., Wurzer, G., & Stouffs, R. (Eds.), *eCAADe 2022: Co-creating the Future - Inclusion in and through Design* (pp. 133–142)., DOI: 10.52842/conf.ecaade.2022.1.133

Akçayır, M., & Akçayır, G. (2017). Advantages and challenges associated with augmented reality for education: A systematic review of the literature. *Educational Research Review*, *20*, 1–11. DOI: 10.1016/j.edurev.2016.11.002

Akgun, S., & Greenhow, C. (2022). Artificial intelligence in education: Addressing ethical challenges in K-12 settings. *AI and Ethics*, *2*(3), 431–440. DOI: 10.1007/s43681-021-00096-7 PMID: 34790956

Akkaya, B., Özkan, A., & Özkan, H. (2021). Yapay zeka kaygı (YZK) ölçeği: Türkçeye uyarlama, geçerlik ve güvenirlik çalışması. *Alanya Akademik Bakış*, *5*(2), 1125–1146. DOI: 10.29023/alanyaakademik.833668

Alaçam, S., Güzelci, O. Z., Bacınoğlu, S. Z., Kızılyaprak, H. N., Uzun, C., Coşkun, E., & Karadağ, İ. (2025). Artificial intelligence 101 for architectural education. *Öneri Dergisi, 20 (MX Yaratıcı Endüstriler Çalıştayı 2024: Yapay Zeka Çağında Yaratıcı Endüstriler Özel Sayısı)*, 219-237.

AlAli, R., & Wardat, Y. (2024). Opportunities and challenges of integrating generative artificial intelligence in education. *International Journal of Religion*, *5*(7), 784–793. Retrieved May 30, 2026, from. DOI: 10.61707/8y29gv34

Alanzi, T. M., Arif, W., Aqeeli, R., Alnafisi, A., Qumosani, T., Alreshidi, A., Alhawsawi, S., Alnakli, R., Alotaibi, A., AlOthman, M., Khamisi, M., & Alanzi, N. (2024). Examining the impact of digital detox interventions on anxiety and depression levels among young adults. *Cureus*, *16*(12). Advance online publication. DOI: 10.7759/cureus.75625 PMID: 39803084

Alasadi, E. A., & Baiz, C. R. (2023). Generative AI in Education and Research: Opportunities, concerns, and solutions. *Journal of Chemical Education*, *100*(8), 2965–2971. DOI: 10.1021/acs.jchemed.3c00323

Alatrash, R., Chatti, M. A., Ain, Q. U., Fang, Y., Joarder, S., & Siepmann, C. (2024). "ConceptGCN: Knowledge concept recommendation in MOOCs based on knowledge graph convolutional networks and SBERT" *Computers and Education Artificial Intelligence*, *6*, 100235. DOI: 10.1016/j.caeai.2024.100235

Aldamen, H., Alnemrat, A., Al-Deaibes, M., & Alsharefeen, R. (2026, April). Using AI to adapt reading input for mixed-proficiency EFL learners. [). Frontiers Media SA.]. *Frontiers in Education*, *11*, 1737903. DOI: 10.3389/feduc.2026.1737903

Aldowah, H., Al-Samarraie, H., & Fauzy, W. M. (2019). Educational data mining and learning analytics for 21st century higher education: A review and synthesis. *Telematics and Informatics*, *37*, 13–49. DOI: 10.1016/j.tele.2019.01.007

Aler Tubella, A., Mora-Cantallops, M., & Nieves, J. C. (2024). How to teach responsible AI in Higher Education: Challenges and opportunities. *Ethics and Information Technology*, *26*(1), 3. DOI: 10.1007/s10676-023-09733-7

Ali, N. A., Sadiq, M. H., Albabawat, A. A., & Salah, R. M. (2022). Methods and applications of augmented reality in education: a review. In *2022 international conference on computer science and software engineering (CSASE)* (pp. 175-181). IEEE. DOI: 10.1109/CSASE51777.2022.9759807

Alkan, F., & Mustafaoğlu, F. M. (2023). Using web tools in lecture: example of micro teaching lesson. In Queirós, R. (Eds.), *Fostering Pedagogy Through Micro and Adaptive Learning in Higher Education: Trends, Tools, and Applications* (pp. 261–286). IGI Global., DOI: 10.4018/978-1-6684-8656-6.ch012

Almaz, A. F., El-Agouz, E. A. E., Abdelfatah, M. T., & Mohamed, I. R. (2024). The future role of artificial intelligence design integration into architectural and interior design education: Improving efficiency, sustainability, and creativity. *Civil Engineering and Architecture*, *12*(3), 1749–1772. DOI: 10.13189/cea.2024.120336

Alshahrani, A., & Mostafa, A. M. (2025). Enhancing the use of artificial intelligence in architectural education: A case study of Saudi Arabia. *Frontiers in Built Environment*, *11*, 1610709. Advance online publication. DOI: 10.3389/fbuil.2025.1610709

Altundağ, C. K., & Koçer, M. Y. (2023). Web 2.0 tools supported innovative applications in science education based on the context-based learning approach. In Braun, J., & Trajkovski, G. (Eds.), *Designing Context-Rich Learning by Extending Reality* (pp. 179–204). IGI Global., DOI: 10.4018/978-1-6684-7644-4.ch010

Al, U., & Tonta, Y. (2004). Atıf analizi: Hacettepe Üniversitesi Kütüphanecilik Bölümü tezlerinde atıf yapılan kaynaklar. *Bilgi Dünyası*, *5*(1), 19–47. DOI: 10.15612/BD.2004.497

Al-Zahrani, A. M. (2025). Evaluating the impact of inclusive and accessible learning technologies on student engagement and academic performance in higher education. *International Journal of Inclusive Education*, •••, 1–29. DOI: 10.1080/13603116.2025.2593563

Ansell, C., & Torfing, J. (2016). *Handbook on theories of governance*. Edward Elgar Publishing. DOI: 10.4337/9781782548508

ARETE Project. (2023). D6.5 Pilots performance analysis. *Zenodo*. DOI: 10.5281/zenodo.7940994

Arrojula, S. P., Bhaskaran, D., Lekkala, S., & Gurijala, P. (2025). Bridging Augmented Reality and Ai for Secure and Personalized Educational Experiences. In *2025 IEEE International Conference on AI and Data Analytics (ICAD)* (pp. 1-7). IEEE. DOI: 10.1109/ICAD65464.2025.11114028

Arslan, K. (2020). Eğitimde yapay zeka ve uygulamalari. *Batı Anadolu Eğitim Bilimleri Dergisi, 11*(1), *71-88.* https://dergipark.org.tr/en/pub/baebd/issue/55426/690058

Arztmann, M., Domínguez Alfaro, J. L., Hornstra, L., Jeuring, J., & Kester, L. (2024). In-game performance: The role of students' socio-economic status, self-efficacy and situational interest in an augmented reality game. *British Journal of Educational Technology*, *55*(2), 484–498. DOI: 10.1111/bjet.13395

Asio, J. M. R., & Gadia, E. D. (2024). Predictors of student attitudes towards artificial intelligence: Implications and relevance to the higher education institutions. *International Journal of Didactical Studies*, *5*(2), 27763. DOI: 10.33902/IJODS.202427763

Asio, J. M., & Soriano, I. D. (2025). The State of Artificial Intelligence (AI) Use in Higher Education Institutions (HEIs) in the Philippines. In Mobo, F. (Ed.), *Impacts of AI on Students and Teachers in Education 5.0* (pp. 523–552). IGI Global Scientific Publishing., DOI: 10.4018/979-8-3693-8191-5.ch01

Azizoğlu, B., & Çakır, R. (2025). Özel eğitim öğretmenlerinin BİT tutumları, dijital materyal tasarımı yeterlikleri ve üretken yapay zekâ okuryazarlıklarının incelenmesi. *Necmettin Erbakan Üniversitesi Ereğli Eğitim Fakültesi Dergisi*, *7*(1), 231–257. Retrieved May 30, 2026, from. DOI: 10.51119/ereegf.2025.129

Azuma, R. T. (1997). A survey of augmented reality. *Presence (Cambridge, Mass.)*, *6*(4), 355–385. DOI: 10.1162/pres.1997.6.4.355

Bacca, J., Baldiris, S., Fabregat, R., Graf, S., & Kinshuk, K. (2014). Augmented reality trends in education: A systematic review of research and applications. *Journal of Educational Technology & Society*, *17*(4), 133–149.

Bagunaid, W., Chilamkurti, N., & Veeraraghavan, P. (2022). Aisar: Artificial intelligence-based student assessment and recommendation system for e-learning in big data. *Sustainability (Basel), 14*(17), 10551. DOI: 10.3390/su141710551

Baidoo-Anu, D., & Owusu Ansah, L. (2023). Education in the era of generative artificial intelligence (AI): Understanding the potential benefits of ChatGPT in promoting teaching and learning. *Journal of AI, 7*(1), 52–62. DOI: 10.61969/jai.1337500

Baker, R. S. (2016). Stupid tutoring systems, intelligent humans. *International Journal of Artificial Intelligence in Education, 26*(2), 600–614. DOI: 10.1007/s40593-016-0105-0

Baker, R. S., & Hawn, A. (2022). Algorithmic bias in education. *International Journal of Artificial Intelligence in Education, 32*(4), 1052–1092. DOI: 10.1007/s40593-021-00285-9

Bandura, A. (1997). *Self-efficacy: The exercise of control.* W. H. Freeman.

Barteit, S., Lanfermann, L., Bärnighäusen, T., Neuhann, F., & Beiersmann, C. (2021). Augmented, mixed and virtual reality-based head-mounted devices for medical education: Systematic review. *JMIR Serious Games, 9*(3), e29080. DOI: 10.2196/29080 PMID: 34255668

Bayly-Castaneda, K., Ramirez-Montoya, M.-S., & Morita-Alexander, A. (2024). Crafting personalized learning paths with AI for lifelong learning: A systematic literature review. *Frontiers in Education, 9*, 1424386. DOI: 10.3389/feduc.2024.1424386

Beach, D., & Pedersen, R. B. (2019). *Process-tracing methods: Foundations and guidelines* (2nd ed.). University of Michigan Press., DOI: 10.3998/mpub.10072208

Becker, B. (2017). Artificial intelligence in education: What is it, where is it now, where is it going? In Mooney, B. (Ed.), *Ireland's yearbook of education 2017-2018* (pp. 42–46). Education Matters.

Beer, D. (2017). The social power of algorithms. *Information Communication and Society, 20*(1), 1–13. DOI: 10.1080/1369118X.2016.1216147

Benavot, A., Hoppers, C. O., Lockhart, A. S., & Hinzen, H. (2022). Reimagining adult education and lifelong learning for all: Historical and critical perspectives. *International Review of Education, 68*(2), 165–194. DOI: 10.1007/s11159-022-09955-9 PMID: 35668894

Bender, E. M., & Gebru, T. (2021). On the dangers of stochastic parrots: Can language models be too big? *Proceedings of the 2021 ACM Conference on Fairness, Accountability, and Transparency*, 610–623. https://doi.org/DOI: 10.1145/3442188.3445922

Benvenuti, M., Cangelosi, A., Weinberger, A., Mazzoni, E., Benassi, M., Barbaresi, M., & Orsoni, M. (2023). Artificial intelligence and human behavioral development: A perspective on new skills and competences acquisition for the educational context. *Computers in Human Behavior, 148*, 107903. DOI: 10.1016/j.chb.2023.107903

Bezen, S. (2023). Challenges of motivating students in online learning platforms: an analysis through the eyes of teachers. In Bilodeau, J., & Hughes, L. (Eds.), *Handbook of Research on Creating Motivational Online Environments for Students* (pp. 59–81). IGI Global., DOI: 10.4018/978-1-6684-4533-4.ch004

Black, P., & Wiliam, D. (1998). Assessment and classroom learning. *Assessment in Education: Principles, Policy & Practice, 5*(1), 7–74. DOI: 10.1080/0969595980050102

Blonder, R., & Feldman-Maggor, Y. (2024). AI for chemistry teaching: Responsible AI and ethical considerations. *Chemistry Teacher International : Best Practices in Chemistry Education, 6*(4), 385–395. DOI: 10.1515/cti-2024-0014

Bogoslov, I. A., Corman, S., & Lungu, A. E. (2024). Perspectives on artificial intelligence adoption for European union elderly in the context of digital skills development. *Sustainability (Basel), 16*(11), 4579. DOI: 10.3390/su16114579

Bovens, M., & Zouridis, S. (2002). From street-level to system-level bureaucracies: How information and communication technology is transforming administrative discretion and constitutional control. *Public Administration Review, 62*(2), 174–184. DOI: 10.1111/0033-3352.00168

Bowen, G. A. (2009). Document analysis as a qualitative research method. *Qualitative Research Journal, 9*(2), 27–40. DOI: 10.3316/QRJ0902027

Bower, M., Howe, C., McCredie, N., Robinson, A., & Grover, D. (2014). Augmented reality in education: Cases, places and potentials. *Educational Media International, 51*(1), 1–15. DOI: 10.1080/09523987.2014.889400

Braun, V., & Clarke, V. (2006). Using thematic analysis in psychology. *Qualitative Research in Psychology, 3*(2), 77–101. DOI: 10.1191/1478088706qp063oa

Braun, V., & Clarke, V. (2021). Thematic analysis: A practical guide. *Sage (Atlanta, Ga.).*

Broek, S., Linden, J. V. D., Kuijpers, M. A. C. T., & Semeijn, J. H. (2023). What makes adults choose to learn: Factors that stimulate or prevent adults from learning. *Journal of Adult and Continuing Education, 29*(2), 620–642. DOI: 10.1177/14779714231169684

Brougham, D., & Haar, J. (2018). Smart technology, artificial intelligence, robotics, and algorithms (STARA): Employees' perceptions of our future workplace. *Journal of Management & Organization, 24*(2), 239–257. DOI: 10.1017/jmo.2016.55

Brown, T. B., Mann, B., Ryder, N., Subbiah, M., Kaplan, J. D., Dhariwal, P., . . . Amodei, D. (2020). Language models are few-shot learners. *arXiv preprint arXiv:2005.14165*. https://arxiv.org/abs/2005.14165

Caena, F., & Redecker, C. (2019). Aligning teacher competence frameworks to 21st century challenges: The case for the European Digital Competence Framework for Educators (DigCompEdu). *European Journal of Education, 54*(3), 356–369. DOI: 10.1111/ejed.12345

Capogna, S., Pellegrini, S., & Sebastiani, R. (2025). Transition and artificial intelligence: The case of student professionalisation. *European Journal of Education, 60*(1), e12866. DOI: 10.1111/ejed.12866

Carbonell, J. R. (1970). AI in CAI: An artificial-intelligence approach to computer-assisted instruction. *IEEE Transactions on Man-Machine Systems, 11*(4), 190–202. DOI: 10.1109/TMMS.1970.299942

Çelik, T. (2024). The effect of artificial intelligence on creativity in conceptual design in architectural education: The motion of biomimetics and futurism. *AI & Society*. Advance online publication. DOI: 10.1007/s00146-024-02042-7

Cerezo-Martinez, P., Nicolas-Sanchez, A., & Castro-Toledo, F. J. (2024). Analyzing the European institutional response to ethical and regulatory challenges of artificial intelligence in addressing discriminatory bias. *Frontiers in Artificial Intelligence, 7*, 1393259. DOI: 10.3389/frai.2024.1393259 PMID: 38983275

Chalkiadakis, A., Seremetaki, A., Kanellou, A., Kallishi, M., Morfopoulou, A., Moraitaki, M., & Mastrokoukou, S. (2024). Impact of artificial intelligence and virtual reality on educational inclusion: A systematic review of technologies supporting students with disabilities. *Education Sciences, 14*(11), 1223. DOI: 10.3390/educsci14111223

Chan, C. K. Y. (2023). A comprehensive AI policy education framework for university teaching and learning. *International Journal of Educational Technology in Higher Education, 20*(1), 38. Advance online publication. DOI: 10.1186/s41239-023-00408-3

Chang, J. H., Wang, C. J., Zhong, H. X., Weng, H. C., Zhou, Y. K., Ong, H. Y., & Lai, C. F. (2024). Artificial intelligence learning platform in a visual programming environment: Exploring an artificial intelligence learning model. *Educational Technology Research and Development*, *72*(2), 997–1024. DOI: 10.1007/s11423-023-10323-z

Chen, M. A., Hwang, G., & Chang, Y. (2019). A reflective thinking-promoting approach to enhancing graduate students' flipped learning engagement, participation behaviors, reflective thinking and project learning outcomes. *British Journal of Educational Technology*, *50*(5), 2288–2307. DOI: 10.1111/bjet.12823

Chen, X., Xie, H., & Hwang, G. J. (2020). A multi-perspective study on artificial intelligence in education: Grants, conferences, journals, and patents. *Journal of Educational Technology & Society*, *23*(4), 1–18.

Chen, X., Xie, H., & Hwang, G.-J. (2020). A multi-perspective study on artificial intelligence in education. *Education and Information Technologies*, *25*(3), 1819–1842. DOI: 10.1007/s10639-019-10069-9

Chen, X., Xie, H., Zou, D., & Hwang, G.-J.CHEN. (2020). Application and theory gaps during the rise of Artificial Intelligence in Education. *Computers and Education: Artificial Intelligence*, *1*, 100002. Advance online publication. DOI: 10.1016/j.caeai.2020.100002

Chih-Ming, C., & Ying-You, L. (2020). Developing a computer-mediated communication competence forecasting model based on learning behavior features. *Computers and Education Artificial Intelligence*, *1*, 100004. DOI: 10.1016/j.caeai.2020.100004

Chiu, T. K. F. (2023). The impact of generative AI (GenAI) on practices, policies and research direction in education: A case of ChatGPT and Midjourney. *Interactive Learning Environments*. Advance online publication. DOI: 10.1080/10494820.2023.2253861

Chiu, T. K. F., Xia, Q., Zhou, X., Chai, C. S., & Cheng, M. (2023). Systematic literature review on opportunities, challenges, and future research directions of artificial intelligence in education. *Computers and Education: Artificial Intelligence*, *4*, 100118. DOI: 10.1016/j.caeai.2023.100118

Choo, J., & Liu, S. (2018). Visual analytics for explainable deep learning. *IEEE Computer Graphics and Applications*, *38*(4), 84–92. DOI: 10.1109/MCG.2018.042731661

Christ-Brendemühl, S. (2025). Leveraging generative AI in higher education: An analysis of opportunities and challenges addressed in university guidelines. *European Journal of Education*, *60*(1), e12891. DOI: 10.1111/ejed.12891

Clark, A., & Chalmers, D. (1998). The extended mind. *Analysis, 58*(1), 7–19. DOI: 10.1093/analys/58.1.7

Clark, M. J., Reynders, M., & Holme, T. A. (2024). Students' experience of a ChatGPT-enabled final exam in a non-majors chemistry course. *Journal of Chemical Education, 101*(5), 1983–1991. DOI: 10.1021/acs.jchemed.4c00161

Clark, T. M. (2023). Investigating the Use of an Artificial Intelligence Chatbot with General Chemistry Exam Questions. *Journal of Chemical Education, 100*(5), 1905–1916. DOI: 10.1021/acs.jchemed.3c00027

Cohen, L., Manion, L., & Morrison, K. (2018). *Research methods in education* (8th ed.). Routledge.

Coimbra Group. (2025). Generative artificial intelligence in higher education: Literacy and inclusion. Report from the Sixth High-Level Seminar on Education Policy. https://www.coimbra-group.eu/generative-artificial-intelligence-in-higher-education-literacy-and-inclusion/

Condorelli, F., & Berti, F. (2025). Creativity and awareness in co-creation of art using artificial intelligence-based systems in heritage education. *Heritage, 8*(5), 157. Advance online publication. DOI: 10.3390/heritage8050157

Cooper, M. (2025). Bridging the digital divide in European higher education. LinkedIn. https://www.linkedin.com/posts/matthew-cooper-university_bridging-the-digital-divide-in-european-higher

Copur-Gencturk, Y., Li, J., Cohen, A. S., & Orrill, C. H. (2024). The impact of an interactive, personalized computer-based teacher professional development program on student performance: A randomized controlled trial. *Computers & Education, 210*, 104963. DOI: 10.1016/j.compedu.2023.104963

Cotton, D. R. E., Cotton, P. A., & Shipway, J. R. (2024). Chatting and cheating: Ensuring academic integrity in the era of ChatGPT. *Innovations in Education and Teaching International, 61*(2), 228–239. DOI: 10.1080/14703297.2023.2190148

Council of Europe. (2024). Framework Convention on Artificial Intelligence and Human Rights, Democracy and the Rule of Law. Council of Europe Treaty Series. https://www.coe.int/en/web/artificial-intelligence/the-framework-convention

Creed, C., Al-Kalbani, M., Theil, A., Sarcar, S., & Williams, I. (2024). Inclusive augmented and virtual reality: A research agenda. *International Journal of Human-Computer Interaction, 40*(20), 6200–6219. DOI: 10.1080/10447318.2023.2247614

Creswell, J. W. (2008). *Educational research: Planning, conducting, and evaluating quantitative and qualitative research* (3rd ed.). Pearson Education.

Creswell, J. W., & Creswell, J. D. (2022). *Research design: Qualitative, quantitative, and mixed methods approaches* (6th ed.). SAGE.

Creswell, J. W., & Plano Clark, V. L. (2018). *Designing and conducting mixed methods research* (3rd ed.). SAGE Publications.

Creswell, J. W., & Plano Clark, V. L. (2018). *Designing and conducting mixed methods research* (3rd ed.). SAGE.

Crogman, H. T., Cano, V. D., Pacheco, E., Sonawane, R. B., & Boroon, R. (2025). Virtual reality, augmented reality, and mixed reality in experiential learning: Transforming educational paradigms. *Education Sciences*, *15*(3), 303. DOI: 10.3390/educsci15030303

Crompton, H., & Burke, D. (2023). Artificial intelligence in higher education: The state of the field. *International Journal of Educational Technology in Higher Education*, *20*(1), 22. Advance online publication. DOI: 10.1186/s41239-023-00392-8

Crompton, H., & Burke, D. (2024). The educational affordances and challenges of ChatGPT: State of the field. *TechTrends*, *68*(3), 380–392. DOI: 10.1007/s11528-024-00939-0

Cross, N. (2011). *Design thinking: Understanding how designers think and work.* Berg. DOI: 10.5040/9781474293884

Cudzik, J., Nyka, L., & Szczepański, J. (2024). Artificial intelligence in architectural education: Green campus development research. *Global Journal of Engineering Education*, *26*(1), 20–25.

da Costa, T., Aranda Lopez, L. I., Perussello, C., Quinn, F., Crowley, Q. G., McMahon, H., & Holden, N. M. (2025). Addressing the demand for green skills: Bridging the gap between university outcomes and industry requirements. *Sustainability (Basel)*, *17*(6), 2732. DOI: 10.3390/su17062732

Darling-Hammond, L., Hyler, M. E., & Gardner, M. (2017). Effective teacher professional development. *Learning policy institute.*

Davis, F. D. (1989). Perceived usefulness, perceived ease of use, and user acceptance of information technology. *Management Information Systems Quarterly*, *13*(3), 319–340. DOI: 10.2307/249008 de Viron, F., & Davies, P. (2022). New impulses for a lifelong learning university: critical thinking, learning time, and space. In *Third international handbook of lifelong learning* (pp. 1–20). Springer International Publishing. DOI: 10.1007/978-3-030-67930-9_37-1

Deci, E. L., & Ryan, R. M. (1985). The general causality orientations scale: Self-determination in personality. *Journal of Research in Personality*, *19*(2), 109–134. DOI: 10.1016/0092-6566(85)90023-6

Deinega, I. I., & Deineha, M. A. (2022). Implementation of the Right of Access to Higher Education: Barrier-Free and Inclusive Education Policy in International Documents and Acts of National Legislation. *education, 3*, 135.

Delen, I., Şen, N., Ozudogru, F., & Biasutti, M. (2024). Understanding the growth of artificial intelligence in educational research through bibliometric analysis. *Sustainability (Basel)*, *16*(16), 6724. DOI: 10.3390/su16166724

Demir Dülger, S. (2023). Lise müdürlerinin ve öğretmenlerinin yapay zekânın eğitimde kullanımına ilişkin görüşleri. *Milli Eğitim Dergisi*, *52*(237), 1–20.

Demir, H., Erigüç, G. (2018). Bibliyometrik bir analiz ile yönetim düşünce sisteminin incelenmesi. *İş ve İnsan Dergisi, 5*(2), 91-114. https://doi.org/DOI: 10.18394/iid.395214

Demir, U., & Çelebi, C. (2025). Sınıf Öğretmeni Adaylarının Yapay Zekâ Okuryazarlık Düzeylerinin Çeşitli Değişkenler Açısından İncelenmesi. *Necmettin Erbakan Üniversitesi Ereğli Eğitim Fakültesi Dergisi, 7(Özel Sayı), 142-166.*

Democrat Project. (2026). How AI can shape education for democracy: Opportunities and risks. https://democrat-horizon.eu/how-ai-can-shape-education-for-democracy/

Devi, C. M., Gobinath, A., & Ilango, D. (2025). Artificial Intelligence in Training and Education. In *AI Insights on Nuclear Medicine* (pp. 143–162). IGI Global Scientific Publishing. DOI: 10.4018/979-8-3373-1275-0.ch007

Dias-Trindade, S., & Moreira, A. (2022). Digital competence in Portuguese education: A national perspective. *Education Sciences*, *12*(3), 184. DOI: 10.3390/educsci12030184

Díaz, B., & Nussbaum, M. (2024). Artificial intelligence for teaching and learning in schools: The need for pedagogical intelligence. *Computers & Education*, *217*, 105071. DOI: 10.1016/j.compedu.2024.105071

Dieker, L. A., & Rodriguez, J. A., Lignugaris/Kraft, B., Hynes, M. C., & Hughes, C. E. (2014). The potential of simulated environments in teacher education: Current and future possibilities. *Teacher Education and Special Education, 37*(1), 21–33. DOI: 10.1177/0888406413512683

Dimitrova, V. (2025). Analysis of the Main Factors for the Digitalization of Higher Education. In *ENVIRONMENT. TECHNOLOGY. RESOURCES. Proceedings of the International Scientific and Practical Conference* (Vol. 3, pp. 83-89). DOI: 10.17770/etr2025vol3.8539

Doğan, A. (2002). *Yapay zeka*. Kariyer Yayıncılık.

Domínguez, A., Pacho, G., Bowers, L., Wild, F., Alcock, S., Chiazzese, G., Farella, M., Arrigo, M., Ross, D., Treacy, R., Yegorina, D., Mangina, E., & Masneri, S. (2023). Dataset of user interactions across four large pilots on the use of augmented reality in learning experiences. *Scientific Data, 10*(1), 823. DOI: 10.1038/s41597-023-02743-6 PMID: 38001128

Dorst, K., & Cross, N. (2001). Creativity in the design process: Co-evolution of problem-solution. *Design Studies, 22*(5), 425–437. DOI: 10.1016/S0142-694X(01)00009-6

Dragomir, A. (2025). The role of the European Union in shaping an ethical and legal framework for artificial intelligence (AI) in education. Review of Artificial Intelligence in Education, 6.

du Plooy, E., Casteleijn, D., & Franzsen, D. (2024). Personalized adaptive learning in higher education: A scoping review of key characteristics and impact on academic performance and engagement. *Heliyon, 10*(22), e39630. DOI: 10.1016/j.heliyon.2024.e39630 PMID: 39524879

Duart, J. M., Cufuna, D. S. A., & Rangel-de Lazaro, G. (2024). Augmented reality, a tool to encourage participatory learning and student involvement. Universitat Oberta de Catalunya. https://www.uoc.edu/en/news/2025/augmented-reality-a-tool-to-encourage-participatory-learning-and-student-involvement

Dumont, H., & Ready, D. D. (2023). On the promise of personalized learning for educational equity. *NPJ Science of Learning, 8*(1), 26. DOI: 10.1038/s41539-023-00174-x PMID: 37542046

Duran, V., & Aydın, E. (2024). Eğitimde yapay zekanın kapsamlı incelenmesi: Web of Science veri tabanı üzerinden bir AI destekli bibliyometrik analiz. *Zenodo*. https://doi.org/DOI: 10.5281/zenodo.10737254

Edwards-Fapohunda, M. O., & Adediji, M. A. (2024). Sustainable development of distance learning in continuing adult education: The impact of artificial intelligence. *Iconic Research and Engineering Journals*, *8*(1), 113–114.

El Morr, C., Singh, D., Sawhney, V., Fernandes, S., El-Lahib, Y., & Gorman, R. (2024). Exploring the intersection of AI and inclusive design for people with disabilities. *Digital Health and Informatics Innovations for Sustainable Health Care Systems*, 556-559.

Ellegaard, O., & Wallin, J. A. (2015). The bibliometric analysis of scholarly production: How great is the impact? *Scientometrics, 105*(3), 1809–1831. DOI: 10.1007/s11192-015-1645-z

Ertmer, P. A., & Ottenbreit-Leftwich, A. T. (2010). Teacher technology change: How knowledge, confidence, beliefs, and culture intersect. *Journal of Research on Technology in Education*, *42*(3), 255–284. DOI: 10.1080/15391523.2010.10782551

Ertmer, P. A., Ottenbreit-Leftwich, A. T., Sadik, O., Sendurur, E., & Sendurur, P. (2012). Teacher beliefs and technology integration practices: A critical relationship. *Computers & Education*, *59*(2), 423–435. DOI: 10.1016/j.compedu.2012.02.001

Estevez, J., Garate, G., Guede, J., & Graña, M. (2019). *Using Scratch to teach undergraduate students' skills on artificial intelligence* (arXiv No. 1904.00296). arXiv. https://arxiv.org/abs/1904.00296

European Commission. (2018). *Artificial intelligence for Europe. Communication from the Commission, COM(2018) 237 final*. European Commission.

European Commission. (2019). *A definition of AI: Main capabilities and disciplines*. Publications Office of the European Union. https://data.europa.eu/doi/10.2759/177365

European Commission. (2019). Ethics guidelines for trustworthy AI. https://digital-strategy.ec.europa.eu/en/library/ethics-guidelines-trustworthy-artificial-intelligence

European Commission. (2019). Ethics guidelines for trustworthy AI.: https://digital-strategy.ec.europa.eu/en/library/ethics-guidelines-trustworthy-ai

European Commission. (2020). *Digital Education Action Plan 2021-2027. Communication from the Commission, COM(2020) 624 final*. European Commission.

European Commission. (2020). Digital Education Action Plan 2021–2027: Resetting education and training for the digital age. European Union. https://education.ec.europa.eu/focus-topics/digital-education/action-plan

European Commission. (2020). Digital Education Action Plan 2021–2027: Resetting education and training for the digital age. Publications Office of the European Union. https://education.ec.europa.eu/focus-topics/digital-education/action-plan

European Commission. (2021). *Digital Education Action Plan (2021–2027)*. European Commission. https://education.ec.europa.eu/focus-topics/digital-education/action-plan

European Commission. (2022). Ethical guidelines on the use of artificial intelligence (AI) and data in teaching and learning for educators. Publications Office of the European Union. https://education.ec.europa.eu/node/2285

European Commission. (2022). *Ethical guidelines on the use of artificial intelligence and data in teaching and learning for educators*. Publications Office of the European Union., DOI: 10.2766/153756

European Commission. (2022).Ethical guidelines on the use of artificial intelligence (AI) and data in teaching and learning for educators. Publications Office of the European Union. https://education.ec.europa.eu/news/ethical-guidelines-on-the-use-of-ai-and-data-in-teaching-and-learning-for-educators

European Commission. (2024). The AI Act: First regulation on AI. European Parliament. https://www.europarl.europa.eu/news/en/headlines/society/20230601STO93804/eu-ai-act-first-regulation-on-artificial-intelligence

European Commission. (2025). European approach to artificial intelligence. Digital Strategy. https://digital-strategy.ec.europa.eu/en/policies/european-approach-artificial-intelligence

European Data Protection Supervisor. (2024). AI-driven personalised learning. TechSonar. https://www.edps.europa.eu/data-protection/technology-monitoring/techsonar/ai-driven-personalised-learning_en

European Parliament and Council of the European Union. (2024). Regulation (EU) 2024/1689 laying down harmonised rules on artificial intelligence (Artificial Intelligence Act). Official Journal of the European Union, L 2024/1689. https://eur-lex.europa.eu/legal-content/EN/TXT/?uri=OJ:L_202401689

European Parliament and Council. (2016). Regulation (EU) 2016/679 of the European Parliament and of the Council of 27 April 2016 on the protection of natural persons with regard to the processing of personal data (General Data Protection Regulation). *Official Journal of the European Union, L, 119*, 1–88.

European Parliament and Council. (2024). *Regulation (EU) 2024/1689 of the European Parliament and of the Council laying down harmonised rules on artificial intelligence (Artificial Intelligence Act)*. Official Journal of the European Union.

EUSAiR. (2025). EU Regulatory Sandboxes for AI: Roadmap. Digital Europe Programme. https://eusair-project.eu/

Fachrurrazy, M., Beddu, R., Efendi, E., Firmansyah, F., Jamaluddin, F., & SIliwadi, D. N. (2026). AI policy framework in education for advancing society 5.0 with safe AI implementation. In *AI, Policy, and the Future of Human-Centered Education* (pp. 165-196). IGI Global Scientific Publishing.

Fan, Y., Tang, L., Le, H., Shen, K., Tan, S., Zhao, Y., Shen, Y., Li, X., & Gašević, D. (2024). Beware of metacognitive laziness: Effects of generative artificial intelligence on learning motivation, processes, and performance. *British Journal of Educational Technology*. Advance online publication. DOI: 10.1111/bjet.13544

Fernandes, C. W., Rafatirad, S., & Sayadi, H. (2023). Advancing personalized and adaptive learning experience in education with artificial intelligence. *Proceedings of the 2023 32nd Annual Conference of the European Association for Education in Electrical and Information Engineering (EAEEIE)*, 1–6. DOI: 10.23919/EAEEIE55804.2023.10181336

Flintberg, B. (2022). Digital micro-credentials for upskilling and reskilling in the vocational sector: A study on the potential use of a blockchain-based ICT system for micro-credentials in Sweden.

Floridi, L., & Chiriatti, M. (2020). GPT-3: Its nature, scope, limits, and consequences. *Minds and Machines*, *30*(4), 681–694. DOI: 10.1007/s11023-020-09548-1

Floridi, L., Cowls, J., Beltrametti, M., Chatila, R., Chazerand, P., Dignum, V., Luetge, C., Madelin, R., Pagallo, U., Rossi, F., Schafer, B., Valcke, P., & Vayena, E. (2018). AI4People An ethical framework for a good AI society: Opportunities, risks, principles, and recommendations. *Minds and Machines*, *28*(4), 689–707. DOI: 10.1007/s11023-018-9482-5 PMID: 30930541

Fortuna, A., Prasetya, F., Samala, A. D., Rawas, S., Criollo-C, S., Kaya, D., Raihan, M., Andriani, W., Safitri, D., & Nabawi, R. A. (2025). Artificial intelligence in personalized learning: A global systematic review of current advancements and shaping future opportunities. *Social Sciences & Humanities Open*, *12*, 102114. DOI: 10.1016/j.ssaho.2025.102114

Garg, N., Kaur, A., Ahmad, F., & Dutta, R. (2025). Augmenting education: The transformative power of AR, AI, and emerging technologies. *Human Behavior and Emerging Technologies*, *2025*(1), 5681184. DOI: 10.1155/hbe2/5681184

Gerlich, M. (2025). AI tools in society: Impacts on cognitive offloading and the future of critical thinking. *Societies (Basel, Switzerland)*, *15*(1), 6. DOI: 10.3390/soc15010006

Gero, J. S., & Sudweeks, F. (Eds.). (1992). *Artificial intelligence in design '92*. Springer., DOI: 10.1007/978-94-011-2787-5

Gero, J. S., & Sudweeks, F. (Eds.). (1994). *Artificial intelligence in design '94*. Springer., DOI: 10.1007/978-94-011-0928-4

Gero, J. S., & Sudweeks, F. (Eds.). (1996). *Artificial intelligence in design '96*. Kluwer Academic Publishers., DOI: 10.1007/978-94-009-0279-4

Gero, J. S., & Sudweeks, F. (Eds.). (1998). *Artificial intelligence in design '98*. Springer., DOI: 10.1007/978-94-011-5121-4

Goger, A., Parco, A., & Vegas, E. (2022). *Learning and working in the digital age: Advancing opportunities and identifying the risks*. Brookings Institution.

Goldschmidt, G. (1991). The dialectics of sketching. *Creativity Research Journal*, *4*(2), 123–143. DOI: 10.1080/10400419109534381

Goodfellow, I., Bengio, Y., & Courville, A. (2016). *Deep learning*. MIT Press.

Graham, F. (2023). Daily briefing: AI detects risk of Parkinson's from retinal images. *Nature*. Advance online publication. DOI: 10.1038/d41586-023-02903-z PMID: 37773285

Granström, M., & Oppi, P. (2025). Student engagement with AI tools in learning: Evidence from a large-scale Estonian survey. *Frontiers in Education*, *10*, 1688092. DOI: 10.3389/feduc.2025.1688092

Guo, S., Zheng, Y., & Zhai, X. (2024). Artificial intelligence in education research during 2013-2023: A review based on bibliometric analysis. *Education and Information Technologies*, *29*(13), 16387–16409. Advance online publication. DOI: 10.1007/s10639-024-12491-8

Haleem, A., Javaid, M., Qadri, M. A., & Suman, R. (2022). Understanding the role of digital technologies in education: A review. *Sustainable Operations and Computers*, *3*, 275–285. DOI: 10.1016/j.susoc.2022.05.004

Hallowell, M. (2023). *Educator AI Report: Perceptions, practices, and potential.* Imagine Learning.

Hamilton, D., McKechnie, J., Edgerton, E., & Wilson, C. (2021). Immersive virtual reality as a pedagogical tool in education: A systematic literature review of quantitative learning outcomes and experimental design. *Journal of Computers in Education*, *8*(1), 1–32. DOI: 10.1007/s40692-020-00169-2

Han, X., Luo, H., Wang, Z., & Zhang, D. (2025). Using virtual reality for teacher education: A systematic review and meta-analysis of literature from 2014 to 2024. *Frontiers in Virtual Reality*, *6*, 1620905. DOI: 10.3389/frvir.2025.1620905

Hardt, M., & Barocas, S. (2017, December). Fairness in machine learning. In *Neural Information Processing Symposium, Tutorials Track.*

Hargittai, E. (2002). Second-level digital divide: Differences in people's online skills. *First Monday*, *7*(4). Advance online publication. DOI: 10.5210/fm.v7i4.942

Hariyanto, K., Kristianingsih, F. X. D., & Maharani, R. (2025). Artificial intelligence in adaptive education: A systematic review of techniques for personalized learning. *Discover Education*, *4*(1), 458. DOI: 10.1007/s44217-025-00908-6

Harry, A., & Sayudin, S. (2023). Role of AI in Education. [INJURITY]. *Interdiciplinary Journal and Hummanity*, *2*(3), 260–268. DOI: 10.58631/injurity.v2i3.52

Higher Education Authority. (2025). Generative AI in higher education teaching and learning: Policy framework. HEA Ireland. https://hea.ie/2025/12/22/hea-publishes-national-policy-framework-on-generative-ai-in-teaching-and-learning/

Hinings, B., Gegenhuber, T., & Greenwood, R. (2018). Digital innovation and transformation: An institutional perspective. *Information and Organization*, *28*(1), 52–61. DOI: 10.1016/j.infoandorg.2018.02.004

Holford, J. (2023). Lifelong learning, the European Union, and the social inclusion of young adults: Rethinking policy. In *Lifelong learning, young adults and the challenges of disadvantage in Europe* (pp. 3–39). Springer International Publishing. DOI: 10.1007/978-3-031-14109-6_1

Holmarsdottir, H. B., Ayllón, S., & Lado, S. (2023). Digitally deprived children in Europe. *Child Indicators Research*, *16*(3), 643–668. DOI: 10.1007/s12187-022-10006-w PMID: 36618273

Holmes, W., Bialik, M., & Fadel, C. (2019). *Artificial intelligence in education promises and implications for teaching and learning*. The Center for Curriculum Redesign. https://curriculumredesign.org/our-work/artificial-intelligence-in-education/

Holmes, W., Bialik, M., & Fadel, C. (2019). *Artificial intelligence in education promises and implications for teaching and learning*. Center for Curriculum Redesign.

Holmes, W., Bialik, M., & Fadel, C. (2019). *Artificial intelligence in education: Promises and implications for teaching and learning*. Center for Curriculum Redesign.

Holmes, W., Bialik, M., & Fadel, C. (2019). *Artificial Intelligence in Education: Promises and Implications for Teaching and Learning*. Center for Curriculum Redesign.

Holmes, W., Porayska-Pomsta, K., Holstein, K., Sutherland, E., Baker, T., Shum, S. B., Santos, O. C., Rodrigo, M. T., Cukurova, M., Bittencourt, I. I., & Koedinger, K. R. (2021). Ethics of AI in Education: Towards a Community-Wide framework. *International Journal of Artificial Intelligence in Education, 32*(3), 504–526. DOI: 10.1007/s40593-021-00239-1

Holmes, W., & Tuomi, I. (2022). State of the art and practice in AI in education. *European Journal of Education, 57*(4), 542–570. DOI: 10.1111/ejed.12533

Holstein, K., McLaren, B. M., & Aleven, V. (2019). Co-designing a real-time classroom orchestration tool for teachers. In *Proceedings of the 2019 CHI Conference on Human Factors in Computing Systems* (pp. 1–12). DOI: 10.1145/3290605.3300828

Hong, S., Moon, J., Eom, T., Awoyemi, I. D., & Hwang, J. (2025). Generative AI-enhanced virtual reality simulation for pre-service teacher education: A mixed-methods analysis. *Education Sciences, 15*(8), 997. DOI: 10.3390/educsci15080997

Hopcan, S., Polat, E., Ozturk, M. E., & Ozturk, L. (2023). Artificial intelligence in special education: A systematic review. *Interactive Learning Environments, 31*(10), 7335–7353. DOI: 10.1080/10494820.2022.2067186

Huh, M. B., Miri, M., & Tracy, T. (2025). Students' perceptions of generative AI image tools in design education: Insights from architectural education. *Education Sciences, 15*(9), 1160. Advance online publication. DOI: 10.3390/educsci15091160

Hul, T., Matviichuk, N., & Hodzhal, S. (2025). Integration of AI into learning and education: A comparative analysis of European and Ukrainian experiences. *Journal of Learning for Development, 12*(3), 599–614. DOI: 10.56059/jl4d.v12i3.1675

Hunaepi, H., Sudiatmika, A. A. I. A., & Fadly, W. (2023). Augmented reality in education: A meta-analysis of (quasi) experimental investigations. Retorika. *Jurnal Ilmu Bahasa, 9*(3), 78–91. DOI: 10.22225/jr.9.3.9066.78-91

Hutson, J. (2025). Cultivating Identity, Workforce Readiness, and Heutagogical Lifelong Learning: The Case for Student-Trained AI Agents in Postsecondary Education. FAR Journal of Education and Sociology, 2(3).

Ibáñez, M. B., & Delgado-Kloos, C. (2018). Augmented reality for STEM learning: A systematic review. *Computers & Education*, *123*, 109–123. DOI: 10.1016/j.compedu.2018.05.002

Ifenthaler, D., & Schumacher, C. (2023). Reciprocal relationship between learning analytics and personalized learning. *Journal of Computing in Higher Education*, *35*(1), 1–15. DOI: 10.1007/s12528-022-09343-w PMID: 36714821

Ifenthaler, D., & Yau, J. Y.-K. (2020). Utilising learning analytics to support study success in higher education: A systematic review. *Educational Technology Research and Development*, *68*(4), 1961–1990. DOI: 10.1007/s11423-020-09788-z

Iranmanesh, A., & Lotfabadi, P. (2025). Critical questions on the emergence of text-to-image artificial intelligence in architectural design pedagogy. *AI & Society*, *40*(5), 3557–3571. DOI: 10.1007/s00146-024-02111-x

Ironsi, C. S., & Tian, X. (2025). Examining the impact of augmented reality on students' learning outcomes. *Scientific Reports*, *15*(1), 7213. DOI: 10.1038/s41598-025-20833-w PMID: 41125660

Isukapalli, S., & Srirama, S. N. (2024). A systematic survey on fault-tolerant solutions for distributed data analytics: Taxonomy, comparison, and future directions. *Computer Science Review*, *53*, 100660. DOI: 10.1016/j.cosrev.2024.100660

Ivanova, A. (2025). The Digital Transformation of Education-From Vision to Reality. In *2025 10th International Conference on Energy Efficiency and Agricultural Engineering (EE&AE)* (pp. 1-5). IEEE. DOI: 10.1109/EEAE65901.2025.11273760

Ivković, R., Vučković, D., Ječmenić, M., Ananieva, D., Stanković, M., Petković, M., & Janković, N. (2025). The EU AI act and its contractual and educational implications: AI, education, and the law of obligations. *International Journal of Cognitive Research in Science. Engineering and Education*, *13*(2), 551–562.

Jaimes, M. Á. R., Navarro, Y. T., Castillo, Á. I. D., Morales, T. H. V., Cortes, A. L. B., & Vanoye, J. A. R. (2026). Applications of Artificial Intelligence in Instructional Design and Educational Strategies. In *AI Applications in Instructional Education Strategies* (pp. 189–222). IGI Global Scientific Publishing.

Janssen, M., & Kuk, G. (2016). The challenges and limits of big data algorithms in technocratic governance. *Government Information Quarterly*, *33*(3), 371–377. DOI: 10.1016/j.giq.2016.08.011

Jauhiainen, J. S., & Garagorry Guerra, A. (2024). Generative AI and education: Dynamic personalization of pupils' school learning material with ChatGPT. *Frontiers in Education*, *9*, 1288723. DOI: 10.3389/feduc.2024.1288723

Jeon, J., & Lee, S. (2023). Large language models in education: A focus on the complementary relationship between human teachers and ChatGPT. *Education and Information Technologies*, *28*(12), 15873–15892. DOI: 10.1007/s10639-023-11834-1

Jia, F., Sun, D., & Looi, C.-K. (2024). Artificial intelligence in science education (2013–2023): Research trends in ten years. *Journal of Science Education and Technology*, *33*(1), 94–117. DOI: 10.1007/s10956-023-10077-6

Jin, F. J.-Y., Maheshi, B., Lia, W., & Li, W. (2025). Students' perceptions of generative AI-powered learning analytics in the feedback process. *Journal of Learning Analytics*, *12*(1), 152–168. Advance online publication. DOI: 10.18608/jla.2025.8609

Jin, F., & Zhang, X. (2025). Artificial intelligence or human: When and why consumers prefer AI recommendations. *Information Technology & People*, *38*(1), 279–303. DOI: 10.1108/ITP-01-2023-0022

Jin, S., Tu, H., Li, J., Fang, Y., Qu, Z., Xu, F., Liu, K., & Lin, Y. (2024). Enhancing architectural education through artificial intelligence: A case study of an AI-assisted architectural programming and design course. *Buildings (Basel, Switzerland)*, *14*(6), 1613. Advance online publication. DOI: 10.3390/buildings14061613

Jobin, A., Ienca, M., & Vayena, E. (2019). The global landscape of AI ethics guidelines. *Nature Machine Intelligence*, *1*(9), 389–399. DOI: 10.1038/s42256-019-0088-2

John, B. (2025, January). Personalized Learning through Software Design Critiquing Tools: Tailoring Feedback to Individual Student Needs.

Joint Research Centre. (2017). European Framework for the Digital Competence of Educators (DigCompEdu). [EN, Publications Office of the European Union.]. *EUR*, •••, 28775.

Joint Research Centre. (2022). Digital Competence Framework (DigComp). Publications Office of the European Union. https://joint-research-centre.ec.europa.eu/digcompedu_en

Jordan, M. I., & Mitchell, T. M. (2015). Machine learning: Trends, perspectives, and prospects. *Science*, *349*(6245), 255–260. DOI: 10.1126/science.aaa8415 PMID: 26185243

Judijanto, L. (2025). Beyond access: Cultural, ethical, and infrastructural challenges of AI in marginalised education contexts. *European Journal of Contemporary Education and E-Learning*, *3*(6), 83–98. DOI: 10.59324/ejceel.2025.3(6).07

Kaddouri, M., Mhamdi, K., Chniete, I., Marhraoui, M., Khaldi, M., & Jmad, S. (2025). Adopting AI in education: Technical challenges and ethical constraints. In *Fostering Inclusive Education With AI and Emerging Technologies* (pp. 25–72). IGI Global Scientific Publishing.

Kajamaa, A., Kumpulainen, K., & Olkinuora, H. (2019). Teacher interventions in students' collaborative work in a technology-rich educational makerspace. *British Journal of Educational Technology*, *51*(2), 371–386. DOI: 10.1111/bjet.12837

Kamalov, F., Santandreu Calonge, D., & Gurrib, I. (2023). New era of artificial intelligence in education: Towards a sustainable multifaceted revolution. *Sustainability (Basel)*, *15*(16), 12451. DOI: 10.3390/su151612451

Karagöl, E., & Yıldırım, D. (2025). Türkçe eğitiminde yapay zekâ kullanımı: Türkçe eğitimcileri yapay zekâ hakkında ne düşünüyor? *Ana Dili Eğitimi Dergisi*, *13*(2), 356–374. DOI: 10.16916/aded.1611540

Karasavvidis, I. (2022). Augmented reality in the classroom: A study of teacher adoption and implementation barriers. *Journal of Educational Computing Research*, *60*(3), 720–745. DOI: 10.1177/07356331211045231

Karyağdı, M., & Aydın, G. (2023). Fen bilgisi öğretmen adaylarıyla gerçekleştirilen teknoloji destekli kavramsal değişim etkinliklerinin etkileri. *Mehmet Akif Ersoy Üniversitesi Eğitim Fakültesi Dergisi*, *68*(68), 156–184. DOI: 10.21764/maeuefd.1346077

Kasinidou, M., Kleanthous, S., & Otterbacher, J. (2025). Cypriot teachers' digital skills and attitudes towards AI. *Discover Education*, *4*(1), 6. DOI: 10.1007/s44217-024-00390-6

Kasneci, E., Sessler, K., Küchemann, S., Bannert, M., Dementieva, D., Fischer, F., & Kasneci, G. (2023). ChatGPT for good? On opportunities and challenges of large language models for education. *Learning and Individual Differences*, *103*, 102274. DOI: 10.1016/j.lindif.2023.102274

Kaya, Y. (2025). The potential of artificial intelligence as the learning ecosystem of the future in adult religious education. Eskişehir Osmangazi Üniversitesi İlahiyat Fakültesi Dergisi, 12(Din ve Yapay Zeka), 127-156.

Kelley, M., & Wenzel, T. (2025). Advancing Artificial Intelligence Literacy in Teacher Education Through Professional Partnership Inquiry. *Education Sciences, 15*(6), 659. DOI: 10.3390/educsci15060659

Khalid, S., Tadesse, E., Abdellahi, M. L., Jiali, Y., & Dainkun, J. (2026). AI-integrated professional development for pre-service teachers: A systematic review of impacts on pedagogical strategies and technological self-efficacy. *European Journal of Education, 61*(2), e70547. DOI: 10.1111/ejed.70547

Khan, M. A., ... (2024). Generative AI and its impact on personalized intelligent tutoring systems. arXiv preprint arXiv:2410.10650.

Kitchin, R. (2017). Thinking critically about and researching algorithms. *Information Communication and Society, 20*(1), 14–29. DOI: 10.1080/1369118X.2016.1154087

Kizilcec, R. F., & Lee, H. (2022). Algorithmic fairness in education. In Holmes, W., & Porayska-Pomsta, K. (Eds.), *Ethics in Artificial Intelligence in Education*. Routledge. DOI: 10.4324/9780429329067-10

Köfter, B., Alkan, F., & Yücel, A. S. (2026). AI-based interactive simulation for atomic models: Pilot study. *Periódico Tchê Química, 23*(52), 1–14. DOI: 10.52571/PTQ.v23.n52.2026_01_BILLUR_pgs_01_14.pdf

Köhler, T., & Münster, S. (2021). Digital transformation of higher education in Europe: A review of current strategies and practices. European Journal of Higher Education, 11(Sup1), 211–228. https://doi.org/DOI: 10.1080/21568235.2021.1944410

Kohnke, L., & Zou, D. (2025). Artificial Intelligence Integration in TESOL Teacher Education: Promoting a Critical Lens Guided by TPACK and SAMR. *TESOL Quarterly, 59*(S3). Advance online publication. Retrieved May 30, 2026, from. DOI: 10.1002/tesq.3396

Kok, J. N., Boers, E. J., Kosters, W. A., Van der Putten, P., & Poel, M. (2009). Artificial intelligence: Definition, trends, techniques, and cases. *Artificial Intelligence, 1*, 270–299.

Kolarevic, B. (Ed.). (2003). *Architecture in the digital age: Design and manufacturing*. Spon Press.

Kong, S. C., Cheung, W. M. Y., & Zhang, G. (2023). Evaluating an artificial intelligence literacy programme for developing university students' conceptual understanding, literacy, empowerment and ethical awareness. *Journal of Educational Technology & Society, 26*(1), 16–30. DOI: 10.30191/ETS.202301_26(1).0002

Koper, R. (2020). How do students want to learn in online distance education? Profiling student preferences. *International Review of Research in Open and Distance Learning*, *35*(3), 263–283. DOI: 10.19173/irrodl.v16i1.2000

Koumpouros, Y. (2024). Revealing the true potential and prospects of augmented reality in education. *Smart Learning Environments*, *11*(1), 5. DOI: 10.1186/s40561-023-00288-0

Kruckel, J. (2025). Recalibrating the Social Contract: The Case for Lifelong Free Education in the Age of AI.

Kultan, J., Baimuldina, N., Rakhimzhanova, L., Issabayeva, D., Issabayeva, Z., & Aituganova, Z. (2025). Using augmented reality to teach digital literacy course to primary school children with special educational needs. *European Journal of Educational Research*, *14*(1), 55–71. DOI: 10.12973/eu-jer.14.1.55

Kumari, N., & Patra, B. C. (2025). AI and Inclusive Education: Enhancing Equity, Engagement and Excellence. In *AI Based Solutions for Inclusive Quality Education* (pp. 27-44). CRC Press.

Kumar, J. A. (2025). The global landscape of research on AI literacy: A bibliometric analysis of trends, collaborations, and emerging themes. *Proceedings of the IEEE Frontiers in Education Conference*. DOI: 10.1109/FIE63693.2025.11328420

Lampropoulos, G. (2023). Augmented reality and artificial intelligence in education: Toward immersive intelligent tutoring systems. In *Augmented reality and artificial intelligence: The fusion of advanced technologies* (pp. 137–146). Springer Nature Switzerland. DOI: 10.1007/978-3-031-27166-3_8

Lampropoulos, G., Fernández-Arias, P., Antón-Sancho, Á., & Vergara, D. (2024). Affective computing in augmented reality, virtual reality, and immersive learning environments. *Electronics (Basel)*, *13*(15), 2917. DOI: 10.3390/electronics13152917

Lamri, J., & Lubart, T. (2023). Reconciling hard skills and soft skills in a common framework: The generic skills component approach. *Journal of Intelligence*, *11*(6), 107. DOI: 10.3390/jintelligence11060107 PMID: 37367509

Lawson, B. (2006). *How designers think: The design process demystified* (4th ed.). Architectural Press. DOI: 10.4324/9780080454979

Lee, G.-G., & Zhai, X. (2024). Using ChatGPT for science learning: A study on pre-service teachers' lesson planning. *IEEE Transactions on Learning Technologies*, *17*, 1643–1660. DOI: 10.1109/TLT.2024.3401457

Lee, I., Park, J., & Yoon, H.-G. (2022). Science teachers' theory-based teaching: Connecting a learning cycle model to a lesson plan. *Journal of Baltic Science Education, 21*(3), 462–480. DOI: 10.33225/jbse/22.21.462

Lee, L. K., Wei, X., Chui, K. T., Cheung, S. K., Wang, F. L., Fung, Y. C., Lu, A., Hui, Y. K., Hao, T., U, L. H., & Wu, N. I. (2024). A systematic review of the design of serious games for innovative learning: Augmented reality, virtual reality, or mixed reality? *Electronics (Basel), 13*(5), 890. DOI: 10.3390/electronics13050890

Lens. (2025). *Scholar search: AI in Education.* https://www.lens.org/lens/search/scholar/list?q=AI%20in%20Education

Lens. (2025). *Scholar search: Children Online Privacy Protection Act.* https://www.lens.org/lens/search/scholar/list?q=Children%20Online%20Privacy%20Protection%20Act&p=0&n=10&s=_score&d=%2B&f=false&e=false&l=en&authorField=author&dateFilterField=publishedYear&orderBy=%2B_score&presentation=false&preview=true&stemmed=true&useAuthorId=false

Lens. (2025). *Scholar search: evolving role of AI in higher education.* Family Educational Rights and Privacy. https://www.lens.org/lens/search/scholar/list?q=Family%20Educational%20Rights%20and%20Privacy&p=0&n=10&s=_score&d=%2B&f=false&e=false&l=en&authorField=author&dateFilterField=publishedYear&orderBy=%2B_score&presentation=false&preview=true&stemmed=true&useAuthorId=false

Lens. (2025). *Scholar search: General Data Protection Regulation.*https://www.lens.org/lens/search/scholar/list?q=General%20Data%20Protection%20Regulation&p=0&n=10&s=_score&d=%2B&f=false&e=false&l=en&authorField=author&dateFilterField=publishedYear&orderBy=%2B_score&presentation=false&preview=true&stemmed=true&useAuthorId=false

Li, J., & Huang, Q. (2025). Navigating ethical dilemmas in AI-enhanced education: A critical bibliometric analysis of global research trends and collaboration networks. [IJKM]. *International Journal of Knowledge Management, 21*(1), 1–21. DOI: 10.4018/IJKM.382384

Lin, C. C., Huang, A. Y. Q., & Lu, O. H. T. (2023). Artificial intelligence in intelligent tutoring systems toward sustainable education: A systematic review. *Smart Learning Environments, 10*(1), 41. DOI: 10.1186/s40561-023-00260-y

Liu, Y., Xu, B., Feng, J., & Wu, P. (2025). Analysis of the application of generative artificial intelligence in interior design education. *Ain Shams Engineering Journal, 16*(12), 103757. Advance online publication. DOI: 10.1016/j.asej.2025.103757

Li, Y.. (2025). The effectiveness of augmented reality/mixed reality in medical education. *BMC Medical Education*, *25*(1), 1–15. PMID: 39743510

Li, Z., Wang, C., & Bonk, C. J. (2025). Generative AI for teachers' self-directed professional development: A mixed-methods study. *TechTrends*. Advance online publication. DOI: 10.1007/s11528-025-01123-8

Long, P., & Siemens, G. (2011). Penetrating the fog: Analytics in learning and education. *EDUCAUSE Review (Online)*.

Luckin, R. (2018). *Machine Learning and Human Intelligence. The future of education for the 21st century*. UCL institute of education press.

Luckin, R., Holmes, W., Griffiths, M., & Forcier, L. B. (2016). *Intelligence unleashed: An argument for AI in education*. Pearson. https://discovery.ucl.ac.uk/1475756/

Luckin, R., & Holmes, W. (2016). *Intelligence unleased: An argument for AI in education*. Pearson Education.

Luckin, R., Holmes, W., Griffiths, M., & Forcier, L. B. (2016). *Intelligence unleashed: An argument for AI in education*. Pearson., DOI: 10.1063/5.0129803

Madaio, M. A., Stark, L., Wortman Vaughan, J., & Wallach, H. (2020). Co-designing checklists to understand organizational challenges and opportunities around fairness in AI. In *Proceedings of the 2020 CHI Conference on Human Factors in Computing Systems* (pp. 1–14). Association for Computing Machinery. DOI: 10.1145/3313831.3376445

Makransky, G., & Lilleholt, L. (2018). A structural equation modeling investigation of the emotional value of immersive virtual reality in education. *Educational Technology Research and Development*, *66*(5), 1141–1164. DOI: 10.1007/s11423-018-9581-2

Malta, I. D. P. C. (2025). IDPC raises awareness on AI data protection concerns for students including higher education settings. https://idpc.org.mt/news-latest/idpc-raises-awareness-on-ai-data-protection-concerns-for-students-including-higher-education-settings

Mandiá-Rubal, S. (2026). Artificial intelligence and the library as Third Place: Cognitive automation and the reconfiguration of labour. *The Journal of Documentation*, *82*(2), 1–14. DOI: 10.1108/JD-11-2025-0346

Mansur, S. (2025). AI As A Catalyst in Education, Adult Learning, and Digital Literacy. [IJFMR]. *International Journal for Multidisciplinary Research*, *7*(4), 54198. DOI: 10.36948/ijfmr.2025.v07i04.54198

March, J. G., & Olsen, J. P. (2006). The logic of appropriateness. In Moran, M., Rein, M., & Goodin, R. E. (Eds.), *The oxford handbook of public policy* (pp. 689–708). Oxford University Press.

Market Data Forecast. (2025). Europe Edtech market size, share and growth report, 2033. https://www.marketdataforecast.com/market-reports/europe-edtech-market

Mayer, R. E. (2021). *Multimedia learning* (3rd ed.). Cambridge University Press., DOI: 10.1017/9781316941355

Meço, G., & Coştu, F. (2022). Eğitimde yapay zekânin kullanilmasi: betimsel içerik analizi çalişmasi. *Karadeniz Teknik Üniversitesi Sosyal Bilimler Enstitüsü Sosyal Bilimler Dergisi, 12*(23). https://dergipark.org.tr/en/pub/sbed/issue/70445/1092727

Medel-Vera, C., Britton, S., & Gates, W. F. (2025). The role of generative AI in fostering creativity in architectural learning environments. *Computers and Education: Artificial Intelligence, 9*, 100501. Advance online publication. DOI: 10.1016/j.caeai.2025.100501

Mehrabi, N., Morstatter, F., Saxena, N., Lerman, K., & Galstyan, A. (2021). A survey on bias and fairness in machine learning. *ACM Computing Surveys, 54*(6), 1–35. DOI: 10.1145/3457607

Mejia, C., Wu, M., Zhang, Y., & Kajikawa, Y. (2021). Exploring topics in bibliometric research through citation networks and semantic analysis. *Frontiers in Research Metrics and Analytics, 6*, 742311. DOI: 10.3389/frma.2021.742311

Mikeladze, T., Meijer, P. C., & Verhoeff, R. P. (2024). A comprehensive exploration of artificial intelligence competence frameworks for educators: A critical review. *European Journal of Education, 59*(3), e12663. DOI: 10.1111/ejed.12663

Mikropoulos, T. A., & Natsis, A. (2011). Educational virtual environments: A ten-year review of empirical research (1999–2009). *Computers & Education, 56*(3), 769–780. DOI: 10.1016/j.compedu.2010.10.020

Milgram, P., & Kishino, F. (1994). A taxonomy of mixed reality visual displays. *IEICE Transactions on Information and Systems, E77-D*(12), 1321–1329.

Ministry of National Education. (2023). Yapay zekâ uygulamaları dersi öğretim programı (I-II) (*Ortaokul ve imam hatip ortaokulu 7 ve 8. sınıflar*) [Artificial intelligence applications course curriculum (I-II) (*Middle school and imam hatip middle school 7th and 8th grades*)]. MoNE Publications.

Mitchell, M. (2019). *Artificial intelligence: A guide for thinking humans*. Penguin.

Mitre, X., & Zeneli, M. (2024). Using AI to improve accessibility and inclusivity in higher education for students with disabilities. In *2024 21st International Conference on Information Technology Based Higher Education and Training (ITHET)* (pp. 1-8). IEEE. DOI: 10.1109/ITHET61869.2024.10837607

Molenaar, I. (2022). Towards hybrid human-AI learning technologies. *European Journal of Education*, *57*(4), 632–645. DOI: 10.1111/ejed.12527

Molenaar, I. (2022). Towards hybrid human-AI learning: Technologies to support appropriate student and teacher agency. *Computers and Education: Artificial Intelligence*, *3*, 100054. DOI: 10.1016/j.caeai.2022.100054

Mollick, E. (2024). *Co-intelligence: Living and working with AI*. Portfolio.

Montenegro, N. (2024). Integrative analysis of text-to-image AI systems in architectural design education: Pedagogical innovations and creative design implications. *Journal of Architecture and Urbanism*, *48*(2), 109–124. DOI: 10.3846/jau.2024.20870

Moreira, F. T., Vairinhos, M., & Ramos, F. (2021). Conceptualization of Hypersituation as Result of IoT in Education. In Mealha, Ó., Rehm, M., & Rebedea, T. (Eds.), *Ludic, Co-design and Tools Supporting Smart Learning Ecosystems and Smart Education. Smart Innovation, Systems and Technologies* (Vol. 197). Springer., DOI: 10.1007/978-981-15-7383-5_6

Mosha, N. F. V., Chigwada, J., Ketchiwou, G. F., & Ngulube, P. (2026). A systematic review of artificial intelligence in higher education institutions (HEIs): Functionalities, challenges, and best practices. *Education Sciences*, *16*(2), 185. DOI: 10.3390/educsci16020185

Mousavinasab, E., Zarifsanaiey, N., Kalhori, S. R. N., Rakhshan, M., Keikha, L., & Saeedi, M. G. (2018). Intelligent tutoring systems: A systematic review of characteristics, applications, and evaluation methods. *Interactive Learning Environments*, *29*(1), 142–163. DOI: 10.1080/10494820.2018.1558257

Murari, U. K., & Parmar, H. (2025). Ethical Integration of Artificial Intelligence in Inclusive Education: Addressing Challenges and Advancing Opportunities for Equitable Learning. In *Ethics and AI Integration Into Modern Classrooms* (pp. 439-470). IGI Global Scientific Publishing.

Mustafaoğlu, F. M., & Alkan, F. (2024). An analysis of high school students' laboratory self-efficacy beliefs and perceptions of laboratory applications. *Periódico Tchê Química*, *21*(48), 16–31. DOI: 10.52571/PTQ.v21.n48.2024_02_FATMA_pgs_16_48.pdf

Mustafaoğlu, F. M., & Alkan, F. (2025). Artificial intelligence in education: Attitudes and perceptions of pre-service teachers. *Information Technologies and Learning Tools*, *110*(6), 120–134. DOI: 10.33407/itlt.v110i6.6341

Mystakidis, S., Berki, E., & Valtanen, J. P. (2021). Deep and meaningful e-learning with social virtual reality environments in higher education: A systematic literature review. *Applied Sciences (Basel, Switzerland)*, *11*(2), 694. DOI: 10.3390/app11052412

Natarajan, G., Raja, S. R., Elango, E., & Soman, S. (2025). Augmented Reality and Virtual Reality: Transforming the Learning Experience with AI Tools. *Virtual Reality and Augmented Reality with 6G Communication*, 217-243.

Nazaretsky, T., Ariely, M., Itzhak, H., & Alexandron, G. (2022). Exploring teacher trust in AI-based educational technology. *Scientific Reports*, *12*(1), 18567. DOI: 10.1038/s41598-022-22611-z PMID: 36329160

Nejdl, W. (2024). Fairness awareness training helps researchers reduce AI bias. NoBIAS Project, Marie Sklodowska-Curie Innovative Training Network. https://cordis.europa.eu/article/id/454703-fairness-awareness-training-helps-researchers-reduce-ai-bias

Nevrelova, N., Korenova, L., Lavicza, Z., Bruzkova, N., & Schmid, A. (2024). Enhancing digital literacy in primary education through augmented reality. *Frontiers in Education*, *9*, 1390491. DOI: 10.3389/feduc.2024.1390491

Ng, C., Graham, S., Lau, K., Liu, X., & Tang, K. (2021). Writing motives and writing self-efficacy of Chinese students in Shanghai and Hong Kong: Measurement invariance and multigroup structural equation analyses. *International Journal of Educational Research*, *107*, 101751. DOI: 10.1016/j.ijer.2021.101751

Ng, D. T. K., Lee, M., Tan, R. J. Y., Hu, X., Downie, J. S., & Chu, S. K. W. (2023a). A review of AI teaching and learning from 2000 to 2020. *Education and Information Technologies*, *28*(7), 8445–8501. DOI: 10.1007/s10639-022-11491-w

Ng, D. T. K., Leung, J. K. L., Chu, S. K. W., & Qiao, M. S. (2021). Conceptualizing AI literacy: An exploratory review. *Computers and Education: Artificial Intelligence*, *2*, 100041. DOI: 10.1016/j.caeai.2021.100041

Nguyen, A., Ngo, H. N., Hong, Y., Dang, B., & Nguyen, B. P. T. (2023). Ethical principles for artificial intelligence in education. *Education and Information Technologies*, *28*(4), 4221–4241. DOI: 10.1007/s10639-022-11316-w PMID: 36254344

Nikou, S. A., Perifanou, M., & Economides, A. A. (2024). Development and validation of the teachers' augmented reality competences (TARC) scale. *Journal of Computers in Education*, *11*(4), 1041–1060. DOI: 10.1007/s40692-023-00288-6

Nikou, S. A., Perifanou, M., & Economides, A. A. (2024). Exploring teachers' competences to integrate augmented reality in education: Results from an international study. *TechTrends*, *68*(6), 1024–1037. DOI: 10.1007/s11528-024-01014-4

Nisiforou, E., & Kosmas, P. (2024). Assessing institutional readiness for emerging technologies integration in higher education. *Journal of Interactive Learning Research*, *35*(4), 425–450. DOI: 10.70725/441907jrwrsw

Norris, P. (2001). *Digital divide. Civic engagement, information poverty and the internet world-wide.* Cambridge University Press., DOI: 10.1108/146366903322008287

Nyaaba, A., Mensah, M., & Amponsah, K. D. (2024). Pre-service teachers' perceptions and readiness for integrating generative artificial intelligence in teaching and learning in Ghana. *Cogent Education*, *11*(1), 1–17.

O'Dea, X. (2024). Generative AI: Is it a paradigm shift for higher education? *Studies in Higher Education*, *49*(5), 811–816. DOI: 10.1080/03075079.2024.2332944

O'Sullivan, J. (2025). *Generative AI in higher education teaching and learning: Policy framework.* Higher Education Authority.

Oberdieck, T., & Moch, E. (2024). Lifelong Learning with Artificial Intelligence: Potentials, Challenges, and Future Perspectives. *International Journal of Advanced Research*, *12*(06), 545–555. DOI: 10.21474/IJAR01/18915

Odunga, J. O., Musuva, P. M., & Ndiege, J. R. A. (2025, May). Exploring Emerging Technologies for Inclusive Education in Students with Learning Disabilities: A Systematic Literature Review. In *2025 IST-Africa Conference (IST-Africa)* (pp. 1-13). IEEE. DOI: 10.23919/IST-Africa67297.2025.11060558

OECD. (2021). *21st-century readers: Developing literacy skills in a digital world.* OECD Publishing., DOI: 10.1787/a83d84eb-

OECD. (2022). OECD Framework for the Classification of AI systems. In *OECD Digital Economy Papers, No. 323.* OECD Publishing., DOI: 10.1787/cb6d9eca-

OECD. (2023). *AI and the future of skills.* OECD Publishing., DOI: 10.1787/5e031222-

OECD. (2023). OECD principles on artificial intelligence. https://oecd.ai/en/ai-principles

OECD. (2026a). *OECD Digital Education Outlook 2026: Exploring effective uses of generative AI in education.* OECD Publishing., DOI: 10.1787/062a7394-

OECD. (2026b). *Reimagining teaching in an accelerating world.* OECD Publishing., DOI: 10.1787/d0edfe8c-

OECD. (2026c). *An overview of national strategies and policies for immersive technologies. OECD Digital Economy Papers, No. 380*. OECD Publishing., DOI: 10.1787/2da1d7da-

Ofusu-Asare, Y. (2025). *Guiding the future: Developing an ethical framework for generative AI use in education*. International Journal of Information and Learning Technology., DOI: 10.1108/IJILT-06-2024-0113

Ogbu, E. (2025). Re-skilling for the future: An innovative approach in the nigerian adult education for sustainable development in the era of automation. Journal on Innovation and Sustainability RISUS, 16(1), 04-17.

Okonkwo, C. W., & Ade-Ibijola, A. (2021). Chatbots applications in education: A systematic review. *Computers and Education: Artificial Intelligence*, *2*, 100033. DOI: 10.1016/j.caeai.2021.100033

Open, A. I. (2023). *GPT-4 technical report*. https://doi.org//arXiv.2303.08774DOI: 10.48550

Oruç, T., Yeşilyurt, M., & Kurt, M. (2024). Eğitimde Yapay Zekâ Konulu Çalışmaların Betimsel Analizi. *Temel Eğitim*, *6*(24), 44–60.

Ouyang, F., & Jiao, P. (2021). Artificial intelligence in education: The three paradigms. *Computers and Education: Artificial Intelligence*, *2*, 100020. DOI: 10.1016/j.caeai.2021.100020

Ouyang, F., Wu, M., Zheng, L., Zhang, L., & Jiao, P. (2023). Integration of artificial intelligence performance prediction and learning analytics to improve student learning in online engineering course. *International Journal of Educational Technology in Higher Education*, *20*(1), 4. DOI: 10.1186/s41239-022-00372-4 PMID: 36683653

Oxman, R. (2008). Digital architecture as a challenge for design pedagogy: Theory, knowledge, models and medium. *Design Studies*, *29*(2), 99–120. DOI: 10.1016/j.destud.2007.12.003

Oxman, R. (2017). Thinking difference: Theories and models of parametric design thinking. *Design Studies*, *52*, 4–39. DOI: 10.1016/j.destud.2017.06.001

Özdemir, D., Durak, G., Can, S., & Çankaya, S. (2024). Artificial intelligence in education: A bibliometric study on its role in transforming teaching and learning. *International Review of Research in Open and Distance Learning*, *25*(3), 219–244. DOI: 10.19173/irrodl.v25i3.7757

PAIDEIA Project. (2024). D 3.2: AI&EDcomp Framework: Teacher competence framework for working with AI. Erasmus+ Project 101132955.

Pal'ová, D., & Zoričaková, J. (2025). Digital Transformation of Higher Education Institutions. In *2025 MIPRO 48th ICT and Electronics Convention* (pp. 559-564). IEEE. DOI: 10.1109/MIPRO65660.2025.11132039

Palalas, A., & Ally, M. (Eds.). (2016). *The international handbook of mobile-assisted language learning*. China Central Radio & TV University Press.

Parmaxi, A., & Demetriou, A. A. (2020). Augmented reality in language learning: A state-of-the-art review of 2014–2019. *Interactive Learning Environments*, *28*(6), 686–700. DOI: 10.1080/10494820.2020.1712429

Pellas, N., Kazanidis, I., & Palaigeorgiou, G. (2020). A systematic literature review of mixed reality in K-12 education: A 10-year complementary study of benefits, challenges, and instructional strategies. *IEEE Access : Practical Innovations, Open Solutions*, *8*, 37385–37405. DOI: 10.1109/ACCESS.2020.2975608

Perifanou, M., Economides, A. A., & Nikou, S. A. (2022). Teachers' views on integrating augmented reality in education: Needs, opportunities, challenges and recommendations. *Future Internet*, *15*(1), 20. DOI: 10.3390/fi15010020

Perrotta, C., & Selwyn, N. (2020). Deep learning goes to school: Toward a relational understanding of AI in education. *Learning, Media and Technology*, *45*(3), 251–269. DOI: 10.1080/17439884.2020.1686017

Piqueras, C., Díaz-Noguera, M., & Hervás-Gómez, C. (2022). Use of augmented reality for students with educational needs: A systematic review (2016–2021). *Societies (Basel, Switzerland)*, *12*(2), 36. DOI: 10.3390/soc12020036

Plantin, J.-C., Lagoze, C., Edwards, P. N., & Sandvig, C. (2018). Infrastructure studies meet platform studies in the age of Google and Facebook. *New Media & Society*, *20*(1), 293–310. DOI: 10.1177/1461444816661553

Pokrivčáková, S. (2019). Preparing teachers for the application of AI-powered technologies in foreign language education. *Journal of Language and Cultural Education*, *7*(3), 135–153. DOI: 10.2478/jolace-2019-0025

Popenici, S. A. D., & Kerr, S. (2017). Exploring the impact of artificial intelligence on teaching and learning in higher education. *Research and Practice in Technology Enhanced Learning*, *12*(1), 22. DOI: 10.1186/s41039-017-0062-8

Post, D. G. (2017). How the Internet is making jurisdiction sexy (again). *International Journal of Law and Information Technology*, *25*(4), 249–258. DOI: 10.1093/ijlit/eax019

Precedence Research. (2026). AI in education market size to surpass USD 136.79 billion by 2035. Yahoo Finance. https://finance.yahoo.com/news/ai-education-market-size-surpass-095500912.html

Prinsloo, P., & Slade, S. (2017). An elephant in the learning analytics room: The obligation to act. In *Proceedings of the Seventh International Learning Analytics & Knowledge Conference (LAK '17)* (pp. 46-55). Association for Computing Machinery. DOI: 10.1145/3027385.3027406

Prokopyev, A., Kalmazova, N. A., Molodozhnikova, N. M., Akhmadieva, R. S., Belova, T., & Spichak, V. Yu. (2024). Research trends in the use of artificial intelligence in higher education. *Frontiers in Education*, *9*, 1438715. DOI: 10.3389/feduc.2024.1438715

Radianti, J., Majchrzak, T. A., Fromm, J., & Wohlgenannt, I. (2020). A systematic review of immersive virtual reality applications for higher education: Design elements, challenges, and future avenues. *Information & Management*, *57*(1), 103183. DOI: 10.1016/j.im.2019.103183

Radianti, J., Majchrzak, T. A., Fromm, J., & Wohlgenannt, I. (2020). A systematic review of immersive virtual reality applications for higher education: Design elements, lessons learned and research agenda. *Computers & Education*, *147*, 103778. Advance online publication. DOI: 10.1016/j.compedu.2019.103778

Radu, I. (2014). Augmented reality in education: A meta-review and cross-media analysis. *Personal and Ubiquitous Computing*, *18*(6), 1533–1543. DOI: 10.1007/s00779-013-0747-y

Rajaraman, V. (2023). From ELIZA to ChatGPT. *Reson*, *28*(6), 889–905. DOI: 10.1007/s12045-023-1620-6

Raji, I. D., Smart, A., White, R. N., Mitchell, M., Gebru, T., Hutchinson, B., Smith-Loud, J., Theron, D., & Barnes, P. (2020). Closing the AI accountability gap: Defining an end-to-end framework for internal algorithmic auditing. In Proceedings of the 2020 Conference on Fairness, Accountability, and Transparency (pp. 33–44). Association for Computing Machinery. Regulation (EU) 2024/1689 of the European Parliament and of the Council of 13 June 2024 laying down harmonised rules on artificial intelligence (Artificial Intelligence Act). Official Journal of the European Union. https://eur-lex.europa.eu/eli/reg/2024/1689/ojDOI: 10.1145/3351095.3372873

Rana, V., Verhoeven, B., & Sharma, M. (2025). Generative AI in design thinking pedagogy: Enhancing creativity, critical thinking, and ethical reasoning in higher education. *Journal of University Teaching & Learning Practice*, *22*(4). Advance online publication. DOI: 10.53761/tjse2f36

Rani, J., Guru, R., Santhanam, S., Molla, W. T., Singh, J., & Dutt, S. (2025). AI Revolutionizing Education: Exploring Trends, Technologies, and Ethical Considerations for Future Learning Environments. *Implementing AI Tools for Language Teaching and Learning*, 1-24.

Ravi, M. (2025). Using the TPACK Framework for Gen-AI Enabled Learning Activities: Design, Delivery and Evaluation. *Journal of Engineering Education Transformations*, 175-181.

Redecker, C. (2017). European Framework for the Digital Competence of Educators: DigCompEdu (Pun. Y., Ed.). Publications Office of the European Union. DOI: 10.2760/159770

Ritter, L. A., Barenkamp, M., & Moch, E. (2025). Plattform und Kontrolle: Technischer Datenschutz in digitalen Lernsystemen. *Wirtsch Inform Manag*, *17*(5-6), 251–258. DOI: 10.1365/s35764-025-00571-4

Rowley, J. (2023). E. H. Carr: Imperialism, war and lessons for post-colonial IR. *International Affairs*, *99*(2), 840–841. DOI: 10.1093/ia/iiad045

Ruiz-Ariza, A., Casuso, R. A., Suarez-Manzano, S., & Martínez-López, E. J. (2018). Effect of augmented reality game Pokémon GO on cognitive performance and emotional intelligence in adolescent students. *Computers & Education*, *116*, 49–63. DOI: 10.1016/j.compedu.2017.09.002

Runco, M. A., & Jaeger, G. J. (2012). The standard definition of creativity. *Creativity Research Journal*, *24*(1), 92–96. DOI: 10.1080/10400419.2012.650092

Russell, S., & Norvig, P. (2021). *Artificial intelligence: A modern approach* (4th ed.). Pearson.

Sağlam-Kaya, Y. (2019). Öğretmen adaylarının teknopedagojik eğitim yeterliklerinin çeşitli değişkenler ve öğretmen öz yeterlikleri bağlamında incelenmesi. *Journal of Theoretical Educational Science*, *12*(1), 185–204. DOI: 10.30831/akukeg.420909

Sak, R., Şahin Sak, İ. T., Öneren Şendil, Ç., & Nas, E. (2021). Bir araştırma yöntemi olarak doküman analizi. *Kocaeli Üniversitesi Eğitim Dergisi*, *4*(1), 227–250. DOI: 10.33400/kuje.843306

Saldana, J. (2011). *Fundamentals of qualitative research*. Oxford University Press.

Saltan, F., & Arslan, Ö. (2017). A comparison of in-service and pre-service teachers' technological pedagogical content knowledge regarding self-efficacy for using augmented reality in education. *Contemporary Educational Technology*, *8*(3), 203–217. DOI: 10.30935/cedtech/6198

Samoili, S., Cobo, M. L., Gómez, E., De Prato, G., Martínez-Plumed, F., & Delipetrev, B. (2020). *AI Watch. Defining Artificial Intelligence. Towards an operational definition and taxonomy of artificial intelligence*. Luxembourg: Publications Office of the European Union. EUR 30117 EN. https://eprints.ugd.edu.mk/id/eprint/28047

Santos, J. M., Almeida, M., & Celina, A. A. (2021). Computational thinking in elementary school in the age of artificial intelligence: Where is the teacher? *Review of Education, 14*(2), 55–71. DOI: 10.33947/1980-6469-v14n2-3

Saritepeci, M., & Durak, H. Y. (2024). Effectiveness of artificial intelligence integration in design-based learning on design thinking mindset, creative and reflective thinking skills: An experimental study. *Education and Information Technologies, 29*(18), 25175–25209. DOI: 10.1007/s10639-024-12829-2

Schepman, A., & Rodway, P. (2020). Initial validation of the general attitudes towards Artificial Intelligence Scale. *Computers in Human Behavior Reports, 1*, 100014. DOI: 10.1016/j.chbr.2020.100014 PMID: 34235291

Schleicher, A. (2026, January 23). Designing safe AI systems for education. OECD Education and Skills Today. https://oecdedutoday.com/designing-safe-ai-systems-for-education/

Schleicher, A. (2018). *Valuing our teachers and raising their status: How communities can help*. OECD Publishing. DOI: 10.1787/9789264292697-en

Schön, D. A. (1984). *The reflective practitioner: How professionals think in action*. Basic Books.

Schön, D. A., & Wiggins, G. (1992). Kinds of seeing and their functions in designing. *Design Studies, 13*(2), 135–156. DOI: 10.1016/0142-694X(92)90268-F

Sclater, N., Peasgood, A., & Mullan, J. (2016). Learning analytics in higher education. *London: Jisc. Accessed February, 8*(2017), 176.

Scott, L. M., Wilder, T., Zaugg, T., & Romualdo, A. (2025). Enhancing special education using AI: The intersection of personalized learning and inclusivity. In *Transforming special education through artificial intelligence* (pp. 45–78). IGI Global Scientific Publishing.

Scott, W. R. (2014). *Institutions and Organizations: Ideas, Interests, and Identities* (4th ed.). Sage Publishing.

Seawright, J., George, A., & Bennett, A. (2008). *Case Studies and Theory Development in the Social Sciences*. By Alexander George and Andrew Bennett. (MIT Press, 2005.). *The Journal of Politics, 70*(1), 276–278. DOI: 10.1017/S0022381607080231

Selwyn, N. (2019). *Should robots replace teachers? AI and the future of education*. Polity Press.

Selwyn, N. (2019). *Should robots replace teachers?: AI and the future of education*. John Wiley & Sons.

Selwyn, N. (2019). What's the Problem with Learning Analytics? *Journal of Learning Analytics*, *6*(3), 11–19. DOI: 10.18608/jla.2019.63.3

Shah, P. (2023). *AI and the Future of Education: Teaching in the Age of Artificial Intelligence*. John Wiley & Sons.

Sharma, S. (2025). Empowering Multilingual Learners: A Framework for Technology Integration in Diverse Classrooms. *Schools*, *22*(2), 257–278. DOI: 10.1086/737545

Shneiderman, B. (2022). *Human-centered AI*. Oxford University Press. DOI: 10.1093/oso/9780192845290.001.0001

Siddiqui, S., & Bergquist, E. P. (2021). Family characteristics of female-headed households in Pakistan in the context of health promotion. *Health Promotion International*, *37*(1), daab111. Advance online publication. DOI: 10.1093/heapro/daab111 PMID: 34259864

Simmons, A. B., & Chappell, S. G. (1988). Artificial intelligence: Definition and practice. *IEEE Journal of Oceanic Engineering*, *13*(2), 14–42. DOI: 10.1109/48.551

Singh, S., Kaur, A., & Gulzar, Y. (2024). The impact of augmented reality on education: A bibliometric analysis. *Frontiers in Education*, *9*, 1458695. DOI: 10.3389/feduc.2024.1458695

Skills Upload Jr. (2024). AI in European schools: A European report comparing seven countries. https://skillsuploadjr.eu/docs/contents/AI_in_European_schools.pdf

Skraparli, G., Stefanidis, T., & Tsiatsos, T. (2025, April). Evaluating the Impact of Gamification in ePhos AR: A Comparison of Usability, Engagement, and Motivation. In *2025 IEEE Global Engineering Education Conference (EDUCON)* (pp. 1-9). IEEE. DOI: 10.1109/EDUCON62633.2025.11016547

Slater, M. (2009). Place illusion and plausibility can lead to realistic behaviour in immersive virtual environments. *Philosophical Transactions of the Royal Society of London. Series B, Biological Sciences*, *364*(1535), 3549–3557. DOI: 10.1098/rstb.2009.0138 PMID: 19884149

Smuha, N. A. (2021). From a 'race to AI' to a 'race to AI regulation': Regulatory competition for artificial intelligence. *Law, Innovation and Technology*, *13*(1), 57–84. DOI: 10.1080/17579961.2021.1898300

Sperling, K., Stenberg, C.-J., McGrath, C., Åkerfeldt, A., Heintz, F., & Stenliden, L. (2024). In search of artificial intelligence (AI) literacy in teacher education: A scoping review. *Computers and Education Open*, *6*, 100169. DOI: 10.1016/j.caeo.2024.100169

Stake, R. E. (2005). Qualitative case studies. In Denzin, N. K., & Lincoln, Y. S. (Eds.), *The SAGE handbook of qualitative research* (3rd ed., pp. 443–466). SAGE.

Stamper, J., Xiao, R., & Hou, X. (2024). Enhancing LLM-based feedback: Insights from intelligent tutoring systems and the learning sciences. arXiv. /arXiv.2405.04645DOI: 10.1007/978-3-031-64315-6_3

Stare, J., Klun, M., & Dečman, M. (2023). A case study on the development of digital competences of teachers at the University of Ljubljana. *NISPAcee Journal of Public Administration and Policy*, *16*(1), 138–166. DOI: 10.2478/nispa-2023-0006

Steegh, A., Höffler, T., Höft, L., & Parchmann, I. (2021). Exploring science competition participants' expectancy-value perceptions and identification: A latent profile analysis. *Learning and Instruction*, *74*, 101455. DOI: 10.1016/j.learninstruc.2021.101455

St-Hilaire, F., Vu, D.D., Frau, A., Burns, N., Faraji, F., Potochny, J., Robert, S., Roussel, A., Zheng, S., Glazier, T., Romano, J.V., Belfer, R., Shayan, M., Smofsky, A., Delarosbil, T., Ahn, S., Eden-Walker, S., Sony, K., Ching, A.O., Elkins, S., Stepanyan, A.Z., Matajová, A., Chen, V., Sahraei, H., Larson, R., Markova, N., Barkett, A., Charlin, L., Bengio, Y., Serban, I., & Kochmar, E. (2022). A new era: Intelligent tutoring systems will transform online learning for millions. ArXiv, abs/2203.03724.

Subramanian, S. R. S., Anurekha, G., Gomathi, C., Saha, S., Rajalakshmi, A., Elavarasi, J., & Ezhilvendan, M. (2026). Deep Learning and Transformer Models for Educational Chatbots: Enhancing Intelligent Tutoring Systems. In *Educational Applications of Natural Language Processing, Chatbots, and AI* (pp. 117-146). IGI Global Scientific Publishing.

Suluk, B. (2025). İlkokul Eğitiminde Yapay Zekâ: Türkiye'de Öğrenci ve Öğretmen Odaklı Çalışmaların Sistematik İncelemesi. *Temel Eğitim Araştırmaları Dergisi*, *5*(2), 205–222. Retrieved May 30, 2026, from. DOI: 10.55008/te-ad.1757856

Sumbera, B. G. (2025). The Ethical Use of AI in Education. In *Integrating AI Into Pedagogical Education* (pp. 175–210). IGI Global Scientific Publishing.

Suppes, P., & Atkinson, R. C. (1967). *Computer-assisted instruction: Methods and results*. Academic Press.

Susnjak, T., Ramaswami, G. S., & Mathrani, A. (2022). Learning analytics dashboard: A tool for providing actionable insights to learners. *International Journal of Educational Technology in Higher Education, 19*(1), 12. DOI: 10.1186/s41239-021-00313-7 PMID: 35194560

Swiss Cyber Institute. (2025). The EU AI Act: Implications for ethical AI in education. https://swisscyberinstitute.com/research/eu-ai-act-implications-ethical-ai-education/

Tamer, H. Y., & Övgün, B. (2020). Yapay zekâ bağlaminda dijital dönüşüm ofisi. *Ankara Üniversitesi SBF Dergisi, 75*(2), 775–803. DOI: 10.33630/ausbf.691119

Tammets, K., & Ley, T. (2023). Integrating AI tools in teacher professional learning: A conceptual model and illustrative case. *Frontiers in Artificial Intelligence, 6*, 1255089. DOI: 10.3389/frai.2023.1255089 PMID: 38130325

Tamozhska, I., Lehan, I., Shcherbak, I., Suprun, D., & Hryhorenko, T. (2023). FUNCTIONING AND DEVELOPMENT OF NATIONAL AND EUROPEAN ADULT EDUCATION SYSTEMS: A COMPARATIVE ASPECT. *Conhecimento & Diversidade, 15*(40), 45–61. DOI: 10.18316/rcd.v15i40.11275

Tapalova, O., & Zhiyenbayeva, N. (2022). Artificial intelligence in education: AIEd for personalised learning pathways. *Electronic Journal of e-Learning, 20*(5), 639–653. DOI: 10.34190/ejel.20.5.2597

Teles, R. O., & Moreira, F. T. (2025). Integrating AI in Formative Assessment Under UDL Principles in Diverse Learning Environments. In Moreira, F., & Teles, R. (Eds.), *Improving Student Assessment With Emerging AI Tools* (pp. 95–122). IGI Global Scientific Publishing., DOI: 10.4018/979-8-3693-6170-2.ch004

Terzieva, V.. (2020). The effect of augmented reality on students' learning performance in STEM education. *Information (Basel), 11*(4), 209. DOI: 10.3390/info11040209

Thelwall, M. (2020). Measuring societal impacts of research with altmetrics? common problems and mistakes. *Journal of Economic Surveys, 35*(5), 1302–1314. DOI: 10.1111/joes.12381

Tlili, A., Shehata, B., Adarkwah, M. A., Bozkurt, A., Hickey, D. T., Huang, R., & Agyemang, B. (2023). What if the devil is my guardian angel: ChatGPT as a case study of using chatbots in education. *Smart Learning Environments, 10*(1), 15. DOI: 10.1186/s40561-023-00237-x

Toker, A. (2022). Bir araştırma metodolojisi olarak sistematik literatür incelemesi: Meta-sentez yöntemi. *Anadolu Üniversitesi Sosyal Bilimler Dergisi, 22*(Özel Sayı 2), 313–340. https://doi.org/DOI: 10.18037/ausbd.1227360

Tong, H., Türel, A., Şenkal, H., Ergun, S. F. Y., Orkan, Z. G., & Alaçam, S. (2023). Can AI function as a new mode of sketching: A teaching experiment with freshman. *International Journal of Emerging Technologies in Learning (Online), 18*(18), 234. DOI: 10.3991/ijet.v18i18.42603

Trustworthy, A. I. Project. (2022). Framework for Trustworthy AI Education. Erasmus+ Programme. https://www.trustworthyaiproject.eu/framework-for-trustworthy-ai-education/

Ugli, E. B. S., Vincy, V. B. S., Lakshmikantham, B., & Kizi, M. N. T. (2025). Enhancing pedagogical practice through immersive technology with the transformation of classrooms with AR. In. AIP Conference Proceedings: Vol. 3306. *No. 1* (p. 030076). AIP Publishing LLC. DOI: 10.1063/5.0275886

Ukşul, Ş. (2016). *Türkiye'de eğitimde ölçme ve değerlendirme alanında yapılmış bilimsel yayınların sosyal ağ analizi ile değerlendirilmesi: Bir bibliyometrik çalışma* (Yüksek Lisans Tezi). Akdeniz Üniversitesi Eğitim Bilimleri Enstitüsü, Antalya

UNESCO. (2021). *AI and education: Guidance for policy-makers*. UNESCO Publishing. https://unesdoc.unesco.org/ark:/48223/pf0000376709

UNESCO. (2021). AI and education: Guidance for policy-makers. United Nations Educational, Scientific and Cultural Organization. https://unesdoc.unesco.org/ark:/48223/pf0000376709

UNESCO. (2021). Recommendation on the ethics of artificial intelligence. UNESCO General Conference, 41st session. https://www.unesco.org/en/artificial-intelligence/recommendation-ethics

UNESCO. (2023). *Guidance for generative AI in education and research*. UNESCO Publishing. https://unesdoc.unesco.org/ark:/48223/pf0000386693

UNESCO. (2023). Guidance for generative AI in education and research. UNESCO. https://unesdoc.unesco.org/ark:/48223/pf0000386693

UNESCO. (2023). Guidance for generative AI in education and research. United Nations Educational, Scientific and Cultural Organization. https://unesdoc.unesco.org/ark:/48223/pf0000386693

UNESCO. (2024). AI competency framework for teachers. UNESCO Publishing. https://www.unesco.org/en/articles/ai-competency-framework-teachers

UNESCO. (2024). AI competency framework for teachers. UNESCO. https://unesdoc.unesco.org/ark:/48223/pf0000391104

Ünsal Serim, H. (2019). The effect of gamification on the acceptance of coding education. *Journal of Educational Technology & Society*, *22*(3), 116–128.

Uttal, D. H., Miller, D. I., & Newcombe, N. S. (2013). Exploring and enhancing spatial thinking: Links to achievement in science, technology, engineering, and mathematics? *Current Directions in Psychological Science*, *22*(5), 367–373. DOI: 10.1177/0963721413484756

Uyulgan, M. A., & Akkuzu Güven, N. (2022). Web 2.0 Tools in Chemistry Teaching: An Analysis of Pre-Service Chemistry Teachers' Competencies and Views. *Instructional Technology and Lifelong Learning*, *3*(1), 88–114. DOI: 10.52911/itall.1127618

Vadisetty, R., & Polamarasetti, A. (2024, December). AI-Augmented Skill Development Roadmaps: Tailoring 12-Month Learning Paths for Future-Ready Careers in Education 4.0 and Industry 4.0. In 2024 13th International Conference on System Modeling & Advancement in Research Trends (SMART) (pp. 655-661). IEEE.

Van Dijck, J., Poell, T., & De Waal, M. (2018). *The Platform Society: Public Values in a Connective World*. Oxford University Press. DOI: 10.1093/oso/9780190889760.001.0001

VanLehn, K. (2011). The relative effectiveness of human tutoring, intelligent tutoring systems, and other tutoring systems. *Educational Psychologist*, *46*(4), 197–221. DOI: 10.1080/00461520.2011.611369

Vartiainen, H., Valtonen, T., Kahila, J., & Tedre, M. (2025). ChatGPT and imaginaries of the future of education: Insights of Finnish teacher educators. *Information and Learning Science*, *126*(1/2), 75–90. DOI: 10.1108/ILS-10-2023-0146

Vasou, M., Kyprianou, G., Amanatiadis, A., & Chatzichristofis, S. A. (2024). Transforming Education with AI and Robotics: Potential, Perceptions, and Infrastructure Needs. In *European, Mediterranean, and Middle Eastern Conference on Information Systems* (pp. 3-18). Cham: Springer Nature Switzerland.

Veale, M., & Zuiderveen Borgesius, F. J. (2021). Demystifying the draft EU Artificial Intelligence Act-Analysing the good, the bad, and the unclear elements of the proposed approach. *Computer Law Review International*, *22*(4), 97–112. DOI: 10.9785/cri-2021-220402

Verghis, A. M., Jose, B., Cherian, J., Mumthas, S., Joseph, S., & Varghise, S. M. (2025). The cognitive paradox of AI in education: Between enhancement and erosion. *Frontiers in Psychology*, *16*, 1550621. DOI: 10.3389/fpsyg.2025.1550621 PMID: 40297599

Voogt, J., & Roblin, N. P. (2012). A comparative analysis of international frameworks for 21st century competences: Implications for national curriculum policies. *Journal of Curriculum Studies, 44*(3), 299–321. DOI: 10.1080/00220272.2012.668938

Vrba, J., & Huynh, T. N. Q. (2026). *The impact of universities rankings on academic research.* In Academic Research Challenges for Modern Society., DOI: 10.4018/979-8-3373-0897-5.ch004

Wang, E. Q., & Piper, A. M. (2018). Accessibility in action. *Proceedings of the ACM on Human-Computer Interaction, 2*(CSCW), 1–25. https://doi.org/DOI: 10.1145/3274449

Wang, J., Shi, Y., Chen, X., Lan, Y., & Liu, S. (2025). Teaching with artificial intelligence in architecture: Embedding technical skills and ethical reflection in a core design studio. *Buildings (Basel, Switzerland), 15*(17), 3069. Advance online publication. DOI: 10.3390/buildings15173069

Wang, P. (2019). On defining artificial intelligence. *Journal of Artificial General Intelligence, 10*(2), 1–37. DOI: 10.2478/jagi-2019-0002

Wang, S., Wang, F., Zhu, Z., Wang, J., Tran, T., & Du, Z. (2024). Artificial intelligence in education: A systematic literature review. *Expert Systems with Applications, 252*, 124167. DOI: 10.1016/j.eswa.2024.124167

Wang, W., & Wang, Y. (2019). Factors influencing students' behavioral intentions to use the artificial intelligence-powered chatbot. *Computers & Education, 134*, 113–124.

Wang, X. (2025). A review of the Council of Europe Framework Convention on Artificial Intelligence and Human Rights, Democracy and the Rule of Law. *Journal of Politics and Law, 18*(4), 68. DOI: 10.5539/jpl.v18n4p68

Weizenbaum, J. (1966). ELIZA—A computer program for the study of natural language communication between man and machine. *Communications of the ACM, 9*(1), 36–45. DOI: 10.1145/365153.365168

Wild, F. (2022). *Remarks at CEN/CENELEC Standards+Innovation Award ceremony.* Open University, Institute of Educational Technology.

Williamson, B. (2017). *Big data in education: The digital future of learning, policy and practice.* SAGE Publications. DOI: 10.4135/9781529714920

Williamson, B. (2019). Datafication of education: A critical approach to emerging analytics technologies and practices. In *Rethinking pedagogy for a digital age* (pp. 212–226). Routledge. DOI: 10.4324/9781351252805-14

Williamson, B., Bayne, S., & Shay, S. (2020). The datafication of teaching in Higher Education: Critical issues and perspectives. *Teaching in Higher Education, 25*(4), 351–365. DOI: 10.1080/13562517.2020.1748811

Williamson, B., & Eynon, R. (2020). Historical threads, missing strands, and future directions: A sociotechnical perspective on AI in education. *Learning, Media and Technology, 45*(3), 223–235. DOI: 10.1080/17439884.2020.1798995

Winkler, R., & Söllner, M. (2018). Unleashing the potential of chatbots in education: A state-of-the-art analysis. Academy of Management Annual Meeting Proceedings. DOI: 10.5465/AMBPP.2018.15903abstract

Wolfram, D. (2003). *Applied informetrics for information retrieval research* (New Directions in Information Management, No. 36). Greenwood Publishing Group.

Woodbury, R. (2010). *Elements of parametric design*. Routledge.

Woolf, B. P. (2010). *Building intelligent interactive tutors: Student-centered strategies for revolutionizing e-learning*. Morgan Kaufmann.

Wright, S. (2025). Artificial intelligence and work: A review of the European policy landscape. *The Journal of Industrial Relations, 67*(5), 794–805. DOI: 10.1177/00221856251394780

Yadav, S. (2025). Revolutionizing Classroom Learning With Advanced Technology: Harnessing Augmented Reality (AR) and Virtual Reality (VR) for Immersive Education. In *Blending Human Intelligence With Technology in the Classroom* (pp. 223-246). IGI Global Scientific Publishing.

Yanjin, S., Qian, L., Kun, Z., & Ruirui, Z. (2023). The application of artificial intelligence technology in personalized teaching of vocational education. In *2023 13th International Conference on Information Technology in Medicine and Education (ITME)* (pp. 846-850). IEEE. DOI: 10.1109/ITME60234.2023.00172

Yildirim, B., Sahin-Topalcengiz, E., Arikan, G., & Timur, S. (2020). Using virtual reality in the classroom: Reflections of STEM teachers on the use of teaching and learning tools. *Journal of Education in Science, Environment and Health, 6*(1), 1–18. DOI: 10.21891/jeseh.711779

Yilmaz, F. G. K., Yilmaz, R., & Ceylan, M. (2024). Generative Artificial Intelligence Acceptance Scale: A Validity and Reliability Study. *International Journal of Human-Computer Interaction, 40*(24), 8703–8715. DOI: 10.1080/10447318.2023.2288730

Yin, R. K. (2018). *Case study research and applications: Design and methods* (6th ed.). SAGE.

Yoo, Y., Henfridsson, O., & Lyytinen, K. (2010). Research Commentary: The New Organizing Logic of Digital Innovation: An Agenda for Information Systems Research. *Information Systems Research, 21*(4), 724–735. https://www.jstor.org/stable/23015640. DOI: 10.1287/isre.1100.0322

Yücel, A. S., & Koçak, C. (2010). Evaluation of the basic technology competency of the teachers' candidate according to the various variables. *Procedia: Social and Behavioral Sciences, 2*(2), 1310–1315. DOI: 10.1016/j.sbspro.2010.03.192

Yuriev, E., Wink, D. J., & Holme, T. A. (2023). Virtual Special Issue Call for Papers: Investigating the Uses and Impacts of Generative Artificial Intelligence in Chemistry Education. *Journal of Chemical Education, 100*(9), 3168–3170. DOI: 10.1021/acs.jchemed.3c00829

Zawacki-Richter, O., Marín, V. I., Bond, M., & Gouverneur, F. (2019). Systematic review of research on artificial intelligence applications in higher education: Where are the educators? *International Journal of Educational Technology in Higher Education, 16*(1), 39. Advance online publication. DOI: 10.1186/s41239-019-0171-0

Zekeik, H., Chahbi, M., Sefian, M. L., & Bakkali, I. (2025). Augmented reality and virtual reality in education: A systematic narrative review on benefits, challenges, and applications. *Eurasia Journal of Mathematics, Science and Technology Education, 21*(6), em2616. Advance online publication. DOI: 10.29333/ejmste/16830

Zhu, H., Sun, Y., & Yang, J. (2025). Towards responsible artificial intelligence in education: A systematic review on identifying and mitigating ethical risks. *Humanities & Social Sciences Communications, 12*(1), 456. DOI: 10.1057/s41599-025-05252-6

Zimmerman, B. J. (2002). Becoming a self-regulated learner: An overview. *Theory into Practice, 41*(2), 64–70. DOI: 10.1207/s15430421tip4102_2

Zouhri, A., & El Mallahi, M. (2024). Improving teaching using artificial intelligence and augmented reality. *Journal of Automation, Mobile Robotics and Intelligent Systems*, 57-61.

Zuhra, F., & Iqbal, M.Fatima-tu-Zuhra. (2025). Exploration of the tangible and intangible aspects affecting students' learning in architectural studios: A case study of Lahore, Pakistan. *Nihon Kenchiku Gakkai Keikaku-Kei Rombunshu, 37*(3), 283–299. DOI: 10.33948/JAP-KSU-37-3-4

Zupic, I., & Čater, T. (2015). Bibliometric methods in management and organization. *Organizational Research Methods, 18*(3), 429–472. DOI: 10.1177/1094428114562629

About the Contributors

Jan Vrba, born in September 1990, holds both EU and Czech citizenship. He has been appointed Senior Full Professor ("Profesor Titular C") at Universidad Azteca and holds a Ph.D. in Business Administration, a D.B.A. in Human Resource Management from International American University, a PhDr. in Political Science, and a Master's Degree in Business Analytics. His career includes roles as Vice-Dean and University Lecturer in Europe (Austria, Poland, and the Czech Republic), Academic Expert in Political Sciences in India, and Chief Innovation Officer in Malaysia. He leads international partnerships, global research management, and academic support in multicultural environments. An active contributor to academia, he serves as an Academic Editor and Reviewer for SCOPUS-indexed journals, such as PLOS One and Frontiers, and frequently speaks at international conferences. Jan is fluent in Czech, Slovak, and English, and his research focuses on Educational Management, Higher Education and Learning, AI & AR, and Public Administration.

Enrico Moch studied business administration at the University of Wismar and subsequently completed a degree in business law at Saarland University. Several years later, he completed a doctorate in economics on the topic of the influence of artificial intelligence on the world of work. His main job is as an administrative officer at the DLR Project Management Agency in the Society, Innovation and Technology division, where he is assigned to the AI Applications in Business department. In this role, he deals with the monitoring, evaluation and structuring of research and innovation projects in the context of digital technologies. Enrico Moch also works as a university lecturer at various institutions in Germany, including the Baden-Württemberg Cooperative State University Ravensburg. He also holds the position of Assistant Professor of Economics at the IICUT. He has been Academic Director of the Herford-based GrandEdu Research School for several years. His research focuses on AI governance, technical data protection and the institutional governance of digital platforms. In terms of content, his work focuses on regulatory frameworks, governance structures and the economic impact of artificial intelligence and data-driven systems. Enrico Moch regularly publishes scientific articles, is involved in interdisciplinary book projects and is active in academic peer review. He is also active in knowledge transfer between academia and practice and hosts the podcast "GrandEdu Research School - On the trail of the economy!".

Lars Arnold Ritter is a university lecturer and is currently doing his doctorate at the University of Library Studies and Information Technologies (ULSIT) in Sofia. In his dissertation, entitled Optimising the Organisation and Management of Information Processes for Increasing Motivation and Effectiveness of Adult Education, he is developing his own Learning Management System (LMS), which is geared towards efficiency, motivation and sustainability in adult education. He teaches academic work at several universities and combines academic expertise with practical advice.

Tobias Oberdieck is Managing Director of GrandEdu GmbH, a leading further education institution that specialises in preparing professionals for degrees such as the Bachelor Professional, Master Professional and Master of Business Administration (MBA). In his role at GrandEdu, he drives innovative educational strategies to actively support the recruitment of skilled labour in Germany. During his doctorate, Dr. Oberdieck worked as a research assistant at the Department of Business Administration and Economics at the Niederrhein University of Applied Sciences in Germany. During this time, he deepened his expertise in the areas of education management, labour market research and economic education models, which he now brings to his work at GrandEdu. His research focuses on the interface between continuing vocational training, academic education and the challenges of the modern labour market.

***

Sema Alaçam is an Associate Professor at Istanbul Technical University (ITU), Faculty of Architecture, and the Program Coordinator of the Game and Interaction Technologies Master's Program. She holds her B.Arch. (2005), M.Sc. (2008), and Ph.D. (2014) degrees from ITU's Architectural Design Computing Program. Her research focuses on computational design, digital fabrication, and embodied cognition in architectural design processes. She has been a visiting researcher at TU Delft (Hyperbody), ETH Zurich (Chair of Structural Design), University of Oregon (Department of Philosophy), and Université de Versailles Saint-Quentin-en-Yvelines. Between 2018 and 2021, she served as the Coordinator of the Architectural Design

Computing Graduate Program at ITU. She currently teaches undergraduate design studios and graduate courses on computational design and digital fabrication.

Fatma Alkan is works as professor in Hacettepe University Faculty of Education, Chemistry Teaching Program. She has published many articles in national and international peer-reviewed journals. She works as a field editor in peer-reviewed journals.

Simon Baradziej is a Doctoral Research Fellow at the Department of Technology and Safety at UiT – The Arctic University of Norway, where he is a member of the Maritime Safety Science (MARSCI) Research Group. His research spans artificial intelligence in education, adaptive learning systems, maritime training technology, and AI policymaking. He is a researcher in the EU Horizon Europe–funded i-MASTER project, which develops intelligent adaptive learning systems for maritime simulator-based education. His work bridges empirical research, applied AI system development, and the governance of emerging educational technologies within European regulatory frameworks.

Susanta Das is a seasoned educator with a proven record of teaching and mentoring diverse student populations, working at multiple institutions, and contributing to various organizational initiatives. He received his Ph.D. and M.A. degrees in Physics from Western Michigan University (WMU), USA, and his M.Sc. degree in Physics from Banaras Hindu University (BHU), India. He continued his research as a Marie Curie Postdoctoral Fellow at Stockholm University, Sweden, working on beam diagnostics for DESIREE (Double ElectroStatic Ion Ring ExpEriment) under the DITANET project (Diagnostic Techniques for Particle Accelerators – a Marie Curie Initial Training Network). He also conducted research at the Indian Institute of Science Education and Research (IISER), Kolkata, India, on high-pressure physics as a Project Scientist-B, and at the University of Electro-Communications, Tokyo, Japan, on ion–surface interactions as a Postdoctoral Fellow. Throughout his career, Dr. Das has worked and collaborated with numerous researchers, Ph.D. scholars, master's students, and visiting scholars from different countries. He has visited several countries to present and discuss his research and has participated in international conferences in the UK, Italy, Germany, Greece, Belgium, Bulgaria, Romania, Brazil, and other countries. He worked at several institutions before assuming his current role at Ajeenkya D Y Patil University. He has received several prestigious awards and fellowships, including the Marie Curie Postdoctoral Fellowship (Sweden), the Science Academies' Summer Research Fellowship (India), the Gowen Frostic Doctoral Fellowship, the Department Graduate Research and Creative Scholar Award from WMU, and the Leo R. Parpart

Doctoral Fellowship from the Department of Physics, WMU, among many others. Dr. Das has co-authored several research articles in WoS- and Scopus-indexed international journals, conference proceedings, and scholarly book chapters. He has also co-edited multiple books published by renowned international publishing houses, including IGI Global, Springer Nature, Wiley, Scrivener-Wiley, and Notion Press. Currently, Dr. Das is actively engaged in cutting-edge research with a keen interest in nanotechnology, the United Nations Sustainable Development Goals (UN SDGs), and data science. His multifaceted contributions in teaching, research, and academic leadership reflect a dedicated professional who significantly advances the vision and mission of the institutions he serves.

Putheara Dy is a lecturer at the Royal University of Law and Economics (RULE) in Phnom Penh, Cambodia. He holds a PhD in Political Science and has contributed to Cambodian higher education through teaching and research in political and social sciences. His background includes high school teaching, adding classroom experience to his academic profile. His research spans political and social disciplines, with a focus on advancing education, critical inquiry, and scholarship in Cambodia.

Bulent Gursel Emiroğlu is working at Kırıkkale University. His research interest is Artificial Intelligence, Machine Learning, Deep Learning, Educational technology, Distance education.

Alexandre M. Pereira Figueiredo holds a degree in Mass Communication, postgraduate qualifications in Communication Sciences and in Information and Communication Technologies, a Master's degree in Communication Sciences, and a PhD in Communication Sciences. He is also a specialist in Audiovisual and Media Production. He is currently professor at the Polytechnic Institute of Portalegre and researcher at ICNOVA, Techn&Art, and CIDIUM. He serves as editor of the electronic academic journal artciencia.com, is a member of the Editorial Board of the International Journal of European Studies, and sits on the Advisory Board of the Open Access Asia project. He has authored three books and published approximately 40 articles in specialized academic journals. He has organized one academic event and participated in eight others. His research and teaching activities are focused on the field of Communication Sciences.

Deepak Gupta is a distinguished academician with over 20 years of teaching experience and expertise in Computer Science and Engineering. He holds a Ph.D. in Computer Engineering and has an extensive research portfolio, including many international journal papers, multiple conference proceedings, and several books. His research interests span machine learning, artificial intelligence, and data mining. Currently, Dr. Gupta serves as an Associate Professor and Head of Department of

CSE (Emerging Branches) at ITM Gwalior, MP, India. He has also contributed significantly to the field through patents and copyrights and actively engages as a reviewer, conference chair and editor.

Fatih Kaleci is an Assistant Professor of Mathematics Education at Necmettin Erbakan University (Konya, Türkiye), and serves as the General Director of NEU PRESS (Necmettin Erbakan University Press) and the University's Scientific Publications Coordinator. He has led the institutional development of a university-wide publishing governance model and the NEU PRESS ecosystem, coordinating 32 scholarly journals and overseeing digital publishing workflows, indexing readiness, metadata management, and research output analytics. His expertise spans mathematics education, scientific publishing, big data and analytics, bibliometrics/scientometrics, sustainability, and research performance and university rankings. He was elected to the EASE Council in 2022, is a member of IATUL, and joined the EBSCO Global Advisory Board in 2024.

|Mustafa Kayyali - Contributing Author|I am an ardent advocate for excellence in higher education, driven by a relentless pursuit of quality, recognition, and innovation. My journey in academia started with a Master's in Quality Management and Evaluation in Higher Education from Universitat Oberta de Catalunya, followed by a Ph.D. in Quality Management from Azteca University. These academic pursuits have laid a strong foundation for my expertise in Accreditation, Quality Assurance, and Higher Education Rankings. As an entrepreneur, researcher, translator, and publisher, I am deeply involved in various facets of the academic world. My diverse interests encompass Management, Translation, Interpretation, and Academic consulting, contributing to a well-rounded understanding of the industry. Throughout my career, I have made significant contributions to academic literature, with more than 40 published papers and 30 book chapters to my name. Additionally, I take pride in having translated 6 books, bridging language gaps, and promoting knowledge exchange on a global scale. I am committed to fostering positive change in higher education and contributing to its continuous improvement.

Ayşegül Kıdık, received her B.Arch. from Erciyes University, Faculty of Architecture (2001–2006), and her MSc. in Architectural Design Computing from Istanbul Technical University (2006–2010), with a thesis titled "Cyborg Architecture" advised by L. Dr. Hakan Tong. She is currently pursuing her PhD. in Architecture at Abdullah Gül University (2017–2024) with a dissertation titled "XR Impact on Architectural Design Education" under the supervision of Prof. Dr. Burak Asiliskender. She was awarded the TÜBİTAK 2214-A Overseas Research Fellowship and conducted part of her research at the University of Central Florida,

Orlando, US (2022–2023). Her research interests include computing architecture, technology-based architecture, architectural design education, XR (Extended Reality), and design education. aysegul.kidik@agu.edu.tr kidikaysegul@gmail.com Department of Architecture, Faculty of Architecture, Abdullah Gül University, Kayseri, TURKEY.

|Buket Koçak - Contributing Author|Master's Student, Institute of Educational Sciences, Hacettepe University, Turkey

Kritikka Kunte is an undergraduate student pursuing a Bachelor of Technology degree in Artificial Intelligence and Data Science at the School of Engineering, Ajeenkya D Y Patil University, Pune, Maharashtra, India. With a strong academic orientation toward data-driven problem solving, she has developed a focused interest in the domains of data analytics and data science, supported by both theoretical foundations and applied project experience. Throughout her academic journey, Kritikka has cultivated proficiency in core programming and analytical competencies, including Python, SQL, and Java, along with essential data science methodologies such as data preprocessing, exploratory data analysis (EDA), and machine learning techniques. She is proficient in industry-relevant tools and platforms, including Advanced Microsoft Excel, Matplotlib, Tableau, and Power BI, to derive insights from complex datasets and present them in a structured and interpretable manner. Her practical exposure includes the successful completion of projects such as Ocean Salinity Analysis, which involved analyzing environmental datasets to identify patterns and trends, and Speech Recognition and Translation, where she explored applied machine learning concepts in natural language processing. These projects reflect her ability to translate conceptual knowledge into functional, real-world solutions. Kritikka has further strengthened her technical profile through professional certifications, including the AWS re/Start Graduate credential from Amazon Web Services, a certification in Software Development, and Python training certified by Google. Her engagement in competitive and collaborative academic environments is demonstrated by her participation in the Smart India Hackathon (SIH) and by securing Second Runner-Up in an inter-collegiate Tableau competition, highlighting her analytical aptitude and visualization skills. With a growing interest in advanced transportation systems and data-centric engineering solutions, Kritikka brings a multidisciplinary perspective to the GHC Hyperloop Project Competition hosted at IIT Madras. She aspires to contribute meaningfully to innovative, technology-driven initiatives that integrate artificial intelligence, data science, and sustainable engineering to address complex global challenges.

Filipe T. Moreira is a professor and researcher in the field of Education and Educational Technologies at the Polytechnic Institute of Porto, Portugal. His research interests focus on digital education, artificial intelligence in education, emerging technologies, and teacher training, with particular attention to ethical, pedagogical, and human-centred approaches to technology integration. He has participated in and coordinated national and international research projects and is the author of several scientific publications on digital transformation, innovation in education, and technology-enhanced learning.

Krutika Patre, is an aspiring programmer and technology enthusiast, currently pursuing Engineering in Artificial Intelligence and Data Science. With a passion for learning, she is building experience in a variety of programming languages and technologies, including C, C++, Python, Data Structures (DS), HTML, CSS, and JavaScript, DBMS (My SQL). After learning this programming language, she has created interest in Full Stack Development. She had also attended an Arduino-Based Automation course at Dolphin Labs to improve my software knowledge. There, she learned how to work with sensors, microcontrollers, and circuit design. She has written review paper on Sustainable engineering on build environment. She is doing researching and learning many topics related to AI, Policy and governance and related to my interest. She has taken part in hackathons, workshops, and tech events to explore many fields. She is also working with a group on Hyperloop. Being part of this project has really helped her grow, especially in areas like teamwork, innovation, and systems thinking.

Phearak Pok is Deputy Head of the Department of International Relations at the Royal University of Law and Economics (RULE). He holds a PhD in Economics and a Master's in Business Administration. Since 2010, he has specialized in the interdisciplinary fields of economics, business, and politics, with teaching and research focused on integrating theory and practice. Dr. POK is committed to advancing knowledge and fostering critical dialogue in Cambodian academia.

Sunil Sankathala is pursuing B. Tech Computer Science and Engineering at Ajeenkya D Y Patil University, with a diverse range of interests that bridge technology, sustainability, and innovation. He academic focus lies in computer science fundamentals like programming, data structures, algorithms, and software development. He actively supplements this with hands-on experience in web development and robotics. Beyond the core curriculum, He has a strong research inclination in emerging and impactful fields. He current research interests include Artificial Intelligence in Healthcare, bioplastics, nano bioplastics, e-waste management, and solid waste management—areas where he believes technology can make a meaningful difference in solving real-world problems. He has been publishing research articles and book chapters in reputed national and international journals and books. He is also part of an ambitious Hyperloop project, which involves interdisciplinary collaboration and cutting-edge engineering aimed at revolutionizing transportation. Working on this project has enhanced his skills in teamwork, innovation, and systems thinking. In the tech domain, he has developed proficiency in web development using technologies such as HTML, CSS, JavaScript, and React. He interests in robotics further reflects building smart, responsive systems that interact with the physical world. Throughout his course, he has helped strengthen problem-solving and collaborative skills. He proficient in languages such as Python, C, C++, MySQL, Ubuntu, Machine Learning and familiar with frameworks and tools like React, Git. He actively participates in hackathons, coding competitions, and tech events to challenge himself and learn from peers. He is also a quick learner and highly adaptable, with an eagerness to stay updated with the latest trends in the tech world. He aspires to become a skilled software engineer and contribute to building innovative solutions that have a positive impact on society. The long-term goal is to work in a dynamic environment where knowledge, grow professionally, and make meaningful contributions to the field of technology. Driven by a spirit of exploration and sustainability, he aims to contribute to technological solutions that address both human and environmental needs. The long-term goal is to become a versatile engineer and researcher, working at the intersection of computer science, environmental innovation, and human well-being.

Jakhongir Shaturaev is an Associate Professor working in the Department of International Cooperation at Termez University of Economics and Service, Termez, Uzbekistan.

Doni Sugianto Sihotang is a doctoral student in Marketing at Jakarta State University, Indonesia. His academic background combines a Bachelor's degree in Social Anthropology from Universitas Sumatera Utara and a Master's degree in Marketing Management from Jakarta State University. His research interests focus on consumer behavior, digital marketing, tourism marketing, and behavioral analytics. He has actively contributed to several peer-reviewed publications, exploring topics such as consumer decision-making, destination branding, and electric vehicle adoption. He also serves as a Graduate Teaching Assistant and Research Assistant at Jakarta State University, supporting research in marketing and behavioral sciences. Doni has received several national awards, including the BIMA DRTPM Research Grant from the Indonesian Ministry of Education and the PMDSU Fast-Track Scholarship for outstanding young researchers. His interdisciplinary background in anthropology and marketing enables him to integrate cultural and behavioral insights into the study of consumer decision processes and sustainable tourism development.

Devanshi Soni is currently pursuing a B.Tech. in Computer Engineering at the School of Engineering, Ajeenkya D Y Patil University. Her research interests are metal nanoparticles and their applications and the integration of Artificial Intelligence across various domains. Devanshi is particularly interested in exploring how metal nanoparticles can be combined with AI technologies to address practical challenges and develop innovative solutions. She aims to advance research in these fields and contribute to groundbreaking developments that tackle real-world issues.

Hakan Tong is an architect, researcher, and educator at the Department of Architecture at Istanbul Technical University. He received his B.Arch. degree from Istanbul Technical University in 1986 and completed both his M.Sc. and Ph.D. in Building Science at ITU. His academic work focuses on architectural design, computational and digital design methodologies, design technologies, and information technologies in architecture. Dr. Tong has been involved in architectural education and research at ITU for many years, teaching design studios, computer-aided design methods, multimedia and animation in architectural design, and virtual architectural design studios. His recent studies particularly explore artificial intelligence, digital representation, computational thinking, and emerging technologies in architectural pedagogy and design processes.

Ayşem Seda Yücel is works as professor in Hacettepe University Faculty of Education, Chemistry Teaching Program. She has published many articles in national and international peer-reviewed journals. She works as a field editor in peer-reviewed journals.

Index

A

B

C

D

E

F

G

H

www.ingramcontent.com/pod-product-compliance
Lightning Source LLC
LaVergne TN
LVHW061526290926
849162LV00004B/680

* 9 7 9 8 3 3 7 3 9 8 8 3 9 *